**Foreign Relations of the
United States, 1964–1968**

Volume XXII

Iran

Editor   Nina D. Howland

General Editor   David S. Patterson

United States Government Printing Office
Washington
1999

DEPARTMENT OF STATE PUBLICATION 10614

OFFICE OF THE HISTORIAN

BUREAU OF PUBLIC AFFAIRS

For sale by the U.S. Government Printing Office
Superintendent of Documents, Mail Stop: SSOP, Washington, DC 20402-9328
ISBN 0-16-050085-0

Preface

The *Foreign Relations of the United States* series presents the official documentary historical record of major foreign policy decisions and significant diplomatic activity of the United States Government. The series documents the facts and events that contributed to the formulation of policies and includes evidence of supporting and alternative views to the policy positions ultimately adopted.

The Historian of the Department of State is charged with the responsibility for the preparation of the *Foreign Relations* series. The staff of the Office of the Historian, Bureau of Public Affairs, plans, researches, compiles, and edits the volumes in the series. This documentary editing proceeds in full accord with the generally accepted standards of historical scholarship. Official regulations codifying specific standards for the selection and editing of documents for the series were first promulgated by Secretary of State Frank B. Kellogg on March 26, 1925. These regulations, with minor modifications, guided the series through 1991.

A new statutory charter for the preparation of the series was established by Public Law 102–138, the Foreign Relations Authorization Act, Fiscal Years 1992 and 1993, which was signed by President George Bush on October 28, 1991. Section 198 of P.L. 102–138 added a new Title IV to the Department of State's Basic Authorities Act of 1956 (22 USC 4351, *et seq.*).

The statute requires that the *Foreign Relations* series be a thorough, accurate, and reliable record of major United States foreign policy decisions and significant United States diplomatic activity. The volumes of the series should include all records needed to provide comprehensive documentation of major foreign policy decisions and actions of the United States Government. The statute also confirms the editing principles established by Secretary Kellogg: the *Foreign Relations* series is guided by the principles of historical objectivity and accuracy; records should not be altered or deletions made without indicating in the published text that a deletion has been made; the published record should omit no facts that were of major importance in reaching a decision; and nothing should be omitted for the purposes of concealing a defect in policy. The statute also requires that the *Foreign Relations* series be published not more than 30 years after the events recorded. The editor is convinced that this volume, which was compiled in 1995–1996, meets all regulatory, statutory, and scholarly standards of selection and editing.

Structure and Scope of the Foreign Relations Series

This volume is part of a subseries of volumes of the *Foreign Relations* series that documents the most important issues in the foreign policy of the 5 years (1964–1968) of the administration of Lyndon B. Johnson. The subseries presents in 34 volumes a documentary record of major foreign policy decisions and actions of President Johnson's administration. This volume documents U.S. policy toward Iran.

Principles of Document Selection for the Foreign Relations Series

In preparing each volume of the *Foreign Relations* series, the editors are guided by some general principles for the selection of documents. Each editor, in consultation with the General Editor and other senior editors, determines the particular issues and topics to be documented either in detail, in brief, or in summary.

The following general selection criteria are used in preparing volumes in the *Foreign Relations* series. Individual compiler-editors vary these criteria in accordance with the particular issues and the available documentation. The editors also apply these selection criteria in accordance with their own interpretation of the generally accepted standards of scholarship. In selecting documentation for publication, the editors gave priority to unpublished classified records, rather than previously published records (which are accounted for in appropriate bibliographical notes).

Selection Criteria (in general order of priority):

1. Major foreign affairs commitments made on behalf of the United States to other governments, including those that define or identify the principal foreign affairs interests of the United States;

2. Major foreign affairs issues, commitments, negotiations, and activities, whether or not major decisions were made, and including dissenting or alternative opinions to the process ultimately adopted;

3. The decisions, discussions, actions, and considerations of the President, as the official constitutionally responsible for the direction of foreign policy;

4. The discussions and actions of the National Security Council, the Cabinet, and special Presidential policy groups, including the policy options brought before these bodies or their individual members;

5. The policy options adopted by or considered by the Secretary of State and the most important actions taken to implement Presidential decisions or policies;

6. Diplomatic negotiations and conferences, official correspondence, and other exchanges between U.S. representatives and those of other governments that demonstrate the main lines of policy implementation on major issues;

7. Important elements of information that attended Presidential decisions and policy recommendations of the Secretary of State;

8. Major foreign affairs decisions, negotiations, and commitments undertaken on behalf of the United States by government officials and representatives in other agencies in the foreign affairs community or other branches of government made without the involvement (or even knowledge) of the White House or the Department of State;

9. The main policy lines of intelligence activities if they constituted major aspects of U.S. foreign policy toward a nation or region or if they provided key information in the formulation of major U.S. policies, including relevant National Intelligence Estimates and Special National Intelligence Estimates as may be declassified;

10. The role of the Congress in the preparation and execution of particular foreign policies or foreign affairs actions;

11. Economic aspects of foreign policy;

12. The main policy lines of U.S. military and economic assistance as well as other types of assistance;

13. The political-military recommendations, decisions, and activities of the military establishment and major regional military commands as they bear upon the formulation or execution of major U.S. foreign policies;

14. Diplomatic appointments that reflect major policies or affect policy changes.

Sources for the Foreign Relations Series

The *Foreign Relations* statute requires that the published record in the *Foreign Relations* series include all records needed to provide comprehensive documentation on major U.S. foreign policy decisions and significant U.S. diplomatic activity. It further requires that government agencies, departments, and other entities of the U.S. Government engaged in foreign policy formulation, execution, or support cooperate with the Department of State Historian by providing full and complete access to records pertinent to foreign policy decisions and actions and by providing copies of selected records. Many of the sources consulted in the preparation of this volume have been declassified and are available for review at the National Archives and Records Administration. The Department of State and other record sources used in the volume are described in detail in the section on Sources below.

Focus of Research and Principles of Selection for Foreign Relations, 1964–1968,
   Volume XXII

The editor of the volume sought to include documentation illumi-
nating the foreign policymaking process of the U.S. Government, with
emphasis on the highest level at which policy on a particular subject was
determined. The documents include memoranda and records of discussions that set forth policy issues and show decisions or actions taken. The
emphasis is on the development of U.S. policy and on major aspects and
repercussions of its execution rather than on the details of policy execution.

Lyndon Johnson made the major foreign policy decisions during his
presidency, and the editor sought to document his role as far as possible.
Although the foreign policy record of the Johnson administration is vo-
luminous, many internal discussions between Johnson and his advisers
were not recorded. The record of Johnson's involvement as well as that of
Secretary of State Rusk in the policy process often had to be pieced together from a variety of sources.

The volume focuses on the issues that primarily engaged high-level
U.S. policymakers. Major topics include: 1) the efforts of President Johnson and U.S. policymakers to retain a close relationship with the Shah of
Iran; 2) U.S. attempts to buttress Iran's internal security by encouraging a
far-reaching program of political, social, and economic reform; 3) the
conflict between U.S. support for Iranian economic development and reform as a check against internal upheaval or revolution and the Shah's
insistence on spending more of Iran's growing oil revenues on weapons;
4) increased U.S. support for Iran's military modernization program; 5)
the upsurge of anti-Americanism and opposition to the Shah's government following the October 1964 passage of a status of forces bill granting U.S. military personnel stationed in Iran and their dependents full
diplomatic immunity; 6) U.S. efforts to prevent the Shah from buying
arms from non-U.S. sources, especially the Soviet Union; and 7) U.S. determination to prevent the Soviet Union from gaining a foothold in Iran.

The editor included a selection of intelligence estimates and analyses seen by high-level policymakers, especially those that were sent to
President Johnson.

Editorial Methodology

The documents are presented chronologically according to Washington time or, in the case of conferences, in the order of individual meetings. Memoranda of conversation are placed according to the time and
date of the conversation, rather than the date the memorandum was
drafted.

Editorial treatment of the documents published in the *Foreign Relations* series follows Office style guidelines, supplemented by guidance

from the General Editor and the chief technical editor. The source text is reproduced as exactly as possible, including marginalia or other notations, which are described in the footnotes. Texts are transcribed and printed according to accepted conventions for the publication of historical documents in the limitations of modern typography. A heading has been supplied by the editor for each document included in the volume. Spelling, capitalization, and punctuation are retained as found in the source text, except that obvious typographical errors are silently corrected. Other mistakes and omissions in the source text are corrected by bracketed insertions: a correction is set in italic type; an addition in roman type. Words or phrases underlined in the source text are printed in italics. Abbreviations and contractions are preserved as found in the source text, and a list of abbreviations is included in the front matter of each volume.

Bracketed insertions are also used to indicate omitted text that deals with an unrelated subject (in roman type) or that remains classified after declassification review (in italic type). The amount of material not declassified has been noted by indicating the number of lines or pages of source text that were omitted. Entire documents withheld for declassification purposes have been accounted for and are listed by headings, source notes, and number of pages not declassified in their chronological place. The amount of material omitted from this volume because it was unrelated to the subject of the volume, however, has not been delineated. All brackets that appear in the source text are so identified by footnotes.

The first footnote to each document indicates the document's source, original classification, distribution, and drafting information. This note also provides the background of important documents and policies and indicates whether the President or his major policy advisers read the document. Every effort has been made to determine if a document has been previously published, and, if so, this information has been included in the source footnote.

Editorial notes and additional annotation summarize pertinent material not printed in the volume, indicate the location of additional documentary sources, provide references to important related documents printed in other volumes, describe key events, and provide summaries of and citations to public statements that supplement and elucidate the printed documents. Information derived from memoirs and other firsthand accounts has been used when appropriate to supplement or explicate the official record.

Advisory Committee on Historical Diplomatic Documentation

The Advisory Committee on Historical Diplomatic Documentation, established under the *Foreign Relations* statute, reviews records, advises, and makes recommendations concerning the *Foreign Relations* series. The Advisory Committee monitors the overall compilation and editorial process of the series and advises on all aspects of the preparation and de-classification of the series. Although the Advisory Committee does not attempt to review the contents of individual volumes in the series, it does monitor the overall process and makes recommendations on particular problems that come to its attention.

The Advisory Committee has not reviewed this volume but has considered particular declassification issues.

Declassification Review

The Information Response Branch of the Office of IRM Programs and Services, Bureau of Administration, Department of State, conducted the declassification review of the documents published in this volume. The review was conducted in accordance with the standards set forth in Executive Order 12958 on Classified National Security Information and applicable laws.

Under Executive Order 12958, specific information may be exempt from automatic declassification after 25 years if its release could be expected to:

1) reveal the identity of a confidential human source, or reveal information about the application of an intelligence source or method, or reveal the identity of a human intelligence source when the unauthorized disclosure of that source would clearly and demonstrably damage the national security interests of the United States;
2) reveal information that would assist in the development or use of weapons of mass destruction;
3) reveal information that would impair U.S. cryptologic systems or activities;
4) reveal information that would impair the application of state of the art technology within the U.S. weapon system;
5) reveal actual U.S. military war plans that remain in effect;
6) reveal information that would seriously and demonstrably impair relations between the United States and a foreign government, or seriously and demonstrably undermine ongoing diplomatic activities of the United States;
7) reveal information that would clearly and demonstrably impair the current ability of U.S. Government officials to protect the President, Vice President, and other officials for whom protection services, in the interest of national security, are authorized;
8) reveal information that would seriously and demonstrably impair current national security emergency preparedness plans; or
9) violate a statute, treaty, or international agreement.

The principle guiding declassification review is to release all information, subject only to the current requirements of national security as embodied in law and regulation. Declassification decisions entailed concurrence of the appropriate geographic and functional bureaus in the Department of State, other concerned agencies of the U.S. Government, and the appropriate foreign governments regarding specific documents of those governments.

The declassification review of this volume, which was completed in 1998, resulted in decisions to withhold from publication .2 percent of the documentation selected. No documents were denied in full. The decision on one key intelligence issue was appealed to a High-Level Panel consisting of senior representatives from the Department of State, the National Security Council, and the Central Intelligence Agency, established in 1998 to determine whether or not a covert activity could be acknowledged by the United States. The Panel arrived at a determination on Iran that resulted in the release of most of the appealed documentation. The Office of the Historian is confident, on the basis of the research conducted in preparing this volume and as a result of the declassification review process described above, that the documentation presented here provides an accurate account of U.S. policy toward Iran during the 1964–1968 period.

Acknowledgements

The editor wishes to acknowledge the assistance of officials at the Lyndon B. Johnson Library of the National Archives and Records Administration, especially Regina Greenwell and Charlaine Burgess, who provided key research assistance. The editor also wishes to acknowledge the assistance of historians at the Central Intelligence Agency, particularly Scott Koch.

Nina D. Howland collected documentation, selected and edited this volume, under the general supervision of Harriet D. Schwar. Gabrielle Mallon prepared the lists of names, sources, and abbreviations. Vicki E. Futscher and Rita M. Baker did the copy and technical editing. Juniee Oneida prepared the index.

William Slany
The Historian
Bureau of Public Affairs

July 1999

Johnson Administration Volumes

Following is a list of the volumes in the *Foreign Relations* series for the administration of President Lyndon B. Johnson. The titles of individual volumes may change. The year of publication is in parentheses after the title.

Print Volumes

Contents

Sources

The editors of the *Foreign Relations* series have complete access to all the retired records and papers of the Department of State: the central files of the Department; the special decentralized files ("lot files") of the Department at the bureau, office, and division levels; the files of the Department's Executive Secretariat, which contain the records of international conferences and high-level official visits, correspondence with foreign leaders by the President and Secretary of State, and memoranda of conversations between the President and Secretary of State and foreign officials; and the files of overseas diplomatic posts. When this volume was being compiled, the Department of State records consulted were still under the custody of the Department, and the footnotes citing Department of State files suggest that the Department is the repository. By the time of publication, however, all the Department's indexed central files for these years had been permanently transferred to the National Archives and Records Administration (Archives II) at College Park, Maryland. Many of the Department's decentralized office (or lot) files covering this period, which the National Archives deems worthy of permanent retention, are in the process of being transferred from the Department's custody to Archives II.

The editors of the *Foreign Relations* series also have full access to the papers of President Johnson and other White House foreign policy records. Presidential papers maintained and preserved at the Presidential libraries include some of the most significant foreign affairs-related documentation from the Department of State and other Federal agencies including the National Security Council, the Central Intelligence Agency, the Department of Defense, and the Joint Chiefs of Staff.

In preparing this volume, the editor made extensive use of Presidential papers and other White House records at the Lyndon B. Johnson Library. Numerous White House memoranda, including memoranda to the President, testify to President Johnson's concern with issues relating to Iran, especially the maintenance of personal ties with the Shah. The bulk of the foreign policy records at the Johnson Library are in the country files and other component parts of the National Security File.

The Department of State arranged for access to the many audiotapes of President Johnson's telephone conversations that are held at the Johnson Library. These audiotapes include substantial numbers of telephone conversations between President Johnson and Secretary of State Rusk, Secretary of Defense McNamara, the President's Special Assistant for National Security Affairs McGeorge Bundy, and key members of Congress. The editor of this volume selected for publication one audiotape of a President Johnson telephone conversation dealing with Iran. A transcript was then prepared. Although the transcript gives the substance of the conversation, readers are urged to consult the recording for a full appreciation of those dimensions that cannot be captured fully in a transcription, such as the speakers' inflections and emphases that may convey nuances of meaning.

Second in importance only to the White House records at the Johnson Library were the records of the Department of State. The Department's central files contain the cable traffic recording U.S. diplomatic relations with Iran, memoranda of diplomatic conversations, and memoranda proposing action or providing information. Some important documents are found only in the Department's lot files. The Conference Files maintained by the Executive Secretariat contain briefing materials as well as records of conversations. Documentation on initiatives that were not approved is often found only in desk or bureau files. The Rusk Files contain records of Secretary Rusk's telephone conversations.

The Central Intelligence Agency provides access to Department of State historians to high-level intelligence documents from those records in the custody of that Agency and at the Presidential libraries. This access is arranged and facilitated by the History Staff of the Center for the Study of Intelligence, Central Intelligence Agency, pursuant to a May 1992 memorandum of understanding. Department of State and CIA historians continue to work out the procedural and scholarly aspects of identifying the key portions of the intelligence record. This volume includes a limited number of intelligence records. Among the intelligence records reviewed for the volume were files of the Directors of Central Intelligence, especially Richard Helms, CIA intelligence reports and summaries, and the CIA Registry of National Intelligence Estimates and Special National Intelligence Estimates.

Almost all of this documentation has been made available for use in the *Foreign Relations* series thanks to the consent of the agencies mentioned, the assistance of their staffs, and especially the cooperation and support of the National Archives and Records Administration.

The following list identifies the particular files and collections used in the preparation of this volume. The declassification and transfer to the National Archives of these records is in process. Many of the records are already available for public review at the National Archives. The declassification review of other records is going forward in accordance with the provisions of Executive Order 12958, under which all records over 25 years old, except file series exemptions requested by agencies and approved by the President, should be reviewed for declassification by 2000.

Unpublished Sources

Department of State

Central Files. During 1964–1968 the Department's central files were filed according to a subject-numeric system. The records were divided into broad categories: Administration, Consular, Culture and Information, Economic, Political and Defense, Science, and Social. Within each of these divisions were subcategories. For example, Political and Defense contained four subtopics: CSM (communism), DEF (Defense), INT (intelligence), and POL (politics). The subcategories were divided into numerical subdivisions or, in many cases, country files, with numerical subdivisions. The POL series began with files with numerical subdivisions on international issues, such as issues relating to international rivers, and continued with country files. These files have been transferred to the National Archives and Records Administration at College Park Maryland, Record Group 59.

AID 6 IRAN: Communist bloc aid, Iran
AID (US) IRAN: general policy, U.S. aid to Iran
BG 6 TEHRAN: buildings and grounds acquisition, Tehran
DEF 1 IRAN: defense policy, Iran
DEF 1–4 IRAN: air defense, Iran
DEF 1–5 IRAN: alert measures, Iran
DEF 6 IRAN: armed forces, Iran
DEF 12–5 IRAN: procurement and sale of armaments, Iran
DEF 15 IRAN–US: bases and installations, Iran–U.S.
DEF 15–3 IRAN–US: status of forces, Iran–U.S.
DEF 12–5 US–IRAN: procurement and sale of armaments, U.S.–Iran
DEF 19 US–IRAN: military assistance, U.S. –Iran
DEF 19–3 US–IRAN: defense organizations and conferences, U.S.–Iran
DEF 19–8 US–IRAN: defense equipment and supplies, U.S. –Iran
DEF 19–9 US–IRAN: advisory and training assistance, U.S. –Iran
DEF 19–6 USSR–IRAN: U.S.S.R. military assistance to Iran
E 2–2 IRAN: economic review, Iran
E 8 IRAN: economic conditions, Iran
E 12 IRAN: land use, land reform, Iran
EDU 9–3 IRAN: educational system, institutions, college and university, Iran
EDX 12 IRAN: educational cultural exchange, youth programs, Iran
FN 16 IRAN: revenue, taxation, Iran
ORG 7 S: organization and administration, Secretary's visits
PET 2 IRAN: petroleum general reports and statistics, Iran
PET 6 IRAN: petroleum companies, Iran
PET 17 USSR–IRAN: petroleum trade, USSR–Iran
POL 33 PERSIAN GULF: waters, boundaries, Persian Gulf
POL ARAB–IRAN: political affairs and relations, Arabs–Iran
POL ARAB–ISR: political affairs and relations, Arabs–Israel
POL 27 ARAB–ISR: military operations, Arabs–Israel
POL IRAN: political affairs and relations, Iran
POL 2 IRAN: general reports and statistics, Iran
POL 2–3 IRAN: politico-economic reports, Iran
POL 7 IRAN: visits, meetings with Iranian leaders
POL 12 IRAN: political parties, Iran
POL 13–2 IRAN: students, youth groups, Iran
POL 15–1 IRAN: Iranian Head of State
POL 23–1 IRAN: internal security, counter-insurgency, plans and programs, Iran

POL 23–9 IRAN: rebellion, coups, Iran
POL 30 IRAN: defectors and expellees, Iran
POL IRAN–SAUD: political affairs and relations, Iran–Saudi Arabia
POL IRAN–US: political affairs and relations, Iran–U.S.
POL 17 IRAN–US: diplomatic and consular representation, Iran–U.S.
POL 1 US: general policy and background, U.S.
POL 7 US/HARRIMAN: visits, meetings of W. Averell Harriman
POL 7 US/McCLOY: visits, meetings of John J. McCloy
POL 15–1 US/JOHNSON: Head of State, Executive Branch, President Lyndon B. Johnson
POL 15–1 US/NIXON: Head of State, Executive Branch, President-elect Richard M. Nixon
POL 7 USSR: visits, meetings with Soviet leaders
POL 27 VIET S: military operations, South Vietnam
SOC 13 IRAN: social conditions, population, Iran
UN 6 CHICOM: question of Chinese representation in the United Nations

Lot Files. These files have been transferred or will be transferred to the National Archives and Records Administration at College Park Maryland, Record Group 59.

Conference Files: Lot 66 D 110

> Records of official visits by heads of government and foreign ministers to the United States and international conferences attended by the President, the Secretary of State, and other U.S. officials, 1961–1964, as maintained by the Executive Secretariat of the Department of State.

Conference Files: Lot 68 D 453

> International Conference chronologies, May 10, 1967, through December 29–January 11, 1968, as maintained by the Executive Secretariat of the Department of State.

Conference Files: Lot 70 D 418

> Official visit chronologies, January 1968 through December 1969, as maintained by the Executive Secretariat of the Department of State.

NEA/IRN Files: Lot 69 D 30

> Iran Subject Files for 1964, as maintained by the Office of Greek, Turkish, and Iranian Affairs, Bureau of Near Eastern and South Asian Affairs.

NEA/IRN Files: Lot 69 D 95

> Iran Subject Files for 1964, as maintained by the Office of Greek, Turkish, and Iranian Affairs, Bureau of Near Eastern and South Asian Affairs.

NEA/IRN Files: Lot 69 D 178

> Iran Subject Files for 1964, as maintained by the Office of Greek, Turkish, and Iranian Affairs, Bureau of Near Eastern and South Asian Affairs.

NEA/IRN Files: Lot 69 D 426

> Iran Subject Files for 1965, as maintained by the Office of Greek, Turkish, and Iranian Affairs, Bureau of Near Eastern and South Asian Affairs.

NEA/IRN Files: Lot 69 D 484

> Iran Subject Files for 1965, as maintained by the Office of Greek, Turkish, and Iranian Affairs, Bureau of Near Eastern and South Asian Affairs.

NEA/IRN Files: Lot 69 D 489

> Iran Subject Files for 1965, as maintained by the Office of Greek, Turkish, and Iranian Affairs, Bureau of Near Eastern and South Asian Affairs.

NEA/IRN Files: Lot 69 D 490

> Iran Subject Files for 1965, as maintained by the Office of Greek, Turkish, and Iranian Affairs, Bureau of Near Eastern and South Asian Affairs.

NEA/IRN Files: Lot 69 D 513

> Iran Subject Files for 1964 and 1966, as maintained by the Office of Greek, Turkish, and Iranian Affairs, Bureau of Near Eastern and South Asian Affairs.

NEA/IRN Files: Lot 70 D 330

> Iran Subject Files for 1966, as maintained by the Office of Greek, Turkish, and Iranian Affairs, Bureau of Near Eastern and South Asian Affairs.

NEA/IRN Files: Lot 70 D 552

> Iran Subject Files for 1965, 1966, and 1967, as maintained by the Office of Greek, Turkish, and Iranian Affairs (after July 1, 1966, Country Director for Iran), Bureau of Near Eastern and South Asian Affairs.

Rusk Files: Lot 72 D 192

> Files of Secretary of State Dean Rusk, 1961–1969, including texts of speeches and public statements, miscellaneous correspondence files, White House correspondence, chronological files, and memoranda of telephone conversations.

S/P Files: Lot 72 D 139

> S/P and S/PC Country Files; W. Rostow and H. Owen memoranda.

S/S Files: Lot 68 D 475

> Official State visit chronologies of foreign heads of state and government and ranking foreign officials June–November 1967, as maintained by the Executive Secretariat of the Department of State.

Central Intelligence Agency

Job 78–03805R, U.S. Government, Special Group, CI, and 303

Job 79–R01012A, ODDI Registry of NIE and SNIE

Job 79–T00430A, Current Intelligence Memoranda

Job 79–T00472A, OCI Intelligence Memoranda

Job 80–00105A, Iran

Job 80–B01285A, DCI Files, DCI Helms Chrons

Job 80–R01580R, DCI Files

Library of Congress, Manuscript Division

Harriman Papers
> Special Files; Public Service, Kennedy–Johnson Administrations, 1958–1971.

Washington National Records Center, Suitland, Maryland

Record Group 330, Records of the Office of the Secretary of Defense

OASD/ISA Files: FRC 68 A 306

> Secret and lower-classified general files of the Assistant Secretary of Defense for International Security Affairs, 1964.

OASD/ISA Files: FRC 70 A 6648

Secret files of the Secretary of Defense, Deputy Assistant Secretary of Defense, and Special Assistants, 1966.

OASD/ISA Files: FRC 72 A 1498

Secret files of the Assistant Secretary of Defense for International Security Affairs, 1968.

OSD Files: FRC 70 A 4443

Secret files of the Secretary of Defense, Deputy Assistant Secretary of Defense, and Special Assistants, 1966.

OSD Files: FRC 72 A 2468

Secret files of the Secretary of Defense, Deputy Assistant Secretary of Defense, and Special Assistants, 1967.

OSD Files: FRC 73 A 1250

Secret files of the Secretary of Defense, Deputy Assistant Secretary of Defense, and Special Assistants, 1968.

Lyndon B. Johnson Library, Austin, Texas

Papers of President Lyndon B. Johnson

National Security File

Country File, Iran

Agency File, Department of State

Special Head of State Correspondence File

Files of the Special Committee of the NSC

Memos to the President, McGeorge Bundy, Walt W. Rostow

Files of Robert W. Komer

Files of Walt W. Rostow

W. Howard Wriggins Memos

NSC Files of Harold H. Saunders

White House Central Files

President's Daily Diary

Papers of Robert W. Komer

Transcripts of Telephone Conversations, Alpha Series, Mohammed Reza Pahlavi

Published Sources

U.S. Department of State. *American Foreign Policy: Current Documents, 1961–1967.* Washington, D.C.: U.S. Government Printing Office, 1965–1969.

U.S. National Archives and Records Administration. *Public Papers of the Presidents of the United States: Lyndon B. Johnson.* 5 vols. Washington, D.C.: U.S. Government Printing Office, 1965–1969.

Abbreviations

AC&W, aircraft control and warning
AFP, Agence France Presse
AID, Agency for International Development
AID/W, Agency for International Development Headquarters in Washington
Amb, Ambassador
APC, armored personnel carrier
APQ, Annual Programmed Quantity
ARAMCO, Arabian-American Oil Company
ARMISH/MAAG, U.S. Army Mission in Iran/Military Assistance Advisory Group
Atty, attorney

BAR, Browning Automatic Rifle
BG, Brigadier General
BOB, Bureau of the Budget
BPD, barrels per day

CAS, Controlled American Source
CENTO, Central Treaty Organization
CEP, circular error probable
CFP, Compagnie Francaise des Petroles
ChiCom, Chinese Communist
CI, Counter Insurgency
CIA, Central Intelligence Agency
CIC, Counter Intelligence Corps
CINCMEAFSA, Commander in Chief, Middle East/South Asia and Africa South of the Sahara
CINCSTRIKE, Commander in Chief, Strike Command
CONUS, Continental United States
CT, Country Team
CY, calendar year

DASD, Deputy Assistant Secretary of Defense
DCI, Director of Central Intelligence
DELAWAR, U.S.-Iran military, naval, and air force training exercise carried out under CENTO April 4–11, 1964
DepSec, Deputy Secretary
Dept, Department of State
Deptel, Department of State telegram
DIA, Defense Intelligence Agency
DOD, Department of Defense
DOD/ISA, Department of Defense, International Security Affairs
DOD/ISA/NESA, Department of Defense, International Security Affairs, Office of Near Eastern and South Asian Affairs

ELINT, electronic intelligence
Embtel, Embassy telegram
ERAP, Entreprise de Recherches et d'Activites Petrolieres
EUR/SOV, Office of Soviet Union Affairs, Bureau of European Affairs, Department of State
Exdis, executive distribution
EXIM, Export-Import Bank

FAA, Federation of Arab Amirates
FBI, Federal Bureau of Investigation
FMS, foreign military sales
FonMin, Foreign Minister
FRC, Federal Records Center
FRG, Federal Republic of Germany
FY, fiscal year
FYI, for your information

GNP, gross national product
GOI, Government of Iran
G/PM, Deputy Assistant Secretary of State for Politico-Military Affairs

HIM, His Imperial Majesty

IAF, Iranian Air Force
IBRD, International Bank for Reconstruction and Development (World Bank)
IDP, Internal Defense Plan (Iran)
IFC, International Finance Corporation
IIAF, Imperial Iranian Air Force
IIF, Imperial Iranian Forces
IIG, Imperial Iranian Gendarmerie
IMF, International Monetary Fund
INR, Bureau of Intelligence and Research, Department of State
INR/RNA, Office of Research and Analysis for Near East and South Asia, Bureau of Intelligence and Research, Department of State
IO, Bureau of International Organization, Department of State
IRG, Interdepartmental Regional Group
ISA, Iranian Students Association

JCS, Joint Chiefs of Staff
JCSM, Joint Chiefs of Staff Memorandum
JFK, John F. Kennedy

Komar, Soviet missile-carrying PT boats

LBJ, Lyndon B. Johnson
Limdis, limited distribution
LMG, light machine gun
L/NEA, Assistant Legal Adviser for Near Eastern and South Asian Affairs, Department of State

MAAG, Military Assistance Advisory Group
MAP, Military Assistance Program
ME, Middle East
memcon, memorandum of conversation
MRP, Mohammed Reza Pahlavi

NATO, North Atlantic Treaty Organization
NATUS, series indicator for communications from the Department of State to the U.S. Mission to the North Atlantic Treaty Organization
NEA, Bureau of Near Eastern and South Asian Affairs, Department of State
NEA/GTI, Office of Greek, Turkish, and Iran Affairs, Bureau of Near Eastern and South Asian Affairs, Department of State

NEA/IRN, Office of the Country Director for Iran, Bureau of Near Eastern and South Asian Affairs, Department of State

NEA/NE, Office of Near Eastern Affairs, Bureau of Near Eastern and South Asian Affairs, Department of State

NEA/NR, Office of Near Eastern, South Asian Regional Affairs, Bureau of Near Eastern and South Asian Affairs, Department of State

NIE, National Intelligence Estimate

NIMCOM, National Military Communications Systems

NIOC, National Iranian Oil Company

Nodis, no distribution

Noforn, no foreign dissemination

NPT, Nuclear Nonproliferation Treaty

NRM, National Resistance Movement (Kurdish)

NSA, National Security Agency

NSAM, National Security Action Memorandum

NSC, National Security Council

NYHT, *New York Herald Tribune*

NYU, New York University

OASD/ISA, Office of the Assistant Secretary of Defense for International Security Affairs

OBE, overtaken by events

OCI, Office of Current Intelligence, Central Intelligence Agency

ODDI, Office of the Directorate of Intelligence, Central Intelligence Agency

OPEC, Organization of Petroleum Exporting Countries

OSD, Office of the Secretary of Defense

Pak, Pakistan; Pakistani

PanAm, Pan American Airlines

PGM, motor gunboat

PIW, *Petroleum Intelligence Weekly*

PL, Public Law

PM, Prime Minister

POLAD, Political Adviser

PTT, Postes, Telegraphes, Telephones

RCAP, Royal Canadian Air Force

RCD, Regional Cooperation for Development (formed among the regional members of CENTO—Iran, Turkey, and Pakistan—1964)

R & D, research and development

reftel, reference telegram

Rep, representative

S/AH, Office of the Ambassador at Large

SAM, surface-to-air missiles

SAMAA, Special Assistant for Military Assistance Affairs, Joint Chiefs of Staff

SAVAK, Iranian Intelligence and Security Organization (Sazman-i Ittili'at va Amniyat-i Kishvar)

SC, Security Council (UN)

SCS, Supreme Commander's Staff

SEATO, Southeast Asia Treaty Organization

SecDef, Secretary of Defense

Secto, series indicator for telegrams from the Secretary of State (or his delegation) at international conferences to the Department of State

SNIE, Special National Intelligence Estimate

Sov, Soviet(s)
STRATCOM Strategic Command
STRICOM, Strike Command

TIAS, Treaties and International Acts Series
Topol, series indicator for telegrams to the U.S. Mission in Paris, NATO, and USRO
TUPAIR, economic and cultural cooperation among Turkey, Pakistan, and Iran

UAR, United Arab Republic
UCLA, University of California at Los Angeles
UK, United Kingdom
UN, United Nations
UNEF, United Nations Emergency Force
UNSC, United Nations Security Council
UNSYG, United Nations Secretary-General
UPT, undergraduate pilot training
USAF, United States Air Force
USG, United States Government
USIA, United States Information Agency
USIB, United States Intelligence Board
USSR, Union of Soviet Socialist Republics
UST, United States Treaties and Other International Agreements
USUN, United States Mission to the United Nations

VIP, very important person

Persons

Adams, General Paul D., USA, Commander in Chief, Strike Command (CINCSTRIKE), until November 1966; also Commander in Chief, Middle East/South Asia and Africa South of the Sahara (CINCMEAFSA), until November 1966

Alam, Amir Asadullah, Minister of the Court of the Shah of Iran from 1967

Ansary, Hushang, Iranian Ambassador to the United States from May 1967

Aram, Abbas, Foreign Minister of Iran until March 1967

Ball, George W., Under Secretary of State until September 1966; Representative to the United Nations June 1968–September 1968

Battle, Lucius D., Assistant Secretary of State for Educational and Cultural Affairs until August 1964; Ambassador to the United Arab Republic from September 1964 until March 1967; Assistant Secretary of State for Near Eastern and South Asian Affairs April 1967–September 1968

Bell, David E., Administrator of the Agency for International Development until June 1966

Bowling, John W., Deputy Director, Office of Greek, Turkish, and Iranian Affairs, Bureau of Near Eastern and South Asian Affairs, Department of State, until August 1964

Bracken, Katherine W., Director, Office of Greek, Turkish, and Iranian Affairs, Bureau of Near Eastern and South Asian Affairs, Department of State, until June 1966

Bundy, McGeorge, Special Assistant to the President for National Security Affairs until February 1966

Cameron, Turner C., Director, Office of South Asian Affairs, Bureau of Near Eastern and South Asian Affairs, Department of State, until July 1965

Clifford, Clark M., Secretary of Defense from March 1968

Conway, General Theodore J., USA, Commander in Chief, Strike Command (CINCSTRIKE), from November 1966

Crawford, Franklin J., Officer in Charge of Iranian Affairs, Bureau of Near Eastern and South Asian Affairs, Department of State, August 1965–August 1966

Davies, Rodger P., Director, Office of Near Eastern Affairs, Bureau of Near Eastern and South Asian Affairs, Department of State, until October 1965; thereafter, Deputy Assistant Secretary of State for Near Eastern and South Asian Affairs

Duke, Angier Biddle, Chief of Protocol, Department of State, until December 1964

Ebtehaj, Abol Hassan, Iranian banker and administrator; Managing Director, Plan Organization

Eckhardt, Major General George S., USA, Chief, ARMISH/MAAG, Tehran, June 1964–April 1965

Eliot, Theodore L., Jr., Country Director for Iran, Bureau of Near Eastern and South Asian Affairs, Department of State, from July 1966

Foroughi, Mahmoud, Iranian Ambassador to the United States until 1967

Foster, John W., member of the National Security Council Staff

Fowler, Henry H., Deputy Secretary of the Treasury until April 1965; thereafter Secretary of the Treasury

Freeman, Orville L., Secretary of Agriculture

Fulbright, J.W., Democratic Senator from Arkansas; Chairman of the Senate Foreign Relations Committee

Gaud, William S., Assistant Administrator, Bureau for Near East and South Asia, Agency for International Development, until February 1964; Deputy Administrator February 1964–August 1966; thereafter, Administrator

Grant, James P., Deputy Assistant Secretary of State for Near Eastern and South Asian Affairs until September 1964

Handley, William J., Deputy Assistant Secretary of State for Near Eastern and South Asian Affairs from September 1964

Hare, Raymond A., Assistant Secretary of State for Near Eastern and South Asian Affairs September 1965–November 1966

Harriman, W. Averell, Under Secretary of State for Political Affairs until March 1965; thereafter, Ambassador at Large

Hart, Parker T., Ambassador to Saudi Arabia until May 1965; Ambassador to Turkey October 1965–October 1968; thereafter, Assistant Secretary of State for Near Eastern and South Asian Affairs

Helms, Richard M., Deputy Director of Central Intelligence April 1965–June 1966; thereafter, Director

Holmes, Julius C., Ambassador to Iran until March 1965

Hoopes, Townsend W., Deputy Assistant Secretary of Defense for International Security Affairs 1965–1968

Hoveyda, Amir Abbas, Iranian Minister of Finance March 1964–January 1965; thereafter, Prime Minister

Hughes, Thomas L., Director of the Bureau of Intelligence and Research, Department of State

Humphrey, Hubert H., Vice President of the United States

Jablonsky, Major General Harvey J., USA, Chief, ARMISH/MAAG, Tehran, August 1965–July 1968

Jernegan, John D., Deputy Assistant Secretary of State for Near Eastern and South Asian Affairs until July 1965

Johnson, Lyndon B., President of the United States

Johnson, U. Alexis, Deputy Under Secretary of State for Political Affairs until July 1964; Deputy Ambassador to Vietnam July 1964–September 1965; Deputy Under Secretary of State for Political Affairs November 1965–October 1966, thereafter, Ambassador to Japan

Katzenbach, Nicholas deB., Deputy Attorney General until February 1965; Attorney General February 1965–October 1966; thereafter, Under Secretary of State

Khomeini, Ayatollah Ruhollah, dissident Iranian religious leader

Khosrovani, Khasro, Iranian Ambassador to the United States from 1967

Kitchen, Jeffrey C., Deputy Assistant Secretary of State for Politico-Military Affairs until February 1967

Komer, Robert W., member of the National Security Council Staff until September 1965; Deputy Special Assistant to the President for National Security Affairs October 1965–March 1966; Special Assistant to the President March 1966–May 1967

Kuss, Henry J., Jr., Deputy Assistant Secretary of Defense for International Logistics Negotiations from March 1965

McClellan, John L. Democratic Senator from Arkansas

McNamara, Robert S., Secretary of Defense until February 1968; thereafter, President of the International Bank for Reconstruction and Development (World Bank)

McNaughton, John T., Assistant Secretary of Defense for International Security Affairs July 1964–July 1967

Macomber, William B., Assistant Administrator for Near East and South Asia, Agency for International Development, February 1964–March 1967; thereafter, Assistant Secretary of State for Congressional Relations

Macy, Robert M., Director, USAID Mission, Tehran

Mansur, Hasan Ali, Prime Minister of Iran from March 1964 until his death in January 1965

Meyer, Armin H., Ambassador to Iran from April 1965

Moyers, Bill D., Special Assistant to the President and Chief of Staff at the White House, October 1964–January 1967; also White House Press Secretary July 1965–January 1967

Newberry, Daniel O., Officer in Charge of CENTO Affairs, Office of Near Eastern and South Asian Regional Affairs, Bureau of Near Eastern and South Asian Affairs, Department of State, October 1964–August 1965; Officer in Charge of Multilateral Organization Affairs August 1965–July 1966; Iranian Desk Officer July 1966–June 1967

Nitze, Paul H., Secretary of the Navy until June 1967; Deputy Secretary of Defense from July 1967

Pahlavi, Mohammed Reza, Shah of Iran

Raborn, Vice Admiral William F., Jr., USN (Ret.), Director of Central Intelligence April 1965–June 1966

Read, Benjamin H., Special Assistant to the Secretary of State and Executive Secretary of the Department

Rockwell, Stuart W., Minister-Counselor at the Embassy in Iran until August 1966; thereafter, Deputy Assistant Secretary of State for Near Eastern and South Asian Affairs

Rostow, Eugene V., Under Secretary of State for Political Affairs from October 1966

Rostow, Walt W., Counselor of the Department of State and Chairman of the Policy Planning Council until March 1966; Special Assistant to the President from April 1, 1966

Rusk, Dean, Secretary of State

Samii, Mohammed Mehdi, Governor of the Central Bank of Iran until 1968; thereafter, Managing Director, Plan Organization of Iran

Saunders, Harold H., member of the National Security Council Staff

Schultze, Charles L., Director, Bureau of the Budget, until January 1968

Shriver, R. Sargent, Jr., Director of the Peace Corps until 1966

Sloan, Frank K., Deputy Assistant Secretary of Defense for International Security Affairs until 1965

Smith, Bromley K., Executive Secretary of the National Security Council

Solbert, Peter O.A., Deputy Assistant Secretary of Defense for International Security Affairs until December 1965

Solomon, Anthony M., Assistant Secretary of State for Economic and Business Affairs from June 1965

Spain, James W., Director, Office of Research and Analysis for Near East and South Asia, Bureau of Intelligence and Research, Department of State, March 1964–June 1966; thereafter, Country Director for Pakistan-Afghanistan Affairs

Talbot, Phillips, Assistant Secretary of State for Near Eastern and South Asian Affairs until September 1965

Taylor, General Maxwell D., USA, Chairman of the Joint Chiefs of Staff until July 1964; Ambassador to Vietnam July 1964–July 1965

Tiger, M. Gordon, Officer in Charge of Iranian Affairs, Bureau of Near Eastern and South Asian Affairs, Department of State, until July 1965

Udall, Stewart L., Secretary of the Interior

Vance, Cyrus R., Deputy Secretary of Defense January 1964–June 1967

Walsh, John P., Deputy Director, Office of Near Eastern and South Asian Regional Affairs, Bureau of Near Eastern and South Asian Affairs, Department of State, until May 1965; Deputy Executive Secretary until September 1967; thereafter, Acting Executive Secretary

Warnke, Paul C., Assistant Secretary of Defense for International Security Affairs from August 1967

Wehmeyer, Donald A., Assistant Legal Adviser for Near Eastern and South Asian Affairs, Department of State, until August 1968

Wheeler, General Earle G., USA, Chief of Staff, U.S. Army, until July 1964; thereafter, Chairman of the Joint Chiefs of Staff

Wriggins, W. Howard, member of the National Security Council Staff 1966–1967

Zahedi, Ardeshir, Foreign Minister of Iran from March 1967

Zwick, Charles J., Director, Bureau of the Budget, from January 1968

Iran

1. Letter From President Johnson to the Shah of Iran[1]

Washington, January 2, 1964.

Your Majesty:

I am delighted that my friend Sargent Shriver is visiting Iran, and can deliver this personal message to you.[2] I wish that I could come back to Tehran myself; my heart is warmed even now by memories of the welcome which you, the Empress, and your subjects of high and low estate extended to the Johnsons last year. Unfortunately, the press of work makes it impossible for me to be with you now other than in spirit.

The circumstances which elevated me to the awesome responsibility of this office still weigh heavily upon me. I know that you, too, feel deeply the loss. I was helped in the period of immediate shock and sorrow following the tragedy by your kindness in sending Prince Gholam Reza to extend your sympathy and Iran's.

Since my own trip to Iran I have followed with great interest the strides Iran is making under your leadership toward a new birth of freedom and justice in your ancient land. In freeing the energies of Iran's peasantry and laborers, as well as the women, you have taken a difficult and courageous step. You have proven your faith and confidence in the Iranian people and your resistance to alien pressures. You will be misunderstood and you will be maligned. That is the price of historical movement—the price of progress. But you will also be admired and loved by your people.[3]

I have asked Sargent Shriver to convey to you our deep appreciation for your warm welcome to the 45 Peace Corps Volunteers in your coun-

---

[1] Source: Johnson Library, National Security File, Special Head of State Correspondence File, Iran—Presidential Correspondence. No classification marking.

[2] Shriver visited Iran January 14–20 in the dual capacity of Peace Corps Director and personal emissary of President Johnson. He delivered the President's letter during a personal meeting with the Shah on January 15. (Telegram 648 from Tehran, January 16; Department of State, Central Files, ORG 7 PC)

[3] A January 3 memorandum to Shriver from NSC staff member Robert Komer stated: "One of JFK's unheralded achievements was to con our nervous Shah into stressing reform and modernization at home, instead of constantly bleeding to us about his need for more arms to deter the Soviets and even Nasser. Every time the Shah said 'more arms,' the President came back with 'more reform.' Now we've got the Shah thinking he's a 20th Century reformer (and not doing a bad job of it). You might try the same recipe." (Johnson Library, National Security File, Robert W. Komer Files, RWK CHRON FILE, January–June 1964 [3 of 3])

try. Since its birth under President Kennedy, I have regarded the Peace Corps as one of the most imaginative instruments ever devised for capturing the idealism of youth and putting it to work in the cause of world peace and understanding.

Our Volunteers have benefitted enormously from their experience in your country. The United States will also benefit as they return, with broader horizons and greater understanding of the world, to take their places in our society. They will add a new dimension to American life. I only hope that, while with you, they have contributed in some small way to the well-being of your people and to their understanding of us.

I realize now, even better than I did when last we met, just how heavy is the burden of ultimate responsibility for the security of one's country. In searching for words to convey to you our response to Iran's concerns, let me repeat what I said to your entire nation when I left Iran more than a year ago:

"We of the United States know that a free Iran is vital to freedom everywhere, and that as long as freedom stands, Iran's independence and Iran's control over its own destiny will not be compromised. We shall walk beside you toward the new horizons of human dignity. Let me assure you that as long as you walk this road, you'll never walk alone."

Those words came from my heart and from the heart of my country when I spoke them. They still do.

Sincerely,

Lyndon B. Johnson[4]

---

[4] A handwritten postscript at the end of the letter reads: "Please convey the high regard and warm wishes Mrs. Johnson and I both entertain for the Empress—LBJ."

2. Letter From the Shah of Iran to President Johnson[1]

Tehran, January 7, 1964.

Dear Mr. President,

I have been recalling with pleasure impressions of your memorable but short visit to Teheran, in the company of Mrs. Johnson and your daughter. It was indeed gratifying to have had the occasion to meet you again personally. For the citizens of our capital it was a rare and cherished opportunity to have a glimpse of a kind-hearted and affable personality of your stature, to show their genuine admiration for you and to extend to you, as you no doubt witnessed, their spontaneous and cordial welcome. Such personal contacts and human relationships make for more sincere cooperation, still better understanding and closer ties of friendship between our two countries.

Let me express the earnest hope that the United States, under your wise and capable leadership will further succeed in her continued efforts to usher in a new era of peace and prosperity for mankind.

I am quite confident, Mr. President, that your wisdom and high statesmanship, as well as your long and intimate association with American politics and extensive knowledge and experience of world affairs, will prove invaluable assets in the successful discharge of the heavy responsibilities of your high office both in the United States and abroad.

Since your visit, Mr. President, much has happened in Iran. A comprehensive programme of far-reaching social, political and economic reforms, of which you were then given a brief account, has now been fully implemented. These reforms have transformed completely the entire structure of our society, and placed its foundations firmly upon the enlightened and progressive principles of our time. In their application, varying political slogans which essentially cater for the interests of only a certain class of society played no part. The guiding principle of our national policy is the realization of that which is advantageous to the interests of a free and independent society.

That the Iranian people wholeheartedly supported the cause of our revolutionary reforms was amply manifested at the referendum of January 1963, and during our recent general elections. I am certain that you are already familiar with these events.

Our position today, from the point of view of internal stability, national prestige, and our people's confident hope for a better life has

---

[1] Source: Johnson Library, National Security File, Special Head of State Correspondence File, Iran—Presidential Correspondence. No classification marking. The copy of the Shah's letter in the Department of State is attached to a covering memorandum indicating that the original was delivered by the Iranian Embassy to the Department on January 17. (Department of State, Central Files, POL 15–1 US/Johnson)

reached a point where, if no external dangers should threaten us, gives us reason to look to the future with well-founded optimism and confidence.

Turning to conditions outside Iran, we are thankful that the firm and far-sighted policy of the United States has led the world to the threshold of a period of relaxation of international tension, and that the Soviet Union seems, for the present at least, to have discarded the use of force as an instrument of her foreign policy. In these circumstances, I believe, Mr. President, co-existence with Russia, in the face of the Chinese peril to universal peace, commends itself as the wisest course to adopt; bearing in mind that until such time that complete and general disarmament with full and precise control becomes a reality, the fundamental question of our time, namely the preservation of peace, remains unsolved. Meanwhile, it is a matter of course that we should be well-disposed to undertake any step or action that would contribute to the realization of this goal, provided, of course, that in so doing we do not compromise our principles.

Your illustrious predecessor, in a letter written to me just before his tragic demise, had asked my opinion, in view of our past experiences with the Soviet Union, on the question of the bruited non-aggression treaty between NATO and the Warsaw Pact countries.

You are well aware, Mr. President, that in 1959 we were on the point of signing with the Soviet Union a non-aggression treaty for a period of some 30 or even 50 years. Their rather ridiculous initial conditions, however, delayed the negotiations for a few days. In the meantime, we received messages from the Presidents of the United States, Turkey and Pakistan warning us of the dangers of such a step. We were even reminded of the fate of the Baltic States. The reason they advanced was that if any action of this nature were to be taken, it would have to be on behalf of all the countries of the free world; in other words, that such an action would have to be collective, if the free world's united front were to remain intact.

This reasoning I found convincing, and I believe that it holds true even today. There can be no objection, in principle, to the conclusion of a non-aggression treaty between NATO and the Warsaw Pact countries; it may even be fruitful; but what, may in that case be asked, will be the impact of such a treaty on the regional member nations of the Central Treaty Organization? Where will American and British obligations to CENTO stand? Will Russia, then, be allowed to have a free hand to do as she pleases elsewhere? In such a situation—should it arise—it is not unlikely that the countries thus exposed will have to see how best they can arrive at a bilateral agreement with the Soviet Union and that, certainly at a price.

It is, therefore, highly advisable that the non-aggression pact between NATO and Warsaw Pact countries—if there is to be one—should cover all member countries of CENTO, in particular those bordering on the Soviet Union and not to leave them outside the agreement. We have also heard of a proposal that all countries of the world should sign a treaty of non-aggression with each other.

There are certain countries in the world, the preservation of whose independence and territorial integrity, because of their characteristic geographic position, does not only constitute a service to those countries alone, but a service also to the stability and peace of an entire area. Iran is an instance of such a country.

Mr. Brezhnev paid a visit to Iran about a couple of months ago. In his talks with me he did his best to be friendly and to leave formality aside. So much so, that on the last day of his stay he went as far as confiding to me that, relations between Iran and the Soviet Union having improved considerably, he would permit himself to express Russia's dislike of Iran's participation in military agreements with the West. My immediate reply, of course, was that one did not have to go too far to seek the reasons for the existence of such regional defensive agreements. They would automatically lose their force and validity as soon as the numerous military pacts between countries of the world ceased to exist and the dangers of war and aggression no longer posed a threat to the territorial integrity of smaller nations; and that such an ideal situation could only be brought about when general and complete disarmament with proper controls became a reality.

Permit me to say a few words now about developments in some of the countries around Iran. A matter to which I wish, Mr. President, to call your attention is the danger which threatens this area of the world. I refer to the stockpiles of weapons of aggression in the possession of Egypt and the ever increasing delivery of offensive equipment to that country by the Soviet Union, designed to serve, overtly or under cover, as instruments of Egyptian intervention. Yemen, the Morocco–Algeria conflict and the arming of Somalia for expansion are instances in point. Egypt, in fact, has already prepared an "intervention force" of considerable size, equipped with long-range bombers, missiles, heavy troop transport planes, submarines, ships, and torpedo boats armed with missiles, so that if a "change" should happen to occur in any Arab country and President Nasser be asked to "intervene" he would willingly do so and let the world be faced with a fait accompli. I should perhaps add that even Iran does not seem to be too distant for his designs or immune from his subversive activities.

It is in consideration of these compelling reasons that the security of the Persian Gulf poses for us a source of constant concern, not only in the interest of our own country, but in the interest of the West as well. Indeed, the stakes involved are so great that any lack of vigilance on our parts may have disastrous consequences. To this situation, we have endeavoured to draw the attention of the United States Government.

Last year, the Pentagon prepared a Five Year Plan for Iran which was accepted with some reservations and for want of a more satisfactory alternative.[2] This Plan has already proved inadequate for the requirements of the changing situation in this area. The Iranian Army is capable of serious combat neither in the mountainous regions—for lack of adequate material requirements and logistical support—nor in the plains—for being devoid of the required mobility, and armour for such warfare. Our armoured equipment, the M47 tanks, are of type not in current production whose replacement and spare parts can be found with great difficulty. Now, if such is the condition of our equipment in peace time, it is difficult to imagine how they can be of any serious value at times of emergency. We have no military stockpiles of any kind and no reserves, even of machine guns, automatic rifles and ammunition to meet routine demands. Should unforeseen circumstances require us to put our army in a state of mobilization, we shall hardly be able to place ourselves in a state of readiness for the emergency. All our supplies and equipment have been distributed to provide for the army's current requirements.

The responsibilities of the Iranian Air Force, moreover, have never been equal to even the minimum of the Army requirements. Our airfields are limited in number, and where they do exist we are there faced with deficiencies in radar facilities and anti-aircraft protection.

Furthermore, ships and vessels presently in service with our navy, in number as well as in military value, are hardly adequate to carry out their vital responsibilities.

If our armed forces are to function effectively and to perform their alloted duties, and if Iran, a staunch and steadfast ally of the United States, is to play her full part in the changing political climate of the Middle East, then obviously, Mr. President, these shortages have to be met. Otherwise, we must consider as wasted the funds that are presently allocated for maintaining our armed forces.

In my correspondence with you, Mr. President, I wish to be perfectly candid in dealing with matters of mutual interest. If the United States is not in a position to meet our clear and urgent military needs in addition to the Five Year Plan, in order to be able to fulfil our duties, I thought that we might advisedly arrange for the purchase of our additional needs, under favourable conditions, from the United States of America or from elsewhere.

---

[2] For text of the U.S. Five-Year Military Program for Iran, accepted by Iran on September 19, 1962, see *Foreign Relations*, 1961–1963, vol. XVIII, pp. 105–109.

Of course, the question of CENTO strategy, American engagements and a great many related topics will form the subject of discussions by our representatives at the CENTO Ministerial Council. We hope that this forthcoming meeting, due to be held in Washington, will provide a suitable opportunity for clarifying all these points. In the meantime, it would be useful if you should see fit to appoint someone to discuss with me urgent matters of interest to our two countries and to report the result to you.

In the field of economic activity, it is a source of satisfaction that our own potentials are so great that if we can devote all our planned resources to the implementation of our Five Year Plan, we can envisage an annual growth of 8 per cent, with every hope of raising considerably the material welfare of our people. We have received a number of proposals for economic assistance from Western and even Eastern European countries as well as from the Soviet Union. Doubtless, we would be more than gratified to have offers of loan from the A.I.D. with their very generous terms, and also from the Export-Import Bank and its subsidiary organizations. We would welcome, further, private American investors who would wish to participate in the development of our economy.

To turn once again to the Middle East, the situation in Iraq seems uncertain. With the fall of Kassem's unwholesome regime, we welcomed with relief what we hoped would be closer ties with Iraq, thinking that since the Baathists at once began to purge their country of Communists, we had been rid of a troublesome neighbour. Our optimism was short-lived however, for we soon discovered in Southern Iran centres of Arab espionage, with their covetous eyes on a certain integral part of our country, namely Khuzistan, the main centre of our oil industry.

With the overthrow of the Baathist Government in Iraq, this danger seems to have abated. Uncertainty however, still persists. For our information indicates that Marshal Aref himself had been fully aware of the above activities and had given them his full support.

I regret to say that already Marshal Aref has shown a tendency to turn towards Egypt. If I lay emphasis on this question and express my concern, it is because we are well aware of the developments in this area and the course they are likely to take.

Here, I must state that our attitude towards Iraq has always been a friendly one, and we have always hoped that Iraq will have a strong and stable Government, capable of preserving its independence and of safeguarding its national interests.

The Kurdish question is still unsettled. Agents of international communism are making every endeavour to exploit the situation to their own advantage, and Cairo is anxious to play its dubious role in any development in this situation.

If negotiations between the Government at Baghdad and the Kurds should fail to reach an understanding, we have reason to expect that the fighting will flare up again in the spring.

We have reports to the effect that President Nasser did try, and is still making efforts to "mediate" between the Kurds and the Central Government of Iraq. This, on the surface, sounds quite harmless, even perhaps commendable. However, the contents of one of his messages to the Kurds fully reveals his ill intentions towards Iran. He has said in effect, according to our information, that it was a pity the Kurds were fighting the Arabs. He would have given them full support if their force were directed against Iran.

Thus with the situation prevailing in Iraq and with the UAR adventures in Yemen and elsewhere likely to erupt in other parts of the Middle East as well, my obligations to my country and my people make it incumbent upon me to take all precautions for the safety of the country and of our national interests. We cannot tolerate Egypt's subversive influence at our doorstep; nor fail to regard it seriously. I think, as referred to above, upon the stability of Iran depends the security of the entire Middle East. While we in Iran are seeking to ensure the security and stability of our own country, and that of the Persian Gulf, we are contributing also to the preservation of peace in this entire area—an area in which the United States has vital interests.

Happily, on these as on other matters, we have always maintained close and cordial contact, and our views have never been far apart.

Again, my best wishes for your happiness and success in the service of the United States of America as well as in the cause of the free world.

With high esteem,

Sincerely,

M.R. Pahlavi

3.   **Memorandum From Harold H. Saunders of the National
       Security Council Staff to Robert W. Komer of the National
       Security Council Staff[1]**

Washington, January 23, 1964.

RWK:

Bob Macy came back to plan the phase-out of the Iranian program. Though he originally argued we'd have to continue development lending to retain influence, he's now reconciled to its end.

The big question now is how Macy plans to retain maximum influence in Iran's economic machinery with the few top-level advisers we can keep there. How many people would he need? What kind? Does he have suitable ones on board now? What are his best channels to key points in Iranian decision making? What can we use for leverage (What about MAP?)?

Wheeler doesn't think you'll have to argue with Macy so much as enthuse him. *Why not make your speech about "getting more for less"?* Paint him a picture of how, as Congress cuts our aid resources, we have to find new ways to push our interests in important countries like Iran. We're looking to guys like Macy to come up with new techniques.

May I sit in?

H.

---

[1] Source: Johnson Library, National Security File, Robert W. Komer Files, Iran, November 1963–December 1964. Confidential.

4.   Telegram From the Embassy in Iran to the Department of State[1]

Tehran, January 28, 1964, noon.

669. The following comments may be helpful in connection with preparation of reply to Shah's letter to President of Jan 7.[2]

Important to realize that at time of writing letter Shah was not, and is not now, in one of the depressed moods which have in past resulted in excessive insecurity leading to appeals for military assistance. On the contrary, he is self-confident and self-assured. In addition to his continuing desire for military equipment beyond what we are providing him, Shah has what seems to me legitimate concern over what will happen when five-year military agreement comes to an end, particularly with regard to providing for replacement of equipment, such as M–47 tanks, which will become unsupportable toward end of current agreement. In addition, Iran is now having to assume certain military expenses (spare parts, consumable supplies) which were not commitments in the agreement but which the Military Assistance Program had previously covered. Shah's long existing desire for military equipment beyond that provided in the agreement has not [now] been reinforced by marked improvement in Iranian financial position arising from increase in revenues from oil.

With regard to Shah's attitude to the agreement itself, there is no doubt in my mind, despite language in his letter to President, that he does not consider that he has abrogated agreement or asked for formal renegotiation of it.

We will, of course, wish to stress essential validity of five-year agreement, underline our condition that it adequately provides for defense of Iran, convey our assessment that threat to Iranian security now less, not more, than at time agreement signed, and point out that we are meeting our commitments despite fund stringencies and expect Iran to continue to meet hers. However, Shah's concern for post-agreement military needs is in practical terms by no means premature. I, therefore, think President's response should be positive in sense of expressing our willingness to discuss reasonable on-going program of Iranian acquisition military equipment after expiration of agreement. Appropriate comments regarding possibility of declining US grant assistance or its replacement by military credit could be included as necessary. I would hope that possibility of credit at least could be indicated.

---

[1] Source: Department of State, Central Files, DEF 19 US–IRAN. Secret.

[2] Document 2.

Within this framework I could then explore in less formal manner more specifically what Shah has in mind and ascertain possibility of mutually satisfactory solution. I believe that if I am able to discuss problem of future program with him in reasonably frank terms, we will be able to contain within acceptable bounds his desire to purchase additional equipment now and ensure that such purchases are from us and compatible with our MAP and advisory program. I could also in this context pointedly remind Shah once again of danger that excessive Iranian purchases of military equipment now could call into question agreement itself and result in sharp reduction in US grant military assistance.

Reference should also be made to the Indian Ocean Task Group and to DELAWAR as evidence of US interest and ability to reinforce the security of Iran, and of increasing US capacity to deal with limited war situations.

With regard to Shah's request that representative be sent here, we have since confirmed he had in mind military representative and referred to his November conversation with General Adams. This request probably arises from fact Eckhardt and I have held line firmly with regard to additional military equipment and Shah would no doubt like to attempt to influence such a representative in that direction. I would hope that President's reply might make clear that his civilian and military representatives in Iran have his full confidence and are entirely qualified to discuss whatever the Shah may have in mind. To avoid brushing off request and in interest Shah's personal relation with President, reply might note General Adams will be coming to Iran in March (we understand this is tentative plan) and this will afford opportunity for him to join Eckhardt and me in discussing military matters related to defense of this region.

With regard to international political aspects of Shah's message, Dept will not require lengthy comments from us, but I put forward following.

Unlikelihood of non-aggression treaty should be mentioned as well as fact that such treaty, if it should come to pass, would in no way detract from our CENTO commitments. Question about USSR's being allowed free hand in non-European areas should be vigorously refuted. Ref to USSR's having discarded use of force as instrument of foreign policy could be used to lead to emphasis on need for economic development and social, administrative and political reforms to counter possibility of aggression through subversion, especially in vulnerable areas, which is only weapon available to Arabs at moment and in foreseeable future to cause trouble for Iran in Khuzistan.

Finally, the President would presumably refer at some point to the situation in Iran. Need to keep Shah's attention focused on what remains to be done fully as great as requirement to approve his hopeful start. I believe we should avoid leaving impression that we share Shah's view that his "comprehensive program . . . has now been fully implemented" but rather should indicate we are glad he is aware and actively working on the serious social, economic administrative political problems that beset Iran.

Holmes

---

5.   **Memorandum From Acting Secretary of State Ball to President Johnson**[1]

Washington, January 29, 1964.

SUBJECT

Proposed Unofficial Visit by the Shah of Iran, May–June 1964

The exhibit, "7,000 Years of Iranian Art," which had a highly successful tour of European capitals last year, is now scheduled for a tour of United States cities, beginning in the spring of 1964. The formal opening of the United States tour will take place at the National Gallery of Art in Washington some time between May 25 and June 6, 1964. We think that the value of this event as a landmark in United States-Iranian cultural relations would be greatly enhanced if the Shah of Iran were invited to open the exhibit. This visit might be combined with a trip to Los Angeles, since we have been informed that the University of California at Los Angeles is considering the possibility of awarding the Shah an honorary degree at the commencement exercises in June.

The Shah last visited the United States, in an official capacity, in April 1962. An unofficial visit for the purposes mentioned above would be useful in demonstrating to him continuing United States interest in the welfare of his country and approval of his program of social reform.

If the proposed unofficial visit is made, we would recommend that you and Mrs. Johnson host an informal luncheon for the Shah (and the

---

[1] Source: Department of State, Central Files, POL 7 IRAN. Limited Official Use. Drafted by Tiger; cleared by Jernegan and in draft by Chief of Greek, Turkish, Iranian, and Cyprus Programs in CU/NEA John T. Forbes, Assistant Chief of Protocol for Visits and Public Events Samuel L. King, Special Assistant to the Deputy Under Secretary for Political Affairs Windsor G. Hackler, and Special Assistant for Congressional Relations (Appropriations) to the Deputy Under Secretary for Administration William R. Little. A typed note on the source text indicates that the Department was informed of the President's approval on February 1.

Empress if she accompanies him) and that you also have a private informal talk with the Shah on the same occasion. If it should prove impossible to schedule these events, we would not advise the National Gallery of Art to invite the Shah to open the exhibit and we would discourage the University of California from awarding him an honorary degree.

George W. Ball[2]

---

[2] Printed from a copy that indicates Ball signed the original.

---

6.   **Memorandum From the Acting Assistant Secretary of State for Near Eastern and South Asian Affairs (Jernegan) to the Special Group (Counter Insurgency)**[1]

Washington, March 2, 1964.

SUBJECT

    Progress Report, Internal Defense Plan—Iran

The Country Team's fourth progress report on the Internal Defense Plan for Iran, covering the period September 25, 1963 to February 3, 1964, is contained in Embassy Tehran's Airgram 421 of February 3, 1964.[2] Further detailed reporting on the political situation is contained in Embassy Tehran's Airgram 361 of December 31, 1963,[3] and an appraisal of police capabilities is contained in Embassy Tehran's Airgram 420 of February 1, 1964.[4] These reports have been reviewed and approved for transmittal to the Special Group by the interdepartmental working group, with qualifications and additional comments as indicated in this memorandum.

    1.   *The Threat and Iran's Vulnerabilities.* The interdepartmental working group's last progress report on Iran, dated October 14, 1963, noted

---

[1] Source: Department of State, NEA/IRN Files: Lot 69 D 178, POL IRAN 1964, POL 23–1–a, Internal Defense Plan. Secret. Drafted by Tiger on February 28; cleared in draft by Special Assistant to the Under Secretary for Political Affairs Charles Maechling, Jr., Abe J. Moses (G/PM), Terence T. Grindall (INR), Colonel M.R. Preble (DOD/ISA/NESA), Captain Pollard (DOD), Officer in Charge of Iran Affairs Henrietta Towsley (AID/NESA/GTICC), and Edward A. Padelford, Jr. (NR). Sent through Harriman.

[2] Not printed. (Ibid., Central Files, POL 23–1 IRAN)

[3] Not printed. (Ibid., POL 2 IRAN)

[4] Not printed. (Ibid., POL 23–1 IRAN)

that, while "Iran is subject to the basic political vulnerabilities of a society in transition, . . . no clearly identifiable threat to internal security is likely to develop in the near future except in the event of the demise or abdication of the Shah." The intervening period has been relatively uneventful, and nothing has happened which would cause us to change this basic evaluation. In fact, with the passage of time, the disposition of the important disaffected groups (middle-class dissidents, clergy, tribal elements) to engage in anti-regime adventures has diminished and the Government's control of the country has improved. (See A–361, p. 2 and A–421, p. 2.)

2. *Basic Developments Affecting Internal Security.*

a. The most noteworthy *internal political* development was the formation of the New Iran Party, based on the intellectual-bureaucratic supporters of the Shah's reform program in the new Parliament. This move is part of an attempt to marshal public support for the reform program and prepare the groundwork for the long-planned accession of the Party's leader, Hasan Ali Mansur, to the premiership. (See A–361, p. 6 and A–421, p. 3.)

b. The most significant actions in regard to *internal security* were the arrest of a retired General for "plotting against the regime," and the apprehension of some 40 Arab "subversives" in Khuzistan. The former appears to have been strictly a precautionary move, with no apparent evidence of an actual "plot," whereas the latter appears to have been a response to probably exaggerated Israeli "tips" on alleged Iraqi and Egyptian subversion attempts. (See A–361, p. 2 and A–421, p. 2.)

c. In respect to the *oil problem,* Iran has been successful so far in forestalling unilateral actions by the Organization of Petroleum Exporting Countries against the oil companies. But the issue is not yet settled: Iran faces possible dissension with its Arab neighbors as well as internal political problems if forced to make a unilateral settlement with the companies. On the other hand, if forced to go along with OPEC-voted sanctions, Iran would face financial problems. (See A–421, p. 5.)

d. The developing "normalization" of *Iranian-Soviet relations* was marked by: a visit from Soviet President Brezhnev (marred by the Soviet shooting-down of an Iranian plane near the border); serious negotiations for an Iran-Soviet air agreement; concrete steps toward implementation of an agreement for joint development of a border river; and tentative arrangements for a small contingent of Iranian students in the USSR. All evidence—especially Iranian cooperation in heavy publicity for U.S. assistance during the Brezhnev visit—points to continued wariness as regards Soviet intentions and determination to avoid excessive involvement. (See A–361, p. 2 and pp. 8, 9; A–421, p. 4.)

e. *U.S.-Iranian Relations* were affected by: Iran's decreasing economic dependence on the U.S.; Iran's largely verbal flirtation with "nonalignment"; and an increasing divergence of views between Iran and the U.S. as to the Arab threat. The Shah, moreover, is expressing dissatisfaction with the quantities and sophistication of military equipment being supplied under the Five-Year MAP and has indicated interest in obtaining, by purchase if necessary, equipment not included in the strategic concept of the MAP. There is as yet no reason to believe that these trends and issues portend any essential change in the character of U.S.-Iranian relations. The recent visit of Sargent Shriver afforded an occasion for a ringing affirmation by the Shah of his fundamental commitment to the West. (See A–361, pp. 1, 2; A–421, p. 2.)

3. *Developments Tending to Enhance Internal Defense Capabilities.*

a. The very existence of the *new Parliament* has, as predicted, improved the position of the Government by tempering the constitutional uncertainties about the reform program. (See A–361, p. 3.)

b. The creation of a *"Health Corps"* to use conscripts for an impact program in rural areas is a potentially significant new element in the reform program and, like the already functioning "Literacy Corps," a means of engaging the participation and enthusiasm of urban youth. (See A–421, p. 2.)

c. The *security forces* have continued to work toward improved capabilities in several respects: (See A–421, pp. 5, 6 and A–420, p. 2):

(1) Planning with U.S. advisers was completed for a counter-insurgency Command Post Exercise and three successive Field Training Exercises in the First Army area in west and northwest Iran during the next few months;

(2) Planning also moved forward satisfactorily for the joint U.S.-Iranian exercise DELAWAR, scheduled to take place in southwest Iran in mid-April under the aegis of CENTO;

(3) The Iranian Special Forces have been reorganized from their former status as paratroop forces and have been engaging in active training for the forthcoming counter-insurgency exercises;

(4) With the arrival of most of the AID-programmed riot-control equipment for the Tehran police, plans are now under way for intensification of the training of the police in the use of this equipment. The operational plans, command arrangements, and assigned forces of the police, the Gendarmerie and the army appear sufficient to deal with any likely and foreseeable civil disturbance in Tehran.

d. *Civic action* programs have been given increasing support by the Imperial Iranian Forces: The Air Force has entered more actively into this field, carrying fodder to starving livestock in snow-bound areas and preparing an operation to ferry medical teams and equipment to remote southeastern port areas this month; units of the Iranian Navy participated with a U.S. destroyer in medical assistance calls to southeastern port areas in December and have scheduled further such activities for the near future; two more vocational training centers were opened; and there has been active Iranian discussion of proposals for forming "development batallions" under military supervision. These developments have been receiving an increasing amount of publicity in Iranian media and some favorable public reaction.

4. *Major Areas of Continuing Concern.*

a.   The fundamentals of the *reform program,* while being addressed by the GOI in various ways, still require more vigorous action and forward planning to ensure success. *Civil service reform* is stalled in the Parliament and *budget reform* to achieve fiscal and program control has not passed the talking stage. *Land reform* activities have slowed down considerably, largely because of the increasingly complex administrative problems being encountered in the "Second Stage," although severe winter weather and some potentially beneficial reorganizations in the Ministry of Agriculture have contributed to the slowdown. While programs directed to *labor* and *women's groups,* mentioned in the last progress report, have remained in effect, there has been no great impetus on these fronts. The regime's *base of support,* which is so far largely restricted to the security forces, is too narrow for comfort and has not yet been significantly broadened by reform or political measures. (See A–361, pp. 4–6.)

b.   The *economic recession,* with its consequent large-scale urban unemployment, persists in spite of steady improvement in the government's financial position and the adoption of expansionary credit policies. (See A–361, pp. 2, 3; A–421, p. 4.)

c.   Iran's *Kurdish problem* may well be affected by the recently reported cease-fire between the Iraqi Government and the Iraqi Kurds. At present writing it is too early to judge whether the cease-fire will stick and, if so, whether it will exacerbate or ameliorate Iran's internal security problem.

5. *U.S. Policy and Courses of Action.* All major U.S. assistance programs in Iran except for military advisory services are being considerably affected by Iran's increasing financial strength and, more temporarily, by unexpectedly good crops. Indicated U.S. action in the more important assistance sectors are the following:

a.   *PL–480.* It begins to appear doubtful that there will be sizeable, if any, sales under the Title I wheat program signed in November. Therefore the anticipated rial facilities may not be available for our programs to assist agricultural credit. Title II and III programs remain significant and are having beneficial effects, although the Iranians find great difficulty in administering Title II. We intend to keep in close touch with the GOI on the grain situation to determine, in timely fashion, if the supply factors in the next season will provide scope for a Title I program, but the outlook is not promising now because of the excellent crop prospects for the coming season.

b. *Development Lending.* Although the scheduled reduction of AID development loans and their termination at the end of FY 1965 is commensurate with Iran's improving financial situation, difficulties are being experienced in this transitional period. (A–421, p. 4.) Subsequent to the Country Team's progress report, word has been received that the GOI has finally decided to reject two Export-Import Bank loans on the basis that the terms are unacceptable and the GOI can finance the imports (road and railroad maintenance equipment) itself. In general our Government export-promotion lending programs are running into effective competition from some of Iran's other foreign suppliers. There are only two pending AID loan applications ($7.7-million for the Iranian portion of the CENTO Turkey–Iran rail link[5] and $1.5-million for training assistance to the Iranian national airlines). We plan to take early action on these two requests. For purposes of retaining influence in Iranian development and reform programs and preserving markets for U.S. equipment, we intend to encourage applications for further qualifying projects within our FY 1965 development loan availabilities for Iran.

c. *Police Training.* Within the context of the phase-down of the Development Grant Program as projected in the approved Country Assistance Strategy Statement, AID plans to begin immediately a comprehensive re-evaluation to determine the scope and nature of its police training program in the near future. The recommendations already made by the Country Team (e.g., A–420) will be taken into consideration and further Country Team assistance requested in making this re-evaluation.

Prompt action has been taken to replace about $28 thousand of AID-financed communications equipment (out of the $500,000 AID program) which was lost in transit.

d. *Military Assistance.* As noted above, the Shah is reacting increasingly to what he considers unreasonable restraints on his procurement of military equipment. We think he understands that MAP grants cannot be increased above the amounts necessary to meet our commitments under the five-year MAP worked out in September 1962. In view of Iran's increased financial resources, we are now studying the feasibility of Iranian purchase of certain spare parts and other items not covered in our commitments but nevertheless supplied heretofore under MAP grants.

6. No amendments in the basic Internal Defense Plan are proposed at the present time. Since the insurgency prospects in Iran are now considered latent rather than incipient, it is recommended that the schedule

---

[5] For the interdepartmental working group's position on the Turkey–Iran rail link project, see the previous progress report (Memorandum for the Special Group, October 14, 1963) p. 4. [Footnote in the source text. The October 14 memorandum is ibid., Special Group, Counterinsurgency Files: Lot 68 D 451.]

for consideration by the Special Group (CI) be changed to a semi-annual rather than a quarterly basis.

7. The review of the interdepartmental working group has not revealed any specific requirements for action at this time by the Special Group (CI) or any new resource requirements other than the Development Loan funds mentioned in paragraph 5–b above. It is therefore recommended that the Special Group (CI) approve the Country Team's fourth progress report, as qualified and expanded herein, for planning purposes.[6]

John D. Jernegan

---

[6] On March 16 Tiger sent a copy of this report to the Embassy in Tehran, noting that the Special Group meeting on March 6 had accepted the recommended change to a 6-month basis for IDP reporting, and that Harriman had asked that the Ambassador write to him directly in the interim if there were any particular problem or anything the Special Group could do to enhance the U.S. internal security effort in Iran. (Ibid., NEA/IRN Files: Lot 69 D 178, POL IRAN 1964, POL 23–1–a, Internal Defense Plan)

---

7.   Telegram From the Embassy in Iran to the Department of State[1]

Tehran, March 10, 1964, 5:45 p.m.

783. Re Deptel 617.[2] In audience today I told Shah that delay in President's reply to his letter of January 7 no doubt caused by numerous topics raised by Shah, all requiring study, and pointed out preoccupation of President with domestic program and critical international problems, adding that there was nothing in Shah's communication requiring urgent action. I said that I anticipated a reply within about a week. In circumstances, suggest that reply be sent by telegram which would contain statement that signed letter is to follow.

---

[1] Source: Department of State, Central Files, POL 15–1 IRAN. Confidential.

[2] Telegram 617 to Tehran, March 9, informed Holmes that the Department intended to pouch the President's reply to the Shah's letter of January 7 within 1 week. (Ibid.) In telegram 754 from Tehran, March 5, the Ambassador reported the Foreign Minister's statement that the Shah had exhibited some concern at having not yet received a reply to his letter. (Ibid.)

In calm, unemotional tone, Shah went over again his preoccupations about Nasser and his concern for the security of Persian Gulf. I gave him the obvious counter-arguments. He has focused his attention particularly on the prepositioning of military equipment, pointing out the advantages of the area in the mountains behind Bandar Abbas as an ideal location. He stated that with the development of the port, Bandar Abbas could become both a naval and military base, representing a secure position in terms of its distance from the Russian and Iraqi borders and pointing out the relative ease of preventing naval penetration of the Persian Gulf from this strategic point. His attention continues to be focused on the Persian Gulf and a potential Arab threat to Khuzistan. His fears of overt threat from Soviet Union are very much less than in the past.

The Shah was critical of some of our policies, especially pursuing the same theme he has followed in the past that we do not treat our friends as well as we treat those who are either our enemies or are not committed to us. At the end of about 10 minutes of this, he turned and smiled and said, "but after all, if it weren't for America, none of us would be here", and then restated that he had taken his position with the US and the West and there was no question of abandoning it. He spoke in highest terms of the President, saying that during the latter's visit[3] here he felt that he had developed cordial communication with Mr. Johnson, coupled with admiration and respect for him. He expressed the wish of having further discussions with me after the receipt of the President's reply, preliminary to his conversation with the President in June.

As previously reported, there have been rumors current in Tehran that the Shah's health has deteriorated. He told me that basically his condition had not changed but that the doctor in Vienna had counselled more frequent and longer periods of rest away from his heavy responsibilities. He does bear a heavy burden, works long hours, and is by nature a worrier. He appears to me to be unchanged from when I last saw him prior to his visit to Europe.

Holmes

---

[3] For information on Vice President Johnson's visit to Tehran August 24–26, 1962, see *Foreign Relations, 1961–1963*, vol. XVIII, p. 72.

8.   Letter From President Johnson to the Shah of Iran[1]

Washington, March 19, 1964.

Your Imperial Majesty:

Thank you for your long letter of January 7, 1964,[2] and for the frank comments which it contains. It is just this sort of mutual candor which you and I must always strive to maintain.

Sargent Shriver has told me of the warm hospitality which you extended to him. We are all proud of the similarity between our Peace Corps and your Literacy Corps and recently established Health Corps. Indeed, your whole program of social reform is highly regarded here. Iran seems the brightest spot in the Middle East these days. On all those fronts of greatest concern to Iran—the threat from the north, internal security, and the modernization of Iranian society—the outlook seems most favorable.

The important thing now is to press forward and consolidate the domestic progress so well begun. I am impressed with the support you are giving to civil service, budget, and fiscal reform. Let me urge on you the equal importance of a dynamic and buoyant economy; as you know, I too am devoting much attention to this problem in the United States. We wish all success to your new government, which seems to us to be going in the right direction.

Because of Iran's exposed position, we have always taken quite seriously your military concerns. However, after another thorough look, we have concluded that the basic factors that led our military experts to agree on the current Five-Year Military Plan have not changed significantly. I personally believe the Plan remains practical and adequate. While we can understand your quite natural worry about potential developments in the Arab world, we simply do not yet foresee much likelihood of a substantial Arab threat to Iran. I can assure you, however, that should any such threat develop, we are more than prepared to re-examine the situation with you. Meanwhile, we trust that Iran will continue to do its best to live up to its very difficult tasks under the Five-year Plan.

General Adams will be coming to Iran again in late March or early April, and if you desire he could discuss with you some of the very broad questions you have raised in your letter. Of course, Ambassador Holmes and General Eckhardt also stand ready to discuss at any time the full range of your political and military problems.

---

[1] Source: Johnson Library, National Security File, Special Head of State Correspondence File, Iran—Presidential Correspondence. Confidential.

[2] Document 2.

I much appreciate your comments on the meaning of a possible non-aggression pact between Communist and non-Communist states. They strike a responsive chord, and I can assure you that no East-West pact of this kind is contemplated at present. If such a matter were ever to be seriously considered, I would expect to consult fully with you before any final decisions were made.

Meanwhile I very much look forward to seeing you in June when we can discuss these matters further. Personal discussions between the leaders of our two Governments are important to both our countries, and it will be a pleasure to have you here in Washington again.

Sincerely,

Lyndon B. Johnson

---

9. **Information Memorandum From the Deputy Assistant Secretary of State for Near Eastern and South Asian Affairs (Jernegan) to Secretary of State Rusk[1]**

Washington, March 20, 1964.

SUBJECT

Iran as a Country in Transition from Aid to Self-support

On March 18 we in NEA were surprised to learn for the first time that Iran is one of the fourteen countries described in the President's foreign aid address of March 19 to Congress[2] as in transition from reliance on aid to self-support. Before Iran's inclusion in this group of countries, it had been our understanding that the contemplated transition period was one or two years, and we were thus most concerned that a decision seemed to have been taken without our concurrence to end aid to Iran within so brief a time. We informed A.I.D. of our concern.

---

[1] Source: Department of State, NEA/IRN Files: Lot 69 D 30, Iran 1964, AID 1, General Policy, Plans, Coordination. Confidential. Drafted by Thomas and cleared by Director of the Office of Near Eastern and South Asian Regional Affairs Guy A. Lee. Copies were sent to Bell and Macomber.

[2] For text of the President's foreign aid message to Congress on March 19, see *Public Papers of the Presidents of the United States: Lyndon B. Johnson, 1963–1964,* Book I, pp. 393–398.

We now concur in Iran's inclusion on the list of transition countries, having been assured (1) that the list is not limited to countries to which we plan to end our aid within a year or two and (2) that there has been no change from the position agreed upon in the Country Assistance Strategy Statement for Iran signed by Mr. Bell on December 30, 1963. This statement calls for continuation of Development Loans to Iran through June 1965, after which the further continuation or termination of concessional rate lending will depend upon economic trends in Iran and the availability of U.S. funds. As for technical assistance through Development Grants, our aim is described as termination of this program in four or five years "if, as anticipated, Iran succeeds in obtaining assistance it needs through the international agencies and if our technical assistance activities are successful in building up the competence of the GOI to manage its development drive more efficiently."

We agree, and we are pleased, that Iran does in fact appear now to be in stage of transition which it may be hoped will lead, if present trends continue, to eventual self-reliance. However, we believe it would be a very serious mistake to withdraw our aid presence abruptly from Iran, the most vulnerable country on the Soviet perimeter and the key member of CENTO. The progress of the past eighteen months should not hide the fact that Iran is still a weak country periodically in need of reassurance. It would be short-sighted, possibly tragically so, to become committed too far in advance and without adequate study to a position which would deprive us of an important means of providing such reassurance. Moreover, our assistance strategy should not ignore the fact that strategically located Iran still remains hospitable to our military and intelligence sites at a time when other countries are obliging us to remove or limit such facilities.

10.   **Letter From the Deputy Assistant Secretary of Defense for Regional Affairs (Sloan) to the Commander in Chief, U.S. Strike Command (Adams)**[1]

Washington, March 24, 1964.

Dear General Adams:

The Shah of Iran in a letter of 7 January 1964 (Enclosure 1)[2] expressed dissatisfaction with the present Five-Year Military Assistance Program. He went into considerable detail explaining the ever increasing Arab threat and used this as a basis for requiring more and better military equipment. He suggested that the President appoint someone to discuss with him urgent matters of interest to Iran and the United States.

The President in his reply (Enclosure 2)[3] indicated that the basic factors that led to the Five-Year Military Plan have not significantly changed and that we have not seen any major change in the Arab situation.

The President informed the Shah that Ambassador Holmes and General Eckhardt were ready to discuss the full range of his political and military problems and that you would be coming to Iran and would be glad to join them in discussing the questions raised in his letter.

In your discussions with the Shah you should:

a.   Avoid making any statement to the Shah which could be interpreted as a U.S. commitment of future grant military assistance.

b.   Advise the Shah that the U.S. will continue to assist Iran in planning for the improvement and modernization of its military establishment.

c.   Explain to the Shah that the amount of future Grant Aid to Iran will depend upon congressional action and that the trend is to reduce grant aid and shift to cash and credit sales.

d.   Volunteer to review Iranian requirements developed by the Iranians in coordination with the Country Team.

e.   Reiterate the U.S. evaluation of the Arab threat.

The Department of State has prepared a political evaluation of the situation in the Middle East as it affects the Iranian military policy. This together with a Defense Intelligence Agency evaluation,[4] which will be

---

[1] Source: Washington National Records Center, RG 330, OASD/ISA Files: FRC 68 A 306, 091.3 Iran, 24 March 64. Secret. Drafted by Colonel M.R. Preble of ISA/NESA.

[2] Attached to the source text; see Document 2.

[3] Attached to the source text; see Document 8.

[4] The Department of State evaluation was not found. A copy of the Defense Intelligence Agency evaluation entitled "The Capabilities of Arab Countries Singly or in Concert to Threaten the Security of Iran" is in Washington National Records Center, RG 330, OASD/ISA Files: FRC 68 A 306, 092 Iran, 25 March 1964. The DIA estimate concluded that only Egypt, Syria, and Iraq were expected to possess organized forces capable of significant military action against Iran during the next 3 years, and that current circumstances made concerted military action against Iran unlikely.

forwarded separately, may be used at your discretion in your discussion with the Shah.

Please submit a report of any impressions you may have after you talk with the Shah and any recommendations you may consider appropriate concerning our future policy toward Iran.

Sincerely,

Frank K. Sloan[5]

---

[5] Printed from a copy that indicates Sloan signed the original.

---

11.   Telegram From the Department of State to the Embassy in Iran[1]

Washington, March 25, 1964, 7:48 p.m.

678. Following is outline of principal points which may be used by CINCMEAFSA and by Embassy Tehran as basic guidance in any discussions with Shah which may develop concerning present and future shape of MAP, along with other aspects basic Iranian military policy.

These points neither all-inclusive nor detailed. They may be filled out and supplemented by drawing on previous communications and general information available to USG representatives. Shah, not USG, should take initiative in opening subject, and US side should, under ordinary circumstances, counter initiatives the Shah can be expected to undertake.

1.   US is satisfied with the Five-Year Military Plan and with way it is being implemented on both sides.

2.   Far from doubting validity of assumptions and principles of the plan, US is confirmed in its belief that they continue essentially valid. Iranian military capacity is being improved steadily. Iran's military capacity as compared with that of Iraq and Afghanistan is also continuing to increase.

---

[1] Source: Department of State, Central Files, DEF 19 US–IRAN. Confidential. Drafted by Bowling; cleared in draft by Wheeler, Hirschberg (AID/PC/MAD), Colonel Preble, George L. Warren (G/PM), and Padelford; and approved by Jernegan. Also sent to CINC-STRIKE/CINCMEAFSA and repeated to CINCEUR, Paris TOPOL (by pouch), Moscow, Ankara, and CINCSTRIKE/CINCMEAFSA for POLAD Tampa.

3. As Shah knows, our military assistance appropriations have been drastically reduced and future of such appropriations is uncertain. Despite shortages of funds and pressing needs from areas such as Vietnam, US has managed to continue essential elements of the Five-Year Program as concerns MAP. We hope continue do so though we are aware we have had to ask Iran to take over certain support functions (viz. follow-on spares) which had earlier been a US contribution under MAP.

4. We do not know whether there will be a military assistance program beyond FY 1967, when the Five-Year Plan terminates. If there is one, and if adequate funds are appropriated, US would hope to continue its relationship of military cooperation with Iran. In view of Iran's rapidly improving financial condition, it will probably be necessary for the USG-financed grant MAP portion of such a future program to be for only a portion of the total, and for Iran to cover the remainder with its own foreign exchange resources. The proportion of MAP grant to the total would probably have to be reduced year by year. US matériel would be available for sale to Iran under this program. Depending on Iran's overall financial condition and on other demands on Iran's foreign exchange, credit terms for such sales might be available. FYI. In your presentation of post-FY 67 MAP possibilities, you should take great care not to use language that may be construed as constituting any commitment on our part for any grants or credits in that period. End FYI.

5. We cannot discuss the specifics of such a program, but we are beginning to study the problem and will be able to talk about it in greater detail later.

6. If Shah is unaffected by USG arguments and continues to express a determination to buy additional equipment immediately, USG representatives should, after repeating all the arguments previously used as to equal importance of economic development and social reform in preserving national security, and after defending adequacy and effectiveness of the current plan, inform Shah that:

(a) Certain types of purchases by Iran which would in our opinion result in a net reduction of Iranian military capacity through grossly irrational employment of material and human resources cannot be agreed by the US under any circumstances, and would be regarded by the US as a cause for releasing the US from its obligations under the Five-Year Plan.

(b) Other types of purchases which we feel would have a net positive effect on Iranian military capacity and which would not in themselves cripple Iran's economic development program could be accepted as additional to the present Five-Year Plan, and the US could sell such equipment for cash.

(c) Iran should prepare a study with accompanying rationale which we could discuss together in light of the principles set forth above.

Rusk

12.   Telegram From the Embassy in Iran to the Department of State[1]

Tehran, April 6, 1964, 4:15 p.m.

882. Ayatollah Khomeini, at first imprisoned and later under house detention in connection 1963 Moharam riots and widely regarded as leading contender for position of Shia paramount leader, was released April 5 and returned to religious center of Qom. Press giving minimum play. [less than 1 line of source text not declassified] reports (1) millahs flocking to Qom from all over Iran to "kiss hands", and (2) one tank battalion concentrated Qom outskirts as precautionary measure. No info whether Khomeini reached agreement with govt regarding any restriction on his future activities. Embassy [less than 1 line of source text not declassified] contacts with good connections in religious community view release as victory for Khomeini but also as wise policy decision by regime in preparation for Moharam, period of deep mourning starting May 13.

Request Baghdad and Karachi report any clerical reaction Khomeini's release.

Holmes

---

[1] Source: Department of State, Central Files, POL 23–9 IRAN. Confidential. Repeated to Baghdad and Karachi.

---

13.   Telegram From the Embassy in Iran to the Department of State[1]

Tehran, April 8, 1964, 5 p.m.

890. Embtel 882.[2] Further background on release of Khomeini, obtained from Prime Minister:

1.   Govt made clear to Khomeini that if he engages in political activities, he will be re-arrested. Khomeini allegedly promised behave.

---

[1] Source: Department of State, Central Files, POL 23–9 IRAN. Confidential. Repeated to Baghdad and Karachi.

[2] Document 12.

2. Mansur allowed it to be understood he had had difficulty persuading Shah that Khomeini should be freed.

3. PM felt it was desirable free Khomeini now, rather than just before Moharam, because later release might be interpreted as due to fear of rioting similar to last year's.

4. Govt has "taken steps" with other leading mullahs, notably Milani, Qomi and Shariat-Madari, to prevent Khomeini's position being strengthened as result his release.

Holmes

---

14.   Memorandum From Commander John J. Shanahan to the Chairman of the Joint Chiefs of Staff (Taylor)[1]

Washington, April 11, 1964.

SUBJECT

General Adams' Visit with the Shah of Iran

1. General Adams held a rather extensive conversation with the Shah of Iran during his current visit to the MEAFSA area.

2. A number of significant points contained in the attached tabs[2] follow:

a. The Shah states that the situation in the Middle East has deteriorated since November. He cites:

(1) Pak-Indian relations.
(2) Turkey–Greece problem.
(3) UK withdrawal from bases in Malta and Cyprus.
(4) Bases in Libya are threatened.
(5) Recent strengthening of Arab unity.
(6) Forecast Arab aggression against Israel in 2 or 3 years.

---

[1] Source: Johnson Library, National Security File, Robert W. Komer Files, Iran, November 1963–December 1964. No classification marking.

[2] Attached to the source text are April 6 cables from General Paul D. Adams, Commander in Chief, U.S. STRIKE Command, to the Joint Chiefs of Staff and to Major General Perry B. Griffith, Chief of Military Assistance, STRICOM, reporting on his April 5 audience with the Shah in Tehran.

b. The Shah expressed hope that the April meetings in Washington would make useful progress; felt CENTO was not accomplishing much in a military way because of Pak attitude and US not being a member. Gen. Adams expressed confidence that meetings would be productive and US interest was intense in seeing that CENTO succeeds.

c. Shah stated Iran has more to fear from Soviet-supported Arabs than from Soviets.

d. Shah described Iran's future as bright because of current development of vast resources, and the social and economic reforms that are being implemented. He estimated the country's income from oil by 1970 would reach $1,200 million annually. Accordingly, Iran, the Shah pointed out, should play an increasingly important role in US strategic planning.

e. The Shah expressed his dissatisfaction with the state of his military defenses. (I suggest that up to this point it was all a build-up.)

(1) Defense of oil-rich Khuzistan and the port of Bandar Abbas has been neglected. Gen. Adams agreed to study plans for the defense of these areas.

(2) Need to continue the modernization program.

(3) He is prepared to purchase weapons insofar as the economy will permit.

(4) Desires a replacement for his rifles, wants more BARs and MGs in order to replace the non-standard artillery.

(5) His artillery battalions have only 2 batteries of 4 guns each. Gen. Adams agreed there should be 3 batteries per battalion.

(6) The M–47 tank was rapidly becoming non-supportable and should be replaced with the M–60. Gen. Adams pointed out that he felt sure the US would make available a lightweight tank in the near future, and therefore it might not be wise to expend sizeable amounts on the M–60 and find it out of date. The Shah agreed that perhaps it would only be necessary to replace the M–47 with the M–60 in 2 battalions. Gen. Adams agreed to attempt to determine the dates these conversions could take place. (Tab B, Gen. Adams has directed that this info be available upon his return from the current trip.)

(7) The Shah expressed approval of the F–5 but also pointed out that his F–86's should be replaced with something superior to the F–5. The C–47's must also be replaced by C–130's.

(8) The Shah also felt our air section of the MAAG should be increased, and headed by a Brig. General. Gen. Adams said he would see what could be done. (A BG as head of the MAAG air section has been recommended by the JCS.)

(9) The Shah restated the requirement for an additional airborne battalion.

3. There is little doubt but that Gen. Hedjazi will raise much of the foregoing while he is here. The Shah will do likewise during his visit in June. It seems we should try to draw Gen. Adams into the Washington conversations with Gen. H. as much as is possible. This appears especial-

ly true since Gen. Adams will have Gen. H. at his headquarters on 26–27 April.

J.J.S.[3]

---

[3] Printed from a copy that bears the typed initials of Commander John J. Shanahan, member of the JCS Chairman's staff group.

---

15.   Telegram From the Embassy in Iran to the Department of State[1]

Tehran, April 15, 1964.

922. Re Deptel 678.[2] During Operation DELAWAR I had two hour after dinner conversation alone with Shah.

He went over his discussion with General Adams of April 5 and then referred to statement in President's letter of March 19 that future military programs could be discussed with me. He then outlined his concept of modernization of Iranian armed forces, giving the same reasons for the need of improvement as he has expounded previously, although there was less note of urgency than he had previously expressed. Although Shah did not say it in so many words, I had the feeling that he has to some degree, at least, come to recognize that possibility of aggression in Persian Gulf area or against Khuzistan is less immediate than he had previously maintained. This does not mean that he has changed his view about Arab ambitions but he seems now to feel that he has more time to prepare himself for defense against it. Criticism of our policy toward Nasser was totally absent.

Shah then gave me a series of papers which set forth existing equipment shortages and additional equipment which he desires, some of it on a relatively short term basis and some having to do with long term replacement of items which will become unsupportable, such as tanks and

---

[1] Source: Department of State, Central Files, DEF 19–3 US–IRAN. Confidential. No time of transmission appears on the source text. Repeated to Ankara, Moscow, Paris for TOPOL, CINCSTRIKE for POLAD, CINCMEAFSA for POLAD, and CINCEUR.

[2] Document 11.

F–86 aircraft. On question of aircraft replacement, Shah volunteered statement that he realized perfectly well that it would be some time before Iranian air force could absorb and efficiently operate and maintain any additional aircraft beyond F5As. He added, however, that every effort should be made to improve and expand Iranian capabilities in this connection.

Shah said that he realized the difficulties of our position in furnishing equipment on a grant basis over and above that envisaged in five year program. He pointed out the improvement in Iran's revenues and foreign exchange position and said that what he wanted was to work out a modernization program which would not be extravagant and which would not hamper Iran's economic development program; this should be done without reference to whether the equipment would be furnished by grant from the US or by purchase from Iranian funds. He hoped that purchases could be arranged on an installment basis. I replied that US could make no commitment for the furnishing of military equipment on a grant basis beyond that envisaged in the five year plan. I then described to him the difficulty of sales of military equipment on credit because under our system there were no public funds available from which such sales could be financed, reminding him that the manufacturer in every case had to be paid in cash. Shah then wondered whether or not credit terms could be arranged with American manufacturers. I replied that this might be looked into at some subsequent time.

The series of papers which Shah handed me were part in Persian and part in English and constitute only a list [of] Iranian views of requirements. There is one document in Persian, not yet translated, which apparently contains some rationale with respect to these requirements. Shah admitted that these papers did not constitute a comprehensive approach to the problem, particularly as no attempt at phasing had been made. He made one or two oral statements with respect to time factors which will be reported when we have had a chance to study the character and magnitude of equipment requirements set forth.

I told the Shah that I would ask the MAAG staff to examine the various lists which he had sent me and that after a clearer picture of magnitude, phasing, etc., emerged, discussions might be held with Iranian staff. The Shah readily agreed to this and said that he was sorry the presentation had not been more orderly, expressing the hope that the work could begin without delay as he wished to make as much progress as possible before his visit to Washington in June.

I am refraining from any substantive comment on the Shah's proposals until we are able to examine them here, including getting some idea of cost.

In light of Shah's proposal that a modernization program be discussed without reference to which party should bear costs, I should appreciate confirmation my authority to proceed.

Holmes

---

16.   Telegram From the Department of State to the Embassy in Iran[1]

Washington, April 17, 1964, 6:18 p.m.

774. Re Embtel 922.[2] Joint State–AID–Defense message.

1. We gratified with handling of conversation reported reftel and believe Shah's present approach provides basis for proceeding with constructive discussion of military modernization program of reasonable content and proportions. You authorized proceed discussions, as outlined reftel, without reference to which party should bear costs.

2. We share Shah's hope that material he presented will permit sufficient early discussion with Iranian staff so that general outlines of feasible long-term program, including time-phasing, might be apparent before Shah's talk in Washington. We assume he understands, however, that we would not be able in that time to reach final position on any program, except possibly as regards sales of U.S. equipment for short-term expansion and replacement programs mentioned in third para reftel.

3. We particularly concerned to develop reasonable and flexible criteria for assuring that program would "not hamper Iran's economic development program." To this end we would be interested in examining economic indicators worked out by GOI or Country Team which would permit assessment proposed programs from this standpoint in light of Iran's enhanced economic prospects.

4. Information re availability of credits for sales to Iran will be sent by separate message.

Ball

---

[1] Source: Department of State, Central Files, DEF 19–3 US–IRAN. Confidential. Drafted by Tiger; cleared in draft by Towsley, Preble, and Padelford, and in substance by Victor H. Skiles (AID/PC), and Warren; and approved by Bracken. Repeated to CINCSTRIKE/CINCMEAFSA, and CINCSTRIKE/CINCMEAFSA for POLAD.

[2] Document 15.

17.   Telegram From the Department of State to the Embassy in Iran[1]

Washington, April 21, 1964, 5 p.m.

785. Re Deptel 774;[2] Embtel 922.[3] Joint State–AID–Defense message. While future plans for Iran not sufficiently finalized to allow making any commitment re credit at this time, there are available several sources of credit for military sales without new Congressional appropriation being required. These sources include the MAP reimbursement account (Section 508 of the Foreign Assistance Act) and utilization of Defense stocks (Section 507(a) of the FAA). Also, the dependable undertaking method of payment (Section 507(b) of the FAA), while not credit, may be utilized for procurement of materials. In line with USG policy of gradually shifting MAP recipient countries to a reimbursement basis, GOI would be legitimate claimant for credit during period current five-year plan for spare parts, reimbursement items, etc. For deliveries after FY 67, assuming continued rate of balanced economic growth for Iran, we see no reason at present why Iran should not be a legitimate claimant for larger amounts of credit for military purchases. We should keep credit possibilities in mind in reaching our conclusions about a financially feasible modernization program.

Rusk

---

[1] Source: Department of State, Central Files, DEF 19–3 US–IRAN. Confidential. Drafted by Padelford and Cain in International Logistics Negotiations in DOD/ISA; cleared in substance by Tiger, Skiles, and Towsley and in draft by Preble; and approved by Bracken. Repeated to CINCSTRIKE/CINCMEAFSA, and CINCSTRIKE/CINCMEAFSA for POLAD Tampa.

[2] Document 16.

[3] Document 15.

18.   **Telegram From the Embassy in Iran to the Department of State**[1]

Tehran, April 25, 1964, 5 p.m.

967. While Mansur during first weeks in office has rightly concentrated on economic matters, one major political problem that has arisen to plague him and Shah is how to deal with the recently released Ayatollah Khomeini. As we see it, following factors bear on situation.

1.   Although idea of releasing Khomeini prior to Moharam period originated with previous govt and although ultimate decision was made by Shah, it was Mansur and Pakravan who seem to have precipitated the problem by urging the Shah to let Khomeini go. Mansur thus has certain responsibility for outcome.

2.   Khomeini's latest activities and notably his speech of April 15 (reported NIT–6441) place govt in dilemma. If he is permitted to go on agitating, this will involve loss of prestige to regime and can snowball into serious trouble; but if he is re-arrested, especially during sensitive period just before and during Moharam, this could also cause serious trouble.

3.   There is little reason to doubt that regime is able to control or, if necessary, beat down any manifestations during Moharam period, starting evening May 12. Determination shown by regime during Moharam riots last year is in itself an important factor discouraging repetition of disorders.

4.   One of most interesting features of Khomeini's statements is his appeal for constitutional govt, which intrigues National Front which otherwise has little reason to sympathize with Mullahs. Speech also attacked arms expenditures, relations with Israel, featured xenophobic themes (including claim that govt is "giving away our resources to foreigners") and by implication attacked the Shah himself and the entire reform program. We understand tapes of April 15 speech are circulating in Tehran opposition circles and National Front elements are now considering cooperating with Mullahs.

5.   Although there are signs that economy is picking up, the social background of urban unemployment and misery, especially in Tehran's south side, is essentially unchanged from last year. In bazaar, Khomeini has continued to have many sympathizers, and as far as we can tell his prestige has, if anything, increased in that quarter since his release.

---

[1] Source: Department of State, Central Files, POL 23–9 IRAN. Confidential. Repeated to London, CINCMEAFSA for POLAD, Ankara, Baghdad, Cairo, Jidda, Karachi, and Kuwait.

6. Govt is playing this very carefully so far. Warnings have been sent to Khomeini, and we have no information of political statements by him since April 5 although he made it clear on that occasion that he intends to ignore the warnings. April 23, religious holiday, saw usual large crowds in Qom (estimated by one source at 50,000) and substantial numbers came to "Kisyrand," but it is possible that Khomeini has subsided at least for a while. We understand, however, that recording of his April 15 speech was played at Qom mosque on April 24.

Our tentative conclusion is that, if Khomeini persists, Shah is most likely to order his re-arrest prior to Moharam; that govt is capable of controlling or countering any possible demonstrations stirred up by Khomeini (or his arrest); but that showdown may be postponed until after the holiday period. Will submit another estimate as we come closer to Moharam.

Holmes

19.   Telegram From the Embassy in Iran to the Department of State[1]

Tehran, May 5, 1964, 5 p.m.

1008. State pass Defense. Re Embtels 988[2] and 922;[3] Deptel 744.[4] I had long conversation with Shah aboard aircraft carrier *Bon Homme Richard* evening of May 2. I took position and presented arguments as outlined Embtel 988.[5]

During conversation, it transpired that Shah had not had opportunity to read or study equipment list which he had handed me in reftel. He

---

[1] Source: Department of State, Central Files, DEF 19–3 US–IRAN. Secret. Repeated to CINCSTRIKE/CINCMEAFSA for POLAD.

[2] Telegram 988 from Tehran, April 30, commented on the list of Iranian military requirements that the Shah had given to Holmes during the meeting described in telegram 922. (Ibid.)

[3] Document 15.

[4] Dated April 10. (Department of State, Central Files, CENTO 3 US (WA))

[5] In telegram 988 Holmes reported that he planned to discuss the Shah's military inventory problems with him, emphasize the value the United States attached to Iran's position and role in the area, and say that Iran's needs after FY 1966 would be given serious consideration for military assistance grants—at a reduced level—commensurate with the availability of U.S. funds and Iran's financial position.

immediately disassociated himself from any desire for a full-scale armored division of the usual type in Khuzistan and indicated that he had no plans for an additional armored brigade and an additional infantry brigade in the area. This will make a substantial difference in cost in money and personnel which the first analysis of the papers handed to me in reftel revealed. The paper which ARMISH/MAAG is to present and discuss with Iranian staff is being revised accordingly. Copies of this revision will be sent to CINCSTRIKE and to Department.

He again forcefully stated his determination to build a force capable of defending Khuzistan against any local threat or of stemming a major threat until assistance could be forthcoming. His concept is to convert the eighth division into a unit of three battalions of tanks, three battalions of armored infantry with armored personnel carriers, an armored cavalry unit and normal artillery plus one battery of eight-inch howitzers.

Shah also alluded to need for airlift for two parachute battalions to provide for rapid reinforcement of area. In process of stressing urgency of his desire for more tanks, he emphasized his need to know availability date of M–60 tanks and price and approximate date of availability of projected Sheridan tank equipped with Shillelagh missile (ARMISH/MAAG is seeking this information through CINCSTRIKE).

Shah made great point of vital importance of Khuzistan to Iran emphasizing that this province contains Iran's huge oil reserves and refineries and that other developments, including Dez Dam with electric power, will make Khuzistan thriving industrial region of future. He expressed determination to see that there would be sufficient defensive power on ground to preserve this vital area for Iran. He conceded that he could not describe the immediate military threat but was persuaded that if proper defensive measure is not taken that threat would develop within two years' time.

Shah is very optimistic about increase in oil revenue. Iran's decision to accept consortium's recent offer will, in his opinion, result in revenues this year amounting to 500 million dollars. Discovery of additional large oil reserve makes it certain that Iran will be able to increase its production consistently over foreseeable future. Shah believes that with completion of pipe line and products terminal at Bandar Ma'shur, the cost of production per barrel will be reduced from 26 cents to 32 cents and pointed out that half of this savings will redound to Iran's revenues. He expressed confidence that by 1970 oil royalties from consortium and from other sources, such as PanAm, will amount to a billion 200 million dollars and a modest portion of this income can appropriately be devoted to defense of area whence it comes. He readily agreed that these military expenditures should not be greater than required for a safe minimum defense and felt that this could be achieved without impairing economic development in light of very substantial anticipated increased revenue from oil.

The foregoing will probably be the basis of what the Shah will have to say to the President on June 5. He asked how far he should go in discussing these matters with the President and I replied by saying that only one period of probably an hour's duration had been arranged for conversation with President and that there would certainly be no opportunity for "negotiations." I felt certain the President would be glad to hear of his preoccupations but I felt that the discussions would be in general terms over a broad range of subjects of mutual interest to Iran and the US. I reminded the Shah of the brief and informal character of his visit and that the meeting with the President had developed only incidentally after his acceptance of the invitation to open the art exhibition and to speak at UCLA. The Shah seemed to accept this as reasonable. I took this opportunity of telling him that the Department had not felt it necessary for me to be in Washington at the time of his visit.

I shall expect to discuss military requirements with the Shah at greater length before his departure for the US and hope to be able later to report more specifically on his position.

Holmes

20.   Telegram From the Department of State to the Embassy in Iran[1]

Washington, May 12, 1964, 7:55 p.m.

834. For Ambassador. UCLA officials are receiving increasing number reports to effect many hundreds Iranian students and sympathizers are planning massive, well-organized and well-financed demonstrations on occasion Shah's participation commencement ceremony. They emphasize their primary concern is with outsiders, not with Iranian UCLA students, whom they believe can be controlled.

UCLA now not only has grave doubts that ceremonies can take place with dignity, but is concerned over possible danger to Shah's

---

[1] Source: Department of State, Central Files, POL 7 IRAN. Secret; Priority; Limdis. Drafted by Bowling, cleared by Jernegan, and approved by Talbot.

physical safety. Ceremonies would take place in open field under extremely unfavorable conditions re control of crowds or individuals.

Dept is considering approach to Iranian Embassy to effect that since our analysis indicates danger of assassination attempt at Los Angeles ceremony cannot be completely eliminated, we feel Shah should accept cancellation this ceremony and confine his activities to East Coast, including ceremony at American University, where we can be sure of capacity to protect HIM from any possible assassination attempt by misguided student.

Do not mention foregoing to Iranian officials. Please telegraph your comments, including your estimate official Iranian reactions to such approach, along with any suggestions you may have as to modifications in approach, should we decide to make it. We would plan to base our approach solely on physical safety factor, even though our principal concern is actually over humiliation Shah might suffer in course of really large, well-organized demonstrations. We are aware that Shah's enemies would exploit cancellation as victory.[2]

Ball

---

[2] In telegram 1022 from Tehran, May 13, Holmes responded that the Shah would understand if demonstrations took place despite the efforts of authorities to control them, but would not understand an effort to dissuade him from coming to Los Angeles in the absence of documented and reasoned cause. He pointed out that an April 27 letter from President Kerr had expressed the hope that a small but vocal group of dissident students would not deter the Shah from coming to California. Thus, if the situation had changed since April 27, this would have to be explained with full particulars. (Ibid.)

---

21.   Action Memorandum From the Assistant Secretary of State for Near Eastern and South Asian Affairs (Talbot) to the Under Secretary of State for Political Affairs (Harriman)[1]

Washington, May 13, 1964.

SUBJECT

Request That You Ask the Attorney General to Begin Deportation Proceedings against an Anti-Regime Iranian Leader in the United States

Summary

Our relations with the Shah, and hence our national security interests, have been seriously endangered by increasing activity on the part of

---

[1] Source: Department of State, NEA/IRN Files: Lot 69 D 30, Iran 1964, V—Visas, 21 Deportation. Confidential. Drafted by Bowling and cleared by James J. Hines in L/SCA.

anti-Shah Iranians in the United States, which may culminate in humiliating and perhaps dangerous demonstrations at the UCLA Commencement in June. The effect of these activities is magnified by Iranian suspicion that the anti-Shah Iranians in the United States are being covertly condoned or even supported by the United States Government. We therefore request that you approach the Attorney General, apprise him of the gravity of the situation, and ask him to take deportation action against an anti-Shah leader in the United States, thus restoring Iranian confidence in United States intentions and, hopefully, dampening the ardor of other agitators.

Discussion

For the past six years the activities of anti-Shah Iranians in the United States have been a source of serious friction between the United States and Iran. Anti-American and sycophantic elements in the Imperial Court have fanned the Shah's suspicions that important elements in the United States Government are secretly backing these bitterly anti-Shah Iranians, and that their propaganda activities, including demonstrations against the Shah and members of the royal family on visits to the United States, are condoned by the United States. Unfavorable comparisons are drawn with the actions of other governments, such as that of France, which locked up anti-Shah Iranians during the period of the Shah's visit to France.

The Iranian tendency to suspect the United States Government of involvement in these activities is compounded by such factors as the following: (a) personal friendships between anti-Shah leaders and prominent Americans, such as Justice Douglas; (b) reception by the Attorney General of a delegation of anti-Shah Iranians and his subsequent cancellation of a stop in Tehran on his first trip to the Far East; and (c) suspension by the Department of Justice of deportation proceedings against anti-Shah Iranians in the United States whose passports had expired and were deemed not renewable by the Iranian Government. In two of the latter cases, suspension was continued even after our Ambassador had, at the request of the Department of Justice, obtained the Shah's personal assurance that he would not prosecute the two if they returned.

One of the Shah's top security advisors, who was in the United States a few weeks ago, stated that while the Shah would continue to be annoyed over demonstrations and other anti-regime activities, the real danger to United States–Iran relations was the Shah's growing suspicion that unfriendly elements in the United States were being protected by the United States Government. He begged us to take some symbolic action which would counteract these suspicions.

This problem has been exacerbated by recent information, unconfirmed at present, indicating that anti-regime leaders will mount a very large demonstration against the Shah at UCLA in the course of the Shah's

June visit. We may have to choose between the grave dangers of suggesting that the Shah cancel his appearance in Los Angeles or risking serious humiliation and possible danger to the Shah.

In either case, the possibility of a serious break with the Shah could be greatly reduced by some action which would convince His Majesty that we are not condoning the activities of these elements. Such an action might well also dampen the enthusiasm of other anti-regime Iranians, particularly those without valid passports, and reduce the intensity of such demonstrations as may be held.

The immediate pressing of deportation proceedings against Ali Shayegan (see Tab A),[2] who falsely stated in his visa application that he had never been a member of a communist organization, would appear to be perfectly tailored for the present situation. There is no basis for pity for Shayegan. He informed an NEA officer personally less than a year ago that he intended to dedicate the remainder of his life to the destruction of the Shah. You may remember him as being the most fanatical and anti-Western member of Mosadeq's last cabinet, except for Foreign Minister Fatemi, who was executed.

Recommendation

That you request the Attorney General to examine the case of Ali Shayegan with the view toward immediate pressing of deportation charges against him if the legal basis therefor exists.[3]

---

[2] Tab A, a short biography of Ali Shayegan, is not printed.

[3] The source text bears no indication of Harriman's approval or disapproval. On May 15 Acting Administrator of the Bureau of Security and Consular Affairs Charles Mace sent a memorandum to Raymond Farrell, Commissioner of the Immigration and Naturalization Service, stating that the Department had received "highly disturbing reports" regarding the intentions of anti-regime Iranians to organize demonstrations hostile to the Shah during his visit, which could be highly damaging to U.S. foreign policy and national security. Mace recommended deportation of Ali Shayegan and the extension of warnings to students without valid travel documents to cease their more extreme anti-regime activities or face deportation action. (Department of State, Central Files, POL 7 IRAN)

22.   Telegram From the Department of State to the Embassy in Iran[1]

Washington, May 14, 1964, 6:48 p.m.

842. Embtel 1018. Joint State/AID/Defense message. We regret apparent misunderstanding re Deptels 774 and 826[2] and Embtel 988.[3] Our authorization to you to discuss modernization requirements (Deptel 774) remains in effect. Caution contained in FYI portion para 3 of Deptel 678[4] against any commitment re grants or credits also remains in effect.

Dept did not intend in Deptel 826 raise doubts as to US ability sell for cash tanks or transport aircraft to Iran in future. Discussions as to desirable timing and types of modernization, do not, we feel, imply necessity of commitment at present to supply particular type at particular time, as per second and third proposals contained Embtel 988.

Specific commitments for grant MAP in FY 66 and beyond are simply not possible, though results of your discussions in terms of what would be technically feasible and desirable should be most useful. Specific commitments regardless of payment considerations fall within this category.

FYI. We hope to be able to satisfy Shah re tank modernization through offer of sale to be made in course his visit here. C–130's or other comparable types transport aircraft will be available for sale, and there remains of course possibility some types of transport aircraft and other modernization items under future grant MAP. End FYI.

Ball

---

[1] Source: Department of State, Central Files, DEF 19–3 US–IRAN. Secret. Drafted by Bowling on May 13, cleared by Walsh and in draft by Towsley and Haddad, and approved by Bowling. Repeated to CINCSTRIKE for POLAD Tampa.

[2] In telegram 1018 from Tehran, May 11 (ibid.), Holmes stated that he was puzzled by the apparent contradiction between telegram 774 (Document 16), which had authorized him to discuss with the Shah a reasonable modernization program without regard to financing, and telegram 826, May 8 (Department of State, Central Files, DEF 19–3 US–IRAN), which cast doubts regarding U.S. ability to provide replacement equipment for M–47 tanks and C–47 aircraft, regardless of payment considerations.

[3] Dated April 30; see footnotes 2 and 5, Document 19.

[4] Document 11.

23.   National Intelligence Estimate[1]

NIE 34–64   Washington, May 20, 1964.

IRAN

Conclusions

A. It remains uncertain whether modernization in Iran will proceed relatively peacefully or whether violence and revolution are in store. The Shah's reform effort has already helped to stimulate and shape the forces which must eventually, in one way or another, bring basic changes to Iranian society. Already the strength of the landlord class has been somewhat impaired, the gratitude of the peasants has been enlisted and their expectations aroused, and a new and growing managerial class seems to be acquiring increased responsibilities. However, the Shah, supported by the armed forces, still dominates Iranian political life and seems likely to do so for some time to come. With the self-confidence he has acquired from the relative success of his reform measures thus far, he will probably continue to move forward, though with occasional pauses, like the present one in his land reform program. (Paras. 5, 9, 26–27)

B. Iran is emerging only slowly from a recession which began in 1961 as the result of ineptly applied anti-inflationary measures and the consequent loss of business confidence. The latter was further set back by the uncertainties engendered by the reform measures. But the resources of the country are adequate to sustain a vigorous economic development, and the outlook for ample and growing oil revenues is promising. Within the next few years, Iran will probably be able to overcome the current slowdown and return to a fairly rapid rate of growth. (Paras. 15–16, 18)

C. The reduction in tensions which followed normalization of relations with the Soviet Union in September 1962 has continued, but relations are not likely to become significantly more intimate over the next few years. Though the Shah sees a need to appear more independent of the US, the outlook is for satisfactory US-Iranian relations for at least a considerable time to come. Iran is less dependent than in the past on US economic aid, but in the military and security field continues to rely on US assistance. (Paras. 31–35)

---

[1] Source: Central Intelligence Agency Files: Job 79–R01012A, ODDI Registry of NIE and SNIE Files. Secret; Controlled Dissem. According to a note on the cover sheet, the estimate was submitted by the Director of Central Intelligence and concurred in by the USIB on May 20.

Discussion

I.   Iran's Problems

1. In many respects Iran resembles other backward states ruled by traditional elites and confronted by the many pressures for radical change generated through wider contact with the modern world. There has been a continuing possibility that sooner or later the entire structure of the government and the society would either have to revolutionize itself or be overturned by self-appointed revolutionaries. At one point Mossadeq seemed on the verge of accomplishing such a revolution. Yet his regime collapsed, and the post-Mossadeq era has not seen a resurgence of revolutionary forces. Change has come, but it has been neither radical nor cataclysmic. The social and governmental institutions have been stretched but not rent asunder.

2. The explanation seems to rest in large part with the character of the Shah and the kind of role he has come to play, not only as a symbol but as an active national leader. He has long been aware of the pressures for change and has at various times taken a number of steps toward reform, though none was vigorously pressed. He eventually came to the view that such a slow pace of reform—as exemplified by distribution of crown land to peasants—would not be sufficient to maintain the regime over the long run. By the late 1950's agitation for reform seemed to be evoking a growing popular response; the country was beset with major economic difficulties; and the Shah was vulnerable to charges of reaction which not only offered his external enemies wide scope for attack but also distressed his foreign friends and supporters. In this setting, the government's rigging of the 1961 elections again returned a parliament (Majlis) composed of the traditional elite and created a dangerous situation. In May 1961 the Shah felt it necessary to bring in Prime Minister Amini with a broad mandate for change. Amini's reform measures provided some temporary relief, but they began to alienate the conservative elite without attracting any support from the National Front opposition.

3. Recognizing that Amini's measures were not alleviating opposition to the regime, the Shah allowed his government to fall in July 1962. At this juncture, the Shah evidently came to the conclusion that he must himself take responsibility for a more basic attack on Iran's problems. If this meant radical changes, he was prepared to make them. He also hoped by such measures to take the wind out of the opposition's sails and to broaden his own base of political support. To this end he proposed a six-point program, which was approved in a referendum in January 1963. Land reform, toward which some steps had been taken by the Ami-

ni government, was the main plank in this program and rapidly became the focus of popular attention.[2]

4.   Under the management of the dynamic and ambitious Minister of Agriculture, Arsanjani, the land reform program initially moved very rapidly. But, when Arsanjani seemed to be pressing the land reform too rapidly and to be using it to establish an independent political position, the Shah forced him to resign. Thereafter the pace of land reform was slowed considerably. The government found it difficult to provide agricultural credits and the trained managers for rural cooperatives both of which were necessary for the success of the program. In September 1963, the government publicly claimed that the first phase of the program—expropriation of the largest landholdings—had been completed.[3] Some preparatory work is now going on for the second phase of the reform program, which is to involve roughly 25,000 of the villages held by one or more landlords, but it is not clear whether or when a decision to proceed with it will be made.

5.   The reform program has not yet brought about a basic change in Iranian society or reduced the Shah's domination of political life. However, the Shah may have set in train a process of change which could have far-reaching consequences. Already the strength of the landlord class has been somewhat impaired, the gratitude of the peasants has been enlisted and their expectations aroused, and a new and growing managerial class seems to be acquiring increased responsibilities. Nevertheless, the Shah's regime continues to depend essentially on the army and security forces which have received important favors in return for their loyalty. Much of the urban middle class remains disaffected. The "Thousand Families," though deprived of much of their land, are still wealthy, and many remain entrenched in the Shah's entourage. Finally, the peasantry is not organized and has demonstrated little political consciousness.

6.   One aspect of social change in Iran which holds considerable significance for the future has been the rise of the technically trained managerial and administrative class who now have reached the upper levels of the bureaucracy in substantial numbers. This new breed of foreign-educated intellectual first became prominent in the late 1950's in the Plan

---

[2] The six-point program also included profit sharing for workers, eradication of illiteracy, electoral reform, nationalization of forests, and the sale of government enterprises. The granting of suffrage to women, though not specifically one of the six points, was widely heralded as an essential part of the Shah's reform program. [Footnote in the source text.]

[3] Of the approximately 50,000 villages in Iran, about 10,000 were owned by large landowners—those who owned more than one village. By 23 September 1963 all or parts of more than 8,000 of these villages had been purchased by the government at a cost of $62.2 million. Legal complications had delayed the takeover of the remaining 2,000 villages in this category. Of the villages acquired by the government, about 6,400 had been distributed to 271,000 families, comprising roughly ten percent of the agricultural population. [Footnote in the source text.]

Organization which, being independent of the traditional bureaucracy, provided quick advancement. They are now gradually being distributed throughout the bureaucracy. While many are not enthusiastic about the Shah's style of government, they are sympathetic with much of his reform program and are helping to implement it.

II. Political Situation

7.   Despite the Shah's authoritarian rule, he has generally felt the need for a facade of representative government. In September 1963, after two years of ruling without parliament, he again held elections. Like their predecessors, these elections were rigged; the contending political parties were again cliques attached to certain personalities and not representative of broader population groups. But this time the elections were used by the Shah significantly to increase the number of government officials—including many associated with the land reform program—in the Majlis and to greatly reduce the representatives of the landlord class.

8.   In constituting his most recent cabinet, that of Hasan Ali Mansur in March 1964, the Shah once again turned to the managerial and administrative class. Although Mansur's experience in government affairs is limited, he has a reputation for being a capable administrator. In 1959 he became head of the Progressive Center, a group of pro-government technicians, businessmen, and intellectuals which formed the nucleus of the New Iran Party, founded at the Shah's behest in 1963. Though this party now has about 140 of the 189 deputies in the Majlis, it is an artificial creation without a popular base.

The Role of the Military

9.   Although the reform program in theory threatens the senior officers who have a vested interest in the status quo, thus far they do not seem to have suffered or to be particularly concerned. Some of the middle-grade and junior officers probably share the outlook of the nationalist opposition, but the government is constantly screening the officer corps, and dissent within the military does not appear to be growing. We believe that the overwhelming majority of the officer corps are loyal to the Shah.

10. The Shah continues to rely on the National Intelligence and Security Organization (SAVAK) not only to design strategy for neutralizing the opposition but to organize political support for the government as well. SAVAK has not, however, been able to forestall periodic outbursts of open defiance of the government. On occasion the police and gendarmery have not been able to handle civil disturbances, and have had to call in the military. In these actions, the armed forces have generally performed creditably, and we believe that they can successfully cope with any likely disorders.

The Opposition

11. The opposition has been seriously disorganized and weakened by the Shah's tactics. The leaders of the loosely organized National Front (the remnants of ex-Prime Minister Mossadeq's organization) have been unwilling to support the reform program, since their real objective is not so much benefits for the population at large as it is power for themselves. Yet when they have combined with the conservatives to criticize the Shah's program, they have forfeited popular support. The government has been alert to exploit this dilemma. Moreover, by keeping many of the National Front leaders in detention until just before the elections, the government effectively stifled their chances. As a result of these vicissitudes, the party's political chief has resigned and it is in serious disarray. The danger that extreme and irresponsible elements will gain control is growing.

12. The conservative forces, which until recently supported the Shah, are now largely disaffected. The religious hierarchy in particular sees the reform program as striking at its power and interests. The mullahs have taken the lead and played a major role in agitation against the government which led to widespread popular demonstrations in June 1963. The government's vigorous suppression of these demonstrations and its continuing strong pressure against religious dissidents has severely weakened this segment of the opposition. Furthermore, the mullahs have for some time been hampered by their inability to agree on an overall leader, and their disunity and confusion have been compounded by the government's tactics of alternately arresting and releasing the leading religious figures. While some of the larger landlords have accommodated to the reform program, many of them remain apprehensive and a source of opposition to further development of the program.

13. The Tudeh (Communist) Party has been effectively suppressed. Its main leadership is either in exile or in jail. The party has not made appreciable headway in Iran in recent years and is heavily penetrated by the security forces. Although the discord within the National Front may provide the Tudeh with increased opportunities for infiltration, it appears now to have little chance of coming to dominate the movement.

14. Tribal dissidence remains a potential rather than a present threat to the regime. The Iranian Kurds have yet to overcome their traditional tribal rivalries and lack any widely accepted local leader. Moreover, they have no very serious grievance, and the government is taking some steps to extend to the Kurdish areas the benefits of economic development and to integrate them in greater degree into national life. The Iranian Kurds are unlikely to create serious problems for the government unless Iraqi Kurds win a large measure of autonomy or unless the USSR makes a determined attempt to incite a separatist movement. Neither of these developments now seems likely. While tribal disorders may occur in other

parts of Iran, such conflicts are easy to contain and isolate, and it would be extremely difficult for the diverse tribal groupings to coordinate action against the regime. Though there is almost certainly some Egyptian or Iraqi intrigue among the Khuzistan Arabs, they are unarmed, sunk in poverty and apathy, and therefore constitute no threat at present.

III. Economic Trends

15. Iran's natural resources are capable of supporting extensive economic development. Arable land is more than adequate to support the growing population, and irrigation projects are increasing agricultural productivity and bringing new land under cultivation. Favored by good weather, total agricultural production in 1963 increased some nine percent over that of the previous year. Iran's most important asset, however, is its booming oil industry, which is largely insulated from the vagaries of Iran's domestic economy. The government's rapidly rising revenues from this source are sufficient to provide a solid base for a broad development program, even allowing for continued mismanagement and corruption.

16. Since 1961 Iran has been plagued by a recession which has resulted in considerable unemployment, unused productive capacity, and an unfavorable climate for investment. For a number of years prior to 1961, rising oil revenues, large foreign loans, and good harvests stimulated a high rate of economic activity. Gross National Product (GNP) was rising by nearly six percent annually, and by 1961 annual investment had risen to about 18 percent of GNP. The number of banks and factories doubled, and a start was made toward modernizing the government's economic institutions and practices. By 1960, however, the attempt to carry out such an ambitious—and largely uncoordinated—effort led to serious inflationary pressures, a speculative construction boom, and a sharp decline in foreign exchange reserves. This obliged the government to replace its expansionary policies with a series of anti-inflationary measures, which frightened the business community and proved to be more difficult to rescind than to impose.

17. More recently, the government has been seeking to revive the domestic economy through attempts to increase expenditures under the Third Plan (1962–1968), stimulate private industry, and expand exports. Credit has been made cheaper and more readily available and a trade agreement has been concluded with the Common Market. However, the expansionary effect of such policies has been small, due at least in part to the political uncertainties engendered by the Shah's simultaneous effort to launch his reform program.

18. The advent of the Mansur government and the slowing of the reform program have apparently begun to restore business confidence. Although administrative difficulties continue to prevent the government from rapidly increasing public investment under the Plan, a modest rise

has been achieved in recent months. Nevertheless, many problems remain, and we do not foresee a strong business recovery in the immediate future. Iran's underlying economic strength, however, will probably enable it to overcome these difficulties and within the next few years return to a more rapid rate of growth.

Oil

19. One of the basic reasons for Iran's favorable prospects is its booming oil industry, which provided the government with about $380 million in revenues in 1963, an amount likely to increase by at least 8 to 10 percent annually for the next several years. Since the disastrous experience with nationalizing the oil industry during the Mossadeq era, the Iranian Government has dealt with the oil consortium through negotiations rather than threats. Though the government periodically voices complaints against the consortium's exploration and development programs, the rapid rise of oil production and revenues in Iran and the development of several new deposits have largely allayed these criticisms. Iran will doubtless desire greater oil revenues than in fact it receives, but it will probably continue to take a more realistic attitude than the more extreme members of the Organization of Petroleum Exporting Countries (OPEC),[4] who are interested in gaining greater control of levels of oil production and prices. It is possible that Iran might leave OPEC over this issue; if so, it would probably expect the companies to increase their proportionate offtake of Iranian oil.

Long-Range Planning

20. The concept of comprehensive economic development planning has not yet gained a firm foothold in Iran. The Third Plan, as originally drawn up by the Plan Organization, showed early promise of breaking through the traditional hostility toward planned investment. After the fall of the Amini government, however, the impetus toward meaningful planning was largely lost. Anti-planning elements wielded strong influence in the Alam government and succeeded in weakening the Plan Organization and decentralizing responsibility for project formulation and implementation. Consequently, the Third Plan reflects the constant bureaucratic bickering as to how plan resources should be allocated.

21. Under the Mansur government the outlook for the Third Plan has improved somewhat. Relatively few projects without some intrinsic economic merit are contemplated. Even the "make-work" projects in the program have utility for combatting recession and urban employment. The plan also promises support for land reform and rural development. Thanks to the rising oil income and good prospects for foreign loans and credits, the financing of the Third Plan should not be a serious problem.

---

[4] The members of OPEC are: Saudi Arabia, Venezuela, Iran, Iraq, Kuwait, Qatar, Libya, and Indonesia. [Footnote in the source text.]

Even so, the Plan Organization is passing through a period of trans-formation and is unlikely for some time to have sufficient authority and competence to give effective direction to Iran's development. Thus, the Third Plan, which is supposed to increase development expenditures more than two and a half times, will probably fall considerably short of its goals.

Agriculture and Land Reform

22. Thus far the land reform program has had no discernible effect on agricultural production. Any disruptive effect has been more than off-set by good weather conditions over the past two years, and total agricul-tural production may register a further increase this year. A relatively small proportion of the land has been distributed to date, and most of the government cooperatives which are to play an essential role in agricul-tural management have been formed only on paper. The future of the agricultural sector of the economy will depend in large measure on how successfully these cooperatives fulfill their functions, particularly the management of Iran's complicated irrigation system which has been the traditional task of the landlords. If these management responsibilities are in fact well performed, and if government plans to provide financial and technical assistance are carried out, agricultural production is likely to increase.

IV.   The Domestic Outlook

23. The Shah apparently feels the need for a breathing spell in his re-form efforts in order to consolidate recent gains. The pace of land reform has outstripped the government's administrative capacities, and little new land is likely to be transferred in the near future. Yet it is unlikely that awareness of this fact will arouse significant disappointment among the peasantry, who have yet to display any political initiative of their own. In any event, there is no ready vehicle for them to express their feel-ings, as the Shah has effectively prevented the emergence of any mass leaders. While it does not seem likely that the peasants will become an active force in political life in the near future, it is possible that the Shah has fostered the beginnings of a social transformation in the countryside.

24. The National Front opposition appears to have no great pros-pects at present. Its various leaders will certainly interpret any slow-down of the reform program as confirming their suspicions that the Shah intends no basic reform of Iranian society. Yet they show no signs of being able to overcome the factionalism that has prevented their movement from exerting effective opposition or of developing a positive program of its own. Moreover, even with the slowing of reform, the nationalists are unlikely to be very successful in inducing the technicians, who recog-nize that the regime must modernize to survive in the long run, to risk their government positions by joining the opposition. Pressures for change, stimulated in part by the reform program itself, will probably

grow and bring periodic turbulence. We do not believe, however, that any of the opposition groups singly or in combination, will be able to pose a serious challenge to the regime for the next few years, mainly because of the reliability and efficiency of the security apparatus. In short, the Shah's prospects for retaining control for the foreseeable future are good.

25. In the past the Shah has been unwilling to permit any political personality to consolidate independent power, and Mansur is unlikely to be an exception. His government, however, may be able to provide the administrative and technical talent that the Shah feels is vital to carry out the reform program. In the end he may, like other Prime Ministers, be a convenient scapegoat, should political and economic frustrations build up again to the point of demonstrations or open unrest. Tactics such as these have drawn fire away from the monarchy in the past, and we believe they are likely to succeed again.

Longer Term Outlook

26. Though it seems quite likely that change will continue to be evolutionary for a number of years, it remains uncertain whether Iran will make the ultimate transition to modern life without experiencing a violent revolution. The odds are not as hopeless as they have sometimes appeared when the regime has been faced with crisis. For some years to come it is likely that Iran will pass through a period of consolidation in an effort to assimilate recent changes. During this time the bureaucracy will probably come increasingly to be dominated by the new class of technicians, who offer the best hope for bridging the gap between the paternal administration of the Shah and disaffected middle class elements.

27. As in the past, the Shah will continue to dictate the pace of these developments. It is not certain that he will continue to push the reform program energetically, although he seems now to see it as a design for social and economic advance to which he has a personal commitment. His tendency in the past, however, has been to use reform as a palliative when pressed, and he may draw back once more. Nevertheless, the Shah does appear convinced that his "White Revolution" has thus far been a notable success, and his self-confidence has clearly been enhanced. Hence the chances now seem good that he will continue to move forward, though with some pauses and even retreats along the way.

28. Even if he persists, the success of the Shah's initiative for evolutionary reform will depend in the long run on whether it evokes a response in the country sufficient to be translated into broadened political support for the regime. It is too soon yet to say that this will happen, though if reform is pressed and enlarged in scope, it is not unreasonable to believe that new and more constructive political formations will eventually appear. The test would then be whether the Shah would be willing to share power with the political forces he would have called into being.

On this will depend also his ability to attract and hold the first-class talent so badly needed for the tasks of development. In any case, it seems clear that the Shah's reform effort has already helped to stimulate and shape the forces which must eventually, in one way or another, bring basic changes to Iranian society.

29. It is a basic weakness of Iran that the present equilibrium depends almost exclusively on the Shah. The modernization that has taken place to date has been largely administrative and economic, and little has been done to create political institutions that would survive the death of the Shah. Hence, should assassination or any other event remove him, the monarchy as an institution would be endangered. The 44-year-old Shah has not allowed any other figures to develop power in their own right, and the bureaucracy and the parliament, though somewhat more respected than in the past, have as yet no independent stature. Hence the military would almost immediately be drawn into the political arena. A successor government, if controlled by the senior officers, would probably, without attempting to reverse the Shah's programs, pursue a generally more conservative course. However, if younger officers gain a dominant voice, the government might reflect the more radical outlook of the nationalist opposition. In any event, conditions would be so disturbed that any successor regime would probably find it difficult to consolidate power, and a prolonged period of instability would probably ensue.

V. Foreign Policy

30. Iran's strongly pro-Western orientation represents primarily the will of the Shah. He is supported in this by the bureaucracy, and in particular the military establishment. On the other hand, many of the intellectuals would prefer a neutral course between East and West; indeed, this would be the foreign policy which any National Front government would strive to adopt.

Relations with the USSR

31. The most important development in Iran's foreign relations in recent years has been the normalization of relations with the Soviet Union since September 1962. At that time, Moscow accepted the Shah's pledge not to permit the establishment of missile bases on his soil and shelved its policy of open diplomatic and propaganda pressures to overthrow his regime. Thus, without detracting from his Western ties, the Shah was able to end the strong Soviet pressure which had kept tension high for many years. Soviet acceptance of this gesture may indicate recognition, at least for the near term, of the ineffectiveness of subversive efforts against the regime.

32. Yet neither the Shah nor the Kremlin has sought to do much more than reduce tensions. After an initial flurry of sympathetic articles in the

Tehran press, the Iranian Government intervened to reduce the volume and emphasis of pro-Soviet publicity. For their part, the Soviets have not come forth with the expected proposals for large-scale economic projects, though they have provided a $38.8 million 10-year credit for Iran. Communist propaganda beamed by clandestine radio stations outside Iran still criticizes the regime.

33. The Shah will probably welcome continued improvement in Soviet relations and may even pay increasing lip service to "nonalignment." In any case, it will be difficult for him to reject the friendship of a powerful neighbor that claims to have changed its attitude and whose conduct is correct. A policy of accommodation will also serve to some extent to appease the neutralist and xenophobic sentiments of Iranians who believe their country is overcommitted to the West. It would also counter the Shah's concern that, with signs of a developing East-West détente, the US might lose interest in supporting and defending Iran against increased Soviet influence. Nevertheless, Iranian fears of Soviet designs remain alive and will probably serve to check any significant danger to Iran's Western orientation for the period of this estimate.

Relations with the US

34. Iran's relationship with the US appears to be undergoing a subtle change. Though the American alliance remains the cornerstone of Iran's foreign policy, the Shah, for reasons of domestic politics and international prestige, sees a need to appear more independent. At the same time, the rise of oil revenues, improving agricultural output, and the availability of credits from other free world sources and the Soviet Bloc have reduced Iran's dependence on US economic assistance. Accordingly US influence on economic development is decreasing.

35. The same cannot be said of the security field, where Iran remains heavily dependent on US assistance. The Shah was heartened by a US-Iranian exercise which brought sizable numbers of American troops to Iran. [2-1/2 lines of source text not declassified] The five-year US military aid plan has alleviated to some degree the Shah's dissatisfaction with US military support. Thus we foresee a period of relative calm in US military relations with Iran, probably until near the end of the military aid plan in 1967.

Regional Relations

36. The CENTO alliance is important to Iran as a formal defense link to the West and because it provides an additional claim on the US for aid. This does not mean that Iran is fully satisfied with the alliance. It has been irritated by the refusal of the US and the UK to consider alleged threats from non-Communist regional states as falling within the purview of the alliance and has suspected the US at times of having only a lukewarm interest in this pact. Iran's dissatisfaction with CENTO's economic achievements was greatly alleviated by the recent decision of the US to

finance the Turkey–Iran rail link. Under the circumstances, Iran can be expected to continue to be cooperative in CENTO, although not without criticisms of specific aspects of the alliance.

37. The Shah's chief regional concern is his fear that Nasser is actively plotting to overthrow his regime, working through Iraq and the Persian Gulf Sheikhdoms. Though Nasser has recently made some overtures to improve relations, the Shah remains wary. In fact, he is likely to pursue a more active policy to counter UAR activities directed at the Persian Gulf. Relations with Afghanistan have improved markedly since Iran served as mediator in the Afghanistan–Pakistan dispute, and prospects for the future here are good.

---

24.   Letter From the Ambassador to Iran (Holmes) to Secretary of State Rusk[1]

Tehran, May 20, 1964.

Dear Dean:

Next week I shall be sending a telegram[2] assessing the local situation and the Shah's attitudes, which I hope will be useful to the President and you in discussions with him. There is one important subject which cannot be included because of the circulation such messages receive.

A seldom discussed but vital element in our relationship with Iran is the agreement of the Shah which permits us to continue a series of U.S. technical intelligence operations in various parts of Iran. For the most part, the nature of many of these activities is such that they cannot be concealed from the public, and it is only through the Shah's approval, and in certain instances through direct Iranian participation, that we are able to continue these activities.

More specifically, the activities include

a) The establishment and maintenance of [2-1/2 lines of source text not declassified]. These activities require the presence of upwards of [less than 1 line of source text not declassified] civilian and service personnel, plus dependents.

---

[1] Source: Department of State, Central Files, POL 7 IRAN. Top Secret; Official–Informal.

[2] See Document 27.

b) The establishment and maintenance of [*1 line of source text not declassified*] facilities.

c) The Customs-free importation of technical and other logistic support required for the above activities.

d) The Shah has also given personal approval for [*less than 1 line of source text not declassified*] intelligence [*less than 1 line of source text not declassified*] operations [*3 lines of source text not declassified*].

I should rather not specify the precise objectives or results obtained from these activities which, I am told, are of critical value to us. However, John McCone could inform you of how important they are to our national security.

My point in raising this sensitive matter with you at this time is to make certain that at the top level of our Government, on the eve of the Shah's visit to Washington, there is realization of this particular benefit which we derive from our relationship with the Shah, and of the fact that he, having personally assumed full responsibility for supporting and protecting these activities, has never sought a quid pro quo for them or tried to blackmail us because of them. We should not allow a situation to develop where the Shah would be tempted to resort to such practice. The importance of these facilities in Iran would become even greater if by any unhappy chance, owing to policy changes in Pakistan, we should be deprived of similar facilities in that country.

For these and other reasons our relationship with the Shah and with Iran is an important one and I very much hope it will be possible for us to show a flexible attitude during the Shah's visit to Washington, particularly in relation to his desires for continuing U.S. assistance in the modernization of his military establishment. I should be grateful if you would show this letter to the President.[3]

With warm regards,

Sincerely yours,

Julius

---

[3] On June 12 Secretary Rusk thanked Holmes for his timely letter and noted that it seemed to him that the U.S. Government has been sufficiently flexible regarding the Shah's military modernization and security problems and sufficiently understanding of his economic concerns to obviate the likelihood that he would be tempted to use the intelligence facilities as a basis for undue pressure in the near future. (Department of State, Central Files, POL 7 IRAN)

25.   Background Paper Prepared in the Department of State[1]

SVW–B/4   Washington, May 27, 1964.

SHAH OF IRAN
VISIT TO WASHINGTON, JUNE 5, 1964

THE IRANIAN REFORM PROGRAM

Shortly after Vice President Johnson's visit to Iran in August 1962, the Shah personally assumed leadership of a program of reforms, some of which had been launched by the Amini Government before its fall in mid-1962. In the absence of Parliament, the Shah in January 1963 put to a referendum and won overwhelming endorsement for a six-point reform program, the most significant elements of which were land reform and an Education Corps modelled on our Peace Corps. Subsequently, other elements have been added to the original program, most notably enfranchisement of women and a Health Corps.

While the execution of the program has been spotty, certain aspects have gained considerable momentum and give the impression that some fundamental changes are at last under way in the long-static Iranian society. An election in the Fall of 1963, although carefully controlled by the Shah and barred to the opposition, nevertheless avoided the more blatant rigging of earlier elections. It brought into being a pro-reform Parliament and ended an unconstitutional parliamentary interregnum of more than two years. In March 1964 the Shah appointed a new Government of younger technocrat elements headed by Hasan Ali Mansur, who is concentrating on certain key administrative reforms (budget, civil service) and on attempts to spur a business revival through an increased level of public investments and economic policies favorable to private business.

In espousing basic reforms the Shah alienated the landlords and conservative clergy which had formed the principal base of his support, but failed to overcome the pre-existing opposition of the pro-Mosadeqist "nationalists." While these externally disparate elements have not in most instances joined forces, the conservative groups were powerful enough in the summer of 1963 to incite severe rioting in Tehran and other cities. This was suppressed without great difficulty by the Shah's military and security forces, and a threatened repetition of the rioting this summer has so far been forestalled by precautionary measures. These military and security forces have a high degree of reliability and increas-

---

[1] Source: Johnson Library, National Security File, Country File, Iran, Shah's Visit, 6/5/64. Confidential. Drafted by Tiger and cleared by Bowling, Towsley, Spain, and Jernegan.

ing technical capability. Their methods can be vigorous when necessary and they are feared by some elements of the population. However, they have not been used by the regime to institute an atmosphere of widespread repression, even against the conservative opponents of reform.

The Shah is clearly exhilarated by the initial progress of his reform program, particularly his own success in having overcome his dependence on the anti-reform elements in Iranian society. Although he is undoubtedly sincere in espousing the reforms as an essential feature (along with economic development) of the modernization of his country, he is also acutely conscious of the effect of the reforms on world opinion, particularly in the U.S. In describing the reforms to foreigners, he is apt to exaggerate greatly their success and to confuse promise with fulfillment. We thus find it necessary from time to time, while expressing appreciation for his reform efforts, to remind him that we see them as only a beginning. In order to avoid the appearance of patronizing him, we have couched such strictures in terms of comparisons with the United States, where, in spite of the maturity of economic and institutional development, there remain grave areas of concern, such as poverty and race relations.

---

26.   **Letter From the Deputy Assistant Secretary of State for Near Eastern and South Asian Affairs (Jernegan) to the Deputy Assistant Secretary of Defense for Regional Affairs (Sloan)**[1]

Washington, May 28, 1964.

Dear Frank:

In the course of the Shah's unofficial visit to the United States, he will talk with the President for an hour on June 5. This talk will be followed by a White House luncheon for the Shah.

Briefing papers for the President are being prepared in this bureau of the Department of State, and several of these will be forwarded to ISA shortly for clearance. All of the subjects except one which we expect to come up are non-operational, and we expect no difficulties in obtaining

---

[1] Source: Washington National Records Center, RG 330, OASD/ISA Files: FRC 68 A 306, 333 Iran—28 May 1964. Confidential.

clearances on those portions of the briefing materials dealing with general political and economic affairs or with Persian Gulf problems.

The enclosed drafts,[2] which are to be incorporated in the Talking Paper and Background Paper, respectively, deal with military assistance, which, as you know from recent messages from Tehran and from CINC-MEAFSA, constitutes the critical item which will largely determine the long-term results of the Shah's meeting with the President.

We feel that it is vital for the President to be able to indicate clearly to the Shah that his problems of military equipment are being sympathetically considered at the highest levels of the United States Government. As a minimum, we feel that the President must be able to make a concrete offer to the Shah responsive to the Shah's current primary concern—the replacement during the next few years of aging M–47 tanks.

We are aware that there is some division of opinion in the Department of Defense as to the relative value of the M–48A3 and the M–60 tanks for supply to Iran. We feel quite certain, however, that the Shah greatly prefers the M–60, and that the President's offer should emphasize the availability of the M–60.

We are further aware that there is some difference of opinion as to whether or not the still-experimental Sheridan might be made a part of any commitment to supply tanks to Iran in the future. We are assuming that the stage of development of this tank is such that no such commitment may be made, despite the Shah's known interest in that vehicle.[3]

We would hope that ISA might be able to provide technical tab papers on these tanks and a summary table outlining the current Five-Year MAP Plan for Iran.

Members of your staff have indicated informally to members of my staff that the possibility of a substantial proportion of M–60's being supplied under grant MAP is completely out of the question. We have therefore confined the offer in our draft to one of sale only. However, the Shah, at the time of agreement on the current Five-Year Plan, specifically made reservations in respect to the adequacy of the proposed tank component, and we informed him that we would review this element of the Plan later. Furthermore, we note that thirty grant M–60's for Iran have been included in CINCSTRIKE's MAP submission for FY 66 as a non-commitment item, and that the submission is within the current EUCOM MAP ceiling for FY 64–69. I would therefore appreciate your reviewing the problem to make certain that it will not be possible for the President to

---

[2] Not printed.

[3] On June 3 Sloan responded to Jernegan noting that there were so many variables regarding the Sheridan that it was premature to discuss its being furnished under either sale or grant. (Washington National Records Center, RG 330, OASD/ISA Files: FRC 68 A 306, 333 Iran—28 May 1964)

combine his sale offer with a commitment to supply thirty M–60's under grant MAP before the end of 1967. Should this be possible, the beneficial effect on our military and political objectives of the President's talk with the Shah would be greatly increased.[4]

I am aware that the problem of tank production and supply is at present a delicate one, and that it will not be easy for DOD to make firm and quick decisions. Nevertheless, we feel it is imperative that the President be able to talk to the Shah in specific terms. In addition to the obvious broad political effects of this talk, we are convinced that it may prove to be a major fork in the road determining whether or not we are to continue to maintain our position as the primary source of equipment and military influence in Iran. The Shah's political and financial position is such that he is now capable of shopping in world markets for military equipment. We believe he will do so unless we continue to retain his confidence in us as his primary source of supply.

I would appreciate your clearance and/or comments on the enclosed draft segments of the President's briefing papers.

Sincerely yours,

Jack

---

[4] In his response Sloan pointed out that since no other country had received M–60 tanks as grant aid, the Department of Defense did not want to establish a precedent; therefore, it recommended that they be sold as planned.

---

27. Telegram From the Embassy in Iran to the Department of State[1]

Tehran, May 28, 1964, 5 p.m.

1090. For the Secy from the Amb. The fol summary statement on the Shah and his current concerns may be helpful in connection with the preparations for his forthcoming visit. As I shall not be present, I am submitting this statement, which represents the views of the Country Team, and recommend that it be also submitted to the Pres.

---

[1] Source: Department of State, Central Files, POL 7 IRAN. Secret; Limdis.

When the Shah was last in Wash in April 1962, he was in a depressed and insecure mood and needed to be reassured that we thought he was on the right track with his reform program, that we admired his steadfastness in the face of Sov threats and blandishments, and that he had our continuing political and military support. He has changed a good deal since that time. Now he is in a buoyant mood, convinced (with some justification) that his internal program is a success, that his regime is secure, and that he has managed the foreign affairs of his country wisely. But he is gravely disturbed by recent trends in the Arab world. He still requires reassurance that we are with him, that we admire him, and that we understand his current concerns.

In foreign affairs, the Shah continues to stand squarely with the free world and considers his country the only stable ally we have between Suez and the Sea of Japan. Although he has "normalized" his relations with the Sov Union, he continues staunchly anti-Communist and in fact is sometimes inclined to suspect us of going too far in the direction of a détente. Last year he was acutely worried by talk of a possible non-aggression pact between NATO and the Warsaw Pact countries and felt that this could force him into an unwanted accommodation with the Sov Union; but we managed to convince him that those worries were unfounded.

Today his principal concern in foreign and military affairs is with Arab (and especially Nasser's) designs on the oil-rich Iranian province of Khuzistan which is inhabited by about one million Iranian Arabs. He recognizes that the UAR does not at present have the capability to make serious trouble for him in Khuzistan, but he sees a long-term trend of British withdrawal from the Persian Gulf area and has been especially disturbed by the recent political and military agreements between the UAR and Iraq. At present he is more concerned with the Arab threat than with the threat of Sov expansionism. Persistently misreading our policy, he is inclined to feel—as many of our allies do—that we are too friendly toward neutralists like Nasser, whom he likes to picture as a Sov tool.

On the internal scene, the Shah's control of his country is, if anything, still tighter than it was two years ago. He has recently called in a new team of younger people to run his govt, and that new Cabinet (under Hasan Ali Mansur) is pushing forward with a number of much-needed reforms, including civil service reform, a much-needed new approach to budgeting, and a general overhaul of the administrative machinery. There are also indications that the Mansur govt is managing to gain the confidence of the business community and thus to bring about a much-needed recovery of the private sector. The Shah is probably unwilling to face the fact that in the cities, and particularly among the intelligentsia, his regime has yet to generate enthusiastic support. He continues unable to delegate authority and is probably convinced that past American advice to that effect was proved wrong by events.

Perennially, our problem with the Shah has been to keep his military program in balance with his vitally important programs for social and economic reform. Our five-year program of military assistance, agreed in 1962, has been highly successful in maintaining this balance. Recently he has become concerned with the replacement of items (especially the M–47 tank, but also the F–86 and C–47 aircraft), which will soon become unsupportable, and wanted to discuss what will happen after expiration of the five-year program. In repeated and intensive discussions with him, we have tried here during the past weeks to bring his current requests down to the level where they are reasonable both from the military and from the economic-political points of view, and it now appears that we have had some measure of success; but there is no doubt that the recent UAR–Iraq agreement has made him view the replacement program with even greater urgency. Especially the tank problem is now his central military preoccupation.

Iran's attitude toward U.S. military aid is changing as the country's financial position is improving. A reasonable transition of our MAP from grant aid to a mixture of U.S. grant assistance, extension of credit, and sales for cash—within the limits of a new, jointly arrived, reasonable program—is now the crucial requirement of our continued close relations with Iran.

It would be desirable that the conversation between the President and the Shah not dwell exclusively on military matters. The Shah regards himself as a world statesman and will be flattered by a discussion of world affairs. It would also be useful to remind the Shah in the course of the conversation that, while we will continue to help him in meeting his military problems, we consider his economic and social development programs of fundamental importance for the long-term stability of his country. While much has been done, a great deal more still remains to be done. Since the Shah is currently inclined to be overly optimistic about Iran's future oil income, the President might make the desired point by discussing the problem all national leaders have in allocating scarce resources and by expressing the thought that estimates of future resources are often over-optimistic and that there is no end to the competition between conflicting requirements, so that there is always need for a careful establishment of priorities.

The Shah is a genuine friend of the U.S. He has turned to us for advice on most important problems and cooperates with us in many fields, including some highly classified ones that are of great importance to us. His popular image abroad and at home has improved since he launched his reform program. His current preoccupation with military problems in the Persian Gulf has some justification. We hope that he will feel that he has gained the personal understanding of the President for those problems and particularly that the President understands the need for certain more modern types of equipment for his armed forces, within the framework of a new agreed, long-term program that is being worked out.[2]

Holmes

---

[2] In telegram 906, June 4, Rusk thanked the Ambassador for his telegram, saying that it had proved invaluable in preparing for the Shah's visit, and that it had been submitted to the President as Holmes had recommended. (Ibid.)

---

28.   Telegram From the Department of State to the Embassy in Iran[1]

Washington, May 28, 1964, 1:41 p.m.

889. Embtel 1065.[2] Recognize Shah currently concerned with security situation (Arab threat) and preoccupied with details military modernization but hope he aware that it would be counterproductive to devote hour with President mostly these subjects, particularly technical discussion merits various kinds military equipment. President keenly interested progress Shah's reforms, especially land reform, education and health corps, women's emancipation, administrative reform, etc., and in measures to stimulate Iranian economy. To omit or downgrade these subjects would risk giving impression one-sided preoccupation military-security affairs.

We hope you will find opportunity before Shah leaves to intimate this need for balance in meeting with President. You may wish to refer to opportunity for discussion military problems Iranian Embassy tea June 6 (at which we hope McNaughton, Sloan, and Generals Woods and Adams will be present) and to make it clear again that we expect details concerning timing and equipment content modernization program to be worked out in continuing Tehran discussions with you and General Eckhardt, not during Washington visit.

Ball

---

[1] Source: Department of State, Central Files, DEF 19–3 US–IRAN. Confidential; Priority; Limdis. Drafted by Tiger; cleared in substance by Colonel Taylor and by Komer; and approved by Jernegan.

[2] Dated May 25. (Ibid.)

29.   Current Intelligence Memorandum[1]

OCI No. 1582/64   Washington, May 30, 1964.

SUBJECT

The Visit of the Shah of Iran

1.   The Shah of Iran is due to arrive in Washington on 4 June to open a "7,000 Years of Persian Art" exhibit at the National Gallery. Although he is on an unofficial visit, he is scheduled to see the President, as well as other top officials. The Shah is also scheduled to receive honorary degrees from American University and from the University of California at Berkeley before he leaves the country about 13 June. He has visited the US on four previous occasions, unofficially in 1954–55 and 1958, and officially in 1949 and 1962. The principal problem anticipated during this trip is hostile demonstrations by Iranian students, particularly in California. Such demonstrations against the Iranian Government have been a perennial problem in this country, and a number of sizable ones occurred in Europe during the Shah's visit to Austria and Italy last winter.

2.   The Shah's short title is His Imperial Majesty Mohammad Reza Shah Pahlavi. Now age 44, he is an intelligent and personable individual, fluent in English and French, with a taste for sports—tennis, riding, skiing, flying—and an interest in art and literature as well as in attractive women. He has been married three times: to the sister of ex-king Farouk (1939); to the well-known Soraya, the daughter of a minor tribal chief and a German national (1951); and to the present Queen, Farah, who comes from an old Azerbaijan family (1959). The long-desired heir, Prince Reza, was born in 1960. The Shah has two daughters, one born last year and one by his first wife.

3.   The Shah has been on the throne, ruling most of the time as well as reigning, since 1941, when his father was ousted by the Allies. The father was an army officer who seized the throne to found the Pahlavi dynasty. The Shah's beginning and finishing education was military; in between he spent four years in schools in Switzerland. His interest in the army and in military affairs generally is thus a product of his educational background as well as of a preoccupation with Iran's security problems.

4.   The Shah's family has not been among his assets. His father was disliked and feared, his twin sister leads an uninhibited personal life allegedly engaging in such doubtful business enterprises as opium smuggling and his half-brothers have generally been kept in obscurity. The

---

[1] Source: Central Intelligence Agency Files: Job 79–T00430A, Current Intelligence Memoranda, May 1964. Secret; No Foreign Dissem. Prepared in the Office of Current Intelligence.

political philosophy of many of the Shah's court intimates appears to be late eighteenth century Bourbon.

5. From this background, the Shah has emerged, particularly in the past ten years, as a sensitive, often moody, but nonetheless able proponent of the modernization of his country—under his direction. Since the overthrow of the Mossadeq regime in 1953 he has operated largely as a dictator, with a thin facade of parliamentary democratic procedures. He has confronted, with some considerable skill, a situation in which a rising middle class has agitated restlessly for greater political power and accelerated economic and social change, while vested interests—landed aristocracy, obscurantist clergy, and tribal chieftains—have venomously opposed all attempts at reform.

6. The present phase of the Shah's reform program began in earnest two years ago. Its main points are the redistribution of land, electoral reform including the enfranchisement of women, profit sharing among industrial workers, the nationalization of forests, the formation of a literacy corps, and provision for the compensation of expropriated landlords. Land reform is the key aspect of the program, and substantial progress has been made. There are indications, however, that the program will soon be temporarily slowed to allow the administrative apparatus—surveys, etc.—to catch up. The new cabinet, under Prime Minister Hasan Ali Mansur, is pledged to undertake administrative reforms to consolidate the achievements of the "white revolution." The hyper-skeptical Iranian public, however, is likely to view this development as an indication that the vested interests have gained a round.

7. The Shah's opponents are able to unite only on the issue of his "dictatorial and unconstitutional" methods of governing. The principal opposition vehicle is a National Front, whose core comes from the upper and middle classes. However, the development of a unified opposition is handicapped not only by the disparity of views among its elements—which run from the Muslim mullahs to the Communist Tudeh Party, heavily infiltrated by the government's security organs—but also by the basic appeal that the land reform program has made in an overwhelmingly peasant country. The opposition has been placed in the position of trying to oppose the Shah while avoiding opposition to a popular program with which he is personally identified. There are in fact some signs that younger members of the middle class, who are now taking up their "class positions" in the government bureaucracy, are rallying to the government, at least in the sense that they seem to be working diligently to make the Shah's program a success.

8. This tendency is not evident, however, among the students in the US who are likely to cause trouble during his visit. Iranian young people who study abroad are almost invariably from the upper class, particularly those in the US. Many oppose the Shah because of family memories of

past cruelties committed by his father. Others are genuinely disturbed by the "dictatorship," by the omnipresence of the security police, and probably by their own sense of frustration over the slowness with which Iranian society seems able to change. At the same time, there is evidence that many Iranian student leaders in Europe and in the US are supported in part with funds from Communist sources and/or have become ideologically attached to left-wing movements.

9. The Shah calls his foreign policy "positive nationalism." Its basic pro-Western orientation is a reflection of his personal position rather than of any widespread popular sentiment. Many Iranian intellectuals in fact would prefer a neutralist position, and oppose Iran's membership in CENTO and its 1959 mutual defense pact with the US. Iran's heavy dependence on US aid since World War II is currently undergoing a subtle change as the country's oil revenues improve its financial position. The Shah nonetheless continues to complain that US military aid is insufficient; recent US-Iranian military exercises in southwestern Iran appear to have confirmed in the Shah's mind the strategic importance of Iran to the West as well as reassured him of US support.

10. The Shah's relations with the USSR are diplomatically correct at the moment. Soviet propaganda against him has slackened since Moscow accepted his 1962 pledge not to allow foreign missile bases on Iranian territory. Soviet President Brezhnev visited Iran last year, and the USSR extended a ten-year credit of $38.8 million to finance a project to harness the Aras River, which forms the Iranian-Soviet frontier in northwestern Iran.

---

30.   Telegram From the Embassy in Iran to the Department of State[1]

Tehran, June 2, 1964, 6 p.m.

1109. Dept pass Defense and Eckhardt. Embtel 1065.[2] Following conversation Eckhardt and I had with Shah May 24 (reftel) General Hejazi, Chief Supreme Comdr's Staff (SCS), handed Eckhardt "Study of

---

[1] Source: Department of State, Central Files, DEF 19–3 US–IRAN. Confidential; Priority. Repeated Priority to CINCSTRIKE/CINCMEAFSA for POLAD.

[2] Dated May 25. (Ibid.)

Modernization Program" on May 28. Study rejected ARMISH/MAAG presentation favoring carefully planned and phased replacement program for tanks and transport aircraft and supported in essentials accelerated program proposed by Shah. Study also backed immediate organization naval security battalion and armored personnel carriers for infantry battalions in Ahwaz division. ARMISH/MAAG promptly prepared additional memorandum reiterating and further supporting memo we left with Shah May 24. This memo was passed to SCS May 30 with comment I was available if Shah wished to discuss it. Morning June 1 top SCS officers conferred with General Ash and Col Gildart (Eckhardt in Washington). SCS said MAAG position not satisfactory and more cooperative attitude required in understanding need for accelerated program which SCS then attempted to defend. MAAG said its comments were made in context local discussions of most desirable military program, and represented its best professional views and MAAG officers reiterated considerations supporting them. MAAG added that when GOI had reached position after having MAAG advice, exchange would move to govt level and MAAG would do its best, as always, in support of any GOI–US decisions. In mid-afternoon MAAG was informed SCS wished to consider morning discussion off record. (Text of memoranda of these conversations forwarded by pouch to GTI.)

Evening June 1 I had two-hour audience with Shah. He discoursed along usual lines on Arab threat and Iran's need to prepare for own defense, although calmly and without emotion. I then opened part of conversation covering military requirements with friendly but pointed remarks on value of good professional military advice based on factual analyses, emphasizing particularly the value of sound negative advice, and noted we agreed at Dezful (Embtel 1008)[3] to have exchange of professional views re replacement program without regard to source of financing. All exchanges recent weeks we considered in this context and it now probably time for Shah examine all advice and decide what he wished to propose.

I noted that too rapid introduction of new weapons systems would be likely to overtax facilities for maintenance and utilization, not only for new weapons and equipment, but also for existing equipment. It was judgment our military people that overall combat capabilities of Iranian armed forces would thereby be significantly reduced during immediate future about which Shah appeared most concerned, Shah seemed to be seriously impressed by this consideration.

I once again called Shah's attention to need for balanced use of resources in order not to impair development program. I said it appeared

---

[3] Document 19.

oil revenues were rising nicely but best projections we able make suggested 1970 level not be quite so high as Shah previously indicated. Also foreign exchange projections indicated there would be period of squeeze to fulfill planned development in next few years and for two years or so Iran might well be drawing on foreign exchange reserves. Shah appeared bothered by this but seemed to hoist in its implications.

Shah then said he thought ARMISH/MAAG probably right, SCS program too rapid, it would be wiser to get 17 tanks for training by end Iranian year, March 1965, instead of August 1964 and have six months (instead of four months) program for introduction tanks into each battalion.

I suggested Shah's proposals be set down in writing by SCS and I would send them to Washington with the request that they be considered with regard to availabilities and terms. I said time would not permit answers during Shah's visit and he expressed understanding but hoped there could be some agreement in principle with questions regarding availabilities and terms to be worked out later.

SCS memorandum, delivered to MAAG this afternoon, set forth following requirements (text forwarded by pouch to GTI):

1) 460 M–60 tanks. 17 to be delivered for training by March 1965, 53 to be delivered in each of next three month periods (for three battalions Ahwaz division), then 36 in each of seven following four month periods (for seven other tank battalions).

2) 156 armored personnel carriers for three mechanized infantry battalions Ahwaz division.

3) 130 light tanks or armored cars for seven armored cavalry squadrons.

4) 110 howitzers 105mm to add third battery to 26 field artillery battalions.

5) 28 howitzers, eight-inch, to augment existing batteries and add battery to Ahwaz division.

6) One additional airborne battalion.

7) 1610 A–6 machine guns.

8) 4 C–130 aircraft by mid-1965 (one C–47 squadron to be deactivated).

9) Replacement for F–86 to be discussed later.

10) Level of ammunition reserve increased to six months' supply.

11) High priority to air defense Khuzistan and Bandar Abbas.

12) One additional naval security battalion "when Bandar Abbas port complex completed".

Quantities tanks, APC's, armored cars and machine guns contain attrition factors. Specific time phasing not stated except for tanks and C–130's.

Comment: Shah has accepted substantial validity our views and modified his proposals appreciably to accommodate them, although his proposed deliveries still call for rather tight schedule. However, I believe they now provide basis on which we can work out details of mutually acceptable program and preserve present valuable military relations with Shah.

Immediate problem is tanks. If we can be forthcoming on tanks during Shah's visit, our relations with Iran will be greatly strengthened and success of visit assured. I strongly recommend that we by able to tell Shah we are prepared to sell Iran 17 M–60's for delivery by March, 1965 and to make subsequent deliveries, production rates permitting, at rate approximating his schedule. Would be helpful if we could also indicate we would try to work out some credit arrangements for FY 66 deliveries.

If tanks problem resolved, discussion of program covering other items can proceed here at less rapid pace except for C–130's on which Shah will want early answer. For this discussion we will need to know soon level of credit available for Iran in FY 66.

Holmes

---

31.   Memorandum From Secretary of State Rusk to President Johnson[1]

Washington, June 3, 1964.

SUBJECT

Your Meeting with the Shah of Iran

A.   *Purpose of the Shah's Visit to the United States.*

The Shah's visit is *informal.* He will inaugurate the *exhibit "7000 Years of Iranian Art"* in Washington and receive *honorary degrees* from UCLA, American University, and NYU. The Shah is *fluent in English.* You are scheduled to meet with him for one hour at *Noon* on *Friday June 5.*

The Shah was last in the United States, on an *official visit, in April 1962.* You last saw him on *your visit to Iran in August 1962.* That was shortly before he personally assumed leadership of a *basic reform program* in Iran. He is *exhilarated,* perhaps overly so, about the apparent initial suc-

---

[1] Source: Johnson Library, National Security File, Country File, Iran, Shah's Visit, 6/5/64. Secret. The date is from the Department of State copy. (Department of State, Central Files, POL 7 IRAN)

cesses of that program. Although basically a *moody* man, subject to periods of discouragement, depression, and doubts as to our intentions, he is at present enjoying a high degree of *self-confidence* because of the *consolidation of his political position* at home, as well as Iran's growing *financial strength.* He feels these developments allow him scope for more *independence in foreign policy* (exemplified by *Iran's improved relations with the Soviet Union*), but he recognizes Iran's *dependence on the U.S. for security* and *continues to seek our advice* on all important matters. His principal concerns at the moment are two related ones: his *fears of aggression from the Arab world*; and Iran's requirements for *further military modernization.* A secure, long-range, *close military relationship with the U.S.* is necessary if these concerns are to be satisfied and *our influence in Iran is to be maintained* in the future.

The Shah will leave the U.S. on June 14 for a *visit with the Sultan of Morocco.*

B.   Items for You to Raise.

1. *Military Assistance.* Comment on satisfactory progress of current *Five-Year MAP Plan* and discussions now under way in Tehran for *further modernization* of Iranian armed forces. Offer *sale of* [2] *tanks* on cash or credit terms during next two or three years to fill Iran's most urgent military replacement need.

2. *"Arab Threat."* Indicate *understanding* of Shah's basic *long-range concern* with potential Arab threat to his border provinces. Note, on contrary, basic Arab *military weakness* in spite of supply Sovbloc arms, and continuing *forces for disunity* in Arab world in spite of repeated unity statements and "agreements." Suggest threat to Iran's border provinces *more political and psychological than military* and counsel *internal development measures* and *avoidance of provocation* to neighbors.

3. *East-West Relations.* Reassure Shah on following points: we are *not contemplating* conclusion of an East-West non-aggression pact; we intend to consult with the Shah and our other allies regarding any important development in East-West relations; we will *stand firm* at all trouble spots (Berlin, Cuba, Southeast Asia); we *appreciate Iran's deep understanding* of the reality of the Communist threat; we will *not sacrifice Iran's interests* as part of any East-West settlement.

4. *Miscellaneous "Talking Points."*

a. Express appreciation for growing *U.S.-Iranian cooperation* in all spheres. Make special mention of Iranian provision *facilities for our*

---

[2] The words "up to 150 M–60" are crossed out at this point on the source text, and a handwritten note in the margin reads "Suggest you leave details to DOD." At the end of this paragraph the words "(See Special Talking Papers on Military Assistance.)" are also crossed out. This Special Paper is printed as Document 32.

atomic detection programs and recent Iranian decision in principle to participate in *Free-World aid effort to South Viet-Nam.*

b. Note our satisfaction with Shah's *reform efforts.* Stress also continuing *need for courageous decisions and hard work* to consolidate initial successes of land reform, achieve necessary fiscal and administrative reforms, ensure a healthy economic recovery in private sector.

c. Express satisfaction with *growing Iranian financial strength* and with current promising negotiations for *continued U.S. lending,* on appropriate terms, to assist Iran's development program.

d. In connection with Shah's *trip to Morocco:* ask him to *convey our friendship and sympathy* to King Hassan and Morocco; tell him we commend Hassan's *efforts to establish a viable constitutional system* in face of serious obstacles; *land reform,* to which Shah has devoted so much attention, is a subject worth bringing to Hassan's attention.

C. *Items Which Shah May Raise and Suggested Response.*

1. *Pahlavi University.* The Shah is keenly interested in the development of the recently-established Pahlavi University (at Shiraz) into an American-type institution and might ask that we expand our current assistance. If he raises this, respond that: we also are keenly interested in this project; we intend to *broaden scope of our technical assistance* from medical faculty to the University as a whole; we expect that *principal financial inputs and organizational effort will be made by Iranians* from their growing fund of finances and administrative skills.

2. *Iranian Student Problem.* The Shah may, if he finds time, voice dissatisfaction with our control of *anti-regime Iranian students* in this country who demonstrate against him and other visiting Iranian dignitaries. If he does raise this, tell him: we *do not support* these anti-regime elements but our laws do not allow us to suppress them forcibly in the absence of illegal acts; some of the students with expired passports are under *warning to cease their extreme activities or face deportation;* press and public reaction here are now *so favorable to Iran and the Shah* that antics of these dissident elements arouse scarcely any sympathy.

D. *Background papers have been prepared on all of the foregoing subjects.*

Dean Rusk

32.   Special Talking Paper Prepared in the Department of State[1]

SVW–TP/1   Washington, June 3, 1964.

SHAH OF IRAN VISIT TO WASHINGTON
June 5, 1964

MILITARY ASSISTANCE

The Five-Year Plan for the reorganization and modernization of the Iranian armed forces, drawn up jointly and now being implemented, seems to be working out quite well. Granted adequate Congressional appropriations, we intend to continue to do our part in this program, and we are sure Iran will continue to do its part.

We are pleased that United States and Iranian officers are now discussing the shape of additional measures of replacement, modernization and training which will permit further improvement in Iran's defensive strength through the sixties and into the seventies. These plans should be analyzed carefully by both governments, with the view toward achieving a rational increase in military potential without limiting unduly the resources available for economic development and social welfare, which are also essential components of a broad security concept. Our various Joint CENTO exercises (especially the recent successful Operation DEL-AWAR) and the recent exercises involving the Concord Squadron demonstrate to us all the fact that United States and Iranian military capacities are mutually complementary.

We understand that the Shah's greatest area of concern at present is in the replacement of tanks. In view of the shortage of United States military assistance funds, and Iran's growing economic strength, we will not be able to provide replacements of Iran's needs on a grant basis. We can, however, sell Iran up to 150 of our new M–60 tanks, to come off production lines during the next two or three years, along with the necessary spares and ancillary equipment. These tanks would be delivered to Iran at the same time that they are being put in service with our own forces, and at the same price we must pay, plus handling and transportation.

Iran could pay for the tanks on the same basis that we ourselves make payments to the manufacturers. If this is not possible for Iran, we would be willing to discuss limited credit arrangements. If these tanks are too expensive, the Shah could be offered a rebuilt tank of the M–48 series, retrofitted with the 105-mm gun, the M–48A3, at a cheaper price.

---

[1] Source: Johnson Library, National Security File, Country File, Iran, Shah's Visit, 6/5/64. Confidential. Drafted by Bowling and cleared by Wheeler, John T. Hermansen (AID/PC), Kitchen, Colonel Taylor, and Jernegan.

A radically new tank, the Sheridan, may be produced later in this decade. No decision has yet been made to put it in production, and any discussions of procuring this vehicle are just not possible at present.

---

33.   Memorandum From Robert W. Komer of the National Security Council Staff to President Johnson[1]

Washington, June 4, 1964.

The Shah's visit is mostly an exercise in political massage. Like all our clients, he will be reassured simply to touch base with you (we didn't invite him, but laid on a brief meeting once he decided to come collect a few honorary degrees).

A good personal relationship between you and the Shah is more and more essential to our influence in Iran. We've helped Iran generously ($1.5 billion since 1947) but our aid is dropping sharply as Iranian oil revenues mount ($450 million this year, probably $800 million by 1970—the Shah estimates even higher). For example, we're now in the middle of a 5-year $300 million 1962–66 MAP program, but expect to shift later to a sales basis, because Iran can now afford it. So our chief problem becomes one of periodically reassuring this moody monarch, especially since he actually runs Iran.

Though we've kept telling the Shah that his real problems are internal not external, and that reform is first on the agenda, he keeps reverting to the military toys he loves. We've convinced him there isn't much chance of Soviet attack, so now he's talking up an Arab threat as his excuse. His main interest just now is replacing his aging M–47 tanks. M–48A3s like the Israelis want would be cheaper and more than ample, but he wants our new M–60s. *To avoid a discussion about hardware, you might tell him right off that we can't provide tanks as grant aid but will sell him some* when available; you've directed Defense to work out the details. He'll settle for this, because in his January letter to you he candidly offered to buy such equipment if Congress cut MAP funds too short. Nor

---

[1] Source: Johnson Library, National Security File, Country File, Iran, Shah's Visit, 6/5/64. Secret. The source text is attached to a memorandum to the President from Bundy which reads: "Here is another *excellent* memorandum from Bob Komer, this time on the Shah of Iran, which you may wish to read tonight. He will follow it up tomorrow with a last-minute one-pager on talking points."

do we want to commit ourselves to any MAP grant program for the period after our present arrangement runs out in 1967, but we can assure him we'll continue to work with him.

It's worth telling the Shah that we are beefing up our own strength in the Indian Ocean area by frequent carrier deployments (he recently attended a weapons demonstration on one). This gives us far greater combat power in the area, and is *aimed largely at backing up Iran against the USSR or the Arabs.*

We want to reassure the Shah about the "Arab" threat. He runs scared of Nasser. For example, we don't think the vague new "unity agreement" between the UAR and Iraq adds up to much. Since you've been so heavily immersed this week in Arab-Israeli affairs via the Eshkol visit, you might use that as a handle for expounding *our view that the Arabs aren't much of a military threat.* The Shah also keeps beefing about our making Nasser our "chosen instrument" in the Middle East. It would help if you made clear that: (a) we're not naive about Nasser—we're simply trying to keep him from leaning too far toward Moscow—this is in Iran's interest as much as ours; (b) we aren't really giving Nasser much aid except food which he can't convert into arms; and (c) we are still in effect containing Nasser by our aid to Israel, Jordan, Saudis, Sudan, and Libya as well as Iran.

After rebutting the Shah's security preoccupations, we hope you can shift the conversation to his reform program. We still see this as his best defense against subversion—the real threat from both Moscow and Cairo. We've waged a successful campaign since the economic crisis of mid-1961 to shift his attention from defense to domestic economic progress. His land reform program is going fairly well, and two good harvests have eased initial dislocations. But the economy in the urban areas still hasn't fully recovered (though it's beginning to snap back now that public spending is picking up) and the Shah still needs to get the city people behind him along with the peasants.

So we've got to convince the Shah that he's only begun the modernization process, and has to keep at it. We also want to nip in the bud any notion that he can relax as oil revenues climb. No matter how much money there is, demands are always so great that careful priorities have to be set. The Shah's new government under Ali Mansur has recently taken steps to improve its machinery. But to keep his nose to the grindstone, *you might mention how important you consider his new Budget Agency, his new Civil Service Code, and his plans for tax reform.* You could also explain the rationale of your anti-poverty campaign. *We want him to catch some of your enthusiasm for domestic reform.*

Since the Shah will stop off in Morocco on his way home, I suggest you ask him to convey your regards to King Hassan. You might also enlist his aid to get Hassan too focussed on the need for sound administration and reform.

As background you should read the attached cable[2] from Ambassador Holmes. Also attached are State briefs.[3] I'll give you a last minute reminder on talking points tomorrow.

Bob Komer

---

[2] Document 27.

[3] Not printed. The Special Talking Paper on Military Assistance is printed as Document 32.

---

34.   Memorandum From Robert W. Komer of the National Security Council Staff to President Johnson[1]

Washington, June 5, 1964.

Here are the things *the Shah will like to hear,* interwoven with a few we'd like to get across to him. I'd strongly urge that (as with Eshkol) you get in the first word; it disarms the guest.

1. It's a special pleasure to see Shah, because at time when lots of troubles elsewhere *Iran is brightest spot in ME.*

2. As to US, *we have more troubles but fewer real dangers.* Soviets are behaving, even if Chicoms are not.

3. In fact, one of our biggest headaches today is that our allies are constantly trying to get us to solve their disputes with other friendly countries (for example, Iran's neighbors Pakistan and Turkey are doing so right now). We're glad we don't have this kind of problem with Iran.

4. We recognize Shah's concern over potential Arab threat, but urge he not run too scared. Despite many tries since 1952 revolution, UAR hasn't successfully expanded yet. Nor do we see much likelihood of Iraqi-UAR unity.

5. One of our big problems is to convince allies like Pakistan and Turkey that real way to insure their future security and stability is through nation-building.

---

[1] Source: Johnson Library, National Security File, Country File, Iran, Shah's Visit, 6/5/64. Secret.

6. This is why we're so impressed with Shah's start on reform. We consider especially important his new budget agency, civil service code, and plans for tax reform.

7. But modernization is a never-ending process, even in the US. Look at our urban renewal and poverty problems. Shah must stimulate his economy more too, to provide cushion for shock of reforms.

8. Shah will raise *tanks*, probably after complaining about Arab threat. If so, suggest you tell him we can't provide tanks on top of present 5-year $300 million program. Because of MAP stringency, we'd have to sell him some. He should talk with McNaughton (who sees him this afternoon).

9. Remind Shah that our periodic carrier deployment into Indian Ocean designed largely with Iran in mind. Did Shah like recent carrier demonstration?

10. Finally, when Shah sees King of Morocco give him your regards and stimulate his interest in being reformer too.[2]

Bob Komer

---

[2] A handwritten notation in Komer's handwriting at this point on the source text reads: "Only Shah and his Ambassador, plus Talbot, Komer, and maybe Rusk will be present." An unsigned, undated memorandum for the files in the Department of State files reads: "No Memorandum of Conversation was prepared on the conversation which took place between the President and the Shah of Iran on June 5, 1964." (Department of State, S/S Conference Files: Lot 66 D 110, Vol. II, Visit of the Shah of Iran—Memcons, Sub. & Admin. Misc., CF 2409)

---

35.   Memorandum From the Deputy Assistant Secretary of Defense for International Security Affairs (Solbert) to Secretary of Defense McNamara[1]

I–0109/64   Washington, June 5, 1964.

SUBJECT

Sale of C–130 Aircraft to Iran

The Shah of Iran has included in his most recent statement of military replacement needs a requirement for four C–130 aircraft for delivery

---

[1] Source: Washington National Records Center, RG 330, OASD/ISA Files: FRC 68 A 306, 452.1 Iran, 5 Jun 64. Confidential.

by 1 July 1965. It is proposed that we approve a sale for this requirement totaling $10 million ($2.2 million each, plus spares) and advise the Shah of this approval during his current visit to Washington. The Air Force has indicated that four C–130B's are available and could be rehabilitated and delivered by that date assuming the sale is consummated by 1 July 1964. The Air Force, in turn, would procure four C–130E's for replacement to its inventory within the 22 months lead-time.

The question of credit may arise if the Iranians cannot meet the sale under dependable undertaking, our recommended starting position. In this event, the following credit terms under Section 508 of the Foreign Assistance Act of 1961, as amended, are recommended for your approval (State/AID concur):

Minimum Position

10% down, 3 years repayment in 12 equal quarterly payments, and 3-1/2% interest on the unpaid balance.

Fall-Back Position

10% down, 5 years repayment in 20 equal quarterly payments, and 3-1/2% interest on the unpaid balance.

This amount would be considered to be within the $20–$40 million range for military sales to Iran discussed in background material submitted to the President for the Shah's visit.[2]

Peter Solbert

---

[2] Approved by McNamara on June 6.

---

36.   Memorandum From the Assistant Secretary of State for Near Eastern and South Asian Affairs (Talbot) to the Under Secretary of State for Political Affairs (Harriman)[1]

Washington, June 6, 1964.

SUBJECT

Your Meeting with Shah of Iran, 4:30 p.m. June 6

The Shah's meeting with the President yesterday was warm and cordial. As expected, the Shah devoted considerable attention to the fol-

---

[1] Source: Department of State, NEA/IRN Files: Lot 69 D 30, Staff Studies. Confidential. Drafted by Tiger and cleared by Jernegan.

lowing subjects: Arab designs on Khuzistan, which he said were now backed by Khrushchev, who is anxious to deny Middle East oil to the West; the consequent need for enhanced Iranian defensive capabilities; the suitability of Bendar Abbas for use by the United States for a base; and the Shah's fears that the oil companies would give preferential treatment to Arab producing countries now that OPEC had become what the Shah called an "instrument of Arab imperialism".

In connection with the latter point, the President told the Shah that we would speak to the oil companies about the Shah's misgivings. At the White House luncheon, following the private meeting, both the President and Secretary Rusk spoke to Mr. Howard W. Page of Standard Oil of New Jersey and Mr. George Parkhurst of Standard Oil of California, emphasizing United States Government interest in seeing that the companies treat Iran fairly. Later in the afternoon Messrs. Page and Parkhurst called on Mr. Talbot and reiterated their appreciation of Iran's situation and the agreement of the companies to ensure fair treatment for Iran in the OPEC negotiations. Details of this discussion are included in the attached memorandum of conversation. It would be very helpful if you would reassure the Shah further on this point and convey to him the assurances expressed by Messrs. Page and Parkhurst.

It is expected that the discussions with the Shah at the 5 p.m. "tea" will be concerned mainly with military affairs, specifically the Shah's program for military modernization and the possibilities of United States sales of modern tanks and transport aircraft to Iran to cover the most urgent replacement needs. Mr. Talbot will be present at the "tea", and the other guests will be:

DOD—

    Mr. Sloan

JCS—

    Major General J.T. Kingsley (Special Assistant for Military Assistance)
    Major General Perry B. Griffith (Chief, Military Assistance, STRICOM)
    Major General George M. Eckhardt (Chief, ARMISH/MAAG, Tehran)

White House

    Mr. Komer

State—

    Mr. Rostow
    Mr. Kitchen

AID—

    Mr. Macomber
    Mr. Robert M. Macy (Director, USAID, Tehran)
    Mr. Bartlett Harvey (Acting Assistant Administrator for Program)

37.   Memorandum of Conversation[1]

I–8729/64   Washington, June 6, 1964.

SUBJECT

> Working Tea with Shah 6 June 1964 (Representatives of State, Defense, AID &
> White House Staff in attendance)

1. *Background Briefing*—The Shah gave a detailed description of his reform program, covering past accomplishments and his hopes for the future. He concluded by stressing the importance of his security forces to the success of his program and his concern with the military assistance being rendered the Arabs by the USSR and the aggressive nature of Nasser's policies and propaganda toward Iran.

2. *U.S. Intentions re Military Modernization*—Mr. Harriman (State) expressed the importance that the U.S. attached to its relationship with Iran and asked Mr. Sloan (Defense) to discuss the matter of continued support in the military field. Mr. Sloan referred to the Shah's conversation with the President and stated it was the intention of the U.S. to respond favorably to the military needs of Iran as recently received in the Pentagon.

a. *C–130 Transport Aircraft*—Mr. Sloan announced that the U.S. was prepared to consummate arrangements for the sale of 4 of these planes to Iran as replacements for a squadron of C–47s. Favorable credit terms were available. In order to meet the desired delivery date of July 65 and to provide the same model plane that the IAF already has in its first squadron of C–130Bs, it was proposed to have the USAF rehabilitate 4 C–130Bs for delivery to Iran. These would later be replaced in the USAF inventory by 4 C–130Es from production. Iran would pay the price of the C–130E which is less than the C–130B price. The Shah expressed his appreciation for the rapid consideration of his needs but gave no view concerning the relative desirability of the C–130B and E.

b. *Tank Replacement*—Mr. Sloan reiterated the statement of the President that we wanted to provide him the tanks that he desires but it was felt that, in all fairness, the various alternative possibilities should be described together with their implications. As a result of a cutback in production schedules the cost of the M–60 had escalated to about $270,000 including spares and handling charges. They could be made available starting in March 65 as requested. The U.S. Army had developed two A–3 modifications of the M–48 which were felt to be about equal to the

---

[1] Source: Johnson Library, National Security File, Files of Robert W. Komer, Visit of Shah of Iran, June 1964. Confidential. Drafted on June 9.

M–60 in performance and about $100,000 cheaper per tank. The first modification was being applied to 1000 tanks for use by the U.S. Army and Marines. It has the same engine and operating range as the M–60. The 90mm gun is retained in order to permit the use of large stocks of 90mm ammunition for training. Also a HEAT round has been developed that gives the gun about the same range as the 105mm gun of the M–60. The second modification has the same engine and gun as the M–60. The principal advantage of the M–60 is in a slightly smoother silhouette. Since this latter modification is not presently contemplated by the U.S. Army, it could not be accomplished as rapidly as the first, which is now underway.

The Shah expressed concern that spare parts would become a problem with the M–48 as they have for the M–47. Mr. Sloan stated that the M–48 would be in the inventory of the U.S. Army as long as the M–60 and until a main battle tank was developed and available, estimated to be in the early 1970s. The Shah expressed concern that this conversion to a new tank would not be completed until 1969 which would not leave much useful life if spare parts became short in the early 70s. Mr. Sloan assured him that it was U.S. present policy that spare parts would be maintained for all military equipment provided to allies as long as the equipment was in use. Mr. Komer (White House) spoke up in strong support of the M–48 A–3 as being comparable to and more economical than the M–60. The Shah asked that he be given a detailed comparison of the three possibilities with a revised cost figure for the M–60 that would reflect the increased production schedule to accommodate Iran's requirement.

c. *Other requirements for Iran*—Brief discussion was held concerning the remaining items in the modernization plan: machine guns, artillery, M–113, and scout cars. No one brought up any problem areas and it was concluded by the Shah that these items could be made available, in the context of an *overall plan*.

d. *Air Defense for Southern Area*—The Shah spoke of the absolute necessity of defending the strategically-important oil fields and the Bandar Abbas Port complex. He inquired as to the status of the air defense study being prepared by General Adams (CINCSTRIKE); General Griffith (STRIKE Command) stated that he had turned over to General Eckhardt (ARMISH/MAAG, Iran) this study for further discussion with the Shah.

e. *Cooperative Sales Agreement*—Mr. Sloan stated that when the requirements are completely definitized, it would be possible to draw up an overall agreement that would indicate what Iran desired to buy from the U.S. and the lesser amount that the U.S. would try to provide under MAP during the period in question. MAP, of course, was always subject to Congressional approval. The Shah expressed the opinion that this was the only way to carry forward our mutual efforts in an orderly and businesslike manner.

3. *Economic Modernization*—Mr. Rostow (State) introduced the problem that he had observed in other developing countries and which he thought was probably applicable to Iran. This was the difficulty in getting industry to develop in such a way as to support and complement the agricultural development. This was directly related to the stimulation of proper marketing practices that are necessary if much agricultural produce is not to be lost in the marketing process. Specifically he mentioned the requirement for industry to take the emphasis from production for Teheran and other cities and to concentrate in producing things the farmers need and want: textiles, farm implements and machinery, cheap radios, electricity, etc. Otherwise the farmer will find that his increased productivity and income have brought him no realization of his aspirations.

The Shah admitted this was a basic problem in Iran with which he needed help from the U.S. Dr. Macy (AID Iran) stated that some work was being done on improving the marketing. The Shah asked that additional technical assistance be provided in solving the larger problem described by Mr. Rostow. In the economic field he also expressed the desire that a combination of AID and Ex.Im. Bank loans be considered for Iran.

4. *Conclusion*—Mr. Harriman assured the Shah of continued U.S. assistance in strengthening Iran. As the meeting was breaking up, the Shah asked General Eckhardt to meet with him at 1000 hours Monday to discuss the Air Defense Study prepared by CINCSTRIKE and go over in more detail the other items in the modernization plan, particularly the price of the M–60 to reflect the procurement by Iran of the first 176 tanks.[2] He inquired concerning the light tank he had discussed with General Adams. General Eckhardt advised him that there was no available information on the availability and price of the Sheridan tank.

G.S. Eckhardt
Major General, USA
Chief, MAAG, Iran

---

[2] A memorandum for the record of the meeting on June 8 is ibid.

38.   Memorandum of Conversation[1]

Washington, June 8, 1964, 12:30 p.m.

SUBJECT

Conversation with Shah of Iran on OPEC and Oil Matters

PLACE

Car riding between Department of State and Washington National Airport

PARTICIPANTS

Howard W. Page, Vice President, Standard Oil Company of New Jersey
George L. Parkhurst, Vice President, Standard Oil Company of California
M. Gordon Tiger, Officer in Charge, Iranian Affairs GTI
Edward H. Thomas, Desk Officer, Iranian Affairs GTI

Mr. Tiger referred briefly to the Alphonse–Gaston type of confusion about whether or not the Shah really wanted a serious talk with Page and Parkhurst during his U.S. visit. After the initial negative finding, Governor Harriman had got the impression Saturday that the Shah did want such a talk, and this was confirmed the next day, the appointment being made for 11:30 a.m. Monday, June 8.

Messrs. Page and Parkhurst then described the conversation they had just had with the Shah. He had brought up nothing new, but merely emphasized how important it was that the oil companies not submit to Arab "blackmail." The Shah, of course, would not be opposed to further concessions by the companies, but they should first be offered to Iran.

Page and Parkhurst had reassured the Shah, explaining that they had already told Dr. Fala that the companies would make no deals with the Arabs behind Iran's back. Discussions had been going on with Yamani of Saudi Arabia. Aramco's Brougham, who had just been talking with Yamani, was due back in the U.S. tomorrow. The Brougham–Yamani talks were only exploratory, of course, since Brougham was not empowered to negotiate for the oil industry. If these talks indicated there might be some possibility of reaching agreement with Saudi Arabia within the general framework of the oil companies' offer, the companies had promised to inform Fala immediately.

There had been some discussion of petroleum economics, which the Shah introduced by remarking that, in Iran at least, oil was no longer a political problem, but solely an economic one. The Shah indicated that he knew something of this subject, being aware, for example, that posted

---

[1] Source: Department of State, Central Files, POL 7 IRAN. Confidential. Drafted by Thomas on June 9.

prices were somewhat artificial and that the companies make much of their profit in other operations—transport, refining, etc. Page and Parkhurst had explained that it all depended where one began. If one began on the basis of posted price, then the companies made nothing on the other operations. But in reality they were able to realize overall gains which, while less than those of many other industries, were sufficient to keep them in business. They hoped by improving efficiency to increase their margin of profit. Page and Parkhurst had also explained to the Shah why the competition from other fuels made it impossible to raise oil prices.

Returning to Arab affairs, the Shah had said that it was in Iran's interests to remain on good terms with Saudi Arabia and Kuwait. He thought the companies shared this interest with Iran and that the U.S. Government's interest paralleled that of the companies. The Shah thought highly of Faysal. The big danger, in the Shah's mind, was Nasser and Nasserism. And behind Nasser was Khrushchev.

The Shah had also encouraged the oil companies to invest in non-petroleum activities in Iran. Page and Parkhurst had said the companies were indeed in the process of studying possibilities for such investments.

---

39. Telegram From the Department of State to the Embassy in Iran[1]

Washington, June 8, 1964, 6:07 p.m.

914. Shah's Visit. Presidential meeting and White House luncheon proceeded in atmosphere great warmth and cordiality. In meeting, Shah devoted considerable attention to: Arab designs on Khuzistan, which he said now backed by Khrushchev, who anxious deny oil to West; consequent need enhanced Iranian defensive capabilities; suitability Bandar Abbas for U.S. base use; fears that oil companies would give preferential treatment Arab producers now that OPEC an "instrument of Arab imperialism." President complimented the Shah on his reform measures, calling Iran "brightest spot in the Middle East". He urged on Shah need to keep up pace of modernization which never-ending process even in US.

---

[1] Source: Department of State, Central Files, POL 7 IRAN. Confidential. Drafted by Tiger on June 5, cleared by Department of State Deputy Executive Secretary John A. McKesson and Komer, and approved by Talbot.

He also sought to play down extent of Arab military threat. President told Shah we would speak to oil companies about Shah's misgivings. Shah's luncheon toast consisted of ringing reaffirmation firm commitment to West.

Harriman

---

40.   **Telegram From the Department of State to the Embassy in Iran**[1]

Washington, June 8, 1964, 8:25 p.m.

916. Joint State/AID/Defense message. Military modernization program discussed with Shah by DOD, State and AID reps on 6 June. Shah was told USG intends to be responsive to his military modernization requirements. DOD reps suggested consideration Cooperative Logistics Sales Agreement. Regarding tanks, Shah's attention directed to M–48A3 as better priced substitute for M–60, which now very high priced because of curtailed procurement schedule. Regarding transport aircraft, we offered sale of four C–130's on favorable credit terms for delivery by July 1965. There was less concrete discussion concerning other modernization items. Shah was pleased with general approach, requested further meeting with working level DOD on Monday, June 8, for more detailed discussion modernization plan, particularly possibilities for reduction in price of M–60 as result possible procurement by Iran.

At June 8 meeting, main emphasis was on tanks with Shah questioning sharply price and characteristics data. Shah requested another meeting in New York on 12 June at which time he would like to have firm information as to the availability of the M–48A3 tank with the 105[mm] gun and, if possible, to discuss a draft Cooperative Logistics Sales Agreement covering the entire modernization program. Shah at no time asked for details about credit availability or terms but assumed that this would be included in the discussion of a Cooperative Logistics Sales Agreement.

---

[1] Source: Department of State, Central Files, DEF 19–3 US–IRAN. Confidential. Drafted by Tiger and General Eckhardt, cleared by Colonel Taylor and Bartlett Harvey (AID/PC), and approved by Talbot. Repeated to CINCSTRIKE/CINCMEAFSA, and CINCSTRIKE/CINCMEAFSA for POLAD.

Other subjects covered in meetings (CINCSTRIKE Air Defense Study, Iranian economic development) to be covered in memcons.

Rusk

---

41.   Telegram From the Department of State to the Embassy in Iran[1]

Washington, June 9, 1964, 5:57 p.m.

918. Shah's Visit. Official, social and public aspects Washington portion Shah's visit highly successful. Welcoming delegation headed by Secretary, Duke and Talbot; farewell delegation headed by Duke and Talbot. Shah made excellent impression at Mellon dinner and also at private dinner Washington Institute of Foreign Affairs, where he answered off-the-record questions about world affairs and Iranian domestic problems in frank and informed manner before very distinguished group. Publicity relatively small in volume, prevailingly favorable to Shah, concentrated on cultural-educational aspects of visit with hardly any speculation substantive content official meetings.

Students, numbering 25–30, demonstrated quietly at Dulles, White House, American University, Sulgrave Club, and Mass Ave near Embassy. Missed departure National Airport because of last-minute change in locale from Andrews. In each case picketing was kept at considerable distance, and Shah's party was routed in such ways that it doubtful he saw pickets. Students held press conference at National Press Club, June 5, covered in *Post* inside page, low-key story.

There were several late additions to schedule, as follows: meeting with State, AID and DOD reps June 6, followed up by more detailed discussions military modernization with DOD reps June 8 (Deptel 916);[2] private meeting June 8 with oil executives Page and Parkhurst, at Shah's request (memcon follows);[3] "tea" June 8 with officials Eximbank, IMF,

---

[1] Source: Department of State, Central Files, POL 7 IRAN. Confidential. Drafted by Tiger; cleared by Billings and Deputy Chief of Protocol William J. Tonesk, and in substance by Sidney T. Telford of the Office of Security, Welk of the Export-Import Bank, and Colonel Taylor; and approved by Bracken.

[2] Document 40.

[3] See Document 38.

IBRD, IFC; wreath laying Kennedy grave Arlington, June 8; and brief visit Washington Cathedral as guest Dean Sayre, June 8. We have also heard that Shah spent considerable time June 6 and 7 at Embassy holding levees for various categories of Iranian residents, including some students who sought, and in some cases received, passport renewals.

Aside from military modernization discussions (Deptel 916), most significant addition to schedule was Monday meeting with bankers, which arranged hastily on Sunday, presumably at initiative of Shah. Attended by: Linder, Sauer, and Welk of EXIM; Knapp, Reed, and Khosropour of IBRD; Rosen of IFC; Southard and Gunter of IMF; Foroughi and Amuzegar. Shah addressed this group on Iranian economic problems, reform program, political outlook. EXIM group was well impressed with his informed, balanced approach, particularly his grasp of economic affairs, and believes international org reps were similarly impressed. Shah acknowledged Iran's greatly improved economic prospects but stressed need for continued foreign lending in interim in order to support adequate pace economic development. He referred in appreciative terms to new IBRD road loan and expressed hope for combined AID–EXIM lending for electric power network. Appears this session initiated on basis advice and briefing from Samii and provided most beneficial follow-up recent Samii mission.

Shah has accepted invitation from Northrop to visit USAF base Los Angeles area June 10 for operational demonstration F–5B.

Rusk

---

42.   Memorandum of Conversation[1]

New York, June 12, 1964.

SUBJECT

Military Modernization Discussions with the Shah of Iran

PARTICIPANTS

The Shah of Iran

Defense
Major General George, Eckhardt, Chief MAAG/Tehran
Colonel W.B. Taylor, DOD/ISA
Colonel Ray W. Hodgson, DOD/ILN

State
John Patrick Walsh, NEA/NR

---

[1] Source: Department of State, NEA/IRN Files: Lot 69 D 178, Iran, 19–4–a, Five-Year Agreement, 1965–69. Secret. Drafted by Walsh.

At the request of the Shah, Defense/State representatives met with him in New York on June 12. The meeting was held in his suite in the Waldorf Astoria. It began at 6:45 p.m. and lasted about an hour and twenty minutes. Since the DOD group arrived at about 6:40, we only had a few minutes to discuss our position and no opportunity to see the specific position papers which General Eckhardt utilized throughout the session.

The atmosphere was friendly. The Shah had just arrived some minutes before from Los Angeles. He appeared tired and somewhat melancholy. One had the impression that the demonstrations in Los Angeles had depressed him. There was a huge crowd in front of the Waldorf. According to the police, it was entirely friendly with no demonstrators present. Nevertheless, the fact that he had once again been confronted with a large crowd may have recalled to his mind some of his irritation about what happened in Los Angeles. At one stage in the discussion, the Shah said that he was subject to what one might call an international conspiracy led by the communists with the active assistance of Nasser and the Arabs. In one demonstration in Los Angeles, according to the Shah, there were only six Iranians and the other demonstrators seemed to have been American communists and Arab students. He spoke with manifest irritation about an incident in Los Angeles; apparently a plane flew over the ceremony at UCLA carrying a banner that said "If you want a fix, see the Shah." He said he asked people "What is a fix?" and they told him it was heroin. He said with bitterness that this smearing attack was made against him despite his efforts to kill off this dirty drug. If I am involved in heroin, he added, one should say that I am a terribly poor salesman and that I am working against my "sales interest."

He went on to say that he was going to stop off and see King Hassan who had invited him to talk about Nasser. He said Hassan was having trouble with Nasser, which is a common experience. He said Nasser was giving arms to the Algerians to kill Moslem Moroccans; he was giving arms to Greek-Cypriots to kill Turkish Moslems; he was threatening the life of the Shah, a Moslem.

In accordance with the position agreed upon in Washington, the Shah was informed that the United States is prepared to conclude a sales agreement in FY 1965 for 176 M–60 tanks and four C–130 transport planes with deliveries to occur on a phased basis. He was also informed that we are prepared to begin negotiations at an early date in Tehran of a broader program covering the FY 1965–69 period, which would include both credit and grant equipment elements. Subject to Congressional authorizations, grant MAP would be continued in the three years after the end of the current Five-Year Plan, namely in FY 1967, 1968, and 1969. It was emphasized that the United States participation in the proposed negotiations would be under the direction of Ambassador Holmes who would be assisted by technicians from Washington to the degree deemed necessary.

The Shah was clearly pleased by United States responsiveness in respect to the modernization requirements of the Iranian military structure and by the decision to continue MAP grants. He indicated that he would begin preparations for negotiations as soon as he returns to Tehran this week.

General Eckhardt was under direct instructions from Secretary McNamara to inform the Shah that we would be prepared to begin the negotiations within a week's time. I told General Eckhardt before the meeting started that he should carry out his instructions, but that we would have to inform the Shah that other elements of the American Government doubted our ability to hold the discussions that quickly. Both these points were conveyed to the Shah and it was evident that there was not a problem involved insofar as he was concerned because he himself will not be ready as quickly as the Secretary had hoped. It seems probable that a target date of about July 8 would be logical. If a Team arrives much before that date, it is likely to cool its heels waiting for the Iranians.

It will be recalled that the Department of Defense had strongly desired the preparation and submission to the Shah of a detailed memorandum of understanding which ostensibly would have been initialed by him. We had opposed this proposition and of course it did not take place. For what it is worth, it is my opinion, and I believe the opinion of General Eckhardt, that the Shah would not have been pleased had we followed that plan and that he would not in fact have initialed that paper or any other paper. He was not prepared, in my opinion, to negotiate while in the United States.

Tanks

In opening the subject of tanks, General Eckhardt informed the Shah that Secretary McNamara had looked very closely at the question of the desirability of furnishing the M–60 and/or the M–48A3. It was the viewpoint of the Secretary that, taking a variety of factors into account, it would be desirable to furnish M–60's. The indicated price per unit with one year's spares would be $220,000. This would be about $70,000 more than the indicated price for an M–48A3. On the other hand, the M–60 is a better piece of equipment. It could be maintained for a longer period of time and it would be better from a supply, maintenance, and operating viewpoint to concentrate on one tank instead of having a combination of M–60's, M–48's and M–47's. In response, the Shah said he was pleased by this decision. He felt it was wise. He said he wanted a tank that was good for eight or ten years, and that the M–60 was best for this purpose. He, too, had been worried about the proliferation of models.

On the subject of the proposed M–41 light tank, General Eckhardt said that the United States Army had looked at this question very carefully and recommended that the Shah not take M–41's. The General said that there would be a maintenance problem with the tank within several years and that its adoption would again create proliferation problems. He said that the Army felt the Shah would be better advised to use the in-country M–47's for the purpose he had in mind with respect to the M–41 and, if this recommendation were adopted, there would be a net indicated savings for Iran of about $12 million. The Shah again said that this seemed wise to him and he believed that it was the proper course for Iran to pursue.

The Shah then raised the subject of armored cars. In reply he was informed that the United States Army recommended he not enter this field. We do not use armored cars in our own Army. There are none produced for United States Government account although both Cadillac and Chrysler produce this equipment for export purposes. It was pointed out that their products are competitive with the products produced by other countries but again to the extent that this type of equipment was needed the requirement could be covered by a judicious use of M–47's. The Shah said he was inclined to accept the recommendation in this respect, but he would wish to review this subject in the course of the Tehran discussions.

Other Equipment

The Shah raised the question of certain other equipment that he had inquired about at the meeting on June 8, such as machine guns, APC's, and howitzers. He was informed these would be available and details would be provided in Tehran. Furthermore, it is quite possible that these would be supplied under MAP grant. He said he was grateful for this information, and nothing more was said about it.

Air Defense

The Shah asked what information was available in respect to the various elements of the air defense problem that had been discussed at the two earlier meetings in Washington. In reply, the Shah was asked what his reaction had been to his experience in flying the F–5A on the West Coast. The weary Shah brightened up at this point and for a few minutes we maneuvered an F–5A very high in the sky. He said it was a beautiful plane, highly maneuverable, very easy to fly, and with substantially better characteristics than he had understood. He said he was much impressed with the way the Northrop people had dealt with him when he was in their capable hands. He said as a Persian he had certain knowledge of the tactics of salesmanship. In this instance, he honestly felt that they had not overstressed or oversold their case and he greatly appreciated their approach to him. He then asked General Eckhardt if he had statistics available on the relative characteristics of the various Russian bombers. The General supplied this information with indications that the F–5A was quite capable of handling these bombers in a combat situation. The General went on to point out frankly that a MIG–21, which has quite high air defense characteristics, was in some respects clearly superior to an F–5A. On the other hand, its very short range would indicate that it could not effectively operate against an F–5A very deeply within the territory of Iran. The Shah appeared impressed by these points. He said that he now felt that he should not plan on utilizing the F–4C. He said the F–4C is a superior airplane; on the other hand, it would be terribly expensive in money terms and again would involve a proliferation of aircraft models and would be hard for his people to handle. He therefore was coming to the conclusion that he ought to plan in the years ahead on replacing his F–86 squadrons with F–5A's. He said that he was hopeful that the armament people would be successful in their efforts to produce a better missile for the F–5A, but this of course would remain to be seen. General Eckhardt said that we noted with satisfaction the Shah's feelings about the F–5A and agreed there would be a very substantial savings in terms of money and men, if he would continue with this fine plane. The Shah said this was his point of view at this moment.

He went on to say that the modernization program for all his forces would have to go on. He very much doubted, however, that they would be able to make very much in the way of gains relative to the great strength of their potential enemies from the north. They would of course do their best. On the other hand, he was convinced they had a growing threat from the west. He was confident that Iran, within its resources, could make a positive improvement in its posture in this respect. He was determined to do this. He said that Iran and the United States had made very substantial investments in the Dezful and Hamadan airfields. These are very fine facilities which are of very great importance in a military sense both to Iran and to the United States. At this moment, however, they literally have no defense. It would be a very great pity if nothing were done about this problem and at some future time these facilities were knocked out. He said it was important to establish Hawk facilities at these airfields, and he wished now to obtain American views on the availability of such equipment. In reply he was told that we did have a Hawk battalion which could be made available and that we would be prepared to discuss this in greater detail in the course of the negotiations in Tehran. It was indicated that this particular battalion could be made available at about $21 million. The price of a battalion at a later date would probably be significantly higher. He said he would be interested in obtaining this battalion and that he would contemplate possibly splitting it with two batteries at each airfield. He then asked about the characteristics and potential availability of Nike Hercules. In reply he was told this of course was very good equipment. However, we had not made it available under MAP and it was very doubtful that we would. It is extremely expensive and very difficult to man in an effective sense. He seemed to accept this as a logical and negative reply. He asked if there might be some equipment that could be made available to provide at least a low-level air defense capability for his airfields in the interim before the Hawks were in place, recognizing that this might be three years. He was told there were some twin M–40 "Dusters" available and that they might run about $50,000 a unit. He asked what the status was of the in-country 20 and 40 mms. which have been phased out of the Iranian force structure. The General replied that they were in very bad shape, but that it might be possible to find enough of them in usable condition to provide at least a modicum of defense and training equipment for these two airfields. If this were done, the General felt they probably should be turned over to the Iranian Air Force. The Shah thought this was a good idea and requested the General to look into it when he returned to Tehran and to discuss it with him at a later date. This was agreed.

The Shah said that at some time in the future he felt that Iran would need a second Hawk battalion and he wondered if it might not be possible and feasible to train simultaneously the manpower that would be necessary to handle two battalions instead of just one. He said he was thinking in part about the future need for some air defense about Bandar Abbas. He estimated that the Bandar Abbas port and navy "base" would be completed in about 1968. He also said that he very much hoped that the airfield at Bandar Abbas would be operational before that date. He said he had instructed the Plan Organization, which has the necessary funds, to proceed with this as fast it feasible. In this respect he recalled that he had mentioned the possibilities of pre-positioning American equipment in this area. General Eckhardt told him that there would of course be considerable strain in the training process in regard to the Hawks and this was something that would have to be discussed at a later date in greater detail. The Shah said he understood this and would look forward to further discussion in Tehran.

As a final comment in respect to aviation, the Shah said that he was pleased about the decision in respect to the four C–130's and that he hoped that in the course of negotiations in Tehran decisions could be arrived at in respect to the additional four that would be required to complete their air transport force. He would ultimately wish to replace all his C–47's with twelve C–130's.

Navy

The Shah inquired if we had been able to accumulate information he had requested in respect to the possible purchase of a DD or a DE. He was told that we felt we could ultimately make available either a DD or a DE in a completely rehabilitated condition. The destroyer probably would be in excess of $3 million and the destroyer escort would be in the vicinity of $2 million. In each case Congressional authorization would be required for the transfer and it would be unlikely that either could be made available short of two or three years. The Shah said that this was all right because it would take some time for his people to be ready to utilize units like this effectively. He was also told it might be possible to make available a new frigate. This would not require Congressional authorization but the price would be in excess of $4 million. While the Shah did not appear to be much interested in the frigate, he did indicate a desire to discuss this matter further in the coming discussions in Tehran.

In sum, the Shah was informed that (1) we were prepared to sell him 176 M–60's and four C–130's; (2) MAP grant assistance would be continued in FY 67–69; (3) that we were prepared to begin negotiations in Tehran in one week, although we had doubts about the feasibility of such an early date; (4) these negotiations would cover the modernization requirements of the Iranian forces in the FY 65–69 period; (5) that a Hawk battalion would be available at about $21 million; (6) that his other requirements, such as machine guns, howitzers, and APC's, would be provided. He was manifestly pleased.

---

43.   Memorandum From the Acting Assistant Secretary of Defense for International Security Affairs (McNaughton) to Secretary of Defense McNamara[1]

I–25, 193/64   Washington, June 13, 1964.

SUBJECT

　　Five Year MAP for Iran

The Five Year Military Assistance agreement between the Government of the United States and the Government of Iran, consummated by the Memorandum of Understanding of September 1962, provided for furnishing certain defense items of matériel and services. Some items were to be furnished in specified quantities, other items were described in general terms, without specifying quantities, such as: Ammunition for

---

[1] Source: Washington National Records Center, RG 330, OASD/ISA Files: FRC 68 A 306, 381 Iran—13 June 1964. Secret. Attached to a control sheet with a typed notation by Lieutenant Colonel W.A. Forbes indicating that at a meeting on Five-Year MAP for Iran on June 11, Secretary McNamara requested a memorandum stating that all MAP commitments to Iran expressed in the September 1962 Memorandum of Understanding would be delivered by June 30, 1967, the terminal date of the agreement.

training and a 30-day stock level, communications equipment, combat support equipment and civic action support. The total value of the 5-year package was not to exceed $298.6 million, but the Iranians were not informed of this dollar limitation. Deliveries were to be accomplished by 30 June 1967.

Programming actions provided $53.1 million in FY 62, $70.0 million in FY 63 and $53.2 million in FY 64 which have been applied against the commitment. Future programs have been prepared which will provide $41.1 million in FY 65 and $46.1 million in FY 66 for a total cost of $263.5 million for the 5-year program.

All items pertaining to the Memorandum of Understanding commitment have been included in these yearly programs. Deliveries already accomplished and those projected against future programs will permit delivery of all commitment items by 30 June 1967.

John T. McNaughton[2]

---

[2] Printed from a copy that indicates that McNaughton signed the original.

---

44.   Telegram From the Department of State to the Embassy in Iran[1]

Washington, June 16, 1964, 6:44 p.m.

931. Shah's Visit. Following is summary security, publicity aspects New York, Los Angeles portions Shah's visit:

At New York stop 9 June, 30 to 50 anti-Shah pickets, shouting loud and abusive protests, were allowed within 15 feet of entrance to East 78th Street premises where NYU honorary degree awarded. Proximity pickets was result admitted error New York police and situation was corrected before party's return visit to New York 12 to 14 June, when there

---

[1] Source: Department of State, Central Files, POL 7 IRAN. Confidential. Drafted by Tiger; cleared in draft by Chief of the Division of Protective Security Keith O. Lynch, Deputy Chief of Protocol Chester C. Carter, Joseph W. Reap (P), Donald A. Wehmeyer (L/NEA), and Deputy Administrator of the Bureau of Security and Consular Affairs Charles H. Mace; and approved by Bracken.

were no serious disturbances at Waldorf Astoria or World's Fair. About 15 pickets were near the hotel. Shah and Empress upset by 9 June episode and Foroughi cites it as only really disturbing episode entire US visit. N.Y. press treatment not overly sensational and prevailing tone favorable to Shah.

During Los Angeles visit, pro-Shah demonstrators, evidently organized by official Iranians (Naficy and Kowsar) outnumbered anti-Shah demonstrators at airport and Ambassador Hotel, were overly boisterous in their welcome, and engaged in some fisticuffs with anti-Shah demonstrators; at least one anti-Shah demonstrator arrested but released on bail.

UCLA commencement ceremonies 11 June proceeded with dignity in spite of major attempts to cause disturbances. There were about 75 anti-Shah demonstrators, of which only 12 Iranians, remainder being "other nationalities" (no further information yet available). These were kept on sidelines, some 150 yards away from ceremony, and their shouts did not disturb proceedings. When Shah started to speak, 5 students walked out but were not able to create disturbance. When some anti-Shah students attempted to unfurl banner, two were removed bodily by pro-Shah student group, which numbered about 50. During ceremony, hired airplane made two runs toward area carrying streamer reading: "Need a fix? See the Shah" (reference was to heroin addiction). Los Angeles police helicopter, which standing by in case serious riot, ascended and drove plane from area. Shah outraged by reference narcotics addiction but deeply impressed effective police action; at 12 June departure ceremony, he asked to see helicopter pilot and presented him with gift. No info yet available re renters of plane except they said to be "students" and paid $250 for rental.

Los Angeles press publicity, while predictably sensational (referring to "dogfight" in air over UCLA, stressing Empress's extravagant shopping sprees) probably not, in sum, detrimental.

On balance, it appears from info presently available that Shah, though upset with New York picketing and L.A. plane episode, does not hold USG responsible or suspect these incidents result of any official policy protection anti-Shah elements. This does not however preclude strong representations by GOI officials both here and in Tehran, and foregoing details are provided to help you deal with such approaches following Shah's return to Tehran 17 June. We shall attempt to run down further specific details of anti-regime activity and investigate possibilities of legal or administrative action.

Rusk

45.   Memorandum From Robert W. Komer of the National Security Council Staff to the President's Special Assistant for National Security Affairs (Bundy)[1]

Washington, June 27, 1964.

Mac—

Iran Problem. Though 5-year $300 million Iran MAP plan (a real break-through) still has three years to run (FY63–67), Shah recently got all fired up about buying some fancy new hardware. He alleges growing Arab threat to oil-rich Khuzistan, but more likely his rapidly growing oil revenues have gone to his head (he told LBJ he expected $1.2 billion annually by 1970—he gets $400 plus million now).

We're happy to sell for hard currency, since otherwise Shah will simply buy elsewhere. However: (a) chief threat to Iran's stability is still internal, not external—so nation-building remains the basic need; (b) since Iran is oil-rich, we want to phase out AID money and let it finance its development through oil revenues; (c) ergo, we want to limit Shah's overall military outlays to reasonable figure, using MAP credit sales plus some continued MAP as the lever.

So we've cooked up a so-called Cooperative Logistics Agreement under which we: (a) promise Shah good credit terms for some $250 million in sales of M–60's, C–130s, F–5s, etc. during FY65–69; (b) as a sweetner promise to continue a MAP grant program through FY 69 ($53 million beyond present agreement); (c) want in return a promise that Iran will restrict its own military outlays to what we think reasonable so that development program is not short-changed.

McNamara is pushing hard for closing this deal immediately, saying he's discussed it with LBJ. One story is that LBJ told him either to sell $1.5 billion a year in hard goods to balance our payments or to cut troops in Germany. Bob pressed Bell and Alex Johnson last week.

Whatever the cause, Bob has panicked his people, and seems to be listening only to his salesmen, not to politico-military types. For example, he reversed his OK to Sloan to steer Shah to M–48A3 (our Israeli ploy) and plugged M–60s. This will cause havoc with Turks, Paks and others, who will now want M–60s and can't pay for them.

AID and I can't see cause for rushing in so fast (Shah is quite happy with promises of M–60s and C–130s he got here). But above all we think this military carrot (to which we've no objection) should be used to get an *agreed ceiling* on Iran's overall hard currency military outlays, so Iran's

---

[1] Source: Johnson Library, National Security File, Country File, Iran, Vol. I, Memos & Miscellaneous, 1/64–12/65. Secret. Copies were sent to Talbot and Macomber.

future isn't jeopardized to satisfy Shah's military whims. Embassy Teheran says Shah wouldn't like any attempt to impose ceiling (Teheran 1188)[2] and promises to achieve same result through provision for *annual* reviews of Iran military program, upon which each year's MAP and sales increment would be contingent. But I don't trust Embassy or DOD here, and would prefer a real stab at an agreed ceiling, à la the successful Indian exercise we just went through. At least let's make a try for an agreed ceiling, before retreating to annual reviews as a fallback.

We still have control of this, because a 1550 Determination is needed. I'm sure BOB will agree with us, and probably AID too. So I hope we won't let Rapid Robert's passion for promptitude panic us into premature pusillanimity. Saunders will keep you clued.

HHS[3]

---

[2] Dated June 23. (Department of State, Central Files, DEF 19 US–IRAN)
[3] Saunders initialed for Komer.

---

46. Memorandum From Harold H. Saunders of the National Security Council Staff to the President's Special Assistant for National Security Affairs (Bundy)[1]

Washington, July 2, 1964.

McGB:

We have reached a compromise on our new *5-year MAP agreement with Iran.* RWK has dropped his idea of writing a foreign exchange ceiling into the memo of understanding provided we send Holmes tough instructions to tell the Shah our help will continue only so long as his military purchases don't slow Iran's development.

Defense and AID couldn't go along with including a ceiling because (1) they don't have a realistic figure and (2) they don't think the Shah would stand still for such hand-tying. They think an annual US-Iranian review of the effect of arms purchases on the economy would give us bet-

---

[1] Source: Johnson Library, National Security File, Country File, Iran, Vol. I, Memos & Miscellaneous, 1/64–12/65. Secret. McGeorge Bundy initialed his approval.

ter control. They say they'd even be willing to shut off credit altogether if the Shah goes too fast. The key point is to be sure Holmes gets this idea and explains it clearly to the Shah because the memo of understanding doesn't sound that tough.

Kermit Gordon will be looking at the 1550 Determination this afternoon and may talk to you about it. State will also send over instructions to Holmes for clearance, which I'll check.[2]

Hal

---

[2] See Document 48.

---

47.   Telegram From the Department of State to the Embassy in Iran[1]

Washington, July 2, 1964, 8:47 p.m.

6. Joint State–AID–DOD message. Embtels 1188, 1189.[2] Following is new Memo Understanding covering military modernization program now in final process approval. Annexes forwarded separately.[3] Negotiation authorization follows separate cable when approved.[4]

"I. The Government of Iran and the Government of the United States have reviewed the following defense considerations of their respective countries:

A. The Mutual Defense Assistance Agreement between the two Governments of 23 May 1950, as supplemented by the exchange of notes of April 24, 1952, and the exchange of notes of July 12 and October 31, 1957.[5]

---

[1] Source: Department of State, Central Files, DEF 19 US–IRAN. Confidential; Priority. Drafted by Walsh; cleared in draft by Director of the Office of Development and Planning Alfred D. White, AID Near East/South Asia Coordinator Daniel Arrill, Towsley, Stoddart (DOD), and Tiger; and approved by Deputy Assistant Secretary for Near Eastern and South Asian Affairs James P. Grant.

[2] Both dated June 23. (Ibid.)

[3] Annexes A and B were transmitted in telegram 1196 to Tehran, June 25. (Ibid.)

[4] See Document 48.

[5] For texts of the Agreement and supplemental notes, see TIAS 2071. 1 UST 420; TIAS 2967. 5 UST 788; TIAS 3952. 8 UST 2369.

B. The Agreement of Cooperation between the Government of the United States of America and the Imperial Government of Iran of March 5, 1959.[6]

C. The Memorandum of Understanding between the Government of the United States of America and the Imperial Government of Iran of September 19, 1962.[7]

D. The exchange of correspondence prior to, and discussions held in June 1964, between His Imperial Majesty, the Shah of Iran, and the President of the United States of America and other officials of the Government of the United States of America.

II. In the light of these considerations, the two Governments reaffirm the concept for the defense of Iran and the force structure for the Imperial Iranian Armed Forces set forth in the Memorandum of Understanding of September 19, 1962. The Governments also restate their commitments to carry out their respective obligations undertaken in the Memorandum. In particular, the United States Government will, subject to the availability of funds and continued Congressional authorization, deliver on a grant basis the remaining equipment, material and services specified in the 1962 Memorandum. The Imperial Government of Iran will make satisfactory provision for the effective utilization and operation of all equipment provided to and within its military forces and will limit its purchases of military equipment to the requirements of agreed attainable force objectives. The Imperial Government also undertakes to assure that its program of military purchases will not cause undue strain on the nation's foreign exchange reserves or jeopardize plans for the nation's economic and social development.

III. In view of the improved financial situation of Iran and the need for modernizing Iran's military forces on long-range basis, the two Governments agree to an additional program of Mutual Defense Cooperation for the period FY 1965–69 as set forth below. It is understood that, except as specifically modified herein, this new program is subject to those conditions and obligations undertaken by the two Governments in the Memorandum of Understanding of September 19, 1962.

A. The Government of the United States will

1. Extend additional grant military assistance during FY 1967–69 to be programmed as set forth in Annex A for delivery by the end of FY 1970.

2. Subject to the request of the Imperial Government of Iran,

a) Assist in the formulation of long-range plans for the equipping, training and modernization of the Armed Forces of the Imperial Government of Iran;

---

[6] For text, see *American Foreign Policy: Current Documents, 1959,* pp. 1020–1022.

[7] For text, see *Foreign Relations,* 1961–1963, vol. XVIII, pp. 105–109.

b) Provide procurement, contracting and inspection services to the Imperial Government of Iran for the material which Iran desires to purchase in the United States;

c) Provide technical advice and training services to the Armed Forces of the Imperial Government of Iran to enhance the effective installation, operation and maintenance of the equipment concerned.

3. In order to assist the Imperial Government of Iran in financing the purchases referred to in Paragraph III B,

a) Assure credits within 30 days from the date of signing this Memorandum of Understanding for the equipment, spares and services enumerated in Paragraph III C;

b) Assure credits during U.S. FY 1965–69 from available private and Government financial institutions or, subject to the availability of funds, from funds made available under the Foreign Assistance Act of 1961 as amended, in amounts which, including the credits referred to in Paragraph III A 3 a), do not exceed a total of $200 million and are consistent with the foreign exchange and other limitations contained in III C. Negotiations with available private and Government financial institutions to obtain such credits will be conducted by the Imperial Government of Iran in cooperation with the Government of the United States. These credits will be repayable on terms which will allow payment over the ten-year period FY 1965–74 to be negotiated at the time of the conclusion of each credit sales program or contract under this Agreement and shall take into account Iran's repayment capabilities. The interest rate to be negotiated will not exceed an average of 4–5 percent per annum on the unpaid balance.

B. The Imperial Government of Iran will purchase from the United States during FY 1965–69 military equipment, material and services over and above that to be furnished on a grant basis. These purchases have an estimated value of $250 million, including:

1. Cash purchases of an estimated value of $50 million (principally spare parts for equipment provided under military grant aid programs).

2. Purchases, utilizing above credits as necessary, of an estimated value of $200 million (principally new equipment, spares, and related services). Illustrative list is at Annex B.

C. To implement this modernization program, the Imperial Government of Iran will place orders and the Government of the United States will provide credits within 30 days from the date of the signing of this Memorandum of Understanding for the following equipment, at approximately the indicated price:

4 C–130 aircraft with spares and AGE	$12.0 million
176 M–60A1 tanks with spares	39.0 million
Other related items and services including packing, inland transportation, port handling, and ocean transportation to Iran	6.0 million
	$57.0 million

Programming of the other equipment to be offered to Iran under the line of credit cited above will be divided into separate increments and phased over subsequent years. In the course of the negotiation of the credit agreement for each increment, the Iranian balance of payments and budgetary situation and progress of the development program will be reviewed in order to determine the amount of credit to be offered in the increment and a feasible amortization schedule.

IV. The Government of the United States designates the Chief of the United States Military Assistance Advisory Group to Iran, and the Imperial Government of Iran designates (a representative to be specified by the GOI) to meet periodically to perform the following functions:

A. Serve as the focal point for all matters pertaining to the United States–Iran military modernization equipment procurement program.

B. Develop detailed plans and arrangements for the implementation of this general understanding, and to supervise actions relating to the implementation of this agreement.

C. Develop Force Objectives and determine valid military equipment and training requirements for the Imperial Government of Iran which are deemed attainable in future time periods.

V. A ranking representative designated by the Imperial Iranian Government will meet with the United States Ambassador to Iran periodically, but not less frequently than once a year, to review the progress and execution of this understanding and its relationship to Iran's economic and social development program. This will include a joint assessment of the effect of military purchases on the Iranian balance of payments and budgetary situation.

Dated: _____

For the Government of the United States of America

For the Imperial Government of Iran"

Rusk

48.   Telegram From the Department of State to the Embassy in Iran[1]

Washington, July 2, 1964, 8:47 p.m.

8. For the Ambassador. Joint State/AID/Defense message. Deptel 6[2] and DEF 976339.[3] You hereby authorized negotiate with Shah and/or other appropriate Iranian officials additional program of Mutual Defense Cooperation for period FY 1965–69 as set forth Memo Understanding and annexes forwarded reftels. In course outlining to Shah our willingness assist in Military Modernization Program you should emphasize our deep interest in Iran's economic development program and its relationship to fundamental security of his country as expressed by the late President Kennedy and President Johnson. Since we would not wish economic effort to be jeopardized, we strongly feel foreign exchange and budgetary effects of military modernization program must be kept in proper bounds. In this respect we will wish periodically examine jointly with GOI overall economic effects military expenditures as indicated Para III 3 C and Para V Memo Understanding.

FYI. In regard Para III 3 C we have not as yet reached firm conclusions re programming schedule or magnitudes segments other than first $57 million. While we hope last programming segment will not be later than FY 1968, this para meant to cover possibility of stretching out program over longer period if military purchase program tends conflict unduly with economic development program or Iranian balance payments. [End] FYI

Rusk

---

[1] Source: Department of State, Central Files, DEF 19 US–IRAN. Confidential; Priority. Drafted by Walsh; cleared by Solbert (DOD), Macomber, Arrill (AID), G/PM Director for Operations Howard Meyers, Tiger, and Saunders; and approved by Talbot.

[2] Document 47.

[3] Not found.

49.   Telegram From the Embassy in Iran to the Department of State[1]

Tehran, July 4, 1964, 6 p.m.

9. Memo of Understanding without change signed today by me and by Minister of Court "by command of His Imperial Majesty the Shah of Iran". At same time Minister of Court, again by command of the Shah, transmitted a letter which appoints General Hedjazi as the Iranian rep provided for in para IV of the Memo of Understanding. In this same letter it is stated that "In future requirements of the Imperial Iranian Armed Forces will be communicated by General Hedjazi, in accordance with para IV of the memo". Original signed copy of Memo of Understanding and this letter being forwarded by pouch.

Shah said that he recognized the proposed program involving $200 million credit and $50 million cash was the most that should be spent on military modernization under presently anticipated revenues and foreign exchange availability. However, he wishes to be free to bring up possibility of purchasing additional equipment, which he considers desirable, if increased revenues over and above those now anticipated should accrue to the Iranian Govt in such amount as to make it feasible to acquire additional equipment without jeopardizing national economic and social programs. The Shah made a very strong statement that he would not allow military expenditures adversely to affect Iran's economic progress. However, he has high hopes that oil revenues, and hence foreign exchange availability, will increase to a greater extent than presently foreseen. The additional equipment which might eventually be acquired would be:

(1) a second Hawk battalion;
(2) an additional radar station in the Bandar Abbas area;
(3) one or possibly two squadrons of F–4Cs, or other high-performance aircraft, in replacement of two squadrons of F–5As.

Gen Eckhardt considers that the problem of training sufficient Iranian military personnel to man new fighter aircraft, first Hawk battalion and AC and W system will act effectively to defer introduction of this additional equipment prior to 1969. He emphasized this personnel problem very strongly to Shah.

In addition to the foregoing, the Shah wanted to go on record as pointing out that modernization might require some slight upward revision of troop ceilings, although he insisted he had no intention of espous-

---

[1] Source: Department of State, Central Files, DEF 19 US–IRAN. Confidential. Repeated to CINCSTRIKE and Department of Defense.

ing any substantial expansion. He wanted to adhere to the order of magniture of the present force objectives, but, on the other hand, he did not want to be held rigidly to 160,000. A preliminary estimate indicates that any increase required by modernization will not likely exceed the ceiling of 162,000 set in the instructions for the agreement of 1962.

The Shah said that he agreed with Gen Eckhardt that the idea of acquiring destroyers and torpedo boats should be abandoned and said that he would like to add to the program two patrol frigates modified to carry torpedoes. Gen Eckhardt believes that there is enough margin in Annexes A and B to permit this. This addition will be discussed by Eckhardt–Hedjazi.

ARMISH/MAAG will request by cable instructions as to procedure to effect the purchase and credit arrangements within a 30 day period required by para III C.

The Shah expressed himself as being entirely satisfied and pleased with these new arrangements.

Holmes

50.   Airgram From the Embassy in Iran to the Department of State[1]

A–60   Tehran, August 6, 1964.

SUBJECT

Semi-Annual Assessment of the Political Situation in Iran

REF

Embassy A–361 of December 31, 1963[2]

Note: In order that reports of this series may be considered also in connection with the Department's review of our forthcoming Progress Report on the Internal Defense Plan, we have used August 1 as the vantage point from which to survey the political situation in Iran. Therefore,

---

[1] Source: Department of State, Central Files, POL 7 IRAN. Confidential. Drafted by Eliot; coordinated with [text not declassified], First Secretary John A. Armitage; and approved by Rockwell. Repeated to Ankara, Baghdad, Cairo, Dhahran, Jidda, Kabul, Karachi, Kuwait, London, Moscow, Paris, and CINCMEAFSA for POLAD.

[2] Not printed. (Ibid., POL 2 IRAN)

insofar as the present report also contains a semi-annual review of events, it covers the seven-month period from January 1 to August 1. Unless a faster pace of events makes another cut-off date appear more useful for such an assessment, we hope to furnish the next report in this series six months from now, on February 1, 1965.

1. *Summary.* The only important trend that emerges from our assessment is the gradual deterioration of Iran-Arab relations, and especially of relations with Iraq, since the time of our last report in this series. This is now clearly the problem of principal concern to the Shah. Relations with the U.S. are excellent, probably in good part due to our forthcoming attitude toward the Shah's military concerns, which are now primarily related to the Arab claims to Khuzistan. The internal security situation is good, and the regime's control as tight as ever. The economic situation is on balance slightly worse because of the poor crop situation, although business activity is up; but private investment has not revived and real wages for urban workers are probably down.

The Mansur Government appears to be a definite improvement over its predecessor, both in respect to the leadership provided by the Prime Minister and in respect to substantive administrative improvements. The Parliament has not increased in political importance. The reform program has made no particular progress. The New Iran Party is displaying some forward movement and seems to become an asset to the regime. The opposition's capacity for making trouble has probably further declined, and this is also true of the mullahs. Some minor changes have occurred in the "pecking order", but the Shah of course still determines everyone's status. The tribal situation is definitely better in the south, and under control in the west. The slow trend "normalization" of relations with the USSR continues. [*1-1/2 lines of source text not declassified*]

[Here follows the body of the paper.]

For the Ambassador:
Martin F. Herz
Counselor of Embassy
for Political Affairs

51.   Airgram From the Embassy in Iran to the Department of State[1]

A–139   Tehran, September 22, 1964.

SUBJECT

Significance of Khomeini's September 9 Speech

REF

Embtel 278[2]

It now appears that Ayatollah Khomeini's speech of September 9 (NIT–6533)[3] did not include any statement supporting the Mansur Government. The only relatively positive feature of the speech is that, while it criticizes the Iranian regime on numerous counts, it does so somewhat less violently than usual for this dissident clerical leader.

According to more reliable information [*less than 1 line of source text not declassified*], the September 9 speech blamed "world colonialism" for the divisions between Shia and Sunni, and "the West" for differences between Iranians and Arabs and other Moslems. Khomeini termed the RCD a specific instance of such foreign-inspired division among Moslems (although he did not cite the RCD by name). He inveighed against Israeli and Jewish influence in Iran, complained against lack of freedom of public expression for the religious leaders, and took an oblique swipe at the New Iran Party. [*1 line of source text not declassified*][3]

On the whole, qualified observers feel that even though Khomeini continues to remonstrate against the regime and its policies, there has been a slight toning-down in his position. SAVAK believes the religious situation does not for the moment constitute a serious problem for the security authorities.

It is possible that a judicious mix of bribery, conciliatory tactics and the ever-present threat of the regime's mailed fist, has had the effect of lessening somewhat the virulence of Khomeini's opposition—although, as his latest speech is now more reliably reported, he is very far indeed from calling for support of the government.

For the Chargé d'Affaires, a.i.
Martin F. Herz
Counselor of Embassy
for Political Affairs

---

[1] Source: Department of State, Central Files, POL 23–9 IRAN. Confidential; Noforn. Drafted by Political Officer Victor Wolf, Jr., on September 21. Repeated to Ankara, Baghdad, Cairo, CINCMEAFSA for POLAD, Jidda, Karachi, and Kuwait.

[2] Dated September 10. (Ibid.)

[3] Not printed.

52. Telegram From the Embassy in Iran to the Department of State[1]

Tehran, October 14, 1964, 8 p.m.

404. Embtel 398.[2] Majlis yesterday passed Vienna Convention and status bill re US military personnel,[3] by vote 74 to 61. Disappointingly, slim margin was due to number of factors as analyzed below, but what stands out is that New Iran Party leadership lost control over substantial number of its own followers.

There are presently 188 deputies in Majlis, of which 138 are New Iran Party members. Some 50 New Iran Party deputies seem to have been absent, and of those present we estimate at least 12 must have voted against government. This became easier for them when opposition was successful in forcing secret vote, which is highly unusual but can be obtained under Majlis regulations if 15 deputies ask for it.

Sequence of events and factors entering into the vote were as follows: 1. Monday's New Iran Party caucus (reftel) seemingly went so well that Mansur, Yeganeh and Ziai decided to speed up schedule and bring both bills to vote Tuesday. That party leadership was obviously overconfident is shown by fact that majority made no special effort to round up its supporters to secure maximum attendance. (It is difficult to know how many absented themselves deliberately, but certainly not all absent New Iran Party deputies were busy elsewhere.) Mardom and Independents, who make up "opposition", were practically all present.

2. From beginning of debate, PriMin was on the defensive. While Majlis contacts say they admired his composure under fire, Mansur apparently thought he was dealing only with usual "opposition" which could be steamrollered by New Iran Party majority. Fact that government was abandoned by some of its own supporters (either by adverse vote or deliberate absence) came as rude shock after outcome of vote was announced. Before the vote Ziai had told us New Iran Party expected only two or three defections.

3. Government made long and comprehensive statement about purport of bill, and Mansur offered repeated interpretations in course of

---

[1] Source: Department of State, Central Files, DEF 15–3 IRAN–US. Confidential; Priority.

[2] Dated October 12. (Ibid.)

[3] In March 1962 the U.S. Government had proposed that U.S. military personnel and civilian employees of the Defense Department stationed in Iran and their dependents should have the privileges and immunities specified for "members of the administrative and technical staff" in the Vienna Convention, i.e., full diplomatic immunity. See *Foreign Relations*, 1961–1963, vol. XVII, pp. 519–520. Additional documentation relating to the Vienna Convention and status of forces bill is in Department of State, Central Files, DEF 15–3 IRAN–US.

debate. Since these may constitute important legislative history, we will submit separate analysis as soon as full record of debate available. Apparently government was forthright in explaining scope and status of bill and did not hedge in its explanations.

4. Opposition either did not get the word that Shah wanted status bill passed, or else it had license to attack government. In any case Mardom and Independents pulled out all the stops, especially after they were voted down in succession of procedural maneuvers designed to delay vote. Government apparently felt (erroneously) that if opposition did not want bill to be brought to vote, it must be weak.

5. What did not help at all is that yesterday's press reported automobile accident in Tehran in which a US serviceman gravely injured an Iranian taxi driver. Some speakers claimed that status bill would wipe out civil liability in such cases. Among the more scurrilous arguments heard was that, "if status bill was passed, an American non-com could henceforth slap the face of an Iranian General with impunity." Most violent speakers against status bill were deputies Zahtab-Fard and Sartip-Pur. Both independents; but many others also talked against, including Mardom group leader Rambod.

6. With Majlis Speaker Riazi in the US, presiding officer was Shafi-Amin who is unskilled in parliamentary tactics and was weak in controlling debate. (Senate President Sharif-Emami, a seasoned parliamentary strategist, commented to us last night that in similar situation he would have called secret session to "blow off steam" before permitting debate to proceed on the record.)

7. There were clearly anti-American themes employed by some of opposition speakers, some of them quite ridiculous (such as insinuation that PriMin must be an American puppet because he had once rented a house to US Embassy officer who was alleged to be "running the government"). Government seems to have suffered this in silence. There were no enthusiastic supporters of status bill. All the emotion was on the other side.

In conclusion, we find that while it is heartening that long drawnout question of status of US military personnel in Iran is now settled in parliament, not only Mansur but to some extent also the Shah's regime has paid an unexpectedly high price in getting this done. That price was due in large measure to ineptitude of government's handling both in upper and lower house, but it would be idle to minimize the Nationalist reaction which passage of the bill called forth. It will take several days to assess whether this is a temporary phenomenon that will blow over, as now seems likely, or whether it will have some longer-lasting effects on our relations with Iran.

Rockwell

53.   Memorandum From the Director of the Office of Greek,
       Turkish, and Iranian Affairs (Bracken) to the Deputy Assistant
       Secretary of State for Near Eastern and South Asian Affairs
       (Jernegan)[1]

Washington, October 22, 1964.

SUBJECT

Talking Paper on Iran PL–480 Programs for Meeting with Administrator of FAS

Our current experience with USDA in its handling of PL–480 programs for Iran has raised so many troublesome problems that we suggest you schedule a meeting with Mr. Raymond A. Ioanes, Administrator of the Foreign Agriculture Service, to try to reach a meeting of minds on a government-wide approach that would serve both our foreign policy and our commercial interests. At such a meeting you might describe the progress being made in Iran toward efficient economic management and stress the importance of promptness and understanding in our dealings with an important transitional country such as Iran. The following points might be made at such a meeting:

1. *Iran's Progress and Our New Opportunities.* Iran has made such progress in financial management in recent years that we are able gradually to shift our major concern from aid projects to market development. We have made a number of policy changes in the past year to take advantage of growing Iranian financial strength for the benefit of the U.S. balance of payments, including: raising the interest rate on AID development loans and gradually replacing such loans by EXIM lending at commercial rates; shifting our military assistance from an all-grant basis to a combined grant and credit-sales basis; greatly increasing the U.S.-use component of our most recent PL–480 Title I agreement (from 35% to 60%, including Cooley loans); and informing the Iranians that further PL–480 agreements after that of September 29 would be under Title IV (dollar credit sales) rather than Title I. In fact, we may have been overdoing things and making too many changes that impinge on the Iranian balance of payments, which has recently begun to show some unexpected signs of strain. But on balance, we feel that Iran will continue to gain in financial strength over the long term and will offer a growing market for our exports, provided we make the appropriate adjustments

---

[1] Source: Department of State, NEA/IRN Files: Lot 69 D 513, Iran, 1964, AID 15, PL 480 Food for Peace Program. Confidential. Drafted by Tiger and cleared by Deputy Assistant Administrator of the AID Office of Material Resources John W. Johnston, Jr. A handwritten note on the source text reads: "JDJ saw Ioanes 2:30—10/28/64." A memorandum of conversation recording the meeting is ibid.: Lot 69 D 30, Memoranda of Conversation.

in our policies and procedures. As regards agricultural commodities in particular, the rising living standards and the current land reform efforts would seem to portend shortfalls for a number of years in marketable surpluses from domestic production. These opportunities not only offer potential commercial advantages, they also provide what may turn out to be one of our chief means of maintaining U.S. influence in this strategically located country.

2. *Obligations of the Emerging Relationship.* It thus behooves us to manage our new style of financial-commercial relationship with Iran with care. We expect—and to an increasing degree are receiving—more efficient and business-like response from the GOI in our commercial/financial relationships. The GOI, in turn, expects equally business-like and prompt responses from us. During recent months we have encountered hard bargaining in regard to loan terms, and it has been made clear to us that the GOI is in a position and has the negotiating skill to be quite discriminating, for instance, in the choice of foreign suppliers for capital equipment needed in its sizeable development program. So far our PL–480 terms have remained sufficiently concessionary that we have not had to worry about foreign competition in agricultural commodities, although the Iranians have been frustrated by what appears to them as excessive bureaucratic delay.

3. *Current Title I Wheat Program.* This is a good case in point. The Iranians officially requested, on June 29, 1964, an amendment to the FY–1964 Title I wheat agreement (for 80,000 tons) raising the amount to 240,000 tons because of an emergency situation created by an unexpected crop failure. The amendment route was preferred in the interests of speed, because the GOI, facing wheat shortages in parts of the country where land had been distributed to former tenants, felt under political pressure to ensure adequate wheat supplies in the countryside as well as in the cities. A new PL–480 agreement (the amendment route was vetoed) was not signed until September 29, the amount was reduced to 140,000 tons (to allow for Title IV private entity transactions and some increase in usual marketings), and the terms were hardened in many respects. As of the present PA's are being issued for 70,000 tons, whereas the Iranians have been pressing continually for issuance of the full amount. As the Iranians see it, their urgent request for wheat, hopefully to be delivered early in the Fall of 1964, has been whittled down and dangerously delayed. None of the explanations we are able to make about the reasons for these actions is very useful in allaying their irritation and feeling that we have let them down. We think the U.S. Government could have acted much more promptly and responsively if all parties concerned had shared the same appreciation of the urgency of the Iranian request and the policy advantages for the U.S. in responding promptly.

4. *Current Title IV Feed Grain Request.* The GOI on September 8 requested 50,000 tons of feed grains under Title IV to meet unexpected shortages and avoid excessive animal slaughter before cold weather set in. Owing to various delays, we were not able until October 21 to inform the GOI that favorable action was taken on their request, and we still have ahead of us the dispatch of negotiating instructions and the issuance of PA's.

---

54.   Telegram From the Embassy in Iran to the Department of State[1]

Tehran, October 27, 1964, 3 p.m.

451. Embtel 430.[2] On Oct 25 Majlis approved bill authorizing $200 million USG-guaranteed credit from US banks for purchase military equipment. Majlis approval was unanimous following Prime Minister's briefing in closed session and strong statement in open session. Bill sent to Senate for its "observations" (under Article 46 of constitution Majlis has final word on money bills), after which it returns for second reading.

Prime Minister's statement advocating passage of credit bill for improving Iranian military posture referred emphatically [to] the "threats against Iran's interests in the Persian Gulf." This was clear reference, as one paper put it, "the claims to Khuzistan Province by Arab radio stations and newspapers linked the regime of Nasser." Mansur made it clear that GOI regards developments in Middle East as currently posing greatest threat. In contrast, in referring to recent changes in Soviet Union he reportedly described USSR as "our northern neighbor which has for years adopted a policy of peaceful coexistence" and expressed hope that "political, economic and cultural ties would continue to grow strong."

Mansur also expressed appreciation for US aid since World War II and claimed that credit commitments would not detract from development needs and that defense expenditures being kept at lowest possible levels. With reference to CENTO allies he said that "there have not been and will not be any changes in the policies of our CENTO allies."

---

[1] Source: Department of State, Central Files, DEF 19–3 US–IRAN. Confidential. Sent also to DOD for Kuss. Repeated to Baghdad, Kuwait, CINCSTRIKE for POLAD, Ankara, Cairo, Karachi, London, and Moscow.

[2] Dated October 20. (Ibid.)

All major press editorials dealt with subject of credit bill and all follow explicit or implicit anti-Nasser line. For example, English-language Tehran journal headlined "Nasser Forces Military Loan" and made passing reference to UAR "Russian-equipped soldiers."

We understand that deputies who had talked against govt during recent status bill debate went out of their way this time to compliment govt for its handling of country's defense needs. Word has been passed down last week that Shah wanted credit bill passed by Oct 26, and no nonsense.[3]

Rockwell

---

[3] Airgram A–303 from Tehran, December 15, reported that the "coincidence" of having the parliamentary vote on the status of forces bill followed within 2 weeks by the unanimous vote to accept a $200 million credit from U.S. commercial banks for the purchase of U.S. military equipment had contributed to the widespread belief that in some way the passage of the status bill was the price exacted by the United States for the granting of the credits in question. (Ibid., DEF 15–3 IRAN–US)

---

55.   Telegram From the Embassy in Iran to the Department of State[1]

Tehran, November 3, 1964, 1 p.m.

499. Ref Embtels 448, 487 and 495.[2] Vienna Convention—Status Bill. Prime Minister Mansur, in a comprehensive foreign policy speech before the Senate Saturday,[3] for the first time gave public explanations regarding background and coverage of the Status Bill. Speech was prominently featured by press, rebroadcast over the radio, and has perceptibly improved public climate surrounding the status question.

As *Kayhan International* put it, Mansur's speech "in effect made amends for government's handling of the bill, as far as public was concerned. The administration's hush-hush line had provided fuel for flick-

---

[1] Source: Department of State, Central Files, DEF 15–3 IRAN–US. Confidential. Repeated to CINCSTRIKE for POLAD.

[2] Dated October 27, October 31, and November 2, respectively. (Ibid.)

[3] October 31.

ering embers of whatever opposition there is in the country. That fire at one moment threatened to spread, with opposition apparently out to exploit what they thought to be government's Achilles heel. And because exact terms of the bill were not known, and it was not possible to determine the extent of immunity granted, the critics, working from their pulpit sanctuaries or fifth column hideouts, spread the lie that very independence and sovereignty of Iran were being bartered."

Among Deputies and Senators, there is rejoicing that the air has been cleared by Mansur's statement.

Unfortunately, however. PriMin's speech contained not only helpful statements but also number of glaring inaccuracies which look good to the public but apparently involved serious misrepresentation of the bill's coverage. In particular, he was reported to have said three things which are wrong: (1) that, whereas the US had asked dependents to be covered, they are excluded from coverage by the wording of the law; (2) that only on-duty offenses are covered by immunity, apparently without distinction between civil and criminal offenses; and (3) that, although the US had asked all members of advisory missions to be covered, the law actually covers only those who fulfill technical advisory functions.

Ziai, Chairman of Majlis Foreign Affairs Committee, acknowledged to us Sunday that these statements correspond neither to the law nor, in particular, to the legislative history. FonMin told us privately on the same day that he was aware Mansur had said things that were not true; but we could not rely on Aram to set things right.

Accordingly, I sought urgent interview with Mansur yesterday and, while congratulating him on the popular success he had scored with his speech, asked him how we are to report certain apparent mistakes which might be due to misquotation by the press but which could cause future trouble. He backed down all along the way. Regarding families, he said he might have used the wrong word but had meant to refer to members of household who are not members of family. (I believe he really had believed that members of the family were not covered, but realized his error when I pointed out to him the relevant provision of the convention. It is also possible that others beforehand had alerted him to his mistake. He subsequently phoned to say he was arranging to have official record of his remarks amended to make clear he was referring to non-American members of household.) As for on-duty or off-duty distinction, he had clearly said, he claimed, that this applies only to civil liability. And as for coverage of members of advisory missions, he had only meant to say that Iranian employees of those missions cannot enjoy immunities.

I then asked what he intended to do to rectify the erroneous public impression which his remarks had created, adding that I had refused to answer press queries as to whether Embassy agreed with PriMin until I had chance to talk with him. His reply was instantaneous: by no means must there be further public discussion of this matter. Mistakes could be corrected by amending the record. He did not even wish the Foreign Ministry to be brought into the matter for time being. PriMin said he had certain difficulties due to fact that Vienna Convention had inadvertently been submitted to Majlis minus one article. When this and other elements of the record had been tidied up, GOI would formally notify Embassy that law applying provisions of Vienna Convention to members US Military Advisory Mission was in effect. The full provisions of the convention would apply. I said I was glad to hear this, as both US and Iran had suffered from this long drawn-out process, and we must make certain that the goal we have both been seeking is fully achieved. Furthermore, when General Eckhardt had recently discussed matter with Shah, latter had given no indication at all that he had in mind anything but the full application of the provisions of the convention to the US Military Advisory Missions.

This incident clearly demonstrates importance that must be attached to early formal clarification of the coverage obtained through the status bill, and notably the continued validity of our original exchange of notes. It also shows timeliness of our recommendation in Embtel 495, which involves some sweetening of pill to obtain the desired result. If the Foreign Ministry balks at providing the necessary languages we must hold the Prime Minister to his word and if necessary go the Shah. We have been fighting too long to achieve this coverage for our military people, and received too much in the way of unfavorable public repercussions, largely as a result of the ineptitude of the GOI in handling this matter. To risk losing our full goal at this stage of the game owing to lack of precision or effort by some Iranian officials to engage in back-tracking maneuvers.

Rockwell

---

56.   Telegram From the Embassy in Iran to the Department of State[1]

Tehran, November 4, 1964, 4 p.m.

508. Embtel 278.[2] Reliably reported that Ayatollah Khomeini, dissident religious leader, was arrested in Qom yesterday, brought to Tehran,

---

[1] Source: Department of State, Central Files, POL 23–9 IRAN. Confidential; Priority. Repeated to Ankara, Baghdad, CINCMEAFSA for POLAD, Jidda, Karachi, and Kuwait.

[2] Dated September 10. (Ibid.)

and taken across the border to exile in Turkey. As reported NIT–6560, Khomeini clearly over-stepped bounds when, in connection with criticism of the Status Bill according immunities to US military advisors, he not only attacked approval of bill by Majlis as disgraceful, illegal, and "against Islam and the *Koran*" but also called for overthrow of the govt by the Imperial Iranian Army.[3] [*less than 1 line of source text not declassified*] Part of Tehran bazaar closed down, but city quiet. Tehran radio announced exile today without specifying where.

Rockwell

---

[3] A translation of Khomeini's speech on October 26 is attached to airgram A–233 from Tehran, November 10. (Ibid., POL 30 IRAN)

---

57.   Telegram From the Embassy in Iran to the Department of State[1]

Tehran, November 5, 1964, 1 p.m.

515. Deptel 359.[2] ForMinister spoke to me at some length yesterday about Prince Mahmud Reza's difficulties with Gudarzian. He said Shah and Prince are incensed about this matter and cannot understand how things could have developed to point that Prince's account was about to be sequestered, obviously on basis falsified documents since no check given Gudarzian and Prince not in US at time papers allegedly served upon him, and furthermore how this could have been going on without Prince knowing anything about it until very last moment. Aram said did not see how this kind of development could fail have adverse effect on

---

[1] Source: Department of State, Central Files, POL 15–1 IRAN. Confidential.

[2] Telegram 359 to Tehran, October 27, instructed the Embassy to inform the Foreign Ministry that Khaibar Gudarzian had obtained a New York court default judgment against Prince Mahmud Reza for an amount in excess of $1 million, based on Gudarzian's claim that the Prince had given a check for this amount to the World Sport Federation, which was not honored upon presentation. Court records indicated that the Prince had been personally served with papers at Kennedy Airport in New York on August 8, 1963, and had so far presented no defense. Thus, the court was prepared to issue a default judgment against the Prince's Morgan Guaranty Bank account unless he took some effective legal action without delay. (Ibid.)

reputation US banks here, since news bound get around. Amb Foroughi had just cabled recommending that Princess Fatimeh withdraw any funds she might have in US banks lest these be put in danger of blocking. (Aram didn't think she had any deposited in US.)

At same time Aram showed me article from *New York Daily News* of Oct. 29 reporting this whole matter in manner highly unfavorable to Royal Family here, which he said had angered Shah very much. He added both Shah and he convinced that such article would not have appeared, and Gudarzian would not have undertaken this legal action, had USG taken steps to warn Gudarzian of consequences of any further activity against good relations between Iran and US. After it had been so clearly shown that Gudarzian's assertions to McClellan Committee were nothing but falsehoods, why had USG done nothing to prevent Gudarzian from taking further action based on same falsehoods, or at least to make sure that his moves were ineffective?

How did it happen that bank had so easily disclosed amount of Prince's account? Shah and Aram were at loss understand how a crook like Gudarzian should be able get away with all this, apparently so easily. He was even reported as having said that some people in State Dept were not displeased that he was embarrassing Iranian Royal Family. All this having very unfortunate effect on Shah, said Aram.

I made usual points that a Chief of State should not permit himself be disturbed by attacks of man like this, since such developments are part of penalties of being in public life; US political and legal system unfortunately offers opportunities for abuse; courts must take cognizance of complaints brought before them and cannot evaluate substance until these heard; I understood steps to deport Gudarzian underway and perhaps he seeking delay deportation by undertaking new legal action; as Aram knew, Dept had offered provide Prince's lawyer with info concerning Gudarzian's past record. It was clear from Aram's reception of all this that it did not impress him and that he did not believe it would impress Shah.

I do not myself understand how Gudarzian was able to get so far with the New York Court, assuming truth of Prince's statement that he not in US at time papers reportedly served upon him. I would welcome any info Dept can send me which may be helpful in counteracting highly unfavorable impression this matter has created here. Could not Dept take stronger action to warn Iranian troublemakers of this kind against abusing hospitality of US to create trouble for govt with which US maintains friendly relations?[3]

Rockwell

---

[3] Telegram 399 to Tehran, November 10, informed the Embassy that the court had granted a continuation of the case until November 20 and that the Department was actively pursuing with the Department of Justice and INS all possible means of moving against Gudarzian and his associates. (Ibid.)

---

58.   **Telegram From the Embassy in Iran to the Department of State**[1]

Tehran, November 5, 1964, 5 p.m.

521. Embtel 508.[2] Tehran remains quiet following public announcement Khomeini exile. Mass communications media refer fact of exile (but not venue) and also report Khomeini recently "highly critical" Status Bill. Some closure Tehran Bazaar yesterday and [*less than 1 line of source text not declassified*] half Tehran Bazaar closed today at 0900. No incidents reported at Qom Nov. 4 and 5 (to 1100). Special forces group alerted yesterday to full standby status but released from alert 1030 today. One army battalion sent to Qom as precautionary measure. Security authorities do not expect any serious trouble.

Although GOI had watched Khomeini closely since his release from confinement last spring, it probably would have continued to tolerate his speeches and leaflets as long as his political comments avoided outright subversion. However, his reported call for govt overthrow and related attempt suborn armed forces was straw that broke camel's back.

What is unusual is relative moderation of punishment (exile) when considering GOI action against persons committing similar offenses in past. Nevertheless, since govt has not really explained why he was exiled, widespread impression undoubtedly exists that it was only because of his criticism of Status Bill and $200 million US loan. This is unfortunate

---

[1] Source: Department of State, Central Files, POL 23–9 IRAN. Confidential. Repeated to Ankara, Baghdad, Cairo, CINCMEAFSA for POLAD, Jidda, Karachi, and Kuwait.

[2] Document 56.

and further involves US in conflict between govt and opposition, in which privileges for US military personnel have been seized upon as issue on which govt is most vulnerable.

Govt is now making concerted effort to link Khomeini with foreign enemies. After PriMin's reference to "fifth columnists" making trouble over the Status Bill (in his Senate speech last Saturday), press is now rather more explicitly linking Khomeini and Nasser. Thus New Iran Party newspaper in connection with Khomeini exile says "enemies of Iran casting covetous eyes on Khuzistan and the Persian Gulf are trying to disturb the peace in Iran through their paid agents and hirelings." Ajang recalls that last year Khomeini's statements were broadcast over Radio Cairo. Paper even accuses Khomeini of having joined in the call to apply the name Arabian Gulf to the Persian Gulf. *Poste Tehran* says Khomeini was prepared to give Iranian oil to Nasser.

Rockwell

---

59.   Telegram From the Embassy in Iran to the Department of State[1]

Tehran, December 9, 1964, 5 p.m.

643. Deptel 419 and Embtel 630.[2] Vienna Convention. I am pleased to report that we have today consummated satisfactory exchange of notes on immunities and exemptions of our Military Missions in Iran.

There are althogether three notes, texts of which will be pouched:

1.   One Iranian note referring to our note 299 and transmitting text of law passed on October 13 (Emb A–195);[3]

2.   Another Iranian note also replying to our note 299, referring to recent ratification of Vienna Convention, and containing satisfactory statement that immunities and exemptions will apply to "American military and non-military personnel who are in Iran under agreements or arrangements between the two govts."

3.   Our reply, acknowledging the two replies to our note 299 as also constituting favorable and acceptable response to our note 243, and add-

---

[1] Source: Department of State, Central Files, DEF 15–3 IRAN–US. Confidential. Repeated to CINCSTRIKE and CINCSTRIKE for POLAD.

[2] Dated November 16 and December 5, respectively. (Ibid.)

[3] Dated October 27. (Ibid.)

ing waiver provision as per Deptel 419 with restrictive definition (accepted by FonOff) to make sure it cannot be invoked in case of traffic and other minor offenses.[4]

Dept will note that manner in which notes have been drafted also relieves us of need to argue that units such as Gulf district, signal relay etc. come under heading of "advisory" as note two covers everybody not covered under note one.

In difficult and protracted discussions to bring about this result it has been necessary to modify language supplied in Deptel 413, but all our essential requirements are met and in some cases they are exceeded.

Status law has not yet been promulgated. Probable date of promulgation is December 17.

Holmes

---

[4] Telegram 413 to Tehran, November 13, had authorized the Embassy to affirm that U.S. authorities would give sympathetic consideration to a request from Iranian authorities for waiver of immunity in cases where those authorities considered such a waiver to be of particular importance. (Ibid.) Telegram 419 to Tehran, November 16, added a restrictive definition to the waiver provision to ensure that it would not be invoked in the case of traffic or other minor offenses. (Ibid.)

---

60.   Letter From the Assistant Administrator of the Agency for International Development for Near East and South Asia (Macomber) to the Deputy Assistant Secretary of Defense for International Security Affairs (Solbert)[1]

Washington, December 11, 1964.

Dear Peter:

The Country Team in Iran has requested us to clarify for the Department of Defense the possibility of using P.L. 480, Title I, 104(c) funds to finance the local currency costs of MAP projects in Iran. The recent Title I agreements with Iran provide that the proceeds be used for loans to sup-

---

[1] Source: Washington National Records Center, RG 330, OASD/ISA Files: FRC 68 A 306, 121 Iran—11 Dec 64. Confidential. A stamped notation on the source text indicates that Solbert saw it.

port Iran's economic development. No provision has been made to extend grants for defense purposes. Moreover, because of Iran's long term favorable balance of payments position, it is unlikely that further Title I agreements will be concluded. In the future, sales of surplus commodities to Iran will be for dollars under Title IV and not for local currency. In summary, there are no funds available for military purposes under present agreements and future availability is highly improbable.

The Department of Defense will also recall that in the Spring of 1962, the Shah was informed of the United States decision to terminate budgetary support for the Iranian defense establishment. An allocation of P.L. 480 local currency proceeds for defense purposes would represent another form of budgetary support and a reversal of policy which, in our judgment, would not be warranted in view of Iran's improved economic position.[2]

Sincerely yours,

Bill

-----

[2] A handwritten notation on the source text reads: "*General Strickland*—No action called for by us, I take it. PS."

-----

61.   Special Report Prepared in the Central Intelligence Agency[1]

SC No. 00649/64C   Washington, December 11, 1964.

REFORM IN IRAN: PROGRESS AND PROSPECTS

For over two years the Shah has been trying to effect fundamental economic and political reforms in Iran, with the primary aim of building a broad popular base for his regime. The most dramatic changes are oc-

-----

[1] Source: Johnson Library, National Security File, Country File, Iran, Vol. I, Memos & Miscellaneous, 1/64–12/65. Secret; No Foreign Dissem. Prepared in the CIA's Office of Current Intelligence. Attached to a December 14 memorandum from McCone to the President that reads: "Your questions concerning the current situation in Iran prompt me to submit the attached special report, 'Reform in Iran: Progress and Prospects.' This represents the Central Intelligence Agency's most recent appraisal of the situation and reflects in detail points I made briefly in our conversation Saturday [December 12] morning."

curring in the traditional system of land tenure, as villages are taken from individual owners and distributed among the peasants. The program, as expected, is alienating the Shah's supporters among the wealthy classes, whose influence in the country's administration has not lessened significantly. Moreover, the Shah has not yet achieved his desired mass political support; peasants still lack effective instruments to register their approval of his program, and the urban population is skeptical of his motives. Disruptions brought on by the reforms meanwhile threaten an economic crisis and a possible reversal of what he terms his "White Revolution."

[Here follows the body of the paper.]

---

62. **Action Memorandum From the Assistant Secretary of State for Near Eastern and South Asian Affairs (Talbot) to Secretary of State Rusk**[1]

Washington, December 19, 1964.

SUBJECT

    Serious Problem with Iran re the Gudarzian Case

Discussion

    Foreign Minister Aram has requested urgently that you receive him again to discuss the Gudarzian case, which he mentioned to you when he met with you on December 5. I feel strongly that, despite your heavy schedule, you should receive him again while he is in Washington December 21 and 22. There are two major reasons why such a meeting is required at this time:

    1. This affair has incensed the Shah more than any previous incident in U.S.-Iranian relations during the past ten years. He cannot understand how the USG could allow a "known crook" such as Gudarzian first to testify falsely before a Congressional committee regarding corruption in United States aid to Iran, as he did to the McClellen Committee in the summer and fall of 1963, and now obviously to abuse the New York court system for the purpose of harassing the royal family and disturbing U.S.-Iranian relations. Worst of all, the Shah has gained the impression from

---

[1] Source: Department of State, Central Files, POL 15–1 IRAN. Confidential. Drafted by Tiger and cleared by Acting Legal Adviser Leonard C. Meeker and Jernegan.

Aram's reporting from New York that there is insufficient high-level USG interest in bringing Gudarzian to book, as indicated in Tehran's telegram 659. (Tab D)[2]

2. Since you saw Aram on December 5 there has been a new development that has further outraged the Shah and other Iranian officials. Gudarzian's attorneys on December 11 entered an action in the New York courts charging that an Iranian lawyer, Khosro Eghbal, came to this country to remove assets of Princess Fatemeh and was served with a summons which he evaded by leaving the country on the advice of Donald Wehmeyer (L/NEA) and Ambassador Foroughi. Court orders were issued calling upon Wehmeyer and the Ambassador (who however has not been served) to show cause why they should not be held in contempt of court. The charges against Wehmeyer and the Ambassador are groundless, but the Shah has gained the impression that Iranian immunity in this country has been breached by the court's action in entertaining a charge against his Ambassador. This court action was publicized in the *New York Times* of December 12 and is described further in Tehran's telegram 666, (Tab E) and in the Department's telegram 505, (Tab F).

Our foreign policy interests in this problem are substantial. The Shah has just rammed through the Iranian Parliament, at our insistence and with considerable risk to his domestic position, a highly unpopular measure extending immunities and privileges to American military personnel in Iran. He has also responded in very forthcoming manner so far to our suggestions that he take a hand in the affair of Robert Bredin, an American engineer who has been sentenced by an Iranian court to three years for the presumed murder of his wife, in the face of evidence clearly indicating death from other causes. We have ahead of us some possibly delicate representations on the subject of a new oil agreement with the Consortium, negotiations for which are now deadlocked. We will also shortly be wanting to raise the subject of Iran's participation in the supply of military units and equipment to South Viet Nam. We must anticipate difficulties in these endeavors and in all other aspects of our relations so long as the Shah can feel that he has been obliging in meeting all of our requests whereas we do not lift a finger to keep his family from being harassed unjustly in our courts or his Ambassador from being falsely accused, all by one he considers a proven scoundrel whom we do not even expose through publicity channels.

We have, of course, been for months taking measures designed to curb Gudarzian's activities within the limits of our relationship to a state court system. These were described to Aram in some detail by the Department's Deputy Legal Adviser on December 10, as covered in the Department's telegram 486, (Tab G). When Ambassador Foroughi called on me on December 18 to deliver a note of protest about the latest court ac-

---

[2] All of the tabs were attached but not printed.

tion and the entire Gudarzian affair (Tab H), Len Meeker and I assured him in strongest terms of this Government's distress over the affair and our determination at high levels to bring Gudarzian to justice. We also persuaded Foroughi to help us in dispelling the false notion in Tehran that he had actually been served with a subpoena and that Iranian diplomatic immunity here had thereby been breached. I am entertaining Aram at a small luncheon on December 21 and Governor Harriman is scheduled to lunch privately with Aram on December 22. While these meetings will provide further opportunity for expressions of concern and determination, I am certain that nothing less than a direct expression of this kind from you to Aram will suffice to begin repairing the damage.

At a meeting with Aram, you could explain to him that you found, upon looking into the matter after your December 5 meeting, that the Gudarzian affair had been occupying a great deal of attention in various Government Departments for some months. Most recently these included further detailed contacts by Federal Government officials with New York State legal officials.

You could tell Aram that we too are outraged by the latest court action and are determined to take every measure within our power to put a stop to this evident abuse of our state courts by bringing the evidence of possible violations of law forcefully to the attention of the proper authorities. If you agree to send the letters to the Governor of New York, the Secretary of the Treasury, and the Acting Attorney General which are attached as Tabs A, B and C respectively, you could cite these as evidence of our determination to see this matter through. (I do not recommend that you give him copies.) You could also tell Aram that we expect developments in the near future to result in press coverage that will help counteract the embarrassment caused to the royal family and to Ambassador Foroughi by press coverage of the judicial proceedings to date.

Recommendations

1. That you sign the letters to the Governor of New York, the Secretary of the Treasury and the Acting Attorney General, attached as Tabs A, B and C, respectively. I should like to deliver the letter to the Acting Attorney General myself to give him some of the flavor of the whole case and enlist his personal interest and support.

2. That you receive the Iranian Foreign Minister on Monday or Tuesday, December 21 or 22 and discuss the Gudarzian case with him along the foregoing lines.[3]

---

[3] On December 21 Secretary Rusk initialed his approval of Talbot's recommendations and agreed to a meeting with the Iranian Foreign Minister at 3 p.m. on December 22. Telegram 511 to Tehran, December 22, reported that at the meeting Aram pressed for more effort to convict Gudarzian on criminal charges. The Secretary told the Foreign Minister that the Department was in touch with New York authorities and other U.S. Government agencies and was stepping up its efforts in connection with criminal charges against Gudarzian. (Ibid.)

63.   **Briefing Memorandum From the Director of the Office of South Asian Affairs (Cameron) to Secretary of State Rusk**[1]

Washington, January 6, 1965.

SUBJECT

Your Appointment with the Foreign Minister of Iran, Thursday, January 7, 12:00 Noon

Foreign Minister Aram (see attached biographic sketch)[2] is calling, on instruction from his Government, to discuss problems being encountered in the final stages of negotiation for a revised oil agreement with the Iranian Oil Consortium. He will very likely request United States Government intercession with American companies participating in the Consortium to modify certain terms of the offer.

When Iranian officials approached us, here and in Tehran, during the past month to use our influence with the American companies, we have reminded them that our influence is not sufficient to force the companies to abandon a position which they consider important in their operations abroad. While this remains true, our present difficulties with the Shah over the Gudarzian affair would suggest a somewhat more forthcoming approach to Mr. Aram on this occasion. I recommend that, while reminding him again of the limits of our influence, you offer the Department's services in contacting American companies, advising them in detail of the Iranian position, and reporting back to the Iranian officials on the results of these approaches.

Mr. Jernegan will accompany Mr. Aram in his call on you, as will Mr. Ensor (E/FSE) and Mr. Tiger (NEA/GTI).

Background

The proposed agreement, which has been offered by the operating companies to all of the Middle Eastern producing countries participating in OPEC (Organization of Petroleum Exporting Countries), involves an agreement to treat royalty payments as an item of operating expenses rather than as part of the country's 50 percent share of profits. This would net the producing countries substantially higher revenues. The companies agreed to make the offer retroactive for the calendar year 1964 if the producing countries would accept it by December 31, 1964. This dead-

---

[1] Source: Department of State, Central Files, POL IRAN–US. Confidential. Drafted by Tiger and John G. Oliver in FSE; cleared in draft by the Office of International Resources' Chief of Fuels and Energy Division Andrew F. Ensor in the Bureau of Economic Affairs and William D. Wolle (NEA/NE). A handwritten note on the source text reads, "S saw."

[2] Attached but not printed. Secretary Rusk met with Foreign Minister Aram at 12:25 p.m. on January 7. No memorandum of conversation of their meeting has been found.

line has now been extended to January 26, 1965. As of December 31, the offer had been accepted by Saudi Arabia, in principle, and by Kuwait, subject to parliamentary ratification.

On December 31 Iran finally accepted the fiscal provisions of the offer, but it is still balking at other conditions, namely those involving a quit-claim and arbitration procedures. The Consortium wants a quit-claim (waiver) of all additional monetary demands by Iran for the years preceding the new agreement, whereas Iran wants such a waiver limited to questions involving the level of posted prices. As regards arbitration, Iran contends that the current proposal provides the Consortium with a unilateral right to demand arbitration in the event of an alleged breach of the agreement, but denies a similar right to Iran. Iran further claims that there are adequate arbitration mechanisms in its existing agreement and demands special consideration for having helped the companies work out arbitration arrangements with the Arab countries, where no such mechanisms had existed. This special consideration, in the Iranian mind, should take the form of exempting Iran from the arbitration provisions worked out for Arab producing countries.

During ten days of discussions in London (December 20–30) there was apparently some progress on the quit-claim problem, but the arbitration provision remains a sticking point. On December 31 the Prime Minister told Ambassador Holmes that the Consortium's offer was "entirely unacceptable," adding that "it would be utterly impossible for his Government to present anything less than equal treatment to the Iranian Parliament." The companies have taken an equally strong position against retaining unique arbitration provisions for Iran. However, as of December 31 it was evident that both sides had some expectation of being able to settle these differences by January 26. The Consortium was to have despatched three high-level representatives from London to Tehran on January 5 to resume negotiations, but no word has yet been received as to their progress.[3]

---

[3] A supplemental briefing memorandum from Jernegan to Rusk on January 6 reported that the Consortium representatives in Tehran were prepared to yield significantly on the arbitration issue, but that their new proposals would still fall short of the completely reciprocal arbitration rights which the Iranians had been seeking. They also pointed out to Holmes that any modification agreed to with Iran would necessitate renegotiation to grant similar concessions to the Arab countries. (Department of State, NEA/IRN Files: Lot 70 D 552, CHRON FILE, IRAN 1965, Memoranda through S/S (Staff Studies))

64.   Paper Prepared in the Department of State[1]

Washington, undated.

THE SIGNIFICANCE OF KHOMEINI'S OPPOSITION TO THE IRANIAN GOVERNMENT

The opposition of Ayatollah Maj Ruhollah Seyed Musavi Khomeini, the leading Iranian religious figure, is symptomatic of widespread popular opposition to Government policies. One aspect of these policies has been to destroy the power of the clergy. To attempt to weaken the religious structure of Iranian society, as the Shah appears to be doing, believing this necessary to carry on his campaign to modernize Iran, has proven to be a dangerous course of political action. Popular reactions to this policy are already apparent. As reactionary as the present clergy is, the very nature of religion in Iran is such that it is capable of change and adaptation. Khomeini's opposition represents the reaction of traditional Iranian society. As spokesman for the religious community Khomeini's opposition is, in one sense, political protest; more importantly, it indicates the troubled state of Iranian civilization.

During the past two years there has been a reawakened opposition among the religious community to the regime's policies. This antipathy has been extended in recent months to open criticism of American policy in Iran. Speaking for the religious community, Khomeini has said that American policy is responsible for many of Iran's ills and that it is supporting an unpopular regime for its own purposes to the detriment of the people as a whole as did the Russians and British before them. Given this alienation from the regime and this antipathy to the American role in Iran, and given the widespread support Khomeini's views have among the traditional world of bazaar, village and small city, the reasons for Khomeini's rise to political prominence herald resistance from quarters of the Iranian population that have not been in active opposition before.

Khomeini's education, learning and widespread support within the clergy made him eligible to succeed Ayatollah Borujerdi as the leader of Iranian Islam, a position made vacant by Borujerdi's death in 1961 before Khomeini became a political figure. Khomeini's political abilities became evident in 1963 when he first spoke out against the anti-religious policies of the Government. Khomeini's political stand is not an isolated one; it is a view shared by a significant mass of Iranians.

---

[1] Source: Department of State, NEA/IRN Files: Lot 69 D 489, Iran 1965, POL 13–6 Religious Groups. Confidential. Prepared by INR. Attached to a January 7 note that reads: "Rec'd from WGM. This is a copy of an internal paper prepared for Mr. Spain's use." WGM is William G. Miller of INR. The paper was sent to Bracken, Howison, Tiger, and Mulligan in NEA/GTI. Another attachment to the paper makes it clear that it was prepared in 1965.

The religious community and the values they hold play an important part in Iranian society. Because the ulema have expressed disapproval of some of the Shah's goals and condemned almost all of the Shah's methods, the Shah has decided to carry out his plans to change the Iranian social structure without their support or assistance. He has branded the clergy "black reactionaries" who are opposed to reform. He has gone so far as to exile their leader Khomeini for anti-regime speeches and for alleged anti-reform attitudes.

There is no question that Khomeini has opposed certain features of the Shah's program. He has condemned completely the Shah's autocratic methods. There is little question, too, that he is reactionary and provincial in outlook, no matter how learned. Paradoxically, there are few leaders in Iran who by training would be better able to formulate for the devout a religious justification for modernization. Khomeini is recognized as the leading philosophical exponent of ijtehad, the Shia doctrine whereby change can be adapted to an Islamic framework. But it is important to recognize that Khomeini does not speak only for himself. He represents the point of view of traditional Iranian society.

Part of the conflict between the regime on the one hand and the religiously-oriented masses on the other is over the pace and means of carrying out reforms. The clergy has under great pressure grudgingly recognized that reforms in Iranian society must be made. Khomeini says he is not opposed to land distribution and that land distribution is consistent with Islam if just compensation is made. He has opposed, for example, the emancipation of women under present circumstances stating that emancipation without education is meaningless. In almost every instance the principle of a particular reform has been accepted; the challenge has come over methodology. The clergy by its training and philosophical outlook is tradition-bound. The basic changes implicit in some of the Shah's reforms, such as land distribution, require adaptations that will markedly alter the whole religious structure. "What will the position of the ulema be without the waqf?" is the kind of question that has deep philosophical and religious implications for the ulema and Iran as a whole. That there has been opposition on the part of the ulema is inevitable. But within the traditional structure, the power of the ulema might have been used to justify and institutionalize the changes taking place.

Had the Shah consulted with the leaders of the religious community, considered their ideas, and had he given the ulema a limited constructive role to play, opposition to his reforms from the religious would have been considerably lessened. This was former Prime Minister Ali Amini's belief and still is his position. However, these are "might have been's." What is now clear is that Khomeini's exile has aroused dormant nationalist feelings. The Shah and the United States have been branded as both anti-nationalist and anti-religious. This new attitude has tarnished our formerly favorable image, poses a threat to our interests in Iran, and will certainly make our task there far more difficult.

---

65.   Memorandum From the Deputy Director of the Office of Greek, Turkish, and Iranian Affairs (Howison) to the Assistant Secretary of State for Near Eastern and South Asian Affairs (Talbot)[1]

Washington, January 18, 1965.

SUBJECT

Your Appointment with Howard Parsons, AID Mission Director for Iran 10:30 a.m. Tuesday, January 19, 1965

In your meeting with Mr. Parsons you may wish to draw on the following talking points.

1.   Our security interests are too compelling for us to allow favorable indications of Iran's increasing self-reliance to obscure its continuing vulnerability and basic weaknesses or to conclude too early that U.S. objectives can be achieved without significant participation in Iranian affairs. Iran is in transition, deeply engaged in the process of difficult adjustment to the initiation of basic reforms and the effort to achieve rapid modernization. Although progress in this respect is encouraging it is not yet self-sustaining and does not insure continued internal stability.

2.   Our leverage in the past has stemmed in large measure from the inputs of our economic, technical and military assistance. These modes of assistance on a large scale have contributed significantly to the forward movement experienced during the past decade and secured our entree into key administrative, economic and military avenues. Fortunately, there is considerable acceptance among the present ruling society of the value of Iran's ties with the West and increasing agreement with the stress which we have placed on orderly modernization and socio-economic development. Under a continuance of present circumstances therefore we need not look forward to a drastic loss of influence as our material sources of leverage disappear.

---

[1] Source: Department of State, NEA/IRN Files: Lot 69 D 426, AID Iran 1965, AID–1, General Policy, Plans, Coordination. Confidential. Drafted by Mulligan (NEA/GTI). A handwritten note on the memorandum reads: "GTI—A good paper. T."

3. However, apart from military matters, where we may expect some years more of close dependence on U.S. advance and support, we shall be drawn less closely into the government's future decision making process and shall probably adopt more nearly the role of trusted ally rather than that of responsible senior partner.

4. We should exercise the influence and capabilities which derive from our technical and economic assistance programs to lessen the impact of our preponderantly military loan assistance and diminish our vulnerability to the charge that the United States is pursuing a militaristic policy in Iran with little concern for the economic and social betterment of the Iranian people.

5. Although the administration of Iranian economic affairs has improved, we shall want to continue to exercise our available influence to persuade the Iranians to maximize their increasing resource allocations for development and to take the difficult political decisions involved in such critical areas as overhauling the tax system and improving public administration.

6. We should endeavor to maintain flexibility in our aid policy so as to assist in preventing the dissipation of important economic advances, as well as to safeguard our own national interest by developing for U.S. industry an appropriate share of the growing market for capital goods which we have helped to create through our soft loans and other assistance of the past. This is essential not only because of our balance of payments problem but also as a further means of preserving American influence and our presence in key undertakings in the Iranian economy.

7. In the transitional period ahead, with Iran counting heavily upon the success of a land reform program which initially, at least, is adding to a now chronic shortfall of wheat production, our PL-480 programs should assume greater significance. In order to derive maximum benefit from this type of assistance, both as a marketing aid for the United States and as an instrument of foreign policy, we shall have to work hard at both ends in streamlining the bureaucratic procedures associated with PL–480.

66.   Memorandum From the Deputy Director of the Office of Greek, Turkish, and Iranian Affairs (Howison) to the Assistant Secretary of State for Near Eastern and South Asian Affairs (Talbot)[1]

Washington, January 21, 1965.

SUBJECT

Attempt on Life of Iranian Prime Minister

At 10:00 a.m. (2:30 a.m. EST) Prime Minister Mansur was shot and seriously wounded by a young man reportedly carrying a *Koran* and a picture of Khomeini as the Prime Minister arrived at the Parliament to present the new oil agreements. We tentatively infer that the assassin may have been a conservative supporter of Ayatollah Khomeini, who was exiled to Turkey for anti-regime activity at the time of ratification of our Status Bill. Although Khomeini's motivation is primarily opposition to secularist reforms, he thus succeeded in getting official endorsement of his nationalist (in this case, anti-American) pose. The attempt on the Prime Minister's life, if the assassin's sympathy for Khomeini is publicly established, has unfortunate implications of opposition to Iran's relationship with the United States.

Though the event will tend to weaken the regime, it would require genius in mishandling the situation for it to precipitate the kind of chaos which has followed modern assassinations (successful) in Iran. The Shah is in personal charge of the situation, having returned immediately from the ski resort above Tehran.

The wire services have noted that the assassin is young, but have not labelled him a religious fanatic yet. They *have* clearly labelled Mansur a progressive reformist. The wire reports leave room for the almost certainly unjustified inference that the assassin opposed the oil agreements.

---

[1] Source: Department of State, NEA/IRN Files: Lot 69 D 484, Iran 1965, POL 23–8, Demonstrations, Riots. Confidential. Drafted by Howison. A notation on the source text indicates that it was seen by Rusk.

67.   Memorandum From the Director of the Bureau of Intelligence and Research (Hughes) to Secretary of State Rusk[1]

Washington, January 28, 1965.

SUBJECT

The Significance of the Assassination of Prime Minister Hasan Ali Mansur

The Character of Regime Will Remain Unchanged. The death of Prime Minister Hasan Ali Mansur on January 26, five days after he was shot by Mohamad Bokharai, a twenty-year-old ironmonger's assistant, will not alter the character of the regime. Amir Abbas Hoveyda, Minister of Finance in the Mansur Cabinet, was named Prime Minister by the Shah. Hoveyda's appointment may cause difficulties because he is believed to be a member of the Bahai sect, which is deeply disliked by many Iranian Muslims. The Cabinet remains essentially the same as Mansur's, except for the appointment of SAVAK Chief (the Iranian Security Organization) General Hasan Pakravan as Minister of Information. Shortly after Mansur's death, the Shah, in a fiery speech, denounced "black reactionaries" and reaffirmed his support for the reform program formerly directed by Mansur.

Assassination Was Fanatic Expression of Widespread Discontent.[2] There is no evidence that the assassin and his accomplices, all members of a small religious society called Maktab Towhid, were part of a larger movement. On the contrary, the assassination seems to have been planned without outside help. Anger caused by the exile to Turkey by the regime of the leading Iranian religious figure, Ayatollah Ruhollah Haj Musavi Khomeini, seems to have in part motivated Bokharai to shoot Mansur, but there was no known connection between the Maktab Towhid and the movement headed by Khomeini. There are hundreds of small religious groups like Maktab Towhid that could cause religiously motivated violence of the sort that has just taken place. The security measures taken by the regime have prevented the formation of broadly based political or religious opposition movements. At the same time, fragmentation of the opposition and formation of small conspiratorial

---

[1] Source: Johnson Library, National Security File, Robert W. Komer Files, Iran, 1965–March 1966. Secret; No Foreign Dissem.

[2] A February 10 memorandum from Bracken to Talbot noted that GTI considered the use of the phrase "widespread discontent" in the January 28 INR briefing paper unfortunate, allowing as it did for the inference that "discontent" arose directly or solely from misgovernment and/or repressive government. On the contrary, GTI judged that political dissidence in Iran was at a relatively low point, viewed against the experience of the previous 50 years, and it saw the patterns of discontent in Iran as stemming predominantly from the rate of social change that had been taking place. (Department of State, NEA/IRN Files: Lot 69 D 489, Iran 1965, POL 23–8, Demonstrations, Riots)

groups make effective surveillance difficult. The fact that SAVAK was unaware of the activities of Maktab Towhid is a case in point. There is considerable discontent in Iran because of continued repression of opposition groups, exile of Ayatollah Khomeini, unpopular measures passed by the government such as the recent Status of Forces Bill, and the increase in the cost of basic fuels.

Problems Facing the Regime. The appointment of someone as Prime Minister reputed to be a Bahai may arouse additional religious antagonism. There are, however, signs that Mansur's assassination has increased the regime's awareness of the necessity to resolve the differences between the Shah and the religious opposition groups. The circumstances under which an accommodation could be made would require some loosening of political control and a greater measure of participation in government by groups presently in opposition.[3]

---

[3] In telegram 793 from Tehran, January 27, Holmes reported that the appointment of Hoveyda to succeed Mansur would ensure continuity of government policies and practices. He also noted that the Shah's television broadcast had blamed Mansur's assassination on an unholy alliance between Communists and reactionaries, but that the Embassy had no evidence of such an alliance. What evidence it did have pointed to a relatively small group of fanatics motivated by religious and perhaps other factors. (Ibid., Central Files, POL 15–1 IRAN)

---

68.   Telegram From the Embassy in Iran to the Department of State[1]

Tehran, February 15, 1965, 2 p.m.

854. In recent conversations with Eckhardt and me Shah has asked for annual review of military equipment program and acquisitions as provided for in Memorandum of Understanding of July 4, 1964. Shah referred to anticipated increases in oil revenues and indicated his desire to consider purchase of additional military equipment, including high performance fighter aircraft, armored reconnaissance vehicles, increase in war reserve ammunition from 30 to 60 days, and second Hawk battalion.

He accepted my suggestion that review should begin with comprehensive assessment of GOI's projected revenues and outlays, especially

---

[1] Source: Department of State, Central Files, DEF 19–3 US–IRAN. Secret. Repeated to DOD and CINCSTRIKE/CINCMEAFSA.

of foreign exchange, over next several years; review to be carried out by economic officials in consultation with Embassy–USAID economic officers. As first step in consultation we have prepared lengthy questionnaire of matters to be addressed and I will pass it to Prime Minister this week.

Details follow by airgram.

Holmes

---

69.   **Memorandum From the Executive Secretary of the Department of State (Read) to the President's Special Assistant for National Security Affairs (Bundy)**[1]

Washington, February 18, 1965.

SUBJECT

Strong Reaction by Shah of Iran to Gudarzian Affair

A major irritant in our relations with Iran for some months has been the affair of Khaibar Gudarzian, an Iranian national who has been misusing the procedures of both our courts and our Congress. In cases now pending in the New York courts the information available to us indicates he is attempting to obtain money from the Shah's brother and sister by means of false allegations, forged documents, and fraudulent claims of service of process. As long ago as May 1963 he began airing false charges of corruption in our aid program in Iran before the McClellan Committee, through the press, and to the Department of Justice. Investigations of practically all of those charges by the Departments of State and Justice have disclosed that the evidence submitted by Gudarzian consists of forgeries and fabrications, but there has thus far been no public refutation by the Executive Branch or by the McClellan Committee.

This Department has taken a number of steps during the past several months to ensure that justice is done and to counteract the harmful publicity Gudarzian's activities have generated. Late in December, Sec-

---

[1] Source: Johnson Library, National Security File, Country File, Iran, Vol. I, Memos & Miscellaneous, 1/64–12/65. Confidential.

retary Rusk brought the problem directly to the attention of the Attorney General, the Secretary of the Treasury, and the Governor of New York. Background briefings were given to the press in early January. The Department of Justice has been cooperating, within limits imposed by our federal system and by the separation of executive and judicial powers on its capacity to intervene where private litigation is involved. Competent private counsel is defending the Prince and Princess and there is good prospect that the default judgment previously awarded to Gudarzian will be set aside. The New York Court has ordered that its referee go to Tehran at an early date to hear witnesses who will testify that the Prince and Princess were in Iran on the date they are alleged to have been served with process in New York. A Federal grand jury investigation into Gudarzian's activities was launched in December to determine whether sufficient evidence could be obtained to try him on criminal charges for some of his questionable activities.

Throughout these developments, the Shah has become increasingly frustrated over our inability to halt Gudarzian's machinations once and for all, bring him rapidly to book, and dispel in some dramatic fashion the adverse publicity generated about the royal family and Iran in general. On February 13, the Shah's anger erupted violently in the decision to discharge his excellent Ambassador to Washington who has, in fact, done all any Ambassador could have done. The Shah is clearly over-reacting, and we cannot be sure that he will not take further and even more extreme steps before there is any very decisive resolution of the Gudarzian affair. Our relationship with the Shah must be maintained at a tolerable level as it is a key factor in our efforts to extend the stability and progress shown by Iran in the past decade.

The Department of State is exploring with the Department of Justice whether there might be any extraordinary steps the Department of Justice could take at this point that would quickly extricate the Prince and Princess and end Gudarzian's abuse of our judicial system.[2]

Benjamin H. Read[3]

---

[2] A February 22 memorandum from McGeorge Bundy to Attorney General Kennedy reads: "The so-called Gudarzian case is causing great distress and no little annoyance to our good friend, the Shah of Iran. Therefore, the President hopes that the Justice Department will do what it can to help bring about a prompt resolution of this matter, of course with all due regard for our judicial processes. I understand that Secretary Rusk will also be in touch with you with the same plea." (Ibid., Robert W. Komer Files, Iran—Gudarzian Case, 1965)

[3] Signed for Read in an unidentified hand.

70.   Telegram From the Department of State to the Embassy in the United Kingdom[1]

Washington, February 26, 1965, 7:58 p.m.

5386. Embtel 4118.[2] CENTO—Shah's London Visit.

1.   US continues regard CENTO alliance as integral part security structure of Middle East area. We would look upon any change not carefully tailored to meet requirements all parties as greatly weakening position of all.

2.   We somewhat more sanguine than British appear to be that Shah will continue regard CENTO as vital part of alliance security shield. He has important domestic political investment in CENTO and we believe he is well aware that security of area vis-à-vis Soviets is in large part dependent on atmospherics. No element—whether CENTO or US bilateral guarantee—can be removed from structure constituting posture of determination defend Iran without weakening credibility of entire structure.

3.   US-Iranian agreement of 1959 (TIAS 4189; 9 UST 1077) states that "in case of aggression against Iran" USG will, in accordance constitution, "take such appropriate action, including use of armed forces, as may be mutually agreed upon and as is envisaged in Joint Resolution to Promote Peace and Stability in Middle East, in order to assist Govt. of Iran at its request." Shah is aware of falsity of longstanding rumor in Iran that secret codicil to 1959 agreement includes more explicit guarantees to Iran.

We are looking into question of whether Bilateral Agreement would continue to be fully operative in event of dissolution of CENTO or change in Iran's relationship thereto.

4.   Under these circumstances, British in talks with Shah should not discuss question bilateral US-Iranian arrangements. Aside from inappropriateness such discussion in our absence, to reopen question of US position on defense of Iran might create new problem in our relations with Iran and might exacerbate rather than minimize Iranian tendency to reappraise security relationship with West. Fact these issues again moot would almost certainly become known to Russians, with resultant diminution credibility of our security arrangements even if no structural change in these arrangements had occurred.

Rusk

---

[1] Source: Department of State, Central Files, POL 7 IRAN. Secret; Limdis. Drafted by Howison; cleared by Meeker, Lee, Frazier Meade in EUR/BNA, and Officer in Charge of Pakistan–Afghanistan Affairs L. Bruce Laingen; and approved by Jernegan. Repeated to Ankara, Kabul, Karachi, and Tehran.

[2] In telegram 4118 from London, February 25, Ambassador Bruce reported that the British Foreign Office suspected that if the Shah felt absolutely sure of a U.S. bilateral security guarantee, he might be tempted to jettison CENTO. (Ibid.)

71.   Memorandum From the Assistant Legal Adviser for Near
       Eastern and South Asian Affairs (Wehmeyer) to the Assistant
       Secretary of State for Near Eastern and South Asian Affairs
       (Talbot)[1]

Washington, March 25, 1965.

SUBJECT

Secretary's Call on Senator McClellan re Gudarzian

The Secretary called on Senator McClellan on March 24, accompanied by the Attorney General, Mr. Kearney, and Mr. Rostal of the Department of Justice.[2] The Secretary and the Attorney General outlined the nature of the problem from the standpoint of the two agencies.

Senator McClellan indicated that he recognized that Gudarzian was making false statements regarding the AID program. He indicated that he was disposed to set further hearings on the subject of the Gudarzian allegations and to pose questions to Gudarzian which would result in his either commiting perjury or withdrawing the charges. Unfortunately, insofar as timing is concerned, the Senator indicated that his committee has just received additional "documentation" from Gudarzian with respect to certain charges and this material has not been checked out. The Senator indicated that he would like to have someone from the Justice Department and the State Department work with members of his staff in reviewing this material. (Mr. Saridakis (IGA) and Mr. Wehmeyer are meeting with members of the committee staff and a representative of the Department of Justice at 10:00 a.m. Thursday to examine the "new material".)[3]

---

[1] Source: Department of State, Central Files, POL 15–1 IRAN. Confidential.

[2] On March 8 Talbot sent a memorandum to the Secretary suggesting that there was now a good chance that Senator McClellan, if approached carefully on the subject, might be willing to make a public statement to the effect that his investigation of Gudarzian's charges of corruption in U.S. aid to Iran had been completed and the charges found to be false. He noted such an action would be of immense value in meeting the understandable Iranian dismay over the Gudarzian affair and would create a better atmosphere for the Secretary's talks with the Shah and other Iranian officials during the CENTO Ministerial Council meeting in Tehran in April. (Ibid.)

[3] Presumably April 1. Telegram 888 to Tehran, April 5, informed the Embassy that Senator McClellan had announced in the Senate that day that the Permanent Subcommittee on Investigations had made exhaustive inquiries into Gudarzian's allegations that there had been a large-scale diversion of U.S. aid funds intended for Iran and had discovered no evidence substantiating the truthfulness of those charges. On the contrary, the preponderance of the evidence pointed to their deceptiveness and falsity, and a complete transcript of the hearings had been turned over to the Department of Justice for its determination as to whether there had been any violation of Federal law and for appropriate action. (Ibid.)

72.   Telegram From Secretary of State Rusk to the Department of State[1]

Tehran, April 8, 1965, 6:30 p.m.

Secto 25. Secretary's conversation with Shah—Iranian reforms and general foreign policy.[2] Secretary, accompanied by Talbot and Rockwell, had one and one-half hour audience with Shah last evening which marked by extreme cordiality and frank exchanges of views. This is the first of six messages reporting conversations. Subjects concerned are: 1) Iranian reform program and general foreign policy (including Vietnam); 2) Iran's military policy; 3) Gudarzian case; 4) Bredin case; 5) Fairhurst problem; 6) Iran-Arab relations.

Secretary began by conveying President's greetings to Shah and stating he knew President would be interested to learn Shah's views concerning progress of reform program in Iran. Shah gave brief exposé along lines familiar to Dept, reiterating such points as that White Revolution is supported by nation with exception minor groups such as reactionary mullahs and dispossessed landlords; that revolution had been achieved without bloodshed and without dispossessing landlord group of their wealth other than land; that land being paid for; that partnership between workers and employers had been established; that literacy corps had been a tremendous success; and that Shah was confident White Revolution would continue to succeed.

During discussion of Literacy Corps, Secretary conveyed message from Sargent Shriver, saying latter would welcome any comments or suggestions Shah might have regarding operations of Peace Corps in Iran. Shah made very favorable comments on Peace Corps volunteers, noting their dedication to duty and the good reception many of them had achieved in this country.

Secretary then took up South Viet-nam, setting forth problems faced by us and factors which made us determined not to be driven out of that country or to abandon its commitments there. Said he believed that maintenance integrity of American commitment to South Viet-nam was important for world peace.

Shah said he completely agreed with Secretary and was delighted to receive this reaffirmation of US determination to stand by Viet-nam. He recalled he had told Pres Johnson that if US pulled out of Viet-nam, free world would lose confidence in US policy and promises, that progress of

---

[1] Source: Department of State, Central Files, E 12 IRAN. Confidential; Priority.

[2] Secretary Rusk was in Tehran April 7–8 attending the 13th CENTO Ministerial Council session. Briefing material for the CENTO meeting is ibid., NEA/IRN Files: Lot 69 D 490, 1965 IRAN, DEF 4–e–1, Papers for CENTO Ministerial Session in Tehran.

deterioration would begin in other non-Communist countries of Southeast Asia, Shah added: "In Viet-nam you are doing what you should do."

Secretary said that he had found Policy Planning Group in the Dept to be extremely valuable. He outlined the advantages of having a group of people who were disconnected from the daily problems and had the time to devote themselves to consideration of long-range issues. He said he would appreciate the privilege of receiving the Shah's views on long-range problems affecting the Middle East. The Shah was clearly very pleased to have been offered this opportunity for consultation and said that he would be delighted to take advantage of it.

Discussion then turned to specific Iranian and Middle Eastern topics which are being reported separately.[3]

Rusk

---

[3] See Documents 73–75.

---

73.   Telegram From Secretary of State Rusk to the Department of State[1]

Tehran, April 8, 1965, 10 p.m.

Secto 26. Secretary's conversation with Shah—Iran's military policy. During Secretary's audience with Shah April 7, Shah said that Iran's military policy was entirely defensive and reflected the determination not to be taken by surprise from any quarter. He said that there was complete agreement between Iran and US as to the menace of Communist aggression from the north. If this occurred, it would provoke international conflict. He added that there might be disagreement between us as to dangers to Iran from other quarters, and he thought the US should welcome a situation wherein it would not be required to become involved militarily in defending Iran in the event of an attack from a country other than the USSR. Iran could not afford to be weak in the face of Arab claims against a part of Iranian territory and in view of the uncertainty as to the

---

[1] Source: Department of State, Central Files, DEF 1 IRAN. Secret; Priority. Repeated to CINCSTRIKE/CINCMEAFSA.

future of the Persian Gulf State. Accordingly, Iran had sought and obtained a loan of $200 million for military purchases from the US and it was now time to consider the need for additional such purchases.

The Shah then said that the answers to the economic questionnaire which had been prepared by the Embassy were now ready and would soon be turned over. The study which had been undertaken showed that there would be $680 million available to Iran for borrowing in the next 10 years, even after the establishment and maintenance of an eight percent economic growth rate. One of the future sources of foreign exchange income to which the Shah attached particular importance was the establishment of ammonia plants. He made clear that he was confident that Iran would have no trouble in assuming an additional loan burden for the purchase of military equipment.

The Secretary said that Iran was right in being sensitive about threats to its territorial integrity. If a firm attitude was taken at the very beginning against aggressive tendencies, the danger of aggression was greatly reduced.

Rusk

74.   Telegram From Secretary of State Rusk to the Department of State[1]

Tehran, April 8, 1965, 10 p.m.

Secto 27. Secretary's conversation with Shah—Gudarzian case. During his audience with Shah April 7, Secretary discussed Gudarzian case at some length. He told Shah that only other matter which had recently been taking up more of his time than this affair was Viet-nam. He expressed opinion that although it has taken a long time, Gudarzian's days are now numbered. Secretary thought it possible that Gudarzian might flee the country.

Shah expressed pleasure with statements in Senate but revealed that he still lacks comprehension of US legal procedures. Secretary men-

---

[1] Source: Department of State, Central Files, POL 15–1 IRAN. Confidential; Priority; Limdis.

tioned importance of presence and suitable testimony of Iranian witnesses in US, if Gudarzian is to be successfully tried on criminal charges. Shah made no substantive comment but Aram inquired whether all witnesses had to go. He was told only key individuals would be needed.

Rusk

•

75.   Telegram From Secretary of State Rusk to the Department of State[1]

Tehran, April 8, 1965, 11 p.m.

Secto 30. Secretary's conversation with Shah—Iranian-Arab relations. Major part of audience which Secretary had with Shah April 7 was concerned with Iranian-Arab relations and developments in Arab world. Shah outlined his well-known concern with subversive and aggressive policies of the UAR, with particular reference to Arab claims on Khuzestan and the danger of Nasser's taking over the Persian Gulf States. Secretary said that US had been very patient with Nasser but that this patience now running out and US relations with UAR now hanging by a very slender thread. Secretary thought it was encouraging, however, that other Arab States had clearly shown unwillingness to submit to Egyptian hegemony. He thought these states would be supported in that attitude. Shah said he entirely agreed and remarked he had been surprised by the determination not to be pushed around by the UAR which President Bourguiba had exhibited during his recent state visit to Iran.

Shah said attitude of Saudi Arabia was also very constructive. Relations between Iran and Saudi Arabia had grown extremely close. He hoped, however, that Saudis would not press Iran too hard about Israel. Iran desired good relations with Saudi Arabia, but would not abandon Israel to achieve them. Israel was in existence as a sovereign state and its relations with Iran were good. Besides, there was the saying that "the enemy of my enemy is my friend".

Shah asked what US would do if Nasser attacked Saudi Arabia. Secretary replied that Saudi assistance to Yemeni Royalists created difficult

---

[1] Source: Department of State, Central Files, POL ARAB–IRAN. Secret; Priority. Repeated to Damascus, Rabat, Tunis, Tripoli, Baghdad, Jidda, Beirut, Amman, London, Tel Aviv, Taiz, Dhahran, Cairo, and Algiers and passed to the White House at 4:20 p.m.

problem for US, which had been made clear to Saudis. In Viet-nam US was resisting the infiltration of men and war material across the border, and was itself attempting to stop this by military action in the guilty country. If UAR should attack Saudi Arabia in area other than Yemeni border region where staging of Saudi aid to Royalists taking place, US would support Saudi Arabia.

But if border staging area a•.acked by Egyptians, this would be another matter. Secretary added that US would like to see the Yemenis get their own country back.

Secretary asked Shah about Iran's relations with Iraq. Shah reiterated his well-known concern over desires of Iraqi leaders to make Iraq subservient to Nasser. Iran's only policy was that Iraq should be truly independent. There was the problem of the Shatt al Arab between the two countries and also that of subversive activity in Khuzestan originating in Iraq. With regard to the Kurdish problem, the Shah said that, while it was helping them, Iran was not encouraging the Kurds to resume hostilities. At the same time, Iran considered that in its relations with Iraq it held a trump card in the Kurds, which it would not relinquish as long as a "truly national" government was not established in Iraq. The Shah said: "We are not going to let the Iraqi Kurds down until a national government is established in Baghdad".

In a discussion of Arab-Israeli relations, Secretary said that Israel seems only matter on which Arabs can achieve any degree of unity. The Palestine issue was valuable to the Arabs for this political purpose, but Secretary did not believe it likely that Arabs would engage in military action against Israel. At the same time, US had made very clear to Israelis that they would receive no US support should they undertake military action against Arab States because of latter's operations to divert Jordan waters. There was, however, danger of Arab or Israeli military action if either side became prey of fear that it was about to be attacked by the other. Therefore, it was important that there not be created an armaments imbalance in the Near East and that was reason why US found itself in the distasteful position of participating in an arms race in the area as result of its efforts to prevent such imbalance.

Shah mentioned his forthcoming trip to Morocco and said that while there he would endeavor to persuade King to embark on a reform program.

Rusk

76.   Information Memorandum From the Deputy Assistant Secretary of State for Near Eastern and South Asian Affairs (Jernegan) to Secretary of State Rusk[1]

Washington, April 10, 1965.

SUBJECT

Attempt to Assassinate the Shah

The most recent reports on the shooting incident which took place at Marble Palace in Tehran on Saturday[2] morning indicate that a member of the Imperial Guard shot his way into the palace with a submachine gun in an apparent attempt to reach the Shah. Two guards and the assailant are reported killed. In announcing the incident the Government has attributed the shooting to a quarrel between a conscript soldier and a regular member of the palace guard. No mention was made of the location where the shooting took place. Tehran has remained quiet and the Shah, who was apparently in his office throughout the episode, is said to have continued with his regular appointments for the day.

Comment:

A [*less than 1 line of source text not declassified*] report indicates that security records disclosed no prior adverse information regarding the assailant and that it is not yet known whether or not the assassination attempt was a plot. The fact that the assailant had made a trip to Meshed in 1962 would indicate that he had probably made a religious pilgrimage to the Shrine of Imam Reza, which is customary for devout Muslims of Iran's predominantly Shia belief. On the basis of information reported thus far, we do not anticipate any immediately significant political effect or threat to the continued maintenance of internal stability in Iran. We do not discount the possibility however that further investigation may disclose the motive for this attempt at assassination and that it may be found related to the desperate frustration of certain minority elements of the Shah's reform opposition, which led to the recent assassination of Prime Minister Mansur.

---

[1] Source: Department of State, NEA/IRN Files: Lot 69 D 489, Iran 1965, POL 23–8, Assassination Attempt—Shah. Secret. Drafted by Mulligan.

[2] April 10.

77.   **Memorandum From Robert W. Komer of the National
Security Council Staff to President Johnson**[1]

Washington, April 15, 1965.

Your meeting with our new Ambassador to Iran[2] seems to me most important, because it is essential he get a clear sense of what we really want in Iran. You in 1962 and then JFK in 1963 preached reform to the Shah. Now he takes it as his own idea, and wowed his UK hosts recently by a 45-minute peroration on the subject.

But the Shah's palaver is better than his performance. With rapidly rising oil revenues ($750 million last year), he's tempted to spend far too much on fancy military hardware and not enough on meeting his own people's rising expectations. He's got a good *land reform* program but lags badly on the credit facilities and marketing arrangements to help the peasants out. In a word, he doesn't pay enough attention to his own economy, but loves (now that we've stopped the Soviets for him) to worry about the piddling Arab threat.

Given Iran's wealth we've practically disengaged from major aid programs, but are still getting his military purchases through some skillful MAP credit deals. So without aid leverage, keeping the Shah steered right will depend largely on Armin Meyer. I hope you'll tell him:

1.   When you visited Iran in 1962 you tried to impress on the Shah that good economics is good politics, and that modernizing their countries was the way for monarchs to keep their thrones. You still feel the same way.

2.   Meyer should impress on the Shah that you watch closely the results of his *reform program*, which we regard as an impressive achievement.

3.   Just as we are trying to expand output and purchasing power to provide the resources for all we want to do, so the same principle might hold good for Iran.

4.   Meyer should carry your warm best wishes to the Shah and express your pleasure he escaped last week's assassination attempt (we sent a private message in your name[3] and got a very grateful reply).

---

[1] Source: Johnson Library, National Security File, Country File, Iran, Vol. I, Memos & Miscellaneous, 1/64–12/65. Secret.

[2] Armin H. Meyer was appointed Ambassador to Iran on March 18; he presented his credentials on April 27. The President met with Ambassadors Meyer and Holmes from 12:15 p.m. to 12:17 p.m. on April 15. No record of their discussion has been found.

[3] A copy of the President's April 11 message to the Shah is in the Johnson Library, National Security File, Special Head of State Correspondence, Iran, Shah Correspondence, Vol. I.

5.   Meyer should use all his arts of persuasion to influence the Shah in the right direction. If you can help, just let you know.

R.W. Komer

---

78.   Telegram From the Embassy in Iran to the Department of State[1]

Tehran, April 20, 1965, 1215Z.

1171. Reference: Deptel 957.[2] Basic estimate security situation not significantly altered by recent assassination attempt. That attempt high-lighted, however, the fact, which has long been apparent, that stability in Iran is unduly dependent on the life of one man.

We have had no further information to add to interesting psycholog-ical phenomenon reported Embtel 1136,[3] that after the recent assassina-tion attempt another such attempt is now regarded as more likely. There is no evidence to support belief that another attempt will follow soon, but somehow there is impression that cost of life insurance policy on Shah must have gone up. This phenomenon will bear watching, but cannot be developed further at this time.

There certainly are efforts under way to plug gaps in arrangements for personal security of Shah; otherwise there are no indications at pres-ent time that regime is further tightening up after the assassination at-tempt. It has been keeping tight control of any opposition activities all along. We continue to believe that regime is capable of dealing with any disorders that might be fomented by opposition groups. Assassination by fanatics who are willing to die in the process is another matter, but as Shah will be better protected we do not on balance see any deterioration.[4]

Meyer

---

[1] Source: Department of State, Central Files, POL 23–1 IRAN. Secret.

[2] Dated April 19. (Ibid.)

[3] Dated April 14. (Ibid., POL 15–1 IRAN)

[4] In telegram 1203 from Tehran, April 27, Holmes reported that the Shah had repeated to him a statement he had previously made to others, i.e., that the April 10 attempt on his life had been part of a plot inspired by pro-Communist Iranian students centered in Lon-don. (Ibid.)

79.   Current Intelligence Memorandum[1]

OCI No. 1109/65   Washington, April 23, 1965.

THE SITUATION IN IRAN

1. Iran, as it has for the last decade, continues to present a picture of relative peace and stability. Ruled by a pro-Western monarch who permits no organized open opposition, the country is making slight but visible progress in all fields without the revolutionary convulsions which have struck much of the Middle East.

2. The basic weakness of the situation has been heavily underscored in the last month, however, by the attempt on the Shah's life by a conscript member of the Imperial Guard. Both supporters and opponents of the Shah expressed great concern at the incident—supporters because to insiders the Shah is indispensable, opponents because the Shah has not permitted the development of persons or institutions capable of continuing an orderly government if he were suddenly removed. The Shah's reaction to the incident has been mild, considering that it came less than six months after the assassination of Prime Minister Mansur. There has been no widespread and indiscriminate crackdown on all opposition elements as would have been the case a few years ago. The Shah appears firm in his belief that he has widespread popular support for his "White Revolution" and that any opposition may be irritating but not dangerous. Coupled with this is his frequently expressed belief that he is under divine protection until he accomplishes his mission.

3. The opposition to the Shah is so disorganized and fragmented as to be powerless. A substantial portion of the Moslem clergy disapproves of his reform program because it involves redistribution of lands they have depended on, and suffrage for women. The clergy are reluctant to force a showdown, however, because the Shah has demonstrated that he is willing to destroy this group as a political force if he is pushed too far. The nationalist opposition—the National Front followers of former Prime Minister Mossadeq—are likewise in disarray. Watched and harried by the security services, there is little they can do that is not known to the government. The leadership has split between the older and more cautious who have advocated waiting until the right time to make a bid for power, and the younger radicals who insist that such an opportunity will never come and the only solution is violence. Nationalist students in the United States contend that an underground movement divorced from the old leadership and devoted to violence is getting under way.

---

[1] Source: Central Intelligence Agency Files: Job 79–T00472A, OCI Intelligence Memoranda, 1–30 Apr 1965. Secret. Prepared in the Office of Current Intelligence.

4. There are few major problems between the US and Iran. The American image has held up better in Iran than in most countries in the Middle East. Within recent months, however, this image has been tarnished by a clumsy presentation of the Status of Forces bill to the Iranian parliament, which raised memories of the hated "capitulations" formerly imposed by European powers. In an unfortunate bit of timing, a $200-million US military credit bill was presented to parliament a few days later, giving rise to charges that Washington had bribed the Iranian Government to grant widespread immunities to US personnel. Although the Shah has increased his room for maneuver by a series of friendly gestures toward the Soviet Union, he remains firmly committed to the West. His main external concern is expanded pro-Nasir activities in the Persian Gulf area. This has given rise to greater Iranian activity in the Middle East in the form of providing aid to Kurdish rebels in Iraq, aid to Yemeni royalists, and cooperation with Israel on security matters and in connection with land reform.

5. The Shah's "White Revolution"—distribution of landlord-owned villages to the peasants, the Literacy Corps to educate the villagers, and a medical and development corps to work in the villages—has started a trend that probably can never be reversed. Whether a bureaucracy that is noted for its inefficiency and corruption can maintain sufficient momentum to keep up with the rising expectations of the population is questionable. At this juncture the death of the Shah would probably produce a period of chaos from which a military dictatorship would be likely to arise.

---

80.   Memorandum on the Substance of Discussion at a Department of State–Joint Chiefs of Staff Meeting[1]

Washington, April 23, 1965, 3:30 p.m.

There was one item on the agenda—a discussion of the Iranian situation by Ambassador Holmes. The substance of his remarks was as follows:

---

[1] Source: Department of State, NEA/IRN Files: Lot 69 D 490, Iran 1965, POL 1 Gen. Policy, Background. Secret. The meeting took place at the Pentagon. Chairman of the Joint Chiefs of Staff General Earle G. Wheeler headed a 15-man delegation from the Department of Defense; Captain Zimmerman, Rivinius, and Lieutenant General Spivy represented J–5; and Brigadier General Strickland and Deputy Assistant Secretary of Defense for International Security Affairs William Lang represented OSD/ISA. The Department of State was represented by Ambassador Llewellyn E. Thompson, Ambassador Holmes, Kitchen, and Colonel Evans. Bromley Smith represented the National Security Council and Jack Smith represented the CIA. The source text indicates that it is a State draft that has not been cleared with the Department of Defense.

As an introduction, Ambassador Holmes stated that Iran has a 1200-mile border with the Soviet Union and has a long border with a stirred-up Arab World. If the Soviets again try to take over Iran, they would get Iranian oil and outflank all other sources of Middle East oil—a heavy blow to Western Europe. By taking over Iran, the Soviets would also have an open shot to East Africa. We, therefore, have to retain our influence over Iran, and it should not be too costly for us to do so.

In September 1959 Iran agreed not to permit any Thor missile bases on its soil. From the Cuban crisis to date the Soviets have followed a change of tactics. Radio Moscow has been relatively mild in its propaganda attacks on the Shah's regime (although clandestine radio attacks continue). Natural trading patterns continue and the Soviets have increased slightly the numbers of their people in Iran—e.g., more cultural missions. Joint enterprises on border area irrigation and Caspian Sea fishing also have been developed. The Iranians, however, are very sensible and very suspicious of the Soviets.

The Shah is worried about his people's becoming too complacent about the Soviets. He has asked the U.S. and the U.K. for recommendations to improve his security police. He has never made a move on a problem dealing with the Soviets without consulting the U.S.

The Shah is also very concerned about the Persian Gulf and the Arab minorities in the oil lands of southern Iran. There is considerable agitation of Arab minorities by the UAR-subsidized newspapers in Kuwait.

But the Shah is a Commander-in-Chief in fact, and he worries about various things a great deal, especially Arab unity. He uses his concerns to push us for more aid. He has stated he is concerned about CENTO. He is disillusioned, but in his own mind he has stopped worrying about military problems because he knows he can be assured of U.S. support. The modernization of the armed forces, a program agreed to in July 1964, is progressing well.

He is happy that the U.K. presence in the Persian Gulf continues, but the Shah worries about the day when the U.K. pulls out of the Gulf and he will have to fill the vacuum.

The Shah's government reform program is going ahead—in a Persian way. The human materials in Iran are good. The literacy rate is still low but growing. Ambassador Holmes was impressed with the basic intelligence of the Iranian people and stated that the Shah now has a government he never had before.

The one great danger to continuing progress and stability is that some one will kill the Shah. Each year that passes, however, will decrease the chaos following the demise of the Shah. The main factor contributing to this improved situation is the improvements being made in the Iranian armed forces.

The present Chief, MAAG (Major General Eckhardt, USA) has done a superb job. Ambassador Holmes hoped that his successor (Major General Jablonsky, USA) would have similarly high qualifications to permit continued effective influence. Chief, MAAG serves as a military adviser to the Shah; he goes to the Shah and sees him alone; but he still has managed to maintain excellent relations with the Iranian General Staff. On the latest military shopping list of the Shah, Ambassador Holmes has talked to the Finance Minister to give the Shah the facts; it is a constant struggle to keep the Shah's appetite within bounds—e.g., he is talking about getting one squadron of F–111's by 1970. Nevertheless, so long as we recognize that the Shah is moody and he stays alive, the U.S. will be able to handle him.

General Wheeler commented that, when General Abdul Hassain Hejazi, Chief of the Iranian Supreme Commander's Staff, visited the U.S., the Iraqis were getting more support from the UAR than we had estimated at the time. Nevertheless, General Wheeler argued that Arab unity was a long time in the future, and noted that General Hejazi was a mirror of the Shah and probably never has an original idea of his own. General Wheeler also noted that improved Iranian relations with the Soviets are all to the good. Ambassador Holmes replied that most officials in the Iranian Government are realistic. Only some of them appear to be complacent about the Soviets and they are really preoccupied with their own problems.

General McConnell[2] stated that a USAF Brigadier General will be assigned as Deputy Chief, MAAG this coming summer. He then asked if the Kurds are currently a problem to the Iranian Government. Ambassador Holmes stated that the Iranian Army still occupies Kurdish areas, but that the government is now beginning to treat the Kurds as Persians and is instituting an aid program for them.

Ambassador Holmes noted that the Shah was very interested in the Concord Squadron, and was impressed with his visit to the Bon Homme Richard. He has talked with General Adams, CINCSTRIKE, and would be willing to have a floating U.S. reserve to be located in his ports.

Mr. Kitchen asked about Iran's relations with Israel. Ambassador Holmes stated that the Israelis frequently force feed the Shah with raw information on the Arab threat. Israeli technical assistance men also aid and abet this in the oil areas of southern Iran.

Ambassador Holmes stated that in 1958 we did not live up to our MAP commitments. Ambassador Holmes urged that, in the current five-year modernization program for the armed forces, we do not arouse the Shah's suspicions by permitting MAP slippages to develop. General

---

[2] General John P. McConnell, Chief of Staff, U.S. Air Force.

Wheeler stated that there has been a great effort by all services to overcome MAP slippages—a problem not unique to Iran.

General Wheeler stated that the JCS were delighted to get such a favorable and encouraging report on Iran—such was not the case several years ago. Mr. Kitchen observed that a lot of the credit for the improved situation in Iran belongs to the Mobile Training Teams who served with the Iranian armed forces. Ambassador Holmes added that the training of Iranian officers in the U.S. also must be recognized as a reason for the improved situation, although it was agreed that a "Nasser" might well have been trained in the process.

---

81.   Telegram From the Embassy in Iran to the Department of State[1]

Tehran, April 27, 1965, 1700Z.

1205. Shah's Interest in Arms. After giving me build-up re economic and social progress Iran is making and his philosophy how Iran must be capable of coping with war by proxy,[2] Shah twenty-seventh stressed importance of prompt and favorable U.S. response to his recent requests for more modern military equipment.

I pointed out U.S. disposition toward Iran has been uniquely friendly, there being no other country where U.S. has involved itself in five-year arms program. More than that equipment in that program is well advanced over equipment which we providing most other countries in this part of world.

Referring to economic review currently under study, I said Shah was on right track in seeking "balanced program" of economic and military progress. Shah said that he hoped following his return from forthcoming month-long journey, economic review and subject of his arms needs can be brought to successful conclusion, e.g., end of May.

---

[1] Source: Department of State, Central Files, DEF 19–3 US–IRAN. Confidential. Repeated to CINCSTRIKE and DOD.

[2] In telegram 1204, April 27, Meyer reported that during a private talk following presentation of his credentials the Shah had discussed his "White Revolution" at length, and had made the point that the more successful his revolution became, the more desperate were his enemies. (Ibid., POL 15–1 IRAN)

Shah said main point is that it takes such long time from date of order to date of delivery. Meanwhile, area threat (Nasser) is increasingly imminent. He, therefore, must have early decision as to whether he can have advanced equipment, so adequate training and planning can be undertaken in years intervening before equipment is actually delivered.

Having made his major pitch to General Eckhardt (being reported separately) re his desire for F–111, Sheridans and more Hawks, Shah said he wanted to mention to me one further "detail." Originally he had asked for destroyers for defense of Persian Gulf. USG had demurred, on basis destroyers beyond Iran's capabilities. His request for motor torpedo boats had also been turned down. Mention had been made, however, of "bull-pup" air to surface missiles. It obvious, he said, that if Iran had capability deliver its own weaponry, it much preferable to time-consuming maritime vehicles. I told Shah this was new subject as far as I was concerned and I would have to look into it.

Shah made clear his greatest defense concern is Persian Gulf area. He said he had to have suitable weaponry and would like to get it from the U.S. if possible.

Meyer

---

82.   Memorandum From Secretary of State Rusk to President Johnson[1]

Washington, May 10, 1965.

SUBJECT

Telephone Call to the Shah of Iran During New York Stopover

Recommendation:

I suggest that you telephone the Shah of Iran during his one-day stopover in New York on Tuesday, May 18. The Shah and the Empress left Tehran on May 2 for state visits to Brazil, Argentina, and Canada. On the New York stopover they will be en route from Buenos Aires to Ottawa. The Shah will be residing at the Waldorf Towers, and according to his

---

[1] Source: Johnson Library, National Security File, Special Head of State Correspondence File, Iran, Presidential Correspondence. Confidential.

present schedule he could be reached there by telephone at 11:00 a.m. on May 18.

Background:

The Shah is important to the United States as the reform-minded ruler of one of the most stable countries in the Middle East. He considers, not without justification, that Iran has been our most dependable ally on the southern periphery of the Soviet Bloc. In spite of some issues that have arisen recently (most notably our differing assessment of the Nasser threat to Iran and the Shah's irritation at our inability to bring rapidly to justice an Iranian who has been abusing our Congress and Courts with false charges of corruption against the royal family), there remains a broad consensus between us and the Shah on the really fundamental issues of foreign and domestic policy. As our posture toward Iran changes gradually in keeping with the country's increasing financial strength, administrative capabilities, and broadening foreign ties, the Shah is watchful for signs of our continuing sponsorship of Iran's welfare and security and, most particularly, our regard for his counsel on key world issues. I believe that the proposed telephone call from you on May 18 would be an important step in maintaining our fruitful relations with Iran.[2]

Dean Rusk

---

[2] A typewritten notation on the source text reads: "He made the call."

---

83.   Memorandum From Robert W. Komer of the National Security Council Staff to President Johnson[1]

Washington, May 17, 1965.

We have a massage problem with the Shah of Iran, who has a 24-hour *stopover in New York Tuesday, 18 May,* en route from Brazil and Argentina to Ottawa and Paris. We naturally evaded feelers that he come down here, so Rusk urges five minute phone call from you. It would be worth weeks of lower level diplomacy.

---

[1] Source: Johnson Library, National Security File, Special Head of State Correspondence File, Iran, Shah Correspondence, Vol. I. Secret. This memorandum was attached to a May 18 transmittal note from Jack Valenti to the President that reads: "Mr. President, I thought you'd want to see this."

The Shah has been very good on Vietnam and the Dominican Republic, and we don't want De Gaulle to talk him out of those positions. Harriman will be talking to the Shah in the Waldorf Towers from 10:30 to 11:30, so you'd have no problem getting through to him then. Here are a few suggested talking points:

1. Happy to have Shah and Empress on American soil again, even if only briefly. You are especially relieved that the Shah escaped the recent attempt on his life (you wired him). You know from your own role at the time of President Kennedy's assassination what a shock such an experience is.

2. You are glad he was so well received in Brazil and Argentina. Did he pick up any interesting reaction to our handling of the Dominican crisis? Vietnam?

3. You appreciate the Shah's support for our Dominican and Vietnamese positions. You are especially concerned that the *Afro-Asian Conference* in Algiers next month will degenerate into an anti-US orgy unless responsible delegations like Iran's stand up against the Communist steam-roller. Could the Shah help?

4. You'll be anxious to hear Gov. Harriman's report of his talk with the Shah (we hope the Shah doesn't bring up the Gudarzian case, of an obvious swindler who's sought to implicate the Royal Family).[2]

If you can't call, telegram at Tab[3] would be useful (but not half as good).

R.W. Komer

---

[2] See Document 84 for a record of Harriman's meeting with the Shah.
[3] Not printed.

---

84.   Memorandum of Conversation[1]

New York, May 18, 1965.

SUBJECT

Call on the Shah of Iran

PARTICIPANTS

The Honorable W. Averell Harriman
Mr. Phillips Talbot, Assistant Secretary, NEA
Mr. Chester Carter, Deputy Chief of Protocol

---

[1] Source: Department of State, Central Files, POL 15–1 IRAN. Confidential. Drafted by Talbot on May 21. Approved in S/AH on May 26.

Governor Harriman and Mr. Talbot met with the Shah for one and a quarter hours at the Waldorf Towers. Mr. Chester Carter of Protocol was also present.

The Shah in discussing his recent visits to Brazil and Argentina said that it had seemed quite useful to tell them of Iran's experiences in facing land reform problems frankly and in undertaking rigorous battles against corruption. He also had had opportunities to state publicly his strong endorsement of United States positions on Vietnam and the Dominican Republic. This seemed to him important, because the President is taking just the right line in a very difficult period and deserved the public support of those who agreed with him. The pity was that many others agreed but were unwilling to say so except privately.

Governor Harriman congratulated the Shah on the position he had taken and expressed our appreciation for his firm and forthright backing of our efforts to meet difficult situations. The Governor then explained in considerable detail the course of developments in Vietnam and the Dominican Republic, and the specific aspects of our policy in each situation. The Shah reiterated his support of United States firmness in dealing with Communist-directed challenges of these sorts. He inquired whether any results had been achieved by five day stop in bombing and expressed approval of decision to renew operations.

Talk turned to the forthcoming Afro-Asian Conference in Algiers. The Governor expressed the hope that the Shah's representatives could play a useful role in preventing the conference from being captured by extremist delegations. The Shah stated this to be his intention, and recalled he had discussed the matter with the Secretary of State during the latter's visit to Tehran in April. The Shah said he had not decided who would lead the Iranian delegation but it might be the Prime Minister. The Governor encouraged the Shah to send the Prime Minister, whose official position and personal qualities would enable him to deal effectively with the heads of government present at the conference. The Shah said he would welcome continuing discussion with the United States and exchange of information on preparations for the conference. He suggested that the American Ambassador in Tehran might be armed with reference material. Governor Harriman and Mr. Talbot assured the Shah that our Ambassador in Tehran would be equipped to discuss all aspects of preparations for effective participation in the Afro-Asian Conference.

Turning to his own region, the Shah referred to Iran's complete alliance with the United States against the "ultimate Communist danger." At the same time, he said, it would be regrettable if the major powers entered into limited area disputes. Therefore, he felt it important that Iran should strengthen itself to deal with any problems that might arise in, for example, the Persian Gulf. He expressed confidence that the situation could be kept manageable with the military strength Iran was building.

He was concerned about the situation in Iraq. Iran had substantial assets there, with the Kurds, Shiahs, etc., but he was not using them at this time. Governor Harriman and Mr. Talbot encouraged the Shah in a policy of restraint toward the Arab nations. The Governor added that strength for Iran obviously needs to be based first on social and economic modernization. He hoped the Shah would always keep his military outlay in balance with these other objectives. The Shah said this was his intention.

A brief discussion of the situations in various Arab countries developed no new points.

The Shah spoke of relations with his close neighbors along the Soviet periphery. The Governor noted that the King of Afghanistan had been warm in his comments about the Shah. The Shah recalled the assistance Iran had given to Afghanistan and suggested he would like to strengthen their relationship, "even though I don't understand how a country can call itself neutral," he said "we must protect Afghanistan's neutrality against Soviet pressures." The Shah expressed his desire to help persuade Ayub of Pakistan to be careful in his dealings with Communist China. He said that he was broadening Iran's relations with India, now through cooperation in oil extraction and in the future perhaps in such things as aluminum. Looking westward, the Shah expressed concern about the mood in Turkey, which he found badly shaken by the Turkish inability to get a favorable solution to the Cyprus issue.

The Governor and Mr. Talbot congratulated the Shah on escaping harm when the attempted assassination occurred on the night after the CENTO delegates had dined with the Shah. The Shah described the incident as a near thing and expressed his concern at the Communist encouragement of Iranian students in Western countries, particularly in Germany, Austria and Great Britain. He identified the assassination ring as developed and directed by students in Britain.

In the middle of the conversation, the President telephoned the Shah from Washington.[2] It was clear that the Shah greatly appreciated this gesture of friendship and interest. The President asked the Shah to take an active interest in the Afro-Asian Conference.

---

[2] See Document 85.

85.   **Telephone Conversation Between President Johnson and the Shah of Iran**[1]

May 18, 1965, 11:01 a.m.

LBJ: Hello?

MRP: Hello

LBJ: Your Majesty, how are you?

MRP: Mr. President, I'm so glad to hear you.

LBJ: Well, it's wonderful to hear your voice, and we're so happy to have you and the Empress back in our country again, even if it's very brief.

MRP: Yes. Unfortunately, we could not pay you our respects.

LBJ: Oh, I would like so much to see you. I was, oh, so relieved, though, that you escaped the recent attempt. You know from your own role at the time of President Kennedy's, what a shock such an experience is.

MRP: Yes, it was rather close this time.

LBJ: Well, we were so pleased that you were so well received in Brazil and Argentina.

MRP: Yes, they have been very nice to us. And I hope that this is a new era between our part of the world and this continent of South America.

LBJ: I sure hope so. Did you pick up any interesting reactions to our handling of the Dominican crisis or Vietnam?

MRP: Oh, well, I think that all of them in their inner heart were in favor of it. Some of them dared to say so openly and some others refrained to. But I suppose they all agree in their inner hearts.

LBJ: Well, we certainly are grateful to you for your Dominican and Vietnamese position, and I'm very concerned that the Afro-Asian Conference in Algiers next month will degenerate. I'm afraid it will be an anti-US operation unless some responsible delegation like Iran stands up against these steamrollers.

MRP: Yes. We shall do our duty, and we are grateful to you to have taken this attitude, Mr. President.

LBJ: Well, we have to take this when our liberty is at stake—

MRP: Oh, yes.

---

[1] Source: Johnson Library, Recordings and Transcripts, Recording of Telephone Conversation between President Johnson and Mohammed Reza Pahlevi, May 18, 1965, 11:01 a.m., Tape 6505.17, PNO 4. No classification marking. The Shah was in New York; the President was in Washington. This transcript was prepared by the Office of the Historian specifically for this volume.

LBJ:—and I'm going to be anxious to have Governor Harriman report his talk with you, and if you have any suggestions for me, let me know, and please give Mrs. Johnson's high regards to the Empress and yourself. We look forward to seeing you before too long.

MRP: Thank you very much. Would you please be kind enough as to give Mrs. Johnson our best regards?

LBJ: We enjoyed our visit in your home so much. You don't know how much it meant to both of us and how close we feel to both of you.

MRP: Well, we have the best of recollections, really, of your visit.

LBJ: Everyone tells me you have just made phenomenal progress.

MRP: Yes. We have been very lucky.

LBJ: Well, no. You've been very courageous, that's what. And the very best of everything to you.

MRP: Thank you, Mr. President, I wish you all the success.

LBJ: You tell Governor Harriman I want him to report to me. Y'all talk confidentially [about] every problem you have so I can get a full report.

MRP: All right, thank you very much.

LBJ: And I look forward to—you help us out in Algiers now and you get on top of that.

MRP: All right. Thank you very much.

---

86.   Excerpt From Memorandum for the Record[1]

Washington, May 20, 1965, 2 p.m.

SUBJECT

Minutes of the Meeting of the Special Group (CI) 2:00 p.m., Thursday, May 20, 1965

PRESENT

Governor Harriman, Admiral Raborn, Mr. Bell, Mr. Anderson vice Mr. Rowan, General Anthis vice General Wheeler, Mr. Friedman vice Mr. Vance

Ambassador Holmes and Messrs. Jernegan and Maechling were present for the meeting

---

[1] Source: Department of State, NEA/IRN Files: Lot 69 D 489, Iran 1965, POL 23–1 Plans, Programs—POL 23–1–a, Internal Defense Plan. Secret. No drafting information appears on the source text. The excerpt was prepared as an enclosure to an airgram to Tehran, but a handwritten notation on the source text reads: "Note: this not included in airgram as Maechling says sending minutes of CI outside of country prohibited. dg 6/1/65."

2.   *Progress Report on Internal Defense Plan for Iran*

Mr. Jernegan briefly reviewed the Progress Report on the Internal Defense Plan for Iran[2] saying that there is essentially no great change and that the situation has vastly improved despite recent assassination attempts on the Shah. He said that there is always danger of assassination of high level officials in Iran but that there are no indications of major plots to threaten the regime. He informed the Group that local internal security forces have improved their ability to handle internal security situations and that the Army has enough personnel trained in counter-insurgency to begin training themselves.

He briefly reviewed some of the reform programs such as the Literacy Corps, female emancipation and administrative and fiscal reforms. He said that the Youth Program is progressing well but that there is a shortage of operating funds for the Student Center. Messrs. Bell and Anderson said *that USIA has agreed to provide the funds that the Country Team has requested; if there is a problem in providing more funds, AID is prepared to take another look.*

Mr. Jernegan concluded by saying that no new actions by the Special Group are called for and suggested that in light of the current stability of Iran the requirement for semi-annual progress reports on the IDP be suspended and reports be submitted on an ad hoc basis. The JCS and DOD representatives did not concur, stating that the police have probably improved but are not yet capable of handling a situation such as that of June 1963; also there is unrest among the ethnic minorities. *The Group agreed with the Chairman's recommendation that, since there is a new Ambassador in Iran, he be asked to submit one more report by October 1, together with his recommendation on further reporting.*

The Chairman reported that in his discussions with the Shah on Tuesday, the Shah had expressed concern over student activities. The Shah said that he had evidence that the recent attempt on his life was planned by students recently returned from England. Mr. Jernegan informed the Group that the Shah's information is from an Iranian source, but we do agree that students are involved. Ambassador Holmes pointed out that there are indications of Chinese Communist influence among the students in Iran.

Mr. Bell brought the attention of the Group to the recent report of a Youth Committee Survey Team asking if not more could be done in this field. *The Chairman suggested that the Interdepartmental Youth Committee*

---

[2] Governor Harriman's April 28 memorandum for the Special Group (CI) summarizing the Country Team's fifth and sixth progress reports on the Internal Defense Plan for Iran is ibid. Airgram A–81 from Tehran, August 22, 1964, containing the Embassy's fifth progress report and airgram A–501 from Tehran, March 29, 1965, containing its sixth report are ibid., Central Files, POL 23–1 IRAN.

take a look at our programs in Iran to see what useful things we might do to assist.

In reply to a question by the Chairman, Mr. Bell explained that the phase-out of AID in Iran, tentatively scheduled for FY–68, will be reviewed annually, and if there is need for continued CI programs they will not be phased out.

The Director of Central Intelligence asked if there is a contingency plan on what should be done in case the Shah is removed from the scene, and if there is one, is it adequate? Ambassador Holmes replied that there has been a contingency study. He said there are constitutional provisions for a regent, but not for a regency council, and that it has been suggested that perhaps there could be a council of advisers for the Prince, acting as regent, until such time as he reached his majority. He reported that he had discussed this subject with the Shah but nothing specific has been done. *It was agreed that the Ambassador should be requested to bring this contingency study up-to-date.*

The Director of Central Intelligence asked if there is any new action that we should take to expedite and support such programs as Youth, Literacy Corps, and land reform, etc. *The Group agreed with the Chairman's recommendation that the Ambassador be asked to observe these programs closely to insure that all steps are being taken to improve their effectiveness.*

The Director of Central Intelligence asked if the USIA is initiating or assisting in any psychological operations in support of western-oriented youth and labor groups. *Mr. Anderson answered by saying that USIA will prepare a report on this subject for the Group.*

The Director of Central Intelligence stated that he would like to have the Country Team's views on the adequacy of Iranian security measures to protect the Shah. *The Group agreed with the Chairman's recommendation that we request the Country Team's views on this subject.*

87.   Memorandum From Harold H. Saunders of the National
       Security Council Staff to Robert W. Komer of the National
       Security Council Staff[1]

Washington, June 8, 1965.

RWK:

FYI. Here's a cable[2] approving the second tranche of Iran's five-year military purchase. Chief issues decided this way:

1. Shah asked us to lift the $200 million ceiling to $230m. to raise war reserve ammo from 30 to 60 days. Our military go along with this (Greece, Turkey, 90 days; Korea, Thailand, China, small arms 90, other 60; Pakistan, India 60). However, decision recommended in this cable is to go ahead with the ammo but not raise the ceiling yet. Since this $90 million brings two-year total to about $140 million, we'll be pressing the ceiling well before five years. Embassy says greatly improved revenue prospects warrant slight increase in ceiling. But leaving it intact now maximizes our leverage later.

2. Iranians want to go back up to 172,000 man force level. DOD goes along, and even AID isn't ready to fight over this.

3. Stall on advanced aircraft, Hawk and Sheridan (which is still in R & D anyway). The planes will be the toughest to handle, and there's some thought of putting the Bullpup missile and F–5 together but not this year.

AID feels the economic review this spring was a major step forward. Iranians worked from sound economic projections for the first time. The Shah is still working on the principle of putting hardware above everything else, but AID feels this is the resurrection of a useful economic dialogue.

So while the Shah is probably pushing reasonable economic ceilings, we may make progress by going along on the war reserve and force level in order to drag our feet on less reasonable requests. Any objection to the attached?

HHS[3]

---

[1] Source: Johnson Library, National Security File, Robert W. Komer Files, Iran, 1965–March 1966. Confidential.

[2] Not found attached; see Document 88.

[3] Printed from a copy that bears these typed initials.

88.   Telegram From the Department of State to the Embassy in Iran[1]

Washington, June 12, 1965, 11:03 a.m.

1124. Joint State/Defense/AID message. Embassy A–590;[2] Embtels 1311,[3] 1346,[4] 1359,[5] 1402[6] and DEF 2212.[7] Concur your analysis US policy objectives and evaluation Shah's position outlined A–590. While we share CT's concern about Shah's long-term military spending plans, we agree that so long as he convinced Iran's economic prospects will allow both meeting these plans and financing ambitious development program, there is probably little we can do directly at this time to curtail his military spending without risking impression we reacting completely negatively his desires purchase additional US military equipment and thereby jeopardize what influence we have. We have therefore worked out approach outlined below, which we believe sufficiently responsive to Shah without posing present threat Iran's economic welfare. We trust that you will find further opportunity to impress on Shah that factors affecting control and growth of the economy demand action as urgently as do military requirements. Believe presentation to Shah should be designed: (1) avoid any suggestion advance commitment specific military equipment; (2) exploit opportunity offered by annual review procedure to interest Shah further in administrative improvements required minimize inflationary dangers and threat to development effort inherent proposed military expenditure increases.

Specific points for discussion with Shah follow:

1. *Second Tranche.* Approve second tranche in range $85–$90 million covering items as proposed Enclosure 2, A–590. This decision may be communicated to Shah in general terms, including our willingness help Iran secure 60-day war reserve ammunition by combination various means now being explored (including credit), as proposed Embtel 1402. Re other items in tranche, they may be catalogued, but details im-

---

[1] Source: Department of State, Central Files, DEF 19–3 US–IRAN. Confidential; Priority. Drafted by Tiger, Mulligan, R. Murray (DOD/ISA), and Henrietta Towsley (AID/NESA); cleared in substance by Solbert and Captain Cain of SAMAA, and in draft by Komer, Arrill, Bunte, and Chief of AID's Military Assistance Division Robert B. Black; Charles Mann of the Bureau of the Budget was informed; and approved by Jernegan. Repeated to CINCMEAFSA.

[2] Airgram A–590 from Tehran, May 15, transmitted the Embassy's first annual review of the July 4, 1964, Memorandum of Understanding. (Ibid.)

[3] Dated May 24. (Ibid.)

[4] Dated June 1. (Ibid., E 2–2 IRAN)

[5] Dated June 3. (Ibid., E 8 IRAN)

[6] Dated June 10. (Ibid., DEF 19–3 US–IRAN)

[7] Not found.

plementation must await clarifications discussed paras 7 and 8 below. Details second tranche items should be developed by MAAG with GOI and submitted Military Departments info OSD for preparation Letters of Offer and disbursement schedule. Based on disbursement schedule, instructions for negotiation second tranche credit will be provided by DOD.

2. *Five-Year Credit Ceiling.* Do not perceive any utility broaching at this time change in over-all credit ceiling ($200 million for five-year period) as specified July 4, 1964 Memo of Understanding. Since approved new items second tranche consistent 1964 illustrative list and since sum first and second tranches does not approach over-all five-year figure, we believe it premature raise issue now. Consideration ceiling change would also cause time-consuming procedural hurdles (new 1550 determination, etc.) which unnecessary face at this time. We would hope Shah would be satisfied this year with second tranche as proposed and our undertakings re other problems as outlined below and would not question five-year total. If he should question, you may refer at your discretion to above points.

FYI. Believe we will be in better position to address problem at later date, giving us more time to urge Shah in direction higher priority for economic development and take advantage later reading Iran's economic situation. In any event, you should be aware that, owing present and prospective tightness MAP funds and especially in view Iran's improved financial condition, it unlikely we could modify agreement in any way requiring more MAP resources for Iran than originally foreseen. Sales additional to $200 million in five-year period could, of course, be accommodated without more MAP resources if they were for cash or if unguaranteed commercial credit could be provided. End FYI.

3. *Aircraft.* Argumentation against F–111 as previously provided: no present or future military requirement for Iran to have an aircraft of this capability, too sophisticated, costly, still in R&D stage. In your discussions with Shah you may note that we recognize that Iran may need at some point aircraft of greater capabilities than F–5. We would be prepared discuss GOI aircraft requirements at greater length with IIAF during course of year if Shah so desires. FYI. DOD plans undertake unilateral study of Iran's aircraft requirements and U.S. aircraft availabilities. End FYI.

4. *Second Hawk Battalion.* On both Hawk and Sheridan we believe offer "sympathetic consideration" at time next annual review is too strong. On Hawk, we do not wish to convey to Shah idea that we will say "yes" next year only to find that none are available. (See DEF 2212 re problem availability.) Conversely, we do not wish to tell Shah outright that we will not have any available and risk his turning elsewhere at this early stage. Recommend you place chief stress on absorption difficulties,

but also refer possible improvements we contemplating to Hawk, and suggest further discussions during coming year.

5. *Sheridan Tanks.* Principal arguments already known to you: Sheridan still in R&D, none are available, problem of absorption, and—as in case of all other items—problem of cost. We suggest GOI be informed of problems, that it is premature for commitments, that we recognize their requirement for improved armor capabilities and that we should also watch this over course of year and see where we stand at time next annual review.

6. *Bullpup.* FYI. While agree your position, we willing consider sale Bullpups at some future time provided they are available and releasable to Iran from security standpoint; and if in your judgment this will help dampen Shah's desires for more sophisticated aircraft. At present time there are none available from U.S. production, although may be available from European consortium. We have not looked into this in great depth, and will not do so unless you so recommend after your discussions with GOI. End FYI.

7. *Other Items.* Other items recommended for financing under 2nd tranche approved, subject to availability. ARMISH/MAAG should define requirements for Military Depts. so that Letters of Offer can be prepared. DOD now taking steps authorize Military Depts. proceed in advance of funding with supply actions for second 4 C–130s, radio test equipment, 163 APCs and 1610 LMGs.

8. *Price and Availability.* Prices and delivery schedules cannot be determined in detail at this time. MAAG must first define requirements more precisely for Military Depts. before deliveries can be projected and prices as stated A–590 confirmed. In any case, there would appear to be no obligation determine this type detail in connection with annual review.

9. *Force Level.* We recognize additional units called for in 1964 Memorandum of Understanding will require some additional personnel; nevertheless, principle that economic development Iran's first need and that military establishment must be forced sort out priorities within reasonably economic ceiling remains key consideration. Ceiling 160 thousand was accepted by Shah only after President Kennedy personally pressed principle during Shah's 1962 visit and ceiling was finally reached only recently. Accordingly, prior to any decision re breaching personnel ceiling which subject high level decision, wish your views on how Iranians might meet modernization needs through reshuffling within 160 thousand ceiling perhaps through cutback non-essential units. We are prepared if GOI considers desirable to assist in personnel survey, to include availability of personnel with requisite skills. In any case, we doubt it necessary broach this subject in connection annual review 1964 Memo of Understanding (which limited by terms of agree-

ment essentially to questions financing and training readiness for equipment purchases) and we gather from Embtel 1402 that you do not expect Shah raise issue June 19 audience. If he should inquire, you may refer in general terms to our concerns as expressed above.

10. *Allocation of Economic Resources.* We wish stress importance your continued emphasis on value careful economic projections and allocation resources as set forth Embtels 1346 and 1359. Appreciate we must take care not to nip in bud dialogue begun between Shah and economic planners this subject or create suspicion in his mind that economists are "sabotaging" military program, but we will need to reiterate at appropriate opportunities necessity facing hard questions if Iran is to carry out effective development program and attain satisfactory growth rate. Certainly US will have gained important advantage from annual review procedure if continuing dialogue can be established with Shah concerning application competent economic analysis to problem military purchases. You might consider introducing your top economic advisers into high-level discussions military/economic problem, as supplement to ongoing discussions technical military matters between Shah and MAAG chief.

We realize discussion this subject with Shah must proceed slowly and carefully. Although projections on which Shah bases optimistic plans for development and military programs probably unrealistic many critical respects, we recognize little advantage debating merits these projections with Shah. Trouble could well ensue if Iran accelerates volume public expenditures at rates foreseen without commensurate increases public savings, but fact remains development program not now competing against military for resources due slowness preparation sound development projects. Since qualitative discussions economic projections apt appear academic to Shah, suggest you strive focus his attention for time being on fact that projections appear indicate that a bright future attainable, but this will not come about automatically merely because resources available, but will require continued and accelerated actions to upgrade economic administration (along lines represented by initial steps toward modern budgeting system) in order to achieve maximum growth rate under conditions minimal inflation.

Rusk

89.   Telegram From the Department of State to the Embassy in Iran[1]

Washington, June 17, 1965, 2:12 p.m.

1144. Deliver the following orally and confidentially to the Shah on the President's behalf. Or if this not practical in view of his imminent departure you may deliver orally to FonMin. Report Shah's response and comments.

The President was delighted with the Shah's understanding interest in the Algiers conference when they discussed it in the brief but gratifying telephone chat at the time of the Shah's stop in New York.[2]

The President notes that the prospects of the forthcoming conference of Asian and African leaders in Algiers have struck some of our friends with dismay, but he is encouraged by the constructive efforts which Iran is making to the end that the responsible voices of Asia and Africa may have a full and effective hearing at Algiers. The President is impressed to learn from Ambassador Meyer that Iran will seek to focus the main attention of the Asian-African conference on a consideration of ways and means of improving the social and economic conditions of the peoples of Asia and Africa.

The President hopes that other responsible delegations will recognize the wisdom of this conception of the "Afro-Asian movement" and not fall prey to those forces of confusion and subversion which cynically seek to betray the deeply felt longings of Asians and Africans to enjoy the fruits of independence and human dignity.

The President sees hopeful signs that more and more leaders of Africa and Asia are learning to distinguish their real interests from the lure of slogans and the transitory satisfactions of belaboring the phantoms of ancient animosities. The kind of leadership and example Your Majesty is giving has already done a great deal to bring awareness of these lessons to other governments. If other responsible delegations at Algiers recognize how much may be gained from coordination of their efforts with their real friends, the conference will have a more constructive atmosphere than some of our friends have feared. So the President hopes that the Iranian Delegation will provide leadership to this end.

The President expresses again how much it meant to him to be able to have that all so brief chat with the Shah. The Shah's friendship, under-

---

[1] Source: Department of State, Central Files, POL 15–1 IRAN. Confidential; Immediate; Limdis. Drafted by Newberry and Tiger; cleared by Special Assistant to the Ambassador at Large Rollie H. White, Handley, and Komer; and approved by Rusk.

[2] See Document 85.

standing, and support are of the greatest importance to President Johnson personally and to the American nation in these difficult days.

The President sends the warmest good wishes to the Shah and the Imperial family.

Rusk

---

90.   **Telegram From the Embassy in Iran to the Department of State[1]**

Tehran, June 18, 1965, 0930Z.

1450. Annual Econ-Military Review. Re Deptel 1124, June 12.[2]

General Eckhardt and I had two and three-quarter hr session with Shah 17th formally reviewing econ-military picture pursuant to US-Iran Memorandum of Understanding of July 4. Shah was in good mood, no major problems developed. He went along with our various positions (Deptel 1124) except that he wishes one squadron F–5's equipped with Bullpups. Gen Eckhardt who ably handled discussion military procurement is writing up memo for record[3] of understandings reached which will be supplied to Shah for his approval prior to his departure for USSR. Details of military aspects will be reported by separate message.

Nearly hr was spent re econ framework. I led off by reiterating econ development is as important as military. Noted Iran has excellent income but also large deficits projected for future. Added Shah's reform programs apt to add to GOI financial burden and cautioned unless rising expectations met frustration of Iran masses could cause real problem. Concluded that while redoubled effort is going to be required in econ filed over long run, prospects for immediate future satisfactory and, therefore, we prepared proceed with second tranche of military program.

Shah then expatiated at length. First he expressed his personal cynicism re economists, noting Iran has had sad experiences with experts

---

[1] Source: Department of State, Central Files, DEF 19–3 US–IRAN. Confidential. Repeated to DOD and CINCSTRIKE.

[2] Document 88.

[3] Not found.

who claim to know all answers and who disagree among themselves. Happily Iran econ sitatuion has now recovered from handiwork these economists. He particularly pleased by what he considers overwhelmingly favorable impact of his recent attack high cost living thru setting prices for certain basic commodities. He confident his reform programs will greatly improve welfare Iran masses, e.g. by increased production from farms which they now own and by sharing profits from expanding industrial sector. Meanwhile, great strides being made Khuzistan and elsewhere. Thus in general picture good one.

From this point, Shah launched into his usual contention that this future prosperity meaningless if Iran not secure. He simply has been able cope with regional threats. Viet Nam is graphic example, according Shah, of what could happen Iran. US despite its might now compelled seek "unconditional discussions," which Shah means negotiating with and making concession to aggressor. He went on to express concern re future of Kuwait, Aden and Bahrain. He believes Nasser frustrated in Yemen and elsewhere bound to launch adventure some where, probably against Libya, much less probably against Israel. Nasserist threat in Gulf area cannot be ignored.

Thus his principal foreign policy consideration is safety and security Gulf area where Iran's wealth concentrated. He said no responsible leader facing threat this kind can afford be too cautious. After seeking downplay Nasserist threat, I pointed out threat very likely be more subversive (as in Viet Nam) than open military attack. Thus more attn to counter-insurgency was desirable. Shah recognized this and said that his interest in counter-subversion explains his emphasis on total "positive program." He cited new dams being built in Khuzistan and other efforts toward econ and social improvement.

After he had delivered himself of remarks obviously previously planned, Shah agreed my summation that he and his govt are determined accelerate econ progress and that GOI will dedicate its resources to extent necessary to achieve that objective.

Meyer

91.   Telegram From the Embassy in Iran to the Department of
State[1]

Tehran, June 22, 1965, 1130Z.

1470. Personnel Ceiling—Iranian Armed Forces. Emb A–590,[2] Deptel 1124,[3] Embtel 1468.[4] In accordance 1962 agreement, personnel of Iranian Armed Forces had to be reduced to 160,000 "within two or three years." This was achieved March 1, 1965. However, events subsequent to 1962 have, in our view, made a higher ceiling necessary. Based on the following considerations, Country Team therefore again recommends that ceiling be established at 172,000 for period of 1964 Memorandum of Understanding. We consider such ceiling necessary to success of modernization program.

Principal reason for need to increase ceiling is fact that July 4, 1964 Understanding provides for additional equipment and units which must be manned and supported. In particular additional personnel requirements are necessary for new airborne battalion, Hawk battalion, increased number of aircraft, AC&W equipment, additional tanks and reorganization of 8th Armor Division, new patrol frigates and other equipment.

In addition, IIF has undertaken greater responsibilities in connection Literacy, Health and Development Corps and vocational training program. These responsibilities, added to requirements for modernization program, render 1962 personnel ceiling obsolete.

ARMISH/MAAG and IIF have completed comprehensive and detailed joint study of manpower requirements, including TOES/TDS. Study encompassed all possibilities reducing non-essential units while instituting modernization program. Starting point of study was IIF estimate of 188,000 for new ceiling. As result of study, this figure reduced to 172,000, and Shah has reluctantly concurred in lower figure. It could be reached by yearly increments through 1969. We do not think further personnel survey necessary. ARMISH/MAAG will continue insure ceiling reflects essential requirements. Stress will be placed on bringing only trained manpower into regular forces and elimination of unfit from present personnel.

---

[1] Source: Department of State, Central Files, DEF 19–3 US–IRAN. Confidential. Repeated to DOD and CINCSTRIKE.
[2] See footnote 2, Document 88.
[3] Document 88.
[4] Dated June 22. (Department of State, Central Files, DEF 19–3 US–IRAN)

In conclusion, as stated above and in A–590, we believe ceiling of 172,000 justified and necessary and recommend its approval.[5]

Meyer

***

[5] Telegram 43 to Tehran, July 16, authorized the Ambassador to exchange notes with the Iranian Government amending the September 19, 1962, and July 4, 1964, Memoranda of Understanding so as to increase the agreed personnel ceiling of the Imperial Iranian Armed Forces to 172,000. (Ibid., DEF 6 IRAN)

***

92.   Telegram From the Department of State to the Embassy in Iran[1]

Washington, June 24, 1965, 2:33 p.m.

1166. Gudarzian Criminal Case. US Attorney's Office Southern District New York has completed presentation witnesses to Grand Jury and is prepared ask indictment Gudarzian on charge conspiracy to commit fraud by mail. Check forgery aspect not under consideration at this time because of technical difficulty making such case without presence Prince and Princess as principal witnesses. Fraud case would be based obtaining money from various individuals in US by false assertions re construction sports arena in Iran. Prior requesting indictment, however, US Attorney needs to ascertain availability following Iranian witnesses for testimony jury trial, listed alphabetically and not in order importance:

Reza Ansari, Ahmad Chafik, Gen. Mohammad Daftari, Dr. Amir K. Diba, Abolhassan Ebtehaj, Mohammad Vali Meshkatti, Ardeshir Zahedi.

FYI. Believe you should press hard for appearance all witnesses. Although Ebtehaj probably most important of these, you should not disclose this fact to GOI nor give regime impression case could not be made without him. We know Ebtehaj violently opposed to testifying and believe important for internal political reasons Iran seek avoid having issue develop into open clash between him and regime with possible side ef-

***

[1] Source: Department of State, Central Files, POL 15–1 IRAN. Confidential; Limdis. Drafted by Tiger, cleared by Kearney, and approved by Bracken.

fects, important bureaucrats who remain loyal Ebtehaj. End FYI. Therefore unless you perceive objection, we believe best course is simply include his name on list of desired witnesses and await GOI response. We will pouch for your consideration alternative courses of action we might pursue if GOI announces Ebtehaj unavailable and if US Attorney reaches conclusion conviction cannot be obtained without his testimony. Judgment latter respect will depend in part on availability other witnesses above list.

Rusk

93. Telegram From the Embassy in Iran to the Department of State[1]

Tehran, July 4, 1965, 1350Z.

9. Shah's Trip to USSR. During Fourth of July reception today Aram told me briefly that Shah's trip to USSR had been extremely interesting and marked by unusual warmth of reception. There were many discussions but no important substantive decisions were taken. Specifically, no final decision was taken about possibility of Soviets constructing steel mill here, although Soviet Ambassador quoted in press this morning as saying USSR ready to go ahead if Iran will agree. Aram said this matter would be further explored with Soviets.

Aram stated that Shah had explained and defended US policy in Viet-nam "even better than President Johnson." This had made Russians very angry. They had pressed hard to have their point of view on Vietnam included in final communiqué, and when Iranians refused, discussion of communiqué almost terminated. I thanked Aram, and said I was sure President would be very grateful to Shah for what he had done.

Aram promised to fill me in later in more detail.[2]

Rockwell

---

[1] Source: Department of State, Central Files, POL 7 IRAN. Confidential; Priority. Repeated to Moscow.

[2] Telegram 36 to Tehran, July 14, instructed the Ambassador to ask Aram to inform the Shah of the fact that the President had taken a personal interest in his Soviet visit. The President was particularly heartened by the Shah's strong stand on Vietnam and asked that the Shah be told of his personal pleasure at this further example of the aims shared by their two governments. (Ibid.)

94.   Telegram From the Department of State to the Embassy in Iran[1]

Washington, August 25, 1965, 1:38 a.m.

193. For Ambassador. President has approved unanimous recommendation SecState, SecDef, and DCI that we proceed as matter of urgency to develop alternative facilities for our intelligence installations and activities now in Pakistan. He has asked for a firm recommendation on this as soon as feasible. Intelligence community here now hard at work on this problem. Secretary has expressed desire Department play major role in view important political aspects involved in our relations with several countries.

Technical studies have already indicated that preferred alternatives would involve in addition to things elsewhere [less than 1 line of source text not declassified] in Iran: [1 line of source text not declassified]. In eventuality that Pakistan forced withdrawal all our facilities there would be immediate heavy pressure for introduction Iran as much as possible of this burden. Everyone here aware enormous political problems which would be involved and fortunately chances Pakistan's insisting early and complete withdrawal do not now seem great. Nevertheless, possibility exists and in any event there is desire over longer run reduce our present high degree dependence on Pakistan in intelligence field.

Department's problem now is to determine politically feasible background within which technical planning for both short and long terms can be done. It may turn out that best approach will be effort to develop embryo installations at technically suitable sites which would be susceptible to expansion should a critical need develop. This could be done in an austere, inconspicuous, and gradual manner. Department keenly aware political liabilities *any* expansion or additions facilities in Iran and of likelihood relatively short lifespan of [less than 1 line of source text not declassified] intelligence installations there as in many other countries. We are determined hold requests for them to minimum absolutely necessary. However, every additional year of coverage counts, and state technology does not provide much hope that other forms collection can relieve burden on [less than 1 line of source text not declassified] facilities your area for next few years.

Department would appreciate by August 30, if possible, your best effort help us define political parameters within which we must work in

---

[1] Source: Department of State, Central Files, DEF 15 IRAN–US. Top Secret/Sensitive; [distribution indicator not declassified]. Drafted on August 23 by Spain and Director of INR's Office of Current Intelligence Indications William M. Marvel; cleared by Deputy Director for Coordination William McAfee (INR/DDC), Handley, and Howison; and approved by Hughes.

Iran, including time elements involved (i.e., possibilities in six months, possibilities in a year), possible developments in US-Iranian and Soviet-Iranian relations which might affect receptivity, Shah's basic attitudes, potential [*less than 1 line of source text not declassified*] arrangements, etc.

Specifically, what is your estimate prospects for success present proposal [*less than 1 line of source text not declassified*] which provides for introduction some collection personnel. What is maximum number and kind (military or civilian) personnel which could be introduced in [*less than 1 line of source text not declassified*]? Is any other relatively large [*less than 1 line of source text not declassified*] installation feasible elsewhere? What are prospects for modest expansion existing [*less than 1 line of source text not declassified*] covert activities in [*less than 1 line of source text not declassified*]?

Rusk

---

95. **Telegram From the Embassy in Iran to the Department of State**[1]

Washington, August 28, 1965, 11:35 a.m.

229. Re Deptel 193.[2] While urgency reftel apparent, believe in interests providing more valid response it highly desirable familiarize myself firsthand with on-ground realities of existing facilities and geography of suggested expansions and new sites. This I propose to do in coming days.

As reftel notes, there no question proposed additional facilities can be political dynamite, particularly after our pyrrhic victory last fall in obtaining legislative approval for immunities for Americans here. Question is how much official American presence can Iran tolerate (it is already one thousand five hundred plus families).

Before attempting to provide answers I should among other things like obtain firsthand reading of Shah's present temperature. Accordingly hope Dept will concur in my desire to postpone for fortnight our specific response to reftel.

Meyer

---

[1] Source: Department of State, Central Files, DEF 15 IRAN–US. Top Secret/Sensitive; Roger Channel.

[2] Document 94.

96.   Telegram From the Embassy in Iran to the Department of State[1]

Tehran, August 31, 1965, 1610Z.

244. In nearly two and half hour session thirty-first, Shah told me he has been spending many sleepless hours meditating re orientation Iran's policies. These meditations obviously sparked by his recent visit to Moscow. Highlights of this discussion follow:

1. US friendship. Shah gratified by personal greetings from President and Secretary which I conveyed. He said his pronouncements in support of our Viet Nam policy based on friendship for US and even more on his conviction in principles.

2. Viet Nam and US. Shah pleased by firm US policy re Viet Nam. He convinced situation is taking turn for better. Soviets, he believes, anxious to avoid escalation to major confrontation. He admits, however, that Chinese not peace-minded.

3. Viet Nam and Soviets. When Soviet leaders expressed horror at American bombing attacks in North Viet Nam, Shah pointed out if Viet Nam falls to Chinese, rest of Southeast Asia including Indonesia will also fall under Chinese control. Shah also alluded to Soviet-supported activities by Nasser in Yemen. Soviets, he says, made little effort to defend Chinese or themselves re Yemen. Shah confirms Soviet-Chinese rift is deep. It was particularly evident when he needled Soviets about question their being invited to Algiers Conference.

4. Soviets' southern neighbors. Shah tried to write off current Soviet attention to Turkey, Iran, Afghanistan, and Pakistan as "series of coincidences." He contended that Soviet friendliness toward these countries is not something new; they tried in 1965, at which time they asked him to intercede with Turks for better relations. Major Soviet purpose, according to Shah is to have friendly cordon of states around Soviet Union so USSR can get ahead with its major task of developing its economy. He added, however, there undoubtedly is added incentive for Soviets of rallying as many non-yellow countries as possible behind Soviets in long-term struggle with ChiComs.

5. Stand-on-own-feet policy. Shah's central theme was that Iran must stand on its own feet, militarily and economically. "Intervention" by outsiders is increasingly outmoded, he said. In maintaining Iran's independence vis-à-vis Soviets no one (not even Americans) could be more "patriotic" than Iranians, he added.

---

[1] Source: Department of State, Central Files, POL 15–1 IRAN. Secret; Limdis. Repeated to Ankara, Kabul, Karachi, Moscow, and London.

6. "Moribund" CENTO. In most disparaging description he has yet made of CENTO, he described it as "moribund" and as "masquerade" that meets to little effect every six months, although he mused "we better keep it." When Soviets said they did not like CENTO, he told them he would be glad to see it terminated when all other pacts are terminated, e.g. NATO, Warsaw, etc. He said he told Soviets they had little to fear militarily from CENTO.

7. Soviet-Iran non-aggression pact. Shah said Soviets proposed to him an un-registered "non-aggression pact for 200 years." He had turned conversation aside and has "not yet" given Soviets an answer. He wondered whether having such a treaty might not serve Iran's purposes by assuring that Soviets would spare Iran if world-tensions break out in hostilities. When Soviets had made proposal of this kind in 1959, he had turned it down, mostly because US and UK urged him to reject it. *Note:* This is first indication Embassy has had of this proposal. In interests maintaining dialogue with Shah, Embassy hopes there will be no leakage.

8. Regional entente. Commenting that Afghan policy seems to be successful, Shah at one point mentioned possibility Iran, Afghanistan, and Pakistan getting together in common policy of independence.

9. Grievances vs US. During conversation, Shah uncorked whole set of personal grievances against US, including:

a. Bevan–Byrnes and Molotov in 1944 or 1945 made an agreement pointing to autonomy in Iran for Kurds, Azerbaijan, and Khuzistan. Ambassador Wallace Murray had been commissioned to bring him this unhappy news. *Note:* This is surprise to me. Wonder if Dept can shed light on this.

b. During Azerbaijan crisis of 1946, Ambassador Allen had been instructed to make clear that USG would not support Iranian cause militarily.

c. While US economic aid has been deeply appreciated, virtually all of it has been extended only after agonizing wrangling. Specifically, Americans sabotaged British-German steel mill project seven years ago. President Eisenhower spoke to Shah sneeringly of countries insisting on having "damn steel mills." Friendly countries like Iran naturally are bitter when they see American critics like Nasser and India receiving aid on more generous terms and at time when aid to Iran is being curtailed.

d. Similarly Shah deeply appreciative of US military aid but there have been many delays and continued resistance even when he is obtaining it through purchase. He said he has only recently realized that loans for military equipment are not on favorable basis. Meanwhile, while Iran has virtually no air defense equipment, even Afghanistan has SAM sites and MIG–21's.

e. US steadfastly refused to join CENTO, Lincoln White stating publicly that it was in deference to Arab world (read Nasser) sensitivities.

f. Among list of other irritants, Shah particularly bitter about Gudarzian case which in his view has dragged on an unnecessary eighteen months.

10. Therapy. Several times underscoring our impressive record of friendship and help for Iran. I sought to straighten Shah up at various appropriate points including such arguments as: a) since Iran increasingly becoming model for progress in Mideast it would be sad for Iran and for free world if its leadership now tries to follow a route taken by leadership in countries not doing so well; b) since as Dean Acheson once said treaties are mere pieces of paper registering an existing situation there is no assurance that piece of paper would deter Soviets from over-running Iran if they felt impelled to do so; c) masses of Afro-Asia including Iran take their cue from on high and tend to stampede in direction leadership points them and leadership then no longer in control; d) as Dulles once said at SEATO meeting US aid is limited and is not reward for good behavior but is deployed where it can do most good in life-and-death struggle between free world and slave; e) Shah's great strength has been that he is man of principle and this is no time for him to shirk the principles which both our countries uphold. I specifically discouraged any moves toward dismantling CENTO or toward non-aggression pact with USSR. Shah seemed get some lift when I told of how home leave was valuable in reassuring me that American system can outstrip any other, e.g. burgeoning business and industry establishments in Manhattan where Shah also had been amazed by new construction, verdant prairies of central Illinois which producing more food than ever, and Gemini 5 space feat which gives indication that we ready compete with Soviets even when they get head start.

Comment. Obviously Shah had prepared himself to pave way for possible shift in his future policy. Also obviously his talks with Soviet leaders have made marked impression. He may be in one of those moods re which Ambassador Holmes talked to me about. Hopefully he can surmount it without going too far toward Soviets. Meanwhile, our attention must be as cordial and cooperative as possible without being panicky.

Meyer

97.   Telegram From the Embassy in Iran to the Department of
       State[1]

Tehran, September 9, 1965, 1215Z.

319. Re Embtel 244.[2] In discussion eighth Shah remarked that Soviet economic delegation currently visiting Tehran is manifesting almost unbelievable cordiality. This followed cordiality he (Shah) had experienced during his recent Moscow visit when Soviets offered 200-year non-aggression pact and MIG aircraft. Shah had not responded to these two Soviet offers but he said he could not help wondering whether he should not be more responsive to Soviet offers, particularly since his generally pro-Western orientation seemed to be having less value. He noted Ayub finding CENTO membership useless. As for himself, he had only recently realized when there was an alarm re an air attack by Iraqis that Iran has no early warning or other anti-aircraft equipment. He said Iran's airfields and aircraft could be wiped out in one raid. Current attention, he said, is being given to dispersal of aircraft.

Referring to well-known Soviet objectives vis-à-vis Iran, I pointed out what Shah had termed "Soviet smiles" were clearly tactical. He should give credit, I said, to CENTO for deterring Soviet bully tactics and compelling Soviets to be more friendly.

Comment: Shah's irritation re lack of air-defense equipment is increasing.

Meyer

---

[1] Source: Department of State, Central Files, AID 6 IRAN. Confidential. Repeated to Moscow.

[2] Document 96.

98.   Telegram From the Embassy in Iran to the Department of State[1]

Tehran, September 10, 1965.

332. Reference: Deptel 193 and Embtel 229.[2] While I have not completed my survey of all our sensitive installations in Iran, I have visited a sufficient number to be tremendously impressed by what is already being accomplished here. I wonder if many authorities in Washington are aware of the extensiveness of our sensitive operations here by [*less than 1 line of source text not declassified*], Army, Navy, Air Force, etc. (some of them of a duplicating nature).

My conclusion is that there is little being done in Pakistan that is not already being done adequately here. Under these circumstances, piling on an additional [*less than 1 line of source text not declassified*] Americans atop [*less than 1 line of source text not declassified*] in Iran (not counting dependents) would in my view be inconsonant with President Johnson's injunctions re economy in government.

The importance of the Pak facilities is their geography. They afford an additional bearing on target areas. This advantage cannot be transplanted to Iran where bearings are already being taken. Unless someone can demonstrate otherwise to me, transferred personnel from Pakistan will be able to do very little more than is already being done in Iran.

[*less than 1 line of source text not declassified*] communications, I find that both [*less than 1 line of source text not declassified*] already have first-class installations. Obviously any radio man, and I am one myself, is always dreaming of a more extensive antenna system. But as far as I can see both [*less than 1 line of source text not declassified*] are handling traffic with maximum speed and effectiveness. For neither system is volume of traffic more than one-third its capacity.

General Meyer who visited Tehran last week agrees that proposed site at [*less than 1 line of source text not declassified*] for [*less than 1 line of source text not declassified*] is unsuitable for various reasons. He would like to find more favorable location. He concurs that until that day is reached an extension of present [*less than 1 line of source text not declassified*] site is required. It is adequate, if not ideal. I favor indefinite stay at present location.

Foregoing conclusions reached even without political considerations. As recent Embassy telegrams have confirmed, Iran is in process of

---

[1] Source: Department of State, Central Files, DEF 15 IRAN–US. Top Secret/Sensitive; Priority; [*distribution indicator not declassified*]. No time of transmission appears on the source text.

[2] Documents 94 and 95.

adjusting its foreign policy so as to avoid image of being "American stooges." Basically Shah and his government will continue to be with US. At same time, from standpoint of keeping them in power, we must understand value of their improving their image. Nationalistic sentiment is virulent in most of Africa and Asia. It is on upswing in Iran, particularly as Pakistan [*less than 1 line of source text not declassified*] loosen their ties with us. Sensitive US operations here as well as burgeoning US official presence are tailor-made targets for anti-Shah and/or anti-American elements. If such elements were to succeed in stirring up passions against US and Shah remained cooperative with US, his own future would be in jeopardy. If he responded to popular sentiment, which he would probably be forced to do, it would mean ouster of great bulk of American presence here, including our existing sensitive operations.

Since we already have well established facilities [*1 line of source text not declassified*], I think it would be most unwise to tempt fate by importing additional hundreds of Americans. Camel's back is already heavy laden, from standpoint of what is politically tolerable here. Why risk destroying extensive facilities already in being for minimal additional product?

While recommending against transfer of Pak facilities or any substantial part of them to Iran either now or in forseeable future. I do not preclude squeezing in an extra technician or so in facilities already established here. I am impressed by present efficiency and compactness of these facilities. My vote goes for keeping them that way.

Meyer

99.   Telegram From the Department of State to the Embassy in Iran[1]

Washington, September 11, 1965, 7:04 p.m.

292. For Ambassador. Appreciate deep thought and effort devoted Embtel 330.[2] Keenly aware political problems you point up. Fear however there is misunderstanding nature of situation we now face. Following factors must be accepted as valid and determinative:

(1) The highest authority has directed that the USG proceed as a matter of urgency to develop alternative facilities for those now in Pakistan. The question of economy in government, while always pertinent, is in this case clearly subordinate to the protection of critical US national security interests.

(2) Top US intelligence authorities concerned, supported by most competent technical experts in USG, have reviewed requirements and capabilities this field in detail and have concluded that Iran is technically most suitable site for relocation major portion collection activity now in Pakistan. Geographic and other factors related to target areas have been thoroughly taken into account.

(3) Same top US intelligence authorities know well nature and scope present sensitive operations in Iran. While uniquely valuable in its own right, Iranian facilities cannot compare with operations in Pakistan. Assumption that there is little being done in Pakistan that is not already adequately being done in Iran is not correct.

(4) Question of adequacy existing [*less than 1 line of source text not declassified*] facilities in Iran in terms US [*less than 1 line of source text not declassified*] communications needs now under study here but is separate from that with which we now seized except insofar as new [*less than 1 line of source text not declassified*] facility might [*less than 1 line of source text not declassified*] intelligence collection personnel.

We can assure you that no one here has any desire to burden you with additional problems in Iran. We now face, however, the possibility of exclusion from Pakistan at short notice and even if we weather the present crisis, the future viability of the facilities there is in grave doubt. Our job is to try to determine (A) what could be done in Iran right now should we suddenly be excluded from Pakistan and (B) what can be done in the months ahead to prepare the way for a more gradual transfer of at least some of the activities now carried out in Pakistan to Iran.

---

[1] Source: Department of State, Central Files, POL IRAN–US. Top Secret; Sensitive; Priority; [*distribution indicator not declassified*]. Drafted by Spain and Curl; cleared by Talbot, and in substance by Bracken and Komer; and approved by Hughes.

[2] Reference is to telegram 332, September 10, (Document 98), initially transmitted incorrectly as telegram 330.

Department and White House must therefore ask in the most urgent terms your immediate further consideration in the context set forth above of the questions put in Deptel 193,[3] including the specifics requested in the last two paragraphs of that message.

Rusk

---

[3] Document 94.

---

100.   **Telegram From the Embassy in Iran to the Department of State[1]**

Tehran, September 13, 1965.

355. Re Deptel 292.[2] Department and White House may be confident I wish cooperate to utmost in meeting critical intelligence requirements. Fully understand gravity of problem. If Embtel 332[3] seemed unresponsive, it is simply that I do not want our interests here to follow same ill-fated course they have in Pakistan. Reftel suggests USG prepared to take greater risks here than would normally be wise. With that assumption, following views are submitted:

A. Scope of Facilities

1. Existing sites. Although I have not visited all sensitive sites here, and in particular I have not been to [*less than 1 line of source text not declassified*], observations to date indicate that current quarters are being quite fully utilized. Small additional amount of extra equipment, however, can probably be installed in each of them (with possible exception of [*less than 1 line of source text not declassified*]). My hope would be that transfers from Pakistan could be limited to such modest expansion.

2. New [*less than 1 line of source text not declassified*]. Previous thought has already been given to [*1 line of source text not declassified*]

---

[1] Source: Department of State, Central Files, POL IRAN–US. Top Secret; Sensitive; Priority; [*distribution indicator not declassified*]. No time of transmission is given on the source text.

[2] Document 99.

[3] Document 98.

building much needed warehouse. If additional housing is needed for facilities transferred from Pakistan, least risk would of course occur if they housed on compound. Proposed warehouse might be converted into [*less than 1 line of source text not declassified*]. Such new construction might however take minimum six months. I do not favor construction new ostentatious installations elsewhere than [*less than 1 line of source text not declassified*]. However, if Washington decides there is no alternative perhaps best [*5-1/2 lines of source text not declassified*]. This might make project palatable to Shah. As general rule any major new installations [*less than 1 line of source text not declassified*] should be discussed with Shah.

3. Consultations. While burgeoning American presence is indeed problem here, it is less explosive than new [*less than 1 line of source text not declassified*] installations. With all due respect to "top US intelligence authorities concerned" it would seem to me that an Ambassador is entitled to know specifics of additional facilities contemplated [*2 lines of source text not declassified*]. Accordingly, I would appreciate consultations here within next week or ten days with "top US intelligence authorities" who can describe in detail each project desired and how it does not duplicate something already existing. As soon as their ETA received I will gladly reserve whole day for these mutual consultations. Incidentally, I would appreciate their bringing clarification whether [*1-1/2 lines of source text not declassified*] is functioning in accordance with money invested.

B. Political Parameters

1. Bird's eye view. As Dept knows, particularly during present Indo-Pak tension, Shah is badgering us re West's lack of appreciation his friendship. He appears to be shifting Iranian policy so as to reduce his image as "American stooge" and give impression Iran has "independent" policy more consonant with mainstream of Afro-Asian nationalism. His subjects, taking cue not without some relief, inevitably tend to swing too far. There is current trend in government circles, press and public opinion treat Western interests much more critically and coolly. While both Shah's shift and public allergy been developing over long period of time, they have developed markedly within past six months, and most specifically after red carpet treatment he received in Moscow. Much of this change is rooted in series of grievances re which Iran has felt lack of US attention.

2. Need for total policy. From my own experience, I know how Washington is compartmentalized. Issues between US and Iran during recent months been handled pretty much without full realization their effect on total US-Iran relationship. Impression around Washington is Iran is now "rich" country and, therefore, we can shift our attention elsewhere. As a result, most of these individual issues have not received sympathy in Washington which Shah and Iranians feel they deserved.

Ergo, the US-Iran relationship is not as healthy as it was. Shah asked me again last night, "Does Washington really care for Iran?"

3. Grievances. Since Iran's grievances inevitably bear a relationship to Iran's receptivity to what we might wish to do here, it may be worth reviewing some of key irritants. If these can be gotten out of way, climate for introduction of at least some part of needed facilities would be somewhat improved.

A. Military Aid. Shah has become increasingly resentful re our military aid program. While extending grant aid to countries less faithful to our cause than Iran, we are requiring him to pay for high percentage his procurement from us. We agreed on 4–5 percent interest and promptly applied 5 percent rate. He must repay in dollars. (Meanwhile Soviets are offering steel mill, and MIGs, at much lower rate with repayment in Iranian products.) There are other aspects of our military program which because of their restrictive nature tend to offend Shah's sensitive pride but they stem from our legislation and there is little we can do about them, e.g. limitation on his helping Iran's ally Pakistan.

B. Economic Aid. Because Iran is "rich," we understandably have tapered off grant aid and are phasing out technical assistance programs. Loans via Eximbank and commercial banks are still available, but stand in stark contrast to Soviet blandishments, i.e. long term loans at 2-1/2 percent interest with repayment in Iranian products notably natural gas (exploitation of which has long been futilely asked by Iranians of oil consortium).

C. Gudarzian. Shah, his family and his govt simply cannot understand how a crook like Gudarzian can in highly civilized US perpetrate gigantic hoax as Gudarzian has against Iran Prince and Princess. Nearly hundred thousand dollars already been spent by Iranians to free $200,000 in funds attached via Gudarzian's hoax. USG been working hard in both civil and criminal suits, but it is difficult to convince Oriental mind like Shah's that after 18 months something more could not have been done in matter so close to friendly Chief of State.

D. Fairhurst Case. As Iranians see it American businessman who invested only $200,000 is using blackmail of Congressional pressure to extort $5,500,000 for his personal profit.

E. PL–480 Food. Iranian requests for from 100,000 to 300,000 tons of PL–480 Title IV wheat have apparently gotten stalled in notorious red tape of Agriculture Dept.

F. Iranian Students. Re-stimulated by his recent New York stopover, Shah remains aggravated by apparent USG inability to do something re anti-Shah "students," some of them over 40 years old who have already been in US decade or more.

G. Steel Mill. Iranians complain that for number years they been relying on Western interests for steel mill but response was always evasive.

Now that Soviets have made attractive offer Iranians somewhat irritated by Western admonitions re dangers of dealing with Soviets. Shah points out to virtually every listener that students in US demonstrate against him, students trained in England almost assassinated him this spring, so what worse can happen if he sends technicians to be trained in Russia in connection with steel mill.

H. Literacy Conference. Current UNESCO Literacy Conference in Tehran is spectacle dear to Shah's heart. He is less than pleased by our understandable coolness to his pet idea of devoting military funds to World Literacy Program.

4. Symptoms of coolness. Recent evidences of cooling Iranian attitude toward US:

A. Shah's limited responsiveness to our appeals not to jog surgeon's (UNSYG's) arm in current Indo-Pak crisis.

B. Clear indications that Shah will accept new Soviet economic offers, including probably steel mill.

C. Shah's increasing disaffection with CENTO.

D. Resentment over breakdown of Fairhurst negotiations and Congressional pressure in connection therewith.

E. Restoration of three years' hard labor sentence on American engineer Bredin for the alleged murder of his wife. Higher court had earlier reversed this verdict and milder sentence was anticipated.

F. [1-1/2 lines of source text not declassified]

G. GOI turndown of our Embassy's appeals for diplomatic exemption from gasoline taxes. This relatively minor matter but is straw in wind.

H. Similarly $2,000,000 GM contract with Ministry Water and Power for mobile generators was voided by higher authorities.

C. Recommendations

While I do not believe that even if these current irritants are removed, traffic here will bear introduction of full complements from Pakistan envisaged in Deptel 193,[4] I do believe that if we want to expand our facilities in Iran and obtain approval as appropriate from Shah, we will have to improve climate as soon as possible. Following steps recommended:

1. Enlist White House assistance in calling off Senators McClellan and Kuchel from exerting ill-considered public pressure in Fairhurst case. There is not a moment to lose in making them aware that they risk endangering very important facilities here.

---

[4] Document 94.

2. A suitable memento and really forthcoming warm message from President on the occasion of 25th anniversary of the Shah's reign, as already recommended.

3. Action to ensure that Iranians obtain truly concessional interest rate for second tranche of military sales agreement. If we say that 5 percent is already concessional, why can we not give evidence of greater effort to produce greater concession? Our military sales are pivot of our military relationship with Iran. More can and must be done here to improve climate.

4. A high level push to come through with decision re PL–480 wheat. We could really make points both with Shah and public opinion if at least some part of transaction would be in Title I. Increased foreign exchange crisis here should provide justification.

5. A clean-cut steel mill proposition. While prospects are that Soviets have this project almost in hand, our only hope will lie in tidy package which has some attractive features to counter-balance favorable Soviet interest rate and repayment in natural gas.

6. Continued USG pushing for expeditious judicial verdicts against Gudarzian.

7. Court action against at least one or two vagrant Iranian students. Also reply to Shah's frequent requests that we investigate where these "professional students" get their means of support.

8. Over long range, high level USG review of treatment of countries where aid programs being curtailed. We seem to swing between extremes. Once we decide a country, e.g. Iran is off list, it casts pall over almost every tangible tie. Specifically, we should have means to counter attractive loan terms offered by Soviets who gleefully pick up credit projects in countries we deserting.

9. Also over long range do something about US laws which permit crooks so easily to attach stateside bank accounts of foreign leaders. Certain New York lawyers are making good living by these nefarious practices. Not only is there Gudarzian case, but Saudi bank accounts are being attached and also accounts of Hashemite family, all under most flimsy grounds and all to detriment our national interest.

While this is bit lengthy, it seemed appropriate to paint picture on wall. Such understanding is necessary to obtain receptivity of both Shah and Iran people for closer relationship reflected in installation of additional [*less than 1 line of source text not declassified*] facilities here. Believe specific questions asked in last two paras Deptel 193 are all answered in this full presentation.

Meyer

101.   Memorandum From Robert W. Komer of the National Security Council Staff to President Johnson[1]

Washington, September 16, 1965, 10 a.m.

The whole purpose of your exercise with the *Iranian Ambassador at 11:45 this morning* is to make a big splash over the 25th anniversary of the Shah's coming to the throne.[2]

While the Shah didn't compromise much of his pro-Western virtue in Moscow, the Soviets made handsome enough offers (steel mill, non-aggression pact) to start the Shah worrying again. He's stood foursquare behind us on Vietnam, but Meyer is sure he's worried by our seemingly slow progress there. He doesn't want to become another Diem, and whenever he worries about his destiny he begins to see rust on his westward anchor. So this, like your call to him in New York, is mostly massage.

However, you could add a specific touch by asking the ambassador to relay your thanks for Iranian help with American evacuees from Lahore. Also, the Shah has just gone out on a legal limb to grant clemency to an American who got wound up in the Iranian courts and was recently sentenced. So a word of thanks for this personal favor in the "Bredin case" would be a nice touch.

Lloyd Hand is sending you separately a memo on details of the ceremony.[3]

R.W. Komer[4]

---

[1] Source: Johnson Library, National Security File, Country File, Iran, Vol. I, Memos & Miscellaneous, 1/64–12/65. Confidential.

[2] Shortly before noon on September 16 in the Oval Office, President Johnson presented Iranian Ambassador Khosro Khosrovani with a message and gift for the Shah commemorating the 25th anniversary of his accession to the throne. For text of the message, see *Public Papers of the Presidents of the United States: Lyndon B. Johnson, 1965*, Book II, p. 1002.

[3] Not found.

[4] McGeorge Bundy initialed under Komer's signature.

102.   Telegram From the Embassy in Iran to the Department of State[1]

Tehran, September 24, 1965, 1110Z.

469. Pass Komer White House. DOD for Kuss. US-Iran Military Cooperation. As Embassy has previously reported, Shah has become increasingly unhappy with his virtually complete dependence on US for military supplies. He considers there have been intolerable delays, too much back-seat driving "from 10,000 miles away", undesirable gaps such as in air defense, and discrimination in sense that Iran, one of few Afro-Asian countries to support us in foreign policy matters (like Viet Nam), is forced to pay for its supplies on virtually commercial basis while other less friendly nations receive both military and economic aid at more generous terms. Just prior to Central Bank Governor Samii's departure for US to negotiate financing of "second tranche." Shah was startled to learn that while our agreement envisaged interest terms between four and five percent we at outset immediately jumped to five per cent figure.

With this background, a crowning irritation for Shah has been discovery that when he wanted to send token military help to Pakistan to assist Iran maintain dialogue with Ayub during recent Indo-Pak crisis, USG bluntly and categorically put its foot down, not just re MAP supplied hardware but also supplies purchased via USG guaranteed credit and even straight sales which require USG licensing. In bitter tone, he spoke exasperatedly to PriMin Hoveyda in front of me, "We are not free." When signing various military agreements with US, Shah was, of course, aware restrictions incorporated. They were, however, at time somewhat academic. Now full meaning has come sharply to his realization. This comes at time when in general foreign policy is tending toward move designed to alter what he considers his "American stooge" image in Afro-Asian world.

There is no doubt in my mind Shah will make definite effort to decrease his military dependence on US. In fact, there is already evidence coming to Embassy that he intends to do it promptly. He will be seeking procurement from non-American sources. Even Iranian procurement from Soviets cannot be ruled out (Shah has told me Soviets offered him MIGs during his recent Moscow sojourn).

While we may not be able completely to forestall Shah's move to loosen his military cooperation ties with US (including CENTO), there is much to be said for our maintaining that cooperation to the maximum

---

[1] Source: Department of State, Central Files, DEF 19–8 US–IRAN. Confidential; Priority. Repeated to CINCSTRIKE. Passed to DOD and the White House at 8:45 a.m.

extent possible. Certainly we should seek to avoid having pendulum swing too far in other direction. With this end in view Embassy once again appeals to Dept and DOD to conjure up some means (perhaps through appropriate component of USG financing) for reducing interest rate for "second tranche" purchases as close as possible to four percent figure.

In addition to Samii, Iran FinMin Amuzegue also now in Washington. Advising them that more favorable terms have been arranged would do great deal to shore up our position in Iran, specifically as far as military cooperation is concerned.

Meyer

103.   Letter From President Johnson to the Shah of Iran[1]

Washington, October 5, 1965.

Your Imperial Majesty:

I greatly appreciate your recent letter on the conflict between India and Pakistan,[2] and welcome its words of wisdom. I am wholly in agreement with you that the resolution of the Security Council obliges all of us to seek a settlement of the underlying political problems that divide those two great nations.

The firm policy of the United States Government is to search for a peaceful settlement between the two countries through the United Nations which is the instrument we have agreed should act in these matters. We stand ready to lend our best efforts through the Security Council to assist as we can. As you and I are well aware, this task will not be easy. The issues between India and Pakistan have resisted solution for some

---

[1] Source: Johnson Library, National Security File, Special Head of State Correspondence File, Iran—Presidential Correspondence. Confidential. Sent to the President for signature under an October 5 memorandum from Komer calling it a "friendly but carefully noncommittal reply" to an attached message from the Shah appealing for U.S. support in getting a Kashmir settlement. (Ibid., Memos to the President, McGeorge Bundy, Vol. 15)

[2] The text of the message, sent by telegram, was delivered to the Department of State with a September 27 covering letter from Ambassador Khosrovani to Assistant Secretary Hare. (Ibid., Special Head of State Correspondence File, Iran—Presidential Correspondence)

eighteen years already, and I hope that the recent fighting has not made them harder rather than easier to resolve.

I am aware of and admire the statesmanlike roles played by Your Majesty, Prime Minister Hoveyda, and Ambassador Ansary in support of the successful efforts of the United Nations to achieve a ceasefire. Your thoughts on how we can move forward to lasting peace as relayed by Ambassador Meyer have been interesting and useful. It is clear to us that as the United Nations seeks solution to the problem, Iran can provide constructive support by encouraging and strengthening Pakistan's ties to the Free World.

Because of our deep mutual interest in a stable subcontinent, I look forward to continued close consultations and exchanges of views with you as India and Pakistan seek, with the help of the United Nations, a solution to the troubles which have plagued them for so long.

Sincerely yours,

Lyndon B. Johnson

---

104.   Telegram From the Embassy in Iran to the Department of State[1]

Tehran, October 27, 1965, 1100Z.

650. For General Taylor. Ref: Deptel 509.[2] Threat of insurgency in Iran is in latent rather than active stage. Thus, our efforts and those of GOI are directed as much towards prevention as towards improving capability to deal with insurgency if it occurs. Overall US objective in Iran (preservation this country from domination by elements inimical to US interests) is at present best served by furthering progress already made in economic, social and political development while recognizing that Shah represents vital element of stability. Thus, our unremitting efforts are directed toward development and implementation number courses of action many of which have counter-insurgency implications.

GOI authorities, from Shah down through military, security, and police echelons, are all aware of importance counter-insurgency opera-

---

[1] Source: Department of State, Central Files, POL 23–1 IRAN. Secret; Exdis.
[2] Dated October 22. (Ibid., POL 23–1 COL)

tions, and GOI has improved its posture by launching own programs in fields of health and sanitation, literacy, land reform, vocational training and civic action. Since inauguration civic action programs in Iran (1962) there has been noteworthy change in public image of Iranian military and gendarmerie and attitude of general public toward gendarmerie and military has altered visibly for better; similar changes have taken place in attitude military toward civilian population. Civic action thus has played material role in decline of insurgency threat and pacification of tribes.

Greatest danger to stability, as brought out by events of this year, comes from small groups of fanatics who might assassinate Shah but who have no significant capability for insurgency themselves. (Embassy's A–105)[3] Second major problem, in my opinion, is narrowness of base of regime. (Embassy's A–281)[4] However, this is not insurgency problem but tied to personality of Shah. In short while due attention is given by Country Team to potential insurgency threats from tribes, mullahs, and dissatisfied urban elements, Iran in my judgment is a situation where further refinement of counter-insurgency programs is less important than encouraging well-conceived economic development and broader based institutionalized government.

Am satisfied with progress being made in Iranian counter-insurgency preparations and at moment I see no major problems. This is why in our last progress report on IDP I recommended that Iran be taken off special group list requiring periodic review. As reported in Embassy's A–281 current situation here better than it has been for some time.

However, in our regular and continuing process of analysis Iranian political environment we are, of course, constantly alert to any signs of increase in counter-insurgency threat or its potential. I am fully aware of advantages for prompt attention at highest levels USG which special group provides and would seek assistance promptly this channel should changing conditions here seem to justify.

I regard our IDP as adequate and geared to Iran's present requirements. I consider that I have authority to utilize all resources of US agencies within mission to insure efficient execution of US responsibilities under IDP. Country Team fully effective in counter-insurgency field and there are no conflicts between US agencies regarding roles and missions. I believe attitude of local authorities towards insurgency threat is healthy one. GOI appears to be increasingly aware of importance of counter-insurgency programs and local authorities are susceptible to advice on that score.

---

[3] Dated August 17. (Ibid., POL 2 IRAN)
[4] Dated October 20. (Ibid., POL 23–1 IRAN)

With regard to our ability to evaluate local conditions in sufficient time to take preventive action against a subversive threat, our sources appear to be adequate. [2 *lines of source text not declassified*] US and GOI interests in this field are almost identical and I consider GOI sources as reasonably satisfactory. Embassy, Consulates, [*less than 1 line of source text not declassified*] have certain capabilities in this field, [1 *line of source text not declassified*].

In general, I am satisfied with level of training of my staff in counter-insurgency theory and practice. However, since Iran poses problem like many other countries where we are endeavoring strengthen economic and social fundamentals of regime over long run against possible insurgent or subversive forces, suggest training courses stress particularly appropriate utilization positive techniques aimed at encouragement of constructive evolutionary forces. Officers all agencies should be trained accordingly to approach whole issue with constructive mentality rather than as simple matter fire-fighting after open conflagration has commenced.

Meyer

105. Telegram From the Embassy in Iran to the Department of State[1]

Tehran, November 12, 1965, 0950Z.

715. Iran Military Build-up.

1. Build-up Urgent. In discussion with Eximbank President Linder and me 11th, Shah stressed once again that successful economic development of Iran is useless unless Iran has adequate military security. Reiterating many points made previously and those disclosed by FinMin Amuzegar 3 days ago, Shah made clear that in wake of Pak-Indian crisis and procurement by Iraq of new MIGs and British aircraft he considers augmentation his military establishment an urgent necessity. His fears center particularly on vulnerability of Khuzistan and Kharg Island to

---

[1] Source: Department of State, Central Files, DEF 19–8 US–IRAN. Confidential. Repeated to CINCSTRIKE, London, Bonn, Baghdad, Ankara, and Karachi.

surprise attack. He said he realized US and Iran have agreement on military program but new facts require additional $200,000,000 expenditures envisaged in request made this week and approved by parliament.

2. US–Iran Cooperation. Pointing to cooperative aspects of US-Iranian military relationship, I said I felt we had formulated effective program for Iran's military security as envisaged in our respective agreements, latest being that of July 1964. If there were certain weaknesses which required amendment it struck me they should be worked out by ARMISH/MAAG Chief Jablonsky and Iranian top military.

3. Alleged Delays. Shah said problem is delay. He said he had been waiting two months for paperwork to be completed re second tranche including determination of interest rate. It not possible with urgency facing him militarily to countenance such delays. I assured him that delay of second tranche paperwork in no way deliberate nor with ulterior motive. Meanwhile, as General Jablonsky has already assured him, we been meeting time schedule for our commitments with remarkable success.

4. Anti-aircraft needs. Shah stressed his anxiety over lack of air defense. He asserted that USG itself considered certain anti-aircraft guns obsolete and pursuant to US advice Iran disposed of them. Now, however, he realizes that he needs such guns or others to defend his defenseless installations. I noted that General Jablonsky had told him a week ago in their monthly meeting that whole question of anti-aircraft weaponry is under review in US as result of Viet Nam and some definitive decisions expected in December. As he did to Jablonsky, Shah said he would wait until December before he makes any final decisions re this equipment. In talking with me, however, he prefaced his statement emphatically with the word "maybe".

5. Unhappiness re Hawks. When I suggested that in long-range program Hawk missiles were to play a key role in Iran's air defense, Shah virtually exploded in complaining we are limiting him to one battalion. He said it impossible to fragment one battalion and try to defend each of his installations with only one or two Hawk launchers. In addition to his irritation over fact that Iraqis, Egyptians and others have more and faster planes, Shah voiced his unhappiness that Egypt already has eight SAM sites and that both his neighbors Iraq and Afghanistan have such Russian equipment.

6. Decision re $200,000,000 is Firm. Stating he wanted no misunderstanding, Shah said "It has been decided" that additional $200,000,000 worth of urgent military equipment will be obtained. He said he hoped bulk of it would be available from US. At same time he gave indication that Iran will be shopping other places and said some military training for Iranians is already planned for Germany.

7. Inadequate Human Resources. I took occasion once again to point out inadequacy of trained human resources in Iran Armed Forces. I

said I concerned at prospect of Iran importing more highly technical equipment, when already some supplies not being handled properly. Shah acknowledged this deficiency but asked for examples. This prompted further emphasis on my part that his military and General Jablonsky should be in close consultation.[2]

Meyer

---

[2] Telegram 591 to Tehran, November 13, noting that any substantial increase in defense expenditures would have a long-range impact on economic development, asked for the Embassy's judgment regarding the Shah's motivations and whether he would seriously contemplate proceeding with a procurement program even if it jeopardized Iran's MAP relationship with the United States. (Ibid.)

---

106.   Telegram From the Embassy in Iran to the Department of State[1]

Tehran, November 18, 1965, 0720Z.

743. Shah's Moodiness. FinMin Amuzegar evening 17th told me that following our conversation 9th (Embtel 702)[2] he sought to explain to Shah valid reasons for delay in US decision re second tranche interest rate. Amuzegar said he found Shah unreceptive. According to Amuzegar, Shah is in glum mood, convinced that Washington is determined to retaliate for his having made steel mill deal with Soviets.

Amuzegar said that in addition to second tranche interest rate issue, Shah cited "What Americans are doing to my brother and sister" in Gudarzian case. According Amuzegar, Shah simply cannot conceive that top USG leadership could not, if it really wanted to, secure prompt justice for Prince and Princess.

I told Amuzegar that by coincidence two USG attorneys, Kearney and King, presently in Tehran with purpose of explaining to Shah extent to which USG has gone to clear Prince and Princess.[3] I noted it boils down

---

[1] Source: Department of State, Central Files, POL 15–1 IRAN. Confidential; Limdis.

[2] Dated November 9. (Ibid., DEF 19–8 US–IRAN)

[3] Telegram 759 from Tehran, November 20, reported that the Ambassador, Deputy Assistant Legal Adviser Richard D. Kearney, and Assistant U.S. Attorney Robert King had had a 1-hour audience with the Shah that morning, during which they had emphasized that the U.S. Government had expended great efforts in seeking to put Gudarzian in jail but would not be able to proceed on fraud charges if Ebtehaj and Daftary were not available as witnesses. The Shah expressed his inability to understand why the American system of criminal justice could not convict Gudarzian of forgery or perjury, but he did not indicate willingness to relieve Ebtehaj's apprehensions about testifying. (Ibid., POL 15–1 IRAN)

to our determination to have Gudarzian locked up, but this requires necessary Iranian witnesses. Amuzegar said this is precisely what irks Shah, who is convinced that Ebtehaj, as great and good friend of top American leaders, would not fail to testify if that were truly USG's desire. Fact that Ebtehaj has refused can in Shah's view, according to Amuzegar, only mean that USG really suggested Ebtehaj not testify and all this is aimed at making Shah squirm because of steel mill transaction.

Amuzegar emphasized that he himself realizes all this is pure moodiness on part of Shah but it exists nevertheless. He pleaded that USG make some gesture, as for example quick word re second tranche interest rate, to help break intensified feeling Shah has that USG is determined to take punitive measures against him. Amuzegar said Shah's belief that USG is undertaking punitive measures is heavily influenced by his brooding over Pakistan's plight vis-à-vis US.

Meyer

---

107. Memorandum From Robert W. Komer of the National Security Council Staff to the President's Special Assistant for National Security Affairs (Bundy)[1]

Washington, November 22, 1965.

Mac:

Iran interest rate on arms sales. I've held this up for over 8 weeks now, in order to keep it tied to Peshawar package. But we're going nowhere fast, and heat is mounting (see Tehran 743 attached).[2]

Case for holding up has been that giving away a goodie too long before we ask for something in turn vitiates the leverage. But State and DOD think the Shah would still remember, and also argue the case for going ahead now anyway on general grounds of keeping Iranians happy. Also Iran is talking about purchasing arms elsewhere at cost to our balance of payments. Past rate has been 5%. State/DOD want to cut it

---

[1] Source: Johnson Library, National Security File, Country File, Iran, Vol. I, Cables, 1/64–12/65. Secret.

[2] Document 106.

to 3-1/2–4% (ultimately about $350 million in sales over next several years may be involved).

Other problem is that McNamara wants to lay off this paper with Ex-Im, thus freeing MAP credit fund for other sales. It will take a WH whip, of course, to get Linder to do this.

I favor going ahead now at 4%, so long as I have your backing in beating up Harold when necessary.[3]

.RWK

---

[3] Next to this paragraph Bundy wrote "OK" with his initials.

---

108.   Telegram From the Embassy in Iran to the Department of State[1]

Tehran, November 25, 1965, 1550Z.

776. Shah and US. At outset Thanksgiving Day conversation, Shah agreed with me that time had come for mutually frank discussion. Two-hour session resulted with following highlights:

1. Incipient Divergence. Shah said he had uneasy feeling growing estrangement between US and Iran. Agreeing, I said purpose my audience was obtain better understanding Iran's policies and seek provide him better understanding of USG problems.

2. Rehash of Grievances. Obviously planned, Shah rehashed what he considers unhappy developments in US-Iran relations. This time instead of harking back to Azerbaijan days, he began with mid-fifties and US refusal join CENTO. He also contended USG sought to dictate Iran's policies from days of Gerry Dooher (who "wanted to be Lawrence of Iran") to Amini days of early sixties. He recalled President Kennedy, during Shah's Washington visit in 1962, had gone out of his way to inform Shah that USG had two favorite Prime Ministers, Amini and Karamanlis. Amini's premiership had been disastrous. Stating publicly Iran

---

[1] Source: Department of State, Central Files, POL IRAN–US. Confidential. Repeated to CINCSTRIKE, Ankara, Baghdad, Cairo, Jidda, Karachi, London, Moscow, and USUN.

was bankrupt, Amini precipitated tremendous flight of capital and eco-nomic depression. More recently USG has sought to dictate in minutest detail what his military establishment may and may not have. In all hon-esty he felt Iranian authorities here are in best position to assess Iran's se-curity needs.

3.   Relations with Soviets. In rehashing grievances, Shah recalled how in 1959 at insistence his Western allies he rejected offer of non-ag-gression pact with Soviets. Subsequently whole world witnessed USG attempts to relax relationship with Soviets. When Test Ban Treaty was signed, large US Congressional contingent appeared in Moscow with all sorts of prophecies re new era in US-USSR relations. It was only natural, Shah said, that Iran would not want to be left out in cold. Accordingly, Iran began probing Soviet expressions of interest in relaxed Iran-USSR relationship. Until now evidence is that Soviet intentions are reasonably honorable. Accordingly, as long as Soviets behave themselves, Shah said he sees no objection to neighborliness particularly in economic field.

4.   Steel Mill. Among grievances, of course, was long-standing Western rejection of Iranian aspirations for steel mill. Shah said steel mill had become dream of all Iranians, dramatic symbol of Iran's movement into modern world. So when Soviets made attractive offer, Shah accept-ed. He acknowledged recent active interest of Western consortia but said their efforts were to no purpose for they could not possibly compete with Soviet offer unless they would make gift of steel mill. He was referring to his well-known thesis that by paying for steel mill with natural gas, until now wasted by flaring, Iran is in effect getting steel mill from Soviets for nothing.

5.   US Reactions to Steel Mill. I pointed out to Shah our understand-ing of Iran's acceptance of steel mill. Realized it had political advantages for Shah as well as economic (he demurred slightly). Noted that during my Washington consultations number of officials had pointed out there benefit to US as well as Iran in relaxed Iran-USSR relationship. Shah said he knew this but some "junior officers" have been "critical." I took occa-sion to point out that number Iranians misquote Americans to Shah feel-ing they can improve their own standing with him by relaying sensational reports. Shah said he fully cognizant of this racket.

6. $200,000,000 Military Build-up. Shah expressed deep gratitude for close US-Iranian military cooperation. He felt, however, that there had been serious USG misunderstanding of his true needs and this has resulted in glaring weaknesses in his security establishment. He stressed throughout conversation his need for anti-aircraft capability and naval units in Persian Gulf. He did not mention aircraft (General Khatemi has made clear to US that he wants hold to USAF cooperation).

7.   Less Favorable Treatment. Shah complained we had supplied military equipment more generously to number countries, including

many who have been less staunch friend of US than Iran. Again he recalled his support for US policy in Viet Nam. Shah also said Turks being more favorably treated, e.g. $160,000,000 this year in MAP grant aid, twelve destroyers (to Iran's none), etc. Indicating his figures exaggerated, I pointed out USG still has sizeable $45,000,000 grant component in Iran program and Turkey does not have $500,000,000 annual oil income. Shah agreed, saying he glad Iran has increasing capability to purchase its military requirements. Problem is USG unwillingness to supply even when he is willing to pay.

8.   Military vs Economic. I pointed out to Shah that from purely selfish standpoint USG is doing itself disservice. US could use $200,000,000 foreign exchange in view our increasing gold outflow. Fact is our Washington colleagues put Iran's interest above our own. They sincerely believe Iran should limit Iran's military expenditures in favor economic development. Shah said no one excels him in desire for Iran's economic development, paid for with Iranian funds. This launched him on description of progress to date. Including success of his dramatic reform program which, he said, has taken wind out of sails of Communists as well as opposition elements inside Iran.

9.   Revised Program. Referring to our 1962 and 1964 agreements Shah said even at time of signature Iranians had indicated their fears that envisaged program would be inadequate. In fact, in letter approving agreements they had noted that situation could change and modifications required. Stressing need for both countries adhere to agreements, I acknowledged that nothing in life is immutable. If threat has altered and if weaknesses have developed in program, they could be talked out and appropriate revisions made. What was hard to explain was sudden unilateral Iranian action.

10. Anti-aircraft Plight. Shah said he had several times sought to make clear to US his deep concern re anti-aircraft defense. He had highest regard for US military but even they can make mistakes. In Viet Nam only eight percent American aircraft being shot down by missiles; 92 percent by ground-fire. This has precipitated total revision US military thinking re anti-aircraft defense. Unfortunately, previous erroneous evaluation is partly responsible for Iran's lack of air defense.

11. Naval Units for Gulf. Noting vulnerability Kharg Island, vital importance Khuzistan and increasing number off-shore drilling operations, Shah said he simply must have naval capability in Persian Gulf. US has steadfastly denied him destroyers. He is determined to obtain that type vessel. He feels his need is as valid as is that of Turkey.

12. Arab Threat in Gulf. Shah said he realizes USG does not consider Arabs as threat to Iran. I corrected him to say that we consider threat less formidable than does he. Re Iraq, Shah said just last week four Iraqi tanks crossed Iranian border and captured small Iranian mule train falsely sus-

pected of carrying arms to Kurds. Nasserism could without too much difficulty take over Kuwait or other Gulf principalities. Syria has openly advocated Arab move on Khuzistan. Iraq has same objectives, even though only Qassim stated them publicly.

13. British Withdrawal. Shah predicted by 1968 British will have withdrawn from Aden and by 1970 probably from Gulf principalities. I called his attention to fact that Iran Del at UN had joined wolf-pack in voting resolution against British in Aden. Shah said Iran had no alternative but to vote against colonialism. Meanwhile, since British influence one way or other will be withdrawn, Iran remains single constructive free world power capable of protecting commerce and peace in Gulf area from predatory elements including Communists.

14. Saudi Potential. Shah said he looks forward to Faisal's forthcoming visit to Tehran. While disturbed that Saudis seem be able obtain substantial equipment from US and UK in contrast to his own less successful efforts, Shah said he welcomes military strengthening of Saudis. Asked whether Saudis might play role in security of Gulf principalities (as for example by federation), Shah said he saw no objection, provided such consolidation was definitely non-Nasserist. Shah added Iran has no territorial aims on Gulf's southern shore (he did not even mention Bahrain).

15. Syria. Referring to Syria, I expressed view that Damascus pronouncements are chronically so wild that no one pays any attention to them. By reacting as Iranians did to Syrian PriMin's statement re Khuzistan, it merely convinces Arabs this is an issue re which to make more noise. Shah professed to agree.

16. Shah in President's Shoes. In trying explain US problems, I asked Shah to put himself in President's shoes. I expressed opinion that Presidents are products of their times. Eisenhower was chosen over very able Stevenson because Americans at that point wanted complacency and approved Eisenhower's father image. Kennedy captured American imagination with theme that he wanted get US on move again. World liked Kennedy because of his quivers and arrows foreign policy. (I noted in passing that Shah's complaints re US intervention via Amini stemmed from days when under Kennedy leadership US was trying play more active role in world affairs. In any case, Amini was Shah's choice not that of US. Shah said Amini had been intriguing for job since his days as Ambassador in Washington.) I said US people have become increasingly disillusioned. After two world wars and $110 billion in foreign aid, all to preserve freedom abroad, there is epidemic anti-Americanism in numerous foreign countries. We know it only represents minority who loudmouthed and who by melodramatics capture press headlines. Pity is that some leaders cater to such demagoguery. Americans too are human beings. They resent failure of other people appreciate their endeavors. They doubly resent indignities such as having their SecState spat

upon. They want their President take hard look at foreign relations. This is what President Johnson is doing. Where there is aggression as in Viet Nam, President takes vigorous action and US people overwhelmingly support such policies. But fact that they have to do this thankless job (240 lives lost last week alone) virtually alone causes them to pause. Shah recalled his own support in world capitals for US policy in Viet Nam and expressed apparently sincere view that American boys are "fighting gallantly" in Viet Nam.

17. Hard Look at Aid Projects. With above background, I said it not surprising Congress been increasingly critical foreign aid program. It is my understanding President himself is personally checking all foreign aid commitments. Shah said he understands this natural American attitude. He felt problem with foreign aid was "way it was handled", e.g. too many strings, etc. I said reason Congress injected one proviso after another was increasing public concern at lack of foreign appreciation.

18. Second Tranche Paper-work. During conversation Shah spoke with utmost seriousness re delay in completing second tranche paper-work, which was to have been finished when Samii was in Washington two and half months ago. What worries him most, Shah said, is that if Washington can delay paper-work in this way, same "uncertainty" can apply to Iran's supply of military equipment. I reiterated that until now there been no interruption in supplies as scheduled. Shah again referred to Pak experience. He realized we would say Iran is different but even if there is "only one chance in million" that Iran would find itself in same plight if Pan-Arab dispute arose, he could not take that chance. He said some of his military are now in Europe checking on anti-aircraft and naval equipment. He sincerely hoped early answer would be received from Washington re second tranche since he would "hate to move" in direction which would neither be in US or Iran's interest. He reiterated his desire to work in close harmony with us and to "buy American."

19. Soviet Aim; Rupture US-Iran Military Cooperation. I called Shah's attention to current output of Communist-bloc anti-Iranian clandestine broadcasting stations. Major attack is on US-Iran military cooperation. Noting that he has chosen to go along with first stage of classic Communist strategy, i.e. alliance of Communists with national aspirations, obviously Soviets now concentrating on second stage, i.e. disrupting Iran's ties with West. I sincerely hoped Shah would block this Soviet move. Shah said it is US which by second tranche delay is aiding Soviet objective. I closed conversation by quoting Arab proverb "You can't clap with one hand" and expressed hope nothing would intervene to disrupt basic friendship which exists between our two countries including our military cooperation. Shah cordially agreed.

Meyer

109. Telegram From the Embassy in Iran to the Department of State[1]

Tehran, November 25, 1965, 1830Z.

778. Personal for Secretary. FonMin Aram tells me that after my two-hour session with Shah Thanksgiving Day (Embtel 776),[2] Shah told him he and I had laid all our cards on table. But Shah, according to Aram, still asks, "Why don't Americans understand we want to be their friends?"

From Washington, world situation may look different, but from here I (hopefully not just due to localitis) believe that Shah remains true friend of everything in which we believe and that we can ill afford disaffection of another country. Accordingly, I would appreciate your personal intervention with White House to break loose long-delayed paper-work re second tranche of our military program with Iran. It should be with interest rate of four percent. If this unsalable please get it out whatever the rate but hopefully less than five percent.

Aram also recalled your conversation with Shah last April in which you proposed periodic (three to six months) reviews of all subjects of mutual interest. Shah and I are getting along fine. But in his present blue mood, Shah needs evidence that Washington still loves him. Therefore, please do your best to assure that in foreseeable future some high ranking USG official drops in at Tehran to hold Shah's hand. Aram suggested you yourself during one of your travels. He agreed, however, that George Ball or Averell Harriman could do the job.

I cannot stress too strongly that our relations with Iran are at crossroads. Shah wants to go on same course with US. I am sure this is in our country's interest.

If feasible, show this message to President. Despite poison of Gudarzian fiasco, Shah trusts President, recalling his visit here in 1962. Shah asks little. Can't we keep this country in free world camp?

Meyer

---

[1] Source: Department of State, Central Files, POL IRAN–US. Confidential; Limdis.
[2] Document 108.

110. Telegram From the Embassy in Iran to the Department of State[1]

Tehran, November 28, 1965, 1730Z.

789. Country Team message. Shah and US.

1. Fathoming the Shah. To understand Iran one must understand Shah. This is not one-shot undertaking. Shah's personality undergoes steady metamorphosis. To understand current developments, such as authorization to borrow up to $200,000,000 for military purposes it is therefore necessary to fathom present state of Shah's mind.

2. Becoming more like father. Shah today is no longer ward of foreigners as in 1941–45, nor vacillating youth of late forties. Mosadeq era effected major conversion. While for decade leaning heavily on Uncle Sam's shoulders, Shah has increasingly become self-sufficient authority. Iran has been making remarkable strides. Shah believes it is because he knows better than anyone else how to handle his people. Former Ambassador George Allen[2] aptly observed, "he is becoming more like his father." Old Reza Shah was tough, independent-minded, impulsive and autocratic. But he modernized Iran of his day. Shah is determined to do same.

3. 1965 Model Shah. While it difficult dissect complex personality such as Shah's, following traits noteworthy at this stage his development:

A. Hard worker. Shah is indefatigable worker. There is no tint of play-boy. Virtually every waking moment is invested in progress and security his country. This is dulling and can tend to foster sense of infallibility. Shah should have more diversions.

B. Pretensions. Convinced that he has mastered job of pulling his listless and backward people forward, Shah knows that he is more firmly in saddle in Iran than ever before. This is fact which we must also recognize. It is not surprising that Shah feels his talents can have wider usefulness. Hence recent moves to build up his image in Afro-Asian world. At this point, however, his political ambitions in area do not include territorial aggrandizement, even Bahrain. On the whole his ambitions are constructive and responsible.

C. Independent-mindedness (see Embtel 611).[3] Even as he himself has learned to stand on own feet, Shah wants independent stance for his

[1] Source: Department of State, Central Files, POL IRAN–US. Secret. Repeated to CINCSTRIKE for POLAD, Ankara, Baghdad, Kabul, Karachi, London, Moscow, and USUN New York.

[2] George V. Allen was Ambassador to Iran May 11, 1946–February 17, 1948.

[3] Dated October 19. (Department of State, Central Files, AID 6 IRAN)

country. (As George Allen observes this is precise goal of USG policy since Azerbaijan days.) Soaring oil income makes independent policy possible economically. Politically, he is having inner tension between his basic beliefs which coincide with those of West and expediency of enhancing his image in unprincipled Afro-Asian political milieu. Shah cherishes his ties with US, but Viet-nam and Pakistan have shaken him badly. In Viet-nam, Diem was murdered and despite American military power, Shah fears end result may be negotiated settlement which in Iran's case could mean loss of wealthy Khuzistan. For Shah lesson of Pakistan is that Iran must have reasonably adequate military resources in event military supplies are shut off during regional conflict. Beyond these selfish considerations, Shah sincerely believes it is in US, as well as Iran's interest, that Iran itself be able cope with regional threats. Hence, his desire to have adequate military capability.

D. Surprise tactic. Over years Shah has learned that hesitation permits intrusion of opposing forces. When Soviets proposed non-aggression pact in 1959, delay in following it up permitted Western Ambassadors to block agreement. FonMin Aram tells me same thing happens in cabinet changes, i.e., Shah stages fait accompli. Steel mill transaction was initially [apparent omission] even before terms decided. Thus $200,000,000 borrowing authorization was rushed through before inevitable resistance could buildup either from within or from outside Iran.

E. Congenital weaknesses. Shah's two greatest weaknesses stem from his father. He has obsession for things military. He is intolerant of criticism. These weaknesses require almost daily treatment.

4. Guilty conscience. Shah is self-confident and even a little cocky because of recent successes. He tells me his White Revolution has "taken wind out of sails" of Communist and National Front movements. Steel mill transaction, like eating of forbidden fruit, has given populace big lift. Yet Shah knows he is treading on dangerous territory. He, therefore, engages in rationalization and self-justification.

A. Feigned grievances. As Dept knows, Shah has been dredging up whole set of grievances which are based on distortion (Embtels 244 and 776).[4] Obviously he wishes to rationalize to us, and particularly to himself, his recent moves.

B. Sensitivity re small things. Shah has become increasingly sensitive to Iranian student criticism abroad, anti-regime articles in foreign press, Cuyler Young, etc. This past month PriMin Hoveyda, trying to be more royalist than Shah, threatened Turk Ambassador to recall Iran Ambassador from Ankara unless Turkish student who had criticized Shah were brought to trial. Fortunately FonMin Aram has throttled this stu-

---

[4] Documents 96 and 108.

pidity. Similar case was Syrian PriMin's statement re Khuzistan re which Hoveyda made mountain of molehill.

C. Alleged US infidelity. Shah is fully aware how US saved his regime in Azerbaijan crisis and in Mosadeq days. He also knows extent of our financial assistance. Yet in present state of mind he conjures up all sorts of spectres, e.g., USG could put Gudarzian in jail but really does not want to; McCloy letter to Ebtehaj[5] shows USG is abetting Shah's enemies; no one in Washington appreciates really how in Kremlin Shah (alone among Afro-Asians) supported US policy in Viet-nam; delay in second tranche paper-work is retaliation for steel-mill transaction with Soviets: US supports Iraqis on Shatt-al-Arab; while economic aid to Iran is being terminated and military aid rapidly diminishing, USG continues subsidize generously those who undermine Western cause, e.g. Nasser and India; US is discriminating Iran on interest rates, etc.

5.   Shah feels misunderstood. Not all of Shah's complaints are due to self-rationalization. He is basically on our side. He is affording US facilities of tremendous strategic importance. He has spoken up for us on Viet-nam when others have spit on us. He is piloting his country on an economic take-off. His efforts in this connection are gaining wider support and participation from skilled Western-trained civil servants. Shah's security problems cannot be dismissed lightly. Soviet-backed neighbors are receiving some military equipment superior in quality and quantity. Despite all that we have done in past, Shah feels US today does not appreciate him nor understand his needs.

6. $200,000,000 Motivation. Shah is military expert. There is little doubt his present military posture is weak in air defense. While we may not agree, he understandably believes that Kharg Island and virtual forest of off-shore oil installations in Persian Gulf require security protection, including destroyers. In Shah's view, other countries in this area, whether US allies like Turkey or Soviet-supported outfits like Egypt, Iraq and Afghanistan, have equipment better both in quantity and quality, notably SAM's and MIGs. A pilot himself, he is envious of Mach 2.3 MIG speeds. Since he now has financial resources of his own, Shah is determined to maintain parity, hopefully via supplies from his closest friends, the Americans; but if not from whatever sources available. He has mentioned to me several times that while he was in Moscow Soviets offered him MIGs. As Shah sees it, greatest need is in anti-aircraft and naval equipment. (We have impression that General Khatemi, who is realist as well as admirer of US Air Force equipment, has toned Shah down for moment re more highly supersonic aircraft.) In any case, Shah himself has

---

[5] Telegram 568 to Tehran, November 8, transmitted a letter from John McCloy to Ebtehaj stating that it would not be possible to take the latter's testimony by deposition. (Department of State, Central Files, POL 15–1 IRAN)

indicated that about $80,000,000 of new $200,000,000 authorization will have to go for increased costs of already agreed US-Iran military program.

7. Our monopoly is cracking. I am convinced we no longer have ability dictate Shah's policies, including details his military establishment. Our agreement of 1962 was intended to do that. It lasted only until 1964, when revision was unavoidable. But even 1964 agreement was signed under Iranian protest. We hoped our grant aid "sweetener" would retain our dominance. It has not. He has told me he would hate to change American pattern in which his military establishment is molded but unless US recognizes his security requirements he has no choice. Thus his move to obtain $200,000,000 additional authorization from Majlis is not ploy to obtain favor from US (Deptel 591).[6] He is deadly serious. If US were to denounce our 1962–64 agreements, in his present mood, Shah could just as easily obtain additional authorizations from Majlis to replace American military program. In fact, it could be portrayed as another triumph for Iran's independence. Such a move might be foolhardy on Shah's part, but as Ambassador Grady[7] observed years ago, "One cannot assume that Iranians will not cut off their nose to spite their face."

8. Soviet potentiality. While I know my Washington colleauges are weary of Ambassadors raising Soviet bogey, I must place on record these possibilities:

1) Soviet readiness to supply Iran with military equipment even MIGs
2) Shah's interest, revived from 1959 days when he turned Soviets down because West insisted, in non-aggression pact as replacement for onerous Soviet-Iran 1921 treaty. At present Commie clandestine radios are concentrating heavy attack on US-Iran military relationship, urging ouster of ARMISH/MAAG. This is all part of perennial Czarist-Soviet aim of penetration to warm water port. Worth reading is authentic Tudeh document (CAS NIT–6894) where Soviets themselves describe present phase as "cultivating the land" before overthrow of Shah and "imposition of socialism".

9. Art of possible. Given foregoing, it strikes us that most sensible course is for USG to adjust its relationship with Shah to "be responsive to his basic security needs" (Deptel 561).[8] To be rigid and insist on compliance to letter with unaltered 1964 agreement (and his withdrawal of $200,000,000 bill) would defeat very objectives we sought in those agreements. We would lose our influence on Shah in military field and other fields as well. It is much better in our view to hold Shah to aims of those agreements by recognizing that modifications are possible. This will per-

---

[6] See footnote 2, Document 105.
[7] Henry F. Grady was Ambassador to Iran July 2, 1950–September 19, 1951.
[8] Dated November 3. (Department of State, Central Files, AID 6 IRAN)

mit us to retain considerable leverage in his military planning. It will also permit us to use solid citizens like General Khatemi to curb some of Shah's extreme desires (Khatemi has told us of his annoyance that other supreme commanders and sycophants fail to air with Shah Iran's limitations such as trained manpower). Incidentally, it may be that some diversification in sources of Shah's military procurement would be of value to US by removing onus that US is Shah's exclusive support in vital military field. In any case, by maintaining dialogue with Shah re things military we can retain influence in whole spectrum of our relations. Furthermore, by picking up large portion of $200,000,000 business we could help our dollar balance, which we gather is still problem of major concern in Washington.

10. Top priority: second tranche. At moment, our military relationship with Shah, and much of our political relationship, is stymied by lack of response from Washington re second tranche documentation. As indicated in Embtel 611, favorable response with 4 percent interest rate can help us retain fruitful relationship with Shah. In our conversation 25th (Embtel 776), Shah made clear this one problem is fateful road-block in pathway of continued friendly US-Iran relations. In his present mood Shah considers delay as proof positive that Washington has lost interest in him. It is my sincere hope Washington will give us speedy indication that paper-work is cleared, hopefully with 4 percent interest rate. On our end, we can make clear that such rate would not necessarily apply to purchases under new $200,000,000 authorization.

11. Have money, will buy. IBRD has indicated Iran highly creditworthy with capability assume additional $200,000,000 worth of debt annually through 1967 (Embtel 724).[9] Shah is going to buy additional equipment (in effect $120,000,000 more than what we have agreed). To extent possible he wants to "buy American." We think favorable attitude on our part is in our interest: a) to maintain our military cooperation (including strategic facilities); b) to help our gold outflow problem; and c) to maintain friendly political relationship which has until this year been thriving between our two countries. First step is breaking second tranche log jam.

12. Protection of investment. Foregoing is not to suggest that we cater to Shah's every whim. Until now we believe our differences re scope of military program here have been honest differences of judgment. Iran's shift on ChiRep issue, I am convinced, was not premeditated move by Shah. In fact we have every hope of repairing Iran's position to large extent. To influence his behavior re this and other issues we need maintain friendly dialogue which has characterized our relations over years.

---

[9] Dated November 16. (Ibid., DEF 19–8 US–IRAN)

Vast sums we have invested in Iran have succeeded in saving this country from chaos and Communism and Shah knows this. Our help has assisted Iran to stand on its own feet. USAID economic assistance is being terminated. Our technical assistance program is being phased out. Our military aid program is also tapering off. In recommending that we unfreeze second tranche and maintain military cooperation on adjusted basis, our conviction is that this will help insure that after take-off Iran will still remain member of our flying club.

Meyer

---

111.   Telegram From the Embassy in Iran to the Department of State[1]

Tehran, December 2, 1965, 0950Z.

808. Shah and US.

1. In phone call Dec. 01 FornMin Aram said Shah had instructed him to express to us his gratification for USG's favorable response on second tranche interest rate.[2] Aram said Shah is extremely pleased this problem finally settled and happily so. Shah told Aram to reaffirm his desire for continued close harmony in military matters and his wish to "buy American."

2. Since Pak FornMin Bhutto visiting here 2nd, I took occasion to refer Aram to Assistant Secretary Hare's talk with Khosrovani, particularly re important and useful role which Iran is playing in keeping channel open for exchanging information and ideas (Deptel 637).[3] Aram welcomed this word and again indicated Shah and he hope to do some useful missionary work on Bhutto particularly vis-à-vis Pak-ChiCom relations.

Comment: Hare–Khosrovani hand-holding exercise was very helpful.

Meyer

[1] Source: Department of State, Central Files, DEF 19–8 US–IRAN. Confidential. Repeated to Karachi.

[2] Telegram 629 to Tehran, November 29, informed the Embassy that the U.S. Government had approved a 4 percent interest rate to be applied to the second tranche of the $200 million military credit sales program. (Ibid.)

[3] Dated November 30. (Ibid., POL IRAN–US)

112.   Memorandum From the President's Special Assistant for National Security Affairs (Bundy) to President Johnson[1]

Washington, December 4, 1965.

The Shah has promised to send a medical team to Vietnam, and we recommend the attached note thanking him.[2]

He has been in one of his gloomy moods lately, fearing that we're backing away from him. (Ayub's experience has shaken him badly.) But his heart is in the right place; he approved the team almost on the spot because he knows of your personal interest. So this is an inexpensive way of showing you haven't deserted him.[3]

McG.B.

---

[1] Source: Johnson Library, National Security File, Special Head of State Correspondence File—Iran, Shah Correspondence, Vol. I. Limited Official Use. A handwritten notation on the source text indicates that it was received at the LBJ Ranch on December 10 at 9:30 a.m. A second handwritten notation reads: "Passed to Bromley Smith 12–11–65, 3:45 p. JJ."

[2] Attached to the source text is a copy of telegram 683 to Tehran, December 13, transmitting the President's message of thanks to the Shah.

[3] The approval line is checked on the source text.

---

113.   Memorandum for the Record[1]

Washington, December 21, 1965, 2 p.m.

SUBJECT

Minutes of the Meeting of the Special Group (CI); 2:00 p.m., Tuesday, December 21, 1965

PRESENT

Governor Harriman, Mr. Marks, Mr. Komer, Mr. Gaud vice Mr. Bell, Mr. McNaughton vice Mr. Vance, Mr. Karamessines vice Admiral Raborn, General Anthis vice General Wheeler

Messrs. Sayre, Davies, and Maechling were present for the meeting

---

[1] Source: Central Intelligence Agency Files: Job 78–03805R, US Govt—Special Group CI & 303. Secret. Drafted by C.G. Moody, Jr., Executive Secretary of the Special Group (CI).

[Here follows discussion of other subjects.]

3.   *Progress Report on Internal Defense Plan for Iran*

Mr. Davies briefly reviewed the memorandum, explaining that the recent agreement with the Soviet Union for the construction of a steel mill is another manifestation of the Shah's desire for a more independent posture. He explained that an increasing ruble balance over the years would bring closer economic ties between Iran and the Soviet Union.

The Chairman asked if we are prepared to sell the ships and planes requested by the Shah. Mr. McNaughton replied that the question of ships is out. Mr. Komer suggested that we sell planes to the Shah and let the British sell them ships.

The Chairman pointed out that the Shah is concerned over our reliability as a supplier of spare parts for military equipment in light of our recent stand in Pakistan.

Mr. Davies said that the Bureau of Near East Asia supports the Country Team's recommendation that future progress reports be submitted on an Ad Hoc basis. Mr. Komer expressed concern over the complacency of recent reports and apparent concentration on short term factors. He suggested that the Group keep a close watch on Iran.

The Group agreed with the Chairman's recommendation that the Ambassador report quarterly by letter on the situation rather than through an IDP progress report and endorsed Mr. Komer's suggestion that the letter report reflect concern for future contingencies.

[Here follows discussion of another subject.]

C.G. Moody, Jr.
Executive Secretary
Special Group (CI)

---

114.   Telegram From the Embassy in Iran to the Department of State[1]

Tehran, December 29, 1965, 0835Z.

929. US-Iran Military Cooperation.

1. Shah's Purposes. In conversation 28th, Shah made studied effort to persuade USG of: a) what he considers need for $200,000,000 augmentation Iran's military establishment, and b) his desire to maintain US supply pattern to maximum extent possible.

---

[1] Source: Department of State, Central Files, DEF 19 US–IRAN. Confidential. Repeated to CINCEUR, CINCSTRIKE, London, and Paris.

2.   Reasons for Revision. In citing reasoning behind augmentation Shah cited:

A. 1964 Reservations. When 1964 Memo of Understanding was signed Iranian authorities, according to Shah, had made clear their belief that joint military program envisaged was inadequate, particularly since circumstances might change. Furthermore, Iran as independent country had reserved right to alter program if it determined it to be necessary for national self-defense.

B. International Developments. Since 1964, there have been various international developments which have left their imprint on Iran's judgment of its defense needs: (1) Vietnam where USG intervention is necessary but not particularly desirable course of action; (2) Indo-Pak hostilities with lesson that a small nation must have sufficient independent defense capability to handle itself in regional quarrel for up to three months; (3) Cyprus where Soviets playing chameleon role but people of country still suffer; and (4) instability and uncertainty of Arab world as witness collapse of Haradh Conference, Nasser's non-withdrawal from Yemen, Iraq's subservience to Nasser and ever festering Arab-Israel question.

C. Persian Gulf Vulnerability. More specifically Iran's attention is increasingly riveted on Persian Gulf because of: (1) almost inevitable British withdrawal; (2) Syrian and Iraqi agitation re Khuzistan; (3) development of Kharg Island which makes Iranian crude oil exports almost totally vulnerable to one surprise attack; (4) King Faisal's increased interest in cooperating with Iran, but until both have military establishment of reasonable respectability such cooperation is ephemeral; and (5) Iran's obvious destiny along with Saudis, as heirs to British, to protest security and tranquility of Gulf not only from predatory regional threateners but in interest of whole free world.

D. Unfavorable Comparisons. As far as Iran's defense is concerned, Shah believes that USG has "built two-thirds of dam" and should complete it if Iran's defensive role is to be useful. Shah again noted Saudis, who have much less need than Iran, are being allowed to purchase $400,000,000 or more from Western sources, including three battalions of Hawk missiles. He wondered why we continue to "beef up" Turkey in much more favorable way than Iran, e.g. nine destroyers, submarines, etc. (I noted: his impression of US MAP program in Turkey is exaggerated, Turkey has always had much larger military establishment, Turkey has no $500,000,000 annual oil income, and in US public opinion Turkey still ranks high for its effective role with US in Korean War.) Shah went on to point out Soviet-supplied neighbors, notably Iraq, continue to get MIG–21's and other equipment more efficient than what Iran has.

E. US Ally. Making clear his continued dedication to US-Iran alliance, Shah once again said if Soviets cross frontier it would be world war and Iran would count on US support. He believed however that Soviets at least for present have peaceful intentions. If regional hostilities were to develop, Shah added, he doubted, as he had observed to *NY-Times* man Brady, that Iran could "count on" active US military help. Conclusion, therefore, was clear: Iran itself must be in position to cope with such trouble.

3. Nature of Augmentation. Shah listed his additional military needs as follows:

A. Anti-aircraft Defense. Shah said he anxious to have US military expert survey Iran's air defense needs, so as to determine where various items such as Hawks and early warning equipment can most efficiently be installed to give Iran best protection. He said he is considering British bloodhounds but seemed interested when I suggested his greatest threat is from low-level attack which is better countered by Hawks.

B. Aircraft. Shah said there is no question Iran will need higher performance aircraft than F–5. Question is which one. He disclosed he is giving serious consideration to Mirage, which he considers equal to MIG–21. There is also possibility of F–4C but price is probably $2,500,000 or $3,000,000 which is almost twice as much as Mirage. TFX would be best plane but Iran cannot afford aircraft which costs $5,000,000 or more per copy. Shah said his first choice F5X if and when it ever goes into production. As Shah sees picture, two squadrons of one of these higher performance aircraft should replace the eighth and ninth F–5 squadrons which according 1964 agreement Iran would purchase from US. Meanwhile, Shah feels that for efficiency purposes size of present F–5 squadrons should be increased from 13 to 16 planes each. He said Iran is prepared to purchase 21 F–5's necessary to enlarge seven MAP F–5 squadrons to this size.

C. Naval Vessels. Shah said present key question is whether in expanding his naval security capability in Gulf he should get three small vessels (presumably recommended by British to General Toufanian) or one modern destroyer which Chief of Italian Navy recommended (at cost of $40,000,000). Noting problems of manning ships when present Iranian Navy already understaffed, I told Shah he wise in taking careful look before he leaps.

D. Tanks. Shah said his M–47 tanks will eventually be phased out and he remains interested in possibility of Sheridans as their replacement.

4. US Attitude. After appropriate remarks concerning longstanding friendly US-Iran relationship in military field, I told Shah his explanation of situation would be helpful in Washington. It no secret that recent $200,000,000 authorization had caught his US friends by surprise. It not our intention to back-seat drive, but we did have close relationship translated into mutual commitments in 1964 agreement designed to pro-

vide Iran with biggest bang per buck. He must realize questions would inevitably arise in Washington, notably on Capitol Hill, as to need for US-MAP grant component in that program if program ignored by Iran. I acknowledged it is difficult to argue that 1964 circumstances immutable, but at same time we would need valid explanations such as he had just given in order persuade Congress to continue providing necessary funds. It was good particularly to hear, I said, that he continues to respect 1964 agreement, even though he considers modifications necessary.

5.   US Pattern. Shah said it obvious Iran has every interest in continuing to obtain military equipment from US. To change pattern of supply would only compound Iran's military problems. He therefore sincerely hoped that USG would consider his revised needs promptly and let him know at an early date prices, financing terms and availability. He emphasized that while decisions must be made in near future, point is that in most cases it would be two or three years before equipment would actually be delivered.

6.   Economic Frame-work. While appreciating Shah's eagerness to make decisions, I noted that important element in our 1964 agreement was fitting Iranian military program into Iran's economic capability. Shah reiterated his usual points that economic development is useless if it is not secure and that Iran's income is continually rising (again he mentioned $2,000,000,000 target by 1970). Moreover, his Chief Financial Advisor, Central Bank Governor Mehdi Samii, had noted that recent parliamentary authorization for $200,000,000 in fact made it possible for Iran to contract for more than that amount of military equipment if necessary. Shah again noted that 1964 program would cost $280,000,000 or $80,000,000 more than anticipated (including addition of 60 to 90 day supply of ammo. Ninety day supply is necessary, Shah said, because in any case it requires three months to transport matériel from US and offloading of explosives is impossible in heat of Persian Gulf summers.) Shah said his economists had recently produced economic data which made clear Iran's capability for proposed military purchases but he did not seem clear whether this was last annual review or something subsequent. In any case, Shah said he realized USG's interest in economic aspects of his military program and he would assure that appropriate consultations would take place.

Comment. Believe this conversation has been helpful in restoring to some degree dialogue re Iran-US military relationship. At same time it is clear Shah is determined to make early decisions, specifically re anti-aircraft equipment, high performance aircraft, and naval vessels. Re anti-aircraft equipment, we can gain time and keep Shah content by favorable response to request for experts' survey which he has now thrice made (Embtel 850[2] and Shah's talk with Jablonski 23d). Re naval craft, I am sure

---

[2] Dated December 10. (Ibid., POL IRAN–US)

Shah would similarly appreciate some expert US advice. Even though he has not made specific request. Most troublesome item will be aircraft. For year now, Shah has been eager because of long lead-time to make decisions with respect to post F–5 period. Obviously French salesmen have gotten to him glamorizing the Mirage and such representations by French and others will undoubtedly whet his appetite further. One way of forestalling precipitate action in this field would be to provide info re prospects of an F5X. If Shah felt there were hope of his buying F5X, we would not need to worry about Mirages, Lightnings or even MIGs.

Meyer

115.   Editorial Note

When Averell Harriman met with the Shah in Tehran on January 3, 1966, he conveyed President Johnson's greetings and warm appreciation for his support on Vietnam. The Shah said that he had made his position clear on trips to various world capitals, i.e., that stopping aggression in Vietnam, as elsewhere, was a matter of vital principle. Emphasizing the need to recognize world opinion, however, he also stated that he unqualifiedly supported the President's initiative in the bombing pause. He pointed out that resuming the bombing too early would lend credence to Soviet propaganda claiming the U.S. peace moves were a "facade" before further escalation. (Text of telegram 954 from Tehran, January 4; Johnson Library, National Security File, Memos to the President, McGeorge Bundy, Vol. 18, 1/3–2/23/66. Another copy of telegram 954 is in Department of State, Central Files, POL 27 VIET S)

116.   Special Defense Intelligence Agency Intelligence Supplement[1]

SIS–281–66   Washington, January 28, 1966.

ASSESSMENT OF NON-SOVIET THREAT TO IRAN

Conclusions

Iran's Ability to Cope with the Real Non-Soviet Military Threat

The arms inventory of the Arabs continues to increase in quantity and quality, but reportedly for use against Israel. The Arab's capacity to absorb sophisticated equipment is limited, however. Such equipment could be employed on a selective basis against Iran, e.g., Iraqi fighter aircraft, Iraqi and UAR bombers, and UAR naval craft. Its use en toto against Iran is unlikely in the next five years in view of inter-Arab rifts, Arab fears of an Israeli preemptive attack, and of current Arab commitments in Yemen and against the Kurds. Neither the Iraqi ground forces nor the estimated projected improvement of the Iraq Air Force pose a very formidable threat to Iran. The source of Iran's wealth and subsequent ability to develop itself has been and is likely to remain its oil-rich southwest. Iran has recently realized that its concentration at Abadan and the supplying oil fields must be spread out, and it has taken steps to accomplish this dispersion. Additionally, it is developing other capital investments—and potential targets—throughout Iran. Although this dispersion will make each target relatively less important if it is destroyed, concurrently they will become more difficult to defend and will require ever-increasing amounts of defensive equipment—which the Iranians do not have the trained personnel to operate. The Iranian AC and W System currently faces north. Regardless of how tight the Iranian defense system may become, however, some aggressive segment of an attacking force is more than likely going to reach its objective.

Iran's Ability to Cope with the Real Non-Soviet, Non-Military Threat

The urbanization likely to follow the increase in capital development will bring with it the problems already evident in other areas of the world—problems of housing, jobs, and food shortages which provocateurs will attempt to use to their advantage. The mullahs used these problems in June 1963 to instigate the urban riots which were strongly repressed by military forces and which can and probably will be re-

---

[1] Source: Washington National Records Center, RG 330, OSD Files: FRC 70 A 4443, Iran 381, 28 Jan 66. Secret; No Foreign Dissem. The study was prepared in response to a request from the Assistant Secretary of Defense for International Security Affairs.

pressed in the future. The bad effects of the traditional landlord-peasant relationship and the tribal nomadism have been broken, in part, by the land-reform program. This program will continue, but it will be phased so as to disrupt as little as possible. Social reforms will likewise be continued, but at a pace which will not alienate the conservatives. The Medical Corps and the Literacy Corps will receive more emphasis to implement these reforms.

A more literate public will expect a larger share of the economic and social benefits from Iran's oil wealth. This is reported to be true in Khuzistan, the source of the oil, not only of the sizable Arab population there but of the other inhabitants as well; some tribes claim that the oil fields were taken from them. The exact number of Arabs in the population of the province is not known, although reports indicate that at least 100,000 Arabs live in the sugar cane area north of Abadan and another 100,000 live in the date groves to the south. The latest census of Iran (1956) counted about 2,000,000 people in the entire province. An estimate of the number of Arab-speaking people in the province is about 500,000, half of Iran's Arabs.

In line with the historic aversion of the Persians to the "late-coming" Arabs, the Government of Iran until recently had not given much thought to the far-off Khuzistanis, especially the Arabs. Currently, however, it has indicated the district's importance and the potential for subversion of its Arab population. It has increased the amount of government funds spent there and has instituted some repressive measures against the Arabs. Although reports indicate that the Arabs have become less apathetic than heretofore, continued interest in the area by Tehran should preclude the start of the type of terrorism that changed British policy in Palestine and Cyprus and is working against UK presence in Aden.

Possibly a greater danger to the government's operation of the oil fields will occur if the labor unions which are planned there get out of hand. The government is attempting to permit the laborers to "let off steam" by establishing several tightly controlled unions. These unions might merge and subversive elements could inflame attitudes as they did recently in Bahrein. The government appears to have recognized this potential problem. Whether it is willing to mend its autocratic and bureaucratic ways and satisfy the aspirations of the laborers and the other Khuzistanis, including the Arabs, however, is open to question.

[Here follows the body of the paper.]

117. Memorandum From the Joint Chiefs of Staff to Secretary of Defense McNamara[1]

JCSM–67–66   Washington, February 1, 1966.

SUBJECT

1966 Military Survey Team—Iran (U)

1. (U) In response to a memorandum by the Deputy Assistant Secretary of Defense (ISA), I–20358/66, dated 18 January 1966, subject: "Constitution of a Military Survey Team, Iran,"[2] the Joint Chiefs of Staff have requested CINCSTRIKE/USCINCMEAFSA to activate such a team to proceed to Iran by mid-February 1966.

2. (S) As requested, the team will be tri-Service to permit a comprehensive assessment of the full range of the Shah's stated requirements in air defense and for improving the Iranian Navy. The team also will be prepared to address other requirements which may emerge during the course of its in-country survey.

3. (S) The team will be headed by a general officer and such additional technically qualified officers as may be required to examine the following areas:

a. The air threat to Iran and the minimum essential requirements for meeting that threat by a balanced air defense system, composed of a proper mix of air defense aircraft and missiles, supported by an adequate ground environment.

b. The threats to Iranian ports, installations, and shipping in the Persian Gulf and the minimum essential naval surface forces required to counter those threats and to assist in the enforcement of Iranian law in its territorial waters.

c. The minimum essential requirements for meeting other matériel needs; e.g., armor.

4. (S) The team is setting aside two full days prior to departing for briefings as requested by and at the convenience of the Assistant Secretary of Defense (ISA). Additionally, CINCSTRIKE/USCINCMEAFSA has been requested to submit the "US Eyes Only" and sanitized versions of the report to the Joint Chiefs of Staff within ten days after the team has

---

[1] Source: Washington National Records Center, RG 330, OSD Files: FRC 70 A 4443, Iran 091.3 MAP. Secret.

[2] Not printed. (Ibid.) Telegram 992 from Tehran, January 10, reported that the Shah had requested that a U.S. group of experts be sent to Iran to make a long-range air defense study. Meyer urged a prompt affirmative response. (Department of State, Central Files, DEF 1–4 IRAN) On January 20 Meyer and Jablonsky informed the Shah of U.S. readiness to send a tri-service military survey team to make a professional appraisal of Iran's security needs. (Telegram 1040 from Tehran, January 20; ibid., DEF 19–9 US–IRAN)

returned to the CONUS, with advance copies of both reports to be submitted concurrently to you and to the Secretary of State. The views of the Joint Chiefs of Staff on the findings and recommendations of the team will be submitted within three weeks after the team returns.

5.   (S) Detailed terms of reference (see the Appendix hereto)[3] for the survey team have been tailored to center on maintaining the primacy of the US military presence in Iran at a moderate cost to Iranian resources. The objective of keeping Iranian military procurement at a level consistent with legitimate military requirements against the spectrum of threats to Iran, while minimizing the impact of military procurement on Iranian economic development, has been emphasized in the terms of reference and is further reflected in the US Government-approved background data provided in the Annexes hereto. Finally, the terms of reference accommodate the fundamental reality that future military equipment assistance to Iran should be related to its ability to absorb and maintain that equipment.

For the Joint Chiefs of Staff:
Earle G. Wheeler
Chairman
Joint Chiefs of Staff

---

[3] Not printed.

---

118.   **Memorandum From the Assistant Administrator for Near East and South Asia of the Agency for International Development (Macomber) to the Deputy Assistant Secretary of State for Politico-Military Affairs (Kitchen)**[1]

Washington, February 2, 1966.

SUBJECT

Iran's Proposed $200 million Purchase of Military Equipment

I have discussed with Dave Bell Iran's intention to purchase $200 million of military equipment. It is our view that this action by Iran is

---

[1] Source: Department of State, Central Files, DEF 12–5 IRAN. Secret.

contrary to the spirit of the 1962 and 1964 agreements. We believe such a purchase will have an adverse impact on Iran's economic development.

We realize that the U.S. probably cannot prevent Iran from making such a purchase. Moreover, any attempt to do so would likely damage the national and security interests of the U.S. in the Middle East.

Nonetheless, we believe the following steps should be taken:

1. An analysis of the impact on Iran's economic and social development be highlighted in the annual review under the terms of the 1964 agreement, and a) this review in Tehran be attended by a senior representative from AID/W, b) the time for the review be moved up to occur before final agreement on the sale.

2. The Country Team should argue to the GOI that the threat the Shah envisages is not great, but the impact on Iran's economic development would be severe. Iran would be better off to shift its expenditures to capital investment and social progress.

3. In arriving at final agreement, the U.S. should seek to reduce the actual amount purchased and stretch out the delivery time over the longest possible period of years.

4. AID should concur in and help prepare the instructions given to the military team to be sent out in mid-February.

Meanwhile, while discussions are continuing among State, DOD, AID, and the White House Staff, I would propose that no commitment be made to the Government of Iran.

WM

---

119. **Memorandum From the Assistant Secretary of Defense for International Security Affairs (McNaughton) to Secretary of Defense McNamara**[1]

I–21036/66   Washington, February 16, 1966.

SUBJECT

Military Survey for Iran

I. *Problem:*

The Shah of Iran has become increasingly concerned over what he views as a mounting Arab threat to Iran's security. We have accordingly

---

[1] Source: Washington National Records Center, RG 330, OSD Files: FRC 70 N 6648, 381 IRAN 16 Feb 1966. Secret. A stamped note on the margin of the source text reads "Mr. McNaughton has seen."

agreed, after several months of discussion, to conduct a survey of Iranian military requirements against the non-Soviet threat. The Survey Team will arrive in Iran on 16 February.

The Survey Team's Terms of Reference direct that all recommendations be in full consonance with the U.S. objective of maintaining our position as primary arms supplier to Iran, while limiting equipment purchases to legitimate requirements and minimizing the impact on Iran's economic and social development. The Team does require, however, supplemental guidance as to specific items of U.S. equipment it can consider in formulating a response to Iran.

II. Discussion:

As you will recall, the 1964 U.S.-Iranian Memorandum of Understanding called for Iran to purchase two squadrons of F–5 interceptors during the late 1960s to supplement the seven squadrons provided by MAP grant aid. Soon after the agreement was signed, the Shah informed us that the introduction of Soviet-built MIG–21 aircraft into neighboring Arab countries, particularly Iraq, made it "imperative" for him to buy a higher performance aircraft than the F–5. In this context he has mentioned an improved F–5, the F–4 or the F–111 as possible substitutes.

In a study of Iran's air defense requirements prepared for ISA last fall, the Joint Chiefs of Staff indicated their belief that Iran had a genuine need for a higher performance aircraft than the F–5 and recommended that the U.S. sell the Iranians two squadrons (UE–13) of F–4s in the 1967–1973 time frame.

Another of the Shah's felt needs is an anti-aircraft system to defend key air bases and oil installations in western and southwestern Iran. The Shah deferred his decision on choice of weapons pending a U.S. decision on what we intended to procure for U.S. forces. When informed in December that the U.S. had chosen the gun (Vulcan)/Chaparral mix, the Shah expressed interest in procuring the system, providing that price and availability were reasonable. Although I understand U.S. requirements are expected to saturate Vulcan and Chaparral production capacity until FY 70, it might become politically desirable to be prepared to offer Iran one or two battalions from current production before U.S. requirements for 22 battalions are fully satisfied in 1970.

The Shah also wants a tank to replace the M–47s now in inventory, and expressed keen interest in the Sheridan during last year's Annual Review of the 1964 agreement. Army production of the Sheridan is scheduled to peak at 50 a month in FY 68 and a phased delivery to Iran, beginning in the last half of CY 68, could be worked into the Army's production schedule.

In the naval area, the Shah believes he needs destroyer types to meet the threat to his oil installations in the Persian Gulf area, and an Iranian purchase team recently visited Western Europe to secure price and avail-ability data on various equipment items, including new-construction de-stroyers.

In general we believe the Shah exaggerates the non-Soviet threat to Iran, and would like to discourage his purchase of highly sophisticated weaponry. We concede that Iranian air defenses in the southwest could be strengthened and a follow-on tank deserves consideration, but we re-gard the Persian Gulf naval threat as minimal. On the other hand, the Shah has purchasing power and a determination to modernize his forces, so our continued political relations depend on a moderately forthcoming response.

III.   Recommendations:

That you authorize the U.S. Survey Team, Iran, in assessing Iranian requirements, to consider the following U.S. matériel for possible sale to Iran. This authorization would be for planning purposes only.[2] The find-ings of the Survey Team will be subject to a careful interagency review before a commitment is made.

1.   Sale from new production of up to two squadrons (U/E, 13 each) of F–4 aircraft, in lieu of two F–5 squadrons, for delivery in approximate-ly CY 70.[3]

2.   Sale of up to two squadrons of F–5C aircraft, in lieu of F–5A/Bs, for delivery in CY 1968.[4]

3.   Sale of the sanitized Sparrow (AIM–7–N).

4.   Sale from new production of up to two battalions of Gun/Chap-arral for phased delivery between CYs 68–70.

5.   Sale from new production of up to 150 Sheridan tanks, with Shil-lelagh missiles, for phased delivery between CYs 68–70.[5]

6.   Sale from new construction of one DE or DD-type ship (Hull class DD, Dealy Class DE, DEG or DDG) for delivery in CY 70–71.[6]

John T. McNaughton

---

[2] The words "for planning purposes only" are underlined and initialed by McNama-ra.

[3] McNamara initialed his approval of this recommendation on February 19 and add-ed "reluctantly & for planning only."

[4] McNamara initialed his approval of recommendations 2, 3, and 4.

[5] McNamara initialed his approval of this recommendation and added "or earlier if he wishes."

[6] McNamara initialed his disapproval of this recommendation.

120. Letter From the Counselor of Embassy for Political Affairs in Tehran (Herz) to the Director of the Office of Greek, Turkish, and Iranian Affairs (Bracken)[1]

Tehran, February 21, 1966.

Dear Kay:

Your letter of February 4, about obtaining more information on rightist or opposition groups has given us a great deal of trouble.[2] Frankly, the difficulty is that these opposition groups are essentially clandestine, and the national police are hunting for the very kind of information that you are asking us to procure. I know Alan is working on this too, but the Counselor for Political Affairs really has to be very careful not to promise you too much.

On the positive side, we do try to keep contacts with various exponents of the religious milieu, but I must confess that in respect to the kind of information that the Department is seeking these contacts are not too productive. We see [*less than 1 line of source text not declassified*] who is really a government stooge; [*2 lines of source text not declassified*] a highly vocal religious critic of the regime but not a very useful source of information on particular groups; [*less than 1 line of source text not declassified*] a religious-oriented right-wing politician, [*3 lines of source text not declassified*] who is sometimes interesting.

In addition, Archie Bolster has developed a fairly productive contact with [*less than 1 line of source text not declassified*] who seems to know some of the as yet unarrested members of the Islamic Nations Party which was uncovered late last year, but even [*less than 1 line of source text not declassified*] who are obviously against the regime are exceedingly careful to cover their tracks. Because of the inherent interest of Archie's conversations with [*less than 1 line of source text not declassified*] I enclose two copies of recent MemCons[3]—even though they do not really answer the question that you have raised.

You are of course quite right that we learn of the existence of small obscurantist rightist cells or groups only when they find themselves in an "acting" posture, but in this respect it is very difficult for us to be better

---

[1] Source: Department of State, NEA/IRN Files: Lot 70 D 330, Iran 1966, POL 12, Political Parties (general). Secret; Official–Informal.

[2] On February 4 Bracken had written Herz, saying that INR/RNA and GTI were both concerned with the need to obtain more information about the nature and scope of the activities of rightist and conservative opposition groups, including religious groups, in Iran, and their interaction (if any) with each other. This concern had been highlighted by the recent arrests of 55 opponents of the regime. (Ibid.)

[3] Not printed.

informed than SAVAK and the National Police who were taken equally unaware by the Mansur assassination, a fact that still rankles with the Shah and has caused him to ride the internal security people rather hard of late.

The difficulty of getting really deeply into the rather amorphous clerical opposition stems in part from the fact that a Christian foreigner really has little chance of taking its pulse by meeting just a few mullahs and ayatollahs. Also, since Khomeini was banished in the aftermath of the status bill furor, clerical oppositionists are even less pro-American than before. Direct approaches are sometimes rebuffed and the most glaring case of such a counter-productive effort was provided last year by Bill Clevenger when he tried to sound out Ayatollah Qomi in Meshed. Not only did Qomi rebuff him but the rather innocuous conversation seems to have been tape-recorded by SAVAK. All in all, we will try to do better in the future, but we really cannot be too sure.

Incidentally, when the question of the religious opposition was raised at the Consular Conference here last week, I felt that the responses that we got from our consuls were equaled in their inconclusiveness only by the responses to our questions about the Development Corps and the Bakhshdar program. We may be groping in the dark, but I promise you that we will continue to grope and "try harder" to grope a little more effectively in the future.

With warm personal regards,

Sincerely yours,

Martin

121.   Telegram From the Embassy in Iran to the Department of State[1]

Tehran, March 2, 1966, 1250Z.

1185. "Turmoil Gap" in Iran. Shah's speech to Majlis deputies (Embtel 1181)[2] brings together number of significant elements of his thinking, and thus of Iranian policy, on which we have recently reported on basis of private conversations (Embtels 789,[3] 1040,[4] 1041[5]), but some of these ideas have been sharpened and fact that he is making them public shows extent to which his attitudes are hardening.

1.   Pressure on West. It is clear that there is now concerted campaign to increase oil offtake and obtain wanted military equipment from West, coupled with threat to reorient trade patterns if traditional orientation does not yield desired results. That this is campaign is apparent from number of conversations Shah has had with American visitors recently, and from candid comment we received from one of his subordinates who cited recent reports of U.S. aid to UAR and Turkey to conclude that "apparently the only way to get one's way with the Americans is to be difficult."

(Comment: We are of course not rising to this bait and adopting studied attitude of business as usual.)

2.   Pride of Accomplishment. Shah pointed to ten percent growth in Iranian year now drawing to close, stable prices, and two and one half percent population growth, contrasting this with lack of progress in neighboring countries. He sees Iran booming, investments picking up, reform program paying off, prices stable, labor satisfied, farmers working harder. All this ascribed to "the inborn Iranian genius" (for which one may read the genius of Mohammed Reza Shah Pahlavi Arye Mehr).

3.   Critics Have Been Proved Wrong. Both in his speech ("We take no orders") and in recent conversations, Shah has lashed out against foreign and domestic critics and pessimists who have been proved wrong by events. Privately, he has zeroed in on "Harvard economists" (to which one may safely add Iranian economists trained in US who are skeptical about growing Iranian commitments) and served blunt notice that determination of what is best for Iran will henceforth be made by Iranians alone.

---

[1] Source: Department of State, Central Files, POL 15–1 IRAN. Confidential. Repeated to London, Ankara, Karachi, Baghdad, Kuwait, Jidda, and CINCMEAFSA for POLAD.

[2] Dated March 2. (Ibid., FN 16 IRAN)

[3] Document 110.

[4] Dated January 20. (Department of State, Central Files, DEF 19–9 US–IRAN)

[5] Dated January 20. (Ibid., PET 6 IRAN)

4. Guns and Butter. Speech was an emphatic reaffirmation that tempo of economic and social developments will not be reduced and that neither will defense measures be slighted. Shah spoke pointedly of national duty to defend Khuzistan and south Iran "Even if there were no single oil well and no commercial ship passed through (Persian Gulf)" and referred to "various affronts to Iran's position, status, dignity and interests" in Gulf area.

5. Non-dependence on Allies. Evidence that experience of Pakistan during last fall's crisis still deeply troubles him was given when Shah said: "There have been developments in world recently which have been an exemplary lesson to US, that Iran cannot surrender its destiny to whims of foreigners even if they are very close friends... We cannot subject our destiny entirely to decisions of others who can one day help us and another day not help us. This is not only from national point of view. Internationally also it is not dependable."

Comment: We interpret latter point as argument that Iran is really acting in interest of its allies and of world peace by becoming less dependent on West for its defense. He has often pointed out that if US were required to intevene militarily to protect Iran, conflict would be wider and potentialities greater for Communists to create Vietnam type of situation. At same time Shah gave assurance that "Iran still retains the same importance in regard to preservation of regional security which could be interpreted as guarded reaffirmation of CENTO.

While speech contains nothing new, tone is getting shriller and sense of self-satisfaction and grievance somewhat stronger. It is apparent that recent resumption of US aid to Nasser despite his postponement of withdrawal from Yemen, and reports of additional US military assistance to Greece and Turkey pursuant to McNaughton's visit to those two countries (and not to Iran) have added to feeling of Shah and his ranking subordinates that Iran is once more being taken for granted by West, that "papa knows best" attitude of Americans toward Iran's military requirements is an affront to national dignity, that Iran has the means to purchase what it needs for its defense, that present US balance of payments policies threaten Iran's remarkable economic progress, and that best way to deal with Uncle Sam is to make a public scene.

As Art Buchwald would phrase it, there has been a "turmoil gap" in Iran recently. The Shah is aware of this, and would like to fill it; but we still believe that despite certain threats, for instance that he would resort to Soviets for arms procurement, there are prudent limits to any "reorientation" which he is not likely to transgress under present circumstances. Point of concern is when and whether Shah and Iran become captive to "reorientation" speech-making.

Meyer

122.   Telegram From the Department of State to the Embassy in Iran[1]

Washington, March 7, 1966, 3:18 p.m.

903. Following is text of message dated February 26 from Shah to President. Reply in preparation.

"Dear Mr. President,

During my short stay in Austria, I had the pleasure of receiving your letter of January 31, 1966 delivered to me by your Ambassador to that country. I gratefully acknowledged it by a letter sent to you through my Ambassador in Washington.[2]

Some time before that your esteemed and able envoy, Mr. Averell Harriman, whom you had entrusted with the mission to explain the American aims and objectives paid a visit to Tehran and gave me a full account of his mission. We had a long and fruitful exchange of views.

It would be appropriate to observe, Mr. President, that the evil of aggression which has plunged South Vietnam into the miseries of a ruinous war, may also engulf other areas of the world, if adequate measures are not taken in good time to forestall it. The developing course of events in this region clearly shows that my predictions of these past years have not been far wide of mark. Let me add, Mr. President, that unfortunately disruptive elements in the Middle East, in utter disregard of morality, principle and human life are constantly on the look out to carry out their destructive activities in order to be able to maintain their position which they could not otherwise do so in a healthy and orderly community. We are at present face to face with dangers coming from directions which, though clearly foreseen by me, we could not for reasons I would not elaborate here, take adequate measures to provide against them.

I need hardly stress, Mr. President, that my cherished aim in this region is the safeguarding of peace and stability—factors so essential to the implementation of our reforms and further enhancing the prosperity of our people. And perhaps, it will be no exaggeration to say that the political and economic stability of Iran, as so far maintained, has proved to be not only to the advantage of our own country but also of great value to the security and continued stability of the whole region.

---

[1] Source: Department of State, Central Files, POL 15–1 IRAN. Secret; Exdis. Drafted by Crawford, cleared by Bracken and Komer, and approved by Hare.

[2] Telegram 967 to Vienna, January 30, transmitted a message from the President to the Shah informing him that the U.S. and South Vietnamese Governments were ending the suspension of bombing attacks against North Vietnam. (Ibid., POL 27 VIET S) The Shah's February 2 response is in the Johnson Library, National Security File, Special Head of State Correspondence File, Iran—Shah Correspondence, Vol. I.

But we can hardly maintain this situation if we fail to provide ourselves with the necessary facilities and requirements. Recently, however, diminishing United States military assistance coupled with the exchange requirements of our growing population are placing unduly heavy burden on our limited foreign exchange resources, further aggravated by the fact that in comparison with other oil-producing countries of the Middle East, our oil production figures bear no relation to the needs of our greater and growing population.

Faced with this situation and feeling more than ever the grave danger gathering in the direction of our Western and Southern borders, our national interests demand that we lose no time in preparing ourselves to cope with any threat by purchasing our military requirements with our limited foreign exchange at a reasonable price from the United States or look out for other suppliers who are in readiness to offer us better terms and conditions. I earnestly hope that this vital question of our approaches in the United States will receive favourable consideration. I take this opportunity to offer you my heartfelt and sincere wishes for the success and fulfilment of your great task. May God Almighty's blessings be with you in the pursuit of your high ideals and noble work.

Sincerely, Mohammad Reza Pahlavi"

Rusk

---

123. Telegram From the Embassy in Iran to the Department of State[1]

Tehran, March 14, 1966, 1420Z.

1244. Iranian Military Program.

1. Security Preoccupation. During course of lengthy discussion 14th Shah bore down heavily re his military needs and his desire maintain collaboration with US.

2. President's Response Awaited. Shah said he awaiting reply from President Johnson after which he wishes proceed promptly with addi-

---

[1] Source: Department of State, Central Files, DEF 19 US–IRAN. Confidential. Repeated to CINCSTRIKE.

tional military procurement. He stressed hope USG would be responsive, for Iran has every reason to continue in pattern set by long-standing US-Iran military cooperation. He said urgency problem increasing and there no need delay because of annual economic review in June or July. He gratified by expert military advice which is emerging from General Peterson's military survey mission. He confident findings will support his own conviction that Iran does have justifiable additional military needs because of increasing vulnerability of Iran's vital source of wealth, i.e. Persian Gulf region.

3. Shah Determined. Shah said he wanted to make clear that his public as well as private statements re Iran's critical needs and his determination to have them supplied elsewhere if West is unresponsive is not bluff, threat or blackmail. He said UAR receiving SU–9 (Fishpot B) aircraft which superior even to MIG–21's of which Egypt already has goodly supply. Nasser also has 12 destroyers, 9 submarines and number of deadly KOMAR boats, all from Soviets. Iraq recently acquired 20 MIG–21's and now Shah hears they acquiring KOMAR boats. If latter report true Shah said it clearly accentuates Iranian requirements in Gulf area. Urging reasonable terms from USG, Shah said he has heard that price of F4C's is from $3,000,000 to $5,000,000. By contrast, MIG's are available for $600,000. He hopeful US response will be such as to enable him to maintain US-orientation as in past.

4. No Viet-Nam Here. Noting I not aware what President Johnson's response might be, I told Shah he should nevertheless keep in mind US has problems also. We currently carrying thankless burden of stopping aggression in Viet-Nam and American people heavily preoccupied this matter. Congress also leary of USG military programs following sad experience of Indo-Pak conflict. Shah said it is precisely because he does not want Viet-Nam story repeated here that he is pursuing policy of making Iran self-reliant as far as regional security concerned. He noted US in any case not member of CENTO and its bilateral agreement with Iran is directed exclusively at Communist threat. Shah reiterated complete support for what US doing in Viet-Nam and recounted how he had made this clear to Sov Dep FornMin Kuznetsov during latter's visit here week ago. He reiterated his long-standing view that it is in US interest for Iran be able take care of itself.

5. Nature of Collaboration. I told Shah I felt US friendship for Iran was well proven. We delighted country is able stand on its own feet, an objective to which we had made substantial contribution. Our cooperative relations in military field were particularly noteworthy. I felt confident that USG will continue to do what it can to be helpful but he should not build false expectations. If what we might do was not enough, Iran is, as he has emphasized an "independent" country, and it would have to make its own decisions re wisdom of reorienting its philosophy.

6. Agreed Program. Specifically, I said Washington demonstrated responsiveness in sending Peterson mission. While mission's findings still not completed, my impression is that there is growing US awareness of increasing vulnerability of Persian Gulf installations, and this is without regard to who possible aggressor might be. Referring to 1962 and 1964 Memoranda of Understanding, I made clear that whatever emerges from Peterson survey would require revision of 1964 memorandum and coordination with annual economic review. I expressed view consideration of revised military program in connection with annual economic review did not necessarily mean delay in efficient and effective defense program in Iran. Shah was a bit taken aback because he apparently hoped to place orders, either with US or elsewhere, in month or two. However, he recognized validity of 1962 and 1964 memoranda and reluctantly agreed to procedure I had outlined.

7. *Comment.* Shah was in dark mood, particularly at beginning of audience. Again he recounted list of grievances against us, specifically expressing hope that our defense collaboration would not experience same end reached after several years of discussing what he said President Eisenhower called "damn steel mill." He stressed time and again Iran's new policy of "independence" and what an obvious success it is with people of Iran. After my rather frank and strong responses, he mellowed a bit. Upon departing, he expressed appreciation and welcomed further such frank exchanges between "two friends."

In speaking as strongly as he did, Shah no doubt was putting on pressure for favorable response from us re things military. Danger is that endeavors of this type can ultimately become national crusade.

One of problems here is that few people have courage to speak to Shah except in terms he wants to hear. Thus sitting in his regal isolation he conjures up without restraint various illusions and distortions of reality. Continuing dialogue with US officials is therefore desirable. We continue to hope that Secretary Rusk's plans for visit with Shah during CENTO trip will materialize.

Meyer

124.   Letter From President Johnson to the Shah of Iran[1]

Washington, March 15, 1966.

Your Imperial Majesty:

Your letter of February 26th[2] shows how clearly you, too, understand the lesson so vividly confirmed in Vietnam—that "a healthy and orderly community" is the best defense against disruptive elements. That is why I am sending my Secretary of Health, Education and Welfare to see how we can speed progress in helping the Government of Vietnam bolster this first line of defense.

The military campaign there must go on; yet its ultimate purpose is to enable the Vietnamese leaders to press the war against hunger, disease and ignorance. The problem in Vietnam is that both of these campaigns must be waged at the same time, and there are scarcely enough resources—human or otherwise—to go around.

This is the tragic backdrop of so many of our hopes for the security and well-being of free men everywhere. I fully understand your own preoccupation with decisions as to what resources you will allocate to preparing your military forces in case they are needed and your determination that those forces be as effective as you can make them. I myself have been deeply impressed since assuming office with the difficulty, even in a country as bountifully endowed as mine, of making constant choices between programs, all of which are worthwhile. I am coming to believe that the essence of great leadership is the ability to pick from an impressive field the few that are truly crucial.

Every leader must make those choices for himself, but I am pleased that you have sufficient confidence in us to seek our opinion as to how we can most effectively work together. Happily, the findings of the military survey team which has just completed its work will be available for discussion with you in the course of the annual military-economic review later this spring. I might say that Secretary McNamara has been my mainstay in developing revolutionary analytical tools for weighing cost factors in the tremendously complicated choices I must make. I hope that our joint military-economic talks will give us an opportunity to bring that kind of analysis to bear on your problems in whatever ways may prove helpful.

I am reassured by the knowledge that, for many years, our countries have worked together extensively to safeguard peace and stability in the

---

[1] Source: Johnson Library, National Security File, Memos to the President, McGeorge Bundy, Vol. 21. No classification marking. The letter was transmitted in telegram 932 to Tehran, March 15. (Department of State, Central Files, POL 15–1 IRAN)

[2] See Document 122.

Middle East. Wherever our discussions lead, we can be certain that our mutual respect and common goals will enable us to move ahead in honorable cooperation. I look forward to continued close consultation with you as we do our utmost to solve those problems which touch the heart and marrow of people everywhere—the preservation of national security and the search for the best possible lives for our countrymen.

Sincerely,

Lyndon B. Johnson

---

125.   National Intelligence Estimate[1]

NIE 34–66   Washington, March 24, 1966.

IRAN

The Problem

To estimate the main trends in Iranian foreign policy and domestic affairs over the next two to three years.

Conclusions

A. Iran is adopting a more active and independent foreign policy as a result of the Shah's increased confidence in Iran's economic situation, his declining fear of the USSR, and his increasing anxiety about Nasser and other Arab nationalists. Iran's new international stance will provide opportunities for the USSR to expand its presence in the country and will cause difficulties for the US. However, the Shah is well aware that his domestic position and Iran's security depends heavily on US support. Thus he is unlikely to move deliberately to alter the alliance or reduce US activities in Iran. (Paras. 1–10, 13–15)

B. Domestic considerations are unlikely to alter Iran's foreign policy to any great extent over the next two to three years. The Shah will

---

[1] Source: Central Intelligence Agency Files: Job 79–R01012A, ODDI Registry of NIE and SNIE Files. Secret; Controlled Dissem. According to a note on the cover sheet, the estimate was submitted by Raborn and concurred in by the U.S. Intelligence Board on March 24.

probably remain firmly in control, though the bulk of the educated middle class probably will remain estranged from the regime. (Paras. 16–19)

C. Iran's rate of economic growth may be adversely affected by the Shah's ambitious military expansion program. Oil revenues, which are Iran's main source of foreign exchange, are not rising as fast as in the past; the reform program is unlikely to have much effect on the pace of economic development. If, as is likely, the Shah gives priority to his military program, the economic growth rate would probably slow somewhat, accompanied by periods of inflation and recession. (Paras. 21–24)

[Here follows the body of the paper.]

---

126.   Letter From the Shah of Iran to President Johnson[1]

Tehran, March 25, 1966.

Dear Mr. President,

I thank you for your letter of March 16, 1966.[2]

It is a source of satisfaction to see that both of us hold identical views on the best defense against disruptive elements—which, to the detriment of our peace and security, are not wanting in this part of the world.

This region needs nothing more than peace, tranquility, and a healthy political climate. A favorable atmosphere must prevail in order to bring lasting and fundamental solution to centuries-old problems. This truth has been well recognized in Iran, as it is reflected in the pattern of our comprehensive economic and social reforms.

Back in 1963 it was decided that the great reservoir of talents and energies of young men who had finished their secondary school or university education and become eligible for military service should, instead of serving in barracks, be mobilized and effectively employed for economic and social purposes. These young men, upon completion of the first four months of their military training, and initiation in their respective fields, are organized into various corps such as literacy, health and rural development, and sent to the various parts of the country to serve in distant villages and townships. They carry out their allotted duties with great

---

[1] Source: Department of State, Central Files, POL 15–1 IRAN. Secret; Limdis. Attached to a March 28 memorandum from Read to Bromley Smith stating that it had been delivered to the Department under cover of a note from the Iranian Ambassador on March 28.

[2] Document 124.

devotion and play a constructive role in the improvement of social and economic conditions of the rural areas. They have proved to be a transmission vehicle for bringing leadership, guidance, and badly needed services and skills to the remotest areas of our land.

I take pride in saying that in my estimation no other country in the world, with conditions similar to our own, has been able to achieve this remarkable progress in combatting illiteracy and helping provide a better life for its rural citizens. In fact Iran with a population of 25 million has been generally recognized as a pilot country in this field.

In the year past, members of the Literacy Corps have built 4649 schools and taught over 320,000 illiterate adults and children. Our ultimate goal is to stamp out illiteracy from our land within the next ten years.

Similarly, the Health Corps has had a distinguished record of accomplishment in the course of the past year. The medical units of this corps have risen from 117 to 471. These units are scattered in villages all over the country and their services have reached at least 5 million people of our rural areas.

Our country has extraordinary potential for industrialization and for genuine economic and social development. In one of our provinces alone, namely Khouzestan, we are able to bring under cultivation no less than one million hectares of land by utilization and application of modern agricultural methods. The vast land of this province will be irrigated by dams already constructed or in the process of construction. In the same province, plans are under way to produce more than seven million kilowatt-hours of energy.

Plans are also under way for the vast development of petrochemical and chemical fertilizer industries whose products are estimated to meet the growing needs of our own economy as well as the needs of great neighbouring markets like the sub-continent of India, and even the continent of Africa.

I need hardly refer to the immensity of our oil production potential. In the Consortium zone alone the potential proven reserves would permit us to produce some four million barrels of oil per day over the next 50 years.

The increase in oil exports together with the development of our gas and petrochemical industries, no doubt, are bound to expand our foreign exchange earnings by 1970. But evidently the importance we attach to the economic development of the country and the necessity of making utmost use of our foreign exchange resources for this purpose would make it difficult for us to meet all of our security needs from our foreign exchange earnings for the period 1966–70.

It is our confident hope that by 1970 our total revenues from the oil consortium agreement, and income accrued from petrochemical and gas industries and other sources would exceed the annual sum of $1,500 million. In the meantime, that is between now and 1970, however, we might experience some difficulty in making our limited foreign exchange meet the growing deffense requirements.

We are allocating, at present, 70% of our oil revenues for development purposes. In the course of the past year our economic growth has risen by 10%, while general price stability has been maintained and in some cases the prices have shown a downward trend. In order to keep up this pace of growth and to assure the continuation of our revolutionary programs, we are making every effort to accelerate the economic development of the country.

We are strongly determined to stand on our own feet and to undertake the responsibilities of an independent and peace-loving nation with vital interests in the security and stability of this area—a policy which should be welcome to our friends. Thus in the present uncertain conditions and in the face of real dangers in this part of the world we cannot ignore the defense needs of the country. We should be well prepared to cope with any eventuality. If we are strong enough to face these dangers, they may even fail to materialize.

It was in consideration of these facts that our Parliament, in addition to the $200 million agreement with you, authorized a further amount of $200 million, and if necessary authorization for additional amounts would be forthcoming.

Since we have to decide on the utilization of the amounts authorized by our Parliament, I shall be pleased to receive the findings of the military survey team and to be kindly informed of your readiness in securing the necessary requirements with interesting prices. It is our desire to make our purchases in the United States of America and would like to know the extent to which we can be accommodated. I would also be pleased to have your military experts evaluation report.

Upon receipt of the above reports we shall study them and decide on our needs, informing Washington accordingly. We will then await Mr. McNamara to inform us of the quantity of matériel we can purchase with these additional amounts.

We are most grateful to you for the generous material and moral assistance you have so far extended to us.

Let me say in conclusion that I am in complete agreement with you in that wherever our discussions lead, we can be certain that our mutual respect and common goals will enable us to move ahead in honorable cooperation.

Sincerely

M.R. Pahlavi

127.   Memorandum Prepared in the Central Intelligence Agency[1]

Washington, March 30, 1966.

THE SHAH OF IRAN'S CURRENT OUTLOOK

1.   After twenty-five years on the throne of Iran, the Shah is for the first time acting like an independent monarch. He is fashioning his own image as a modern-minded, progressive ruler, no longer in the shadow of the memory of Reza Shah, his iron-willed and despotic father, founder of the dynasty.

2.   Reza Shah abdicated in 1941 in the face of British and Russian invasion of his country. The 22-year-old Mohammad inherited a discredited dynasty, the victim of a shameful defeat, and obviously dependent upon foreign support. There was no national unity. Courtiers and self-seeking politicians confused the frustrated young monarch, and bad advice came from all sides. His first two marriages produced no male heir, a failure which he took as another symbol of his weakness.

3.   The showdown with Premier Mossadeq between 1951 and 1953 was a turning point. When Mossadeq fell, the Shah triumphantly returned from brief exile and began taking direct, forceful charge of his country. His confidence has grown constantly since then. There is today no challenge to his throne, the political opposition is in disarray, and his third wife has produced a Crown Prince, now five years old.

4.   Economically the country is in good shape, and the Shah is confidently proceeding with what he calls his "White Revolution," a broad program of modernization and reform. Concurrently, he has broken his exclusive reliance on the US and is well on his way toward a more independent position between the US and the USSR. He is convinced that this course will enhance his image both domestically and internationally, but in following it he risks moving further away from the US than he now intends.

5.   The Shah's recent acceptance of a Soviet steel mill—a project on which the West had dragged its feet for many years—is a testimony to his new feeling of confidence. But it is also a major breakthrough for the USSR. The mill will be the core of Iran's industrial development program, and will result in the influx of hundreds of Soviet technicians over the next few years. It nonetheless gives substance to the Shah's repeated warnings that, while he does not intend to change his country's pro-Western orientation, he will not hesitate to go elsewhere if the US cannot meet his needs, and has been warmly welcomed by the Iranian public.

---

[1] Source: Central Intelligence Agency, DOD/NE Files: Job 80–00105A, IRAN, Historical File for Chief ME (J.R. Critchfield), Book 1. Secret; No Foreign Dissem.

6.　The Shah acknowledges the danger from the USSR, but insists on his ability to deal with Moscow without serious risk. In his eyes, the only immediate threat to Iran comes from those Arab states, including Iraq, which he sees as dominated by Nasir. For defense against this threat, he believes Iran needs faster fighter aircraft, better air defense, and a stronger navy in the Persian Gulf, primarily to protect the vital southern oil regions. The Shah is no longer willing to listen to US arguments that Iran cannot afford such equipment. Oil revenues are increasing, and he is pressing the foreign oil companies for even greater production. He has received a credit authorization from parliament for $200 million to buy arms.

7.　For logistical reasons, the Shah prefers to buy US equipment, but will probably turn instead to Western European countries if the US is not forthcoming. He has intimated that as a last resort he might turn to the USSR. Such a move would represent a turning point in his relations with the West and could, if carried out on a large scale, accomplish a major current Soviet objective, the withdrawal of the US military mission in Iran.

128.　Memorandum From the President's Special Assistant (Rostow) to President Johnson[1]

Washington, April 7, 1966, 4:30 p.m.

The Shah answered your last letter[2] almost immediately. He obviously wants to assure you that he is not neglecting his economic revolution in pressing for more arms. He details his achievements—combatting illiteracy, improving rural life and public health, bringing new land under modern cultivation, development of a fertilizer industry. Then he explains how growing oil earnings should put Iran on its feet by 1970. Between now and then, however, he will need help in building an effective military while continuing to devote most of his resources to development.

We're walking a tightrope between bowing to his intention to be master in his own house and keeping his military spending within rea-

---

[1] Source: Johnson Library, National Security File, Memos to the President, Walt W. Rostow, Vol. 1, 4/2–5/26/66. Secret.

[2] Documents 124 and 126.

son. JCS is now reviewing our recent survey of the Shah's military requirements. You will have a crack at the final package (much of it will be credit sale), and we will thrash it out with him in our annual military-economic review.

The attached reply, *for signature if you approve*,[3] reassures him that we will not dismiss his security needs lightly but it does not prejudice your final decision.

Walt

---

[3] An unsigned copy of the letter sent on April 11 is attached; see Document 129.

---

129.   Letter From President Johnson to the Shah of Iran[1]

Washington, April 11, 1966.

Your Imperial Majesty:

Iran's signal progress in education and literacy, in health, in social and economic development, and in agriculture, recounted in your letter of March 25, is most impressive. I sense your pride and I share your pleasure in these accomplishments.

I fully understand the importance that you attach to making the necessary defense decisions that will protect and promote Iran's security and progress. To that end my government is earnestly making a careful examination of the defense and security situation as it affects us both—what Iran's needs are and how the United States can help to meet them. The report of the military survey team is now under review by the Joint Chiefs of Staff and the Department of Defense. One purpose of this review, the necessity for which I am sure Your Majesty can appreciate, is to determine the most favorable prices that can be offered for the equipment recommended by the military survey team. Once this is completed, the report will be forwarded to you to permit thorough study by your government before the Annual Review.

---

[1] Source: Johnson Library, National Security File, Special Head of State Correspondence File, Iran—Shah Correspondence, Volume II. No classification marking.

Ambassador Meyer has informed me that he expects to receive soon from your government the economic data needed for the Annual Review. Once both military and economic data are in hand and have been analyzed, I believe our two governments should be able to reach a prompt conclusion as to our future military cooperation.

Let me assure you, Your Majesty, that the United States Government wishes to promote the dual objectives of economic advance and national security which you have outlined so effectively in your letter. And we mean to do this as expeditiously as possible.

Sincerely,

Lyndon B. Johnson

---

130.   Telegram From the Embassy in Iran to the Department of State[1]

Tehran, April 12, 1966, 1355Z.

1370. President's Message re Iran-US Military Cooperation. Re Deptel 1002.[2]

1.   Handed President's message to Shah during audience 12th. After reading it intensively, Shah agreed with me that it reflects healthy progress. He asked me to convey his gratification to President. He thought for time being no further correspondence required since matter appears to be on rails.

2.   Shah noted, it has been five months since he received emergency authorization from Parliament for $200,000,000 augmentation. He said although there is certain amount of urgency he will defer purchasing little while longer but he hopes USG can expedite matters so that survey report and economic review can be completed prior to his departure May 27 for three state visits. I said my impression is Washington desirous cooperating provided Iranian economic data is promptly provided.

---

[1] Source: Department of State, Central Files, POL IRAN–US. Secret; Limdis.

[2] Telegram 1002 to Tehran, April 11, transmitted the President's message (Document 129) to the Embassy for delivery to the Shah. (Department of State, Central Files, POL IRAN–US)

3. Shah said economic data being expedited. He wanted to make clear however, as he had in his most recent letter to President, that Iran's future earnings must be taken into account when determining security program which Iran can afford.

4. Shah added that while he supposed President not in position to do so, it would be helpful if USG authorities could as occasion permits impress on oil consortium members point he has been trying to make that it is in interest of oil industry and free world generally to assure that Iran has adequate income to support appropriate security program as well as Iran's highly successful economic development (as over against furnishing vast sums of money to tiny sheikhdoms who are not as dependable nor influential as Iran in preservation of stability of Gulf region in interests of free world).

5. Shah gratified that in first two months of 1965 consortium offtakes were up over 20 per cent that of year ago but noted in March they only 13 per cent. Average is 17 per cent. He anxious that at least 17 per cent be sustained as year's average.

Comment. We will continue to press Iranians for economic projections. Central Bank Governor Samii indicates they are prepared and before PriMin for consideration. At same time, we hope Washington can cooperate in processing of Peterson Report with view to May 21 as target date for annual review. Our comments on latter forthcoming next day or two.

Meyer

---

131.   **Telegram From the Embassy in Iran to the Department of State**[1]

Tehran, April 18, 1966, 0745Z.

1397. Hare Talks with Shah and PriMin.

1. In wide-ranging 1-1/2 hour talk 17th with Asst Sec Hare, Shah rehearsed well-known themes. They included: unpredictability of Iraq and readiness of Arabs to serve as Commie tools require Iran's being able

---

[1] Source: Department of State, Central Files, POL IRAN–US. Confidential. Repeated to Ankara, Karachi, London, and CINCSTRIKE/CINCMEAFSA.

cope with regional military threats; even if available, foreign intervention as by friendly US not desirable except of course in event of Soviet aggression which unlikely; Soviet objectives remain unchanged, i.e. penetration of Mideast leap-frogging Iran; specific Soviet objective which is clear from regular Moscow broadcasts is interdiction of West's oil supply from Mideast; Soviet arms are continuing to pour into UAR, Iraq and Syria; Soviet penetration of UAR and Red Sea area already well advanced; Iran must protect its wealth-bearing Khuzistan area; disarmament is ideal but only possible if Arab military establishments controlled; Shah hopes to continue receive his military equipment from US and hopes USG won't let this issue turn into another "steel mill business" and in general Shah urged US (and oil consortium) should support Iran's "command position" in Gulf and Mideast areas.

2. Asst Sec Hare conveyed Secretary Rusk's greetings (which Shah reciprocated); volunteered some observations of Iraqi scene as he had just observed it; complimented Shah on success to date of his various reform programs including literacy corps; discounted Shah's alarmest assessment of Soviet penetration of Arab world but said we maintaining alert observation of situation; assured Shah USG giving expeditious attention to its part of current military-economic deliberations; and stressed that economic development and adequate security must go hand in hand.

3. Of particular interest were Shah's views re CENTO. While acknowledging CENTO's value in economic and communications matters, Shah felt it had not met expectations as military organization, e.g. no command structure, etc. Its collapse, however, would be victory for CENTO's critics. Shah said alternatives for replacing CENTO should be carefully studied. As for himself, he would like to see grouping of Afghanistan, Pakistan and Iran, with Iran because of its wealth and effective leadership playing key role. Form of this grouping not clear and Shah has not broached subject to Paks or Afghans. It doubtful if Turkey could be included because of its NATO affiliation. Nevertheless, Shah been giving some thought to revivification of Saababad Pact. He frankly admitted there no ready-made alternative to CENTO but all alternatives should be seriously studied. Asst Sec Hare agreed future of CENTO deserves thorough study but at same time pointed out CENTO has had and continues to have significant value. Shah indicated Iran does not intend to cause any controversy at forthcoming CENTO Ministerial conference since he believes intimate discussions more feasible and useful.

4. Later in lengthy dinner discussion, PriMin Hoveyda emphasized Iran's need to continue its remarkable economic progress. He said economic projections for our Annual Review before him for consideration and they will show Iran's determination to maintain 8 percent growth rate. He made usual plea for American investments and USG in-

fluence on oil consortium for increased offtakes from Iran (noting that French are taking active interest in financing Iran-Soviet pipeline and in securing new oil concession in Iran). At same time PriMin echoed Shah's views re essentiality adequate military establishment, Asst Sec Hare pointed out it was not simply matter of determining military needs but for USG it was practical problem of what USG can do, pursuant to Congressional authorization, to meet those needs.

5. On departure Shah asked that his best wishes be conveyed to President Johnson and Secretary Rusk.

Comment. While not much new emerged from these conversations they were very useful in allowing Iran's two top leaders to present their case first-hand to a top USG official. Shah had obviously given his presentation forethought for it did not require more than a few minutes for him to swing into an appeal for USG forthcomingness in current discussions re Iran's military needs. Once he had delivered his preordained words, Shah loosened up and latter part of discussion, particularly re CENTO, was natural and mutually responsive. PriMin Hoveyda, as usual, was informal and friendly throughout, pleading his case from depth of a heart thoroughly dedicated to economic progress of his country. All in all visit was successful as timely manifestation that USG continued to value Iran's friendship.

Meyer

---

132.   Memorandum of Conversation[1]

Ankara, April 19, 1966, 7:05 p.m.

PARTICIPANTS

United States	Iran
The Secretary	Foreign Minister Aram
Assistant Secretary Hare	
Mr. Patricelli	

SUBJECT

United States–Iran Relations

The Foreign Minister, noting that he was speaking at the Shah's request, raised the question of "the purchase of arms, which was very dear

---

[1] Source: Department of State, Central Files, POL IRAN–US. Secret. Drafted by Robert E. Patricelli on April 21 and approved in S on May 3. The source text is labeled "Part VI of VIII." The meeting took place at the Ambassador's residence. Secretary of State Rusk was in Ankara heading the U.S. observer delegation to the 14th Ministerial Council session of the Central Treaty Organization. Briefing material and other memoranda of conversations from Rusk's trip are ibid., S/S Conference Files: Lot 67 D 305.

to His Majesty's heart." He referred to the recent exchange of correspondence between President Johnson and the Shah, and said that His Majesty had been very pleased with the last reply from the President. He stated that the Shah was waiting anxiously to see what General Peterson's report on Iranian arms requirements would conclude. His Majesty felt that Iran was a stable country in the midst of a number of less stable nations, and that it was to the advantage of Iran's friends that she remain stable. She had to be strong, therefore, but in fact she was weak in the Persian Gulf and her air force was inferior to Iraq's. Thus, His Majesty wants very much to purchase arms from the U.S. on favorable terms, but if the terms were unfavorable Iran would have to look elsewhere. The Foreign Minister hoped that the U.S. would not take offense at this kind of statement, for Iran remained a staunch friend of the U.S. Rather it was a matter of the independence of the country and of her stability.

The Secretary said we understood and would examine carefully the Shah's proposals in a helpful spirit. The Secretary said that we did not take offense. His Majesty is responsible for Iran and we are responsible for the U.S. And we are two strong, independent, self-respecting peoples. The Foreign Minister stated that he would like to have something to carry back to the Shah about the possibility of purchase of arms in the U.S., and the Secretary asked Assistant Secretary Hare to cable Washington to determine the status of the Military Mission's report. We will try to have something soon for the Foreign Minister.

The Secretary observed that His Majesty was a remarkable man, always looking ahead and anxious to achieve great performance. If the Shah reflected back ten or fifteen years, he might well conclude that Iran had never been more secure or economically sound and might feel reassured at her success, for which he himself had been largely responsible. We understood his nervousness about Baghdad and Egypt, but those were minor league threats compared to the Soviet threat which had been much more serious.

133.   **Telegram From the Department of State to the Embassy in Iran**[1]

Washington, May 3, 1966, 4:21 p.m.

1094. Joint State–Defense message. Embtel 1481.[2]

1.   Sanitized version Peterson Report[3] pouched to you by separate means for delivery to General Aryana and Shah. Total package recommended by report is estimated to cost approximately $308 million. While it is possible that cost may be reduced by such factors as greater equipment austerity, lower usage rates, lower maintenance requirements, reduced volume of supporting equipment, greater in-country maintenance and overhaul, and later delivery dates, these factors have already been partially applied to original cost-out which was substantially higher than $308 million. Therefore major further reductions may be difficult to achieve.

2.   An additional factor is requirement for about $80 million to fund remaining items in Annex B to 1964 Memorandum of Understanding (Hawk battalion, M–60 tanks, and electronics gear) as against a remaining $60 million of uncommitted credit. Therefore to fund both these agreed items and total Peterson package would require new credit of about $328 million. This in turn would require raising Iranian credit ceiling from present $200 million to $528 million.

3.   State, AID and Defense agree that Iran's total credit should be held within a $400 million ceiling, given Iran's foreign exchange position, estimated future revenues, and economic development needs. Also, MAP funds required to guarantee loans by other institutions are expected to be relatively stringent. Therefore, even if Team report is considered to reflect legitimate military requirements, it will be necessary inform Shah that credit limitations will force a deferment of substantial elements of package beyond 1971. We concur in proposed priority items for deferments as set forth in sanitized version of report, but would expect give Shah wide discretion in determining mix of US-approved items. They would reduce new credit requirement by about $144 million or down to approximately $184 million. When added to present credit of

---

[1]   Source: Department of State, Central Files, DEF 12–5 IRAN. Secret; Immediate; Limdis. Drafted by Hoopes; cleared by Director of the AID Office of Greece–Turkey–Iran–Cyprus–CENTO Affairs John H Funari, Deputy Assistant Administrator for Programs in AID's Office of Program Coordination Gordon Chase, Warren, and Bracken; and approved by Davies. Also sent to ARMISH MAAG, IRAN and repeated to CINCSTRIKE.

[2]   Dated May 3. (Ibid.)

[3]   A copy of the Report of the U.S. Military Survey Team to Iran, March 22, is in the Johnson Library, National Security File, Robert W. Komer Files, Iran—Report of U.S. Military Survey Team (Peterson Report), February 16–March 3, 1966.

$200 million, this would hold total credit within desired $400 million ceiling. At same time, we believe these particular deferments would not adversely affect planned improvement of Iran's air defense and naval capability which we understand is Shah's primary concern.

4. While firm USG position not yet established, it probable that all items recommended in Peterson Report will be approved for sale except US destroyer. DOD likely take negative position on either US reserve fleet DD or new construction DD. In that event, there would probably be no USG objection if Shah wished turn to UK for destroyer type vessel (either new or used), but USG would have to be satisfied that aggregate of US and UK purchases were sustainable by Iranian economy.

5. Economic review now underway here should shed additional light on capability of Iranian economy. We are certain however that USG will be unable to support an add-on package exceeding $150–$200 million over next five years.

6. In handing Shah Peterson Report it important you make clear that it does not now represent USG position, that its proposals appear to involve in aggregate a cost which exceeds feasible credit limits, and that deferment of some items beyond 1971 is unavoidable and subject review at that time. Suggest you do not raise matter of a probable negative US position on destroyer sale, and give noncommittal answer if pressed.

7. Firm USG position on all issues will be established in time for annual review on May 19.

Rusk

---

134. **Telegram From the Embassy in Iran to the Department of State**[1]

Tehran, May 4, 1966, 1000Z.

1485. Iran Military Purchasing. Ref Deptel 1094.[2]

1. Peterson Report handed to Shah morning 4th. Meanwhile General Jablonsky has made it available to General Aryana.

2. Without discussing report itself, I conveyed to Shah key points of reftel. I pointed out augmentation recommended by Peterson estimated total $308 million, although there some possibility shaving few dollars

---

[1] Source: Department of State, Central Files, DEF 19–8 US–IRAN. Secret. Repeated to CINCSTRIKE/USCINCMEAFSA.

[2] Document 133.

here and there via routes suggested in reftel. Shah said while Iran might not require equipment of too much sophistication, as far as spare parts, training and usage concerned he could not treat his military personnel with less care than US treats its military personnel.

3. Pointing out USG desires maintain total ceiling of $400 million ($200 million envisaged in 1964 Memo of Understanding plus $200 million authorized last fall by Iran Parliament), I noted that some items would have to be deferred but Shah would have discretion in determining mix of US-approved items. Shah said he has no intention of spending dollar more than is necessary, but he cannot "play with fate" of his country. Once again he called attention to billions of dollars of wealth in southern Iran and said it would be foolish to risk its loss for few million dollars. He considers these expenditures as "insurance." In this connection, he said "recent developments" (Nasser's threats against territory of Saudi Arabia) prove that his concern is not idle and that possibility cannot be ruled out that Nasser's influence will reach Persian Gulf area. I, as usual, expressed view he is overestimating imminence and nature of such danger.

4. Later in discussion, Shah said he has report that Turks are seeking $2,000 million in new military assistance from US, including 3,000 tanks, I expressed doubt. *Comment:* In Shah's mind there is obviously contrast re what USG providing Turkey via grant as over against much lesser amount we willing to permit his more opulent country to buy. Pri-Min yesterday also asked me re Turk aid, noting GOI has received report from its Embassy Washington giving various military aid figures deduced from Congressional reports.

5. Shah concluded conversation by expressing hope USG will realize importance of "solidifying" its relations with those countries who still want close and friendly ties with us. I assured him it remains our desire to have healthy relationship with Iran, noting, however, at same time that America is bearing heavy burdens notably Viet-Nam which sometimes limit what we are able to do elsewhere.

6. *Comment:* Audience was short one for until Shah has had opportunity to study Peterson Report I saw no purpose in getting into details or going beyond general observations set forth in reftel. Shah agreed we would discuss specifics during annual review exercise following my return from Washington.[3]

Meyer

---

[3] In telegram 1500 from Tehran, May 6, Meyer reported that the Shah's initial reaction to the Peterson Report centered on two points: 1) queries regarding the price of each item in the proposed program; and 2) the need for expediting and increasing the number of all-weather high performance aircraft. (Department of State, Central Files, DEF 19–8 US–IRAN)

135.   Intelligence Memorandum[1]

No. 0813/66   Washington, May 6, 1966.

US-IRANIAN RELATIONS

1.   US-Iranian relations may reach a critical point this month over the issues of Iranian military purchases and the Iranian drive to increase oil revenues. An annual joint survey of the Iranian economy is under way now, and the report of the US Military Survey Team to Iran (Peterson Report) has been completed and was submitted to the Shah on 4 May. Analysis of these two reports in Washington will determine the extent to which large Iranian military expenditures in the US are economically feasible. In addition, the Oil Consortium will determine this month how much to increase its oil offtake (exports) from Iran. The Shah considers a large increase essential to finance his military and economic programs.

2.   The Shah is determined to make major military purchases in the near future to bolster defenses in oil-rich southern Iran and in the Persian Gulf, which he believes are endangered by the ambitions of Egyptian President Nasir. The Iranian parliament in November approved additional military expenditures of up to $200 million. The Shah would prefer to make these purchases in the US, but has made it clear that he will turn elsewhere if this proves too difficult.

3.   The US takes the position that these purchases can be approved only in the context of an annual joint review of the Iranian economy. The annual review grows out of a US-Iranian Memo of Understanding in 1964. In essence, the review provides economic information which Washington will analyze to determine whether Iran can afford increased military expenditures and still maintain rapid economic development. The Shah finds such limitations irritating and insulting, particularly in the light of his new "independent" foreign policy.

4.   The arms issue is complicated by the completion of the Peterson Report. This report appears to be more in line with the Shah's thinking—it acknowledges the Arab threat to Iranian security and recommends stronger defenses in the southern provinces and the Persian Gulf. The additional recommended armaments would require a credit of $328 million over the $200 million credit extended under the 1964 agreement.

5.   However, the State Department has tentatively determined (pending completion of the annual review) that the new credit must not

---

[1]   Source: Central Intelligence Agency, DDO/NE Files: Job 80–00105A, IRAN, Historical File for Chief ME (J.R. Critchfield), Book 1. Secret; No Foreign Dissem/CIA Internal Use Only. Prepared by the Office of Current Intelligence in the Central Intelligence Agency's Directorate of Intelligence.

exceed $184 million, thus requiring that the Shah postpone a substantial portion of the arms purchases until after 1971. In addition, the US Embassy in Teheran has expressed its concern over the magnitude of the prices listed in the Peterson Report, and fears that the Shah will be disturbed also. Thus, although all the Shah's wished-for purchases except a prestigious destroyer apparently will be approved in principle, the Shah may well find the delay on some items, and the prices, unacceptable. Completion of the annual review probably will not substantially alter the US position. It is quite conceivable that the Shah will use the Peterson Report to counter State Department arguments against immediate heavy expenditures.

6.   The oil issue is locked in closely with the foregoing. Members of the Oil Consortium may reach a decision this month on the rate at which they will increase oil offtake. As of late April, the member companies were thinking in terms of a 10.5-percent, or at most 12-percent, increase over 1965 production. The Shah insists, however, that the rate must be at least 17 percent if Iran is to carry out its economic and military programs without "reorienting" its trade pattern. Both the US and British companies in the consortium argue that they are producing as fast as possible, and each group accuses the other of holding back production. A final meeting was scheduled for 10 May, but apparently has been temporarily postponed because the Shah has invited some company heads to Teheran for discussions later in May. The US fears the consequences of a major confrontation between Iran and the consortium, and has been encouraging US companies to raise their production as much as possible.

7.   The Shah, bolstered by his rapprochement with the Soviets and by political stability and economic growth at home, has exhibited an increasingly independent spirit in the past year. He is determined to obtain new military equipment soon, and there is little doubt that he will turn elsewhere if the US does not sell quickly and on favorable terms. He has felt for some time that the US takes Iranian friendship for granted, and he regards the arms question as a crucial test of US support and sincerity. He is equally determined to increase oil revenues, and may well be serious in his threat to shift at least part of Iran's trade to the East, where export prices are lower and terms are easier. This could, in turn, put a brake on the growing US private investment in Iran, as well as affect our general politico-military relationship with the country.

136. Memorandum From the President's Special Assistant (Rostow) to President Johnson[1]

Washington, May 12, 1966, 11 a.m.

Ambassador Meyer asked to see you *tomorrow*[2] chiefly to get your personal greetings for the Shah. However, he is here to work out our position on a new $200 million arms sales package, which he will be discussing with the Iranians next week at our annual joint economic-military review. You will get a formal recommendation shortly. AID feels the Shah should not spend his money on arms because the purchase could strain his resources to the point of requiring renewed U.S. budget support. State believes the Shah is determined to buy—he has told you so in his last two letters—so our best bet is to try to control his buying by selling ourselves. So you may want to hear Meyer's views firsthand.

Suggested talking points:

1. Meyer should carry *your personal greetings to the Shah.* You especially *hope the new Prince is doing well.*

2. He should express *your appreciation for the Iranian medical team in Vietnam.*

3. He should also give the Shah *a private message from you:* You are concerned about reports that the Shah feels we are trying to run Iran for him. You want to assure the Shah of your fullest respect for him as a leader. When you express your views, you are not advising him. But you are deeply interested in the progress of his economic revolution and often want to share your thoughts, as only friends can.

4. You are *worried to hear that new arms sales will create a serious debt burden. You are interested in Meyer's views.*

5. You *count on Meyer to make serious business of the annual economic military review.* (He feels it has already accomplished its purpose by forcing the Iranians to face up to shortage of resources and to set priorities. But we ought to continue to press them on economic issues in next week's talks rather than just negotiating the arms package.)

6. Meyer should understand that *if these arms purchases cause a financial crisis, it will be very difficult for us to justify bailing Iran out.* You count on Meyer personally to make sure the Iranians fully understand

---

[1] Source: Johnson Library, National Security File, Country File, Iran, Memos & Miscellaneous, Vol. II, 1/66–1/69. Secret. A notation in the President's handwriting on the source text reads: "Put on my desk—L."

[2] On May 5 Rostow sent the President a memorandum suggesting that he meet with Ambassador Meyer while he was in Washington in order to get his first-hand analysis regarding the new military credit sales package for Iran, which was going to be the biggest issue in U.S.-Iranian relations that year. The President agreed. (Ibid.)

the economic consequences of these purchases and to raise the red flag at the first danger signal.[3]

Walt

---

[3] Johnson held an off-the-record meeting with Ambassador Meyer and NSC staff member Howard Wriggins on May 13 from 1 to 1:28 p.m. The President's Daily Diary notes that the discussion centered on the hopeful changes in Iran in the past 2 years as well as the problems associated with the Shah's desire for large military imports. (Ibid.)

---

137. Memorandum for the Record[1]

Washington, May 12, 1966, 2:30 p.m.

SUBJECT

Near East–South Asia IRG Meeting;[2] Thursday, 12 May 1966 at 2:30 PM

1. The general subject was U.S. relations with Iran; the specific problem was the proposal to respond to the Shah's request to buy additional arms from American manufacturers with favorable credit terms underwritten by Defense.

2. *Background:*

a. In 1964 negotiation, USG agreed provide $200 million arms aid, 10 years @ 4% terms. Currently under negotiation are final arrangements of third tranche of this 1964 package.

b. Several months ago the Iran Parliament authorized the Iran Government to expend an additional $200 million on foreign arms procurement.

c. 1964 agreement included provision that USG would annually review the viability of Iran economic development to ensure defense spending did not undermine economy.

---

[1] Source: Central Intelligence Agency, DCI Executive Registry Files: Job 80–R01580R, IRG. Secret. Drafted on May 13 by Chief of the Near East and South Asia Division in the Directorate of Operations James H. Critchfield.

[2] The Interdepartmental Regional Group for the Near East and South Asia (IRG/NEA) consisted of members from the Departments of State and Defense, the Central Intelligence Agency, the Joint Chiefs of Staff, the Agency for International Development, the U.S. Information Agency, and the White House.

d. In February 1966, General Peterson of STRICOM visited Iran and reviewed (1) the character of the military threat to Iran and (2) a proposed arms package that would meet this threat.

e. When costed out, General Peterson's package adds up to well over $300 million, i.e. more than $100 million more than Iran Parliament provided.

f. General Peterson's report for the first time included USG recognition of the threat to Iran as the result of massive Soviet involvement with and support of a variety of revolutionary elements in the Middle East. (Footnote: This estimate was written in Tampa and included in a document signed by U.S. and Iran military prior to consultation with either the Ambassador or the intelligence community. After expressing some irritation, Ambassador Meyer and the State Department elected to live with this fait accompli. Indeed, Ambassador Meyer is now exploiting it.)

g. The CIA member of the IRG/NEA transmitted a proposal to Ambassador Hare on 22 March 1966 proposing an early IRG consideration of the dangers apparent in the present state of our relations with the Shah. Ambassador Hare responded by calling to the attention of the CIA representative NIE 34–66[3] on Iran (basically reassuring), but agreed to put Iran on the IRG agenda at an early date.

h. During late April and early May, Ambassador Hare visited the Middle East, including Iran.[4]

i. NIE 34–66 approved by USIB on 24 March 1966 concluded:

(1) that the Shah was unlikely to move deliberately to alter the alliance or reduce U.S. activities in Iran.
(2) that Iran's rate of economic growth could be adversely affected by the Shah's ambitious military expansion program.

j. An OCI Memorandum (CIA Internal Use Only) dated 6 May 1966[5] observed that:

(1) U.S.-Iranian relations may reach a critical point this month over the issues of Iranian military purchases and the Iranian drive to increase oil revenues.
(2) the Shah would prefer to make military purchases in the U.S. but has made it clear he will turn elsewhere if this proves too difficult.
(3) the Shah found the insistence on the part of the USG that any agreement to provide additional military purchases be related to the annual review "irritating and insulting, particularly in light of his new 'independent' foreign policy".

---

[3] Document 125.
[4] For a report on Hare's meeting with the Shah on April 17, see Document 131.
[5] Document 135.

3. *IRG Discussions:*

a. Ambassador Hare provided a lucid analysis of the long history of USG involvement in the internal affairs of our military and aid clients, concluding with the observation that we are in a new phase; we have seen the end of the "client relationship". The close relationship must be modified, he said; it will be different but it will not disappear. His assessment of the Shah's attitude coincided with that which has been reported [*less than 1 line of source text not declassified*] by Ambassador Meyer.

b. Mr. Hoopes (ISA/Defense) reviewed the status of the old 1964 agreement (third tranche of $60 million under negotiation of credit terms) and summarized the history of the new proposal. Regardless of Defense agreement with the Peterson Report, limitations on MAP resources would, he thought, limit a new package to approximately $180 million); the 10-year and 4% credit would be difficult to arrange but Defense would attempt it. Hoopes thought this package would, with luck, barely meet the Shah's requirement; Ambassador Meyer agreed.

c. AID was entirely negative, deprecated the threat to Iran (rather incompetently), argued for tough handling of the Shah (shades of the 1961 Iran Task Force!) and stuck to the position that the Iran economy could not support the $200 million additional arms purchase. State, falling back on IBRD and IMF judgments, disputed some of the AID premises. Ambassador Meyer also challenged AID. Ambassador Hare acknowledged that the AID position was probably sound but unrealistic and wishful thinking; Ambassador Meyer agreed.

d. I said that the Agency supported both the assessment of Ambassador Hare and that of Ambassador Meyer (as I understood them). In describing the Agency position I use the language (*but made no reference to*) the OCI Memorandum dated 6 May 1966. I acknowledged this reflected an adjustment from the conclusions of the 24 March 1966 NIE. The threat to Iran from the areas of her Near East neighbors had never, I thought, been the subject of an intelligence community estimate; State had, however, occasionally offered judgments, to the Shah, on this subject. I referred to the dangers inherent in the practice of reacting to the exaggerated "estimates" from the Shah and others by calming them with watered-down estimative judgements deprecating the long-term Soviet indirect threat in the Near East. I expressed the opinion that these "bogus estimates" tended to gain currency and validity within the USG and unnecessarily complicated the task of developing a USG consensus for action when it was needed. I noted the need for better intelligence on the changing situation in the Gulf and the Arab Near East.

e. *Alternatives to USMAP*—The question of alternative free world military sources was discussed. Ambassador Meyer categorically opposed any sacrifice of our monopolistic position. ISA/Defense, the White House representative and I all expressed some enthusiasm for a reappraisal of this established USG position. I noted, for example, that the UK alternative to the USG in the field of naval equipment for the Gulf might be positively approached. I also observed that the Shah's representatives had been shopping in German shipyards.

f. *The Shah's new status*—I noted that we had not indicated any real interest in the Shah's offer to assume a greater responsibility in his part of the world in order to reduce the load on the USG. Regardless of the obvious question of his real capability, I thought that the Shah's offer should be viewed as an opportunity which could be exploited. A smaller military package could be made palatable to the Shah if it were wrapped in the trappings of a real gesture from the President recognizing the Shah's offer. ISA/Defense and the White House favored this and recognized it would take some careful thought. Ambassador Hare and Ambassador Meyer listened attentively to this discussion.

4. *IRG Action*—Ambassador Hare summarized the discussions as reflecting a consensus that we should, within the limits of available resources, react positively to the Shah. He noted that Defense had not yet formulated a precise proposal.

5. Following the meeting, Ambassador Meyer and Mr. Hoopes departed for the Pentagon for a meeting with Secretary of Defense McNamara. I have been reliably but informally advised that the meeting went badly. Secretary McNamara did not appear to be aboard on the otherwise positive Defense position. His reaction was reportedly very discouraging; he emphasized the troubles he was having with Congress on MAP and the great demands elsewhere for our limited resources.

6. Secretary Rusk, advised late 12 May 1966 of Secretary McNamara's negative attitude, reportedly withdrew to a non-committal position. Ambassador Meyer was, however, given a free hand to present his case to the President.

7. Ambassador Meyer saw the President at noon on Friday the 13th. The President, I have been advised by State, listened carefully to a thirty-minute presentation. The President said that he would defer making a decision. Ambassador Meyer has cancelled his reservation to depart for Iran on 14 May.

James H. Critchfield[6]
Chief, Near East and
South Asia Division

---

[6] Printed from a copy that indicates Critchfield signed the original.

138.   Telegram From the Embassy in Iran to the Department of State[1]

Tehran, May 18, 1966, 1015Z.

1550. For Secretary.

1. As you may know, my efforts last week in Washington to assure responsive USG position to Shah's military needs, as confirmed by General Peterson's military survey, unexpectedly met resistance from Secretary McNamara. Despite Peterson findings, he reluctant proceed with additional military sales here. His understandable reasons: a) general Washington antipathy to military programs particularly following Indo-Pak conflict last year: and b) concern that military expenditures will jeopardize Iran's economic development.

2. Even without Peterson confirmation, Shah is convinced Iran needs additional equipment. It not possible to dissuade him from securing adequate air defense for wealth-bearing southern region of Iran and some additional naval craft to assure stability of Gulf as traditional British power diminishes. Economically, Shah tends to bite off more than he can chew but recent history demonstrates projects never progress as rapidly as anticipated and this tends to relieve financial indigestion. In any case at present Iran is thriving and generally justified optimism prevails here re future.

3. There is no doubt Shah means it when he says he will buy elsewhere if USG not forthcoming. British told us last week they undertaking intensive military sales campaign here. French, Italians and others also in wings. Soviets also a possibility that cannot be excluded. Our conviction is that maintenance of US-Iran military relationship is best bet for keeping Shah from going off deep end economically or otherwise.

4. Aram 17th quoted Shah as expressing hope that his five months' wait would be followed by adequate US responsiveness but if not he determined make other arrangements. Shah cited Kosygin's visit to Cairo as compounding concern engendered by Nasser's threats against Saudi Arabia and Nasser's announcement that UAR will continue in Yemen in anticipation of British withdrawal from Aden in 1968. While Shah no doubt sent this word in part to pressure us, Aram is genuinely concerned re Shah's attitude.

5. Turk Ambassador Kent sought me out evening 17th to report that during 1-1/2 hour conversation previous day Shah had at one point stated that if US fails to respond to his additional military needs Kent

---

[1] Source: Department of State, Central Files, DEF 19–8 US–IRAN. Secret; Priority; Exdis.

should "not be surprised to see Malinovsky here." Such talk is, of course, obnoxious and may also have had purpose of influencing our views. At same time, I remember Ambassador Henry Grady telegraphically commenting before breakdown of oil industry here that some people think Iranians will not cut off nose to spite face but those people are wrong.

6.   All this does not mean we should jump through hoop when Shah snaps fingers. Peterson Mission reduced Shah's demands to justifiable requirements. Beyond this, equipment recommended by Peterson will exceed in cost $200,000,000 supplementary loan authorization which Shah has received from Parliament. This means that within Peterson program, Shah is going to have to make some choices. In any case, during our discussion of these matters I intend to bear down heavily on need for keeping military expenditures from wrecking economic progress which Iran is making.

7.   Military package which we propose should above all honor promise made in President's letter to Shah of April 11,[2] i.e. credit sales within additional $200,000,000 ceiling at "most favorable prices." It seems every time DOD takes another look at the figures, prices go up further. Hope they can be kept to minimum cost to USG and with waiver of research and development percentage (my impression such waivers not at all uncommon). As to interest rate, we continue to hope that for important political reasons (climate for augmented special facilities) one percentage point can be shaved from 5-1/2 percent going rate for additional $200 million credit.

8.   In general, our colleagues in DOD appear to want to be as forthcoming as circumstances permit. Ray Hare would know present status of their thinking and whether a word from you might be helpful. If such word needed, I can assure you it is in our nation's interest.

Meyer

---

[2] Document 129.

139.   Intelligence Memorandum[1]

No. 1355/66   Washington, May 21, 1966.

THE ARAB THREAT TO IRAN

1.   Iranian foreign and military policies are heavily influenced by the Shah's belief that Arab nationalism, personified by Egyptian President Nasir, is striving to dominate oil-rich and vulnerable south-western Iran and the Persian Gulf area. His concern has been heightened by the diminishing role of the UK in the Persian Gulf shiekdoms.

2.   From a geopolitical standpoint, the Shah's fears for the security of southwestern Iran and the Persian Gulf are not groundless. The oil facilities in Khuzistan Province and the offshore islands provide nearly 75 percent of Iran's foreign exchange earnings, and hence are the primary source of Iranian economic development funds. These highly concentrated facilities provide extremely vulnerable targets for sabotage.

3.   Iranian transportation routes to the Western world are also vulnerable. The major ocean port, Khorramshahr, can be reached only through the Iraqi-controlled Shatt-al-Arab waters. A hostile Arab sheikdom at the Strait of Hormuz—the mouth of the Persian Gulf—could endanger all Iranian shipping into the Indian Ocean. Iran is attempting to decentralize the oil industry, and to open new ports along the Gulf beyond Iraq's control. The most important new facility will be the port at Bandar Abbas, on the Iranian side of the Strait of Hormuz. This will also be Iran's main naval base. Bandar Abbas is not expected to be completed before 1968, however.

4.   Psychological and political factors have led the Shah to believe that Arab nationalism presents a "clear and present danger" to Iranian security. He bitterly resents Nasir's claim to leadership of "progressive forces" in the Middle East against "reactionaries" (including the Shah), especially in view of his ambitious social "revolution" in Iran. The Shah feels that he has been insulted by the UAR's break-off of diplomatic relations in 1960 and by Nasir's subsequent propaganda attacks against his country and himself. He may fear, too, that Nasir's brand of aggressive and neutralist nationalism, and his charisma, will prove infectious to some Iranians.

5.   The Shah holds Nasir responsible for claims occasionally voiced by various Arab leaders to Khuzistan ("Arabistan") and for their presumption in terming the Persian Gulf the "Arabian Gulf." The Shah

---

[1] Source: Johnson Library, National Security File, Country File, Iran, Memos & Miscellaneous, Vol. II, 1/66–1/69. Secret; No Foreign Dissem. Prepared by the Office of Current Intelligence in the Central Intelligence Agency's Directorate of Intelligence.

probably is convinced that Egypt, Iraq, and Syria—which the Shah lumps as one malevolent force—are actively plotting to take over Iranian territory, and fears that the nearly 500,000 Arabs living in Khuzistan—a majority of the province's population—could become a "fifth column."

6. Iraq's close relations with Egypt since the coup of November 1963, and the presence of Egyptian troops in Iraq, have convinced the Shah that the Iraqi Government is a tool of Nasir and that the web of Arab nationalism is tightening around Iran. [3 lines of source text not declassified] In addition, actual border incidents between Iranian and Iraqi troops in the course of the Kurdish rebellion have added fuel to the fire in the Shah's mind. There have also been reports of arms shipments from Iraq to dissidents among the Qashqai and Baluchi tribes. The Shah's predilection to believe the worst of Nasir leads him to put all available facts, rumors, intelligence reports, and suspicions into a pattern which proves to him that Nasir is out to overthrow his government.

7. The pattern he sees is an exaggerated version of what Nasir in reality has done and is doing in the way of "threatening" Iranian security. Nasir may well be giving encouragement and some form of covert aid to Arab nationalists conspiring against the Shah. Egypt regularly beams propaganda to Iran—Cairo radio broadcasts in Persian for two hours each day, and a clandestine "Voice of the Iranian Nation" emanates from Egyptian territory for four hours daily. Moreover, Nasir has attacked the Shah directly in recent speeches. Nasir is actively engaged in subversive activity in the Persian Gulf sheikdoms, and his efforts eventually to succeed Britain as the dominant influence among them could be construed with some validity as posing a long-range threat to Iranian transit through the Strait of Hormuz.

8. Other information indicates that the over-all danger Nasir poses for Iran is at most only potential, and indirect at present. [3 lines of source text not declassified] The small 350-man Egyptian force in Iraq, which worries the Shah, is but a token force in the narrowest sense of the term and is designed to influence political developments in Iraq. There are no plans to use it against Iran. The regime of Iraq's late premier Arif, who died in a helicopter crash early this spring, was clearly pro-Nasirist, but did not menace the Shah or his domains. The Arabian majority in Khuzistan is generally inactive politically, [1 line of source text not declassified]. A "Khuzistan Liberation Front," based in Kuwait with an office in Syria, probably receives some support from both Cairo and Baghdad, but does not appear to wield much influence in Khuzistan.

9. In responding to the Arab "threat," the Shah has followed a policy of supporting governments, elements, and activities which might keep his enemies distracted and occupied. The Iranian Government has directed a hostile—sometimes shrill—propaganda campaign against Nasir, both in Iran and abroad. Iran has given military equipment and

financial assistance to the Kurdish rebellion, which keeps a large percentage of Iraqi troops tied up in northern Iraq. [*3-1/2 lines of source text not declassified*] The Iranians have attempted openly to win support among leaders of the Shi'a minority Islamic group in Iraq. Iran has purchased arms for Saudi Arabia to pass on to the Yemeni royalist forces, and has maintained close liaison with Nasir's primary enemy, Israel. Among the more conservatively ruled Arab states, the Shah has attempted particularly to woo Saudi Arabia and Jordan and has given sympathetic attention to Saudi King Faisal's proposal, which Nasir opposes, regarding Islamic solidarity. There is even evidence that the Shah hoped that his rapprochement with the USSR would cause the Soviets to exercise some restraint over Nasir—although Premier Kosygin's recent visit to Egypt may have dashed those faint hopes.

10. The Shah lays most emphasis, however, on bolstering Iranian defenses, particularly naval and air, in the Persian Gulf and southwestern Iran. A considerable defense build-up would be necessary to provide a credible deterrent for hostile Arab countries—which presently have substantial military superiority, at least in an order-of-battle sense—were they in fact bent on attacking Iran. The Shah suspects, moreover, that in the event of an attack, the US might be caught in the middle and might even stop selling arms, as it did to Pakistan during the conflict with India last fall. US economic assistance to Nasir tends to bolster the Shah's conviction that he would have to stand alone against the Arabs. He gives every sign of being determined to add substantially to his country's armaments, whether or not the US Government agrees with his assessment of the Arab threat, and has made it clear that he will go elsewhere if he cannot purchase additional military equipment quickly and on desirable terms from the US. (MAP)

140.   Memorandum From W. Howard Wriggins of the National Security Council Staff to the President's Special Assistant (Rostow)[1]

Washington, May 21, 1966.

WWR:

McNamara has won the battle over the new $200 million *Iran arms sale,* so the Rusk–McNamara recommendation (attached)[2] comes out as close to the hard line as possible. The Shah may scream. So we could face a tactical review of our negotiating line later, though we think it unlikely.

The *two main issues* were: (1) State argued hard for slices of $100 million in FY 67 followed by $60 million and $40 million tranches. McNamara stood firm on four tranches of $50 million each to spread out the burden on his MAP budget (MAP funds must cover 25% of these credit deals). (2) Meyer pushed hard for 4% interest, but even State eventually agreed that this doesn't make sense. A 4% rate on a $200 million credit would cost $42–48 million more in MAP funds over five years than for the same deal at the market rate (now 5.5%).

Hal has fully staffed this out with Budget. Schultze's memo to you (attached)[3] is fully reflected in the memo to the President he drafted for your signature.

Schultze feels very strongly (as we do) that it's essential to keep control of this program in the President's hands.

—First, the economics really are disturbing, as Schultze says. Bringing the President down hard on that point will help keep Meyer on his toes (I wasn't too impressed with his grasp of this problem last week). We also want to avoid making this an irrevocable commitment and are underscoring (as Schultze suggests) that this is a planning figure subject to annual review.

—Second, we regarded the joint annual economic-military review as a major achievement when the Shah agreed to write it into the 1964 Memo of Understanding. It's an excellent device for keeping our voice alive even after AID phases out, and this year's exercise showed that we really have succeeded in bringing the Shah face to face with his economists.

This is why the last paragraph in our memo.

---

[1] Source: Johnson Library, National Security File, Country File, Iran, Memos & Miscellaneous, Vol. II, 1/66–1/69. Secret. The source text bears a stamped indication that it was seen by Rostow.

[2] The undated memorandum from Rusk and McNamara to the President is not printed.

[3] Schultze's May 21 memorandum is not printed.

The touchy element is timing. Meyer begins the economic review Sunday and should present this package to the Shah as soon after that as possible. However, tactically I assume you feel it's bad to rush the President. So we've only alluded to the timing problem in the memo. We'll rely on you to get it onto his desk quickly and give him a chance to get to it before nudging.

Howard

---

141.   Memorandum From the President's Special Assistant (Rostow) to President Johnson[1]

Washington, May 21, 1966, 1:30 p.m.

Secretaries Rusk and McNamara recommend you approve $200 million in new *arms sales to Iran,* which Ambassador Meyer will discuss with the Shah this week. This would extend our 1964 agreement through FY 1970, raising the total arms credit to $400 million. State proposed bunching these sales in the early years but gave in to McNamara's plan for $50 million a year FY 67–FY 70. They finally agreed that our Military Assistance budget is too tight to cover the 4% interest rate Meyer asked for and propose sticking to the market rate (now 5.5%), except for one last sale under the 1964 agreement.

Most of us believe the *Shah is foolish to spend his money this way.* AID forecasts a rapidly growing balance of payments deficit if he pushes both development and heavy arms purchases too hard. His oil revenues will not rise as sharply as he hopes, and AID fears he will end up asking us to bail him out of a foreign exchange bind just when we are phasing out of economic aid.

But since he is determined to buy arms somewhere, the best we can do is to lean on the brakes. His parliament appropriated $200 million last fall, and only by sending a survey team have we delayed him this long. We will probably want him to let us set up in Iran a partial alternative to our intelligence facilities in Pakistan (we will re-open this with you soon). Anyway, if we cannot dissuade him, no point in losing a good sale.

---

[1] Source: Johnson Library, National Security File, Memos to the President, Walt W. Rostow, Vol. 3, May 16–31, 1966. Top Secret. A handwritten note on the margin of the source text reads, "Rec'd 3:20 p."

While on balance this package makes sense, we want to be flexible in case Iran's economy sags. We want Meyer to keep a close eye on the economics and not tie you too firmly to a long-range commitment, thereby losing the leverage of a short leash.

So I recommend you approve but authorize me to read back to State this indication of your feelings: "The President is deeply concerned over Iran's worrisome economic prospects. He wants each slice of this new program submitted to him for approval only after searching review of Iran's economic position. He regards the new $200 million as a planning figure subject to annual review. He asks that Ambassador Meyer tell the Shah of this concern, while reassuring him of the President's full respect for his judgment." Charlie Schultze concurs. Attached is a rather legalistic justification.[2]

Walt

Approve[3]

See me

---

[2] Not printed.

[3] This option is checked on the source text.

---

142. Telegram From the Department of State to the Embassy in Iran[1]

Washington, May 23, 1966, 4:53 p.m.

1158. For Ambassador. Subject: Annual Review. Refs: Deptel 1155;[2] Embtel 1572.[3]

1. President has approved following instructions (which take place of refdeptel) for your audience with Shah in connection with second

---

[1] Source: Department of State, Central Files, DEF 19–8 US–IRAN. Secret; Immediate; Limdis. Drafted by Crawford; cleared by ISA Regional Director for Near East and South Asia Lieutenant Colonel Fred E. Haynes, Jr., Howison, and Wriggins; and approved by Hare.

[2] Dated May 21. (Ibid.)

[3] See the attachment to Document 143.

annual review. You should inform Shah US willing, subject to availability of funds and continued Congressional authorization:

a. Provide credit financing for remaining $60 million under 1964 Memorandum of Understanding at 4 percent.

b. Provide additional credit sales up to $200 million in annual increments of $50 million through FY'70 at interest averaging between 5 and 6 percent, repayment within ten years from date of agreement.

c. Provide credit financing in FY'67 of $50 million (in addition to $60 million remaining under 1964 Memorandum of Understanding).

d. Make every effort complete deliveries of items opted for by Shah by end FY'71, but because this involves new procurement we cannot now predict with certitude that this will be possible. FYI. Almost certain some items will spill into FY'72; extent of spill-over will depend on priority GOI assigns to weapons systems and which ones it wants to negotiate first. End FYI.

2. You should also inform Shah orally as follows: It is our view total amount of US credit contemplated for FY'65–'70 period ($400 million) together with $70 million in cash purchases could prove overly heavy burden for Iran's economy. For this reason we continue attach great importance to our joint annual military/economic review which will allow us to form economic conclusions bearing on release of annual tranches. These reviews will necessarily consider, among other things, substantial additional military purchases. FYI. We assume annual review already agreed to would allow for consultations on magnitude and terms of major purchases outside this arrangement and therefore specific amendment of 1964 Memorandum of Understanding to provide for consultations on this not necessary. President considers new $200 million as planning figure, a commitment in principle on condition that our joint economic review confirms feasibility in light Iran's economic position. You should impress concern re economic burden on Shah, in context above, while reassuring him of President's full respect for his judgment. End FYI.

Rusk

143.   Memorandum From the President's Special Assistant (Rostow) to President Johnson[1]

Washington, May 23, 1966, 6 p.m.

SUBJECT

Iran Military Purchase Loan: Information

Attached is a cable from Armin Meyer, objecting to the State–Defense Iranian package.

Setting aside rhetoric he has two pleas:

1. *Getting Deliveries on Schedule.* Because of long delivery lead times, he wants more funds at the beginning and smaller amounts toward the end of the five-year period. DoD insists on equal slices for budgetary reasons, but in reply to his cable has agreed to make a special effort to speed deliveries.

2. *Eliminating the Strait Jacket.* Because of the Shah's growing sense of confidence and independence, Meyer objects to insisting that the Shah must agree to revising our 1964 Memorandum of Understanding to include consulting with us prior to making purchases of military equipment from third countries. Anticipating this problem, we put a paragraph in our memorandum to you, providing that you would review each tranche of the loan in the light of Iran's economic position. This gave the flexibility required to meet Meyer's point; that is, our commitment is a target figure, subject to regular review; but he doesn't have to ask us every time he wants to buy equipment somewhere else. We have agreed, therefore, to eliminate this part of Meyer's instructions, though we shall tell the Iranians we expect such purchases will be part of the annual military/economic review agreed to by the Shah in 1964 and a regular cooperative exercise since then.

Walt

Attachment

TEXT OF CABLE FROM TEHRAN (1572)[2]

For the President from Ambassador Meyer.

Iran and U.S.

The problem of U.S. military sales to Iran which I was privileged to discuss with you on May 13 has reached a critical juncture. A package

---

[1] Source: Johnson Library, National Security File, Country File, Iran, Memos & Miscellaneous, Vol. II, 1/66–1/69. Secret. A handwritten notation on the source text reads: "OK—L".

[2] Telegram 1572 from Tehran, May 23, is in Department of State, Central Files, POL 1 US.

proposal has been formulated by our associates in Washington. It is to be presented to the Shah as soon as your approval has been obtained.[3]

While considerably more restricted than is compatible with protection of our interests, the package proposal reflects careful attention and an effort to be as forthcoming as Washington circumstances and the U.S.'s view as to Iran's capabilities permit. As your Ambassador to this country, I am nonetheless concerned that we are about to alienate the Shah and his country with whom we have had a long and mutually beneficial friendship. My concern is of sufficient depth to warrant taking a few minutes of your valuable time to request relatively small modifications which may be able to reduce adverse repercussions to manageable proportion.

My week in Washington made clear the antipathy which exists both in our legislative and executive branches to military programs, particularly following the Indo-Pak debacle last fall. This is fully understandable. But it makes very difficult the maintenance of healthy relationships with true friends like Iran with whom we have a long-standing military relationship. Due to massive Soviet arms shipments to this region, the vulnerability of Iran (like Israel) has sharply increased. The Shah six months ago became so concerned he obtained authorization from his Parliament for an additional $200,000,000 borrowing authority to build up his air and naval defenses. His purpose is to deter aggressive action against Iran's vulnerable oil producing areas or to cope with such aggression if it takes place. Deeply impressed by the Vietnam situation, the Shah believes such self-reliance is in U.S. as well as Iran's interest. A seven-man team of U.S. military experts under Brig. Gen. Peterson assessed the situation in March. In a report (which the Shah has in his possession) Peterson confirmed that a threat truly exists and recommended a rational program for augmentation within the $200,000,000 added ceiling. Thus, the judgment that early measures should be taken is not only the Shah's but our own.

A main concern in Washington is the effect of military expenditures on Iran's economic development. At present, Iran is thriving. With his profound sense of mission, the Shah is making Iran a show-case of modernization in this part of the world (8–10 percent growth rate, utilization of 75 percent of the $500,000,000 annual oil income for development purposes, land reform, literacy corps, etc.). The problem is he may bite off more than he can chew. It is the Embassy's view, however, that as in the past, major projects (and their financing) will stretch out over a considerably longer period than planned. While we, of course, regret any diversion of Iran's resources to military expenditures, we are convinced

---

[3] Telegram 1155 to Tehran, May 21, transmitted the package proposal. (Ibid., DEF 19–8 US–IRAN)

favorable economic factors are such that Iran can meet the financial burdens of a military program along lines envisaged in the Peterson Report without courting disaster. In any case, economic difficulties are more apt to be forestalled if we at this Embassy are enabled (by adequate responsiveness to the Peterson recommendations) to maintain a healthy dialogue with the Shah and his Government.

This brings me to my greatest concern with the proposed package. The underlying assumption appears to be that the U.S. Government can compel the Shah to obtain only such equipment as we decide he can have. This is altogether unrealistic in 1966. Time and again over the past few months the Shah has said, privately and publicly, that Iran is its own master. He has made this clear (again in a lengthy talk with us yesterday) specifically as far as arms purchasing is concerned. I do not foresee the possibility of attaining his agreement to a documentary amendment, as presently proposed, requiring him to consult with us "on the magnitude and terms of major purchases outside this arrangement." It is true he will only with greatest reluctance give up the benefits of a package proposal but he will in my view balk at being put in a strait jacket. Even if it proved possible to obtain his concurrence, rancor would be deep and he would inevitably violate this injunction. Then we would be faced with a showdown in our total relationship here.

Instead of a "Papa knows best" attitude, excessive manipulation of which is in my view to a considerable extent responsible for anti-Americanism in this part of the world, I believe we would get much further by treating the Shah like an adult. In our 1964 Memorandum of Understanding we already have provisions similar to the one proposed. We can refer to them if necessary. In any case, I feel strongly that in the realm of human affairs one gets farther by reasoning together than by coercion.

I will, of course, try my best to sell whatever final package you authorize. It would have been helpful to have a concessional interest rate, particularly to induce a favorable climate for installation of augmented special U.S. intelligence facilities. That apparently is not possible. What should be possible, however, in addition to "favorable prices," which you mentioned to the Shah in your letter of April 11,[4] are the following two proposals:

A.   On-schedule deliveries. According to the proposed package, the $200,000,000 credit will be phased in $50,000,000 tranches over four years. The problem is that there is usually a two or three-year delay in delivery after credit funds are arranged. It would be important to be able to assure the Shah:

1.   While funding is being held at $50,000,000 per annum level because we want to assist Iran in keeping its debt burden manageable,

---

[4] Document 129.

2. Delivery of equipment will nevertheless hold to the phased five-year schedule set forth in the Peterson military survey report (in effect this means in most cases funding would be delayed until just prior to delivery dates).

If such telescoping of leadtimes is not possible, it is recommended as an alternative that the FY 67 new credit tranche be increased to $200,000,000 by advancing the final $50,000,000 tranche (FY 70) to FY 67.

B. Elimination of the strait jacket. If we hope to retain our military cooperation with Iran, including discouraging the Shah's purchasing elsewhere, we are more likely to do so (although complete control is unlikely) by informal consultations as we go along, based on provisions which already exist in the 1964 Memorandum, than if we try to coerce him by further documentation in effect requiring him to seek our permission before he can purchase elsewhere.

Certainly treating the Shah like an adult is the best long-range policy if we are to continue to play a role in Iran's moving ahead and if we wish to maintain our rather extensive assets here of significant importance to our national security.

---

144. Memorandum for the Record[1]

Washington, May 23, 1966.

On June [May] 23, 1966 the President approved the $200 million military purchase loan for Iran. He signed it with the proviso that we would communicate orally to the Department of State the following caveat:

"The President deeply concerned over Iran's worrisome economic prospects. He wants each slice of this new program submitted to him for approval only after searching review of Iran's economic position. He regards the new $200 million as a planning figure subject to annual review. He asks that Ambassador Meyer tell the Shah of this concern while reassuring him of the President's full respect for his judgment."

While the paper was on the President's desk, a telegram addressed to the President came from Ambassador Meyer[2] expressing his profound misgivings at the package as it had been communicated on a hold basis awaiting the President's signature.

---

[1] Source: Johnson Library, National Security File, Country File, Iran, Memos & Miscellaneous, Vol. II, 1/66–1/69. Secret. Copies were sent to NSC Executive Secretary Bromley K. Smith and Chief of the Bureau of the Budget's International Division James W. Clark.

[2] See the attachment to Document 143.

1. He was particularly concerned that each year's tranche would be equal to the others, instead of the first one being larger, since the long lead time necessary for certain items would put their delivery well into the 70's. As a result, DoD agreed to pay special attention to the problem of speeding deliveries.

2. He was also deeply concerned that the GOI would be asked to consult with us before it made any military purchases in addition to those made possible by this loan. The instruction sent to him had insisted that he explicitly seek a revision of the 1964 Memorandum of Understanding to include such prior consultations.

NSC staff members Wriggins and Saunders revised the language of paragraph three of the instructing telegram so that it read as follows:

3. It is our view total amount of U.S. credit contemplated for FY 65–70 ($400 million) together with $70 million in cash purchases may prove overly heavy burden for Iran's economy. That is why we attach importance to our joint annual military/economic review on which the future release of annual tranches will depend. These reviews will necessarily consider, among other things, substantial additional military purchases. FYI: We assume annual review already agreed to would allow for consultations on magnitude and terms of major purchases outside this arrangement and therefore specific amendment of 1964 Memorandum of Understanding not necessary. The President considers the new $200 million as a planning figure, a commitment in principle on condition that our joint economic review confirms the feasibility of Iran's growing economic commitments. End FYI.

This was intended to be consistent with the staff's understanding of the President's intent in regard to our relations with the Shah, to the substance of the economic review without requiring such an explicit denigration of Iranian independence as the original language represented. Rostow informed the President by memo of 23 May (attached)[3] of our approach, and the President did not object. Therefore, that part of the Rusk–McNamara memo[4] which says we will deduct from future sales an amount comparable to the value of purchases in third countries should be read in the light of this later exchange (including Tehran 1572 attached).[5]

The record should note that the President approved this program via the covering memo from Walt Rostow. He probably did not address specifics in the Rusk–McNamara memo. Therefore, his decision should be understood more in terms of these memos than in terms of every last legalistic detail in the Rusk–McNamara memo.

Howard Wriggins[6]

---

[3] Document 143.

[4] See footnote 2, Document 140.

[5] See footnote 2 above.

[6] Printed from a copy that bears this typed signature.

145. Telegram From the Embassy in Iran to the Department of State[1]

Tehran, May 24, 1966, 1635Z.

1585. Annual Review. Reference: Deptel 1158.[2]

1. Annual review with Shah took place evening 24th. Two-hour discussion went reasonably well. Shah agreed that Jablonsky and SCS sketch out phased program of procurement within credit limitations set forth in reftel. We made clear all Shah's expectations cannot be accommodated, but did not discuss price details. Shah gave his views as to which items should have priority.

2. Bore down heavily on economic burden, as well as complications which would result for US if Shah makes substantial purchases elsewhere. Only outside purchasing Shah seemed seriously interested in is naval package from British.

3. Threshing out detailed program, which will require Shah to make some hard choices, will still be difficult, but believe at least until his return from three state visits situation here is under control.

4. Appreciate expeditiousness which our Washington colleagues accorded this problem. More detailed report tomorrow.[3]

Meyer

---

[1] Source: Department of State, Central Files, DEF 19–8 US–IRAN. Confidential; Priority; Limdis. Repeated to CINCSTRIKE/USCINCMEAFSA.

[2] Document 142.

[3] Telegram 1594 from Tehran, May 25, transmitted a detailed account of the annual review session on May 24. (Department of State, Central Files, DEF 19–8 US–IRAN)

146. Memorandum From the President's Special Assistant (Rostow) to President Johnson[1]

Washington, May 27, 1966, 4:30 p.m.

In November you tentatively approved a recommendation from Rusk, McNamara and Raborn for establishing contingency alternatives for our intelligence facilities in Pakistan. But you felt we ought to hold final decision until after you talked with Ayub. Then we held further until after Tashkent and the Indian visit.

Now State, Defense and CIA have reviewed their October recommendations and (with minor updating) feel we should go ahead. They emphasize that this is not a proposal to relocate most of the present activities from Pakistan or to duplicate them. They propose to develop minimum space and install basic equipment so we can diversify some of these activities and be in a position to move them all on short notice with little intelligence loss if need be.

To refresh your memory, they recommended we: (a) increase existing [1 line of source text not declassified] (b) add one floor to a planned warehouse in the embassy compound in Tehran; (c) acquire land outside Tehran for eventually developing a more satisfactory permanent installation (including dependent quarters) if needed; and [1 line of source text not declassified].

Costs of (a) and (b) would be about $1.5 million; time about 9 months. Cost of (c) is approximately $5 million with eventual cost depending on how extensively we develop that site; time about 18 months. [3 lines of source text not declassified]

As general guidelines, they recommend (a) no further investment in Pakistan; (b) as new facilities come into being, we transfer some of those now in Pakistan to reduce the leverage any one country holds over us; but (c) unless you decide otherwise or the Paks kick us out, we retain a substantial portion of our present Pak activities.

They also recommended certain sweeteners for Iran to develop the favorable political climate essential to expansion. Your recent approval of the new military sales package has brought those up to date.

The balance of payments impact would be minimal; all equipment would be US-built. One-time real estate and construction costs would be about $6 million, and annual recurring costs about $750,000 (much of which would be offset by reduction of Pak facilities).

---

[1] Source: Johnson Library, National Security File, Memos to the President, Walt W. Rostow, Vol. 5, May 27–June 10, 1966. Top Secret; Sensitive.

I believe it makes sense to go ahead with this program now. Since we no longer have the kind of close relationship with Pakistan we had prior to the Chinese attack on India, we would be well to reinsure.

If you still approve, I recommend you *sign the attached*.[2]

W.W. Rostow[3]

---

[2] Attached was a draft National Security Action Memorandum for the Secretaries of State and Defense and the Director of Central Intelligence entitled "Alternatives to US Facilities in Pakistan" that reads: "I have reviewed your 22 October 1965 Memorandum to me in response to NSAM 337 as updated by the Department of State's 17 May 1966 Memorandum to Mr. Rostow and by my approval on 23 May of the new military sales package for Iran. I approve your recommendations as updated subject to the usual review by the Bureau of the Budget before expenditures are authorized." This was issued as NSAM 348 on May 30, 1966. A copy of NSAM 348 is in Department of State, S/S–NSAM Files: Lot 72 D 316. NSAM 337, "US Intelligence Facilities in Pakistan," August 10, 1965, is printed in *Foreign Relations, 1964–1968,* vol. XXV, Document 168.

[3] Printed from a copy that bears this typed signature.

---

147.   Research Memorandum From the Director of the Bureau of Intelligence and Research (Hughes) to Acting Secretary of State Ball[1]

RNA–38   Washington, June 3, 1966.

SUBJECT

    Shah of Iran Demands Greater Oil Offtake

The Shah has expressed disappointment with Iran's 1965 crude oil export figures and considers a substantial increase during 1966 necessary to finance his plans for economic development and an expanded defense establishment. This paper explores the background of recent discussions on this subject and its relationship to the Shah's attitude toward the US.

Abstract

The Shah considers the 1965 increase in crude oil offtake inadequate in view of Iran's financial needs for its economic development and de-

---

[1] Source: Johnson Library, National Security File, Harold H. Saunders Files, Iran, 4/1/66–12/31/67. Confidential; No Foreign Dissem; Controlled Dissem.

fense. Iranian officials assert that the Organization of Petroleum Exporting Companies (OPEC) authorized a 20 per cent increase in offtake for Iran in 1966 (almost twice the 1965 increase). However, OPEC has not made a public announcement of allotments, and the oil Consortium (which insists that OPEC allotments are not binding on the producing companies) notified the Iranian Government on May 25 that it planned to increase oil liftings by about 9–11 per cent in 1966. Prime Minister Hoveyda has already termed this increase "unsatisfactory" and "unacceptable." The Shah has threatened to go elsewhere for military and economic assistance if the US does not provide what he wants, and Iranian officials have the impression that the Consortium could have promised greater oil offtake had the US applied pressure on the American companies who are members. As a result of the Iranian dissatisfaction, the Shah is likely to become more intransigent in his dealings with the US. However, if the Consortium maintains a unified position on the issue of oil offtake, it is possible that the Shah will be obliged to proceed in a more pragmatic fashion toward a resolution of the conflicting demands of military modernization and economic development on Iran's limited resources.

[Here follows the body of the paper.]

---

148.   Telegram From the Embassy in Iran to the Department of State[1]

Tehran, June 29, 1966, 1400Z.

1762. Military Sales to Iran.

1. Jablonsky and I spent one hour and three-quarters with Shah morning 29th. It was rough.

2. Noting in our meeting previous to his departure we had been able to inform him of USG readiness to provide additional $200,000,000 in credit for military purchases over next five years, I said we had during Shah's absence worked on pricing with view to minimum financial burden. We now had data which we believed could be worked into program acceptable to him. Important point was to get on with job of figuring out third tranche bearing in mind HIM's priorities.

---

[1] Source: Department of State, Central Files, DEF 19–8 US–IRAN. Confidential; Limdis. Repeated to CINCSTRIKE/USCINCMEAFSA.

3.   Shah said he had every intention being "reasonable." He repeatedly expressed appreciation for what USG has done for Iran in military field in past and his desire that healthiness this relationship will continue. At same time, he referred to predicament in which Pakistan had found itself last fall and since that time due to suspension of US military supplies. He considered USG's policy misguided for in his view US has driven Paks as regards military procurement into arms of Chinese and also Russians, Pak military mission currently being in Moscow. All this, he said, has given him much cause for thought. He has, he said, reached a conclusion as far as Iranian military procurement policy is concerned. If USG shows itself responsive, Shah said he wishes to maintain maximum supply relationship with traditional US supplier. This is particularly true, he said, for lethal and sensitive items such as aircraft. He pointed out that once a pilot is in air he is beyond control and can in fact turn against his country. Hence Shah wants aircraft program in safe American hands. Other items such as anti-aircraft equipment do not present same opportunities for subversive potential. Therefore, if USG unwilling supply such items at reasonable prices and terms, they can be procured elsewhere.

4.   Turning to spread sheet of Peterson approved items (except destroyer) and their costs, Shah quickly concentrated on items he wants to order from US without delay: Blue Shark system, remaining 209 M–60 tanks, F–4 aircraft, and 30-day war reserve for three services. Later in discussion, Jablonsky was able to persuade Shah at least for this year to limit additional war reserve to air force only.

5.   Shah laid greatest emphasis on F–4 aircraft. He was particularly upset by limitation to one squadron. One squadron, he observed, would only be enough for two or three planes at each airfield. This was totally unacceptable. Also unacceptable, he said, is 1970 target date. Noting how Soviets have already supplied and are continuing to supply MIG–21's to their friends, notably Iraq, Shah said, "We are faced with the problem right now."

6.   As to F–4 pricing, Shah considers price of $39 million for 12 aircraft high, although he did not describe it as unacceptable. He said French Mirages have been offered at $1.1 million per copy "naked" and $1.6 million "complete." French have guaranteed to have first Mirage in country in 20 months and total order within 32 months. He noted he could buy at least two Mirages for price of each F–4. At same time, he said, he realized F–4 is much better aircraft. He indicated he would think about this offer for "a week or ten days" (later he said until July 4) but his interest ultimately dependent on obtaining two squadrons and earlier delivery.

7. Question of destroyer never came up during conversation. Shah, however, at one point gave clear indication that he is tending toward British deal (Embtel 1594).[2]

8. Later in discussion when I urged Shah to keep in mind that his F–5 is good aircraft, which is doing yeoman work in Vietnam, Shah disclosed "in confidence" that an Israeli pilot had been here recently, had flown the F–5, and contrasted it disparagingly with Mirages which Israelis possess.

9. When we noted Shah had not indicated interest in anti-aircraft equipment, Shah said he thought he could get such equipment, as opposed to "sensitive" aircraft, from elsewhere, probably from Russians. He asked re effectiveness of Russian SAM's in Vietnam and Jablonsky reported they only having limited success. Shah noted that until now he has not approached Russians, only British and French. (Implication was that British and French offers not very attractive.) Re Tiger Cat, Shah acknowledged it had only limited value.

10. When I expressed personal hope that Shah could avoid arms procurement from Russians and indicated how it would complicate matters for us, Shah took firm stand. Rest of conversation was heavily punctuated with his insistence that Iran simply must have "liberty of action." He said he hoped USG would understand that his ideals are same as ours and that "even behind our backs he supports US on Vietnam" but Iran's main concern is to "stand on its own feet," from security as well as economic and political standpoints. Instead of acting irritated, USG should realize that Iran's independent stance is best possible roadblock to Communist influence.

11. Shah went on to say that USG has had no compunctions about providing arms to other countries which also procure arms from Soviets. He noted specifically India, Iraq and Yugoslavia. I mentioned those were different circumstances. India was faced with Chinese aggression. Shah retorted India used American arms against Paks. I noted equipment to Iraq was limited and cash sales. Shah said bitterly USG always finds "excuses" for such deals with countries which persistently side against US in world affairs while at same time making life as difficult as possible for US's true friends.

12. Re Pakistan, I noted we apparently assess last fall's episode somewhat differently. I said USG considers it acted in Pakistan's "higher interest" by inducing an early end to conflict instead of fueling war further. Shah retorted tartly all US did was to hurt Pakistan, its ostensible ally, while Indians continued to receive arms from other suppliers.

13. I assured Shah USG welcomes Iran's ability to stand on its own feet, and there is no divergence of opinion in Washington on this score. In

---

[2] See footnote 3, Document 145.

fact, most Americans are so gratified they are concerned that Iran's remarkable progress not be jeopardized by excessive expenditures for arms.

14. Expressing full confidence in Shah's ability to keep situation on even keel, I noted clandestine Soviet broadcasts and wondered about wisdom of opening further opportunities for Soviets via arms procurement, non-sensitive or sensitive. Shah was quick to emphasize that broadcasts are aimed at him and his regime. This all more reason, he said, why Iran's best hope lies in "independent" stance which frustrates Communist atempts to drive wedge between Shah and his people. I took occasion also to note that extent of shift in Iranian policy is already misleading some of Iranian opinion, e.g. almost daily attacks in some of lesser Iranian newspapers and a general cooling of atmosphere here against Americans. This too, is Soviet aim, I added. Shah said Russians are paying some newspapers. He added that any unfriendliness of Iranian opinion is at least part due to America's past mistakes. He cited what he considers virtually public USG support for Amini as "last chance for Iran," and alleged USG opposition to Iran's acquisition of steel mill. He said he felt that this trend in public opinion would pass within next few months, just as American press attitude toward his own endeavors has undergone favorable change.

15. Throughout discussion, Shah referred in bitter terms re US policy toward Nasser, and to India. Re latter, he reluctantly agreed that it would be calamity for such sizeable nation to "go down drain." Re Nasser, I reiterated previous argumentation that USG policy is based not on reward for good behavior but on what is in general interest of blocking communism and facilitating Mideast stability. He remained unimpressed.

16. Shah complained how USG treats its friends as "commercial" clients. All my efforts to explain what preferential treatment Iran has received in past and continues to receive failed to change his mind.

17. In summing up, Shah reiterated he wishes to proceed with purchase of: remaining M–60 tanks, Blue Shark, and air force war reserve. He will await further word re F–4's, particularly whether two squadrons available and delivery prospects. Cost factor will also be taken into consideration when comparing offers. He said he would like to make foregoing purchases, but under clear understanding re his "liberty of action" re procurement elsewhere if USG intends to attach "strings." He said he would like to know now so that alternative arrangements can be made now rather than two or three years later when it may be too late. Shah closed by reassurance that whatever happens to our military relationship his ideals are always those of US and free world.

Meyer

149.   Telegram From the Embassy in Iran to the Department of State[1]

Tehran, July 3, 1966, 1210Z.

31. 1. Having conveyed indication to Shah re unfeasibility of pre-July 4 response to our conversation 29th (Embtel 28),[2] FonMin Aram called me in evening 2nd. He had sheaf of notes substance of which emanated from Shah.

2. Main theme was that Shah wanted USG continue supply "sensitive" equipment like aircraft. As for non-sensitive material USG should show no concern if such items purchased from Soviets. Aram indicated there was possibility Shah had already approached Russians, i.e. in his talk with Semyon Skachkov, Chairman of Soviet State Committee for External Economic Relations, who was in Tehran this past week signing formal steel mill agreements. In any case, according to Shah via Aram, Americans should not react except cheerfully.

3. Expressing concern, I told Aram Shah should realize Americans are human also. There no question in my mind there will be American reaction if Shah initiates any kind of military procurement from Soviets. Americans will be particularly hurt because Americans have considered Shah tried and true ally and friend.

4. Aram contended USG has not been sufficiently forthcoming. "For seven months" (since passage of additional $200,000,000 credit authorization by Parliament) Shah has waited, Aram said, but only result is USG insists on treating Iran no better than ordinary commercial client.

5. Noting I was getting tired of this line, I said it is grossly unfair. Over years US MAP assistance has been tremendous. Aram agreed, saying Shah deeply appreciative. Despite what was presumably close military relationship, I said, Shah sprang $200,000,000 credit gambit in Parliament without any hint to us. We read about it in newspapers. I could assure Aram effect in Washington was not good. Nevertheless, at Shah's prodding, USG had agreed provide additional credit.

6. It seems incredible to me, I said, that Shah fails appreciate extent of USG military assistance still under way. We had only two years ago agreed provide $200,000,000 credit for military purchases, of which $60,000,000 still available at 4 percent. Recently USG agreed to additional $200,000,000 at between 5 percent and 6 percent. Meanwhile, tens of millions of dollars worth of grant material (including five squadrons of F–5

---

[1] Source: Department of State, Central Files, DEF 19–8 US–IRAN. Confidential. Repeated to CINCMEAFSA/CINCSTRIKE.

[2] Dated July 2. (Ibid.)

aircraft) still undelivered, and tens of millions of dollars are programmed as grant component for our supposed joint program in years
ahead. I said I could not comprehend Shah's jeopardizing all these millions for a few dollars of ephemeral savings and a 2-1/2 percent interest
rate.

7.   Aram asked if I have explained all this to Shah. I said these points
been conveyed to Shah time and again but he not in listening mood. Furthermore, when one gets explicit, Shah immediately gets offended,
makes accusation we threatening him, and is propelled in opposite direction.

8.   I went on to speculate that there is something more in all this than
meets the eye. (*Comment.* My hunch, not indicated to Aram, is Shah
wants to announce his abortive talks with consortium moguls next week
that as he warned his Western friends Iran is shifting its trade pattern, including arms, to Eastern Bloc. This would turn defeat of consortium
summitry exercise into cheap political victory.) Aram insisted Shah is
honest and guileless friend of US with no ulterior motives.

9.   Aram re-emphasized Shah wishes purchase only non-sensitive
relatively unimportant military wares from Soviets. I alluded to incom-
prehensibility of Shah's hastiness. I said I convinced adequate staff work
not been done re purchases Shah proposing to make. In our talk 29th, I
noted, he completely disinterested in PGM's Hawk Missiles, etc. They
best equipment available but apparently for political or other reasons,
Shah eager to purchase elsewhere what may turn out to be junk. With
Russians, Shah obviously doesn't even know what he wants to purchase,
but is "hell-bent" to purchase something probably for political reasons
and also because he like other Iranians is mesmerized by 2-1/2 percent
interest rate, totally disregarding other factors such as quality, value, etc.
I added Shah's military advisors tend to be sycophants who lack courage
to question any whim Shah may have.

10. Another point, I said, is that by introducing Russians into Iranian
military establishment Shah is inviting security problems for US. US military survey team some months ago checked Iranian security effectiveness and was able to give tentatively favorable report, thus permitting
US to go forward with program for Iran's acquisition of Hawks. Now
Shah wants F–4 aircraft, one of most sophisticated pieces of equipment. It
would not be surprising to me if USG would find it impossible to supply
such equipment if Russians in any way involved in Iranian military establishment.

11. Another refrain we been hearing so frequently, I said, is that Iran
is "independent" and will tolerate no "strings." (Aram had earlier said
Shah tends to feel USG treats him like "lackey.") I noted how delighted
US is that Iran is standing on its own feet but added US is also independent. Just as Shah is free to purchase from wheresoever he wishes, includ-

ing Soviets, US is also free to determine when, how or where it will sell equipment, or even extend grant aid. Question is not one, therefore, of strings. I added that Shah had demonstrated his "independence" in steel mill deal and visits to East Bloc countries. There appeared no urgent need to do so in something as risky as military field.

12. Aram again urged that I have another go at Shah. Reiterating Shah's quickness to take offense, I said he would probably as he did 29th try to back us into corner to state categorically whether F–5's will or will not be forthcoming if he turns to Soviets. I assured Aram that while some sort of reaction is sure neither I, nor President Johnson himself, could in advance state precisely what nature of extent of American reaction will be. Such things as security factors, Congressional reaction, as well as Executive Branch determinations would all play a role.

13. Somewhat taken aback by this blunt talk, Aram said both he and I as diplomats would have to buckle down to confine damage if Shah turns to Russians. I said that was both our jobs. Nevertheless, even aside from direct repercussions on USG military supply program in Iran, by opening door to Soviets in military field Shah in every way stands to lose much more than he can gain. I noted in this connection troubles Pak President Ayub is having in putting lid back on Pandora's box.

14. In closing I urged Aram to seek to curb precipitate action by Shah so as to permit productive US-Iranian dialogue to continue on matters of such vital consequence to this country. I said I ready talk again with Shah or Aram any time they felt it would be useful.

15. At his request ex-PriMin Alam and I discussed arms procurement situation morning 3rd. Covered most of same points covered with Aram but more in context of providing Alam with ammunition in his intimate discussions with Shah. Although considerably more worried than heretofore, Alam retains hope Shah can be dissuaded from involvement with Soviets in military matters.

Meyer

150. Letter From the Deputy Under Secretary of State for Political Affairs (Johnson) to the Deputy Secretary of Defense (Vance)[1]

Washington, July 6, 1966.

Dear Cy:

Ambassador Meyer informed the Shah of Iran in late May of the U.S. proposal for an additional military credit sales program to Iran of up to $200 million. The Shah left almost immediately for state visits in Romania, Yugoslavia and Morocco. Since his return to Tehran the Shah has conveyed to the Ambassador directly, and through his aides, some serious misgivings about our offer. His dissatisfaction stems from his almost obsessive concern for the security of Iran's oil-rich province of Khuzistan and his conviction that equipment for the defense of this vital area must be obtained in the shortest possible time.

The Shah has mounted major pressure campaign to bring us around to his point of view, using a number of high-level Iranians and the British Ambassador in Tehran as channels of information as to what he might do if the United States is not more responsive to his needs. This has been in addition to his own personal contact with Ambassador Meyer. The principal spectre raised in this war of nerves has been the possibility that Iran would buy arms from the Soviet Union, if the United States could not offer Iran what it feels it needs at this time.

Obviously, the bargaining element is very strong in this dialogue, which is reminiscent of many exchanges with the Shah in the past. Times have changed, however, and Iran is receiving large oil revenues and is experiencing steady economic growth. The Shah, who more than any single individual is responsible for this progress, is riding high. Al Friendly's article in the *Washington Post* gives a balanced picture of the Shah's present strengths and weaknesses.

With this as background the question arises, if we are to preserve our special relationship with Iran, how far we need to go to meet the Shah's demands. To accede completely is probably unnecessary, even if it were possible from the point of view of the resources available to support a military program in Iran. Nevertheless, the Shah has got himself committed publicly to an independent arms procurement policy. It will be impossible for him to retreat without some face-saving device. Should this be lacking, I fear the Shah could easily take steps which would jeopardize our position in Iran and which would be contrary to our national interest.

In the light of all this, we have concluded that present political hazards are great enough to call for a little "give" in our military proposal.

---

[1] Source: Department of State, Central Files, DEF 19–8 US–IRAN. Secret.

The Embassy in Tehran has suggested a number of possibilities, including the sale of rehabilitated F4C's at a cost substantially lower than the F4D's now being offered the Iranians and the waiver of R & D costs in connection with the new credit program. A third possibility, in line with the Peterson Report proposal, might be increasing the size from 12 to 16 of the F4D squadron now being offered.

I would very much appreciate your reaction to these suggestions and your own judgment as to how we might best seek to keep our relationship with Iran on an even keel.

Sincerely,

Alex

---

151.   Telegram From the Embassy in Iran to the Department of State[1]

Tehran, July 7, 1966, 1350Z.

80. Military Sales to Iran.

1. In hour-long talk morning 7th, I told Shah that time had come for frank conversation on arms procurement problem. Shah said he welcomed opportunity and wanted make clear that steps he taking in no way intended as "threats." I said what I had to say should also be considered in framework not of threats but facts.

2. I opened by expressing full USG support for Iran's "independent" policy, emphasizing we delighted Iran able stand on its own feet. Similarly, we can understand Iranian desire in military field to get best buys and to diversify sources of supply. We had been aware of Toufanian's shopping tours to Western Europe and this gave us no serious concern. What was cause for concern, however, would be turning to Soviets for arms. At least three times during conversation I stated categorically that move to Soviets will inevitably have serious "impact" as far as US concerned, but added that precise nature that impact uncertain.

3. Shah professed failure to comprehend why there should be any US reaction. Contact has been made with Soviets, he affirmed, but ac-

---

[1] Source: Department of State, Central Files, DEF 12–5 IRAN. Secret; Priority. Repeated to CINCSTRIKE/USCINCMEAFSA.

quisitions would be limited in quantity and quality. I pointed out Americans are human and there not slightest doubt they would be deeply hurt that valued and admired friend like Shah has decided to trade in arms with our adversaries. This particularly true, I added, at this time when whole American nation is gripped by anxiety over Vietnam.

4.   Shah said problem is one of basic economics. As he had publicly stated in convocation of Deputies March 1, if oil income not stepped up to meet Iran's requirements Iran would have no choice but to look to sources of supply other than traditional suppliers. Problem was purely and simply one of foreign exchange.

5.   On same occasion, Shah said, he had publicly stated his desire maintain traditional sources of arms supplies if those sources would offer acceptable terms. He had made same point in his personal appeals to President Johnson. Meanwhile, he had "waited seven months" for US to understand and respond sympathetically. R and D costs were being assessed and in case of Hawk Missiles this alone represented $2,000,000. I tried to explain that "accessorial charges" included number of elements. Crowning blow, Shah said, was limiting Iran to one squadron of 12 F–4 aircraft. Clearly, Shah said, USG not interested in according Iran favorable treatment compatible with investment US has put into this country or with traditional friendship between our two countries.

6.   [garble—USG?] deeply devoted to Iran's higher interest, I said, USG, unlike certain other countries, not sending arms peddlers around even though we have serious balance of payments problem. We abhor arms races and overriding desire of President and others has been keep military expenditures to minimum adequate level so that economic progress can go forward. I went on to describe his assessment of our hardware response as grossly unfair. Stressing framework of our 1962 and 1964 agreements, I pointed out generous USG cooperation over years which continues to this very moment. Despite surprise nature of additional $200,000,000 authorization which Shah requested and received from parliament, USG had come forward with offer of additional $200,000,000 credit. Military costs are high these days, I said, and US equipment is best available. Prices had been shaved as best we could. Noted in this connection Hawk Missile battalion was offered at $28.8 million when earlier it had been $30, yet Shah in our conversation week ago scarcely noticed Hawk item. Shah said originally we had talked of $22 million price. I noted that was "naked" Hawk battalion.

7.   Shah said total cost of items Iran required was over $400 million according prices USG offered. I said on contrary I continue to have conviction we could work out acceptable procurement program of USG purchased items, providing efficient and adequate military security.

I went on to say that indicative of USG's general forthcomingness, there is today over $200,000,000 worth grant assistance either undelivered or contemplated over next three year period. It difficult to understand, I said, how our Iranian friends overlook something of such importance and appear ready to jeopardize it. Noted in this connection difficulties in obtaining grant funds to support such assistance from Congress.

8.   Referring to inevitability of impact as far as USG is concerned, Shah said if USG held up on planned military supplies it would naturally produce a chain reaction. Among other repercussions, Iran would procure equipment elsewhere. Because of sensitivity of aircraft, he would not consider MIGs. Shah said if F–4 aircraft unavailable he would buy Mirages, adding that French are ready at any time to conclude transaction including credit. When I recalled his aversion to single engine aircraft Shah noted again that Israeli Air Force Chief of Staff had been here and had recommended Mirages enthusiastically.

9.   Agreeing with Shah that chain reaction unfortunate, I asked why in order to save a few dollars by purchases from East Bloc he so ready to risk so much. Noted in this connection how Russians are duping so many Mideast countries by handing out MIG–21s "like lollipops" and mesmerizing Iranians and others with 2-1/2 percent interest rate. Shah said problem was not so much savings as it was Iran's shortage of foreign exchange, caused by lack of responsiveness of oil consortium. It was because of this that Iran must turn to barter arrangements with Soviets.

10. Shah said he knew we would lecture him re iniquities of dealing with Soviets. No one knew them better than he, he said. He fully aware their aims, including his own overthrow. I assured him we fully realize Iranians have had more firsthand experience this subject than even we. Shah said we should realize that by getting Soviets to contribute to Iran's strength, he was in fact improving Iran's capability of resisting Commie penetration.

11. This prompted discussion of implications of Commie involvement in Iranian military establishment as far as US security considerations concerned, vis-à-vis Hawk, Sidewinders and F–4's. Shah tried argue security penetration capability of Soviets would not be significantly increased, but this point seemed at least make slight dent. When he emphasized Soviet involvement would be carefully circumscribed, I told him it is difficult "to be little bit pregnant."

12. Shah returned to old argument how Paks had been hurt by cutoff in US supplies last fall. I reiterated previous arguments. Shah agreed Paks had fomented conflict. He also reluctantly agreed that USG policy of stopping hostilities was wiser than fueling them with more arms. Noting that Arabs were his rivals, I questioned his depending on Soviets if Iran-Arab conflict were to arise. Shah said he aware this point and would lay in adequate spare parts, etc. in advance.

13. Shah obviously actively interested in Soviet SAMs. When I suggested their inferiority to Hawks, noting morning's news that US planes in Vietnam undertook all missions successfully yesterday despite SAMs, Shah insisted effective altitude of Soviet SAMs to possibility of Soviet tanks if Sheridans not available. He was very critical of what he contended is $500,000 per copy price for Sheridans, noting again he being assessed R and D costs. Shah did not contest strongly when I pointed out M–47's still useful and question of Sheridans deferrable at least until 1970.

14. Even more disturbing than "impact" on US-Iran military relationship, I said, is general effect turning to Russians will have on Shah's image and confidence in Iran. I pointed our Western world considers him enlightened, progressive and responsible leader. Some people would inevitably feel he now becoming another De Gaulle or even Nasser. Noted sad shape of other countries who started down arms procurement path with Soviets, i.e. Egypt (whose move to buy Soviet arms came under circumstances not entirely dissimilar from Shah's complaints), Ghana, Indonesia, and even Afghanistan. Shah promptly cited India. When asked whether he envied India's plight, Shah said no, but contended that Iran is much more responsibly and intelligently led than all those countries. I emphasized Iran is doing very well indeed and that is precisely reason we hate see policies which have produced its prosperity put in jeopardy. Shah insisted policy of procuring arms even from Soviets would be fully supported throughout Iran. I said undoubtedly it would be popular with street elements but I would have thought he might have learned from Ayub's present troubles difficulty of putting lid back on Pandora's Box. Shah said all Iranians, not just street, would be content.

15. At one point, Shah warned that when he turns to Soviets USG should not set in motion political movement in Iran. Very thought, I said, is ridiculous. Nevertheless, Shah went on to point out what we would lose if he were to lose his throne. *Comment.* Obsession of this type is incomprehensible to us, but it is in Shah's full character.

16. At one point Shah plaintively expressed wish for opportunity to have two or three days to talk out his problems with President Johnson. He said he very much shares President Johnson's concern for preserving Iran's economic progress. He reemphasized problem is primarily one of foreign exchange. It was because of this serious problem that he had hoped USG could find it possible to accord Iran reasonable prices and terms as it had with M–60 tanks. Pointing out President recalled favorably his personal visits with Shah and to Iran and has high regard for Iran's progress and Shah's leadership, I noted that during my half hour talk with President this came through as did President's personal concern that military expenditures be minimal within framework of adequate security.

17. Each time question Soviet procurement came up, Shah made clear contact been made and transaction with Soviets will fail materialize only if Soviets themselves refuse be responsive. Like Aram (Embtel 61),[2] he recalled trouble he got into with Soviets in 1959 when he retreated from negotiations which had already begun.

18. Shah said he is convoking Senators and Deputies next week to "report" to them on state of affairs as he did on March 1. He said he planned not to go into "details." Before departure, I referred to this and urged that such public pronouncement refrain from making situation any worse. Public blow-up of this issue, I said, would make useless our continuing diplomatic dialogue on a subject with such vital consequences for Iran. Shah indicated concurrence.

19. *Comment.* Give and take was frank and friendly, as Shah had promised Alam it would be. I wish I could say I am encouraged that Shah will not turn to Soviets but I cannot do so. At same time, fact that USG reaction is inevitable is now clearly on record, and room is left for maneuverability as to what our reaction will actually be.

Meyer

---

[2] Not printed. (Ibid., DEF 19–8 US–IRAN)

---

152. Telegram From the Department of State to the Embassy in Iran[1]

Washington, July 8, 1966, 8:41 p.m.

4417. Joint State/Defense.

1. Your statements to Shah, Aram and Alam (Embtels 1762, 31, 80)[2] have covered essential points on US-Iranian political and military relationship, our desire continue that relationship to our mutual benefit (provided GOI action does not make it impossible for us to do so), and political and security problems inherent in any Iranian decision to buy

---

[1] Source: Department of State, Central Files, DEF 19–8 US–IRAN. Secret; Priority; Limdis. Drafted by Crawford, Eliot, and Reed (DOD/ISA); cleared in draft by Warren, Colonel Haynes (DOD/ISA), Macomber, Wriggins, John G. MacCracken (EUR/SOV), and Hare; and approved by Acting Secretary Ball. Repeated to CINCSTRIKE and Moscow.
[2] Documents 148, 149, and 151.

arms from Soviets especially if introduction of Soviet military advisors or technical personnel involved. We were particularly refreshed by your blunt conversation with Shah on seventh and Aram earlier. Trust you will feel free to use with Shah points in paras 5, 6 and 9 in Embtel 31 if you deem them useful.

2. You should seek audience with Shah and make following points:

A. You have reported conversation of July 7 in detail to USG which confirms views you expressed to Shah.

B. In light of Shah's sense of urgency regarding defense of vulnerable industrial and military installations, US actively considering sale of 2 F4 squadrons for delivery commencing in FY'69, sale to be within available $200 million proposed credit and remaining credit under 1964 Understanding. FYI. We are looking at squadrons of 12 to 16 each in C, D, and E series from point of view of pricing, availability and impact on US inventory. Prices and availabilities will follow shortly by septel. End FYI.

C. We believe it would be mistake for Iranians cancel plans purchase Hawk missile units. Hawk would play important part in any credible Iranian air defense capability and could not effectively be replaced by other types of surface-to-air missiles.

D. US willing move ahead on sale of PGM's with first delivery about December 1968 if at least partially funded in third tranche.

E. USG recognizes final decision on arms procurement is matter of Iran's sovereign choice just as furnishing of military assistance is US sovereign choice. We earnestly hope that it will remain in our mutual interest to continue the intimate military relationship we have had in the past.

F. USG urges that Iran not take steps which could damage this relationship. Shah well aware need for public and Congressional support for foreign assistance programs; there is no doubt that Iran's entering into a military relationship with the USSR would produce a negative reaction in the US which would adversely affect this support. It is impossible to predict the future but the Shah can surely understand inevitability of such reaction to attempts to justify a concessionary military program (grant or sales) for Iran if Iran obtains arms from USSR, given the facts that the USSR is the only major long-term threat to Iran's security, that our military assistance to Iran has been predicated primarily on that threat and that Soviets are opposing us and our Free World friends including Iran on Viet Nam. Additionally, there are security considerations affecting sensitive US equipment (FYI, such as F4's end FYI) which would have to be weighed in the light of any Soviet or Eastern European arms program with Iran. FYI. If Shah again raises US-Soviet arms co-existence in India, Iraq, you should note that no sophisticated US equipment involved in either case. End FYI.

G. We note that Ambassador Khosrovani has asked to see Secretary this coming week which will provide further opportunity for discussion these matters.

3. FYI. We are looking into matter of all administrative costs, including R & D. End FYI.

Ball

---

153. Telegram From the Embassy in Iran to the Department of State[1]

Tehran, July 11, 1966, 1400Z.

145. Military Sales to Iran. Ref: State 4417.[2]

1. Pursuant to reftel, I discussed with Shah eleventh each of points set forth in para 2. Left with him written paraphrased version.

2. Re point A, Shah now knows USG endorses fully views which I have previously expressed to him.

3. Re point B, Shah obviously gratified by prospect of two F–4 squadrons being considered for Iran, as well as earlier delivery date. I noted phrase "within available credit" signifies Washington's uninterrupted desire that military expenditures be kept in perspective.

4. Point C opened up whole subject of proposed dealing with Soviets. Disinterest in Hawks, Shah said, is due to fact Iran has approached Soviets for anti-aircraft guns and SAMs. I showed him clipping from July 8 NYHT describing ineffectuality of Soviet SAMs in Viet-Nam. Having had considerable background in capability of Hawks (during days when Israelis first sought them from us), I pointed out superiority this weapon: a) entirely different from Nike–Bloodhound–SAM flashlight ray types; b) radar much more sophisticated; c) catches aircraft at low altitudes, which is what Shah has to fear, as over against SAMs which are not good at low levels; and d) enemy aircraft have more difficulty dodging Hawks than SAMs.

---

[1] Source: Department of State, Central Files, DEF 19–8 US–IRAN. Secret; Limdis. Repeated to CINCSTRIKE/USCINCMEAFSA.

[2] Document 152.

5. Shah showed lively interest in these arguments but countered; a) it's too late; Iran has already approached Soviets and to reject Soviets without hearing them out would be impossible demonstration of his being "US puppet"; and b) it is all question of money; Hawks are too expensive to shoe-horn into available US credit. Re latter point, I said it remains to be seen what we can finally shoe-horn into joint program we had envisaged. Re Soviets, I expressed assumption Iranians would do better staff work than obviously been done to date and decisions re military equipment would be influenced by quality of product as well as low pricing and political considerations. I suggested that inferiority of SAMs might well prove to be loophole from which to get out of transaction with Soviets. While Shah gave no indication, my impression is that this thought was tucked away in his mind for potential but not probable use.

6. Re point D, Shah still attracted to four British Vospers, hovercraft and battle-class destroyer (which while not new will be adequate for time being, he said, particularly as trainer. He likes idea of 1,100 ton Vosper "pocket destroyers" with their 40 knot speed and electronic guns. (He confided in strict confidence Vospers would be equipped with surface to surface missiles to be acquired from a small nonCommie country.) Shah said PGM's are lighter craft, but I stressed earlier delivery date possible than for British vessels which still largely gleam in designer's eye. Shah said destroyer is not essential to British sales package; any or all items availiable in accordance Shah's wishes. Cost of Vosper is 4,000,000 pounds per copy. Once again I urged Shah to assure complete staff work had been accomplished before rushing headlong into a transaction. Throughout discussion I [garble] clear that some well-conceived diversification of his supply sources provided they not Communist is not objectionable.

7. Shah smarted somewhat over assertion in point E that furnishing of military assistance is a choice just as sovereign for US as is procurement for Iran. He himself began adding up figures and found something like $460,000,000 in USG grant and credit is at stake. He suggested this is something we should think about (meaning gravity of chain reaction), but quickly drew obvious point it is even more important for Iranians to think about. I of course, once again emphasized how incredible it is that Shah would jeopardize so much for so little gain. Changing supply pattern in itself would be costly business. Nonetheless, Shah undauntedly professed confidence Iran would one way or another be able fulfill its military needs if complete break in US-Iran military relationship occurs.

8. Re point F, Shah with considerable conviction expressed view Congress could be persuaded to see wisdom of his purchasing some arms from Soviets. He argued: a) by contributing to Iran's security strength, Soviets will in fact be contributing to Iran's ability to resist Communist endeavors against Iran. I said obviously Soviets have other

purposes of which we only too well aware. His second argument: b) Soviets are building up image as being [garble] and peaceful nation whose only interest is to build up Iran's economic strength as by steel mill. Last evening he had heard clandestine broadcast emphasizing this theme. Wouldn't it be more intelligent, he asked, to tarnish Soviet image by diverting to them allegations presently being made against Americans to effect our only interest is monetary profits via peddling of arms? I said latter thought had occurred to us. "Intellectual critics" of Shah's regime (whom Shah loathes) have for long time condemned USG's over-identification with Shah in military field. I said I did not believe day would come when Shah would concur with those critics. He quickly added that such criticism exists in Washington as well as Iran.

9. I went on to say that popular opinion does not usually charge Soviets with same criticism it employs against US. Fact is most Iranians would be impressed and quite a few dismayed by what is becoming virtual stampede in direction of Soviet Bloc, e.g. steel mill, barter agreements, HIM's visits to five Commie countries, etc. My own impression is Soviets and many Iranians would consider this as sign of weakness on Shah's part, particularly if pell mell rush to Soviets is now topped off with arms deal. I pointed out what a triumph all this would represent for Soviet policy in Iran and in Middle East. Shah said it was USG's fault e.g. high prices, R and D costs, etc. Once again I reviewed what we have done to be responsive.

10. Although acknowledging there many different circumstances particularly in economic field, I drew parallel of "red prince" Badr in Yemen. He too had been impatient with West, had gone to Moscow, been wined and dined, and delightedly embarked on arms procurement road with Soviets. Months later, when he was murdered by recipients those arms, Soviets shed no tears but cynically and quickly recognized his successors. Shah opined that Soviets had also worked through Nasser, but then went off on tangent re American recognition of Sallal regime. Shah made clear he intends to purchase five years' supply of spare parts for equipment acquired from Soviets.

11. Shah contended by proper instruction American people could be persuaded of wisdom his buying non-sensitive arms from Soviets. I said this simply not realistic. On contrary, fact that he has been such an admired and responsible friend likely cause added bitterness of jilted lover. Emphasized, as in point F, impossible predict future of concessionary military programs, both grant and sales.

12. Referring to Al Friendly articles, I said Shah has always had good image in US and particularly recently. This highly gratifying. I said it incomprehensible why he wishes tarnish this image in such dramatic fashion. I quoted Shakespeare re money being trash but good name is all-important.

13. When making point re security complications (noted in point F), Shah insisted Soviets would be kept in check. There would be no Iranians trained in Soviet Union and Soviet technicians training in anti-aircraft usage would be kept apart and returned as soon as possible. Again, I said, Shah is being unrealistic. In any case, there no question in USG minds that opportunities for Soviet penetration and subversion would multiply and would effect our willingness-supply equipment. Shah said USG seeking "excuses." I pointed out India and Iraq are examples where US furnishing no sophisticated arms.

14. Shah said he wants proceed with procurement those items he ready purchase from US. He wondered re next move, e.g. letter from Minister of Court to us. I said it not possible make such move until total picture is clear. For example, how could we make an agreement without knowing whether Iran will order Hawks. Shah said he would in any case require three battalions and that would eat up too big a chunk of available credit. He simply wants order from US those items which he clearly wants. If USG unwilling sell F–4's Shah said, he will turn to French Mirages, and there is, he added, some urgency re this matter. I reminded him that when prior to his departure we expressed readiness to provide additional $200,000,000 credit it was made clear that if substantial purchases made elsewhere this would reduce total available from USG. It was obviously time to make this point again for Shah was visibly shaken by it.

15. Shah went into inequities of "strings" and "taking orders." He referred to our "puppets" elsewhere which he did not care to emulate. I asked him to name one. He couldn't. I said even General Ky in whose country USG is investing $20,000,000,000 is, sometimes to our pain, his own boss. Human beings everywhere, including Americans, have same instincts as wish of wanting be "independent." There is no attempt, I said, for USG to give Shah "orders." There is, however a great challenge to both our countries to translate former aid-dependent relationship into something normal, natural, constructive and durable. I said I was sure this was his intention, even as it ours, but it is something that must be done gradually and may not survive drastic move as his turning to north. Irritated by phrase "turning to north," Shah reiterated his old line that over these past months USG has failed to respond satisfactorily to his appeals including indications that he would, if necessary and as much as he disliked it, increase trade, including initiation of some arms procurement, from East Bloc if USG and oil companies persisted in their disinterestedness.

16. Throughout conversation I stressed to Shah importance of his maintaining his maneuverability. This is true in his handling of opinion in Iran, I indicated, (having in mind his forthcoming session with Parliament members). Shah said he is refraining from airing details of issue be-

tween our two countries, even in his deliberate efforts to fashion US opinion as via Al Friendly and via Tom Brady who is currently here with *New York Times*. Shah agreed our diplomatic dialogue continue.

17. *Comment.* There is no longer question Shah has approached Soviets for Ack Ack guns and SAMs. He indicated several times curiosity re what Soviet response will be, even manifesting a little impatience over failure of Soviets to reply in past ten days or fortnight. He thought it might be their preoccupation with Warsaw Pact. Questions now are whether Shah can be persuaded to extricate himself from joint business (using technical loopholes) with Soviets, and if not how to shape our own response considering among other factors undesirability pushing him further into Soviet embrace.

Meyer

---

154. Telegram From the Department of State to the Embassy in Iran[1]

Washington, July 12, 1966, 6:02 p.m.

5931. 1. Following summary July conversation is FYI and Noforn. It is uncleared and subject to amendment upon review of memcon.

2. Khosrovani began by stressing Iranian friendship for US, hope that close relationship would continue and gratitude for past and present US aid. He said he instructed explain that momentum of development and reform programs must be sustained while at same time defense program requires attention in light Egyptian trouble-making in Persian Gulf. If US not able assist as much as before, Iran hopes it will understand if Iran procures what it needs at cheaper prices from elsewhere. Iranian military cooperation with US will be maintained and there should be no US apprehension.

3. Secretary replied he familiar with talks Ambassador Meyer has had on this subject with Shah and Aram. He said we have always held Shah in highest esteem and continue do so. Under his leadership Iran has

---

[1] Source: Department of State, Central Files, POL 17 IRAN–US. Secret; Limdis. Drafted by Eliot, cleared by Hare, and approved by Walsh. Repeated to CINCSTRIKE.

never been more stable, secure and progressive. We have greatly valued relationship and hope it will continue. We understand what we have offered may not be as much as Shah wants, but it very large in light US fighting war and other burdens on US taxpayer.

4. Secretary said Iran is of course as sovereign as US, but we are concerned about path on which Shah may be embarking because we do not see where it will lead. If there is trouble in area, it comes from USSR through its provision of arms to UAR and Iraq and its encouragement of trouble-making. Secretary said it difficult understand what Iranian arms purchases from Soviets will mean for Iran or for USSR. Soviet attitude to Iran well known, and Aram himself has in past commented on his concern about "friendly Soviet subversion." It not surprising Soviets might want sell arms cheaply, for example SAM's after their experience with them in Viet Nam. Of over 300 fired in Viet Nam only 14 on target, and head of Soviet missile program is in Viet Nam to see what is wrong.

5. Secretary added it difficult perceive longer-term effects on US-Iranian relations of contemplated Iranian steps. Since 1946 we have given strong support to independence and security of Iran. We don't know what Congress and American public will think about Iran's turning for arms to the principal source of trouble in area. This not something which executive branch alone can control. Hence reaction cannot be predicted, but we hope our relations will remain intimate as they have been of mutual benefit for past twenty years. In short, we concerned about future.

6. Secretary also pointed out we might have serious security problems if Iranian purchases from Soviets expose our sensitive equipment such as F-4's to penetration.

7. Khosrovani responded by saying admittedly USSR a threat, but immediate danger comes from elsewhere. He said Iran feels need as independent nation be able defend itself and stronger Iran will be better friend of US. He twice expressed hope we would make clearer in Tehran what it is we are prepared to offer, saying that Iran must make best use of its limited financial resources.

8. Ambassador Hare mentioned that we have been pursuing in Tehran question of program for our available credit and that Ambassador Meyer has told Shah we are considering second F-4 squadron.

9. Secretary said if there are problems about amounts of money and delivery dates this is because we are demonstrating in Viet Nam, by among other things spending extra billion dollars per month, that friendship of US is important to security of our friends. Most important security asset Iran has is friendship of US.

10. Khosrovani, saying he speaking personally, commented that there is a psychological factor involved in that at certain stage of development countries feel they should have independent means of defense.

11. Secretary responded Iran's armed forces are for defense of Iran and Iran's policy is independent but repeated we do not understand what it means for Iran to turn for arms to the source of trouble in the area.

12. Khosrovani asked if this would not neutralize Soviet policy, to which Secretary replied it works other way too and Soviets may want have important influence on Iranian policy. Replying US should not worry about that as GOI will maintain close ties with US military mission, Khosrovani said Iran wants to be free to procure in any available market. Iran understands, he said, value of US friendship and is grateful and hopes any new steps will not be misunderstood.

13. Secretary concluded conversation by once again stressing US has respect for Shah's great service to his country and has continuing desire for friendship but does not have complete understanding because we do not see where contemplated steps lead.

Rusk

---

155. Memorandum From Vice President Humphrey to President Johnson[1]

Washington, July 13, 1966, 10:30 a.m.

Over the years I have gradually developed an increasing appreciation for what Iran does in the world. The Shah has worked closely with Israel. Iran is the only country in the Middle East contributing directly to South Vietnam.

Recently I met the Shah's brother socially, as well as several other well informed friends of Iran. Their story is always the same: Please tell the President that unless something happens to change his mind, the

---

[1] Source: Johnson Library, National Security File, Country File, Iran, Memos & Miscellaneous, Vol. II, 1/66–1/69. No classification marking. Attached to a July 14 draft memorandum from Rostow to the President noting that the Vice President had hit the nub of an Iranian problem they had been struggling with: "When the Shah feels cut off from you, he reads our every act as a rebuff." It is not clear whether this memorandum was sent to the President. Another copy of the memorandum (ibid., NSC Files of Harold Saunders, Iran 4/1/66–12/31/67), is attached to a July 13 note from Bromley Smith to Wriggins noting that it was for a memorandum from Rostow to the President. A notation in Wriggins' handwriting on the note reads: "See WWR memo for President 7/19/66" (Document 157).

Shah is going to buy a package of Soviet arms on the relatively easy credit they dangle in front of him.

Our executive departments are struggling to come up with the right answer; since April they have wrestled each other without decision.

I know how overcrowded your calendar is and I would only suggest adding to it for the most important reasons.

In the present circumstances I feel it would be wonderful if you would invite the Shah to come talk to you. He wants to hear from you personally what a grand guy he is, and how much you love him. He wants to tell you his fears and he needs to be reassured by you. Only the President, himself, can persuade the Shah against taking the step he is now contemplating.

---

156. Memorandum From Harold H. Saunders of the National Security Council Staff to W. Howard Wriggins of the National Security Council Staff[1]

Washington, July 14, 1966.

Howard:

Jim Critchfield called to explain the two tacks the Agency is going to take with the Shah:

1. In the next few days [less than 1 line of source text not declassified] will be giving the Shah a rather complete technical commentary for his eyes only on the performance of the Soviet missiles. He feels this will thoroughly demonstrate that the Soviet missile is a third rate product which will be increasingly obsolete in the next couple of years, especially as the countermeasures to it will become as widespread as the missile itself.

2. [less than 1 line of source text not declassified] will tell the Shah that no one of his friends [less than 1 line of source text not declassified]—though they have sympathized with the Shah's viewpoint for many years—agrees that he is doing the right thing now. First, he will set off a train of events here in Washington where everyone is preoccupied with Vietnam

---

[1] Source: Johnson Library, National Security File, NSC Files of Harold Saunders, Iran, 4/1/66–12/31/67. Secret.

that no one can see the end of. If he can just be patient, Washington is increasingly aware of the Shah's legitimate interest in the Persian Gulf and is working its way to encouraging him to take a larger role there. On the Middle Eastern theme, with recent developments in Iraq, the gap between the Shah and his potential adversaries is narrowing. Moving to the Soviet Union now would just undermine this very hopeful trend.

Critchfield reiterated his feeling that the chief ingredient of this problem is the Shah's sense of being cut off from the President. The Shah believes that the letters the President sends him are drafted in the State Department and, therefore, he has had no direct communication with Lyndon Johnson since the President took office.

Critchfield says he argued with Bill Moyers and others in the White House discreetly that during the Shah's recent trip we should invite him to fly over from Morocco for a few hours to see the President. Moyers and others felt the President should not be involved, so we missed that opportunity for a quiet morale boosting exercise which would have stopped this whole Soviet ploy in its tracks.

I commended Critchfield for the private approach he is planning to have made. I told him what we had in mind to proliferate the impression that Washington is deeply disturbed by the Shah's move. Critchfield feels we missed a golden opportunity to have the Shah here back in June but is not sure that now, in the wake of Brady's article, we could do this. He promised to keep us posted.

HHS[2]

---

[2] Printed from a copy that bears these typed initials.

157.   Memorandum From the President's Special Assistant (Rostow) to President Johnson[1]

Washington, July 19, 1966, 6 p.m.

We are down to the wire in our arms negotiations with the Shah. He still feels that the $200 million package we offered does not include all the air defense he needs; and he has approached the USSR for surface-to-air missiles and anti-aircraft guns. We included both our Hawk missile and some AA guns in our package, but Soviet prices are lower.

Part of the Shah's move is traditional Persian bargaining. But there are other elements:

—He feels neglected and taken for granted; and he rightly sees these negotiations as a way to gain attention.

—He genuinely fears that the UAR and Iraq have designs on his oil-producing southern provinces. Our cutting off Ayub's military aid last fall left him suspicious that we would do the same to him in a fight with local non-Communist enemies.

—He sees short-run domestic political advantage in showing he is not a U.S. puppet.

We are trying through both formal and informal channels to dissuade him from buying Soviet equipment. If he wishes to diversify his sources of hardware, Western Europe would make more sense and be acceptable to us.

Defense says security would prevent our selling advanced equipment if Soviet technicians come to Iran.

Congress would also give us a hard time if another ally turns to Communist arms supply, although the problem arises in good part because military aid funds are too low.

Most important, while the Shah's reform program is going well, Iran is far from out of the woods politically. We wish to avoid his inviting the Soviets into Iran to meddle in what may still be a turbulent process of evolution.

On balance, we would rather not see the Shah buy equipment on the scale he contemplates. Though oil revenues are good, we fear he is over-reaching his ability to repay in the years ahead without cutting into development. We have set up an annual joint review to keep the military-economic balance firmly before the Shah.

But the fact is that he believes the Arab threat is urgent; and he believes security comes first. With the British pulling out of South Arabia

---

[1] Source: Johnson Library, National Security File, Special Head of State Correspondence File, Iran, Shah Correspondence, Vol. II. Secret. A handwritten "L" on the memorandum indicates that it was seen by the President.

and retrenching in the Persian Gulf, I'm not sure he isn't right. He is dead earnest when he says he will buy this hardware somewhere if we refuse to sell it. Soviet equipment is the cheapest, though Soviet missiles are poor in quality, at least when manned by North Vietnamese.

Our choices now are to:

—Tell him that we have gone the limit and that if he buys Soviet hardware he will jeopardize our continued military aid. Chances are that he would go ahead anyway if only to underline his independence, and we would have to make up our minds to adjust to an increasingly neutralist Iran.

—Offer one more concession in substituting 32 rehabilitated F–4C aircraft for the 12 new F–4D's in our initial offer. Secretary McNamara could take these out of our inventory in late 1968 and pass them on at second-hand prices, so the cost to us would be the difference between that price and our cost of replacing those planes with newer models for our own inventory.

I share the judgment of Secretaries Rusk and McNamara that we should make this final offer.

We would still try to keep the Shah within the total credit ceiling you approved, but we would have to absorb about $30 million in additional costs to the USAF via our FY 1967 supplemental. This would round out our effort to meet his most legitimate air defense and other needs at good prices.

Secretary Rusk also recommends you send the Shah a letter.

I have thus far resisted involving you directly in the bargaining which has been going on. But now that we are about to make our final move, I think a letter is a good idea. Part of our trouble is the Shah's familiar feeling that he is cut off from you. This letter would show that you fully understand his real worries and have personally tried—within the limits of your problems—to accommodate him.

Attached is for your signature, if you approve.[2]

Walt

---

[2] Document 158.

158.   Letter From President Johnson to the Shah of Iran[1]

Washington, July 20, 1966.

Your Imperial Majesty:

I have followed closely Ambassador Meyer's reports of his recent conversations with you. He has told me of your concern over Iran's defense requirements, and I want to share with you my own views on the developing situation before us. Candor between friends is essential to mutual understanding and my views are offered in that vein.

The total relationship between the United States and Iran, and particularly our cooperation in military matters, has been cordial and it has met the interests of both our countries. The U.S. for its part sincerely hopes that circumstances will permit this to continue in full effectiveness.

For we share a common view of certain basic problems. Thus we both understand that, while the immediate threat of Soviet military aggression has receded, indirect pressures continue and the Soviet aim of communizing Iran remains the same. I know clandestine radio broadcasts remind you daily of this long-range threat. You have shown your understanding of Communist aims by sending an Iranian team to Vietnam, and I am strengthened by this demonstration of your faith in our purpose there.

We also share the realization that the Middle East is undergoing rapid change. The unfolding situation, particularly in the areas south of Iran, demands our close watchfulness, as it embodies both potential opportunity and potential danger. At a time when the United States is heavily engaged in the defense of freedom in Asia, we are no less interested in continued stability in the Persian Gulf area. We welcome your determination to help maintain that stability. As responsible leaders, we share the awareness that our task is to make inevitable change as orderly and constructive as possible.

It was thus against a background of continuing comradeship between our two nations in facing together a complex and dangerous international environment and of concern for Iran's security that we have offered an additional $200 million credit for the purchase of military equipment. We have been seeking by all means to develop fair and reasonable terms. We are also urgently working further on the particular questions of price and delivery dates for two squadrons of F–4 aircraft.

---

[1] Source: Johnson Library, National Security File, Special Head of State Correspondence File, Iran, Shah Correspondence, Vol. II. Secret.

Our resources are, of course, burdened by the defense of free world interests in Vietnam. And they are limited, for military assistance purposes, by the Congress. Nevertheless, it remains our intent to respond to your security needs; and I believe we have done so.

You should have no doubt of our desire to help Iran. But you should also understand that if Iran were to enter into an arms arrangement with the Soviet Union or with other Communist countries, this would confront us with serious problems in carrying forward our military assistance.

While you may see short-term advantages to such a step, I see major long-term disadvantage, both political and technical.

First, I cannot believe that any of us will profit by the Soviets' coming any closer to the Persian Gulf than they already are. I would not guess that they regard it as in their interest that the stability of this area be increased.

Second, it would confuse our Congress and our people concerning Iran's intentions. I cannot predict precisely what the reaction here would be; but it would certainly be unfavorable to the interests which we share in strengthening Iran's defenses.

Third, on the technical side, I am certain you can appreciate our intent to protect sensitive American equipment from compromise by Soviet military technicians.

Our purpose in aiding Iran has been to preserve and strengthen your country's independence. We are proud to have contributed to the gathering political and economic strength of Iran under your wise and skillful leadership. If Iran should turn to the Communist nations for arms, we will not be so shortsighted as to turn from our close relationship. But I do fear the impairment of our military assistance program.

Therefore, I hope that you will look only to Free World sources of arms in meeting your security requirements.

You will, of course, weigh this matter in the light of Iran's basic interests as you see them. I did, however, want you to receive my views personally and with the complete candor our partnership requires and deserves.

I look forward to going more deeply into this and other problems of common concern when it becomes possible for us to meet. I will also very much want to hear directly from you more about the heartening economic and social progress Iran has made under your skillful leadership. Unfortunately, with our coming elections, I doubt we can manage to get together in the next several months. Perhaps early in the new year we could find a mutually agreeable time for direct discussion. In the meantime, I wanted to share with you now—in the spirit of the partnership I feel—the problems which might arise.

Sincerely,

Lyndon B. Johnson

---

159.   Memorandum From W. Howard Wriggins of the National Security Council Staff to the President's Special Assistant (Rostow)[1]

Washington, July 22, 1966.

SUBJECT

McNamara turns down planes at concessional prices for Iran

McNamara and Vance have decided that we cannot add $30 or $40 million to the nearly $1 billion supplemental in order to provide planes for the Shah at concessional prices (and simultaneously modernize the U.S. air force more rapidly) by taking 2 squadrons of F–4's out of inventory for the Shah in 1968.

McNaughton tells me that there were three reasons for this:

(1) FYI, the F–4C's are not as maneuverable as they should be, and he doesn't want the Shah to have them because this fact would then become widely known.

(2) He does not want to decide *now* whether and at what pace he wants to permit the air force to replace the F–4C's. This decision will not be coming up for six weeks to two months. (These reasons have nothing to do with the Shah or Iran.)

(3) He thinks that if the Shah wants to be so foolish as to go to the Russians for equipment and risk cutting off his supplies from us, as was made unambiguously but delicately clear in the letter to the Shah, he should feel free to try it. McNamara does not think it the end of the world for the Shah if he does procure something from the Soviets. What is important is what he procures and our own reaction to it.

McNaughton has warned McNamara that he should expect flak from State on this. And he admits he might be amenable to the argument that

—the Shah is unusually nervous and in a particularly irrational season; this has been accentuated by the action we took last year vis-à-vis Pakistan to bring them in line;

---

[1] Source: Johnson Library, National Security File, NSC Files of Harold Saunders, Iran Military, 4/1/66–12/31/67. Secret.

—the Shah is now particularly anxious about the Persian Gulf, Nasser and the British pull-out;

—we are seeking to ensure rights for intelligence facilities;

—by the Shah's peculiar chemistry, the prices and quantity of planes have become for him the touchstone of whether or not the President is his friend.

I would add:

—the political climate here, in an election year, may or may not permit us to control our own reaction to an Iran which appears to be following Ayub off the reservation, however understandable this may be to us specialists;

—you will recall the President's hope, expressed to Armin Meyer and you, that "his people" would "do their best" to meet the Shah's needs;

—a forthcoming offer now may well direct the Shah's purchases to purely token acquisitions of ack ack. No offer now maximizes the chances of a substantial lurch toward the Soviets as the Shah broods over the Gulf and Nasser-in-Iraq.

I would therefore urge a call to Alex Johnson to see how hard he weighed in (probably not very hard) on political grounds yesterday, and then a call to Vance or McNamara to express the President's concern. This should wait till Secretary Rusk makes a personal push with McNamara tonight or tomorrow.

Howard Wriggins[2]

---

[2] Printed from a copy that bears this typed signature.

---

160.   Telegram From the Embassy in Iran to the Department of State[1]

Tehran, July 23, 1966, 1430Z.

365. Ref: State 12039.[2]

1.   Delivered President's letter to Shah at Caspian morning 23rd. After careful perusal, Shah expressed appreciation for warm tone but observed that contents were identical with what I have been telling him.

---

[1] Source: Department of State, Central Files, DEF 19 US–IRAN. Secret; Priority; Exdis. Repeated to Moscow.

[2] Telegram 12039 to Tehran, July 21, transmitted the President's letter to the Shah. (Ibid.) The letter is printed as Document 158.

2. Almost resignedly, Shah said everything depends on Russians. It was Iran which took initiative and it simply not possible for Iran call off approach made.

3. Shah said he first to recognize Russians "are my enemies." At same time, in his opinion USG cannot "reproach" him for what he did. He reiterated usual line about waiting many months for American responsiveness but, while he appreciated $200,000,000 credit, USG prices were high, terms were harder than they should be, and delivery dates were far off. Particularly indicative of USG lack of sympathy, he said, was limiting sale of F–4 aircraft to 12 (which would mean 3 per airfield). This reflected persistent Washington disposition to make decisions which Shah feels are within his competence.

4. Once again I pointed out USG had indeed been responsive. In addition to credit, we agreeing to make available best military equipment in world, e.g. F–4 aircraft, despite fact that we fighting major conflict in Viet-Nam which requires full complement such equipment. Moreover, as President's letter indicates, we continuing to review possibilities, e.g. F–4 situation. I made clear President's personal interest in Iran and current problem in particular.

5. Reiterating he on spot with Russians, Shah insisted that he would reject any Soviet proposals if there any conditions attached. This led to assessment, which Aram had conveyed (Embtel 319),[3] that Soviets have so much to gain from mere disruption of US–Iran military relationship that other considerations, including conditions, are of secondary importance. Shah agreed with that assessment, but opined that USG seems ready to leave, "luggage packed and with first class tickets."

6. While recognizing that Shah may have gotten himself "in a box" with Russians, I expressed confidence he could extricate himself if he truly wished. Expressing assumption he "free man," I said I did not see why just because he had approached Russians he required effect purchases, particularly since it possible to demonstrate that most of Russian equipment could be refused on quality grounds, e.g. SAMs. Shah assured me he "under no obligation" but it also clear he is so psychologically. I questioned economics of buying "cheap" SAMs with 5 percent efficiency when Hawks, though more expensive, have many times effectiveness.

7. Shah had received from General Khatemi info we had passed along re Hawks vs SAMs (State 8922).[4] To this I added additional info, e.g. SAMs been diagnosed by our specialists, their vulnerabilities determined, and counter-measures developed which in not too distant future

---

[3] Dated July 21. (Department of State, Central Files, DEF 12–5 IRAN)

[4] Dated July 15. (Ibid.)

will be available through normal arms channels; that 82 SAMs been fired in Viet-Nam in last 90 days without a hit; that Soviets withhold some of the SAM data so as to maintain key control; and that SAM ineffectiveness in Viet-Nam is despite fact they manned by Russians. Shah said Pak mission which recently in Moscow was told by Soviets SAM problem was due to incompetent Vietnamese manning them. (*Comment:* Any sure info Washington has on this point would be helpful to us.)

8.   Of parenthetical interest, Shah said Pak mission to Moscow at first ran into Soviet jibes re their American friends, their relations to CENTO and SEATO, etc. Subsequently, however, Paks were shown SAMs, a high quality tank with two anti-aircraft guns, truly remarkable mobile radar, etc. Asked if transaction concluded, Shah said no it is under Pak study. He implied Paks are worried about effect on their improving relations with USG. Shah said ChiCom equipment been provided to Paks completely "free of charge" (he agreed it is obviously for ulterior motive). Shah took occasion to emphasize importance Iran's keeping door open to Paks to avoid further entanglement with Commie countries.

9.   Asked what specifically Iranians have asked of Russians, Shah said anti-aircraft guns, SAMs and "other things" not coverable via USG or British credit. Reluctantly he indicated tanks cannot be excluded. He said plans must be made for replacing M–47's. He had hoped for Sheridans. Reiterating no response yet received from Soviets, Shah said only clue was Soviet Military Attaché recently asked an Iranian officer why Iran not interested in Soviet aircraft. Shah again assured that under no circumstances will he purchase MIG's.

10. Shah insisted he will tolerate no Soviet "conditions," e.g. ouster of ARMISH/MAAG, withdrawal from CENTO, or even stationing of Soviet technicians in Iran. Under interrogation, however, he appeared less sure that he could hold the line at just "some training of few students." To illustrate his firmness re "conditions" Shah said Soviet Ambassador when Shah was in Europe called on For Ministry UnderSec Qarib, and referring to *NYTimes* article, protested USG strategic installations in northern Iran. Shah said he sent word back to tell Soviet Ambassador to "mind his own business." Shah noted that in 1962 Iran had promised Soviets not to have foreign missile bases and Soviet Ambassador was told that no interference in Iran's internal affairs would be brooked from any quarter. (*Comment:* This is first time Shah has referred to subject of our installations in any conversation on arms sales.)

11. Shah was greatly impressed by two phrases in President's letter, i.e. US "will not be so shortsighted as to turn from our close relationship". And President's fear that our "military assistance program" will be impaired. Shah bemoaned why would USG undertake "strong reaction" which would so clearly serve Soviet aim. Noting that it was not

USG which has produced present situation, I said President in his letter gave three clear reasons why USG reaction inevitable. Even if Executive Branch were not involved, American people and Congress are. Moreover, potential compromise of highly classified equipment should certainly be understood by him. Observing that Soviets not bothered by such things as "this Congress business," Shah again said USG can always find "excuses." I said sharply this not question of "excuses." Then went into lengthy explanation of how USG does not want its Hawks, Blue Shark and F–4's compromised after example of Soviet SAMs. Pursuant to last para Embtel 311,[5] I noted how difficult it would be to shield Soviet technicians from Blue Shark control, etc. Shah said he suspects Soviets already know much re US equipment, and in my case he would shield US equipment, as for example by keeping Soviet technicians within walled compound way out in country.

12. Shaken but seemingly undaunted by Presidential declaration that US military program here will be adversely affected, Shah reiterated his earnest desire that US–Iran military relationship not be disrupted. He added, however, that if that came to pass, Iran would be able fill void from other sources. I reiterated that as long as Iran arms procurement is from non-Communist sources, USG does not object. Except for Soviet procurement, I agreed with Shah that there may even be advantage in diversification as a principle in order for Iran to have a more independent image.

13. Shah contended that while he turned to Soviets only because of USG's insufficient responsiveness, there may even be one or two good points favoring the move. For one thing, it would demonstrate to the people of Iran that Soviets are arms peddlers (a criticism heretofore reserved only for Americans) as well as peaceful steel mill providers. Secondly, Shah said that by his dealing with Soviets it may help "break Soviet offensive in building up a bloc of so-called progressive states" in Mideast.

14. This provided occasion expound my theory that Soviet motives are diabolical. Soviets have no qualms about fueling regional conflicts, I said, probably realizing that as with Pak–India conflict last fall those conflicts will run out of gas in couple of weeks and both sides welcome UN truce order. Meanwhile, Soviets pour arms into countries friendly to them to assure their friendship. Shah himself interjected that in process they wean America's friends and make them ripe for Soviet blandishments. Shah added that behind these moves Soviets are desperately trying shore up waning fortunes of Socialist-Communist system which is failing wherever it exists and which is doomed unless Soviets can divert attention from its failures. He cited Syria as product of these Soviet en-

[5] Dated July 20. (Ibid., DEF 19–8 US–IRAN)

deavors. I said this was precisely my main point, i.e. by loading up Mideast countries with arms Soviets can keep them weak and dependent. I said Soviet propaganda re "progressive" Mideast states, i.e. Syria, UAR and Egypt, is hollow as long as Iran, Saudi Arabia, Lebanon and even "unviable" Jordan are doing so much better than "progressives." Obviously, I said, Soviets want to reduce all Mideast states to be Syrias. Shah agreed, but, of course, insisted that Iran has no choice but to build up adequate defense, as even Peterson mission, he added, had determined is necessary. Saying he doubted USG capable of handling several Viet-Nam situations at once, Shah said he continues to believe it is in USG interest to have Iran adequately equipped to deter or cope with regional threat in Persian Gulf area.

15. During course of conversation I pointed to President's warm hope that Shah and he could talk things out. Shah showed gratification at this point but at same time made clear that his decisions re military procurement cannot wait until early next year.

16. *Comment:* There was no indication whether or not Shah will reply to President's letter. Letter, however, was very timely both to get on record from highest US authority likelihood of significant USG reaction to Iran's purchasing from Soviets and at same time placing on record President's own desire to maintain close US–Iran ties. My point in delivering letter personally was to provide additional info re SAMs and press point that if Shah really wants to he can find technical or other reasons for retreating from Soviet embrace. My impression is, however, that complete retreat is almost impossible, unless Soviets play their hand badly or unless USG comes through with some new proposals markedly more favorable in terms.

Meyer

161.   Telegram From the Embassy in Iran to the Department of State[1]

Tehran, July 25, 1966, 1230Z.

378. For Hare NEA. Ref: State 13889.[2]

1. Even before we informed Shah we "considering" second F–4 squadron (State 4417),[3] he insistent on need for two squadrons of 16 each. He himself had figured on basis one squadron of 12 or 13 for $39 million that two squadrons of 16 would cost circa $100 million. He considered this cost high but he might conceivably pay this sum: a) because he knows F–4 is best of its kind; and b) he and General Khatemi want keep air force in US hands. As to delivery, Shah's target date for completion of defense build-up is 1968, when British leave Aden and in his view Nasserist threat will become more serious. He will, therefore, be disappointed at prospect of delivery in 1969–70.

2. In President's letter, as earlier, we have indicated possibility two F–4 squadrons. Since Shah has had no reason to reckon cost at other than $100 million, proposal in reftel would represent nothing new nor special. It would, therefore, by itself not dissuade Shah from buying other things from Soviets. Meanwhile, French are pressing hard, and if his hopes for F–4's falter, Shah apt move quickly to purchase of Mirages (which he been offered at half F–4 price and better credit terms). He has made this clear in conversations with me.

3. My talk with Shah 23rd,[4] as well as comments from numerous top Iranians, have convinced me that if we hope have any chance keeping Soviets out, we are going have to offer something which clearly indicates extraordinary move by USG. As minimum, it means: a) noteworthy mark-down in F–4 price (probably on order 50 percent which is attractiveness of rehab F–4 proposal); b) reduction of $2 million in battalion price of Hawks (which Shah considers R and D surcharge); c) scaling down of surcharges on other equipment; d) expeditious schedule of deliveries; and e) ultimate availability under USG credit of Sheridan tanks.

4. Above is tall order, but should be within USG competence. Underneath bargaining lies something more fundamental. Sahah remains obsessed with idea that since 1961 USG has shifted its affection from traditional friends and allies (he probably has read Schlesinger) to court-

---

[1] Source: Department of State, Central Files, DEF 12–5 IRAN. Secret; Priority; Limdis.

[2] In telegram 13889 to Tehran, July 22, Hare asked for the Ambassador's judgment as to the probable Iranian reaction to a U.S. offer of an aircraft package of two squadrons of new F–4s (up to a total of 32 aircraft) at new aircraft prices with rough cost estimate of $50 million per squadron and probable delivery in late 1969 or early 1970. (Ibid.)

[3] Document 152.

[4] See Document 160.

ing "third world." He is, therefore, looking for unmistakable sign that USG values Iran's friendship. For his simple barometer is prices, terms and delivery dates we offer for military equipment which he is prepared to purchase (instead of receiving as grant as heretofore) and which he considers essential for Iran's role, particularly in Gulf area after 1968.

5.   Current Soviet aim, manifest in daily clandestine broadcasts, is ouster of US influence in Iran, particularly US military presence and our strategic facilities which military presence covers. While Embassy cannot guarantee that special move as suggested in para 3 will preclude all arms purchases from Soviets, we can guarantee that without such move Soviets will make major inroads and US interests will suffer accordingly. By making such a move, with attractive F–4 proposition at its heart, USG will: a) demonstrate to Shah USG's continued interest in assisting Iran to meet its reasonable defense requirements; b) provide Shah with bridge for retreating from excessive military involvement with Soviets; c) thwart Soviet efforts for ousting our facilities and other interests here; and d) assure healthy maturation of US–Iran relationship. If despite friendly USG move Shah still becomes entwined with Soviets, we remain free to adjust our policies as circumstances require.

Meyer

162.   Memorandum of Conversation[1]

Washington, July 26, 1966, 11:30 a.m.

THOSE PRESENT

Ambassador Khosro Khosrovani (Iran); Howard Wriggins

I first expressed Mr. Rostow's regret for not being able to meet with the Ambassador, but that he had unexpectedly been called upstairs by the President before a Cabinet meeting that was to follow about 12:15. I suggested we have our discussion, and then if Mr. Rostow returned, he could carry on.

---

[1] Source: Johnson Library, National Security File, Country File, Iran, Memos & Miscellaneous, Vol. II, 1/66–1/69. Secret. Copies were sent to Rostow, Hare, and Saunders.

Ambassador Khosrovani made six main points:

1. Iran is America's closest friend in the Middle East; it is the only one which has stood with us on behalf of our policy in Vietnam. The Shah argued for three days in Bucharest in order to water down a sharp Rumanian communiqué. We have stood side by side in the anti-Communist struggle.

2. However, Iran has found that the direction of the threat to Iran has been changing somewhat over the past two or three years, as Soviet policy toward Iran has become more civil while Soviet military support for the Arab countries has radically increased. This has happened at a time when British power is withdrawing from the area, particularly the Persian Gulf. The Shah believes that America's reaction to this changed situation has not been as responsive as the threat from the Arab countries has required.

3. While he has great respect for our military experience and the competence of our military specialists, the long discussions preceding each decision on military support have sometimes appeared like foot-dragging and have often been humiliating as foreign advisors tell him that they know better what he needs than he does—a contention the Shah is unwilling to accept.

4. With the U.S. switch from grant assistance to credit sales, the unwillingness of the oil companies to increase Iran's oil liftings, and the Shah's need to channel resources into development, the Shah was having increasing difficulties in meeting his rising defense requirements. He therefore found it necessary to seek out the cheapest source of supply, which is now the Soviet Union. This is regrettable, but the Shah has seen no alternative.

5. While the United States is understandably fearful of any Soviet presence in Iran, the Iranians have been dealing with the Russians for many generations. They have a "feel for the real dangers." Now, the more immediate danger is from the revolutionary Arab world.

6. Ambassador Khosrovani is not at all convinced that "all is lost." So far as he knows, the Shah has not been pressing Moscow hard for an answer. The Ambassador believes that if we can provide fairly promptly a forthcoming answer to the present negotiations, the Shah may not feel it necessary to go forward with his Russian explorations. He hopes very much that whatever misunderstanding that appears to have come between us will easily be overcome. He knows the Shah has no desire to change in any way the essential relationship between our two countries. He hoped very much to be able to see Mr. Rostow personally.

Mr. Wriggins' main points were:

1. We ourselves have been puzzled and frankly somewhat annoyed by the Shah's approach to this problem. In 1964 we provided $200 million for a 5-year defense program.

2. Within less than two years the Shah raised another $200 million for defense purposes; and then appeared to expect us to immediately respond. We did provide a special military mission to examine the problem.

3. While the Shah may have felt that this was not entirely sufficient, it made substantial recommendations which we actively pursued toward another $200 million—more than doubling our assistance within a five-year period. While we were examining this problem, we were suddenly informed that he is seeking assistance from the Soviet Union. (The Ambassador replied we should not have been surprised—we had had plenty of warning from the Shah's advisors.)

4. We have never argued that he wasn't independent or that he didn't have the power to make his own decisions. Of course he did. Indeed, as a long-time student of politics outside of North America and Western Europe, I fully understood the desire of governments to demonstrate their independence. All we were attempting to do was to make quite sure that the Shah understood that in choosing this way of demonstrating his independence, there could be serious consequences, however unpredictable. As the Secretary and I have pointed out before, it was impossible to predict how the Congress would react if Iran, an old and close ally against Communism, began to accept substantial quantities of military equipment from the Soviet Union. It also raised the problem of protecting the security of our advanced equipment. This was not like India, where no advanced equipment had been sent. The fact of the presence of Soviet technicians in Iran would pose us considerable difficulty. The Shah, I knew, would take these considerations into account as he attempted to add up what he considered to be to the best advantage of Iran.

We both expressed our pleasure at seeing each other again and discussing this matter once more. We both hoped nothing would stand in the way of continued close collaboration between our two countries.

He expressed the hope that he could greet Mr. Rostow before he went on leave tomorrow afternoon—simply a courtesy call of a few moments, if that were possible. (He had obviously reported home he was seeing Mr. Rostow, and wanted to be able to report home that he had seen him.)

I told him I would do my best to arrange a convenient time, though I made it clear it would be difficult to arrange on this short notice.

HW

163.   Letter From Vice Presidential Aide George Carroll to Vice President Humphrey[1]

Washington, July 27, 1966.

SUBJECT

Conversation with Kermit Roosevelt

You know Kermit Roosevelt. He is Vice President, Gulf Oil Company. He is also President, Middle East Institute. No American knows the Shah of Iran as well as does Kim. While he was still abroad he communicated with his secretary here in Washington and asked her to arrange a meeting with me upon his arrival. Therefore, the meeting which I now report was held with some sense of urgency.

I learned its urgency as soon as we sat down to talk. The Shah saw Roosevelt for over three hours. Roosevelt's main conclusion is that the Shah feels that his special relationship with his closest friend, America, is coming to an end. The Shah feels that it is coming to an end because of the indifference of his American friends. American indifference hardly balances the scales because the Shah's input includes Iran's contribution to South Vietnam, Iran's recognition and assistance to Israel, Iran's standup fight against the incursions of Nasser, etc. The Shah feels that it has been a one-way street and that the United States does not really care any more what happens to Iran. He concludes that America does not care because what concerns the Shah does not concern the United States. The Shah is tired of being treated like a schoolboy, particularly by officials of the Agency for International Development. He believes that AID has no legitimate claim upon his right to his own views and to his own policies. The Shah cites, also, Secretary McNamara's handling of his arms package. This is a story in itself.

The story is that the Shah feels that the United States is charging him more money in interest for a Hawk Battalion than anybody else. He feels that the money Secretary McNamara wants to charge him for other military items is usurious and discriminatory.

Because of this maltreatment the Shah concludes that America does better by its enemies than it does by its friends. The Shah is certain that Nasser is given quicker and fairer treatment than is Iran. He spells out chapter and verse to show that the United States has shown no gratitude for his support in South Vietnam.

Concerning the current withdrawal of British power from the Middle East, the Shah has led the way in realizing that this power vacu-

---

[1] Source: Johnson Library, White House Central Files, EX FO–5, 6/30/66–8/31/66. No classification marking.

um must be filled and that Iran can relieve the United States of an appreciable part of the cost. Roosevelt says the Shah believes that Iran, Saudi Arabia, Pakistan, and perhaps Iraq can hold the line against Nasser and the USSR, but they must have the support and understanding of the United States.

The Shah realizes that the reason why the Soviets have not yet responded to his overtures for arms is because the Shah wants SAM–2's and the Soviets do not want these missiles placed in a country which has an American military mission. The Shah knows that the Russians would like to respond positively but must hesitate over the question of missiles for Iran. The Shah wondered aloud to Roosevelt over how the United States and Iran could have arrived at a parting of the ways. Heretofore, the United States had realized the importance of Iran and its geographic location. The Shah's relations with the United States have been confidential, cooperative, and rewarding for both sides. The Shah could not understand how the United States could charge him more interest than it charged others. This seemed to be the last straw.

Roosevelt said he had reported this conversation to Ambassador Meyer. He had also seen Walt Rostow early this morning. Rostow did not seem convinced of the seriousness of the situation, Roosevelt thought, and told Roosevelt that he thought the acceptance by Iran of Soviet arms represented an inevitable step in the "normalization" of U.S.-Irananian relations. Roosevelt said he planned to see Assistant Secretary Ray Hare this afternoon or tomorrow.

---

164.   Letter From Vice President Humphrey to Secretary of Defense McNamara[1]

Washington, July 28, 1966.

Dear Bob:

I hestitate to draw your attention away from other serious matters but I would like to call to your attention a situation of immediate danger to our relations with Iran. As a member of the Senate Foreign Relations

---

[1] Source: Washington National Records Center, RG 330, OSD Files: FRC 70 A 4443, Iran 091.3 MAP 1966, 28 Jul 66. Secret. A stamped notation on the source text indicates that McNamara saw it on August 2.

Committee I was charged with the duty of studying the Middle East, including Iran. Throughout the years I learned that nothing is certain in that area except trouble, and that only quick footwork at the right time can avoid serious pitfalls.

I know you share my deep appreciation for the Shah's contribution to the struggle in Vietnam, for his staunch defense of our policies during his recent swing through the Satellites, and for his unfailing support of the United States in the field of mutual defense. The fact that he is now turning to the Soviet Union to purchase arms is regrettable. Our intelligence services report that his movement toward the Russians could be far more serious than the immediate issue at hand. I wonder if the situation is correctable?

I think we all would feel much better knowing that you had taken a personal look at the commercial details we are proposing to the Shah and hearing from you that you believe it proper to accept the high risks we are informed are involved.

Sincerely,

Hubert H.

---

165. Memorandum From the President's Special Assistant (Rostow) to President Johnson[1]

Washington, July 29, 1966.

Mr. President:

Herewith a final call for help from our Ambassador to Iran.[2] The Iranians threaten to buy some Soviet military equipment from the Soviet Union unless we alter the prices and terms we have offered.

---

[1] Source: Johnson Library, National Security File, Country File, Iran, Memos & Miscellaneous, Vol. II, 1/66–1/69. Secret.

[2] Attached to the source text is a typed copy of telegram 451 from Tehran, July 28, which conveyed a message from Meyer to the President arguing that before the Shah got inextricably involved in an arms deal with the Soviets, the United States should make one last effort to avoid a serious set-back for U.S. interests in the area. Meyer stated that the only hope of avoiding excessive Iranian military involvement with the Soviets was an indication from the U.S. Government of better prices and terms. The Ambassador regretted bringing this matter to the President's personal attention, but because there was so much at stake—not the least of which was U.S. strategic installations in Iran—he felt compelled to appeal personally to the President. (Department of State, Central Files, DEF 19 US–IRAN)

I have checked with Secretary Rusk[3] and with Secretary McNamara. Sec. Rusk believes we should not try to impose this extra $30 million military aid burden on the Department of Defense and that, on balance, it might be good for us to see some slight loosening in our ties to the Shah. He has always been a little uneasy about our commitments to him.

Secretary McNamara believes that we should stand on our present position; although he is willing to consider helping marginally if his military aid is fully restored. But basically he does not wish to give in to the Shah's "blackmail."

I have a feeling that, whatever we do, the Shah is likely to buy some Soviet equipment because it would be good for him domestically, indicating that he is not wholly "subservient" to the U.S. and "normalizing" his relations with the USSR.

As Ambassador Meyer points out, there are certain risks in our present position. The Shah might behave irrationally and get in much deeper with the Soviets than we now calculate. On the other hand, he is asking to be treated like a grown up. Your letter to him was in a mature mood of partnership. I agree, therefore, that we should stand on our present position.

It seems to me possible—but not sure—that if we stand on your letter and do not go rushing in with an additional "carrot," the Iranians may come back to us with a specific proposition which we might look at.

Let the situation rest as it is

Put on agenda for Tuesday lunch[4]

Organize a further "carrot"

See me

Walt

---

[3] Rostow had telephoned Rusk concerning Meyer's cable at 5:20 p.m. on July 29, saying that he did not want to send it to the President until he had Rusk and McNamara's final position. Rusk said that State's position was that they should not ask McNamara to take on another $30–$40 million in defense spending for this, and that it would not be proper for the United States to be blackmailed. The Secretary said that he was nervous about the behind-the-scene U.S. commitment from previous years and would not object to a little loosening up there. (Memorandum of telephone conversation between Rusk and Rostow, July 29; ibid., Rusk Files: Lot 72 D 192)

[4] The President checked this option.

166.   Memorandum From the Joint Chiefs of Staff to Secretary of Defense McNamara[1]

JCSM–498–66   Washington, August 1, 1966.

SUBJECT

    Military Sales to Iran (U)

    1.   (S) Reference is made to JCSM–240–66, dated 15 April 1966, subject: "Report of US Military Survey—Iran (C),"[2] wherein the Joint Chiefs of Staff informed you of their concurrence in the conclusions and recommendations of a tri-Service team which surveyed the equipment needs of the Imperial Iranian Armed Forces. This concurrence was based on a recognition of the need to maintain the primacy of the US military presence in Iran.

    2.   (S) The Joint Chiefs of Staff are concerned that the Shah of Iran is dissatisfied with current US offers to sell military equipment he deems essential for Iran's defense. He already has initiated action to procure certain equipment including SAMs from the Soviets. Recent messages from the Ambassador, CINCSTRIKE/USCINCMEAFSA, and the Chief, ARMISH/MAAG, indicate that the US offers must be more forthcoming if a major Soviet entry into Iran, with all its attendant disadvantages, is to be prevented.

    3.   (S) In view of this possibility and the serious deterioration in US/ Iranian relations which could result, the Joint Chiefs of Staff:

    a.   Reaffirm their judgment that it is essential to maintain the primacy of US military interests in Iran and that every effort should be made to prevent the Soviets from gaining a foothold through the introduction of military equipment and technicians into Iran.

    b.   Recommend support of reduced costs, to include the waiving of R&D costs on all items contained in the approved equipment requirements, in order to make this judgment meaningful in light of the circumstances mentioned.

    c.   Further recommend an offer of two squadrons of sixteen each F–4C aircraft at reduced cost with delivery to commence late in calendar

---

    [1] Source: Washington National Records Center, RG 330, OSD Files: FRC 70 A 4443, Iran 091.3 MAP, 1 Aug 66. Secret. A stamped notation on the source text reads: "SecDef has seen Brief."

    [2] Not printed.

year 1968. This offer requires inclusion of additional procurement funds for F–4E aircraft in the Air Force supplemental FY 1967 budget.[3]

> For the Joint Chiefs of Staff:
> **David L. McDonald**
> *Acting Chairman*
> *Joint Chiefs of Staff*

---

[3] On August 23 Acting Secretary of Defense Vance sent the Chairman of the Joint Chiefs of Staff a memorandum noting that he shared the JCS concern over the implications of the Shah's dissatisfaction with U.S. unwillingness to sell Iran military equipment he deemed essential for Iran's defense. Vance said that following a Defense–State–White House review, they had decided to offer the Shah several new concessions, including waiver of R and D charges on all items and two squadrons of F–4s. These had been conveyed to the Shah the previous week by Hoopes, and it appeared that the Shah now felt that the U.S. offer met most of Iran's needs, although it was not certain that this would forestall his purchase of Soviet anti-aircraft missiles. (Washington National Records Center, RG 330, OSD Files: FRC 70 A 4443, Iran 091.3 MAP, 23 Aug 66)

---

167. Memorandum From W. Howard Wriggins of the National Security Council Staff to the President's Special Assistant (Rostow)[1]

Washington, August 2, 1966.

Walt.

Tuesday[2] lunch discussion of military sales for the Shah.

　1.　The attached cables (Tehran 492)[3] point out:

　(a) Soviets reportedly have responded positively to Iran's request for military equipment, but no details agreed on yet;
　(b) Shah finally aware purchases from Soviets will present us with security problems;
　(c) Shah assures us he can deal with these;

---

[1] Source: Johnson Library, National Security File, NSC Files of Harold Saunders, Iran Military, 4/1/66–12/31/67. Secret.
[2] August 2. No record of the Tuesday lunch discussion has been found, but see Documents 168 and 169.
[3] Dated August 1. (Department of State, Central Files, DEF 19–8 US–IRAN)

(d) Armin believes a forthcoming U.S. position will keep the Shah's purchases to a minimum;

(e) the President's letter was very helpful in reassuring the Shah of the President's personal interest.

2. By a "forthcoming" position, Meyer means (Tehran 378):[4]

(a) mark-down of F 4's;

(b) reduction of $21 million in batallion price of Hawks—Shah believes this to be the R & D add on which he thinks should long ago have been amortized;

(c) scaling of surcharges on other items;

(d) expeditious schedule of deliveries;

(e) USG credit available for Sheridan tank in the future.

3. This is obviously a very tall order. We can't do all this, but now to fall back positions. Having seen the Secretary of State cave on prices for the planes, Hare is still hoping to remove R & D costs on the Hawks. I hope you can persuade McNamara to do *at least* that.

4. Attached is a memo from DOD[5] on price variations in the military equipment purchased by Iran.

Howard Wriggins[6]

---

[4] Document 161.

[5] Attached but not printed.

[6] Printed from a copy that bears this typed signature.

---

168.   Memorandum From the President's Special Assistant (Rostow) to Secretary of State Rusk and Secretary of Defense McNamara[1]

Washington, August 2, 1996.

This is to record the decision made by the President today that:

1. Mr. Townsend Hoopes would proceed to Tehran to explain to the Shah the budgetary limitations on our military aid; the nature and rationale of our administrative procedures in military aid; the non-dis-

---

[1] Source: Johnson Library, National Security File, Country File, Iran, Memos & Miscellaneous, Vol. II, 1/66–1/69. Secret. A handwritten notation on the source text indicates that a copy was sent to Hoopes.

criminatory character of our price offers to Iran in the present package; and other elements which determine our position as set forth in the President's letter to the Shah of July 20, 1966.

2. Mr. Hoopes would be empowered to tell the Shah that we shall deliver military equipment to him under our various agreements on an accelerated basis.

3. He would be empowered also to say that, in response to the Shah's request, we are prepared to eliminate from the price of the Hawks the R&D costs imputed in our original offer.

W.W. Rostow

---

169.   Memorandum From W. Howard Wriggins of the National Security Council Staff to the President's Special Assistant (Rostow)[1]

Washington, August 5, 1966.

SUBJECT

Iran Military Sales

Attached are draft *instructions for Hoopes and Meyer*[2] in presenting our final offer to the Shah. Vance and McNamara have cleared, but we want to be sure this reflects your understanding of the agreement reached Tuesday in the President's presence.

In addition to outlining our positions on F–4's and Hawks, and offering to begin detailed negotiations, this reiterates the line we took in the President's letter:

—U.S. considers its Iranian relationship important (sending Hoopes underscores this).
—We want Shah to understand fully that our procedures and prices are not discriminatory (Hoopes will explain).
—Our offer to sell F–4's and missiles conditional until Iran clarifies its position on buying from the USSR.

---

[1] Source: Johnson Library, National Security File, Country File, Iran, Memos & Miscellaneous, Vol. II, 1/66–1/69. Secret.

[2] See Document 170.

—We consider our annual economic-military review important and will take into account the effect of Iran's third-country purchases in determining later credits.

This is a fair statement of where we have come out. Since we can't meet all the Shah's requests, this states our limits while relying on Hoopes to make them as palatable as possible.

This looks O.K.[3]

See me

_____

[3] The options are handwritten and the first one is checked.

_____

170. **Telegram From the Department of State to the Embassy in Iran**[1]

Washington, August 5, 1966, 8:14 p.m.

23183. Joint State/Defense message.

1. Basic US-Iran relationship and impact thereon of Shah's flirtation with Soviet arms purchase have been subject of highest level USG discussions during past several days. We now ready state our position in more definitive framework with aim of achieving forward movement. The President had directed DASD Townsend Hoopes proceed immediately to Tehran to participate with you in putting our position before Shah. Hoopes presence with you during audience will underline importance USG attaches to relations with Iran. He will be prepared help you set our position in context of present realities in Washington—specifically to restate the financial terms of the new $200 million credit as approved by the USG, to explain budgetary limitations on military sales as they relate to size of loan and interest rate, nature and rationale of our administrative procedures in military sales, character of our price offers to Iran in present package, and other elements which underlie our position as set forth in President's letter to Shah of July 20. Accordingly you should seek early audience for yourself and Hoopes with Shah. FYI. Hoopes arrives Tehran Monday August 8 at 2030 hours via Pan Am 114. End FYI.

_____

[1] Source: Department of State, Central Files, DEF 19–8 US–IRAN. Secret; Priority; Limdis. Drafted by Colonel Haynes in DOD/ISA on August 4; cleared by Hare, Eliot, McNaughton, and Wriggins; and approved by U. Alexis Johnson. Repeated to London, Moscow, Paris, and CINCSTRIKE.

2. Following are basic elements of USG position which you and Hoopes should convey to Shah:

(a) After study at highest government level, USG prepared open detailed technical discussions of further Iranian military purchases from US. As indicated by President's letter, we place great value on US-Iran cooperation in military matters and sincerely hope circumstances will permit this cordial relationship to continue in full effectiveness. We therefore trust Shah will recognize that our proposals are based on genuine desire continue in that military relationship without impairment.

(b) We prepared discuss with him and his military advisers, within purchasing power of new credit, full range of equipment items reflected in Peterson Report, except destroyer (DD). We now in position offer two squadrons (up to 32 aircraft) of F–4's for delivery in CY '68 or earlier. These will be new production aircraft whose cost, while not firm, will be in neighborhood of $50 million per squadron. FYI. This probably minimum figure but there is some prospect for reduction. End FYI. Final price must be determined after thorough technical exploration with Iranians as to detailed configuration of aircraft and support elements. You should stress that our willingness increase total aircraft from 12 to 32 and to promise early delivery are important concessions. Furthermore, we are prepared make concessions on R&D charges with respect to the two Hawk battalions; these would put price of first Hawk unit at about $27 million and of second unit at slightly above $30 million, an aggregate reduction of approximately $3 million. Moreover, Secretary McNamara has indicated his willingness to deliver military equipment to Iran on an accelerated basis where possible. We are prepared proceed with sale of PGM's, even though we are not able offer a destroyer (DD). FYI. To summarize, USG offering three concessions: 1) Increase from 12 to 32 F–4 aircraft; 2) Accelerate deliveries of these aircraft and where possible other items; 3) Waive R&D charges on Hawks approximating $3 million. End FYI.

(c) Our offer sell major sensitive, sophisticated items (FYI—F–4 aircraft and Shillelagh missile system at minimum—end FYI) must remain conditional until Iran has clarified its position with respect to possible military procurement from the USSR. As the President's letter stated, we cannot believe that either US or Iran will profit by an increase of Soviet influence in Persian Gulf area; we believe an Iranian arms deal with the Soviet Union would confuse our Congress and people concerning Iran's intentions; and on the technical side, we are determined to protect sensitive US equipment from compromise by Soviet military technicians. FYI. Concerning the relationship between an Iran-USSR arms deal and US willingness to offer certain items, we wish to keep above caveats in general terms. You should accordingly refuse be drawn into specific arguments in this regard, particularly on technical and security issues. End FYI.

(d) USG hopes that the Shah will look only to Free World sources of arms in meeting his security requirements; but in any event, we continue attach great importance to the annual economic review; and during each review we will wish to take account of impact on Iran's foreign exchange and debt servicing position of any major third country military purchases, and we will determine US military credit availabilities in light of that impact.

(e) Assuming there is clear understanding that new US credit limit is $200 million at 5–6 percent plus $60 million of old credit at 4 percent, we are prepared send DOD team immediately to open negotiations on item content and Iranian repayment schedule for the $60 million remaining under the old credit arrangement and on first $50 million of new $200 million. US negotiators would reserve position on sensitive items as indicated Para (c). Prior to negotiating detailed financial arrangements, we would require appropriate amendments to 1964 Memorandum of Understanding. FYI. USG position on amendments will be cabled shortly. End FYI.

Rusk

---

171.   Telegram From the Department of State to the Embassy in Iran[1]

Washington, August 5, 1966, 8:15 p.m.

23184. Ref: State's 23183.[2] Subject: Additional MAP Agreement.

1.   Embassy is authorized negotiate amendment to 1964 Memorandum of Understanding on basis text para 2 and to sign if no changes made. Any changes must be approved by Dept.

2.   Negotiating text: "Excellency: I have the honor to refer to the Memoranda of Understanding between the Govt of the United States of

---

[1] Source: Department of State, Central Files, DEF 19–8 US–IRAN. Secret; Priority. Drafted by Newberry on August 4; cleared by Saunders, Colonel Haynes, Wehmeyer, Eliot, and Warren and in draft by Funari; and approved by Hare. Repeated to USCINCMEAFSA.

[2] Document 170.

America and the Imperial Government of Iran of September 19, 1962, and of July 4, 1964, and to the exchange of notes in amendment thereof signed Aug. 18, 1965.[3] The said agreements provide for the Military Assistance Program during Fiscal Years 1962–66, and for an additional Program of Mutual Defense Cooperation during 1965–1969.

I have the honor to propose that the Memorandum of Understanding of July 4, 1964 be amended as set forth in the Annex hereto so as (1) to extend the period for the additional program of Mutual Defense Cooperation through Fiscal Year 1970, (2) to provide for additional cash purchases of an estimated $20 million principally for maintenance matériel and services, (3) subject to availability of funds, to provide additional credit for purchases up to $200 million in annual increments up to $50 million at interest averaging between five and six per cent, and (4) to provide that the additional amount of credits will be repayable over the ten-year period FY 1967–76.

I further have the honor to propose that this note and Your Excellency's reply thereto concurring therein shall constitute an amendment of the Memorandum of Understanding of July 4, 1964 between our two Govts and shall enter into force on the date of Your Excellency's reply.

Accept, Excellency, etc.

Annex of Amendments:

The Memorandum of Understanding of July 4, 1964 between the Imperial Govt of Iran and the Govt of the US is hereby amended as follows:

1. In the first sentence of para III, substitute "FY 1965–1970" for "FY 1965–1969."

In Para III.A 3(B):

A. In first sentence, substitute "$250 million" for "$200 million"; delete "and are consistent with" and substitute therefor the following: "and subject to satisfactory mutual conclusions being reached in the reviews provided for in para V, additional amounts not to exceed $50 million each for US FY 1968, 1969 and 1970, all of such credit being subject to".[4]

B. Delete the last two sentences and substitute therefor the following: "these credits will be repayable on terms which allow payments for the first $200 million over the ten-year period FY 1965–74, with addition-

---

[3] See Document 47 and footnote 6 thereto. The August 18 notes were not found.

[4] In telegram 570 from Tehran, August 6, Meyer argued that rewording the 1964 memorandum with reference to Iran's sovereign right to determine what it would devote to its defense was unnecessarily provocative and strongly urged that he and Hoopes be authorized to provide the interpretation intended by this new wording orally. (Department of State, Central Files, DEF 19–8 US–IRAN) Telegram 23991 to Tehran, August 8, authorized Meyer to change the proposed annex to the amendment as follows: "In Para, III A 3 (B) in first sentence following the phrase "including the credits referred to in Paragraph III A, 3 A," substitute for remainder of sentence "do not exceed $250 million and additional credits not to exceed $50 million each for US FY 1968, 1969, and 1970, consistent with the foreign exchange and other limitations contained in Paras III C and V." (Ibid.)

al terms to be negotiated and contained in each detailed credit sales arrangement under this agreement, taking into account Iran's repayment capabilities. The interest rate on the unpaid balance to be negotiated will not exceed an average of 4 to 5 per cent per annum for the first $200 million and an average of 5 to 6 per cent per annum for such additional amounts."

3. In Para III.B. substitute:

A. "FY 1965–70" for "FY1965–69",

B. "FY up to $470 million" for "$250 million",

C. "$70 million" for "$50 million", and

D. "Up to $400 million" for "$200 million".[5]

Rusk

---

[5] In telegram 639 from Tehran, August 11, Meyer reported that he had handed the official note with the proposed amendment to the 1964 Memorandum of Understanding regarding military sales to the Foreign Minister that morning. He noted that he had emphasized again, as he and Hoopes had the previous day, the abiding U.S. concern that Iran's outlays for military equipment not overburden its economic development effort. Aram had agreed to reemphasize this to the Shah when he secured his approval to a favorable Iranian response to the U.S. note. (Ibid.)

---

172.   Memorandum From the President's Special Assistant (Rostow) to President Johnson[1]

Washington, August 10, 1966.

SUBJECT

Ambassador Meyer's and Tim Hoopes' Talk with the Shah about the Defense Package

They had a good talk with the Shah[2] which may have gone a long way toward moderating his somewhat irrational feeling that we have been neglecting him. The Shah expressed his deep regard and affection

---

[1] Source: Johnson Library, National Security File, Country File, Iran, Memos & Miscellaneous, Vol. II, 1/66–1/69. Secret. A handwritten "L" on the source text indicates that it was seen by the President.

[2] Telegram 634 from Tehran, August 10, reported on Ambassador Meyer's and Assistant Secretary Hoopes' discussion the same day with the Shah regarding U.S. military sales to Iran. (Department of State, Central Files, DEF 19–8 US–IRAN)

for you and asked Hoopes to convey his sincere appreciation for your interest and for all the U. S. has done for Iran since World War II. He reiterated his desire to maintain a close relationship with us.

Hoopes led off with a detailed exposition of our interest in Iran, our problems and what we could do to help. After a lengthy discussion, they succeeded in persuading the Shah willingly to make some hard choices, cutting out some of the less important items of equipment which would not fit under his financial ceiling. This in itself is a gain, since the Shah has talked recently as if he were going off the deep end buying everything in sight.

They believe that they dissuaded the Shah from buying Soviet SAMs but expect that he probably will buy a few anti-aircraft guns and trucks which he can get there at much lower prices. They explained to him quite frankly that our offer of F–4 aircraft was conditional on how far he went in getting equipment from the USSR. The Shah vowed that he would not allow Soviet technicians in Iran, and Hoopes and Meyer believe he will not permit serious penetration of his country.

The Shah summarized the discussion as "constructive, comprehensive and expensive." The upshot of it is that we will send a technician to Tehran to negotiate some of the military details while the Governor of Iran's Central Bank, who will be here next week on another project, will negotiate financial details in the Pentagon.

I think we have come out of this pretty well. I would not be personally worried if the Shah were to buy a few minor Soviet items, although every breach in the wall makes it more difficult for other leaders like King Hussein to resist Soviet blandishments. Nevertheless, I think both your letter and your sending Hoopes out there have gone a long way toward keeping the Shah from going overboard. We will undoubtedly have to adjust to his increasingly independent tendencies, but for the moment we have managed to keep the worst we had feared from happening.

Walt

173. Letter From the Shah of Iran to President Johnson[1]

Tehran, August 15, 1966.

Dear Mr. President,

The opportunity you have so kindly afforded me with your warm and cordial letter of July 20, 1966,[2] to discuss some questions of mutual interest is greatly appreciated, particularly as there has been a lapse of some time between our correspondence. I entirely agree with you on the necessity of candor between friends.

I am in full agreement with you, Mr. President, that our co-operation in military matters has been cordial and to the interest of both countries. Indeed, it is my strong feeling that this co-operation has been of much greater service in that it has contributed effectively to the maintenance of the peace of this region—a region fraught with danger and which, in my opinion, merits closer, deeper and more sympathetic attention, if we are to preserve, at least, the semblance of peace it now enjoys.

It gives me much satisfaction to note your interest in the continued stability of the Persian Gulf area. This area and my deep concern over its security have occupied my attention for some years. I have often discussed the problem with high American officials who must have reported my views to you. I feel that a strong and stable Iran can serve as a deterrent to any country around, which would, with scant respect for human or material loss, keep the region in a condition of constant turmoil only to further its own expansionist policy.

The unfolding situation in the area and its potential danger, as you have well put it, Mr. President, requires close scrutiny in order to provide against it before it is too late.

It is essential for Iran to enjoy peace and tranquility in order to be able to carry through her social and economic reforms now well under way. A strong Iran can, not only ensure such a condition, but also avert the spreading of conflicts in the region, guarantee the smooth and orderly flow of oil to the west and, what is of vital importance and worthy of serious consideration, forestall the repetition of current tragic and costly involvements. I therefore make no apology for repeating that the advantages of a strong and friendly Iran to the west should not be denied or minimized. It is my ardent hope that with our community of feeling and interest this co-operation and the happy and cordial association between our nations will continue to grow stronger and be consolidated.

---

[1] Source: Department of State, Central Files, POL IRAN–US. Secret; Exdis. Attached to the source text is an August 22 memorandum from Read to Rostow stating that the enclosed letter had been delivered to the Department on August 22 under cover of a note from the Iranian Ambassador.

[2] Document 158.

I fully realize that your resources are burdened by your heavy commitments in other parts of the world and I feel grateful to you, Mr. President, for your concern for Iran's security and for your continued intent to respond to Iran's needs despite these commitments.

While I was writing this letter to you, Mr. Hoopes, the U.S. Assistant Secretary of Defense arrived in Tehran and called on me with Mr. Armin Meyer your Ambassador and Major General Jablonsky. We had a long and useful discussion on various aspects of Iran's military requirements. He gave me an account of your difficulties and limitations which I fully realize.

I do not intend to go over what we discussed since Mr. Hoopes will certainly make a full report to you. What I would like to stress here is the great responsibility I feel towards my people in this troubled area of the world. My most sacred duty is the safeguarding of my country's independence and territorial integrity. Unfortunately, I can see little relief in the troubled Middle East situation, and future generations will not forgive me if I fail to pay every attention to my country's defense requirements.

I have given instructions to my government to sign the necessary documents for the 200 million dollars credit, though this figure, I must say, still falls short of meeting Iran's needs.

We have always maintained that from all standpoints, political, economic, strategic and also from the standpoint of helping Iran preserve her position as a factor of stability in this region, the production of Iran's oil should be set at a level higher than what it is now. We see people around us who do not even know what to do with their oil revenues.

I fully appreciate your interest in Iran's economic welfare and the progress we have achieved. I am resolved to see that while we make provisions for our defense requirements we do not jeopardize the rate of this progress. It is in pursuance of this policy that I need to husband our exchange resources in order to be able to cover the military requirements without hampering the rate of our economic development.

I welcome the possibility of a meeting between ourselves some time early next year. I have always found these personal contacts highly satisfactory and I look forward with much pleasure to this meeting with you. In the meantime may I express, Mr. President, my high esteem for you and the great importance I attach to the warm and deep friendship which binds our two countries.

Sincerely

M.R. Pahlavi

174. Telegram From the Embassy in Iran to the Department of State[1]

Tehran, August 21, 1966, 1035Z.

791. Military Sales to Iran.

1. Expressing gratification over constructive progress re military sales made during talk which Hoopes and I had with him at Caspian (Embassy 634),[2] I told Shah morning 21st that Washington proceeding with follow-up actions. It is our hope, I said, to have preliminary studies completed so that USG team can come out in second or third week of September to help negotiate details of FY67 tranche.

2. Calling attention to GOI's concurrence in amendment of 1964 Memorandum of Understanding (Embassy 777),[3] Shah also expressed satisfaction that our military relationship moving in more normal course. He noted, as he had via Aram (Embassy 763),[4] that Soviets have suddenly become "enthusiastic" to sell arms to Iran. He wanted to assure us, however, that what he had indicated at Nowshahr remains valid. Specifically, Shah said he has made decision not to buy any SAMs from Soviets. He noted that he had earlier suggested isolating SAM contingents from American sophisticated equipment. Now, however, he could assure us he would not buy any Soviet SAMs at all.

3. Asked re Soviet military reps' prospective visit to Tehran, Shah said it is not clear at this point whether Soviet team would arrive before his departure for Eurpoean visits September 1 or after his return circa Sept. 20 or 21. As he had to [line(s) missing from the source text] Hoopes and me, Shah indicated possibility purchasing minor non-sensitive items like Ack Ack, trucks or personnel carriers. He reiterated what he had told us at Caspian that he would "never" have Soviet military advisors.

4. Shah said there seems to be some doubt in USG's mind re necessity of any kind of SAM weaponry, whether Soviet or American (Hawks). We reviewed what Hoopes had explained re cost effectiveness and that instead of investing large sums in anti-aircraft missilery it might be better to base air defense plan primarily on warning system and aircraft.

5. Shah said he been giving this matter much thought, particularly as it would affect vital and highly vulnerable Kharg Island oil installa-

---

[1] Source: Department of State, Central Files, DEF 19–8 US–IRAN. Secret; Priority; Limdis. Repeated to CINCSTRIKE/USCINCMEAFSA and Moscow.

[2] See footnote 2, Document 172.

[3] Dated August 20. (Department of State, Central Files, DEF 19–8 US–IRAN)

[4] Dated August 19. (Ibid.)

tions. Choice, he indicated, boils down whether to invest $25,000,000 in one Hawk battalion (he aware that it could be funded with holding payment of $9,000,000, for black boxes, in FY67 tranche) or purchase additional F–5 squadron at $15,000,000 which would be based at Bushire and would be equipped with Sparrow missiles. He asked that DOD experts provide soundest advice possible re this choice.

6. After discussion number of other subjects, discussion returned to arms procurement and Shah again gave categoric assurances that he would buy no Soviet SAMs. I said this welcome news for as he knew purchase of any major sophisticated sensitive weaponry from Soviets would be incompatible with US sale of F–4. Shah expressed gratification that circumstances have developed so as to permit him to rely on traditional US supply of sophisticated equipment. He recalled how from start he anxious maintain maximum US procurement and that in any case air force should remain completely American oriented. Although again mentioning that F–4's "very expensive," Shah gratified to be able purchase such high quality aircraft.

7. *Comment:* Undoubtedly due to Aram's spadework (Embassy 763) Shah knew precisely two key issues of moment. Although Shah asked that we consider his commitment to us as confidential, his assurances re non-purchase of Soviet sophisticated equipment and specifically SAMs were categoric and explicit. Re Hawks, his request for advice re defense of Kharg strikes us as intelligent and worthy of prompt and honest Washington response.

8. DCM Thacher accompanied me. Shah was told that if during my absence any significant problems arise Thacher and General Jablonsky well equipped to handle them. Shah agreed avail himself their assistance if necessary.

Meyer

175.   Memorandum From the President's Special Assistant (Rostow) to President Johnson[1]

Washington, August 31, 1966.

SUBJECT

Letter from the Shah

The Iranian Ambassador had just delivered the Shah's answer to your 20 July letter[2] and to your sending Tim Hoopes to talk about his arms purchases. We do not recommend a reply now because his letter completes the circuit for the moment. However, if you approve, we will ask Ambassador Meyer to tell him at an appropriate moment that you appreciated his letter and will be in touch with him later. Unless something unexpected comes up, your next letter would probably be later in the fall, confirming arrangements for a talk early next year.

The Shah has taken heart, I think, from our explicit recognition of the importance of stability in the areas surrounding Iran. He uses that recognition as an excuse for underscoring the importance of his security needs. He is appreciative of our help, which he realizes is a strain in view of our Vietnam commitment, but he states frankly that our $200 million credit still falls short of meeting Iran's total requirements. He welcomes the prospect of a meeting with you early next year but does not sound as if he will press for more aid then.

We have come out of this exercise pretty well. Hoopes spelled out our problems in detail but couched them in sympathy for the Shah's aims. The Shah has since assured Ambassador Meyer that he will buy no Soviet missiles and allow no Soviet military technicians into Iran. A Soviet military mission is in Tehran for talks this week, but he says he will buy only vehicles and maybe some simple ack-ack guns, if anything. He is buying some naval equipment from Britain, but our only objection to that is the possible impact on his development program. On that, we'll just have to wait and keep an eye open to how the economy shoulders the burden of these arms purchases.

So while the Shah will increasingly move toward a position more independent of us, we have managed to keep him from jumping too quickly this time. Some independence is to be expected and is healthy. We just

---

[1] Source: Johnson Library, National Security File, Special Head of State Correspondence File, Iran, Shah Correspondence, Vol. II. Secret.

[2] Documents 173 and 158.

want to be sure he doesn't go too far too fast and get us all in hot water. For the moment, we've succeeded.

Walt

Approve verbal acknowledgment[3]

See me

_____

[3] This option is checked. In telegram 1277 from Tehran, September 21, Meyer reported that he had expressed to the Shah that morning the President's appreciation for his August 15 letter. He also reminded the Shah that a DOD team was currently in Tehran negotiating with his officials and pointed out that the proposed military package should certainly meet with his satisfaction. (Department of State, Central Files, DEF 19–8 US–IRAN)

_____

176. Memorandum From the Deputy Assistant Secretary of Defense for International Security Affairs (Hoopes) to Secretary of Defense McNamara[1]

I–26118/66   Washington, September 13, 1966.

SUBJECT

US Military Sales to Iran—Status Report

This memorandum is for information.

You will recall that in early August, as a result of a decision reached at the Tuesday lunch with the President,[2] I traveled to Iran to reinforce and amplify the President's letter of 20 July,[3] to make clear to the Shah the dangers to US-Iran relations if Iran should purchase "major, sophisticated and sensitive" military equipment from the Soviet bloc, and to make further proposals regarding F–4s and Hawks. Tab A[4] is the cable of instruction governing my mission. Tab B is a copy of my remarks to the Shah. Tab C is the reporting cable on the conversation with the Shah. Tab D is the President's letter of 20 July.

_____

[1] Source: Washington National Records Center, RG 330, OSD Files: FRC 70 A 4443, Iran 091.3 MAP 13 Sep 66. Secret.

[2] See Document 167.

[3] See Document 158.

[4] All of the tabs were attached to the source text; Tab A is Document 170.

At the conclusion of the conversation, the Shah said that a purchase of sophisticated equipment from the Soviet bloc was "improbable." A week later we were able to obtain categorical assurances that Iran would make no purchases of Soviet SAMs or other sophisticated equipment. Also, in the course of the conversation, the Shah decided that Iran required only one Hawk battalion instead of two; subsequently, he told Ambassador Meyer that he intends to purchase no Hawks, but to base his air defense on an early warning radar system, fast-reaction interceptor aircraft (F–4 and F–5), and simpler, less expensive antiaircraft guns. As a face-saving gesture in view of his overtures to the Soviets, the Shah restated that he would probably buy a few "lorries, APC's and ack-ack guns" from USSR.

Agreement was also reached during the conversation on the major components of a sales program for FY 67. This would total $110 million (comprising $60 million from the original 1964 credit and the first $50 million of the new $200 million credit). The agreed elements of this tranche are: Blue Shark radar system, one F–4 squadron, four C–130s, additional air force war reserve, and about 100 M–60 tanks. Draft Letters of Offer have been prepared on these items and will be carried to Iran by an ILN team for negotiations beginning on 19 September.

We now have evidence that Iran has just about concluded the purchase of a naval package from the UK, including 4 Corvettes, 6 hovercraft (fast patrol boats), and a refitted (but not modernized) WW II destroyer. In addition to the naval items, the package includes 18 additional Tiger Cat antiaircraft missile launchers and appropriate missiles. The total cost is estimated at $60 million. This purchase has been anticipated. It will confront the US Government over the coming months with the need to determine the extent to which this third country purchase by Iran will affect the total of the new US credit. The FY 67 tranche will not however be affected.

On balance, we believe the situation is now well in hand.

Townsend Hoopes

177.   Telegram From the Department of State to the Embassy in Iran[1]

Washington, October 15, 1966, 10:49 a.m.

66833. 1. Following summary October 12 conversation between Secretary and Aram is FYI and Noforn. It is uncleared and subject to amendment upon review of memcons.

2.   Conversation was long and most cordial. Much time devoted to review current status Viet Nam, Iran-Arab, Iran-Pak relations. Memcons being pouched.

3.   Following bilateral matters discussed:

a. Aram said Shah pleased with recently concluded military negotiations. Only remaining problem is need for early delivery of aircraft as British may depart Persian Gulf before aircraft scheduled arrive in 1968–69. Secretary replied that we have procurement and budgetary problems resulting from war in Viet Nam but that within framework our past discussions we will do our best on deliveries to Iran. Secretary suggested in meantime necessary training of Iranian air force personnel begin in case emergency should develop requiring assistance earlier than planned.

b. Aram inquired about status Iran's request for PL–480 wheat. While pointing out US no longer has surplus Secretary assured Aram within limits our short supply there is every disposition in USG to do best we can for Iran.

Rusk

---

[1] Source: Department of State, Central Files, POL IRAN–US. Secret; Limdis. Drafted by Eliot on October 14, cleared by Walsh, and approved by Hare. Repeated to CINC-STRIKE.

178.   Letter From the Ambassador to Iran (Meyer) to the Assistant Secretary of State for Near Eastern and South Asian Affairs (Hare)[1]

Tehran, October 22, 1966.

Dear Ray:

Set out in the paragraphs below is the Embassy's assessment of the internal security situation in Iran prepared in accordance with instructions from IRG/NEA (Department Airgram A–11 of July 21).[2] You will note that since last October when we submitted our last formal report on the counter-insurgency situation here (A–281 of October 20, 1965),[2] no major changes have taken place in the situation as we viewed it at that time. However, the moves toward settlement of the Kurdish revolt in Iraq this year and some evidence that the growing number of Soviet technicians is outrunning the capacity of the security services for effective surveillance, point to possible longer-term problems. There has also been a negative development in the reorganization of the Army's Counter-Intelligence Corps (CIC), hitherto regarded as the most effective counter-intelligence force in the government, which will bear continuous close scrutiny.

As noted in the Embassy's recently-prepared semi-annual assessment of the political situation in Iran (Embassy's A–104 of August 23, 1966),[3] the period since our last assessment has been characterized once more by the relative placidity of the internal scene. It has been years since the political atmosphere has been as sluggish, as self-satisfied, or as resigned to the status quo. This is related only partly to the effectiveness of political controls. It is in large measure attributable to economic prosperity and to the Shah's success in giving the impression that a reorientation has taken place in Iran's international position. There is more popular confidence in the regime and less carping criticism. A rising new middle class is on the march economically and, in the short run at least, appears to be developing an interest in political stability. This situation could change, of course, if the Shah should be assassinated, or if a serious slowdown in present economic momentum should take place.

The favorable economic situation and the reduced level of popular dissatisfaction have had the effect of dampening political activities of all kinds. The Communists are in disarray, their fortunes probably at the

---

[1] Source: Department of State, NEA/IRN Files: Lot 70 D 330, Iran 1966. Secret; Official–Informal. A handwritten note on the source text indicates that it was received on October 27.

[2] Not printed. (Ibid., Central Files, POL 23–1 IRAN)

[3] Not printed. (Ibid., POL 2–3 IRAN)

lowest ebb in years. They certainly can take little heart in the increasingly obvious efforts of the Soviets and the Communist orbit of Eastern Europe to deal directly with the Shah himself on a government-to-government level. The religious opposition remains unreconciled to Iran's increasing modernity and, while there have been rumors of an unholy alliance between the right-wing religious oppositionists and left-wing elements, so far nothing actually has materialized. With the surrender of the Qashqai bandit Bahman Khan earlier this year the last vestige of rebellion among the southern tribes disappeared from the scene, at least for the time being.

However, there is some evidence of increasing activity on the part of the Iranian Kurds. The apparent negotiated settlement of the Kurdish revolt in Iraq reached late last June was generally well-received by the Kurds in Iran. The end of hostilities, however, also set in motion a latent nationalist fervor among this minority group due primarily to the expectation that the Iraqi Kurds would gain certain advantages and privileges from their acceptance of the cease-fire. This tendency probably is best reflected in what has been described by Embassy sources as a general increase in political activity, particularly among Kurdish groups in the Mahabad area. The Iranian Government appears to be watching this unsettled situation warily and has developed a renewed interest in the National Resistance Movement (NRM). So far, however, we have no evidence of any major shift in GOI policy vis-à-vis the Kurds.

Although some Iraqi leaders continue to believe to the contrary, the GOI appears to have discontinued purely military assistance to the Iraqi Kurds, and has closed the Iraqi-Iranian border in the Kurdish area. So far, although there are the usual cases of smuggling and banditry, Iranian Kurdistan appears peaceful. We do not believe that political activity on the part of Kurds in Iran which might affect drastically Iranian Kurdistan will develop in the near future. Iran's central security organizations appear quite capable of handling any situation likely to develop.

While Iranian security forces appear capable of handling any political activity likely to develop in Kurdistan, they are having their difficulties elsewhere. At the present time, the greatest security problem is of a *long-term character*. The Iranian security forces clearly are unable to keep the steadily rising number of Soviet technicians in Iran under effective surveillance. The number of Soviet personnel in Iran in connection with the steel mill, pipeline, and other projects is approaching 600 and likely to surge beyond that figure. The Iranians, however, have taken a number of administrative steps to aid in controlling more effectively the movements of Soviet officials more or less permanently stationed in this country. The Embassy also hears that a number of dossiers concerning suspicious activities on the part of the Soviets are piled up on the desk of the Shah. We believe that Iranian security forces are keeping especially careful tabs on possible contacts between Soviet technicians and Iranian Communists.

Speaking once more of the Communists, Savak is showing interest in long-term threat posed by the Chinese Communists. The latter have not been able to form any organization within Iran, but have been successful in their propaganda activities among Iranian students in Europe. An increasing number of these students have begun to show Communist Chinese sympathies and some of them apparently have even visited China. The Chinese have flooded Europe with publications which are having an effect on Iranian students some of whom can be expected to return to Iran and to attempt to conduct subversive activities. Savak believes that students returning from abroad will have to be checked very carefully lest the Chinese Communists get a foothold in Iran. Although Savak believes that the pro-Soviet group now dominates the Tudeh party, it feels that the Chinese Communists, considering that they have been laboring under the double disadvantage of being newer in the field than the Soviets and of having no official representation in Iran, have done very well to date. For this reason, Savak will continue to observe closely the activities of Chinese Communist elements.

The decentralization of the Counter Intelligence Corps (CIC) of the Iranian Armed Forces has reduced its effectiveness markedly. CIC units in the field have been transferred from the administrative and operational control of CIC Headquarters in Tehran to the units to which previously they had been attached only. Thus, all reporting on security matters now must pass through channels via the unit commander who, if he sees fit to do so, may suppress the reports rather than forward them to the Supreme Commander's Staff (SCS). Given the well-known Iranian penchant for not reporting matters which superiors do not wish to hear, security reports are more often suppressed than forwarded to headquarters. In addition, decentralization takes away the capability of CIC units in the field to respond quickly to an urgent request from CIC Headquarters for operational support on an espionage or subversion case. Under the new arrangement such requests must be despatched through command channels to the lower CIC unit. In the past CIC Headquarters sent a message directly to the unit concerned. A study is now underway, however, to determine how to retain such support from the field without taking away the prerogative of the major commander concerned. The decentralization has had a deleterious impact on the morale of the CIC as has also the fact that it is still smarting from the incompetence of its previous commander. Although a new commander, a professional intelligence officer, has been recently appointed, it is problematical whether he will be able to restore the CIC to the level of its previous effectiveness when it was regarded as the top security organization in Iran.

We continue to find valid the judgment made at the time of our last report (March 19, 1966 letter to Governor Harriman)[4] that there are no disturbing elements in the present situation requiring counter-insurgency measures. On the program side we continue to be interested in support for the National Police and in communications for the Imperial Iranian Gendarmerie (IIG). In this latter connection we have obtained from the IIG an idea of the program it desires and have forwarded to DOD via Genmish channels our comments and suggestions. The IIG has obtained from the GOI a pledge of support which we believe approaches 50% of the total cost. The total cost of this communications project is $10.2 million. With the GOI apparently prepared to put up $5 million and with $2.2 million already in the program for IIG communications, this means that $3 million needs to be financed over a five to six year period. We would be grateful for any help you feel you might provide in getting this project on the rails. We think it is of the utmost importance in any counter-insurgency situation likely to develop in Iran that we have an effective command and control system for operations in the countryside.

With all best regards,

Sincerely,

Armin

---

[4] Not found.

---

179. **Briefing Memorandum From the Assistant Secretary of State for Near Eastern and South Asian Affairs (Hare) to Acting Secretary of State Ball**[1]

Washington, October 25, 1966.

SUBJECT

Iranian Oil Consortium: Your Dinner with Iranian Foreign Minister, Tuesday, October 25, 1966 at 8:00 p.m.

Recommended Position

At a meeting yesterday in London, the Iranian Government gave the Oil Consortium one month in which to present proposals in response to

---

[1] Source: Department of State, Central Files, DEF 6 IRAN. Confidential. Drafted by Eliot and cleared by Solomon and in draft by Director of the Office of Fuels and Energy John G. Oliver.

the Government's demands. Officials of American companies belonging to the Consortium told us yesterday afternoon in Washington that, while they continue to hope we will help restrain the Iranians from precipitate and unilateral action, they would prefer that we not become involved in the substance of the issues as they are working on their position.

In the light of the attitude of the American companies, we do not recommend that you raise this subject this evening with Iranian Foreign Minister Aram. If he, however, raises the subject, you might say that we continue to view the situation with concern and believe that it was a wise decision to allow a month's time for further discussion.

We anticipate that Ambassador Meyer will speak to the Shah along these lines today in Tehran.

Background

At the annual Consortium-Iranian meeting two weeks ago in London, the Iranians asked for a 17 percent increase in Consortium production for each of the next two years. If the Consortium could not achieve this rate of increase, the Iranians requested an advance payment based on the difference between a 17 percent increase and the actual increase. The Consortium has declined to agree to this demand, pointing out that it is unable to predict in advance any rate of increase in the light of changing market conditions. The Consortium has told the Iranians that it hopes to increase its production 10–11 percent this year. The Mideast average increase will be 7–8 percent.

After receiving the Consortium's negative reply to their first proposal, the Iranians asked that the Consortium make available to Iran to market on its own account, presumably to Eastern Europe, crude oil at cost. The Iranians suggested that the Consortium guarantee an annual production increase of 12 percent and deliver to them an amount of crude oil annually for the next four or five years equal to the difference between the actual increase and a 17 percent increase. At yesterday's meeting, the Consortium declined to agree to this demand, but requested and obtained a month's time in which to consider possible alternative proposals.

The Iranians have informed the Consortium and the British and American governments that they are considering another proposal under which they would ask the Consortium to relinquish all its Iranian reserves of oil except those required to meet a minimum acceptable annual increase in Consortium production. The Shah has indicated that Iran will if necessary take legislative action to achieve this end. Such a move would be contrary to the Consortium-Iranian agreement of 1954.

Iranian motives appear to be a combination of two elements. One is a need for increased foreign exchange receipts to meet the needs of a vigorous development program and to cover the costs of rising military imports. The second is a desire to get into the business of marketing oil for their own account.

It is not certain what new proposals will be developed by the Consortium. The oil companies will seek a solution within the 1954 agreement. They will not consent to an arrangement under which they would guarantee a specified rate of increase in offtake from Iran because they would then be subjected to similar demands from other producing countries. They will also not consent to an arrangement under which the Iranians obtain oil at cost to market in competition with the Consortium. They believe that the Iranians intend to market any such oil not only in Eastern Europe and that Iranian oil exports to Eastern Europe would permit the Soviets to increase their sales to existing Consortium markets.

The Consortium operates in Iran under an agreement reached in 1954 which terminated the crisis set off by Mossadeq's nationalization of the Anglo-Iranian Oil Co. in 1951. The members of the Consortium are British Petroleum (40%), Shell (14%), Standard of New Jersey (7%), Standard of California (7%), Texaco (7%), Mobil (7%), Gulf (7%), French Oil Co. (6%), and eight independent American companies (5%).

---

180. Telegram From the Embassy in Iran to the Department of State[1]

Tehran, November 2, 1966, 1150Z.

1964. Shah–Harriman Talk.

1. Noting he coming at behest of President Johnson, Ambassador Harriman in two hour session evening Nov. 1 outlined to Shah purport of Manila Conference. He stressed it was impressive demonstration of unity of purpose of seven countries with troops fighting in Vietnam to repel aggression. At same time conference concentrated on pacification program as well as determination for negotiated peaceful settlement. Harriman stressed we want South Vietnamese left free to make their own decisions and referred to six months withdrawal pledge. He noted that appeals for US to stop bombing come from same sources which prompted 37-day pause year ago with only result being increase of

---

[1] Source: Department of State, Central Files, POL 7 US/HARRIMAN. Secret; Priority; Limdis. Repeated to Paris for Harriman and to Moscow.

North Vietnamese infiltration and military build-up. He added US ready cease bombing if there any indication willingness on part of NVN achieve just settlement. Unfortunately, such indications lacking. Meanwhile, USG and its six fighting allies determined neither to escalate the conflict nor to shirk their responsibilities.

2.   Shah said USG has no alternative but to continue what it is doing. He reviewed development his own position. In March 1965 during trip to South America he stressed there is clear case of aggression against South Vietnam and USG doing right thing in taking military action to repel it. In June 1965 during his visit to Moscow Shah stressed if Chinese not stopped by Americans in Vietnam all of Southeast Asia would be overrun and in any case Soviets contradict themselves by endorsing Nasser's military actions in Yemen. This past summer in East Europe Shah had stressed that US doing job UN should be doing, that it is unfair and illogical to ask one party to withdraw unilaterally, and that attention should rather be focused on getting all parties to peace table. Shah cited improved situation in Indonesia as tremendous success and reason why solution in Vietnam could be negotiated settlement rather than military victory.

3.   Harriman pointed out that there is no chance of Communists gaining victory and in fact their capability and morale being steadily reduced. Nevertheless Peking and Hanoi give no signs wanting peace, apparently delighted keep US bogged down and hoping one day Americans will become discouraged and pull out. Since there no chance of securing Peking's support for peace, chief hope lies in getting Soviets to bring decisive influence to bear on Hanoi. This hope been slightly reinforced by attitude displayed by Gromyko during his recent Washington talks.

4.   Shah said his trips convince him neither Russian nor East European countries want war. They all determined improve welfare their people because their people demanding it. Moreover, Soviets strongly oppose Chinese expansion. He had that day seen report that Hanoi is asking Soviets and East Europeans to provide "volunteers" as envisaged in communiqué after recent Moscow conference of Socialist countries. Shah convinced this Hanoi ploy is inspired by ChiComs to put Soviets on spot. He said President Ayub describes ChiComs as being motivated by intense nationalism.

5.   Asked by Ambassador Harriman his impressions of attitudes of various East European countries, Shah said Romanians only ones close to Chinese but this is card Romanians playing in their game with Russians. Despite CPR-Romanian ties, Shah convinced Romanians can have no influence on ChiComs re Vietnam. Only hope is, as Ambassador Harriman had indicated, via Russian influence on Hanoi. Shah said he had seen another report to effect special Hungarian envoy is en route to Ha-

noi on peace mission. Shah believes Hungarians, Poles and Czechs so keenly interested in promoting Vietnam peace they might have salutary influence on Russians toward this end. Shah also had strong impression from his East European visits that Poles, and others fear Germans more than Russians and this factor deters them from acting as independently from Moscow as they would like.

6.   Ambassador Harriman commended Shah for 25-member medical team in Vietnam and said they doing outstanding job. Shah said he been receiving reports from team and is gratified that they able to assuage suffering, even of some Communist casualties.

7.   Ambassador Harriman said Americans delighted that Iran making such fine economic and social progress under Shah's leadership and also believe his developing fruitful relationships with East Bloc countries is useful. Word of caution, however, is in order, Ambassador Harriman said, noting that while communism as a system is no longer marketable commodity, Soviets still actively support "wars of liberation." They not beyond dusting off Tudeh Party one day and causing Shah trouble. Thus while détente with East Bloc is good, it well to keep guard up.

8.   Shah fully endorsed Harriman view. Russian objectives he said are historic. He recalled post-war Soviet efforts to get positions in Dardanelles, Libya and Eritrea. Now they seeking bases at Alexandria, Djibouti and Yemen. As far as Iran concerned, Shah said he under no illusions. Daily clandestine broadcasts make clear Soviet designs to oust Shah and his regime. Also indicative are vicious propaganda attacks Moscow is making against Islamic "understanding" concept which Faisal and Shah had discussed. Soviet tactics, Shah said, have, however, changed. Any crossing of Iran's border by Soviet troops would mean world war. Soviets realize this and accordingly are working via Egypt and Syria, both of which wittingly or unwittingly are staging areas for Soviet designs for achieving Mideast warm water ports. Asked if he really convinced Nasser under Soviet control, Shah said Nasser doing better job for Soviets in Cairo than if they had "someone there by name of Popov or Litvinov."

9.   Shah went on to outline his thesis, developed more fully within last year or so, that it is not wise for country like Iran to consider dependence on even as good a friend as US as "essential part of our defense policy." Great power intervention anywhere these days is "more difficult," (he obviously thinking of Vietnam). It therefore imperative for Iran to develop capability of taking care of itself in deterring or coping with regional threats, even though he must pay high US prices for equipment. Danger, he said, will be at its height within next five years, particularly after 1968 when British withdraw from Aden. Ambassador Harriman agreed that British withdrawal was unhelpful, particularly since expense of keeping British forces in place is relatively small. Shah felt Iran's

capability for handling regional disturbance is as much in USG's interest as that of Iran.

10. While agreeing that Iran have adequate self-defense, Ambassador Harriman made strong point of keeping military expenditures down. He stressed that economic development and prosperity are as important if not more so in preservation of Iran's independence and integrity. Shah agreed, provided that minimal defense requirements are met.

11. Shah then launched into his usual argumentation on need for increased revenues from oil consortium in order to maintain 8 percent growth rate for Iran. He noted that while he is told that his demands are exhorbitant oil lifting from several other countries are well above 17 percent annual increase which Iran must have. He added that these other countries have small populations and do not know what to do with their excessive incomes while for Iran, which is largest of these countries, 17 percent increase is critical. Ambassador Harriman repeatedly urged Shah to be reasonable and avoid repetition of 1951 "tragedy." Shah said he did not wish 1951 be repeated but he should not be forced into corner. He alluded to proposals which he had forwarded to US via Alam (Embtel 1932)[2] and expressed hope they would lead way to solution. He noted his request for crude been reduced to 2,000,000 tons. Ambassador Meyer took occasion to refer to likelihood Romanians selling refined Iranian crude to West Germans (Embtel 1952).[3] Noting this would be self-defeating for Iran, Shah insisted it would not occur but he would check into it. Perhaps safeguard provisions, he said, could be incorporated in any agreements. This portion of discussion was closed with expression of gratification that Shah has taken steps to avoid further public discussion of oil problem so that atmosphere most conducive to reasonable negotiation can prevail.

12. Shah spoke of his high hopes for Iran's future. Only Japan and Iran have possibility of attaining within next 20 years state of development reached by European countries, he said, adding Iran has more abundant natural resources than does Japan. Ambassador Harriman congratulated Shah on progress made and expressed delight that so many American firms are entering into joint enterprises here, e.g. petrochemical industry.

13. At conclusion, conversation returned to Vietnam. Ambassador Harriman earlier had noted that so many countries privately support US but refrain for domestic political reasons from coming out openly. In departing he referred to De Gaulle's Cambodia speech which demanded US withdraw but demanded nothing of Vietnam. Similarly, Nasser, Indira Gandhi and Tito had just few days ago in New Delhi made similar

---

[2] Dated October 31. (Ibid., PET 6 IRAN)
[3] Dated November 1. (Ibid.)

public demands. Ambassador Harriman pointed out that such public pronouncements, besides not being impartial, have tragic effect of making Hanoi more intransigent. Shah concurred.

14. At beginning and throughout conversation, Ambassador Harriman made clear that purpose of his visit was to exchange views with leader whose special friendship President Johnson and USG have long valued. Shah was obviously gratified. He asked Ambassador Harriman to convey his warm wishes and abiding friendship to President Johnson.

15. *Comment:* Discussion was everything hoped for. Shah obviously delighted that USG still considers him important friend. Having known Ambassador Harriman since 1942, he was speaking with trusted friend. At times, he sounded almost like Shah we knew in days before present ballyhoo about "independent policy." Under circumstances, this talk tended to bring Shah back to moorings which are deeper than vagaries of current Afro-Asian politics. This does not mean there will be any turning back from Iran's present "independent" posture. But it may mean that swing of pendulum may be a little slower than it has been since Shah's East European visits. All in all, stopover here was decided success. For Ambassador Harriman it was a long day, he having started from New Delhi early in morning, lunched with Ayub, and still having four hour journey to Rome prior to heavy round of talks there tomorrow. We grateful he agreed to this extra task which was accomplished so effectively and look forward to his early return.[4]

Meyer

---

[4] Harriman's November 28 report to the President on his trip to Iran and nine other countries following the Manila Conference is ibid., POL 7 US/HARRIMAN.

---

181.   Telegram From the Embassy in Italy to the Department of State[1]

Rome, November 3, 1966, 0941Z.

2364. For the President and Secretary of State from Harriman.

1. With Amb. Meyer I had a two-hour soul-searching talk with the Shah in Tehran Tuesday afternoon (Nov. 1). He exposed his hopes and

---

[1] Source: Department of State, Central Files, POL 7 US/HARRIMAN. Secret; Limdis. Repeated to Tehran. Passed to the White House on November 3. A November 3 report from Wriggins to Rostow on that day's cables noted the success of Harriman's meeting with the Shah as reported in telegram 2364 from Rome. A handwritten notation indicates that the President had seen the cable. (Johnson Library, National Security File, Wriggins Memos, 1966)

fears on Viet-Nam and he now agrees with your policy to seek a negotiated settlement. The favorable developments in Indonesia have changed his more hawk-like previous views.

2.   He takes satisfaction in his new contacts in Eastern Europe but is under no illusion that Moscow would not take an opening of weakness to cut his throat. He no longer fears open aggression from the north but knows that the Tudeh Party is alerted to sieze any opportunity to cause him trouble. He believes Moscow is working through Nasser and now Syria in a flanking maneuver. The foothold in Yemen will be expanded when the British leave Aden through southern Arabia to the Persian Gulf. Iran must be strong enough to face this threat alone without our intervention. However, his military expenditures should not interfere with Iran's economic and social progress to attain a southern European living standard. Iran and Japan are the only two eastern countries that can aspire to this goal.

3.   He pleads for our help to make oil companies realize it is more important to increase Iranian oil production than that of the small princely states in Arabia. I urged caution in military expenditures and patience in dealing with oil companies and not to kill the goose. The Shah takes justifiable pride in Iran's economic growth of over 10 per cent per annum for the last two years without rise in cost of living. He was obviously pleased that you sent me to consult him and looks forward to talking with you personally in Washington, hopefully in June. All in all it was a friendly conversation combined with a glass of excellent scotch and ample of Iran's best caviar.

Reinhardt

182.   Telegram From the Embassy in Iran to the Embassy in Thailand[1]

Tehran, December 8, 1966, 1315Z.

2453. For Secretary Rusk. Following subjects may come up in your talk with Shah:

1. Iran's Orientation. Although still publicly proclaiming "independent policy," Shah has no illusions re Commie aims. His visits to East Europe, steel mill project and stepped up trade with Sov Bloc were hailed as new look in Iran policy. Some of glamour seems be wearing off, however, particularly pursuant to Moscow efforts to roil waters during recent Iranian discussions with consortium. Surveillance of Sov Bloc activities here is intensive and some inevitable frictions developing as Iranians and Sov Bloc reps try to do business. You may wish commend Shah for cautiousness in dealing with Sov Bloc and note that reduction in tensions with his northern neighbor is also of benefit to US assuming, of course, that relaxation not accompanied by diminution in long-standing US-Iran friendship.

2. Iran's Stability. Due to economic boom, internal stability is at new high in Iran. Shah deserves good marks for economic and social progress notably Literacy Corps, Health Corps and land reform program. Shah determined modernize Iran a la Europe before he lays down reins. Hopefully he will not bite off more than Iran can chew. Hopefully also future will include political progress.

3. Viet-Nam. Shah will welcome opportunity exchange views on world's number one problem. Privately he supports USG policy but except for little publicized medical team in Viet-Nam he refrains from public support. Because of improved Indonesian situation, Shah has "shifted" his view from firm military riposte in Viet-Nam to negotiated settlement. He probably favors extended bombing pause. He would be particularly gratified if there were useful role he might play in achieving settlement.

4. Oil Issue. See Tehran 2435[2] re State of play. In general Shah can be commended for his staying within bounds of reason.

5. Military. As you know Shah believes Iran must be capable of deterring or coping with regional threats and he thinks this is in USG interest. He been heavily influenced by Viet-Nam and by Pak plight last fall. He has been publicly critical of CENTO (for unfair reasons) but intends

---

[1] Source: Department of State, Central Files, POL 7 IRAN. Secret; Priority; Limdis. Repeated to the Department of State, which is the source text.

[2] Dated December 7. (Ibid., PET 6 IRAN)

continue membership until acceptable replacement available, i.e. greater regional cooperation including hopefully Afghanistan. Without sales talk re CENTO's future, it might be useful to remind Shah that Iran's CENTO affiliation has had value, e.g. $800 million in US military aid to Iran, while permitting Iran's peaceful development, and cause of shift in Soviet tactics. If subject of our military credit sales comes up, you might point out that despite our preoccupations with Viet-Nam USG did quite well by Iran last summer, e.g. first country except Brits get F–4 aircraft, relatively reasonable credit terms despite stringency of MAP supporting funds, etc.

6. Arab Threat. Shah sincerely concerned that Nasserism will emerge on southern coast of Persian Gulf, e.g. overthrow of Kuwaiti regime or some vague UAR extension from Yemen–Aden base after British withdrawal from Aden. As counter, Shah is less interested in retention British power than in building up his own capability. Without arguing potentiality of threat, it may be useful to point out that while adequate self-defense necessary (and we have recognized that) Iran's best bet is healthy economic and social development which will thwart more sinister forms in which threat likely to occur.

7. Cooperation with Paks. Shah has stayed close to Ayub to prevent too close Pak asociation with ChiComs. Shah may press you for approval of M–47 tank transaction which is part of quiet and small scale effort of Shah to permit Ayub source of supplies other than from Commies. You may wish indicate we realize value in Shah's keeping window open for Ayub but note that our whole policy re Pakistan's military needs is under discussion.

8. Iran–Iraq. Aram will be in Baghdad when you are here. Shah does not expect substantive progress in relations with Iraqis but wants give public indication Iran's friendly disposition if Iraq determined stay out of Nasser's clutches.

9. US–Iran. Relations very good. Main problem is instant transition from large-scale aid to more normal relationships.

10. AID Phase-out. Conceivably the phase-out of AID might be mentioned. Our line is that we are proceeding with a planned AID phase-out in FY 1968 and expect that by November 1967 we will have our mission staff pretty well on its way, although of course we will continue with an orderly conclusion of ongoing programs using Embassy facilities hereafter.

11. PL–480. A proposal for an agreement for 37.5 thousand tons of wheat is pending and is expected to be concluded this month, with another 37.5 thousand tons in January. This is for dollars under present Title IV. It is hoped that rial proceeds will be used for grain storage and processing facilities.

12. As you fly in, big military parade will be concluding in vicinity of airport. Dec. 12 is anniversary of ouster of Russians from Azerbaijan.

Meyer

---

183. Telegram From the Embassy in Iran to the Department of State[1]

Tehran, December 13, 1966, 0800Z.

2499. Secretary's Talk With Shah. Following are highlights of more than three hours' discussion between Secretary and Shah evening 12th:

1. Presidential Greetings. Secretary said he brought personal greetings from President who is always interested in Shah's views on subjects of international import. Shah asked that greetings be reciprocated and expressed hope that President's health is fully restored.

2. China. Secretary explained that with respect to Viet-Nam Soviets are hesitant to play peace-making role because of their relations with China. At Hanoi there is enigmatic situation but chief obstacle is China. Destruction of culture, except for nuclear science activities, is indicative of bellicose and ultra-nationalistic character of present ChiCom regime. Secretary opined that two ChiCom trends are to be feared: a) increasing militancy; or b) accommodation with the Russians which would again unite these two great powers in drive for world revolution. USG hopes, Secretary said, that both extremes can be avoided and this explains our desire for early stabilization of Southeast Asia. Shah said of two alternatives mentioned by Secretary he would prefer former for USSR-CPR rapprochement could only occur if Soviets moved closer to ChiCom policy of belligerence. ChiComs, Shah said, are fanatical ideologists whereas Soviets are adjusting primitive Marxist philosophy to more acceptable system since pure Marxist system has proved failure.

3. Viet-Nam. Secretary reported current situation in Viet-Nam and commended fine work being done by Iran medical team. Re military aspects Secretary emphasized our forces cannot be defeated. He stated USG will persist until a successful outcome is attained for if we fail to do so our commitments elsewhere in the world would in eyes of Commu-

---

[1] Source: Department of State, Central Files, ORG 7 S. Secret; Priority; Exdis. Repeated to Paris for the Secretary.

nists be worthless. Shah agreed and said US should not be deterred by students and other critics. Secretary pointed out there is growing unhappiness in American public opinion at lack of support by our friends and allies. War in Viet-Nam has changed from organized military conflict to primarily guerilla warfare. Particularly needed is assistance in constabulary endeavors. Shah parried this cue by asking why is there Viet Cong. Secretary said Viet Cong in part result of totalitarian tactics of Diem regime, particularly oppressive propensities of Diem's brother. Shah noted Hanoi is equally totalitarian. Secretary pointed out Diem regime was ruthless enough to alienate people but not as ruthless as Hanoi regime in enslaving the populace. Secretary expressed hope that recent elections, constituent assembly and other developments might lead to more wholesome South Viet-Nam political situation. Shah thought key need is strong leadership. (Secretary has asked Ambassador to follow up with Shah matter of constabulary assistance.)

4. East-West Trade. Shah expressed wholehearted approval of current USG policies for building trade bridges with Eastern Europe. From his visits, he could testify that those countries want increased independence. He cited his efforts to sell oil in East European markets which, he is convinced, are noncompetitive with consortium markets. Secretary wondered whether Soviets and Romanians are truly in need of oil. Shah said Romanians wish to use their high quality crude for sophisticated purposes and in any case the amounts of crude Iran will sell are relatively small. While differing in character, all of the satellites in the Shah's view are loosening their ties with the Soviets despite latter's efforts to perpetuate their dependence.

5. Soviet Arms. Recalling what he described as strong Soviet efforts last summer to sell Iran MIG's and SAM's, Shah reaffirmed his decision not to buy any sophisticated Soviet military equipment. To do so he noted would be incompatible with procurement sophisticated American equipment and would require undesirable influx of Soviet advisors. Shah indicated, however, that active negotiations are in progress with Soviets for purchase of anti-aircraft machine guns, noting Soviet equipment this type less expensive than similar American equipment.

6. Relations With Pakistan. While not agreeing with Pakistan's flirtations with ChiComs, Shah declared firm friendship for Ayub. Shah appeared a bit miffed that Paks recently wined and dined UAR's General Amer. Paks have explained that they need Arab votes on Kashmir question but Shah noted no public pronouncements by Amer siding with Pakistan as over against India.

7. RCD. Without expatiating his complaints re CENTO, Shah expressed wish that RCD could be beefed up as alternative. He would like to see Afghanistan included, perhaps even Iraq. However, Turkey's membership in NATO is stumbling block. Secretary said there no reason

why there cannot be interlocking arrangements. Shah's strong view is that Turks in any case are too Europe-centric.

8. Iraq. Shah said Iran has every desire to be on good terms with Iraq and current policy is to be as patient as possible with Iraqis. He claimed 60 percent of Iraqis are Shia and thus specially linked with Iran. There is no reason, Shah said, why Iraq should be submissive to Nasser.

9. UAR. Secretary asked Shah's view whether it better for USG provide small quantities of food to UAR and thereby have some influence on Egyptian behavior or to refrain from providing food supplies and be without any influence. While our achievements had not been great, he said, our PL–480 program had helped US influence Nasser on number of matters, e.g. moderating Nasser re Congo, re Libya and re Arab boycott. Shah said Nasser wittingly or unwittingly serving as Soviet tool and in any case is dissipating his resources on adventures when he should concentrate on doing more for his people. Shah implied that USG food supplies should be resumed only if Nasser gets out of Yemen and stops agitating against King Hussein.

10. Iran Development. Secretary commended Shah for Iran's remarkable economic progress, also for satisfactory resolution of recent oil crisis. At dinner, Shah, PriMin, FornMin and Court Minister Alam spent much time describing successes of what Shah considers his "revolution." PriMin Hoveyda reported GNP increase this year will again exceed 10 percent. To Secretary's request about next steps, PriMin said govt is heavily engaged in formulating fourth five year plan and main emphasis will be on development of agriculture. Shah said he knows that increased world food production is subject of great interest to President Johnson and he (Shah) is already formulating some thoughts on this subject and what Iran is doing about it in anticipation of visit with the President next June.

11. *Comment:* While nothing sensational emerged from the conversations, clearly Shah was delighted to have opportunity to exchange views with Secretary. Shah's constructive purpose and detailed knowledge of what is going on in world and in his own country were impressive. Also heartwarming was his obvious sympathy for what USG is trying to do. In absence of aid programs, which formerly featured US-Iran relationships, intimate talks of this kind with top-level US officials, including sharing of confidences, are highly useful instruments in retention of friendly ties between our two countries.

12. Incidentally, Secretary's visit here was not marred in any way by activities critical of US policy in Viet-Nam. On contrary, while motoring through city Secretary's cavalcade was on several occasions greeted with impromptu applause.

Meyer

184. Letter From the Ambassador to Iran (Meyer) to the Country Director for Iran (Eliot)[1]

Tehran, December 17, 1966.

Dear Ted:

The Secretary's blitz visit to Tehran was a complete success.

It was successful probably more from the standpoint of form than substance. No thorny issues were raised by HIM. He did not play his usual record of grievances against the USG. Nor did he even broach the question of the dates of his forthcoming visit.

However, for three hours the two were on almost exactly the same wave length on world affairs. Not once was the phrase "independent policy" mentioned. On the contrary, the thrust of the whole evening's conversation was thwarting communist efforts everywhere in the world, not excluding Iran.

It was particularly helpful to have this pro-free world dialogue so manifest at the dinner table. While Aram and Alam needed no shoring up, it was good to remind Hoveyda that Iranian and American policies are still fundamentally in step. Sometimes our good friend Amir Abbas tends to be carried away by street plaudits vis-à-vis palsywalsyness with the Eastern bloc.

Even in the public domain one can feel the good effects of the Secretary's visit. The mere fact that HIM welcomed his visitor and spent three hours in intimate conversation belied suspicions that relations between the United States and Iran have cooled. One gets the feeling around here that Iranians generally now realize that the détente with the North has not greatly changed the relationship with our country.

A dividend for you and me was that both the Secretary and Bill Bundy came away more impressed than ever with respect to the Shah's dedication and profundity of knowledge. Like many others who have had audiences, they know of few if any other Chiefs of State who have such a detailed knowledge (tons of rice per hectare, for example) re matters in and outside the country as does HIM. This firsthand recent impression, coupled with the obvious progress which Iran is making, should hopefully stand us in good stead whenever Iran's name comes before the Secretary in future months.

All this does not mean that all of our problems are solved. Naturally HIM would prefer not to harangue the Secretary as he does the Secretary's Ambassador. Nevertheless, for the time being, particularly after

---

[1] Source: Department of State, NEA/IRN Files: Lot 70 D 330, Iran 1966, POL 7, Secretary Rusk's Visit to Tehran, December 12, 1966. Confidential.

the oil settlement, there is somewhat of a turmoil gap. We hope to prolong it as much as possible.

Fond regards of the Season.

Sincerely,

Armin

---

185.   Telegram From the Embassy in Iran to the Department of State[1]

Tehran, January 24, 1967, 1330Z.

2985. Iranian Purchase of Soviet Arms.

1. Hoveyda and I had one hour discussion morning 24th re Iran military program, arms deal with Soviets[2] and impact military expenditures on Iranian economy. I opened discussion by expressing uneasiness, referring specifically to effects of these subjects on USG military credit sales program here.

2. Hoveyda described at some length present favorable economic situation. Country is stable and calm, he noted, two factors without which present economic strides would be impossible. SAVAK Chief only two days ago complained that his work has few challenges. Remnants of old National Front group, Hoveyda said, are dickering with him personally with view to cooperating with "movement" which country is experiencing and which they attribute to relief that present GOI policies are what they been recommending in past.

3. Hoveyda said although Shah tends toward wishing progress more rapid than is realistic, he (Hoveyda) is determined to maintain a realistic "cruising speed." Third plan he said has not attained all its goals because it was too ambitious; unrealized objectives will be incorporated in first year of new fourth plan. Re latter, private sector industrial development is flourishing so well that major portion of fourth plan will be

---

[1] Source: Department of State, Central Files, DEF 19–6 USSR–IRAN. Secret; Limdis. Repeated to Moscow, CINCSTRIKE/USCINCMEAFSA, and Ankara.

[2] Telegram 2820 from Tehran, January 10, reported that Iran had agreed to purchase military equipment including armored personnel carriers, anti-aircraft guns, jeeps, and trucks from the Soviet Union. (Ibid.)

concentrated on agriculture. Hoveyda noted Iran's growth rate has been excellent. Cost of living been held in line and PriMin has recently appointed standing committee to keep an eye on it. As index of strength of Iranian economy, Hoveyda said black market rate for US dollars is now below official bank rate. He said new tax law will be passed in Majlis within week and it will mean more revenues. In addition, GOI planning measures for mobilizing "savings," including a national loan to cover increased defense costs. Behind all this, Hoveyda said, is his determination to govern by persuasion rather than coercion and to rely heavily on private enterprise.

4.   Referring to apparent increasing military budget, I reminded Hoveyda this continues be matter of great concern to USG. Hoveyda said Iran with help of US advisors determined to have effective modernized armed forces. Increased budgetary costs primarily due to building of "infra-structure." One of the difficulties of having thriving economy with burgeoning middle class, he said, is that military personnel, particularly lower ranks, require more amenities in face of soaring salaries of workers in private sector. To train and keep adequate maintenance and operating staff for modern equipment, therefore, requires such things as relatively decent housing, etc.

5.   Discussion turned to Iranian arms deal with Soviets and I expressed concern at magnitude of reported transaction and my impression that prices higher than necessary. Hoveyda said it important keep in mind that except for small component of Iranian-produced refrigerators, etc. repayment will be made entirely in natural gas. Soviets wanted at least 30 percent foreign exchange, but Iranians flatly rejected. While noting that delivery schedule for proposed vehicles remains to be worked out, Hoveyda sketched out repayment schedule extending to 1978. He said Soviets are charging 2-1/2 percent interest. First payments minimal and not significant before natural gas pipeline completed in 1970. Problem, Hoveyda said, is what can Iran safely obtain from Russians in return for natural gas. He solidly against Soviet prestige projects. Steel mill is more than enough. Soviets been pressing hard to build Tehran subway but he steadfastly opposed. Not all of natural gas credit, even in first years after 1970, will go for repaying steel mill. Thus repayment for trucks, APC's and anti-aircraft equipment can be made via natural gas with no strain. He noted that no Soviet advisors will come with equipment.

6.   Hoveyda indicated that magnitude of deal with Russians was heavily conditioned not only by ease of repayment but also by Shah's determination not to be at Soviets' mercy if crisis develops. Iran wants to have adequate quantity of spare vehicles and spare parts should Soviet policy toward Iran change. He noted in this connection that there are no

illusions anywhere in GOI that Soviet ultimate motivations have changed from what they have always been.

7. Hoveyda expressed view that USG should recognize that this deal with Soviets undercuts Soviet propaganda branding USG villain for supplying arms to Iran. Hoveyda also has hope that deal will throw some sticks in wheels of Soviet cooperation with UAR and Syria.

8. Throughout discussion I made clear that there bound to be repercussions on US opinion. While we might understand Iran's rationale there will be some on Capitol Hill who will wonder about Iran's intentions and this could have adverse effect on our military programs which involve MAP funds. More important, however, is the impact on Iran's economy. I reiterated our stipulation of last summer that each tranche of our future annual military sales credit will be reviewed in light of economic picture here and that President himself must give approval. I recalled specifically our having made clear that purchases from other countries would be taken into account. GOI would be well-advised, I said, to keep these factors in mind. In any case, both of us will be going into the total situation thoroughly during our annual economic review.

9. Hoveyda was greatly interested in observations which I brought along re cost comparisons and re what USG has done over past years in supplying trucks and other military items on large-scale grant basis. Noting how GOI has kept us informed re negotiations with Soviets, Hoveyda agreed that Jablonsky and Toufanian continue their dialogue particularly with a view to assuring that military spending in all fields be kept at minimum compatible with efficient military program. He also agreed it will be useful for me to discuss this whole subject with Shah upon his return.

Meyer

186.   National Policy Paper Prepared in the Department of State[1]

Washington, February 2, 1967.

IRAN

PART ONE—US POLICY

I. US Interests and Objectives

A.   The Broad Setting

With United States participation in the Allied occupation (USSR–UK–US) of Iran during World War II, our role drastically changed from an earlier cultural-missionary presence to a growing position of influence in the country's affairs. Our assumption of leadership in post-war affairs was initially a vacuum-filling operation. We replaced the former rivals, Russia and Britain, whose days of shared hegemony ended rather abruptly with the repulse of Soviet efforts to communize northwestern Iran and the demise of Britain's South Asian empire. Britain's weakened role was later confirmed by the conflict and break over nationalization of the Anglo-Iranian Oil Company. Active United States diplomacy in the UN's handling of the Azerbaijan crisis coincided roughly with our assuming a greater portion of the British responsibility in Greece, and in the strengthening of Turkey against Soviet claims to Kars and Ardahan, which led to the Truman Doctrine of March 12, 1947. Economic efforts under Point Four begun in 1950 established United States influence in both the internal and external affairs of Iran. Since that time, the importance of these northern tier countries, not the least being Iran, has increased rather than diminished.

B.   US Interests in Iran

In the short term Iran is important to the United States because of its strategic location and the defense facilities and privileges extended to the United States bilaterally and through cooperation in the CENTO framework. Over the longer term it is of continuing importance to United States security interests that Iran be seriously committed to modernize its political as well as economic and social institutions and thus build the internal strength to foil insurgent attempts, either by discon-

---

[1] Source: Department of State, S/P Files: Lot 72 D 139, Iran. Secret/Noforn. The introduction to the paper states: "All agencies with major responsibilities affecting our relations with Iran participated in the development of this Paper and concur in the objectives, strategy and courses of action which it sets forth." "Execution of the policy set forth in this Paper is the responsibility of the various executive agencies under the leadership of the Secretary of State and overseas under the leadership of the Ambassador." Secretary Rusk approved the paper on February 2.

tented urban and rural elements, the Communist (Tudeh) Party or dissatisfied, unassimilated tribal elements (Kurds in the west or Arabs in the south), or obscurantist rightist groups such as Fedayan Islam opposing any basic reform. The United States and the West have a stake in continuing modernization of the political and economic structure. This is interrelated to our narrow interest deriving from the $225 million in commercial investments (including the American share in the consortium).

C.   US Objectives

United States objectives in Iran are pursued within the framework of our particular relationship with the monarchy of that country. The Iranian monarchy provides the stability not yet available through popular institutions or long popular experience in organized political affairs. It is, at present, the sole element in the country that can provide continuity for public policy. While there are areas of divergence between us and the Shah, they have remained thus far more matters of emphasis than of essence, not particularly significant within the broad consensus we share with him on most of the really fundamental issues of foreign and domestic policy. While the United States is not necessarily committed to the support of any particular form of Government in Iran, the Shah at present affords the best means for the safeguarding of our basic security interests in Iran and is the only personality on the scene who can lead the anarchically-bent Persians. Thus, until another potentially viable power source appears, which we do not expect during the next two to five years, support for the Shah and his reformist programs will form the basic condition of our pursuit of the following objectives:

1.   An independent and increasingly self-reliant Iran, free from any foreign domination or aggression, and motivated to cooperate with the West in:

a.   Taking such measures as lie within Iranian power to frustrate Soviet clandestine activities within Iran and Soviet expansion toward Suez and the Persian Gulf;
b.   Providing access to Iranian soil for Western forces in the event of conflict, including retention of over-flight privileges;
c.   Stimulating developing relations with neighboring countries so that there evolves in the course of time a more friendly relationship between Iran and its non-communist neighbors to promote greater stability and cooperation in the Middle East, particularly Persian Gulf, area.

2.   Evolution of a new but still mutually rewarding relationship between the United States and Iran, in a climate of increasing Iranian public understanding that the United States role is that of assisting Iran in its national development rather than of directing its course.

3.   An effective Iranian Government which, through the increase of strength and the improvement of administrative efficiency, will command the respect and support of broader segments of the population,

especially among intellectuals—teachers, university students, professional men, etc.—and provincial leaders.

4. A sound, well managed economy which properly balances military and development expenditures so that the already large and rapidly growing wealth of the country can be used for orderly, self-sustaining economic growth and steady improvement of the standard of living.

5. The development and strengthening of political, social and economic institutions which will provide the means for orderly and peaceful transfer of power, as necessary, and in the longer term facilitate increased participation of ever-widening sectors of society in their own government.

6. Continued access for the West to Iranian resources, principally petroleum, on acceptable terms.

7. Continued United States access to expanding Iranian markets.

[Here follows Section II, "Problems and Alternatives."]

III. United States Strategy in Iran

A.   General

Our strategy for Iran must take account of the increasingly independent position of the Shah. This limits our area of maneuver. It also defines a major problem to which our strategy must address itself.

The key developments in recent years that underlie this picture of independence are: (1) the Shah's successful concentration of power in his own hands and the internal stability this has achieved at least for the present; (2) the increase in oil revenues that has given the Shah relative financial independence from the United States and, at the same time, has provided a major instrument for his internal control of the country.

In addition to these developments, the Shah's independent position must be understood as part of a longer run trend to which Mossadeq over a decade ago had given new impetus—namely, the emergence of Iran from a quasi-colonial status to one in which Iran would exercise the power over its own affairs that is associated with full sovereignty. Major elements of a strategy designed to move Iran forward in the next five years—politically, economically and socially—toward a more stable base for the longer run must be devised within this framework.

B.   The Independent Posture

Our strategy should be to respond as fully and as positively as we can, consistent with maintaining our special bilateral security arrangements with Iran, to the Shah's thrust toward a fully independent national posture in the country's foreign relations. On the economic front, this would mean adherence to our current policy of phasing out AID assistance. Again, with respect to our military assistance program, we should adhere generally to the present policy of shifting the appropriate pace from grant to credit sales on fairly hard terms and attempt to restrain the Shah's desires for equipment and forces that we consider unjustified by the threat. Although the days are over when we could dictate to the Shah what his military establishment should be, we can continue to play an important role in influencing Iran's military program, and in preserving a balanced application of resources as between the military and economic fields, provided this is done with tact, diplomacy, and a modest application of US resources. While recognizing that the Shah now has the financial means and market options to shift some of his procurement to non-US suppliers, we also recognize that our mutually beneficial relationship with Iran is, to a significant degree, based on our military training and supply activities.

C.   The Means of Leverage

Our influence on both internal and external policy will have to be exercised in somewhat different ways than in the past because our material assistance is declining and because Iran is determined, after many years of almost embarrassing reliance on American advice, to make at least a show of independence. Recently this has been accompanied by an increase in foreign (non-United States) technical experts serving in Iran including some 500 from the USSR and other communist countries, and by more varied offers of financial assistance from non-United States sources. Our leverage in the past has resulted in large measure from our economic, technical and military assistance, which has totaled $1,453.5 [sic] million ($706 million economic, $757.5 military, through FY'66) in the past 16 years.

While not uniformly successful in achieving the stated goals, these modes of assistance have secured entree into the key administrative, economic, and military circles and have contributed notably to the forward movement experienced on most fronts during the past decade. At present our concrete assistance is dwindling because of our resource limitations, Iran's growing financial strength, and Iranian pride—sometimes not fully justified—in the recent advances in domestic administrative capabilities. We ended direct budgetary support in 1961 and completed the shift in our support for development projects from concessional AID lending to Export-Import Bank loans in FY'66. We have gradually reduced our permanent technical advisory staff over the past three years and have put the Iranians on notice that the Development Grant program will end soon. In this transition period, which will come to an end in FY'68, we will concentrate our efforts in such strategic sectors as power and agriculture (rural development). We have shifted our Food for Peace assistance from a local-currency to a dollar-credit sales basis. In the military sphere, we are reducing MAP grants and shifting to credit sales, meanwhile retaining our close advisory relationship.

Fortunately our multifarious operations in Iran since the early 1950's, combined with Iran's reliance on us for fundamental security from Soviet aggression, have established our reputation sufficiently within influential government and private establishments that we need not look forward to encountering blank walls as our material sources of leverage melt away. Especially among the educated circles there is considerable acceptance of the value of ties with the West and increasing agreement with the stress we have been placing on modernization in all spheres of Iranian life. Neutralistic and xenophobic sentiments remain to be exploited by demagogic politicians, but it would take a major mishap to catapult such a one into power.

Nevertheless, as time goes on, we will unquestionably be more on our mettle to keep our advice sound and convincing in Iranian terms. Except perhaps in security matters, where we may look forward to many more years of close dependence on United States advice and support, we will be drawn less closely into the decision-making process in the inner councils of government, i.e., we will move more into the role of a trusted ally (hopefully still the most trusted) and away from the earlier role of responsible senior partner. When we are consulted on non-military domestic and foreign policy issues, we must take increasing care to avoid repeatedly offering advice which, however beneficial in an objective sense it might seem to be, would be disregarded because the Iranians would be unable or unwilling to act on it. It is hard to foresee how much disregarded advice would add up to a general reduction of confidence in United States leadership, but we must keep in mind that this consideration will be more of a problem in Iran in the future than it has been in the past.

It has been a significant irritant in our relations in recent years that as Iran sees it, we appear to take its dependence on us so much for granted that we show greater concern for troublesome and uncooperative allies and even neutrals than for Iran. As Iran's strength and its bent toward independence grow, this type of irritant could well affect our leverage, and it therefore behooves us to keep in mind the deference due, in both tone and substance, to a staunch and increasingly proud ally.

D.   Contingencies

The principal contingency requiring a change of strategy would be the removal of the Shah from a position of power, either suddenly or as a result of a well-coordinated coup. This and other contingencies will be the subject of a separate study.

IV. The Preferred Strategy: Courses of Action

A.   Political Strategy

A limited response by the Shah to the pressures for broader political participation, which are bound to increase during the period ahead, could be an important factor in achieving the objective of a longer run stability that we and the regime both seek. The 1967 elections may provide the opportunity for a limited opening up of the system. Considering the time required for planning and organizing broader political participation, we should, as opportunities arise, continue to urge upon the Shah the desirability of such an approach. He has occasionally indicted an interest in building bridges to some of the more moderate nationalist figures in the opposition. If the Shah could reach, in the next year or so, a decision to permit at least a limited amount of popular choice in the next elections—even if that choice were only between "approved" candidates, this could be an important step forward in Iran's political development. United States influence, diplomatically exercised, would support such a strategy.

1. Courses of Action—Political

a.   Encourage the Shah in his "White Revolution" on a course which is fast enough to broaden the base of support for the regime by whatever means make sense politically and economically in terms of the regime's basic stability.

Action: State

b.   Continue to deal with the Shah on questions of basic national security but do what we can to foster responsibility for Iran's day-to-day foreign and military policies on the part of the government.

Action: State, DOD

c.   Encourage the Iranian Government's efforts to engender a greater degree of popular identification with government affairs, and discourage regime impulses toward unduly harsh and repressive measures against non-communist opposition elements.

Action: State, DOD

d.   Encourage the Shah to enlist both moderate, conservative and liberal opposition elements to support his program of social reform and emancipation.

Action: State, AID, USIA

e.   Encourage the Shah and the Government toward greater efforts to build more permanent and orderly political, legislative, administrative and labor institutions and organizations.

Action: State, USIA, AID, Labor

f.   Persuade the Iranian Government and people that the United States is willing to assist Iran without threatening its sovereignty.

Action: State, USIA, DOD

g.   Persuade the Iranian Government to show maximum understanding of the real problems faced by Iraq and the Persian Gulf Sheikhdoms, to concentrate on real as opposed to merely apparent threats to Iran's vital interests, and to maintain an attitude of dignity and non-provocation even in the face of provocative propaganda from those countries and the UAR.

Action: State, DOD

h.   Encourage the Iranians to maintain an attitude of vigilance in the face of current Bloc blandishments and to take effective measures to thwart the Soviet subversive potential inside Iran.

Action: State, DOD

i.   Seek to maintain and increase the effectiveness of United States-Iranian cooperation on international issues in the United Nations, CENTO, and elsewhere.

Action: State, DOD, USIA

j.   Encourage the increase of responsible mutual interchange between Iran and other nations in the Free World, particularly in the Regional Cooperation for Development (RCD) organization, taking care that our encouragement of RCD not be misinterpreted as interfering or attempting to influence the course of RCD.

Action: State, USIA, DOD

k.   Take whatever administrative and legal steps are warranted to ensure that dissident Iranian political activity in the United States does not damage United States-Iranian relations.

Action: State, Justice

B.   *Security—Strategy*

1. Future United States Role in External Defense

Our military relationship with Iran is now, and will continue for the foreseeable future, to be close and meaningful. Through our support of CENTO and our bilateral security agreement of 1959, we provide a security umbrella for Iran against Soviet aggression. We should continue to support CENTO as an arrangement of positive, if limited, value, whose collapse would have a tangible disruptive effect in the Middle East. Our official public statements have clearly indicated our willingness to oppose by various means aggression in the Middle East, including Iran, from non-Soviet directions, though the Iranians place little reliance on such statements. Our exclusive military advisory relationship dates from 1947, but is based on the groundwork laid by our army mission and Corps of Engineers during World War II. Since 1951 we have supplied military equipment of various degrees of sophistication, as has befitted developing Iranian capabilities. A unique feature of our military supply relationship with Iran has been joint forward planning which we began on a five-year basis in 1962 and which has been useful in securing agreement with the Shah on a reasonable schedule for equipment supply and on the proper strategic mission of the Iranian armed forces.

The September 1962 agreement was amended in July of 1964[2] to extend the period covered through FY 1969. US commitments are stated in Annex A to the 1964 Memorandum of Understanding,[3] and are listed as specific items of assistance with no dollar costs given. The Presidential determination, NSC 1550, No. 65–1,[4] for the agreement indicates that grant assistance in Annex A for the period FY 67–69 shall not exceed $83 million. This figure does not include grant military assistance to the Imperial Iranian Gendarmerie during the period. The memorandum contained assurances by the Government of Iran that its program of military purchases would not cause undue strain on the nation's foreign exchange reserves or jeopardize plans for the nation's economic and social development. The agreement provided for a joint annual review procedure to satisfy the Iranian and United States Government that a proper balance was being maintained between development and defense. In addition, Iran was authorized to purchase over the next five years $200 million of American military equipment for delivery before the end of FY 1970. These purchases will be financed by United States credit institutions backed by US Government guarantees. The credits will be repayable on terms that will allow amortization over the ten-year period FY 1965–74 at interest rates ranging between four to five per cent per annum.

The Iranian Parliament recently authorized the purchase of an additional $200 million worth of military equipment. The US has offered additional credit up to $200 million for purchases in the period FY 1967–70, with no more than $50 million of this amount to be made available in any one fiscal year. A review of the impact of Iranian military expenditures on the economy of the country shall take place before the US makes commitment with respect to the amount of this credit to be made available to Iran in each fiscal year, and the US Government shall deter-

---

[2] See Document 47 and footnote 6 thereto.

[3] Annex A is in telegram 1196 to Tehran, June 25, 1964. (Department of State, Central Files, DEF 19 US–IRAN)

[4] Not found.

mine military credit availabilities in the light of the impact on Iran's foreign exchange and debt servicing position of any major third country military purchases; after the first $50 million, each subsequent annual credit tranche shall be approved by the President.

It has not always been easy in the past for us to secure agreements on military matters. The Shah, reflecting a consensus of high-level Iranian opinion, has tended to regard Iran's 1955 decision to join the Western defensive system as a claim for special consideration of various kinds, especially economic and military assistance. In the early days of this arrangement, the Shah tended to focus mostly on the latter. Obsessed with Iranian weakness and vulnerability, and fancying himself as a military strategist, he pressed us to support, with equipment grants and direct budgetary assistance, a military buildup on a scale that far out-stripped any conceivable progress in Iranian absorptive capacity and that threatened to create a serious imbalance in the allocation of Iranian financial resources. Since those days we have managed to scale down his military establishment and our relationship has matured in many ways. As the Shah has seen his resources increase and as his dependence on us has declined, our negotiations are increasingly conducted on a basis of give and take in which we must take into account the value that we place on our close and cooperative military relationship. More and more he sees himself as a potential purchaser who wishes simply to state his own requirements with the hope that these can be met from US sources—but with alternative sources clearly in mind. During the summer of 1966, for example, Iran negotiated a $60 million credit sale agreement with the UK for naval vessels, Hovercraft, and Tigercat missiles. The Shah momentarily considered buying surface-to-air missiles from the USSR but decided to abandon the idea; he has nevertheless reached agreement for purchase of non-sophisticated equipment from the Soviet Union.

Since 1958 our military relationship has matured considerably. We have seen a noticeable improvement in Iranian capacity and willingness to relate their military effort to their overall economic development. Our task over the next few years will be, within the context of our long-term agreements, to meet the Shah's intense desire for military modernization—for which he is now able to pay—sufficiently so that we can maintain the US as the primary foreign military influence in Iran and to continue the United States advisory services which have already begun to bear fruit in the form of a gradually growing professionalism in the Iranian armed forces. A specific objective would be to forestall any significant military relationship between Iran and the Soviet Union. The Shah gave us categoric assurance in Summer 1966 that he would not acquire any sophisticated military equipment from the Soviet Bloc.

In the years ahead, we will continue to be faced with the Shah's concern about the radical Arab threat to Iran. The Shah has become increasingly concerned with possibilities of Arab attack on vital oil and military installations in southern Iran, a viewpoint which is the result, partly, of his observation of the negative US reaction to Pakistan's situation in the Indo-Pak war and also his fears of increasing UAR penetration in the wake of what he considers to be an inevitable British withdrawal from the Persian Gulf. He has asserted his unmistakable intention to acquire the military equipment to meet this threat. While responding to the extent possible to legitimate defense needs and while seeking to concentrate the Shah's attention on real as opposed to imagined threats to Iran's vital interests, we will have to be careful not to strain his confidence in us by attempting to dissuade him from meeting what he considers to be Iran's real security needs even if we ourselves cannot supply the equipment he desires. The United States too has an interest in the security of the Persian Gulf area, including its security against inroads and pressures from the United Arab Republic. Although the Shah is inclined to exaggerate the nature of the threat, if a real threat develops, our interests lie closer to those of Iran than to those of the United Arab Republic.

2. Future United States Role in Internal Defense

Thanks to effective political and security control, there is no immediate serious threat to Iran's internal security. Iran abounds, however, in classical potentials for insurgency, and the regime realizes the necessity for vigilance against outbreaks, with or without foreign subversion, among the tribes and border nationalities (Kurds and Arabs) and even among the disparate but volatile urban opposition elements.

The United States has and will continue to play both a direct and an indirect role in enhancing the capabilities of the regime to cope with potential insurgency situations. Our most direct role is in the supply of technical assistance to the urban police and the rural Gendarmerie (with whom we have had an advisory mission since 1942). For the urban police, USAID civil-type police assistance and advice have effected marked improvements in police telecommunications, vehicular mobility, records and identification, and in other civil police functions. In the military sphere, some of our equipment grants and a good part of our advisory services have been tailored increasingly to the techniques and theories of counter-insurgency. Iran has formed a Special Forces Group (approximately battalion size) in Tehran. Mobile training teams from the United States Special Forces have instructed regular units of the Iranian army in unconventional warfare and counter-insurgency in field exercises. Our direct role involves also a considerable amount of persuasion toward more enlightened and long-term means of dealing with potential insurgency situations (disaster relief, labor development, economic rehabilitation and development, etc.) in place of the repressive means to which the regime is so often drawn when the chips are down.

Our indirect role embraces virtually all of our other programs in Iran, since they are all designed fundamentally to chip away at the roots of disaffection and hence to increase the strength of the government.

3. Courses of Action—Security

a.   Continue to make clear to Iran, the USSR, and Iran's Arab neighbors, through our military cooperation and general posture of support for Iran, that Iran cannot be attacked without grave risks of direct United States military counteraction.

Action: DOD, State

b.   To the above end, schedule periodic joint maneuvers on Iranian soil with Iranian forces to demonstrate United States capabilities for quick and effective action.

Action: DOD, State

c.   Equip, train, and encourage Iranian armed forces toward maximal capacity to delay a hostile military advance, and to combat indirect communist aggression with a minimum of direct involvement by Free World military sources.

Action: DOD

d.   Work for a steady improvement in the professionalism of the armed forces and the maintenance of their morale and loyalty to the regime.

Action: DOD

e.   Improve the counter-insurgency and riot-control capacities of the military as well as of the rural and urban police forces.

Action: DOD, AID

f.   Monitor carefully the measures, both military and fiscal, being taken to carry out multi-year MAP and MSA agreements reached with the Shah, including size and programming of force structure.

Action: DOD, State, AID

[Here follow C. "Economic Strategy" and Part Two, "Factors Bearing on U.S. Policy."]

187.   Telegram From the Embassy in Iran to the Department of State[1]

Tehran, February 15, 1967, 1345Z.

3258. General Conway's Call on Shah. Ref: Tehran 3202.[2]

1. General Conway, CINCSTRIKE, and I had nearly one hour audience with Shah 15th. We were accompanied by Ambassador Bell, Admiral Blackburn and General Jablonsky. Shah took occasion to reiterate his well-known views re importance Iran having adequate defense capability.

2. Shah discussed changes taking place in the world and in this region. He made clear that Iran continues to value its friendships and alliances. Russian tactics may have altered but until Moscow renounces its desire to see world dominated by communism Iran and other non-Communist countries must remain "attentive."

3. Shah reiterated his usual theme that if Soviets cross Iranian border there will be world reaction. More imminent threat in his opinion is that in Persian Gulf area. British have reaffirmed their determination to leave Aden in 1968 and, although they are increasing their capability at Sharja and Bahrein, these measures are minimal and probably will last only few years. He implied from reductions in MAP aid that USG also has lessened interest in this area. He considered threat as coming from "rectangle" of Cairo, Yemen, Somalia and Ethiopia, noting that latter two countries are going through rather critical phase.

4. Shah reiterated his intention to have modernized adequate defense capability and disclaimed any thought of territorial aggrandizement. He noted that large quantities of Russian arms continue to flow to countries like Egypt, Syria and Algeria. With such build-ups by aggressive neighbors, countries like Iran cannot confine themselves merely "to prayers and saying mass." He had hoped to maintain exclusive US supply pattern, but with obvious reluctance of USG to supply all his needs Iran has had to resort to other sources. Nevertheless, he still values US-Iran military cooperation, including good work of ARMISH/MAAG.

5. In stressing determination to assure security of Gulf area, Shah mentioned Iran is staying in tough with Saudis. Also in interest of regional security, Iranian cooperation is developing bilaterally with both Turkey and Pakistan.

6. General Conway explained purpose of his visit was to gain first-hand familiarity with countries for which CINCSTRIKE has responsibil-

---

[1] Source: Department of State, Central Files, DEF 19–6 USSR–IRAN. Secret; Limdis. Repeated to Moscow and CINCSTRIKE/USCINCMEAFSA.

[2] Dated February 12. (Ibid.)

ities, both from contingency basis and with regard to MAP assistance. He noted that in about one month he will be required to testify on Capitol Hill where opinion is running heavily against military programs, grant or sales. Ambassador Meyer noted that Indo-Pak hostilities had been among the developments which have colored Congressional thinking and there is widespread sentiment in the United States, particularly in Congress, that it is morally wrong for USG to fuel arms races in developing countries when their limited resources were better spent on vital economic development. Shah expressed view that had it not been for USG military cooperation with Pakistan and India hostilities would have broken out earlier and cessation would not have been achieved as quickly as it was. He expressed regret that members of Congress do not see that their attitude endangers countries with peaceful intentions like Iran and Morocco while playing into hands of aggressive ill-intentioned countries. All this led to discussion re possibilities of securing Soviet cooperation re limitation of arms supplies to developing countries. Shah saw no prospect of such Soviet cooperation in foreseeable future.

7. General Conway alluded to Shah's implication that USG interest in this area is lessening and said this not so. He added that contrary to some press speculation re effects of US commitments in Vietnam, USG military capability remains ample to play role in other contingencies should that be necessary. Shah indicated he already aware of this, but he wondered about Washington's political readiness to get involved in future brush fires.

8. There was brief discussion of Soviet interest in natural gas from Iran and more recently a Soviet offer to buy oil. Shah noted that new Soviet pipeline being built to Europe (info supplied via Alam, reftel) but saw some advantage in having power as large as USSR heavily dependent on small country like Iran for commodity like gas. Ambassador pointed out rich foreign exchange rewards Soviets would gain. This obviously on Shah's mind for he spoke vaguely of demanding from Soviets some "triangular" transaction whereby Iran would gain certain additional benefits. He also mused about the costliness of a pipeline direct from Iran to European natural gas market. Shah also noted how Romania in particular and to lesser extent Czechoslovakia are defying Soviet desires for maintaining Soviet economic hegemony over European satellites. In general Shah said efforts at bridge-building with Eastern European countries are desirable provided vigilance is maintained.

9. At conclusion of audience, Ambassador Meyer made brief reference to UPI story revealing Soviet-Iran arms deal. Shah said two things bothered him: a) disclosure should first have been from Tehran; and b) Iran was portrayed as kicking over CENTO traces while Turks are resisting Soviet blandishments. Re latter point, he said answer is simple i.e. Turks still receiving large-scale grant aid from US. He agreed, however,

that UPI leak was not totally without benefit, noting points along this line which I had made to Alam earlier (reftel).

Meyer

---

188.   Editorial Note

Telegram 169774 to Tehran, April 6, 1967, informed the Embassy that the Justice Department review of the Gudarzian criminal case had concluded that the only realistic course of action involved proceedings based on forgery of the two large checks bearing the names of the Prince and Princess. Chances of conviction, however, were not considered good in the absence of testimony from Ebtehaj. In light of previous Embassy arguments that a Gudarzian acquittal would be worse than no trial at all, the Department had concluded that it should not ask the Department of Justice to pursue the criminal case further. The Immigration and Naturalization Service was prepared to commence deportation proceedings immediately upon being authorized to do so by the Justice Department. Unless the Embassy objected to these conclusions, it was requested to advise the appropriate Iranian officials of this decision and the reasons for it. (Department of State, Central Files, POL 15–1 IRAN)

In telegram 3981 from Tehran, April 11, Meyer responded that the Embassy remained convinced that no trial was better than an unsuccessful trial, and that it concurred in deportation proceedings against Gudarzian and Kushan. Meyer expressed appreciation for the Justice Department's all-out attempt to build a case against Gudarzian, and noted that the Embassy would do its best to explain this "failure" to the Shah. (Ibid.)

189.   Telegram From the Embassy in Iran to the Department of State[1]

Tehran, April 12, 1967, 0710Z.

4006. Subj: Shah's Talks in Washington.

1.   Several times during my audience 11th,[2] Shah referred to subjects which he hopes have chance to discuss with President Johnson during his forthcoming Washington visit.

2.   Shah said at top of list are great problems of water and food. He noted topflight Soviet team currently visiting Iran has admitted that even USSR has potential water problem. Re agriculture, Shah believes outstanding American knowhow should be better applied in other countries, including Iran. He is particularly interested in large-scale farming of type David Lilienthal's development and research organization is proposing for Khuzistan area which follows pattern of Imperial Valley.

3.   Shah also wishes to talk about dangers which will beset Mideast when British leave Aden and Nasserism moves in.

4.   On military side, Shah agrees that Washington not be scene of haggling over military credit sales program. At same time, he will wish to discuss his general thesis that it is in USG's interest to have Iran self-reliant.

5.   Shah seems confident that ground can be covered with President Johnson in the one scheduled meeting evening June 12. However, if not he would appreciate opportunity to complete discussion following day.

Meyer

---

[1] Source: Department of State, Central Files, POL 7 IRAN. Confidential; Limdis.

[2] In telegram 4036 from Tehran, April 13, Meyer reported on his April 11 discussion with the Shah concerning Iran's relations with Nasser and Moscow. (Ibid., POL IRAN–UAR)

190. Telegram From the Embassy in Iran to the Department of State[1]

Tehran, April 19, 1967, 1020Z.

4121. Ref: State 176341.[2] Subj: Shah's Washington Talks—Water and Food.

1. At this point we doubt Shah has specific proposals to make re water and food. His interest in these subjects as major world problems has been greatly stimulated by Secretary Udall's visit and by various public pronouncements made by Secretary Freeman, copies of which we have supplied Shah. He knows these subjects are high priority in Washington and is developing his own thesis, still in embryonic form, that world should get its mind off international quarrels and address its united attention to great problems of tomorrow on this planet. Shah is determined limit population growth in Iran.

2. Shah is convinced that water is limiting factor in food production, notably in Iran. In his talk with Rome *Daily* American editor Galling (Tehran A–559),[3] Shah noted that in addition to desalination Iran would have to pump water up to 4,000 foot plateau which doubles cost. He is nationalizing "every drop of water" as tenth point of his "White Revolution," a move which Secretary Udall suggested was as perspicacious as Teddy Roosevelt's nationalizing forests (which already been done in Iran). Beyond these general points, we know of no specific projects which Shah might propose by way of desalination, etc. Our hope, however, would be that some small consultative project might emerge from Shah's discussions with President and our impression is that Secretary Udall and his able aide Frank Diluzio have already given thought to something along this line.

3. Re food production, Shah's basic thesis is that there is no reason why Iran should not be self-sustaining which it already almost is. However, due to limiting factor of water, Iran will not be able to develop into significant food exporter. Shah's belief is that Iran can make salutary contribution to food production in this entire region by supplying fertilizers from large petrochemical industry presently under construction.

4. In talk reported in Tehran 4006,[4] Shah specifically told Ambassador that he is deeply interested in project which is being proposed by William Warne, former USAID Director to Iran, more recently California Water Commissioner, and presently Vice President for Water Resources

---

[1] Source: Department of State, Central Files, POL 7 IRAN. Confidential; Limdis.

[2] Dated April 17. (Ibid.)

[3] Dated April 18. (Ibid., SOC 13 IRAN)

[4] Document 189.

in David Lilienthal's development and resources corporation. Warne is seeking to organize California consortium to develop commercially 100,000 acres of wheat production in Khuzistan. This fits in with Shah's conviction that while his land reform program has been great success, Iran must proceed with larger-scale farming than 4-hectare plots which been awarded peasants. Shah is immensely impressed with large-scale agriculture in U.S. and wishes have Iran follow U.S. pattern. We recommend Department discreetly stay in touch with Lilienthal and Warne.

5. Shah has already decided not to avail himself of political-military briefing (para 3 reftel). If truly worthwhile briefing re food and water problems could be provided and if time available, Shah might be interested.

Thacher

---

191. Telegram From the Embassy in Iran to the Department of State[1]

Tehran, April 29, 1967, 1135Z.

4261. Subj: Annual Review. Ref: Tehran 4253;[2] A–578; A–580.[3] Dept pass DOD for ISA.

1. Following is summary principal conclusions and recommendations contained in Embassy's A–580 on broad political-military-economic aspects of FY 68 increment US military sales program for Iran:

A. As result last year's extensive review Iran's military requirements for next four years, discussions FY 68 tranche can be conducted within much narrower framework. Although Iranians fully understand each annual $50m tranche of USG military credit requires specific Presidential approval after joint US-Iranian review Iran's economic prospects, Shah and his military advisors planning on assumption US will meet commitment given fall of 1966 to supply Iran with two squadrons (32) F–4 aircraft.

---

[1] Source: Department of State, Central Files, DEF 12–5 IRAN. Secret. Repeated to CINCSTRIKE/USCINCMEAFSA. Passed to DOD at 10:30 a.m.

[2] Dated April 27. (Ibid., E 2–2 IRAN)

[3] Both dated April 27. (Ibid., DEF 12–5 IRAN)

B. Iran's friendship is of tangible worth to US. Iran is oasis of success in ME and provides evidence that close collaboration with US can produce stability, progress, and reform, as well as commendable desire to command one's own destiny. Shah has given quiet support to CENTO, has warned Pakistan against too close association with ChiComs, and has sought to act as moderating influence against Pak extremism. Iran's aid to Vietnam is unique in ME and its friendship and cooperation permit refueling stops and overflights for endless stream US military aircraft. Most important of all, Iran provides base for variety US special facilities vital to US security.

C. These valuable assets require continued US support. With US–GOI relationship in "transitional" phase as result growing Iranian prosperity and steady elimination US economic and military assistance, much depends on US response in major dynamic area our relationship—military sales—on which Shah focuses as barometer US intentions.

D. GOI purchases military equipment from other than US sources (e.g., USSR, UK) have been generally consistent with US understanding Shah's intentions at time four-year sales program evolved. Shah still deeply concerned over his exposure to destructive surprise attack on his vital industrial and oil installations in south and elsewhere in border areas where his two most important air bases are located. Iranian fears keyed largely to what they regard as UK intention to withdraw from Persian Gulf area and immutable UAR objective to obtain by whatever means control over all ME oil wealth. Reinforcing these apprehensions is concern over unfavorable balance in Iran's military power compared with that of its Arab neighbors. Iran remains concerned with Soviet threat and considers Nasser as prime Soviet instrument in ME.

E. Shah still welcomes advice on technical matters but vigorously rejects efforts to challenge his estimate fundamental dangers he faces. To be effective US advice must take into account Iranian sensibilities and Shah's own security estimates. Shah continues to rely on US for sophisticated and sensitive weaponry. However, if US not prepared to provide defensive arms as "insurance" for his rich border region, Shah will surely acquire them elsewhere, a move which would have enormous impact on US military presence in Iran.

F. Iran, now in its third year of rapid economic growth under circumstances of impressive price stability, has demonstrated its capacity to maintain momentum of rapid economic development while meeting its economic problems. Economic outlook for Iran presents no reasons for refusing further credit to Iran. Rather it demonstrates constructive role such credit, at long terms and low rates, can play in Iran's future.

G. In up-coming credit negotiations GOI will emphasize GOI's needs for maximum stretch-out repayment dates and minimum interest costs. Iranians will also be mindful of their accommodating response to

US requests for forebearance re purchases of gold for dollars as well as 2-1/2 percent interest rate and over 10-year repayment period offered by USSR. US will not be expected to meet Soviet credit terms but to present tangible proof it values Iranian friendship.

H. It is recommended that: (1) US extend $50m credit for purchase of arms; (2) US agree to sell Iran second F–4 squadron at most reasonable prices possible; (3) we attempt to conclude negotiations on note of general cordiality and satisfaction; (4) we provide concessional interest rate of not higher than 4-1/2 percent; rate higher than 5 percent unquestionably would deprive US of psychological and perhaps political advantage we can otherwise reasonably expect; and (5) we give careful consideration to possibility extending payment period to full 10 years; in no case, however, should payment period be less than eight years.

Meyer

192.   Record of Meeting of Interdepartmental Regional Group for Near East and South Asia[1]

IRG/NEA 67–16   Washington, May 8, 1967.

Record of Meeting—May 8, 1967

The meeting was held to consider the United States position regarding the negotiation of a new annual increment of credit-financed sales of military equipment to Iran. The Group:

Agreed that a review of the favorable Iranian economic and financial situation does not make undesirable on economic grounds the extension to Iran of the second $50 million increment of the $200 million military sales credit approved by the President in May, 1966. At the same time, *noted* the rapid projected increase in Iranian military expenditures and *agreed* that when informing the Shah of the availability of the $50 million, our Ambassador should stress our concern lest these expenditures divert resources from Iran's economic development.

---

[1] Source: Johnson Library, National Security File, NSC Files of Harold Saunders, Iran Military, 4/1/66–12/31/67. Secret. Drafted by Ernst on May 9.

Agreed that Iran's economic and financial situation does not call for concessionary terms for this increment of the military sales credit. After *noting,* however, the importance to vital U.S. security interests of our special installations in Iran and the key importance of Iran in the light of unfavorable developments affecting the U.S. position in the Middle East, *agreed* that for overriding political reasons the credit should be on concessionary terms.

Noted that DOD currently obtains funds for military sales credits from the Export-Import Bank at an interest rate of 5-1/2% with a repayment term of 7 years and that the President last year stipulated that the terms for such credits to Iran should carry an interest rate averaging between 5 and 6% with repayment by FY 1976. *Agreed* that an interest rate of 5% and repayment term of 8 years for the second $50 million increment should suffice to achieve our political objectives by making it possible for us to indicate to the Iranians our special interest in their country. *Noted,* however, that these terms would not fully please the Iranians. Further *agreed* that the credit negotiators be authorized initially to offer a 5-1/2% rate, with the offer of a 5% rate to be made as required in the course of the negotiation. *Noted* in this connection the critical importance of not handling this aspect of the negotiation in such a way as to lose the overall political gain we seek from the transaction.

Agreed that the recommendations to the President should be ready for forwarding to him by May 12 in order that it will be possible for our Ambassador to meet with the Shah on this matter prior to the Shah's departure from Tehran for Europe on May 23 and in order that the credit negotiations can be completed prior to the Shah's arrival in Washington on June 12.

Noted that the "cost" to the U.S. of the concessionary terms would consist of $3.7 million of appropriated DOD funds, which would be recovered when Iran repaid the credit, and the foregone 1/2% interest which, assuming an even repayment schedule over the 8-year repayment period, would approximate $1 to 1-1/2 million. *Agreed* that a statement of the cost to the U.S. should be included in the memorandum of recommendation to the President.

Members Present:

Executive Chairman: Ambassador Battle
AID: Mr. White
CIA: Mr. Critchfield
DOD: Col. Jordan
JCS: Brig. Gen. Sibley
NSC: Mr. Saunders
USIA: Mr. Carter

State (NEA) Messrs. Rockwell, Eliot, Polstein; INR/RNA—Mr. Archie Bolster

ACDA—Mr. Charles Van Dorn

Treasury—Mr. Sam Cross; Mr. Arthur Gardner

Acting Staff Director: Mr. Ernst

DHE
Acting Staff Director

---

193. Telegram From the Embassy in Iran to the Department of State[1]

Tehran, May 10, 1967, 1248Z.

4458. Shah's Visit in Suspense.

1. Upon my arrival at large luncheon given 10th in honor of Ambassador-designate Hushang Ansary, PriMin Hoveyda, obviously in great state of distress, handed me copy of UPI story dated May 9 reporting statements by Chairman Fulbright and Assistant Secretary McNaughton during recent closed-door hearings of Disarmament Subcommittee.

2. Story quotes Fulbright as saying Iran's recent arms purchases from Russia and US "are largely to maintain Shah on his throne." Story says McNaughton agreed arms not scheduled for use "against Russia." Story said remainder McNaughton's explanation was deleted. Fulbright said he had been impressed by recent conversation with "very intelligent young man from Iran" who warned that further repression of freedom in Iran is bound to result in revolution. Fulbright quoted as saying, "We are following a wrong course and very unwise one to encourage Shah to maintain complete political control." McNaughton reportedly agreed Shah has "displayed a good deal of independence."

3. During middle of luncheon PriMin was called to telephone by Shah who had just read story and was highly indignant. He told PriMin

---

[1] Source: Department of State, Central Files, POL 7 IRAN. Secret; Immediate; Limdis. Passed to White House and USIA.

to ask us for text of McNaughton's statements which had been deleted. According to PriMin, Fulbright's allegations were offensive enough but Shah wishes to know what was response of official USG spokesman. Shah told PriMin that until USG attitude is clear his trip to Washington must be considered in suspense.

4.   Both before and after Shah's phone call, I tried my best to calm Hoveyda down and to enlist his cooperation in bringing Shah down from chandelier. I pointed out that criticism leveled at Shah was relatively minor compared to that to which USG officials themselves, including President Johnson, are subjected. Expressed personal opinion that deleted testimony dealt with Shah's reasoning for acquiring adequate defense capability. Went on to say that best way to meet criticism reported in UPI story was for Shah himself to tell his story in his usual impressive manner. I asked Ambassador-designate Ansary to assist also.

5.   Naturally cancellation of Shah's Washington visit can have untold adverse repercussions in our relations with this country. Hope Dept can provide us soonest with gist, if not text, of McNaughton testimony and that it will be of nature to put issues Fulbright raised in better perspective. In addition it would be helpful to have other testimony favorable to Iran given by official USG spokesmen. Finally, it might be worth sending us for relay to Shah some personal words of friendliness from Secretary or even President.

                                                                                    Meyer

---

194.   Telegram From the Department of State to the Embassy in Iran[1]

                                                    Washington, May 11, 1967, 12:29 p.m.

192135. For Ambassador from the Secretary. Ref: Tehran 4458.[2]

1.   Please assure Shah on my behalf that no Executive Branch witness before any Congressional forum has made any statement which

---

[1] Source: Department of State, Central Files, POL 7 IRAN. Secret; Immediate; Limdis. Drafted by Eliot on May 10, cleared in draft by Rockwell and by Battle, and approved by Rusk.

[2] Document 193.

would in any way detract from our view of the Shah as an ally whose friendship and counsel we highly value and a statesman under whose leadership Iran has made tremendous strides. We greatly admire the progress Iran has made in recent years in economic development and social reform and the leadership Iran has displayed in helping to mitigate international disputes. Executive Branch spokesmen have stated these views frequently on Capitol Hill and elsewhere.

2. The reason the President invited the Shah to Washington was stated in the President's letter to him of July 20, 1966.[3] That letter spoke of the "continuing comradeship between our two nations," of "our desire to help Iran," of our pride in having "contributed to the gathering political and economic strength of Iran under (the Shah's) wise and skillful leadership." The President stated that he wanted to meet with the Shah to discuss problems of "common concern" and "to hear directly from (the Shah) more about the heartening economic and social progress Iran has made." It is in this spirit that we look forward to the Shah's visit. We sincerely and deeply hope that the Shah will go forward with his plans.

3. Septel deals with specifics of testimony which has upset Shah.[4]

Rusk

---

[3] Document 158.

[4] Telegram 192205 to Tehran, May 11. (Department of State, Central Files, POL 7 IRAN)

---

195. Telegram From the Embassy in Iran to the Department of State[1]

Tehran, May 12, 1967, 0700Z.

4488. Reference: Tehran 4486.[2] Shah and Fulbright.

1. Obviously eager to discuss his unhappiness over Fulbright hearings, Shah received me only four hours after request for audience. We had 2-1/2 hour session late Friday afternoon 12th. It was rough going.

---

[1] Source: Department of State, Central Files, POL 7 IRAN. Secret; Immediate; Limdis. Passed to the White House and USIA.

[2] In telegram 4486 from Tehran, May 12, Meyer expressed confidence that Rusk's "wonderful message" in telegram 192135 to Tehran (Document 194) would "do the trick." He noted that the message had arrived during their farewell dinner for Ambassador-designate Ansary, and that Prime Minister Hoveyda had rushed to phone the Shah. (Department of State, Central Files, POL 7 IRAN)

2.   Apparently what irked Shah most was injection into public media of unchallenged suggestion by Fulbright that Iran becoming ripe for revolution. Shah was appalled that chairman of such an influential body as US Senate Foreign Relations Committee could believe and make public as his own views those of an itinerant student who walked into his office. He had assumed Fulbright would be fully briefed by USG but if Chairman's judgement to be gauged by this episode, "Heaven help the United States".

3.   Obviously deeply wounded because he considers himself in forefront of world's progressive leaders and is profoundly proud of Iran's successes under his leadership, Shah contrasted Iran's progress and freedom with that of other Afro-Asian countries, particularly so-called "progressive" states which he presumed liberals like Fulbright favor. He said he ready make referendum in Iran tomorrow and all but smallest fraction (mostly few American or British trained maladjusted Iranians) would register enthusiastic approval of Iran's reforms and economic and social development. It is absurd to think that Western-style democracy could be automatically transplanted to countries like Iran, he said, adding that nevertheless Iran is making progress in democratic procedures in accordance with its cultural traditions and state of its economic development.

4.   We went round and round. I recalled Secretary Rusk during his visit here had told Shah there bound to be reaction on Capitol Hill to Iran's closer relations with Soviets. I emphasized freedom to dissent in US and noted that present administration does not have much leverage on Senator Fulbright. Assured him, as Secretary Rusk's message made clear, prevailing US opinion, certainly that of USG, appreciates good work which being done in Iran. It would be shame, I said, if Iranian student who spoke to Senator Fulbright would be allowed to "defeat" Shah. Best counteracting course, obviously, I said, is for Iran's story to be told more widely and there no better opportunity than Shah's forthcoming Washington visit.

5.   I pointed out Secretary's reassuring message represented official USG view. Shah asked I convey his deep appreciation for Secretary's timely and welcome words. He described both President Johnson and Secretary Rusk as great and good friends. Problem, he said, is that Secretary's message is confidential. Meanwhile, Fulbright's charges will presumably get world-wide publicity. I told him I not aware that UPI story has gotten much play. Shah expressed hope some means could be found to counteract via public media implications Fulbright allegations. If these allegations get publicity here, he said, there would be no alternative but counter publicity.

6.   After first-half our of slow going, I found best way to get Shah into normal frame of mind was to discuss other subjects, e.g., Viet Nam,

Turk visit, Hussein's visit, etc. Separate telegrams re these subjects will be sent tomorrow. But without fail Shah would return to bitter subject of Fulbright's unwelcome remarks. I urged Sermon on Mount reaction or that of Lincoln that best way to destroy an enemy is to make him a friend. Shah recognized this as good philosophy but it clearly not an ingredient of Persian mentality.

7.   While Shah never could get himself to give unqualified affirmative, I came away convinced that he will proceed with plans for Washington visit. Tactically, I felt it better to leave with relatively good feeling we had achieved at conclusion our long talk and leave negotiation of further details re Shah's program for later discussion between Court Minister Alam and myself. I have strong doubts, however, that Shah will be willing to go through with planned tea with Fulbright.

Meyer

196.   Telegram From the Embassy in Iran to the Department of State[1]

Tehran, May 13, 1967, 1250Z.

4503. Subj: CIA and Students.

1.   Both Shah and PriMin Hoveyda have mentioned several times to me in past few days their suspicions that CIA has been subsidizing anti-Shah Iranian students in US.

2.   To both I have said USG has no secrets for whole story has appeared in *Ramparts*. Specifically *Ramparts* made clear that CIA refused support to Iranian students when their organization took on an anti-Shah complexion.

3.   Neither Shah nor Hoveyda were convinced, despite all oaths which I offered. Hoveyda referred to article in some German magazine which stated specifically that CIA was offering secret support to Iranian students. Shah conjectured that I as Ambassador might not be aware of all of CIA's activities.

4.   I pointed out there no plausible reason why USG should support movement against regime of country which doing so well. But Shah is so

---

[1] Source: Department of State, Central Files, POL 13–2 IRAN. Secret; Limdis.

upset by Senator Fulbright's allegation re Iran becoming ripe for revolution that it difficult to stamp out his suspicion that there must be linkage between some USG element and the "Iran student" who fed that view to Fulbright.

Meyer

---

197.   **Memorandum From Director of Central Intelligence Helms to Secretary of Defense McNamara**[1]

Washington, May 16, 1967.

SUBJECT

The Shah of Iran

1. The June visit of the Shah may well be a critical point in the history of our relations with modern Iran. [3 *lines of source text not declassified*] In recent years, the Shah has been comparatively cooperative in permitting us to expand exclusively United States facilities in Iran. Also, he has exercised a moderating influence [1 *line of source text not declassified*]. It is because of my concern that the viability of this entire complex may be affected by the conversations that you and others will have with the Shah that I am taking this means of underlining the significance of his visit.

2. This may be the last occasion that we will have to deal with the Shah as a Middle East leader committed to the United States. I have been impressed that, despite his détente with the USSR in matters of aid and trade, his cooperation with us on matters relating to United States intelligence and security interests and his own posture in dealing with hostile Soviet intelligence activities in Iran have remained, among Middle East leaders, almost uniquely unambiguous. But he has become impatient over the years with our insistence that Iran is militarily threatened only by Soviet forces across the Iranian-USSR border. He is genuinely convinced that Soviet support of radical nationalist forces led by President Nasser constitutes a threat to the more moderate elements. He feels that

---

[1] Source: Washington National Records Center, RG 330, OSD Files: FRC 72 A 2468, Iran 091.112, 16 May 67. Secret.

this threat must be met primarily by a coalition of moderate Middle East countries pursuing a new policy of self reliance. He appears determined to assume the leadership in this new regional alliance but will come seeking United States understanding and a level of support necessary to deter the aggressive actions of those regimes supported and used by the USSR and, to a lesser extent, Communist China.

3. The Shah has repeatedly stated that the ultimate answer to Communism is social and economic progress, and he feels that he has demonstrated this in Iran. He may, during his visit, propose a long-range development program for southern Iran and raise the question of a major development program for all the Gulf as the answer to Soviet and UAR support of the "liberation struggle".

4. The Shah, like most of the leaders in the Middle East, is filled with growing anxieties about both the ability and the will of the United States to remain a Great Power and a reliable ally in his part of the world. Determining our intentions will be the objective uppermost in his mind. His appreciation of our position will, I think, become apparent in the course he pursues when he returns to Iran. Other political leaders in the Middle East, not to mention those in Moscow, will be acutely sensitive to his reactions and consider them in contemplating their separate interests and policies in the area.

Dick

---

198. Memorandum From the President's Special Assistant (Rostow) to President Johnson[1]

Washington, May 17, 1967.

SUBJECT

Your Meeting with the Shah

You have already agreed to one office meeting with the Shah after his 5 p.m. arrival on 12 June, and you are having dinner with him that evening. However, the Shah is anxious to budget a second meeting with you the next day.

---

[1] Source: Johnson Library, National Security File, Country File, Iran, Visit of Shah of Iran, 8/22–24/67. Secret. A handwritten note on the source text reads, "5/19/67 Saunders notified."

Normally, I would stand firm against a second meeting on any but a State visit. However, in this case there is a great deal to talk about. Moreover, the Shah is a person you can talk seriously with. We have invited him over here primarily to convince him that you are deeply aware of the great changes taking place in the Middle East as they concern him, and I think it would be worth going along with him.

We could arrange to keep the second meeting off the schedule so it would not create a formal precedent for later visitors, though it would become known. I am sure the Iranians would go along with this.

The alternative is to wait and see how things go at the first talk and schedule a second meeting then if you want. To carry this off, we should probably be in a position to suggest to the Iranians now that we wait and let you and the Shah decide. This tack seems attractive, but if you're likely to agree to a second meeting, we'd probably gain by scheduling it informally now.

Walt

Approve second meeting[2]

Tell them we'll wait and see

Disapprove

---

[2] This option was checked on the source text.

---

199. Memorandum From the President's Special Assistant (Rostow) to President Johnson[1]

Washington, May 17, 1967.

SUBJECT

This Year's Military Sales to Iran

Secretaries Rusk and McNamara recommend that you approve the second $50 million slice of the $200 million military sales credit for Iran

---

[1] Source: Johnson Library, National Security File, Country File, Iran, Memos & Miscellaneous, Vol. II, 1/66–1/69. Secret. A handwritten note on the source text indicates that the Department of State cleared the memorandum on May 18 at 10:35 a.m.; another handwritten note indicates it was seen by the President.

that you approved in May 1966. They would like to get word to the Shah before he leaves on 22 May for a series of State visits that will bring him here 12 June. This credit will finance the second squadron of F–4's that you approved last August.

When you approved the $200 million planning figure a year ago, we were concerned that this might be more than Iran's economy could safely take on. We therefore insisted that each slice be subject to your review and instructed Ambassador Meyer that he and the Iranians should thoroughly review Iran's economic situation before recommending release of further installments.

One of our motives was simply to force the Iranian economists and politicians themselves to look hard at their allocation of resources between defense and development. We think this device has paid off. The Iranians have improved their management of foreign exchange reserves, and their economic homework for this year's review was much better than last year.

Meyer concludes that Iran can handle this additional purchase safely. He does not believe it will cut into the capital investment necessary to keep the growth rate up to at least 7%. The World Bank and Ex-Im have done their own studies and independently reach the same conclusion.

We do not want to be over-optimistic. Therefore, Secretary Rusk recommends that, in informing the Shah of your decision, Meyer reiterate our continuing concern that the Shah keep military expenditures within bounds and keep his military purchases from the Soviet Union to a bare minimum.

Secretary Rusk for political reasons recommends a slightly concessional 5% rate with 8-year repayment (compared with the normal Ex-Im rate of 5.5% over 8 years). Treasury has gone along. The only cost to us is that Defense must set aside an additional $3.7 million in its sales fund. This will be freed again as Iran repays, so the only "real" cost is about $1–1.5 million in lost interest. In view of our extensive intelligence facilities in Iran and the relationship we are trying to maintain with the Shah, I think this is justified.

We are concerned, of course, about increased arms levels in the Middle East. However, we recognize that the Shah has genuine worries about an eventual threat from radical Arab forces in the Persian Gulf area as the British presence diminishes. This will be very much on his mind when he talks with you in June. While we would hate to see him go overboard, we have already argued him down from much higher levels of purchases and believe we have struck the best balance we can. We would rather have him buying from us under some control than buying wildly elsewhere.

Treasury, AID and Budget have participated in the coordination of this recommendation. I recommend you approve.

Walt

Approve[2]

See me

---

[2] This option is checked on the source text.

---

200.   Telegram From the Department of State to the Embassy in Iran[1]

Washington, May 18, 1967, 9:55 a.m.

196786. Embtel 4488.[2] For Ambassador from Battle and Macomber. Subject: Shah and Fulbright.

1.   While we have not approached Sen. Fulbright directly, we consider it most unlikely that he would be prepared make amends to Shah of kind Shah would want. It doubtful in any case that Fulbright intended directly insult Shah; his remarks are directed more against Executive Branch. Only Senatorial alternative to Fulbright as host for coffee June 13 might be Symington as Chairman NEA subcommittee.

2.   Shah's reneging on his acceptance Fulbright invitation[3] would redound strongly to Shah's disadvantage as it would indicate sensitivity not becoming sovereign of a proud, strong and independent nation and would damage his reputation here as it undoubtedly would become known. At present Fulbright's remarks have received no publicity here. Moreover, as you have pointed out to Shah, Iran's story merits telling to key Senators and the Senators want to hear it as is evidenced by Fulbright's invitation.

---

[1] Source: Department of State, Central Files, POL 7 IRAN. Confidential; Limdis. Drafted by Eliot on May 17, cleared by Macomber, and approved by Battle.

[2] Document 195.

[3] Telegram 4520 from Tehran, May 15, reported that the Shah had told Alam that he could not go through with the scheduled tea with Fulbright. Meyer noted that, in the Embassy's view, the clearly best alternative answer would be for the Vice President to host the Senatorial tea. (Department of State, Central Files, POL 7 IRAN)

3.   We therefore believe it desirable for you once again to urge Shah go ahead with coffee with Fulbright as his host. You might wish stress to Shah that this recommendation comes from Shah's friends, who have considered carefully the pros and cons and believe this course is in best interest of US-Iranian friendship and understanding.

Rusk

---

201.   Telegram From the Department of State to the Embassy in Iran[1]

Washington, May 19, 1967, 9:26 p.m.

198765. 1. President has approved second $50 million increment of military sales credit for Iran under the $200 million planning figure he approved for FY 67–70 in May 1966. You should so inform Shah in your audience May 22.

2.   In informing Shah of this approval, you should also:

a.   Inform him that major item being financed in this increment is second squadron of 16 F–4's. Details on the cost, configuration, etc. of this squadron will be contained in the letter of offer which will be prepared for submission to GOI through ARMISH/MAAG.

b.   Invite him to suggest time and place for credit negotiation which we hope can be completed prior his arrival Washington June 12. DOD prepared receive Iranian negotiator in Washington or send negotiating team to Tehran.

c.   State we consider annual review once again to have been useful process. FYI. Among other advantages, it provides bulwark against telescoping of annual tranches. End FYI. State that in our review of Iran's economic situation, we have been greatly impressed at progress Iran has been making. Her economic growth and programs of social reform are impressive evidence of Shah's determination to have his nation modernized. We do, however, remain concerned about number of trends and

---

[1] Source: Department of State, Central Files, DEF 19–8 US–IRAN. Secret; Priority. Drafted by Eliot on May 15; cleared in draft by ISA Regional Director for Near East and South Asia Colonel Amos A. Jordan, Jr., Funari, Wolf, and Saunders; and approved by Battle. Repeated to CINCSTRIKE/CINCMEAFSA.

this concern should be conveyed to Shah: (1) steadily increasing demands of military on Iran's resources, both domestic and foreign, as evidenced by projected 12.9 percent annual rate of increase in military expenditures over next five years and by 6 percent in 1966 to 9 percent in 1972 proportion of GNP to be devoted to military expenditures; and (2) while we are confident GOI capable of handling, we note from projections that inflationary trends with possible effects on balance of payments are likely increase in years ahead. We believe economic improvement and social betterment are best assurance of security in long run against threats to Iran and hope Iran's economic progress will not be adversely affected by her military expenditures.

d.   Believe it useful to remind Shah of our continuing concern over Iran's arms deal with USSR on grounds stated in President's letter of July 20, 1966.[2]

3.   Our negotiators will be authorized initially propose 5-1/2 percent interest, 8-year repayment credit terms but to go to 5 percent. These terms should not be revealed to Shah but should be reserved for disclosure to Iranians during credit negotiations.

Rusk

---

[2] Document 158.

---

202.   **Telegram From the Embassy in Iran to the Department of State**[1]

Tehran, May 22, 1967, 1025Z.

4629. For Battle and Macomber. Subj: Shah and Fulbright. Ref: State 196786.[2]

1.   Talked with Alam again 21st re Senator Fulbright's tea for Shah, reiterating arguments reftel as well as welcome news contained State 198767[3] about Vice President's willingness to participate in tea with Senate leadership.

---

[1] Source: Department of State, Central Files, POL 7 IRAN. Confidential; Priority; Limdis.
[2] Document 200.
[3] Dated May 19. (Department of State, Central Files, POL 7 IRAN)

2.   As clincher, Alam suggests that if Ambassador Ansary could call on Fulbright and obtain some comments on how much Senator looks forward to seeing Shah, and if Ansary were able to report also some favorable remarks by Fulbright about Iran's accomplishments under the Shah's leadership, way would be clear for Shah's being the Senator's guest. Alam notes this course should make things easy for all concerned.

3.   Suggest Department facilitate such interview between Ansary and Fulbright at early date. Ansary may already be aware (if not initiator) of this suggestion. We believe that with Department's coaching he can be counted on to handle this project discreetly and successfully.

4.   If prospects are for smooth sailing between Shah and Fulbright, Department may wish consider returning to original schedule of 3:00 to 4:00 p.m. for visit with Vice President. This, too, can be worked out with Ambassador Ansary.

Meyer

---

203.   Telegram From the Embassy in Iran to the Department of State[1]

Tehran, May 23, 1967, 0955Z.

4655. Annual Review. Ref: State 198765.[2]

1.   Noting conversations we have had with PriMin, as well as GOI financial officials, General Jablonsky and I in discussion with Shah 22nd expressed conviction Annual Review indeed a useful process for all concerned. Projections which been developed, I noted, unusually realistic and valuable in providing statistical indicators of Iran's present and future economic progress.

2.   Shah said Central Bank projections were very much on conservative side. They did not take adequately into account revenues which bound to accrue from budding projects, e.g. in petrochemical and agricultural fields. Basic problem, Shah said, is not so much Iran's economic

---

[1] Source: Department of State, Central Files, DEF 19–8 US–IRAN. Secret; Priority. Repeated to Moscow and CINCSTRIKE/USCINCMEAFSA.

[2] Document 201.

wherewithal as it is trained human resources. I concurred that Iran's absorptive capacity is limiting factor to both economic development and military modernization.

3. After commending Iran's current and projected growth rate, I noted that perhaps Iran's greatest problem is its success. Burgeoning economic development, accompanied by budgetary and foreign exchange deficits, can cause inflationary pressures. Shah noted prices been relatively stable and GOI intends to keep them that way, e.g. by foreign borrowing. We both agreed it is important to keep watchful eye on this problem.

4. Noting that plan organization expenditures this year due to increase by record 34 percent, I emphasized importance of economic development to Iran's stability and security. At same time, noted that military budget increased each of past two years by over 20 percent and while rate is due to decline it will still be 12.9 percent at conclusion coming five-year period. Said PriMin and we had gone into this matter thoroughly and had ascertained that increased military expenditures are due to such reasons as fact that Iran now must buy its spares instead of obtaining them via grant aid. Nevertheless, this too is matter which requires constant control. Shah said problem is to keep military budget down but present developments in Mideast underscore need for Iran's maintaining adequate defense capability. He recalled Senator Fulbright some years ago lecturing him to effect that scarcely any countries except USSR and USA need have military establishments. He said he had asked Fulbright whether USG would guarantee existence via US armed forces support of every nation whose independence comes under threat. Shah said same question is even more pertinent today. Shah's view is that it is in Iran's and USG's interest that Iran have capability of deterring or coping with regional threats.

5. Shah said factor which had impressed him in economic projections was that at present Iran's debt servicing is only around half of what its debt servicing capacity can be. It was noted that present figure is 8.5 percent of foreign exchange receipts and that foreign repayments will not rise to 12 percent level before end of next five year plan.

6. While reiterating points of concern, i.e. rising military budget and inflationary pressures, I reported our conclusion that Iran's economic progress is noteworthy and our conviction that GOI officials will keep it healthy. Accordingly, President has approved FY68 $50,000,000 credit tranche for military purchasing in US. Added that virtually all this amount will go for second F–4 squadron.

7. Shah expressed appreciation. At same time, he called attention to serious and rather urgent need for five additional F–5B's. Need arises from fact that because of Vietnam demands USG not providing extent of training previously provided. He said he has 20 pilots training in Paki-

stan through T–38 level, but additional F–5B's are necessary to train new pilots in gunnery and formation flying. General Jablonsky indicated there may be small amount of money left in FY68 tranche after F–4 squadron financed but it would not finance more than one or two F–5B's. Shah said if USG not prepared to provide additional $3 to $5 million via credit arrangements, need is such that he would be prepared to pay cash for those not fundable under FY67 tranche.

8. Looking to future, Shah said by 1972 Iran would need replacement equipment. He reiterated his determination to preserve his American military orientation, particularly Air Force. He discussed possibility of post-Vietnam rehab F–4 aircraft or F–5 follow-on aircraft which Northrop now considering. I noted this was for future. Shah agreed but pointed out that because of three to four year time lags Iran must get in line. Main question was whether USG is willing, as he hopes, to remain Iran's chief supplier. He noted in this connection that he has more trouble assuring answer to this question now when he is paying for equipment than previously when USG supplied it via grant aid. There was brief discussion few other military matters but they minor in nature. They being reported via General Jablonsky's usual channels.

9. Shah said he would appreciate my advice whether he should discuss his military needs extensively while in Washington or whether they could be handled adequately either via ARMISH/MAAG here or via Ambassador Ansary. Acknowledging that Shah undoubtedly would be explaining his general thesis as to Iran's need for adequate defense capability, I urged Shah not to get into discussion of specific requirements.

10. During course of discussion, I recalled President Johnson's letter of last July[3] and the concern therein expressed re Iran's dealing with Soviets in arms. This subject, I noted, is very much in minds of many key Washington officials. This launched Shah into lengthy rehearsal of rationale for relatively small amount of Soviet military purchasing. He said Soviet Ambassador was in previous day expressing hope that current arms deliveries would be fore-runners of others. Shah gave us clear indication he does not intend to get into any relationship of dependence on Soviets, noting specifically how easily they could undermine him by cutting off supplies.

11. Shah outlined his familiar thesis that Soviets have leapfrogged over southern tier and for all intents and purposes have established base in Egypt. That accomplished, Soviets, according to Shah, are now maneuvering vis-à-vis Iran and Turkey. While it would be "odd," Shah said, to rebuff "smiles and friendship" entirely, he made clear he knows Soviet game is to get Persian Gulf, i.e. Russia's "historic dream." This prompted inquiry from me why he is planning to let Soviets explore for oil in Ker-

---

[3] Document 158.

manshah and Shiraz areas. Shah reiterated what he had told UK Ambassador Wright (Tehran 4574),[4] i.e. dividing Iran into spheres of influence along lines of the 1907 treaty is unthinkable. I said steel mill project is already in central Iran which should disabuse those who might postulate spheres of influence theory. Shah noted Isfahan in 1907 treaty was considered in Soviet sphere of influence. In any case, he said he does not expect substantial oil deposits to be found in Shiraz area. Shah categorically said he would never let Soviets work in coastal or offshore areas of Gulf where they would serve as "scouts" for Nasser.

12. Re negotiations for FY68 tranche, Shah agreed arrangements should be worked out with Central Bank Governor Samii for either Washington or Tehran. He expressed hope that negotiations could be concluded expeditiously.

13. *Comment:* Shah was in entirely different mood from that when I saw him week ago re the Fulbright affair. He was bouyant and seemed be looking forward with eagerness to telling Iran's story to Washington officialdom. Of more direct importance, Shah had obviously done his homework re economic projections which Central Bank had produced. He was conversant with various economic indicators. This in itself is in our view direct evidence that purpose intended by Annual Review has been served.

Meyer

---

[4] Dated May 18. (Department of State, Central Files, PET 17 USSR–IRAN)

---

204.   Memorandum of Conversation[1]

Washington, May 26, 1967.

SUBJECT

Presentation of Credentials by Ambassador of Iran

PARTICIPANTS

The President
Ambassador Hushang Ansary
Ambassador James Symington
Stuart W. Rockwell, Deputy Assistant Secretary, NEA

---

[1] Source: Johnson Library, National Security File, Country File, Iran, Memos & Miscellaneous, Vol. II, 1/66–1/69. Secret. Drafted by Rockwell and approved by the White House on May 31.

The following were the substantive comments made during the conversation which took place between the President and Ambassador Ansary after the latter had presented his credentials.

The Ambassador said that Iran believed that the present crisis in the Near East proved the correctness of Iran's analysis of the situation in the area. Iran felt that it was necessary to resist aggressive forces. Iran counted on continuing United States support for its efforts to promote stability in the area.

The President made no substantive response at this point but in a later reference to the Near East crisis in connection with his appointment later the same day with Foreign Minister Eban remarked that the United States was trying very hard to find a "middle way" to solve the present crisis. "If this could be done", he said, "a catastrophe could be avoided". Ambassador Ansary said he believed a "middle way" would be the best way to solve the crisis.

The President, in a separate comment, remarked that he thought the world was in the midst of a period of "testing". Efforts were being made to get away with acquiring additional territory. He felt it important that this be understood.

Ambassador Ansary referred to the economic progress being made in Iran with special reference to the rate of growth which he described as being exceeded only by Japan.

The President said that he was looking forward to the visit of the Shah and the Empress and that he would very much welcome any views which His Majesty might have on the situation in the Near East.

---

205. Action Memorandum From the Assistant Secretary of State for Near Eastern and South Asian Affairs (Battle) to the Ambassador at Large (Harriman)[1]

Washington, June 2, 1967.

SUBJECT

Your Meeting with the Shah of Iran: Middle East Crisis

During your visit to Paris, I recommend that you meet with the Shah to discuss the Middle East crisis and specifically to increase his understanding of and support for our policy.

---

[1] Source: Department of State, Central Files, POL 27 ARAB–ISR. Secret; Exdis. Drafted by UAR Country Director Donald C. Bergus and cleared by Eliot.

Background

The current Arab/Israel crisis has had repercussions in Iran. At the same time Nasser called for the evacuation of UNEF, he also publicly requested Jordan and Saudi Arabia to intervene with the Shah to stop sales of Iranian oil to Israel. (Iranian oil has been supplied to Israel since 1957 and has been carried by tanker around the Arabian Peninsula through the Gulf of Aqaba to Eilat.)

In response, the Iranian Government issued an official denial that Iranian oil was being sold to Israel. This is technically true, since the transactions are made through third parties. At the same time, the Iranians became concerned about their isolated position among the Islamic nations of the Middle East and about the effects of Iran's ties with Israel on Iran's efforts to establish closer relations with the moderate Arab states. On May 31, the Iranian Government issued a statement supporting "the legitimate rights of Moslem peoples" and saying that it regards "as necessary the securing of the legitimate rights of the Palestinian people as mentioned in the U.N. resolutions." The statement also expressed the hope for a peaceful solution to the present crisis. The Iranian press has from the first attacked Nasser for instigating the crisis.

Iran's concern about its relations with the moderate Arab states has no doubt been increased as a result of King Hussein's flight to Cairo to effect a grand reconciliation and to sign a military agreement with the UAR. At this writing King Faisal is still in Europe, but we do not exclude the possibility that he, too, may in some manner make a gesture toward improving his relations with Nasser in the name of Arab solidarity against the Israel threat.

In their talks with us, Iranian officials have been expressing the hope that we would take a firm line to keep the Gulf of Aqaba open. The Shah undoubtedly believes that we bear much of the responsibility for the crisis for not having acted vigorously to oppose Nasser long since. Some Iranian officials have indicated a concern that we might resume aid to Nasser in order to end the crisis.

Recommendation

Suggested talking points for use with the Shah:

1. The present crisis in the Middle East is grave and highly dangerous.

2. The U.S. is doing its best to urge restraint on all parties to the dispute.

3. We do not believe that Nasser wishes to be the first to shoot in the present situation. Indeed, it would be against his interest to do so. He has again proven his ability as an expert, albeit a malevolent one, in exploiting and building upon the events of each day. He has been able to create

circumstances in which the very firmly held anti-Israel sentiments of most Arabs come to the fore.

4. For the past six months to a year, Nasser had been convincing himself that the U.S. was determined to destroy him and to humiliate Egypt. He viewed the cessation of significant U.S. aid to Egypt in the UAR's growing economic crisis, his failure to achieve a victory in the Yemen, resistance to his designs by Kings Faisal and Hussein, and even the good relations between Iran and the United States in this light.

5. Nasser, therefore, is trying to exploit the current crisis to his advantage. He has consistently sought to identify publicly the U.S. with Israel. He now believes he is in a position whereby the U.S. and Israel face the painful choice of either accepting his "victory" (withdrawal of UNEF, closure of the Straits of Tiran) or committing "aggression" against Egypt. He strongly hopes for the former. He believes, however, that if he is destroyed as a result of Israel/U.S. military action, he can destroy with him a good many Western interests in the area. He considers this a deterrent. There is some speculation that among Nasser's objectives is the resumption of U.S. aid to the UAR. We have told the Iranians that there is no possibility that we will resume aid to the UAR in the foreseeable future.

6. There is good reason to believe that the Soviets may have been instrumental in touching off the present crisis by floating in mid-May in Damascus and Cairo a report that a massive Israel attack on Syria was imminent. Since then, they have attempted to reap full propaganda advantage of the theme that Israel is the aggressor and has U.S. support, that the Soviet Union is the protector of the Arabs and that the Soviet Union hopes war can be avoided if only the U.S. will restrain Israel. The Soviets seem to have been taken by surprise by Nasser's proclaimed closure of the Gulf of Aqaba and have thus far confined themselves to general statements in support of the Arab position that the Straits lie in Egyptian territorial waters.

7. We certainly do not approve of Hussein's early public capitulation to Nasser. Hussein as a sovereign independent ruler has to decide where his best interests lie. He has assured us that this gesture was solely for the purpose of insurance and that his attitude toward and intention to cooperate with the United States is unchanged. Whether Hussein will be able to maintain this position under the pressure of events cannot be predicted with certainty.

8. It would be helpful if the Shah were to let the Israelis know that his attitude toward them is unchanged and that his intention is to maintain the present relationship with them in all its aspects as circumstances warrant. The Shah could also usefully counsel the Israelis to exercise military restraint in order to give the fullest opportunity for multilateral diplomacy to work. We would hope that Iran would take no steps to interrupt the commercial relationships whereby Iran obtains oil.

9. We would also hope that the Shah would get word to Faisal and Hussein indicating that the present crisis should not be allowed to impair the close relationship which Iran has with both countries. This relationship is based on a mutuality of interests which continues to endure.

10. The U.S. position in this crisis has been made clear by the President in his statement of May 23. The United States is firmly committed to the support of the political independence and territorial integrity of all the nations of the area. The United States strongly opposes aggression by anyone in the area, in any form, overt or clandestine. The United States considers the Gulf of Aqaba to be an international waterway and feels that a blockade of Israeli shipping is illegal and potentially disastrous to the cause of peace. The United States is making vigorous efforts to obtain effective United Nations action to resolve this crisis. Concurrently, we are consulting urgently with the maritime nations of the world with a view to multilateral action asserting our right to use this international waterway.

---

206. Intelligence Memorandum[1]

No. 1117/67   Washington, June 5, 1967.

THE SHAH OF IRAN AND HIS POLICIES

Summary

The Shah of Iran and Queen Farah will arrive in Washington on 12 June for a three-day official visit. Since his last visit to the US in 1964, the Shah has been evolving a new foreign policy which entails less reliance on the US and closer relations with the USSR and Eastern Europe. The Shah remains basically pro-US in outlook, but believes that it is advantageous for Iran to broaden its sources of military equipment, economic credits, and trade. He can be expected to press for a firm US policy against his bete noire, Egyptian President Nasir, and to request more fa-

---

[1] Source: Johnson Library, National Security File, Country File, Iran, Vol. II, Memos & Miscellaneous, 1/66–1/69. Secret; No Foreign Dissem. Prepared in the CIA's Directorate of Intelligence. A note on the source text indicates that this memorandum was prepared by the Office of Current Intelligence and coordinated with the Office of Research and Reports, the Office of National Estimates, and the Clandestine Services, all in the CIA.

vorable treatment for Iran in the extension of US military and economic credits. A proud and sensitive man, the Shah will also be expecting recognition for his role as leader of a country which is stable, achieving rapid economic growth, and undertaking widespread social and economic reforms.

Background

1. The Shah's new independence stems from many factors, but probably the most significant is his growing conviction that the immediate threat to Iranian security is posed not by the USSR but by the ambitions of Egyptian President Nasir. He believes that Nasir has designs on the Persian Gulf and on the oil-rich Iranian province of Khuzestan, which has a large population of ethnic Arabs (see map).[2] Iranian security officials claim to have evidence that the exiled Khuzestan (Arabistan) Liberation Front receives encouragement and assistance from Egyptian intelligence. The Shah can certainly be expected to point to the current Middle East crisis as evidence of Nasir's insatiable ambitions.

2. The Shah is also convinced that American officials have underestimated the Egyptian threat to Iran and fears that the US would not support Iran if a Nasirist campaign against him were to lead to hostilities. He was severely shaken by the withholding of US arms from Pakistan during the Indo-Pakistani conflict of 1965 and constantly points to this as evidence that Iran must have other sources of arms and economic assistance. He is determined to bolster his defenses in the Persian Gulf, and is doing so with arms from a variety of sources.

3. In economic terms the Shah is, of course, attracted by the low interest rates charged by the Soviets and Eastern Europeans and by the opportunity to repay Eastern military and economic credits with goods rather than with foreign exchange. Last year's US-Iranian military credit negotiations were marked by bitter Iranian complaints that US terms were strictly commercial and took no note of Iran's position as a good friend of the West.

Rapprochement with the East

4. The real turning point in Iranian-Soviet relations came in late 1965 when the Soviets extended Iran a credit of $289 million for building a steel mill it had long desired. Part of this credit will be used for the construction of a pipeline, through which will pass the Iranian natural gas which the Soviets will accept as payment for the credit. Soviet economic credits to Iran now total at least $346 million. Other projects include construction of the Aras dam on the Iranian-USSR border, an electric power plant in Tabriz, improvement of Iranian ports on the Cas-

---

[2] Not reproduced.

pian, and Soviet prospecting for oil in the Iranian offshore area of the Caspian Sea.

5. During the first five months of 1967 the pace of Iran's rapprochement with the USSR increased. Early in the year, Iran and the USSR signed a $540 million five-year trade agreement. Although this agreement probably will not be completely fulfilled, it still will result in a significant increase in trade. In April, Soviet Deputy Premier Baybakov visited Teheran and apparently offered the Iranians almost every conceivable type of economic assistance. The communiqué issued at the close of Baybakov's visit mentioned industry, communications, electric power, dam construction, irrigation, mining, oil explorations, and metallurgy. It also mentioned increased shipments of natural gas to the USSR and the sale of Iranian oil. The communiqué was only a "declaration of intent," however, and in negotiations on specific projects the Soviets tend not to be as generous as their initial offers would indicate.

6. The most significant development of 1967 was the announcement in January of a Soviet-Iranian arms deal, involving the extension of a $110-million Soviet credit toward the purchase of armored personnel carriers, antiaircraft weapons, and trucks. Arrangements were also made for Soviet technicians and advisers to train Iranians in the use of the equipment. This agreement, together with the purchase of UK naval equipment and Tiger Cat missiles, has broken the virtual monopoly which the US held over the supply and training of the Iranian armed forces.

7. The Shah also informed Western officials in May that he intended to allow the Soviets to prospect for oil in areas in southern and western Iran. The Soviets, however, may be reluctant to undertake expensive prospecting in areas which the Western consortium was willing to give up. Nevertheless, the Shah's willingness to permit a Soviet presence in the southern oil region is indicative of the extent to which his attitude toward the USSR has changed. It is also indicative of his determination to increase Iranian oil production and of his disappointment with the record of the Western oil consortium.

8. Eastern European countries have extended over $158 million in economic credits to Iran—over $100 million of the credits is from Rumania and the rest is from Bulgaria, Czechoslovakia, Hungary, and Poland. Several new trade agreements have been signed, and Iran has already agreed to sell oil to Rumania and Bulgaria. The Shah was in Czechoslovakia in May; the Czechs had previously indicated an interest in expanding Iran's munitions production capability, and this possibility was undoubtedly discussed.

Domestic Developments

9. Iran is stable and continues to sustain a high level of economic growth. This strong domestic base has contributed to the Shah's increasing self-confidence and has further nurtured his ambitions for even more rapid development. It has also provided the backdrop against which he could for the first time decrease his dependence on the US.

10. Parliamentary elections have been scheduled for August, and there are indications that the government may loosen political restrictions somewhat. The opposition Mardom Party may be permitted to win more seats, the parties may have more leeway in the selection of candidates, and two government-approved candidates may be permitted to run in some constituencies. Nevertheless, the Shah is certainly not prepared to allow outspoken opposition, and there is still no legitimate outlet for the expression of antiregime sentiment.

11. The Shah's "White Revolution"—his term for his reform program—is proceeding apace. The distribution phase of land reform is virtually complete, and the program is now concentrating on farm mechanization and the development of cooperatives. The health and literacy corps are considered successful, although there is little information on the impact of the programs on the average Iranian. All of these programs are hampered to some degree by the lack of trained personnel.

12. The Shah's reform program has taken the steam out of the left-wing opposition National Front Party. The already suppressed Tudeh (Communist) Party has been still further weakened by the reform and by the Iranian-USSR rapprochement. Conservative religious leaders continue to oppose aspects of the reform program—such as increased rights for women—but apparently with little impact on the public.

13. The Iranian economy is healthy, and all indications point to a rapid growth rate at least for the next year. Last year's growth rate was about nine percent, prices remained remarkably stable, public and private investment increased, and oil revenues continued to rise. The government has already taken steps to ease pressures on the balance of payments. Iranian officials continue to believe that oil production is not rising fast enough, and this could lead to further confrontations with the Western oil consortium. A serious Iranian-consortium crisis was narrowly averted last fall when the consortium agreed to step up production, to relinquish 25 percent of its concession area to the Iranian Government, and to make oil available for sale by Iran to Eastern Europe.

14. For the first time, the Shah has been willing to face the succession problem and to make contingency plans for the possibility of his early demise. At the request of the Shah, elections will be held in August for a constituent assembly to examine and amend the articles of the constitution pertaining to succession. The assembly is expected to authorize the Shah to appoint a regent to rule if he should die before the Crown Prince

is of age. All indications are that the Shah will appoint Queen Farah. He has absolute faith in her loyalty, and she has proved to be competent, popular, and actively interested in the reform program.

Outlook

15. Despite his new independence, the Shah remains a good friend of the US—he is one of the few third-world leaders who publicly supports the US policy in Vietnam. Iran is still heavily dependent on the West for investment, trade, and military equipment. The Shah constantly insists that his closer relations with the East will strengthen Iran, and will thus make his country a better ally of the US. He claims to have no illusions about the ultimate aims of the USSR, and his internal security forces have been bolstered to maintain surveillance of the growing number of Communist technicians and advisers in Iran. Recently, the Iranian press undertook a campaign—obviously with government approval—to put the rapprochement in "perspective." The newspapers have taken note of continued antigovernment broadcasts from Communist clandestine radios, past Soviet perfidy, and the dangers of accepting the Soviet embrace too enthusiastically.

16. Nevertheless, the danger remains that the Shah will overestimate his capability to control the increased Soviet presence in Iran. He has said several times recently, with some overconfidence, that Soviet "dependence" on Iranian natural gas will give Iran significant leverage over Soviet policy in the Middle East, a doubtful analysis at best. The possibility also exists that, in the event of the Shah's demise, the USSR would be in a better position to influence the course of events.

---

207.   Telegram From the Embassy in France to the Department of State[1]

Paris, June 5, 1967, 1615Z.

19869. Dept pass AmEmbassy Tehran immediate. For the President and the Secretary of State from Harriman. I had a long talk alone with Shah at noon today, interrupted only by news despatches of Arab-Israel

---

[1] Source: Department of State, Central Files, POL 27 ARAB–ISR. Secret; Exdis. Although the Embassy requested that the Department pass the telegram to Tehran eyes only for Meyer, a note on the source text indicates the Department did not do so. There is no indication on the source text that the telegram was passed to the White House.

fighting. I gave him AFP despatch from Moscow to the effect that Russian position would depend on that taken by the US, which he said was most important.

The Shah listened to my explanation of our attempts to restrain Israel and Arabs, possible Soviet encouragement of Damascus and Cairo belligerence, but our belief Soviets did not now want military action and their surprise over Nasser's closing of Gulf of Aqaba. Furthermore, the President believed Shah's interest was to remain as aloof as possible without interruption oil shipments and that he hoped Shah would use his influence, particularly with Faisal. I said the President would be most interested in getting the Shah's opinions and judgment.

He replied that perhaps we should not talk about the past, but only the future. On the other hand, we must learn from past mistakes. He went over the familiar ground of our assisting Nasser, not accepting the inevitability of his aggressive policies. We had missed opportunity to stop Nasser over other issues in the past, over Yemen, and such outrageous actions as use of gas. Now things were difficult since on the issue of conflict with Israel all Arabs would be united. His Ambassador had seen Faisal who, although concerned over Nasser and other issues, stated he would give full support to Nasser against Israel.

He reported that Soviet Ambassador had called on him this morning. Ambassador stated that hostilities should be stopped, and in this the French might be useful. Security Council action should be sought.

The Shah emphasized several times that the long range problem was how to stop Nasser in future. Some other issue than Israel must be found. Although he continued to consider Nasser a dangerous and aggressive dictator, interested only in his aggrandizement, the Shah could not oppose a Moslem cause. He would, therefore, have to give "lip service" support, specifically referring to earlier UN resolutions. The Shah suggested we should give the impression we wanted to stop the fighting, but implied that he hoped Nasser's forces would be humiliated. He considered our long range major objective was "how Nasser could be destroyed".

Although he looked forward keenly to seeing the President in Washington, he feels he probably must return home as his people would not understand his traveling in Paris and visiting the fair in Canada.

He rehearsed again, as he had done when I saw him last November, his belief that Iran must be militarily strong enough to deal with Nasser and Iraq without US intervention. He again expressed regret that we had not done more to strengthen Iran militarily, referring particularly to our extensive aid to Turkey.

I of course went over the familiar ground of Turkey's NATO membership, etc.

He seemed relieved when I offered to call on him tomorrow if there were any further developments of importance, and when I told him that I felt sure we would continue to consult him closely, he repeated necessity that he must give lip service to Moslem solidarity, but his primary concern was how Nasser's influence could be reduced and eventually destroyed. Otherwise, there could be no peace in the Middle East. He indicated that currently oil shipments would continue without interruption as normal commercial transactions, and that he would in other ways attempt to calm situation.

Please instruct if any reason for me to see Shah again tomorrow morning.[2]

Bohlen

---

[2] Harriman's "Further Notes on Conversation with the Shah," June 5, are in the Library of Congress, Manuscript Division, Harriman Papers, Special Files of W. Averell Harriman, Public Service, Kennedy–Johnson Administrations, Shah of Iran.

---

208.   Telegram From the Embassy in France to the Department of State[1]

Paris, June 6, 1967, 1220Z.

19914. For the President and the Secretary of State from Harriman. Ref State 208388.[2] Called on Shah this morning and conveyed message in reftel. He is remaining in Paris today for talk and luncheon with De Gaulle, then returning to Tehran tomorrow, Wednesday June 7. He regrets not having opportunity for talks with the President and hopes to come to Washington at a later date. He agreed to inform our Ambassador

---

[1] Source: Department of State, Central Files, POL 27 ARAB–ISR. Secret; Exdis. Passed to the White House. Although the Embassy requested that the Department pass the telegram to Tehran eyes only for Meyer, a note on the source text indicates the Department did not do so.

[2] Telegram 208388 to Paris, June 5, informed Harriman that the Department believed that it was desirable for him to speak to the Shah Tuesday (June 6) morning and state that the President of course deferred to the Shah's judgment as to whether he should return home, but would be most disappointed not to have an opportunity for personal discussions on many subjects, including especially the Middle Eastern crisis. (Ibid.)

Meyer fully on his talks with De Gaulle and his analysis of where De Gaulle is heading in Middle East.

Shah expressed earnest desire to continue close exchange of views on developments. He believes Nasser's claim of intervention by US and British planes is to have future basis that his forces were not defeated by Israel alone.

The Shah hopes the Soviets will not intervene militarily on pretext to offset US action. I told him that our contacts with Soviet Government led us to believe Soviets would not intervene and had indicated that all should work for cease-fire and return to old positions. I also said we understand Israel had no territorial ambitions, only assurance of free passage to Gulf of Aqaba.

Shah urged that we should now consider long range problem of Nasser. We could not tolerate flare-ups every few years. He said Nasser's aggressive plans must be stopped.

Shah raised question of his initiative regarding Vietnam which I will report in septel.

Bohlen

---

209.   Message From the Shah of Iran to President Johnson[1]

Paris, June 6, 1967.

It is a matter of deep regret that owing to the grave and uncertain situation in the Middle East, the Empress and I are obliged to cancel our visit to the United States and return home immediately. However, Mr. President, I look forward to the opportunity of seeing you again in not too distant a future when we can discuss matters of mutual interest. The Empress and I take this opportunity to express our heartfelt greetings and best wishes to you, Mr. President, to Mrs. Johnson and to your great people.

Mohammad Reza Pahlavi[2]

---

[1] Source: Johnson Library, National Security File, Special Head of State Correspondence File, Iran, 10/1/66–8/31/67. No classification marking. The letter is on letterhead from the Iranian Embassy in Washington.

[2] Printed from a copy that bears this typed signature.

210.   Memorandum of Conversation[1]

Washington, June 6, 1967.

SUBJECT

Middle East Crisis

PARTICIPANTS

The Secretary
His Excellency Hushang Ansary, Ambassador of Iran
Theodore L. Eliot, Jr., Country Director for Iran, NEA/IRN

Ambassador Ansary began by expressing concern about demonstrations in the Arab countries against American citizens and installations. The Secretary referred to malicious and false reports that American planes participated in the Israeli attacks. He said that the UAR knows where our carriers are; Soviet destroyers are in their area. But such reports incite Arab mobs.

The Ambassador mentioned that there have been reports that the Kuwaitis and Iraqis have stopped the flow of oil.

The Secretary said that it is important for as many countries as possible to remain detached. What is involved is the Jehad psychology on one side and the apocalyptic psychology on the other. Mob pressures in the Arab countries make it impossible for Arab governments to be detached. Hopefully, some of them will be able to draw a distinction between what they say and what they do. We are pleased that Israel has said it has no territorial ambitions. Nasser is riding a tiger; it is difficult to see how he can disengage from a holy war which cannot succeed.

Ambassador Ansary commented that the ill effects of the war are likely to last for some time. Iran, which values its progress and stability, is quite concerned and hopes for a settlement.

The Secretary said we want His Majesty to understand that the United States was not involved in the outbreak of hostilities. We had received commitments from both sides not to attack. We had no advance notice from either side. We are making no judgment as to who started the fighting. Our advice to all capitals concerned was to give the Security Council and diplomatic efforts a chance to find an answer.

The Ambassador said that the Israelis had apparently felt that time was running out for them. The Secretary replied they had been touchy as far as the military problem was concerned. They had had a report of 400 Egyptian tanks moving on Elath. Ambassador Ansary commented that

---

[1] Source: Department of State, Central Files, POL 27 ARAB–ISR. Confidential. Drafted by Eliot and approved in S on June 9.

they were also concerned about the Egyptian Vice President coming to Washington. The Secretary replied that we have had no such information from the Israelis.

The Secretary then reviewed the history over the past 10 years of our support for the integrity of the states of the area, mentioning support we had given to the UAR, Lebanon, Saudi Arabia, Algeria, Kuwait, Tunisia and Morocco. We have had a consistent and even-handed interest in protecting the integrity of the states of the area. All this is forgotten when the issue is Arabs against Israel.

Ambassador Ansary said that it was too bad that the Yemen problem had not been solved. The Secretary, mentioning the use of gas by the UAR, said that Nasser's attitude toward the Yemen was not in accordance with usual standards of conduct.

The Ambassador asked if the United States and the USSR would get together on a resolution in the Security Council. The Secretary said that we may get together on a resolution, but that the resolution might be a complicated one which would mean different things to different people and hence might be the beginning rather than the end of a problem. He stressed that we could not persuade Israel to go back to the status quo before June 5. The Israelis have made clear that closing the Straits of Tiran was a casus belli. What is involved for the United States is not only the general principle of freedom of an international waterway but also the fact that in 1957 we persuaded Israel to withdraw from the Sinai peninsula on the condition that there would be freedom of passage through the straits. We cannot forget such a commitment.

---

211.   Memorandum for President Johnson's Diary[1]

Washington, June 7, 1967.

SUBJECT

The President's Meeting with Ambassador Armin Meyer, 6 June 1967[2]

The US Ambassador to Iran, Armin Meyer, visited with the President about twenty minutes on 6 June. Two general topics were discussed:

---

[1] Source: Johnson Library, President's Appointment File (Diary Backup), June 7, 1967. Confidential.

[2] Rostow's June 6 briefing memorandum for the President noted that Meyer was in Washington laying the groundwork for the Shah's visit. (Ibid.)

1. When the President asked how the Shah of Iran was getting along, Ambassador Meyer described the success of the Shah's land reform program and of his economic policies in general. The President was pleased and suggested Mr. Rostow look into ways of translating Iran's experience to Vietnam.

2. Ambassador Meyer described his views on the current crisis between Israel and the neighboring Arab states. He felt that President Nasser, in accusing the US and Britain of involvement in Israeli air attacks, was trying to trigger a cutoff of oil supplies by the oil producing Arab countries, thereby shifting the confrontation on to other shoulders.

The meeting closed with the President expressing his hope that the Shah would be able to reschedule his visit to Washington and asked Ambassador Meyer to convey his warmest wishes to the Shah, the Empress, and their children.

Harold H. Saunders

---

212.   Telegram From the Department of State to the Embassy in Iran[1]

Washington, June 8, 1967, 11:14 p.m.

209548. 1. Please deliver to Shah following message from President dated June 8, 1967:

"Your Imperial Majesty:

I very much appreciate the kind letter you sent me from Paris.[2] I fully understand why you felt obliged to return home directly from Paris, but wish you to know not only how much Mrs. Johnson and I will miss seeing you and the Empress on this occasion but also how disappointed I am not to have this opportunity to discuss our mutual concerns especially in the Middle East. I hope we will be able to get together soon and that you will let me know when it would be convenient for you to come to Washington.

---

[1] Source: Department of State, Central Files, POL 7 IRAN. Secret; Priority; Exdis. Drafted at the White House. Cleared by Bromley Smith and Meyer and in draft by Deputy Chief of Protocol Chester C. Carter and Special Assistant to the Deputy Under Secretary for Political Affairs Stephen Low; and approved by Handley.

[2] Document 209.

Meanwhile, Your Majesty, I assure you that in these troubled times I deeply appreciate your counsel and Iran's constructive position in world affairs. Ambassador Harriman has informed me of his conversations with you in Paris and of your desire to continue a close exchange of views. That is my desire too.

I have just learned that the UAR as well as Israel have accepted a cease-fire. I would greatly welcome your thoughts as to how we might proceed in trying to bring stable peace, prosperity, and regional cooperation to the Middle East, out of the wreckage of this crisis.

Mrs. Johnson and I extend our very warmest personal wishes to you and the Empress and also to the Iranian people whose progress under your leadership is greatly admired by Americans everywhere.

Sincerely,

Lyndon B. Johnson"

Rusk

213. Telegram From the Embassy in Iran to the Department of State[1]

Tehran, June 10, 1967, 1650Z.

4900. Subj: Shah's Desire Assist with Middle East Crisis. Ref: State 209548.[2]

1. Zahedi called me to Foreign Ministry today to discuss Shah's interest in playing helpful role in resolution present Middle East crisis. Shah had taken note of 3rd paragraph President's letter and has been particularly wondering how, in light postponement his own visit to US, we can best arrange exchange of views. Shah has now decided instruct Ansary propose to Department that either US send special emissary to Iran or GOI would be prepared send someone to Washington.

2. Accordingly, Department will no doubt be receiving urgent request for Ansary meeting with appropriate level Department officers discuss this idea.

---

[1] Source: Department of State, Central Files, POL 7 IRAN. Secret; Priority; Exdis. Passed to the White House.

[2] Document 212.

3. *Comment*. Zahedi did not give me any idea what moves or suggestions Shah may be considering but perhaps Ansary may be prepared spell things out in somewhat more detail. It would seem Iranians could be particularly helpful in contacts with Feisal and Hussein. In this connection, see Tehran 4899.[3] Conceivably they could also play some kind of intermediary role with Iraq.[4]

Thacher

---

[3] Dated June 10. (Department of State, Central Files, POL 27 ARAB–ISR)

[4] Telegram 210152 to Tehran, June 10, reported that the Department had told Ansary that in view of the fact that the U.S. Government was still studying all aspects of the Middle East situation and formulating its plans, it would seem premature to send a special U.S. representative to Tehran. On the other hand, if the Iranian Government wanted to send a special representative to Washington, U.S. officials would be happy to meet with him if there were no publicity and he realized that top-level U.S. officials were extremely busy. Ansary replied that he would recommend to his government postponing a decision on whether to send a representative to Washington. (Ibid.)

---

214. Telegram From the Embassy in Iran to the Department of State[1]

Tehran, June 30, 1967, 1330Z.

5266. NATUS for Battle. Ref: State 218169.[2] Subj: Amb Hare's Meeting with Shah: Arab-Israeli Situation. Following discussion of Glassboro Summit, Amb Hare provided Shah detailed presentation Dept's views contained reftel. Shah from time to time interjected comments which led to further mutual elucidation of respective viewpoints, as noted below:

1. Nasser's Threat.

Shah acknowledged substantial benefits gained by Nasser's other neighbors such as Iran or even Turkey, from Israeli victory. On his recent

---

[1] Source: Johnson Library, National Security File, NSC Special Committee Files, Iran. Secret; Limdis. Repeated to Paris.

[2] Telegram 218168 to Tehran, June 29, for Ambassador Hare stated that the principal purpose of his meeting with the Shah was to get his views on the Middle Eastern situation, particularly any ideas he might have for steps which would lead to a permanent, peaceful solution. Hare was also to congratulate the Shah for the constructive steps he had taken during the crisis, such as intervening with Feisal and Hussein not to break with the United States and urging restraint and moderation to the Israelis. (Department of State, Central Files, POL ARAB–ISR)

visit to Ankara he found full awareness that aggressive UAR threat might have been directed against others if not so effectively blunted by Israelis. Nasser remains an evil force and must someday be destroyed. Yet he had been allowed go on too long unchallenged, throwing gas bombs in Yemen and carrying out other nefarious doings. Arab arrogance and aggressiveness repugnant to Iran. Arabs made much of their long subjection to foreign rule, excuse they constantly draw on to explain their own lack of accomplishments in health, education, etc., whereas real responsibility for lack of progress lay with area countries themselves. If they had actually wanted education, they could have had it, and likewise in other fields about which they now complain. In this atmosphere Communists have been provided with fertile ground for stimulating anti-West reaction on every aspect of Arab sensitivities. Shah concluded Russians now "have" Syria, Algeria, Yemen and UAR.

2. Israel.

Shah more vehement if anything in his criticisms of Israelis. Iran's ties with Israel are close but Shah deeply disturbed by their "arrogant" attitudes: "Mouth of General Dayan should be closed." Israelis should be taking line that they merely trying to defend their security and rights. They should be emphasizing simple desire live in peace enjoying security. Instead Israeli spokesmen taking strong positions all over place, annexing Jerusalem, affirming their desires for this and that, proposals obviously aimed using their recent territorial acquisitions as levers remake their surroundings on lines of ambitions they have long harbored. Concept of demilitarized areas, strengthening of frontiers etc. were ideas which might be put forward by Danes or other Israeli friends but should not be propounded by Israelis themselves.

3. Hare replied that we did not, of course, condone Israeli position on Jerusalem as recent Presidential statement[3] had made clear. Fact was hard-liners now getting most publicity. Shah agreed there two schools of thought in Israel but moderates seem unable attract public attention.

4. Ambassador said examination of problem indicated Israelis perhaps not as hard line as they might seem. Thus fundamental Israeli need is security (requirement which Shah readily acknowledged). Hare said to begin with Israelis obviously don't want Sinai and would probably settle for demilitarization. If belligerency problem could be done away with, beginning with UN vote, this would then take care of Straits of Tiran and Suez problem. As to Gaza, this never historically part of Egypt, but not clear what Israelis want or don't want there beyond security. With regard exodus of refugees from West Bank, US has been striving

---

[3] Reference is to the President's address at the Department of State to the Foreign Policy Conference for Educators on June 19; for text, see *Public Papers of the Presidents of the United States: Lyndon B. Johnson, 1967*, Book I, pp. 630–635.

hard persuade Israel adopt enlightened policy permit West Bankers remain and allow return those who have already fled. Hare urged Shah take similar vigorous line with Israelis. Shah said he had already instructed FonMin in New York urge such policy on Eban. Iran would say something further this topic but he wondered whether Israelis prepared to listen. Shah said US must assume principal role for damping down Israeli exuberance. Time will come when US must say flatly, "Stop the nonsense." (Shah's views on UNGA strategic situation reported Tehran 5261.)[4]

5. Other Factors.

Hare mentioned reactions he had encountered in New Delhi talks and myopic Indian tendency view Arab/Israeli question solely in terms India's problems with Pakistan. Talk turned to Tito's role with Hare noting press reports of opposition within Yugoslavia to Tito's strident support of Nasser. Hare said this explainable perhaps in terms evolving internal political patterns with growth "new" guard chafing at dominance of oldsters. Hare also suggested there perhaps some connection between Tito's hard support for Nasser and recent events in Greece. Shah said he did not know the Greek Junta but felt they had done job which had to be accomplished; otherwise Papandreou like Mossedegh would have thrown country into chaos.

6. Middle East Arms Control.

When Hare touched on our interest terminating ME arms race, Shah asked pointedly how, in this context, US defined Middle East. Hare replied he not in position answer authoritively, but, speaking personally he had not understood we intended that restrictive plans should apply countries with whom we in treaty relationship.

7. *Comment:*

Foregoing paragraphs as well as extended discussion UNGA technical problem (Tehran 5261) revealed no major shifts Shah's attitude. He is still committed to public posture generally sympathetic to Arabs but deeply anxious with regard possible resurgence Nasser's power. Both he and Hoveyda would be delighted find way out of present stage of dilemma through vote for resolution strongly supporting withdrawal and also including paras for coming grips with Arab-Israeli fundamentals. Faced with grim facts rapid Soviet replenishment Arab arms, Shah nonplussed. So far he has reacted by making clear he intends prevent if he can any more overflights of Iran but apparently has refrained from any general remonstrances urging Soviets cease and desist from all arms deliveries to Arabs.

---

[4] Dated June 29. (Department of State, Central Files, POL 27 ARAB–ISR/UN)

Shah interested, courteous, and thoughtful throughout 1-1/2 hour meeting and obviously very appreciative Amb Hare's presentation US views. However, recent lengthy ceremonial visits abroad and hard perplexities of ME situation have left him somewhat weary and worried. He now definitely scheduled depart for Caspian July 1.

Thacher

---

215. Telegram From the Department of State to the Embassy in Iran[1]

Washington, July 21, 1967, 6:57 p.m.

11341. For Ambassador from the Secretary. Ref: Tehran 403.[2] Subject: Senatorial Criticism of Iran.[3] In your discussion with Shah of Senatorial criticism of Iran likely be published in next few days, please assure him on my behalf that the Senatorial views expressed do not represent views of executive branch. As the Shah is undoubtedly aware, entire subject US military assistance and sales programs is currently being intensely reviewed by Congress, and Senatorial barbs are aimed at executive branch and not at Iran. You may assure him that we do not like these barbs either. More important, you may assure him that these barbs have in no way diminished the esteem in which we hold the Shah and that we continue to look forward with great pleasure to his forthcoming visit. Our esteem for him and our desire to welcome him to Washington and to seek his counsel have increased in recent weeks as a result of our deep appreciation for Iran's constructive policies in the Middle Eastern crisis.

Rusk

---

[1] Source: Department of State, Central Files, DEF 19–8 US–IRAN. Secret; Immediate; Limdis. Drafted by Eliot, cleared by Handley and in substance by Kathryn N. Folger in H, and approved by Rusk.

[2] Dated July 22. (Ibid.)

[3] The State Department Activities Report in the President's Evening Reading on July 19 stated that the Senate Foreign Relations Committee intended to release on July 24 testimony given before the Symington subcommittee on U.S. military assistance and arms sales to Iran, India, and Pakistan. The testimony included criticism by Senator Fulbright of U.S. military aid to Iran, and by Senator Symington of Iran's military and economic agreements with the Soviet Union and its middleman role as an arms supplier for Pakistan. The report noted that this was likely to annoy the Shah and that the Department was trying to soften his reaction by alerting him in advance. (Johnson Library, National Security File, Agency File, Department of State, President's Evening Reading, 3/1/67, Vol. VII)

216. Telegram From the Embassy in Iran to the Department of State[1]

Tehran, July 24, 1967, 1400Z.

447. Subj: Shah's Washington Visit.

1.   In lengthy discussion with Shah 24th, I conveyed President Johnson's greetings and his anticipation of Shah's forthcoming visit. I pointed out a blue ribbon program has been arranged providing every opportunity for discussion of matters of mutual interest.

2.   Shah said he too looking forward to visit and been giving much thought to discussions which will take place. He gratified by what he considers USG's friendly attitude toward Iran and even looks forward to talking with "those Senators."

3.   This provided occasion to convey to him Secretary's message (State 11341).[2] He deeply grateful. I noted that *New York Times* may be breaking story today and hoped it would not cause difficulties. With certain amount of bravado, Shah said he feels Iran has matured sufficiently so that criticisms such as those by Senators can be taken in stride. *Comment:* We hope such equilibrium obtains after story breaks. In any case, he has been favorably conditioned thanks to Dept's foresight in alerting us and thanks to Secretary's invaluable personal message.

4.   Shah does not believe special discussion with Mideast experts re Mideast details need be scheduled since he hopes essential ground can be covered in discussions at top levels. However, Thursday morning might be left open for Mideast experts briefing, final decision to be made after completion of top level discussions.

5.   Shah indicated again that he hopes to discuss food problems. Delighted that Iran has unusally good wheat crop this year, he wants to concentrate with American help on increased food production in years ahead as contribution to major problems facing world during rest of this century. Shah noted with keen disappointment that Bill Warne's proposal for agricultural project in Khuzestan has now been scaled down to 5,000 acres when Shah wishes major commercial project of one or more hundred thousand acres.

6.   Shah also indicated he will wish to discuss importance of Iran's maintaining adequate defense capability so that if troubles break out in this region American boys will not be shot a la Viet Nam. He said he thinks our countries owe it to each other to let each other know where we stand and implied that Iran will purchase elsewhere to the extent that the USG is unable to meet its needs.

Meyer

---

[1] Source: Department of State, Central Files, POL 7 IRAN. Confidential; Limdis.

[2] Document 215.

217. Telegram From the Embassy in Iran to the Department of State[1]

Tehran, August 3, 1967, 1005Z.

557. Subject: Shah's Washington Visit.

1. In discussing August 2nd his forthcoming trip to Washington, Shah stressed that he considers it a "working visit in depth." He is pleased that program provides wide range of opportunities for talks with USG leaders.

2. Once again Shah stressed his interest in agriculture. He said that at pace Iran is going now, even though it has almost self-sufficient supply of food this year, full development of Iran's resources will take another century. What is needed, he said, is large-scale commercial farming of hundred thousand acres or more and only US has know-how for this. He mentioned not only Khuzistan, but also Jiroft area (where Kim Roosevelt's project has uncovered abundant water supplies), Sistan Basin, and Gorgan where real successes been scored this year with American hybrid corn.

3. Linked with agriculture is Shah's interest in desalination. He wishes to push forward in this field pursuant to talks which Minister of Water Rouhani has had with Secretary Udall and other well-disposed Department of Interior officials.

4. One of most important purposes of Shah's visit will be to get reassurance that we intend to continue our cooperation in military field. Although he will probably not go into detail in his talk with the President (and did not mention such details in the August 2 interview), we know that his greatest interest is in the following, which he will hope to discuss at least in general terms during his Washington visit: (a) filling gaps caused by attrition and other insufficiencies in our jointly agreed program; and (b) planning four and five years ahead in Iran's defense program. Re latter, he will be interested in: (c) possible re-hab F–4's; (d) possible follow-on plane(s) to F–5 (he has appointment with Northrop official); (e) Sheridan tanks; (f) helicopters to make his military mobile enough to counter Viet Nam-type guerrilla activities which are Iran's most likely threat; and (g) communications to assure command control. In this connection, I am pleased that DOD is suggesting ARMISH/ MAAG Chief General Jablonsky be available.

5. Shah indicates he will also wish to make known in Washington his views that since Iran is most stable and trustworthy state in Mideast, Western oil companies should assure that high level of present liftings be

---

[1] Source: Department of State, Central Files, POL 7 IRAN. Secret; Limdis.

maintained and in fact increased. He sees no reason why Arab producers should be allowed to blackball certain markets and still retain production levels higher than Iran.

6. Obviously of major interest will be exchange of views between Shah and USG officials re Mideast situation. Shah is proud that Iran is almost a model of progress and constructivism in this part of world and he ready to play whatever role is feasible in encouraging similar state of affairs in Arab world. He remains convinced, however, that until Nasserism is checked, as in Yemen, there is little hope for progress in Arab world.

7. Since my departure for Washington is only one week away, Shah and I agreed that unless he or Washington had something special to discuss before my departure we would tidy up any loose ends re his trip via either Court or Foreign Ministers.

8. *Comment:* Shah shared my view that on eve of his Washington visit US–Iran relations are as warm and healthy as they have ever been. There is in Embassy's view, however, a dark cloud on horizon, i.e., Senatorial action already taken blocking concessionary credit and sales by Henry Kuss' department in DOD. During our last audience Shah made clear he feels entitled to know where he stands re military supplies from US in future. In August 2nd discussion he pointed out Soviets continue to pump in arms to Iran's potential enemies and at much lower prices and two and half percent interest rate. While we sure he will avoid overdependence on Soviets, we also sure that if USG is unresponsive to his future military needs Shah will without question turn to French, UK, FRG and other suppliers. Embassy has consistently favored some diversification in Iran's military procurement, but we see present situation as somewhat of a crossroads. If we abdicate role of principal supplier, it will be a severe setback to present healthy relationship which we believe can be retained at small cost both financially and even arms-wise. While such setback in itself will not be fatal, we wonder if USG really wishes to alienate such a staunch friend and at same time surrender concomitant benefits we have here, notably our strategic communications facilities.

9. Embassy realizes Executive Branch is making Herculean effort to counter present unrealistic trends among our friends in Senate. Shah has been apprised of Senatorial concerns. We would like to think that via personal testimony he can play a key role in assuring that Iran–US relationship remains healthy.

Meyer

218.   Memorandum From Secretary of State Rusk to President Johnson[1]

Washington, August 15, 1967.

SUBJECT

Your Meetings with the Shah of Iran

Our aim during the Shah's visit will be to strengthen our relations with Iran by convincing the Shah that we recognize the importance to peace, stability and progress in the Middle East of a strong and independent Iran. To help strengthen our relations you might:

1.   Assure the Shah that we share the same goal: to promote peace, stability and progress in *the Middle East:*

—We greatly *appreciate Iran's constructive efforts* to moderate the Arab-Israeli crisis, and to assist the U.S. in its own efforts to this end.

—We hope that Iran will maintain *intimate relations* with Turkey and Pakistan, retain *close ties with Israel and moderate Arab countries,* continue to work for *better relations with Iraq,* and *support moderate forces in South Arabia* after the British leave.

—We appreciate Iran's concern about the possible extension of radical Arab influence to the Persian Gulf and *approve of Iran's efforts to strengthen its position and engage in political bridge-building in the Gulf.*

2.   Take the Shah into your confidence on other *major international problems:*

—*Southeast Asia:* the Shah will expect to be thanked for Iran's contribution of a medical team to South Viet Nam.

—*US-USSR relations:* the strain caused by Viet Nam has been kept within tolerable limits, and we have made progress in other, unrelated fields.

3.   Indicate *our desire to continue to assist Iran* within the limits of our heavy burdens and Iran's growing financial strength:

—We want to continue our *close military relationship.*

—The *Exim Bank* and *private American businessmen* will continue to play a role in Iran's economic development.

4.   Discuss frankly *Soviet-Iranian relations:*

—The *Soviet aim* is to break up the Irano-American relationship and eventually to establish Soviet influence and presence in the Persian Gulf area.

---

[1] Source: Johnson Library, National Security File, Country File, Iran, Visit of Shah (con't.), 8/22–24/67. Secret.

—*Soviet-Iranian military deals* confuse our public and Congress.

—Mutually beneficial *economic relations* do not cause us concern as long as they do not endanger Iran's independence.

5.   Congratulate him on *Iran's progress,* inquiring about his goals for the future—economics, social and political—and expressing the hope that projected increases in Iran's military expenditures will not inhibit economic development.

Dean Rusk

Attachment

POINTS THE SHAH MAY RAISE AND SUGGESTED RESPONSES

1. United States Military Assistance for Iran

a.   *The Shah will seek reassurance* that we intend to maintain our close military cooperation *and is likely to express a desire to obtain additional equipment and advisory assistance.*

b.   *You might respond* that we will *sympathetically consider any requests* he may make for our assistance in developing a long-range military purchase program. Such assistance will have to be considered *in the context of Congressional opinion and action* on arms sales, and Iran is one of the countries we have had in mind in pressing the Congress for authority to continue extending credits for military sales.

2. Oil

a.   *The Shah may ask* that we urge American *oil companies* belonging to the Iranian Oil Consortium to recognize Iran's stability by *greatly increasing their offtake from Iran* and by participating in the construction of an Iranian-Turkish pipeline to the Mediterranean.

b.   *You might respond* by indicating that *these are matters for the companies* and by expressing the hope that Iran and the Oil Consortium will maintain the mutually beneficial relationship they have had in the past.

219. Memorandum From Secretary of State Rusk to President Johnson[1]

Washington, undated.

SUBJECT

Your Meetings with the Shah of Iran: Viet Nam

The Shah has suggested to us that he might attempt to establish a new mechanism for arriving at a peaceful solution of the Vietnamese war. He has been thinking of bringing together a group of countries, such as Iran, Afghanistan, Pakistan, India, Japan and Cambodia, which would have access to the United States, the USSR and Communist China and might open new doors for discussions of a possible solution. Such a group would work discreetly and not make public proposals. The Shah may again raise this idea in his discussions with you.

We have told the Shah that we deeply appreciate his interest and concern and that we are interested in any effort by any government or group of governments to help achieve a peaceful solution. We have indicated that if the governments the Shah has in mind agree that such an effort would be worthwhile and if the effort would be discreet, we would be openhanded and frank in dealing with such a group. We have stressed that explicit approval by us of such an effort would be a kiss of death.

Dean Rusk

[1] Source: Johnson Library, National Security File, Country File, Iran, Visit of Shah (con't.), 8/22–24/67. Secret/Nodis. Filed with the August 15 memorandum from Rusk to Johnson, Document 218.

220.   Background Paper Prepared in the Department of State[1]

SHAH/BP–1   Washington, August 15, 1967.

VISIT OF THE SHAH OF IRAN
August 22–24, 1967

U.S. MILITARY ASSISTANCE TO IRAN

Summary

Our military relationship with Iran is fundamental to our overall relationship, and the Shah will be seeking, during his August visit, a reaffirmation of our desire to continue the close military relationship we have had in the past. Although he is clearly determined to move away from his former complete dependence on us for military assistance, there is no sign that he wishes seriously to disturb the fundamentals of his security relationship with the United States. Despite recent Iranian purchases from the UK and the USSR, the influential position which the U.S. has achieved with the Iranian military establishment will continue as long as we are able to continue our military assistance, sales and related advisory programs. Since the inception of our military assistance to Iran in 1954, we have programmed military equipment and services totaling more than $790 million for Iran's armed forces. We have also conditionally agreed to extend Iran credits up to a total of $400 million for military equipment and services during FY 1965–70. Credit agreements for $300 million have already been signed and the funds earmarked for specific purchases. Our grant military assistance continues on a reduced scale. During his visit, the Shah is likely to express a desire to obtain additional equipment and advisory assistance and to indicate that Iran's security needs will be met by purchases from other sources if the U.S. is unable to respond favorably to his requests for assistance.

Discussion

U.S. military assistance policy toward Iran has evolved significantly during the past few years. Prior to 1964, all U.S. military equipment and services were provided Iran on a grant basis; since that time, Iran has undertaken to pay for an increasingly large portion of its defense needs, and we anticipate that by 1970 the U.S. grant program in Iran will concentrate on training and support unless overriding political exigencies require grant matériel aid.

The impetus for Iran's present military purchase policy was composed of several factors: 1) the fact that U.S. grant military assistance has

---

[1] Source: Johnson Library, National Security File, Country File, Iran, Visit of Shah (con't.), 8/22–24/67. Secret. No drafting information appears on the source text.

been provided exclusively to meet the Soviet threat and not that from other directions which the Shah believes to be more imminent; 2) the Shah's conviction that the principal short-term danger to his country lies in Nasserist Arab ambitions in the oil-rich Persian Gulf area (see separate Background Paper);[2] 3) Iran's growing foreign exchange revenues from oil which now exceed $600 million annually.

Increasingly worried over the radical Arab threat, the Shah approached us in early 1964 with a proposal to make large-scale military purchases estimated at more than $450 million. We were concerned that purchases of this magnitude might seriously impair Iran's economic development program. We eventually persuaded the Shah that a credit of $200 million over a 5-year period would meet Iran's needs. A Memorandum of Understanding covering this $200 million credit, and also extending the U.S. grant aid commitment through FY 1969, was signed on July 4, 1964.[3]

In November 1965, the Shah pressed us for additional credits. A U.S. military survey team was dispatched to reassess the threat to Iran, and we agreed in August 1966 to amend the earlier Memorandum of Understanding so as to make available an additional $200 million for military purchases over the FY 1967–70 period.[4] The new credit was subject to release in four annual increments of $50 million each, with approval of each increment to be made by the President after a thorough review of Iran's economy to ensure that extension of each credit increment would not impair the economic development of the country.

Under the Agreement as amended, Iran is buying two squadrons (32 aircraft) of F–4–D interceptors to complement the six squadrons of F–5 fighters provided under MAP, 460 M–60–Al medium tanks to modernize Iran's armored division, an air control and warning system to protect Iran's oil-rich southwestern region against possible aggression, C–130–E transport aircraft to enhance armed forces mobility and a 60-day war reserve of ammunition.

Our long-term agreement and the virtually exclusive military advisory relationship provided through ARMISH–MAAG should ensure our remaining the primary foreign military influence in Iran if we can continue to provide advisory services and credit on an attractive basis for military sales. We are not trying, however, to sustain a position as exclusive supplier of military equipment. Last year, Iran ordered some $60 million worth of short-range missiles and naval craft from Britain, and in February 1967 the Iranian Government announced a $110 million barter agreement with the USSR for the purchase of non-sophisticated military

---

[2] Not printed. (Ibid.)
[3] See Document 47.
[4] See Document 171.

items (see separate Background Paper).[5] Iran has been negotiating with other European governments for purchases of defense production equipment.

The Shah recently told Ambassador Meyer that he hopes to place his equipment purchase program on a 4–5 year basis, noting that he was thinking of purchasing Sheridan armored reconnaissance vehicles, transport aircraft, helicopters, a follow-on fighter to the F–5 being provided under MAP and, perhaps, rehabilitated F–4 interceptors late in the planning period. The Shah has not broached the issue of additional credits. In view of the continuing increase in Iran's foreign exchange earnings from oil and Iran's probable equipment modernization needs, however, he may well seek an extension of present credit levels into the 1970's, perhaps coupled with an increase in credit availabilities in FY 1968–70.

The Shah has also indicated that he may request more U.S. advisors to assist his Air Force as increasingly complex systems (e.g., F–4D interceptors and an Air Control and Warning System along the Persian Gulf) are introduced. We are not certain as to just what the Shah has in mind, but he may be thinking in terms of U.S. personnel performing actual maintenance on the new matériel. The U.S. Army Mission/Military Assistance Advisory Group (ARMISH/MAAG) has increased its advisory effort with the Iranian Air Force and plans to devote an increasing proportion of its efforts to this area as these systems are introduced. If the Iranians are interested in direct support, they should be encouraged to purchase it from U.S. industry or from U.S. technical advisory groups. The Military Assistance Program is not intended to perform direct support for foreign forces, and a personnel augmentation for this purpose would be extremely difficult, if not impossible, to justify before Congress. Therefore we should urge him to expedite the training of Iranians for such functions and to consider selective purchasing from U.S. sources of personnel services if necessary to complement Iranian efforts.

---

[5] Not printed. (Johnson Library, National Security File, Country File, Iran, Visit of Shah (con't.), 8/22–24/67)

221. Background Paper Prepared in the Department of State[1]

SHAH/BP–3   Washington, August 15, 1967.

VISIT OF THE SHAH OF IRAN
August 22–24, 1967

IRAN'S DOMESTIC POLITICAL/ECONOMIC SITUATION

Political

The internal Iranian political scene has not been as stable as it is today since World War II. The Shah is firmly in control of the government and is in the forefront of the drive to modernize the country. His programs for economic development, land reform, health and education and many other improvements have engaged the cooperation of most Iranians and have outdone the slogans and proposals of the opposition to his rule. Economic growth is creating jobs and investment opportunities and helping to build a middle class with a vested interest in stability. Aside from having the wind taken out of its sails by the Shah's programs, the opposition is divided and impotent.

The Shah's regime is still dependent in the final analysis on the security forces which he commands, and the opposition is still strictly controlled. But, except for a few minor incidents, there have been no demonstrations or attempts at armed insurrection against the regime since 1963. The Shah's reform programs and the growing economy are enlisting the energies of numerous former opposition leaders.

Parliamentary elections were held on August 4, 1967. Although there were efforts to create an appearance of competition among approved pro-regime candidates, the elections were firmly controlled and directed from the Palace. The new parliament can be expected to be completely responsive to the Shah's guidance.

The principal weakness in the Iranian political scene remains its dependence on one man. But the chances for longer term stability, should the Shah suddenly disappear from the scene, are increasing as more Iranians obtain a stake in stability. Although the establishment of democratic institutions as we know them is still a long time off in Iran, the government is relying increasingly on Iran's best trained people as its administrators, and the Shah seeks advice from a broad spectrum of Iranian life. The Shah has also recently decided to establish better procedures for

---

[1] Source: Department of State, S/S Files: Lot 68 D 475, Visit of the Shah of Iran, August 22–24, 1967, Vol. I, Briefing Book, V–39–A. Secret. Drafted by Newberry and J. Patrick Mulligan (NEA/IRN) and cleared by Eliot, Rockwell, Funari, and NEA Regional Affairs Director Sidney Sober.

a regency should he die before his 6-year-old son reaches maturity. Finally, even many Iranians who oppose the regime can conceive of no viable alternative.

Economic

The Shah and his government are proud of Iran's economic and social progress and their economic development plans for the future. The government's annual growth target of 6% for GNP has been well exceeded in the past two years, with relative price stability being maintained in this period. The prospects for the current year again indicate a growth rate of 7–8%. The rate of population growth is estimated to be 3%. Annual per capita GNP is about $230.

Oil revenues finance the greater part of the government's development expenditures. The Fourth Plan, which begins in 1968, will establish priorities in favor of industry and agriculture with less emphasis on infrastructure to which considerable resources have already been devoted. Private industrial investment is increasing steadily.

Iran's capital investment programs have thus far been carried out with only moderate reliance upon foreign capital. This situation is changing rapidly, however, with official foreign credits as well as foreign private investment steadily increasing. Iran's credit-worthiness has continued to improve, and there appears to be no question that further borrowing on conventional terms will be feasible in the foreseeable future.

Annual oil income amounting to over $600 million accounts for approximately three-fourths of Iran's total foreign exchange earnings and about one-half of total government revenues. Although the current outlook indicates there will be continued pressure upon the balance of payments, the long-term foreign exchange prospect is favorable in the light of increasing oil revenues and exports of petrochemicals and natural gas, greater import substitution in manufactured goods, and the government's demonstrated capacity to impose fiscal and import restraints as well as to borrow and usefully absorb greater amounts of foreign capital.

Despite increasing urbanization, the importance of its oil resources and the growth of new industries, Iran's economy is still essentially agrarian. The agricultural sector supports two-thirds of the population and provides nearly one-third of gross domestic product and GNP.

Land reform has been the cornerstone of the Shah's "White Revolution" and since 1962 the government has made substantial progress in dismantling a feudal land-holding system and extending new ownership and farming rights to villagers throughout the country. This has been accomplished with minimal resistance and without impairing agricultural production. The final phase of land reform now underway is aimed at boosting output and expanding local cooperatives. Further progress will depend heavily upon the ability of the government to mobilize additional capital, extension services and local leadership. This key reform effort has been successfully complemented by an imaginative use of military conscripts serving throughout rural Iran in separate literacy, health and development corps. For example, four years ago only 8% of the rural population received any exposure to rudimentary education. The figure is now 20% and rising.

---

222. Background Paper Prepared in the Department of State[1]

SHAH/BP–7   Washington, August 15, 1967.

VISIT OF THE SHAH OF IRAN
August 22–24, 1967

ANTI-SHAH ACTIVITIES IN THE U.S.

Students

Several hundred of the Iranian students in the United States are ardently and volubly opposed to the Shah. Dissidents, working principally through the Iranian Students Association, have for many years carried on an intermittent campaign of protest against the Shah's regime and have succeeded during previous visits by the Shah in provoking public incidents insulting to the Shah. They have also enlisted American civil liberties groups and "ultra-liberals" in publicizing accounts—some factual and some distorted—of restraints on personal liberty in Iran. These activities have caused continuous irritation in our diplomatic relations with the Shah and his Government.

Iranian officials know the limitations on our ability to restrain these anti-Shah activities so long as the Iranian dissidents do not violate U.S. laws. They also know that we have exerted extraordinary efforts to bring to justice or to deport such agitators wherever there is a legal basis for doing so. Fortunately, the number of irritating cases has been on the decline in recent months, but we cannot be sanguine about the prospects for

---

[1] Source: Department of State, S/S Files: Lot 68 D 475, Visit of the Shah of Iran, August 22–24, 1967, Vol. I, Briefing Book, V–39–A. Confidential. Drafted by Newberry and cleared by Eliot and Rockwell.

avoiding altogether some organized protest or other efforts to embarrass the Shah during his current visit.

Gudarzian Case

A spectacular irritant in our relations with the Shah arose out of the activities of an Iranian promoter, Khaibar Gudarzian. "Khaibar Khan," as he calls himself, three years ago published a sensational set of allegations of multi-million-dollar embezzlement including charges against members of the Shah's family and involving AID activities in Iran. The allegations were repudiated by Senator McClellan after detailed inquiry conducted by the Senate Committee on Government Operations. Gudarzian nevertheless succeeded in tying up substantial bank accounts of the Shah's brother and sister for many months until a Federal District Court ruled against Gudarzian last autumn. Gudarzian's appeal to the U.S. Court of Appeals was rejected and his suit against the Prince and Princess has apparently been dropped.

The Justice Department has continued to review the possibility of criminal prosecution against Gudarzian. At the present time, however, Justice does not believe that any of the possible charges can be pressed successfully due to a variety of legal technicalities. The Department of Justice is continuing, however, to evaluate the case and will take action if it appears that an opportunity is presented.

Our immigration authorities have confirmed that Gudarzian is "out of status" and they have initiated proceedings designed to effect his deportation. This can be a lengthy process, taking a year or more, but the matter will be pressed as rapidly as administratively feasible.

223.   Memorandum From Director of Central Intelligence Helms to President Johnson[1]

Washington, August 17, 1967.

1. [5 lines of source text not declassified] We thought the Shah's mood as reflected in the most recent conversation would be of interest to you in light of his visit with you here next week.

2. I have not sent copies of this cable to anyone other than you [1-1/2 lines of source text not declassified].

Richard Helms[2]

Attachment

There follows the text of a cable [less than 1 line of source text not declassified] covering [less than 1 line of source text not declassified] meeting with the Shah of Iran on 15 August 1967:

1. Aside from the perennial subject of demonstrations by Iranian students in U.S., etc., the 15 August meeting with the Shah was standard friendly affair and something of a rehearsal for upcoming visit to the United States. He obviously looking forward to meeting with the President for whom he expressed sympathy and understanding re heavy burden he carries as U.S. top government executive. This after stating he fully understood legislative opportunism and possible irresponsible public performance. Noted however that Export/Import Bank action turned out favorably. In regard to arms he claims to be relaxed, stating he will make his case and if U.S. Government is interested, as they should be, so much the better; if not, he will make other arrangements. No hard feelings—recriminations, etc. He hopeful that at least Air Force support will be forthcoming and that sufficient Air advisors will be available, preferably out of uniform.

2. The Shah was very much concerned over President Ayub's position and Chinese Communist infiltration of Pak forces. States Ayub is old friend but [less than 1 line of source text not declassified] unfortunately has

---

[1] Source: Central Intelligence Agency, DCI (Helms) Files: Job 80–B01285A, Chrons, Aug.–Dec. 1967. Secret.

[2] Printed from a copy that bears this typed signature.

allowed himself to become isolated from realities. He was pleased to note however that Ayub was most responsive to reasoning set forth last regional cooperation for development meeting at Ramsar (resort on Caspian Sea) and in fact indicated appreciation for guidance and "leadership" offered him.

3. King Hussein due Tehran 16 August and the Shah anxious to see him. "A nice chap in an unfortunate position somewhat due to his impetuous nature." The Shah is hopeful he can help King Hussein vis-à-vis the Israelis but essentially finds latter characteristically arrogant, an attitude he feels will be harmful to them in the long run.

4. Aref and Iraq the Shah described as unpredictable and unfortunately not even clever. He had hoped they would see the advantage of cooperation with Iran but this seems beyond their imagination or intelligence.

5. Subject of covert support to Yemen [*less than 1 line of source text not declassified*] touched on lightly. Message being if you fellows want to be in on the act out here get with it, if not, just say so.

6. In summary, we found the Shah relaxed, confident, pleased with his economic successes at home (which he should be) and looking forward to his visit. His story will be that he is offering the cooperation of the only responsible modern progressive country in the area. While he not working against CENTO, which he views as ineffective, but not bad, the regional cooperation for development is more the answer to regional requirements. While most friendly and bland about all of this, we nevertheless estimate that if visit with the President not productive, he will undoubtedly come away with a less friendly attitude than he now professes. What the Shah really wants from the United States Government is recognition as a responsible area leader and, of course, that undefined material something that goes with this recognition.

224. Intelligence Memorandum[1]

Washington, August 18, 1967.

THE SHAH OF IRAN AND HIS POLICIES IN THE AFTERMATH OF THE ARAB-ISRAELI WAR

(Addendum to Intelligence Memorandum 1117/67, 5 June 67)[2]

Summary

The Shah of Iran will arrive in Washington on 22 August for a brief official visit. His visit was originally scheduled for 12 June but was postponed when the Arab-Israeli war broke out. Although Iran publicly voiced support for the Arab cause, Iran's ties with Israel were not affected and most Iranian officials were privately delighted by Nasir's humiliating defeat.

The Shah has not modified his conviction that the Egyptian president poses the most serious long-range threat to Iranian security, and he will continue to press for favorable prices and terms on US military equipment to bolster his defenses in the Persian Gulf. Staunch Soviet support for Egypt and other radical Arab states appears to have resulted in a note of caution in Soviet-Iranian relations, and rapprochement is likely to proceed at a reduced pace.

[Here follows the body of the paper.]

---

[1] Source: Johnson Library, National Security File, Country File, Iran, Visit of the Shah of Iran, 8/22–24/67. Secret; No Foreign Dissem. Prepared by the Office of Current Intelligence and coordinated with the Office of Economic Research, the Office of National Estimates, and the Clandestine Services, all of the CIA.

[2] Document 206.

225.   Memorandum From Harold H. Saunders of the National Security Council Staff to President Johnson[1]

Washington, August 18, 1967.

SUBJECT

Your Talks with the Shah—5:30 P.M. Tuesday and Wednesday[2]

The main purpose of your meeting is once again to reassure the Shah that you regard him highly and believe the U.S. has a stake in the success of his kind of reform. But as you know, he is a thoughtful man and is looking forward to serious talk. He will be flattered by any confidences you can share on your talks with Kosygin, your thoughts on Vietnam, your interest in Ayub, your feelings about the Middle East, and even your analysis of our own urban problems.

The new factor in the U.S.-Iran equation since his 1964 visit is his increasing independence. After long dependence on U.S. aid and years of feeling that only the U.S. could protect him against Nasser and the USSR, the Shah for better than two years has been feeling his way toward a more independent policy.

No one cause prompted this shift. Our cutoff of military supply to Ayub during the Indo-Pak war upset him. He has watched the changing temperature of U.S.-Soviet relations, which has made him re-think his own relations with Moscow. Domestic pressures have forced him to appear less "the American puppet," especially as Iran becomes economically more self-sufficient.

As a result, he has eased into a limited relationship with the USSR. He has strengthened his relations with Pakistan and Turkey. He has supported the Yemeni Royalists and elements in South Arabia working against Nasser. He has—almost alone among the Moslem states—maintained a respectable relationship with Israel.

He is still feeling his way, and you may want to talk over the pitfalls in going too fast with the USSR. The Soviet role in the Middle East war has probably given him second thoughts, but your own experience with Kosygin might help him sort out the limits of working with the Soviets.

The other side of this coin for him is how heavily he can count on us for future arms supply. Under the current Memorandum of Understanding we are committed to provide another $100 million in credit sales.

---

[1] Source: Johnson Library, National Security File, Country File, Iran, Visit of Shah (con't.), 8/22–24/67. Secret.

[2] August 22 and 23.

Even if the Church Amendment[3] stands, we would be able to meet that obligation if you told Harold Linder to make the loan without a Defense guarantee. But the Shah probably assumes that; his main interest is whether we will go on supplying him beyond the term of the current understanding (1970). While you can say that politically we want a continuing military relationship, we'll just have to wait to see where we stand with Congress. You may want to discuss your Congressional problem with him, since he will be seeing quite a few members of Congress.

More broadly, he will want to know what role we intend to play in the Middle East. One way to explain our position is to say, as you have in the past, that we don't walk out on friends, so we're not about to disengage. But then you might go on to describe the new spirit of regionalism you found on your Pacific trip and your hope that something similar might emerge in the Middle East. While we don't want to commission him for any special job, we do feel he could play an important role in making this happen.

After stating your views, you might be interested to hear from the Shah what role he thinks we can play in the area in the future. A number of our moderate friends tell us frantically that we must do something to preserve the anti-Communist balance in the Middle East, but when we get down to specifics they have little to suggest.

Because of your own personal interest, you will undoubtedly want to hear from the Shah himself about the progress of his reform program. Although AID will be phasing out its activities in the next year, more and more American businessmen are moving into Iran and it might be interesting to ask the Shah how, without a formal aid program, he thinks we can participate constructively.

You will want to read Secretary Rusk's two memos ("General"—Tabs A and B[4] of the attached briefing book). If you have time, I think you would find useful the "Background" tabs on Iran's relations with Communist countries (B);[5] U.S. military aid (C);[6] the Shah's domestic picture with charts on economic progress (D);[7] and our Congress' attitudes toward Iran (K).[5] We'll have a brief talking paper for you Tuesday.

Hal

---

[3] On August 9 the Senate Foreign Relations Committee approved Senator Frank Church's proposed amendment to the foreign aid authorization bill eliminating the "revolving fund" that the Pentagon had been using to finance arms sales to developing countries. On November 6 the House of Representatives Appropriations Committee exempted seven countries (including Iran) from the ban.

[4] Documents 218 and 219.

[5] Not printed.

[6] Document 220.

[7] Document 221; the charts are not printed.

226.   Memorandum From the Ambassador at Large (Harriman) to Secretary of State Rusk[1]

Washington, August 21, 1967.

I am puzzled by one line of your memorandum to the President of August 15 on his meetings with the Shah.[2] In paragraph 4, among the topics for the President to discuss with the Shah is listed: "Soviet-Iranian military deals confuse our public and Congress."

I wonder if this is a matter which the President would wish to raise since we are not presently in a good position to give the Shah any encouragement on more credit purchases of military equipment in the United States.

I understand the Shah has given us assurances Iran will not purchase "sophisticated" military equipment from the Soviet Union. In addition, Iran is paying for this equipment through natural gas sales.

It is certainly true that Symington and certain other Senators have expressed disapproval of the Soviet arms deal (partly because they were not informed in advance), but for my part I think the Shah has developed a more relaxed relationship with the Soviet Union and should not be discouraged from continuing this attitude. He is under no illusions, and yet is attempting to reduce tensions with his difficult northern neighbor through more normal trade and other relationships.

I would hope the President would concentrate his discussion on the other two points listed, namely, Soviet objectives to break Irano-American friendship, and caution not to let economic relations with the Soviets endanger Iran's independence.

Perhaps also caution not to spend too much on military at expense of economic development.[3]

---

[1] Source: Library of Congress, Manuscript Division, Harriman Papers, Special Files of W. Averell Harriman, Public Service, Kennedy–Johnson Administrations, Box 15cl, Shah of Iran. Secret; Nodis. A copy was sent to Battle in NEA.

[2] Document 218.

[3] This last paragraph is typed in all capital letters.

227.   **Memorandum From Arthur McCafferty of the National
       Security Council Staff to the President's Special Assistant
       (Rostow)**[1]

Washington, August 22, 1967.

Lem Johns has just passed on to me the following information which I thought would be of interest to you:

From 4 p.m. to midnight this date approximately 60 to 150 members of the Iranian Students' Association will demonstrate in the northeast corner of Lafayette Park. This is an anti-Iranian group and they originally requested that they be permitted to wear masks to prevent recrimination against relatives still residing in Iran. Legal counsel for the Park Service had no reason to disallow the permit and it was granted, and no one has any objections of a legal nature which would prevent their wearing masks in the District.

This group originally requested to demonstrate right directly in front of the White House on the sidewalk area, and this was denied for security reasons. This means that this anti-Shah group will be in the vicinity of the White House during the arrival ceremony and State Dinner tonight for the Shah of Iran.

Lem also tells me that Secret Service is advising against any walking between the White House and Blair House either after the arrival ceremony or tonight for the State Dinner.

Art

---

[1] Source: Johnson Library, National Security File, Country File, Iran, Visit of Shah of Iran, 8/22–24/67. No classification marking. A copy was sent to Saunders.

228.   Memorandum From the President's Special Assistant (Rostow) to President Johnson[1]

Washington, August 22, 1967, 1 p.m.

SUBJECT

Talking Points for the Shah—5:30 p.m. Tuesday and Wednesday[2]

The Shah would like to see you alone.[3] Since the main purpose of his visit is to develop your personal relationship, this makes sense. You have nothing to negotiate but lots to talk about. Some of these subjects may fall over into after-dinner chat or into your second session. But the following cover the full range of likely topics:

Middle East

1. *Arab-Israel.* You want to see a peace that will last. You are ready to play a constructive role, but you can't force the Israelis to move. The leaders of the region have to face up to the need to end the state of war. Then maybe we can help find the terms of a settlement. You appreciate his constructive stand. What does *he* think chances for a settlement are? (He believes it's important to shore up Hussein.)

2. *Regionalism.* You think it's important for the Middle East to begin acting like a region. On your Pacific trip you saw what regional cooperation promises to do. Iran is a natural to help draw the Middle East together, because the Shah has broader contacts than most leaders. For instance, you understand the Shah, at his recent meeting with President Ayub and the Turkish Prime Minister, kept Ayub from tearing up CENTO.

3. *Nasser.* You know the Shah is concerned about radical Arab influence in the Persian Gulf. We are too. You hope Iran and her neighbors will cooperate in strengthening the Gulf as a little region all its own.

Global

4. *U.S.-Soviet relations.* You'd like to tell him a little about your meeting with Kosygin—your reflections on how far the thaw goes.

5. *Iran-USSR.* You'd like to hear his experience with the Russians. (He has moved toward more open relations with Moscow but had second thoughts since the Middle East war. While we can't keep him from a

---

[1] Source: Johnson Library, National Security File, Country File, Iran, Visit of Shah of Iran, 8/22–24/67. Secret.

[2] August 22 and 23.

[3] The President and the Shah met privately in the Oval Office on August 22 from 5:28 to 7:11 p.m.—interrupted briefly by Rostow and McNamara. (Johnson Library, President's Daily Diary) No record of their conversation has been found, but see Document 236.

business relationship with the USSR, we do want to urge caution. Congress gets upset.)

6. *USSR–Middle East.* You'd be interested in his estimate of the Soviet objectives. Moscow has made some gains but you doubt the Russians will pay the full bill to bail Nasser out. You're still certain Moscow's main aim is to drive us out of the area and undercut non-socialist governments.

7. *Vietnam.* You thank him again for Iran's medical unit. (He will appreciate any thoughts you want to confide on our position.)

U.S.-Iranian Relations

8. *Shah's independence policy.* You frankly recognize that a new era is beginning in our relations and you welcome it. You are pleased that Iran's own income is increasing and that Iran's dependence on outside aid is decreasing. (AID phases out this year.) This is not the end of American participation in the Shah's development program. It's a chance for American private enterprise backed by the Export-Import Bank to enlarge its relations with all aspects of the Iranian economy.

9. *Reform.* You congratulate him on Iran's economic progress and would like to hear how his reform program is going.

10. *Military aid.* You know the Shah is concerned about the state of our military assistance. (There is $100 million in credit still to go under our current sales understanding. This is a firm contract, which we would have to find a way to fulfill even if the Church Amendment stands. The Shah is mainly thinking beyond this.) You want to continue our military relationship and we'll do the best we can within the limits Congress sets. You'd like to tell him about Congressional attitudes because he'll be seeing members of the Foreign Relations Committee Wednesday afternoon and other members of Congress at the Vice President's luncheon on Thursday.

Walt

229.   Telegram From the Department of State to the Embassy in Iran[1]

Washington, August 23, 1967, 2122Z.

25746. Subject: Iranian Oil Consortium.

1. Senior executives American member companies Iranian Oil Consortium called on Shah in New York August 22 and later gave us following report of meeting.

2. Shah made predictable plea that Iran's stability and reliability be taken into consideration in companies' planning and investment. Stressed that Arab-Israeli crisis not ended and may revive.

3. Companies replied that 1967 offtake from Iran not likely far exceed last November's estimate but might prove be 19–20 percent above 1966. Stated not possible at this time estimate increase for 1968. Stressed necessity recognize courage of moderate Arab countries in resisting radical demands against oil companies.

4. Shah concurred fully with latter point saying he would not ask companies do anything else, that if West forced out and others came into moderate Arab countries it would be bad for Iran. While stating that nothing should be done to hurt Saudis, Shah said that potential growth in Saudi oil exports should come instead from Iran. On other hand, Kuwait does not require increased oil income, Libya is weak and any increase in Libyan prosperity would only whet Nasser's appetite take country over. Shah added he knows Iran could not replace any one Arab producer except possibly Iraq. He told companies second export terminal to supplement Kharg is needed and they should step up exploration. He reported French had made no important finds but had found promising seismic structure offshore in Gulf, which, however, may prove dry. He then raised subject of trans-Turkey oil pipeline, saying Iran not willing rely on Suez Canal and that while pipeline might not be economically sensible it was politically necessary.

5. While indicating concern about reliability of canal, companies noted that increasing size of tankers and tanker fleet make pipeline politically unnecessary. (Companies have informed us they will not commit themselves to participate in pipeline project. One of reasons is they question long-term reliability of Turkey.)

6. Shah did not press oil pipeline project and turned conversation to gas, including gas pipeline to Europe and hope that companies would

---

[1] Source: Department of State, S/S Files: Lot 68 D 475, Visit of the Shah of Iran, August 22–24/1967, Vol. II, Admin. & Sub. Misc., Press Releases & Memcons, V–39–B. Confidential. Drafted and approved by Eliot and cleared in draft by Meyer. Repeated to London.

involve themselves in petrochemicals in Iran. He indicated desire make Iranian oil fully competitive and mentioned progress in reducing redundant labor in oil installations in Iran.

7. Companies consider conversation part of useful continuing dialogue which they and Shah find helpful. They found Shah's usual speeches milder than often in past. In sum, they feel results of conversation "not too bad," although they remain concerned that Iranian expectations will continue to exceed realities.

Rusk

230.   Memorandum for the Record[1]

Washington, August 23, 1967.

SUBJECT

Meeting with the Shah of Iran

1. The undersigned met with the Shah of Iran over breakfast from 9:05 to 10:00 o'clock this morning in the upstairs study of Blair House. There was no one else present.

2. After initial pleasantries, the undersigned expressed appreciation for the Shah's assistance in establishing and operating the [*less than 1 line of source text not declassified*] installations in Iran and went into some detail on the value of the take and what it meant to American understanding of [*2 lines of source text not declassified*]. The Shah was clearly interested in hearing these details and asked several questions.

3. We then discussed the Iranian students in the United States, and the undersigned gave the Shah his personal assurance that we were not financing these students and that we would not under any circumstances. The Shah mentioned why he had at one time been concerned, but then readily admitted that in the current context we could have no motive for doing this. I repeated to him, and stated that I had said the same thing to the President, that we had nothing to do with these stu-

---

[1] Source: Central Intelligence Agency, DCI (Helms) Files: Job 80–B01285A, Chrons, Aug.–Dec. 1967. Secret. Copies were sent to DDCI, DD/P, and Chief, NE.

dents, except to try to keep an eye on them in the interest of informing the Iranians of their activities.

4. The next topic of discussion was the [*less than 1 line of source text not declassified*]. After hearing an expression of thanks for this endeavor, the Shah said that he had felt for some time that the Agency should [*1 line of source text not declassified*]. The undersigned replied that we would look into this matter. [*5-1/2 lines of source text not declassified*]

5. There was considerable discussion of the Arab-Israeli war with particular reference to Israeli tactics, the weaknesses of the Egyptian armed forces, and the phenomenon of Soviet miscalculation and mis-assessment. The Shah said that he had never dreamed the Israelis could win the war as rapidly as they did. He was obviously impressed when the undersigned told him that the President had been given estimates from this Agency before the war began, stating, within reasonable limits, exactly what happened.

6. There followed some discussion of the Shah's talk with the President last evening which would not be an appropriate part of this memorandum. He then discussed this theory of arms purchases, his plan for the Iranian air force, and his general philosophy about the military position of Iran. To the extent that the recipients of this memorandum are interested in these points, the undersigned would be glad to present them orally.

7. The meeting ended with a rather lengthy dissertation by the Shah on his view of Iran in the world today, what he is trying to do with his people, and where he would like to end up a few years hence in terms of his country's health and social well-being. Before the undersigned took his leave, he gave the Shah an Agency study entitled "The Outlook for Communist China". The Shah seemed pleased to receive this piece of paper, understood its sensitivity, and promised to guard it with care.

8. Ambassador Ansari greeted the undersigned at Blair House and also saw him to the door after the meeting.

Richard Helms[2]
Director

---

[2] Printed from a copy that indicates Helms signed the original.

231.   Memorandum of Conversation[1]

Washington, August 23, 1967, 11:30 a.m.

SUBJECT

Oil and Gas

PARTICIPANTS

H.I.M. Mohammad Reza Shah Pahlavi, Shahanshah of Iran
H.E. Hushang Ansary, Iranian Ambassador

The Secretary
The Honorable Lucius D. Battle, Assistant Secretary, NEA
The Honorable Armin H. Meyer, Ambassador to Iran
Theodore L. Eliot, Jr., Country Director for Iran, NEA

The Shah said that he had met with oil company officials in New
York and had indicated to them that they should support countries
which are stable and reliable and that they merely caused trouble by giving so much to small desert countries such as Kuwait. He hoped the companies would agree.

Commenting on Arab oil policies, he said it was ridiculous for any
Arab to believe that the West could really be hurt by an Arab oil embargo.
Iranian, Venezuelan and American oil are available. The West could
stand an oil embargo for a couple of years, but the Arab countries could
not. Agreeing, the Secretary commented that he has found it useful to
suggest to our moderate Arab friends that they make this point. The
Shah said he has been doing the same thing. The Secretary said the Arab
countries would not only hurt themselves in the short run by imposing
an oil embargo, but they might cause the West to turn away from Middle
East oil and substitute nuclear power on a crash basis.

The Shah mentioned plans for an oil pipeline across Turkey to the
Mediterranean, for a gas pipeline from Iran to Trieste and for an oil import terminal in Yugoslavia to supply Eastern Europe. On the latter
point, he said that the Eastern European market for oil is of course a limited one. As for gas, he said that he would much prefer to use Iranian gas to
make petrochemical products, especially fertilizers, for Iran and for export. He had urged the oil companies to interest themselves and others in
this possibility. In the meantime, however, Iran was making plans to export gas, and it seemed desirable to have customers in addition to the Soviet Union.

---

[1] Source: Department of State, S/S Files: Lot 68 D 475, Visit of the Shah of Iran, August
22–24, 1967, Vol. II, Admin. & Sub. Misc., Press Release & Memcons, V–39–B. Confidential.
Drafted by Eliot and approved in S on August 30. The meeting took place at Blair House.
This memorandum is Part V of V; memoranda of the other parts of the conversation are
ibid.

232.   Memorandum From the Assistant Secretary of Defense for International Security Affairs (Warnke) to the Deputy Secretary of Defense (Nitze)[1]

Washington, August 23, 1967.

SUBJECT

Shah's Request for Additional Pilot Training

The Air Force has developed what I believe is an ingenious proposal for meeting the Shah's request to the President for additional pilot training for his Air Force. As you know, the Shah asked for a total of 75 spaces for FY 68, but Major General Jablonsky, the US MAAG Chief in Iran, has assured us that the program he has worked out with the Iranian Supreme Commander's Staff (which calls for only 60 pilot spaces per year) is perfectly adequate. (Copy attached.)[2]

The FY 68 jet pilot training program for Iran currently is programmed at 29 spaces, 24 grant and 5 sales. The Air Force has agreed to make 15 more spaces available for FY 68 (recouped from Australia and Saudi Arabia), and proposes to train 16 additional Iranian pilots in its basic T–28 (propeller-driven) program for 9 months and to send USAF instructor pilots to Iran thereafter to give the 16 transition training to jets in country. General Jablonsky thinks this arrangement would be satisfactory to Iran (the Shah learned to fly jets in this manner) and believes that the 60 pilots thus trained in FY 68 would meet the Shah's needs. 24 spaces would be grant aid and 36 FMS.

This does not solve the need for additional spaces in future years, which turns on other OSD decisions now pending. I recommend, however, that you reply to the White House that DOD proposes to handle Iran's FY 68 pilot training requirement in this manner and that the foregoing proposal be discussed with the Shah during his visit.

Paul C. Warnke

---

[1] Source: Johnson Library, National Security File, NSC Files of Harold Saunders, Visit, Shah of Iran, Aug. 22–24, 1967. Confidential.

[2] Not printed.

233. **Memorandum From Harold H. Saunders of the National Security Council Staff to President Johnson**[1]

Washington, August 23, 1967.

SUBJECT

Your Second Meeting with the Shah—5:30 p.m. Today[2]

Secretary Rusk discussed the Middle East, Soviet objectives there, Soviet-Iranian relations, Pakistan and Vietnam. However, they mainly talked about the past in the Middle East. You might want to look to the future. We understand the Shah may raise the following with you:

1. *Future arms purchases.* He will be coming straight from tea with Senator Fulbright so should understand Congress' mood. Secretary Nitze feels the best you can say right now is that you want to continue our close military relationship but you hesitate to make firm promises while Congressional action is uncertain.

2. *Private investment.* You can say we'll encourage it. Governor Harriman's dinner tonight with business leaders will be a good chance for the Shah to argue his own case.

3. *Desalting.* We understand he just wants to discuss general prospects. All you need do is state your strong desire to have a breakthrough. In this connection, you might want to suggest adding a paragraph on water to your joint press release (see attached note).[3]

Beyond these, unless you have something you feel is left over from your talk yesterday, I recommend only these points:

1. Defense Department will substantially meet his yesterday's request for additional jet pilot training in FY 1968 through a combination of U.S. training and final training in Iran. (Nitze programmed for 60 trainees this morning—the Shah's Commander told our military mission this was the number needed—but would raise to 75 if Iran requires.)

2. You think one of the most serious questions in the Middle East is how other leaders can be brought around to following his constructive example. How can we help the Middle East to begin acting like a region?

Hal

---

[1] Source: Johnson Library, National Security File, Country File, Iran, Visit of Shah (con't.), Aug. 22–24, 1967. Secret.

[2] The President held a second private meeting with the Shah in his office from 5:34 p.m. to 5:50 p.m. (Ibid., President's Daily Diary) No record of the meeting has been found, but see Document 236. Following this meeting, a joint statement was released to the press; for text, see *Public Papers of the Presidents of the United States: Lyndon B. Johnson, 1967*, Book II, pp. 806–807.

[3] Not attached to the source text.

234.   Memorandum From Julius C. Holmes of the Special State–Defense Study Group to the Under Secretary of State for Political Affairs (Rostow)[1]

SDG–67–054   Washington, August 24, 1967.

Dear Gene:

In compliance with your request I am furnishing you hereby an account of my conversation with the Shah of Iran this morning.

The Shah received the Board of Governors of the Iranian-American Society of which I am a member. As this short reception was terminating the Shah asked me to stay behind as he wanted to have a word with me. He went straight to the point and said that he had had reports that I had been engaged in a Middle East study and that it included a recommendation for a naval force in the Indian Ocean. The Shah did not indicate the source of his information.

I replied that in fact I had been engaged in a long range policy study for the entire area of the Middle East and that the study included a recommendation that the establishment of such a force be examined as to feasibility, cost, etc. I reminded the Shah of the several conversations we had had in 1964 prior to the visit of the Concord Squadron (I took him to the Gulf of Oman where he spent a day and night witnessing weapons displays aboard *Bon Homme Richard*).

The Shah said that he hoped that such a force would be established and asked what part Iran could play in it. I said that the plans as to composition etc. were not made; but that personally I assumed that if such a force were established that one of its missions would be support for U.K., U.S. and Iranian naval forces in the Persian Gulf and that again, speaking personally, I presumed that Iranian ships might take part in exercises. The Shah said that that was fine and that although, at the present moment, he had no ships capable of forming a part of such a force that he expected to in the near future and hoped that Iranian participation would be considered. He asked to be kept informed as to progress and any future decisions.

I concluded this part of our conversation by reminding the Shah again that the proposal was just that and that it had not been staffed out nor had any decisions been made.

Julius

---

[1] Source: Department of State, S/S Files: Lot 68 D 475, Visit of the Shah of Iran, August 22–24, 1967, Vol. II. Top Secret; Limited Distribution; Noforn.

235. Memorandum From Vice President Humphrey to President Johnson[1]

Washington, August 24, 1967, 1 p.m.

I met privately with the Shah of Iran on Thursday, August 24, 1967, at 1:00 p.m. The conversation lasted 45 minutes, with no staff present.

The Shah told me he was extremely impressed by the President's sincerity and firm grasp. He believed the President when he said, "When a man gives his pledge, that pledge must be kept." He was very pleased with his two private meetings with you. He was deeply touched when you personally escorted him into a meeting that was going on with legislators, and was delighted when Mrs. Johnson came over to sit beside him. The meetings with the President were exactly what he had been looking for.

The Shah said his prime purpose was to explain to the President what he has been trying to accomplish in his own country and in the Middle East, and was pleased that the President understood so clearly.

He assured me of his support of your position in the Near East.

The strategic position of Iran as he understands it is that the USSR is attacking Iran and the Middle East by using Nasser to throw the United Kingdom out of the Red Sea, the South Arabian Sea, and the Persian Gulf. Nasser has seized the Yemen and has the strongest clandestine apparatus present within Aden and the South Arabian Federation. If Nasser and the USSR succeed in controlling the entrances of both the Red Sea and the Persian Gulf, Iran could be cut off.

"It is for these reasons that Nasser must be defeated. This is the primary strategic threat to Iran." The Shah does not believe the United States fully appreciates this threat.

He strongly urged that the United States continue to work with the moderates in the Arab world. He considers himself in Iran as the major counterweight in the Far East to Syria, Algeria, and the UAR, and a reliable associate of the United States.

He was anxious that the United States understand his need to maintain his defensive position. Therefore, he went into detail about his defensive forces. He is proud that Iran is now paying for its own defense. He explained that his reliance upon the USSR for military equipment is on a very low level and that Iran is getting much more from the USSR than it is giving.

---

[1] Source: Johnson Library, National Security File, NSC Files of Harold Saunders, Visit, Shah of Iran, Aug. 22–24, 1967. No classification marking. Drafted on August 30 at 11 a.m. A handwritten "L" on the source text indicates it was seen by the President.

He is fully aware of the danger of Soviet infiltration as a result of this influx of military equipment, and he has therefore very greatly strengthened his intelligence and security system.

On the current situation in the Middle East, the Shah said he had been impressed by Israel's Great Victory. He now worried about the appearance of arrogance he detected in Israel's behavior.

As for the Israelis, he stressed their need to be magnanimous and not arrogant. He was especially anxious that the Israelis move on the refugee problem. If they do not follow such a general line, he feels that Nasser will be able to unify the Arabs once again. He feels that he has a good relationship with the Israelis and wants to continue to be of help on their problem with the Arab states. He specifically indicated that Iran and Tunisia could work together for this purpose.

The Shah spoke quite frankly about Ayub Khan. He said he had spoken "very firmly" to Ayub about Ayub's overdependence on Communist China.

He has told Ayub that the best friend of the Paks is the United States and he warned against a Pakistani relationship with Russia, as well as Communist China.

Concerning the Persian Gulf, the Shah said that as the United Kingdom gradually leaves the Persian Gulf area, the only Free World partners able to fill that vacuum are Iran and Saudi Arabia. He hopes that he can come ever closer to the President in meeting this extremely dangerous situation.

In all these matters I was careful to listen sympathetically, but to confine my remarks to generalities.

236. Memorandum From Harold H. Saunders of the National Security Council Staff to President Johnson[1]

Washington, August 25, 1967, 5:30 p.m.

SUBJECT

Follow-up on Your Talks with the Shah

You will be pleased to know that the Shah left extremely happy. Your taking him over to the East Room Wednesday made a big impression. Ambassador Meyer asked me to thank you.

In Walt's absence, he has suggested that I send you this memo to make sure we issue any instructions that need to be given.

We also want to be sure Ambassador Meyer is able to handle effectively any misinterpretations the Shah may have taken away.

1. *Pilot Training.* Secretary Nitze has arranged jet training for 60 Iranian pilots. He will enter 44 in regular advance jet training school here in the U.S. The rest will go through basic propeller training here and transition to jets under U.S. instructors in Iran. Mr. Nitze has so far arranged for 60, instead of the 75 the Shah mentioned, because our chief of military mission in Tehran understands from the Shah's Supreme Commander that this is the number required this year.

I would propose offering the above program to the Iranians with the understanding that Defense will go to 75 if that turns out to be the number needed. Is this consistent with your promise to the Shah?

Yes. I only promised to meet his need[2]
No. I promised 75

2. *Future Military Aid.* We suggested saying only that you want to continue our military relationship beyond current agreements but can't make any promises until we know what limits Congress has set. Did you go any further than this?

Yes. I said we'd do everything possible to meet his needs[2]
No. I stuck to the above line

3. *Middle East Settlement.* Did the Shah indicate his intention to play any specific role in pressing Hussein to come to terms with Israel?

Yes
No[2]
Didn't come up

---

[1] Source: Johnson Library, National Security File, Country File, Iran, Visit of Shah of Iran, 8/22–24/67. Secret; Nodis.

[2] This option is checked on the source text.

4. *Oil.* We expected the Shah to ask that you urge U.S. oil companies to increase their oil offtake from Iran. Did you give him any encouragement to expect a better response from them?

Yes. I said we'd talk to them
No. I said these are company matters
Didn't come up[3]

5. *Vietnam.* The Shah is considering collecting a small group of responsible countries to hasten a peaceful solution in Vietnam. Secretary Rusk recommended that you simply offer to be open handed and frank in dealing with such a group. Did your discussions with the Shah go beyond this?

Yes. I asked him to press this
No. I stuck to the Secretary's line
Didn't come up[3]

Hal

---

[3] This option is checked on the source text.

---

237. Telegram From the Department of State to the Embassy in Iran[1]

Washington, August 26, 1967, 0159Z.

27532. Subject: Shah's Washington Visit.

1. Shah's August 22–24 visit to Washington was eminently successful in convincing him that U.S. regards him as true friend whose constructive and progressive leadership we greatly admire and whose counsel we highly value. On three public occasions President spoke of Iran's progress and Shah's leadership in glowing terms. Public praise was bestowed by others as well. Shah is unquestionably delighted and refreshed by his visit and found his reception here surpassing his great-

---

[1] Source: Department of State, Central Files, POL 7 IRAN. Secret. Drafted by Eliot on August 24, cleared in draft by Meyer and by Saunders, and approved by Rockwell. Repeated to London, Ankara, Rawalpindi, and Tel Aviv.

est expectations. On his side, he made plain his desire to lead his people into twentieth century, to maintain Iran's independence, and to retain close ties with U.S. In public statements he several times stated his admiration for President Johnson and the inspiration he and Iranian people receive from the President's devotion to American ideals which Iran shares.

2.   Shah had two long and cordial private talks with President Johnson. He also had hour-long meetings with the Vice President and with Secretary Rusk. He had friendly meeting with Senate Foreign Relations Committee in which Senators were hospitable in every respect and in which he made clear he would obtain arms elsewhere if U.S. unable meet Iran's needs. His meetings and dinner with American businessmen gave him opportunity describe Iran's economic progress and goals, and he received warm response, some proposals and considerable adulation from businessmen whose firms already operating in Iran.

3.   Talks with U.S. officials involved no negotiations but were thorough exchanges of views on matters of common concern in the world and on domestic goals, problems and achievements of both countries. Shah raised question of training for jet pilots and received assurance his needs would be met. Joint press release following second meeting with President included statement that two countries will cooperate in studying development of Iranian water resources. In response to suggestion by Secretary Rusk, Shah indicated he would look into establishing fellowships for American students in Iranian universities.

4.   Press coverage of visit included especially thorough reports on arrival and White House dinner. Other aspects highlighted were Shah's interest in Iran-U.S. military relationship, Shah's views on Middle East situation and student demonstrations.

5.   Student demonstrations, which resulted in some scuffling with police and a few arrests, involved at different times number of students varying between 10 and 50 and some anti-Shah and anti-CIA placards and leaflets. Demonstrators were kept well away from Shah except on couple of occasions when they managed to throw leaflets at his caravan. Shah and his party took demonstrations in stride and they certainly did not mar success of visit in any way despite tendency of press to give them more attention than they deserved.

Rusk

238. Memorandum From the Assistant Secretary of Defense for International Security Affairs (Warnke) to Secretary of Defense McNamara[1]

I–11962/67   Washington, October 4, 1967.

SUBJECT

Soviet Arms for Iran and the U.S. Military Advisory Role

I have just approved the broadening of ARMISH/MAAG Iran's role to include advising the Iranian ground forces on the organization, deployment, doctrine and use of anti-aircraft guns recently purchased from the U.S.S.R. The Shah requested such advice earlier this month, and the Country Team, Stricom and State have strongly endorsed the move as a way to minimize the Soviet presence and influence in Iran. Should additional U.S. personnel be required to discharge these new responsibilities, the Iranians are prepared to underwrite the cost of their services.

We plan to inform selected Congressional leaders of this program and the rationale for its adoption at an appropriate time.

Paul C. Warnke

---

[1] Source: Washington National Records Center, RG 330, OASD Files: FRC 72 A 2468, Iran 091.3 MAAG, 4 Oct 67. Confidential.

239. Research Memorandum From the Director of the Bureau of Intelligence and Research (Hughes) to Secretary of State Rusk[1]

RNA–46   Washington, October 9, 1967.

SUBJECT

Iran Designates a Regency Council and Plans a Coronation

By constitutional amendment Iran has provided for a Regency Council to assist the Crown Prince should he succeed to the throne before he is 20. Coronation of the Shah and Empress Farah will take place on October 26. This paper takes a brief look at the history of the Pahlavi Dynasty and analyzes the succession arrangements as they now stand.

Abstract

Reza Shah the Great was crowned the first King of the Pahlavi Dynasty in 1926 and remained on the throne for 15 years until the British forced him into exile and his son Mohamed Reza became Shah. The formal coronation has never taken place, although the present Shah has ruled for just over 26 years. His first two marriages produced no male heir, but a son was born to the Shah and Queen Farah in 1960. Although succession was thus assured, the Shah did not see fit to provide for a Regency Council until he had stabilized the monarch's position and had found a trusted person who could serve as Regent without constituting at the same time a potential rival. Empress Farah's warm personality has proved a definite asset to the Shah's social modernization program, particularly in regard to women's rights, and for the last year she has filled an increasingly official role during various trips inside Iran. On September 7 a Constituent Assembly approved changes in the Iranian Constitution which provide that she will serve as Regent for the Crown Prince in case he assumes the throne before he is 20. The Shah will crown himself and then Empress Farah in splendid ceremony on October 26, his birthday, with Crown Prince Reza Cyrus Ali looking on in implicit emphasis of the planned continuation of the Pahlavi Dynasty.

[Here follows the body of the paper.]

---

[1] Source: Department of State, Central Files, POL 15–1 IRAN. Confidential.

240. Memorandum of Conversation[1]

Washington, November 1, 1967.

SUBJECT

Iranian Oil

PARTICIPANTS

Hushang Ansary, Ambassador of Iran
Anthony Solomon, Assistant Secretary for Economic Affairs
Walter McClelland, NEA/IRN
James Akins, E/FSE

After greetings Mr. Solomon opened by saying our long-standing friendship with Iran made it possible to discuss problems which arise between us in a completely frank manner (the Ambassador concurred) and frankly, the Iranian requests to the U.S. Government both here and in Tehran to insure greatly increased petroleum exports from Iran had caused us considerable difficulty. The Department and the U.S. Government had considerable sympathy for Iran's aspirations and great admiration for its plans for development but this did not mean we were able to translate this sympathy and admiration into pressures on the American companies in the Consortium to comply with the Iranian wishes.

Mr. Solomon said that there should be no confusion about the relationship between American companies operating abroad and the Department of State. We give advice to companies before they go into a country, if they ask for it; we especially want our views known in cases where the companies ask for U.S. Government assistance. But once a company is in a country it is on its own. There are certainly some disadvantages to this but on balance we believe that they are far outweighed by the advantages in our free system where companies act according to their commercial interests rather than in following instruction from the U.S. Government. The host countries can therefore look on local branches of American firms as good citizens, not as tools of U.S. foreign policy.

It is very important to recognize both the very limited nature of U.S. influence over private firms and the reluctance, or even inability of the U.S. Government to set commercial policies of these firms abroad. Venezuela for example has tried for eight years to get special consideration for its oil exports. While the case is not comparable to the Iranian requests

---

[1] Source: Department of State, Central Files, PET 6 IRAN. Confidential. Drafted by Akins on November 3.

there are some similarities. Venezuela is one of our best friends in the Hemisphere and we have a common problem with Castro but nonetheless, we have consistently refused to permit these important political factors to influence our purely commercial policy toward Venezuelan oil.

If the State Department should try to influence companies to favor Iran or any other country, the reaction from companies operating elsewhere and from Congress would be immediate and hostile. We can tell the American companies in the Consortium of the Iranian approaches to us and we can give them our views on the importance of Iran, as we have done repeatedly, but in spite of our warm friendship for Iran we cannot do more and Iran should not think that these mild interventions will outweigh the companies' own purely commercial interests.

There are many complex factors, which the companies have to consider. The comparative cost of oil in Iran and elsewhere is extremely important. And all of the American companies have interests in other oil producing countries which must be protected. (Incidentally it seems to us that it is in the interest of both Iran and the United States for such moderate Arab nations in the area as Kuwait and Saudi Arabia to be strengthened.)

We are very interested in the Consortium activities and note with pleasure that it has shown its willingness to see that Iran gets its fair share of the Middle East offtake, but given the vagaries of the oil industry, it is impossible to make long-term commitments for offtake from Iran for the next five years or even through 1970.

We can also understand why the companies in the Consortium are disturbed by the Iranian desire to revise or even discard the 1966 offtake agreement only ten months after it had been concluded to the apparent satisfaction of all parties. As the Ambassador himself has noted, the continuing Iranian pressure on the Consortium to use all production facilities to their capacity has caused it to be reluctant to enlarge facilities until they are actually needed. This does not seem in the interest of anyone, as surplus capacity in Iran is necessary if Iran is to increase production rapidly during any future oil crisis.

Finally, the Consortium has a vast marketing network which is extremely important to Iran especially during times of a surplus of world oil production. We would hope that the amicable relationship between the Consortium and the Government of Iran, which has proven so profitable to Iran, would continue uninterrupted.

The Ambassador said the points were well made but he feared that the companies were ignoring other important considerations. Iran believes that its special position warrants special treatment; Iran has a development program which increases the wealth and the stability of Iran and thereby benefits the West and the Western oil companies. Iran is particularly disturbed at the increase in production of certain small Arab countries who are given far more money than they can use and who then give or lend this surplus capital to men like Nasser. The Iranians consider it ironic that the Western oil companies are willing to increase production and therefore royalties and taxes to these small countries which are, quite directly, financing a man who is committed to their destruction and to wiping out all Western influence in the Middle East. Such a policy can only aggravate the instability of the area. Iran believes that there is more than short-term economic profit to be considered and the oil companies should look once again at what Iran is doing with its income and compare it with actions of the small Arab countries.

Mr. Solomon said U.S. has investments abroad valued at about $71 billion. The world-wide investment in oil is of course important but it is only a minority of the total. American companies operating abroad act according to their own economic interests as they see them and none serves as a tool of the U.S. Government. Mr. Solomon then said that the American oil companies have important investments in the small Arab countries the Ambassador referred to and if any of the local rulers thought that the American parent companies were shifting their emphasis from the Arab world to Iran—particularly if they suspected it was at U.S. Government instigation—they would certainly retaliate against the American firms.

We must also be aware of the danger that general, undiscriminating pressure frequently results in a reaction quite the opposite from that which is intended.

The Ambassador concluded by saying that it was clear that the Consortium could not make firm commitments for the next five years; Iran had not asked for this but only for an agreement in principle to increase production. The next development plan, starting in March of 1986, is based on a large income from the exploitation of oil and Iran must have this money. The problems might start even before the new development plan; the Ambassador had just been informed that because the increase in oil earnings was less than expected, Iran would probably have deficit of $110 million this year.

A short discussion of Iran's economic development followed.

The Ambassador said Iran had a 9.5 percent growth in GNP last year and expected to have 11 percent this year—and all with a price inflation of only 0.5%. Mr. Solomon commented that oil had made all this possible. The Ambassador agreed, said that income from oil now runs about $700 million per year and provides about 70–75% of Iran's foreign exchange earnings. But this does not mean that more money is not needed.

After leaving Mr. Solomon's office, Ambassador Ansary commented on Mr. Solomon's lucid presentation of the U.S. position and said it was important that it be understood in Tehran. While it is possible to explain some things in letters or telegrams some of the more subtle points may be lost. He said he thought he should return to Tehran to explain the U.S. position directly to his government before the Iranian position hardens to the point where retreat might be impossible.

---

241.   Telegram From the Embassy in Iran to the Department of State[1]

Tehran, November 3, 1967, 1015Z.

1965. 1. Today's Wireless Bulletin reports Senate–House conferees have finally reached agreement on foreign aid legislation. Report says conferees agreed Defense Department's overseas arms sales program should end next June 30.

2.   As Dept knows, military credit sales issue is key factor in our current relationship with Iran. President promised Shah in August that administration continues desire supply equipment to Iran but definitive determination depended on Congressional deliberations then taking place.

3.   Since my return, Shah has three times stated he is awaiting conclusion of Congressional deliberations. He made clear his strong desire to maintain American orientation his military establishment but if there is uncertainty he will purchase elsewhere.

4.   Having provided Iran with most of its military establishment via grant aid, Shah cannot understand USG's unwillingness to provide arms via credit sales now that Iran is in position to pay. Acquiring arms from elsewhere increases costs and decreases efficiency of Iran's military establishment. Thus Shah's incomprehension tends toward resentment.

5.   Realize it may be difficult to sort out where conference committee agreement leaves us as far as arms sales to Iran are concerned. However, we need to have as soon as possible position to take with Shah.

6.   Was there any hope that by June 30, 1968 other avenues might be devised which would permit credit sales to Iran on terms not too unattractive? Would language of legislation permit credit sales to Iran if we determine that Iran is not an underdeveloped country, a determination

---

[1] Source: Department of State, Central Files, DEF 19–8 US–IRAN. Confidential; Priority. Repeated to CINCMEAFSA/CINCSTRIKE.

USG has already made as far as imposing interest equalization tax is concerned? Are there avenues other than that which Congress is terminating as of June 30, 1968 which might be opened for maintaining our relationship with Iran?

7. Needless to say, our first reaction here is that Congress has dealt a crippling blow to our relations with Iran. Tragically, it comes at a time when after Shah's Washington visit and Iran's own remarkable progress relations between our two countries are at a high. Blow also comes at time when it seems to us USG should be preserving friendships with countries like Iran. Aside from friendship, we have at stake number of facilities vital to our national security.

8. Since this is number one problem for Iran and since Shah raised it with President, Dept should not rule out possibility of direct message from President to Shah explaining state of play. Hopefully message could contain some assurance that all hope is not lost for continuing mutually beneficial military cooperation between our two countries.

Meyer

---

242. Letter From the Shah of Iran to President Johnson[1]

Tehran, November 15, 1967.

Dear Mr. President,

It is now almost three months since I had the pleasure of visiting you and your country, and I am still under the very vivid impression of your hospitality and your warm and friendly reception. I also have the best recollection of our talks and I am happy to witness the very close bonds of friendship, understanding and mutual good will which exist between our two countries.

As you know, Mr. President, we are planning for the next five years a development program, starting in March, 1968, which will bring further

---

[1] Source: Johnson Library, National Security File, Special Head of State Correspondence File, Iran, 9/1/67–12/31/67. No classification marking. The letter was delivered to the Department of State by the Iranian Embassy on November 21, according to telegram 74044 to Tehran, November 23, which transmitted the text. (Department of State, Central Files, AID (US) IRAN)

great progress in our economic life. We hope to achieve an annual nine percent increase in our Gross National Product, and we would be delighted to welcome any American firms or private individual participation in our projects, especially in the fields of petrochemicals and agriculture. I remember with pleasure having discussed with you the further development of our agriculture and the great interest you showed in the possibilities in this domain.

This would allow us to develop the agricultural resources of our country more fully, and to provide sufficient fertilizers for the production of more food and thus contribute to forestall and eliminate the danger of hunger and famine, which is one of the key problems threatening the world at large today.

We are also waiting for the America team to study water conservation, and the desalination plan, in Iran, which constitute an essential part of our development programme.

We very much expect the American Oil Companies to try to export the maximum oil they can from our country, with the full knowledge that the stability of Iran helps the maintenance of stability in the whole area, which, in turn, guarantees their oil exports from the other countries in this region as well. Your personal interest in this respect, Mr. President, would be greatly appreciated by us.

As for our military needs, we see modern, and sometimes very sophisticated weapons, pouring into some of our neighbouring countries, which compels us to take appropriate military preparedness measures. We have revised the organization of our armed forces and set ourselves a new five year plan. Since 1964 we have entered into two credit agreements with your country, each for two hundred million dollars, and also obtained credits for approximately three hundred million dollars from other sources. A rough estimate of the requirements over the next five years of military equipment for carrying out the new plan for our armed forces organization is in the order of 800 million dollars.

Although our Air Force, as planned for the future, is still weak in the number of aircraft, we hope that by getting the best and most modern equipment, and by having good and efficient pilots and maintenance, it would carry out the very heavy duty imposed upon it.

I wish the day will come when all of us will only have to think of building schools, hospitals, and homes for old people, and other essentials of civilization. We are certainly working towards that end; but before that day comes we have no other choice but to guarantee the security and independence of our sacred land and nation.

Such are the needs of my country. We would like to buy our needs in your country if your Government could offer the necessary credit arrangements.

I would be most grateful, Mr. President, if you would provide all we need, or at least tell us what we can expect, as we must, in the cases mentioned above, put in our orders now.

Considering the encouraging results already obtained in all branches of our economy, I lay great store in this our next five year development plan, which has been carefully drawn up in order to raise further the standard of living of the individual in my country.

I still recall with pleasure the kind words you uttered, in your address of welcome during my recent visit to Washington, concerning the progress that we, in Iran, have achieved in terms of economic prosperity. It is our firm intention to strive further in this respect.

Hoping, Mr. President, that you will give these matters your considerate attention, I express to you my heartfelt good wishes for your welfare and happiness, and success in your noble task. I seize this opportunity to convey, on behalf of the Empress and myself, our kindest regards to Mrs. Johnson.

Sincerely,

M.R. Pahlavi

---

243. Memorandum From the President's Special Assistant (Rostow) to President Johnson[1]

Washington, November 15, 1967.

SUBJECT

Message to the Shah

Governor Harriman will stop off to see the Shah in connection with his visit to Pakistan to help dedicate the Mangla Dam. Since there has been a minor misunderstanding with the Shah over the proposal for talks on Vietnam he mentioned during his visit here, we felt it would be useful to make a special point of the fact that Governor Harriman is coming on your behalf. While we don't think his idea is a starter, we don't

---

[1] Source: Johnson Library, National Security File, Special Head of State Correspondence File, 9/1/67–12/31/67. Secret; Exdis.

want to be the ones to kill it; he might as well find out for himself how tough this game is.

The following message should serve that purpose:

Your Imperial Majesty:

I am very pleased that you are able to receive Governor Harriman in Tehran on November 22. His visit will come just three months after our pleasant and useful talks here, and I look forward to hearing his report when he returns. I have asked the Governor to inform you fully of our views and the present possibilities for bringing about a peaceful solution in Vietnam. Once again, I want you to know how much we value your constructive position on this as on so many other international problems.

Sincerely,

Walt

Approve[2]

Disapprove

---

[2] This option is checked. Telegram 70589 to Tehran, November 17, transmitted the message to the Embassy for delivery to the Shah. (Department of State, Central Files, POL 7 US/HARRIMAN)

---

244.   Memorandum From the Chief of the Near East and South Asia Division of the Plans Directorate, Central Intelligence Agency (Critchfield) to Director of Central Intelligence Helms[1]

Washington, November 16, 1967.

SUBJECT

Conversation with the Shah on 16 November 1967

1.   This memorandum is *for your information*.

2.   A fortnight after his coronation, the Shah was in a relaxed but sober mood reflecting confidence in his domestic program, his role as a

---

[1] Source: Central Intelligence Agency: Job 80–R 01580R, DCI Files, 10/209—Middle East Crisis. Secret. Sent via the Deputy Director for Plans. Attached to a December 5 note from Helms to the President that reads: "I thought you would be interested to read the highlights of a conversation which one of our senior officers recently had with the Shah of Iran. This officer deals with the Shah in the context of our intelligence assets located in Iran."

leader in the Middle East and his relations with the Great Powers—a confidence mixed with concern and some anxiety about obvious elements in the Middle East situation which continue to threaten his own ambitions for the area.

3.   Although priorities in Iranian foreign policy now rest on his decision to develop regional strengths that will give the Middle East nations a common capability to contain and live with the threat of Soviet pressures, his policy rests on the premise that his special and primary relationship with the United States can be preserved a few years more. Strengthened relations with Pakistan and Turkey remain the basis of his regional policy; as CENTO fades, other military and economic arrangements in which the US and the UK play no direct role are expanding. He has found it necessary to give Ayub "virtually an ultimatum" to get his foreign affairs in order; he sees Pakistan gradually turning more to the West, placing more confidence on regional security arrangements, being less dependent on the Great Powers and emphasizing Islamic rather than radical Afro-Asian associations.

4.   The Shah's relations with the Arab-Israel world remain complicated. In the Cold War context his sympathies lie entirely with Israel; the defeat of the radical Arabs in June dramatically served Iran's interest. [4-1/2 lines of source text not declassified] Denial of the Persian Gulf, the Arabian Peninsula and the lower end of the Red Sea Basin to the Soviet Union and the radical Arabs is the strategic goal that constitutes the basis for this relationship. Arms captured by the Israelis in June are now finding their way via Iran into friendly Arab hands in the Yemen. The expansion of the Soviet fleet in the Mediterranean, the appearance of "Red Beret Russian Marines" and the military implications of the *Elath* sinking were all on the [1-1/2 lines of source text not declassified] agenda.

5.   Overtly, the Shah continues to associate Iran with the Arab, but more particularly the Islamic, cause in the context of the Arab-Israel conflict. He told me that during April 1967 he had advised Hussein to give vigorous armed response to any repetition by Israel of the 13 November 1966 raid on Samu in Jordan's West Bank; this action was essential, in the Shah's view, to Hussein's survival. Since the war, the Israelis have approached the Shah seeking his assistance in mediation efforts with Jordan; the Shah declined because he did not feel that Hussein and moderate forces in Jordan could survive reaction in the Arab world to a unilateral Jordan role. While the Shah has reservations about Hussein's judgement, he argues that Hussein's survival is vital to Iranian and American interests.

6.   The Shah is relaxed about the expansion of French influence in Middle East oil and arms. The Shah takes a positive view of the prospect of some standardization of aircraft—Mirage in the short run—in Pakistan, Jordan, Saudi Arabia and possibly other Arab countries. However,

he is emphatic in his view that the Turkish and Iranian Air Forces must be based on US equipment and doctrine. This was one of two points raised by the Shah in comparatively strong language. The other dealt with the attacks on the President concerning his Vietnam policy.

7. We had examined the likelihood that Moscow, sooner or later, would have to take a hard look at Khrushchev's policy of providing armed support for "just wars of national liberation". In four areas of the world—Southeast Asia, the Arab Near East, Africa and the Western Hemisphere, the Soviets had gained no favorable decision, had suffered several disasters and had seen the price of the game rising steadily. I had said that I thought the time for a Soviet reappraisal of Khrushchev's policy might come after President Johnson was re-elected. A decision by the Soviets to write off the Vietnam War—following the disaster which struck them in the Middle East in June 1967—could, I said, mark the turning point in Soviet policy. In this case, President Johnson would emerge in history as "one of our greatest Presidents". With some vigor the Shah interrupted and corrected my statement—"he will emerge as the greatest President of the United States; the toughness and courage demonstrated by him in sticking to his position when under attack from all those in the US and abroad who oppose his Vietnam policy is inspiring to all of us who know that he is right".

8. The Shah feels that trade with and aid from the Soviet Union is entirely compatible with his basic policy of seeking to build a strong Middle East bloc of nations which will have normal relations with the industrially developed powers, including Russia and all of Europe. He seems confident that a combination of economic and social progress in Iran and an effective and sharply oriented intelligence and security effort keeping track of the Soviets in Iran will limit the dangers of expanding trade and relations with the Soviets to a tolerable level. In this task, he desires to retain his special relationship with the United States. I assured him that in intelligence matters, the United States benefits as much as if not more than Iran in this close cooperation.

9. I saw the Shah alone; the foregoing represents only the highlights of a lengthy conversation.

James H. Critchfield[2]

---

[2] Signed and initialed for Critchfield in an unidentified hand.

245.   Briefing Memorandum From the Deputy Assistant Secretary of State for Near Eastern and South Asian Affairs (Rockwell) to the Ambassador at Large (Harriman)[1]

Washington, November 17, 1967.

SUBJECT

Your Meeting with the Shah on November 22, 1967

The principal matters affecting our bilateral relations with Iran which are likely to arise during your meeting with the Shah are our military credit program, oil, and private American investment in Iran. The following are talking points on these subjects:

1. Military Credit Program (Tab A)[2]

a.   Although the Congressional situation is not yet entirely clear, we intend to do all we can to meet our military credit commitments to Iran and are continuing to attempt to persuade the Congress of the importance of our making military credits available to Iran.

b.   Congressional action so far would probably permit us to make available the next $50 million credit tranche, subject to the usual joint annual economic review.

c.   For the future, we are first going to have to feel our way with Congress during an election year. In this process this Administration like its four predecessors will remain dedicated to the principle of collective security for the free nations of the world. As we proceed, we ask for patience and understanding from our friends and partners in this effort.

2. Oil (Tab B)

a.   The U.S. Government cannot dictate the commercial policy of private American firms.

b.   The American companies of the Consortium have always taken their commitments to the GOI seriously and we have every reason to believe that they will see that Iran gets its fair share of the Middle East increase in production. They have important interests in other countries of the area, and they and we believe that the moderate Arab countries deserve support.

c.   We hope that Iran will continue to deal with the oil companies within its policy of reasonableness that has paid such high dividends to the GOI in the past.

---

[1] Source: Department of State, S/S Conference Files: Lot 68 D 453, Gov. Harriman's Trip, Nov. 1967, Vol. VI, Briefing Book. Secret. No drafting information appears on the source text.

[2] Attached but not printed.

3. Investment (Tab C)

a. We very much appreciate the Shah's kindness to Messrs. Ball, McCloy and Connor during the Coronation.

b. We are pleased to note the Shah's continued interest in obtaining American investment and hope that the steps being taken by the Development and Resources Corporation and by such people as Mr. Ball will lead to the desired results. We will continue to do all we can to assist such efforts.

---

246. Telegram From the Embassy in Iran to the Department of State[1]

Tehran, November 20, 1967, 1330Z.

2210. Augmentation of Soviet-Iranian Arms Deal.

1. From Iranian General Staff, ARMISH/MAAG Chief Jablonsky has received confirmation that Iranians have agreed to 40 million ruble extension of Soviet-Iranian arms deal. Equipment purchased consists of 2200 Zil jeeps for gendarmerie, 200 wheeled APCs, 300 track APCs, 40 tank transporters and five mobile maintenance shops. In training field, about dozen Iranians will go to USSR for brief period to learn how to man mobile maintenance shops.

2. While there was a certain amount of inevitability in this development, given much-publicized Congressional curtailing of US arms sales and attractiveness of getting Soviet equipment "for nothing," i.e. in exchange for Iranian natural gas until now flared, haste with which Iranians have moved is disturbing. As recently as October 19, Shah gave impression (Tehran 1735)[2] that significant purchases elsewhere were being held in abeyance pending the outcome of Congressional deliberations.

3. Via Jablonsky–Toufanian channel, we have already given indication that timing of this new procurement from Soviets can only multiply problems which USG has been having with Congress on whole question

---

[1] Source: Department of State, Central Files, DEF 19–6 USSR–IRAN. Secret; Priority; Exdis. Repeated to CINCSTRIKE/USCINCMEAFSA and Moscow.

[2] Dated October 19. (Ibid., DEF 19–8 US–IRAN)

of military programs abroad. I am seeing Alam tomorrow and speaking more in sorrow than anger I intend to stress how difficult it is to understand why Iran would take such inopportune action when there really no urgency for such add-on military equipment from Soviets. I intend also to note unfortunate damage this causes Shah's image which has reached an all-time high in US pursuant to HIM's recent visit. I will also note disappointment and trouble this causes for those who have been Shah's and Iran's closest friends.

4.   In this post-coronation period, there is certain amount of intoxication apparent in Iranian attitude. Therefore, in taking line mentioned in foregoing para we must be careful to avoid implying Iran is not fully sovereign, etc. Furthermore, we see little chance of deal being recalled and, therefore, must consider it within framework of our actual future relationship with Iran, including specifically limitations on our capability for maintaining special position we previously enjoyed in supplying military equipment.

5.   It is our hope that foregoing attitude will commend itself to our Washington colleagues. This subject may or may not arise during Governor Harriman's forthcoming visit but if it does the above line would seem to us to be most appropriate.[3]

6.   As Dept will recall, when first Soviet-Iranian arms deal was negotiated, news which we had received in confidence from Iranians appeared short time later on front page of *New York Times*. It is our earnest hope that similar leakage will not occur this time. It is for that reason that this telegram is being slugged Exdis.

Meyer

---

[3] Telegram 72956 to Tehran, November 22, concurred with the Embassy attitude expressed in telegram 2210 and approved use of this line if the subject arose during Harriman's visit. (Ibid.)

247. Telegram From the Embassy in Iran to the Department of State[1]

Tehran, November 21, 1967, 1240Z.

2223. Following letter addressed to Secretary of State from Prime Minister may be used if Secretary wishes, at lunch planned November 29 mark close-out of AID–Iran. We not aware if Ambassador Ansary has received copy of letter but Dept. might wish consider consulting with him concerning its use.

"The official termination of the American AID programme in Iran affords me this welcome opportunity to extend to you, along with my very warm personal regards, the sincere thanks and appreciation of the Iranian people.

"The period through which we have been the grateful recipients of your aid stands as an example of the highly successful and cordial cooperation which has always characterized the enriching association of Iran with your great country.

"Today, as we stand on the threshold of our fourth economic development plan, we wish to strengthen our productive economic and commercial relations with the United States. Iran's fourth plan will offer new opportunities to your private sector to participate in the economic progress which we can justifiably expect. American private investors, with their great technical resources and managerial effectiveness, can do much to contribute to our self-sustaining economic development. I hope you will extend a cordial invitation to the American private sector to examine carefully the opportunities which Iran offers and to explore further cooperative ventures mutually beneficial to both countries."

We plan release letter here only as part of story of phase-out ceremonies in Washington.

Meyer

---

[1] Source: Department of State, Central Files, AID (US) IRAN. Limited Official Use.

248.   Telegram From the Embassy in Iran to the Department of State[1]

Tehran, November 22, 1967, 1535Z.

2250. Iranian Military Procurement.

1.   During conversation with Harriman 22nd, Shah said he is writing letter to President re number subjects such as oil, American investment in Iran, and Iran's desire to continue military procurement from the United States. He described letter as follow-up to intimate discussions held with President in August.

2.   Re military, Harriman indicated legislative situation is still murky. He said we hope that we may be able to proceed with next $50 million tranche but what will happen after next June 30 is "in the lap of the gods."

3.   Shah said just as Iran is projecting five-year economic program it is also planning five-year military program. Question is, therefore, important whether US will be in position to continue military supplying during that period. He noted since 1964 he has purchased $400 million from US (including two tranches still not negotiated) and $300 [million] elsewhere. Program over upcoming five-year period, he noted, is being planned at expenditure rate less than past three-year span. Harriman stressed importance of giving priority to economic development.

4.   Once again Shah emphasized his unqualified preference to maintaining relationship with US in military field. Above all, he wants to keep air force American oriented.

5.   Key question, Shah said, is procurement of tanks. He would like additional M–60's and Sheridans so that his total tank force eventually will reach just over one thousand. When challenged re need for so many tanks, Shah said his military is emphasizing mobility, will in fact have fewer divisions, and in any case his goal is merely to place Iran "in balance" with its neighbors. He noted proposed tank complement is only three-fourths what Turks have.

6.   If US unable to supply Sheridans, Shah said he will seek British tanks, i.e. Vickers. He was obviously annoyed that his hopes for tank factory in Iran to supply Pakistan, Saudi Arabia and other countries has fallen through. His impression is that British are to build Vickers factory in Pakistan, but I expressed doubt such deal been consummated. Shah showed some interest in possibility up-grading M–47 tanks but was totally unimpressed with seven-ton British CVRT tanks (Tehran 2193),[2] primarily because he wants tanks with 105 mm guns.

---

[1]   Source: Department of State, Central Files, POL 7 US/HARRIMAN. Secret; Limdis. Repeated to London, Rawalpindi, and CINCSTRIKE/USCINCMEAFSA.

[2]   Dated November 19. (Ibid., DEF 12–5 IRAN)

7. For first time, Shah mentioned possibility of Soviet tanks, if appropriate deal cannot be made with US, British or other Western countries. Later when asked whether Soviets have quoted any tank prices, Shah answered in negative and gave as reason that Iranians have deliberately avoided encouraging Soviets in this sphere. After some thought, he added that GOI would hesitate long time before it would take such dramatic step.

8. To Harriman's question whether any M–47 tanks have gone from Iran to Pakistan, Shah responded negatively but indicated Iran willing to sell up to 100 but this would depend on USG approval.

Meyer

249. Telegram From the Embassy in Iran to the Department of State[1]

Tehran, November 26, 1967, 1515Z.

2248. Russia and Mideast.

1. During course of nearly three-hour discussion with Shah 22nd, Governor Harriman inquired re state of Iran–USSR relations. Shah said as long as Soviets behave themselves relations will continue good. He revealed Kosygin will be visiting Iran, probably in January.

2. Shah said when his arms purchaser General Toufanian was in USSR Soviets fell all over themselves to be gracious. They openly declared that Iranians were with them "in the front trenches," i.e. threatened by ChiComs. To Harriman's request re quality Soviet military equipment, Shah said trucks are satisfactory although they burn more gas than American trucks and some of them have been having trouble with jammed pistons.

3. Re Mideast generally, Harriman expressed view that while there are areas where US–USSR cooperation is feasible, e.g. non-proliferation and China, there are other areas such as Mideast where this not true.

---

[1] Source: Department of State, Central Files, POL 7 US/HARRIMAN. Secret. Repeated to Amman, Jidda, Kuwait, London, Moscow, USUN, and CINCSTRIKE/USCINC-MEAFSA.

Shah stressed view Soviets intent on trouble-making and keeping Mideast pot boiling. This clear from their rearmament of radical Arab states.

4. This afforded Shah opportunity harp on theme that Soviet objectives being facilitated by moderate Arab states who are oil producers, i.e. Saudi Arabia and Kuwait, keeping Nasser afloat via financial subsidies. Asked whether these are dependable sources of UAR revenue, Shah said if Nasser cannot get hostage money from Saudi Arabia and Kuwait he will intensify his endeavors to "swallow them up."

5. Harriman stressed importance of securing passage of meaningful resolution at UNSC, e.g. British resolution, which could serve as base for stabilizing Mideast situation. Three times during conversation, Harriman urged Shah to impress on King Faisal need for giving solid support to moderate course which King Hussein is pursuing.

6. Shah noted he has consistently encouraged King Hussein as well as Saudis to follow moderate course since hostilities against Israel are highly counter-productive.

7. In Shah's view Faisal is progressive leader worthy of encouragement and support even though Saudi Kingdom is still "archaic." Saudi-Iranian relations are good, except for median line problem in Persian Gulf. Re this issue, Shah outlined Iranian position in terms similar to those reported in A–266[2] (following). He expressed hope that two countries and two American oil companies could work out some sort of joint venture solution.

8. Asked by Harrison re British MinState Robert's' recent visit, Shah said affirmation that British will stay in Gulf area was welcome. At same time, he said, clearly British cannot remain there permanently. For this reason, Iran is determined to continue to build up its own military strength so that it will be "in balance" with that of other states in area. It also accounts for Iran's desire to develop closer and cooperative relationships with various Gulf riparian states.

Meyer

---

[2] Dated November 22. (Ibid., POL 32 IRAN–SAUD)

250.   Letter From President Johnson to the Shah of Iran[1]

Washington, November 28, 1967.

Your Imperial Majesty:

This is to let you know that I have received and read with interest your letter of November 15.[2] I am considering the points you raised and will respond soon.

I wish also to add a personal word to my formal statement for the ceremonies here this week marking the closing of our AID mission in Tehran.[3] I am sure from our talks together you know how highly I respect the work you and your people are doing in the development of your nation. Many times—as I face frustrating and difficult problems in various parts of the world—I am heartened to remember what Iran has accomplished under your great leadership. And I would underscore my hope that the end of our AID program will be the beginning of a new era of cooperation and partnership between our countries.

I am grateful for the close relationship that exists between ourselves and between Iran and the United States, and I look forward to continuing and strengthening this relationship.

Mrs. Johnson joins me in sending warmest wishes to you and to the Empress.

Sincerely,

Lyndon B. Johnson

---

[1] Source: Johnson Library, National Security File, Special Head of State Correspondence File, Iran, 9/1/67–12/31/67. No classification marking. Telegram 76981 to Tehran, November 30, transmitted the text of the letter for delivery to the Shah. (Department of State, Central Files, AID (US) IRAN)

[2] Document 242.

[3] For text of statements on November 29 by Secretary Rusk and President Johnson marking the termination of the U.S. AID mission in Iran, see Department of State *Bulletin*, December 18, 1967, pp. 825–827.

251.   Telegram From the Embassy in Iran to the Department of State[1]

Tehran, December 5, 1967, 1410Z.

2410. New Era in US–Iran Relations.

1. Referring to four major economic projects which Shah had inaugurated preceding two days in Khuzistan, I began 90-minute audience with him 5th by suggesting this experience was for me dramatic example of new partnership between US and Iran which President had in mind when issuing statement re conclusion of AID program in Iran. I noted all four projects have some American private sector participation. At same time they fully Iranian in character and foreign contribution is mix of several nationalities.

2. Shah was obviously exhilarated by launching above-mentioned projects. In characteristic mood he said Iran would go on to greater heights in economic development. Noting that natural gas has 2700 possible derivatives, including even aspirin tablets, Shah said petrochemical field is one area where Iran can achieve large-scale success. He looks particularly to Americans who have leadership in petrochemicals to be helpful. He also referred to special relationship with US which he wishes to maintain in desalinization field.

3. There followed philosophical discussion of factors which have caused Iranian spectacular success, e.g. oil income and its wise use, stability stemming from cultural tradition of monarchy, Iran's ability to adjust to changing times and to pick up good points from various societies. When subject of strong leadership was mentioned, Shah quickly described this as an ingredient temporary in nature. He said he looks forward to day not too far distant when Iran will also take off in institutionalized representative government.

4. Referring again to USAID termination celebration on November 30, I noted fine publicity this received in US and my impression that broader segment of American public opinion as well as President and USG grateful that Iran is success story of type envisaged when President Truman began Point Four Program. I said I felt appreciation is all the greater because number of such examples is too few. Shah expressed gratitude for President's kind words.

Meyer

---

[1] Source: Department of State, Central Files, POL IRAN–US. Confidential. Repeated to CINCSTRIKE/USCINCMEAFSA.

252. Action Memorandum From the Assistant Secretary of State for Economic Affairs (Solomon) to the Under Secretary of State for Political Affairs (Rostow)[1]

Washington, December 11, 1967.

SUBJECT

Status of Iranian-Consortium Negotiations

The Consortium maintains that the "negotiations" with Iran ended in agreement among all parties in December, 1966, i.e. there would be an 11 percent increase in offtake in 1967 and 1968. Because of the Middle East crisis, Iranian production in 1967 will actually be over 20 percent above 1966 levels. Although the Consortium emphasizes it is not obligated by the agreement to give any further increase in 1968, it has just assured Iran of an increase in offtake of almost 9 percent over the high 1967 levels.

The Iranians have told the Consortium that this proposal for 1968 is not satisfactory. They say Iran must have $6 billion from oil from now through the end of the fourth development plan in March 1973. (Current production plans and steady growth of about 10 percent per year would give Iran only about $4.5 billion during this period.) The obvious way to get this income would be through increased production but increased payments per barrel of oil or company investment in Iran might also be satisfactory to the GOI.

The Iranians are particularly disturbed by the Consortium over-lift provisions and believe that if they were changed the total offtake from Iran would increase substantially. Last year I recommended to the American participants, through Mr. Henry Moses of Mobil Oil, that they should agree to a liberalization of the Consortium's over-lift arrangements. The Consortium did alter those arrangements. Consortium companies may now over-lift up to 15 percent of their Annual Programmed Quantity—APQ—share at a price halfway between cost and posted price. Previously any volume above the APQ was to be over-lifted at full posted price. But it is clear from our traffic on this problem that the Iranians since last year have become fully informed as to the terms of the over-lift in both Iran and Saudi Arabia and they have demanded specifically that the Consortium adopt a system at least as favorable as the Aramco system. Aramco companies can over-lift as much as they want above the amount their shareholding in Aramco would entitle them to

---

[1] Source: Department of State, Central Files, PET 6 IRAN. Confidential. Drafted by Akins on December 8 and cleared by Eliot and the Economic Bureau's Director of the Office of Fuels and Energy John G. Oliver.

have at a price equal to cost plus one quarter the difference between cost and posted price.

The companies have explained to us that the Consortium as a whole usually takes only about 93 percent of the APQ—the agreed total offtake for the year—and that the crude short companies (Shell, Mobil, CFP and the Iricon group) are thus able to take 7 percent above their "rightful" share at cost—a more favorable arrangement than in Aramco. It is when they exceed this amount that they pay the halfway price. (N.B.: It is in this case when the comparison with Aramco becomes pertinent.) The Consortium companies say they have been unable to explain this adequately to the Iranians without exposing the method of setting APQ and other Consortium rules and regulations; and this cannot be done without causing great trouble for Consortium. However, the companies have consistently told us and the Iranians that the Aramco system would result in lower offtake for the Consortium as a whole.

The Iranians have also demanded specifically that the 6.5 percent OPEC discount be eliminated. If it were, Iran would get about $0.10 per barrel of oil, and if the discount were completely eliminated by January 1968, Iran would get about $200 million extra in the next five years. Negotiations between Aramco and the Saudi Arabian Government are continuing on this subject; Iran and other OPEC members will get whatever Saudi Arabia succeeds in getting from Aramco.

The Consortium members say they cannot increase offtake from Iran without cutting back production in the Arab world and this cannot be done without provoking a reaction from the Arabs. They have not yet been willing to discuss large scale investment in Iran. However, the final Consortium positions have not been established. Its members are now meeting in London to discuss new proposals to Iran and the Iranians have said they can wait at least until January to hear them.

Proposed Action

1. I would recommend that we tell the American companies in the Consortium that we understand their reluctance to discuss internal Consortium arrangements with the Iranians but point out that the GOI already has the essential details of the over-lift arrangements in Aramco and the Consortium. We could tell the companies our view that this has become an important issue with the Iranians and we believe the Consortium would be well-advised to consider adopting something they could call a "quarter-price" for over-liftings. Even if Iran profited little, a troublesome issue would have been eliminated and the Iranians would no longer be able to claim they were being discriminated against.

2. I would recommend that we urge the companies to be as generous as they can in making their next offer to the Iranians. However, we should avoid making any further specific recommendations at this time.

If it becomes clear that the next Consortium offer will not be acceptable to the Iranians we might have to take a more active role in the talks than we have; but we hope GOI–Consortium relations do not deteriorate to this point. While we probably can never get involved in making specific offtake proposals, we might have to tell the companies sometime that we believe there will be serious problems in Iran if, by 1973, it does not reach the same level of exports as Saudi Arabia or, as a minimum, does not enjoy the same *absolute* annual increase as that country.[2]

3. I would recommend that for the time being we do nothing more with the Iranians than repeating our hopes that the talks will continue and that neither side will take rash steps which might be regretted later.[3]

---

[2] A handwritten notation in the margin of this paragraph reads: "Please double check the facts."

[3] Approved by Rostow on December 13.

---

253.   Memorandum From the President's Special Assistant (Rostow) to President Johnson[1]

Washington, December 19, 1967.

SUBJECT

Reply to Shah's Letter

The Shah wrote you describing his military and economic development programs for the five years beginning next March.[2]

In short, he ticks off his own economic plans and hopes for U.S. private investment much as he outlined them to you in August. He also urges you to lean on our oil companies to increase their liftings from Iran—a perennial request.

The main surprise is the size of his military program—$800 million. We think that must be a bargaining figure.

He wants to know what he can count on from us. All we can say is that we are going ahead with the third and fourth slices ($50 million

---

[1] Source: Johnson Library, National Security File, Special Head of State Correspondence File, Iran, 9/1/67–12/31/67. Secret.

[2] Document 242.

each) under our amended 1964 agreement and beyond that will do all we can but have to see what Congress does.

We've consistently tried to keep the brakes on his military spending, but that's increasingly hard to do with his oil revenues rising as they are.

We've tried to strike a balance in the attached reply[3] between the responsiveness I believe you would want and the limitations imposed by uncertainty over what Congress will allow. Our best leverage now is to ride along with him and inject a word of caution where we can.

Attached is a letter for your signature, if you approve.

Walt

For Reference: In 1964, we signed a $200 million agreement to cover 5 years, FY 1965 through FY 1969. It also provided that grant aid would end in FY 1969. In 1966, we amended that agreement to add another $200 million in sales in four $50 million slices through FY 1970—September 1966, June 1967, June 1968 and June 1969. The last two are those referred to in the attached reply. The Shah hasn't yet defined his new program precisely enough for us to know how it would be related to the present program.

---

[3] Document 254.

---

254.   Letter From President Johnson to the Shah of Iran[1]

Washington, December 19, 1967.

Your Imperial Majesty:

I have now studied carefully your important letter of November 15[2] and want to give you the more detailed reply which I promised in my note of November 30.[3]

First let me say that your visit here was one of the bright spots of the year for me. I warmly appreciate the privilege of talking to a leader who

---

[1] Source: Johnson Library, National Security File, Special Head of State Correspondence File, Iran, 9/1/67–12/31/67. No classification marking.

[2] Document 242.

[3] Document 250.

shares our views and approach to the problems of the world and who understands the heavy burdens which those problems place upon this country.

I also appreciate the cordial reception you gave on November 22 to Governor Harriman who has reported to me on his valuable talk with you. I am glad we can maintain our continuing exchange of thoughts through talks like that as well as by letter.

What you tell me of your new five-year development program is indeed good news. The pace of Iran's development arouses deep admiration everywhere.

I am especially heartened that economic development will continue Iran's major goal. We have worked closely with you in this field. Now with the closing of our aid mission in Iran we look forward to a different, but equally productive, kind of economic cooperation between our two countries. We hope this will include increased participation by private American firms in Iran's development, as you suggest, and we will do what we can to support American investment there.

I am also glad that planning is moving ahead on the water resources study on which we agreed in principle when you were here. I hope this will become another important aspect of our continuing economic cooperation. Our team can go to Iran as soon as we receive the preliminary data your authorities will provide and we can complete the Memorandum of Understanding now in Tehran for study.

In view of the importance of the revenues from Iran's petroleum resources to the development of your country, it is natural that you should seek the maximum in exports of oil from Iran. I know that the American oil companies, for their part, take their commitments to the Government of Iran seriously. While the policies of the oil companies are not without some limitations deriving from commercial factors, I have every reason to believe that they desire to assure that Iran will receive as favorable treatment as possible. I was pleased to note Iran's outstanding 20 percent increase in crude production in 1967 over 1966.

An added dividend of this healthy partnership is its encouragement of investment in other fields such as petrochemicals. I hope that this mutually beneficial relationship between Iran and the companies will continue to flourish.

I also want to continue our close relationship with Iran in the military field. We are ready to begin discussions on the third $50 million credit tranche under the amended 1964 Memorandum of Understanding. We intend to seek at the appropriate time the necessary authority and funds from the Congress for the fourth $50 million credit tranche. We cannot, of course, predict Congressional reaction to our worldwide credit sales request at this time.

With regard to the future, you may be sure that the United States continues to regard its military relationship with Iran as mutually important. As I told you when you were here, we will continue to do our best to be helpful. But it is still too early for me to say definitively what we can do beyond what is covered in our existing agreements.

We need, first, to know more specifically what your equipment and credit needs from us will be. I have heard from Ambassador Meyer of his and General Jablonsky's discussions with you and your military authorities, and I suggest that those discussions continue. I hope that we will be able to assist you in assessing your equipment needs and in reducing their costs. We have already begun exploring your credit needs in a preliminary way with Governor Samii of your Central Bank.

In the light of Congressional views, we will also have to consider carefully with you the implications of the substantial military expenditures you project. You are, of course, the best judge of what Iran's security requires, and I know your determination that every rial diverted from economic and social development to military expenditures be spent in Iran's national interests. However, my deep interest in the success of Your Majesty's development program prompts some concern about the contemplated size of your military program as mentioned in your letter and to Governor Harriman, and we will wish to discuss this concern with you.

It remains, Your Majesty, a source of great satisfaction to me to note the example which Iran is setting in the Middle East through its economic and social progress and its constructive position in international affairs. Your statesmanship in the Arab-Israeli crisis and your current efforts to strengthen your ties with the moderate Arab nations, as evidenced by your forthcoming trip to Saudi Arabia, provide rays of hope and encouragement in a troubled area. Americans everywhere are proud to have you and your country as our friends.

Mrs. Johnson and I would also like to take this opportunity to send you and the Empress our warm good wishes.

Sincerely,

Lyndon B. Johnson

255. Telegram From the Embassy in Iran to the Department of State[1]

Tehran, December 29, 1967, 0824Z.

2702. Ref: Tehran 2701.[2] Iranian Oil.

1. My audience with Shah 28th turned out to be one of most unpleasant of my tour here. He was obviously smouldering over devaluation shortfall issue with which he had been preoccupied earlier in day (see reftel).

2. Using terms such as "robbery," "thieves" and some unprintable epithets, Shah professed to be completely disgusted with consortium's behavior. At one point in discussion, Shah said if companies wanted war they could have it. This time it would not be with a Mosadeq but with a united Iran behind Shah himself.

3. When I noted consortium believes it has legal basis for its position and perhaps arbitration might be one possibility for solving devaluation problem, Shah said arbitration is totally unacceptable. As for matter being legal issue, Shah said GOI would take care of that once and for all by immediate passage of legislation which would insure GOI undepreciable payments. *Comment:* Since this is critical point, I later sounded out Shah again and received distinct impression that as of now unilateral legislation which Shah has in mind for dealing with devaluation issue will be limited to insuring value of payments. Question is, of course, re wisdom of having any precedent set for unilateral legislation against consortium.

4. In justification of righteousness his cause, Shah cited fact that both British Ambassador and consortium Chief O'Brien had registered disapproval of consortium's action in reducing December 15 payments.

5. Shah's bitterness splashed over whole oil picture. Re OPEC discount problem, Shah contended companies give with one hand, i.e. agree to phase-out of discount, but then take back with other, i.e. gravity allowance. He said he had doubted wisdom of Amuzegar's going to .52 cents on gravity allowance figure but had gone along with it. *Comment:* [garble] Amuzegar indicated (Tehran 2633)[3] that he had only gone to .45 cents in recent Tehran discussions, Shah's use of .52 cents figure, which he repeated twice, may mean that Amuzegar is prepared to move to that figure in attempt to reach compromise.

---

[1] Source: Department of State, Central Files, PET 6 IRAN. Secret; Priority; Limdis. Repeated to London.

[2] Dated December 29. (Ibid.)

[3] Dated December 21. (Ibid.)

6. Shah went on to berate consortium for its continual maltreatment of Iran, despite Iran's exemplary behavior in comparison with other countries. My efforts to point out that Iran has in fact been treated very well fell on deaf ears. Shah once again contended that consortium is sitting astride Iran's vast reserves and he cannot permit such restraining influences on Iran's welfare.

7. I pointed out problem is one of marketing. In this connection, I suggested Iran may be trying to carry water on both shoulders, i.e. pushing consortium to find greater markets while at same time stealing some of consortium's markets, e.g. recent IPAC deal for providing 18,000 BPD to Philippines which previously been almost exclusively market for American majors in consortium. Shah argued such competition is infinitesimal compared with bonanzas greedy oil companies are throwing to countries like Libya. When I pointed out geographic factor which places Libya in favorable situation with Suez closed, Shah said what really infuriates him is companies' lifting large quantities from sheikhdoms like Kuwait and Abu Dhabi when Iran with its 26,000,000 people needs funds to maintain its progress and play its role in Mideast security. Shah also asserted that Saudi Arabia's production will soon move up to 4,000,000 barrels per day. Since geographic factor a la Libya cannot be applied vis-à-vis Saudi Arabia, this further demonstrates he said, how companies discriminate against [garble—Libya].

8. Shah once again mentioned possibility of legislation which would enable GOI to have oil at well-head for clients which GOI may develop not in competition with consortium. He noted Iraq had long since found companies submissive to such measures. My natural response was to point to Iraq's sorry plight today and how much better off Iran is. I urged Shah "with every bone in my body" not to go down Iraqi road.

9. When subject of Iraq first arose, Shah said derisively, "congratulations." He contended that unhappy developments in Iraq, leading to influx of Soviets into Iraq's oil fields, are primarily due to faulty Western policy over past ten years. Since there was little likelihood of rational discussion, I did not pursue this point further to ascertain what Shah had specifically in mind.

10. I told Shah Washington would be appreciative his views re Soviet intrusion in Iraqi oil industry. Shah said much depends on nature of Soviet involvement. However, danger is real, he said, that perhaps with pipeline through Syria, Soviets can get both Iraq and Syria in their clutches, thus leapfrogging over Turkey and Iran. This would place them in dominating position in Mideast, particularly since they already doing so well in what Shah has often mentioned as triangle (it is somewhat linear) of Cairo, Aden–Yemen, and Djibouti.

11. This provided occasion to pass some of interesting analysis contained in Beirut 5181,[4] particularly ambition of Soviets to become international major. I noted in this connection recent PIW statistics that Soviets last year exported 56 percent of their production, which was 14.6 percent increase from previous year.

12. This led to general discussion on subject, "whither Mideast oil industry?" I took occasion to express concern that increasing Balkanization of this industry has real dangers for Iran, i.e. fall-off in markets available to consortium and unfortunate if not catastrophic repercussions to oil price structure.

13. Once again I reminded Shah that GOI's relationship with consortium likely be much more productive if it continues as partnership than if it is coercive. Shah readily agreed but said companies seem only interested in great profits and fail to take into account broader issues such as encouraging a country like Iran which is moving in positive direction and which has potential for influencing whole area in constructive way.

14. Before closing discussion, I told Shah I had obviously picked a bad day for my audience. He managed to permit himself a brief smile, but added that on any other day he would feel the same way about the oil companies' behavior vis-à-vis Iran.

15. Dept may pass on to companies as much of substance of this telegram as it wishes.

Meyer

---

[4] Dated December 26. (Ibid.)

---

256. Telegram From the Embassy in Iran to the Department of State[1]

Tehran, December 29, 1967, 0950Z.

2704. 1. In opening discussion re arms procurement with Shah 28th, I referred to President's letter.[2] Shah expressed appreciation for warmth of friendship and President's favorable disposition which letter reflected.

---

[1] Source: Department of State, Central Files, DEF 12–5 IRAN. Secret; Priority; Limdis.

[2] Document 254.

2. Shah had President's letter before him and inquired re para which mentions our considering with him economic implications of his proposed military expenditures in light of Congressional views. I noted both Executive Branch and Congress have inherent desire to see developing countries spend less on military hardware and more on economic development. Fortunately, until now Iran's economic progress has been heart-warming and all of us should be interested in keeping it that way.

3. When I noted that $800 million projection had come as somewhat of a shock, Shah reverted to his line that rate of expenditure is less than in past three years. He added, however, that if an adequate program could be developed for $600 million or less so much the better.

4. Noting that specifics re hardware being covered in HIM's talks with Jablonsky, I said problem is to come up with feasible five year program of procurement. Shah agreed, but said that this should immediately be followed by USG determination as to how much credit it can provide for such program. I pointed out that, given situation in Congress, Shah cannot expect President or USG to make categoric credit commitments that far ahead. As is obvious President's letter, I said, disposition of Executive Branch toward maintaining close military relationship is favorable and Shah would simply have to take chance that Executive Branch can secure Congressional support in years ahead. It was regrettable if Shah might not find it possible to have such patience.

5. Shah then came up with idea that after shopping list for next five years has been determined, GOI could proceed with placing orders, perhaps directly with American companies. If USG credit did not eventuate, Iran could secure financing from private American banks. I stressed importance of carefully phased program and re-emphasized point Jablonsky been making that Iran simply unable to find necessary trained personnel for military equipment which Shah has been talking of procuring within next five years. I acknowledged, however, that once practical program been outlined, possibility of credit from private banks is worth consideration. I gathered that Kuss and Samii were already doing some preliminary explorations.

6. Shah once again stressed his desire to keep air force American oriented, even if costs are higher, thus, he said, he would not oppose paying extra percentage point or two to private banks in order to continue American procurement for his air force. Shah also hoped that USG could assist by providing personnel to help maintain his air force. Five year package proposal for McDonnell to provide maintenance, he noted, estimates cost at $67 million. Thus USG by making military technicians available could be of real help. *Comment:* While Shah in discussion interest rates talks a bit cavalierly now, there likely to be resentment if and when American commercial credit terms are in fact proposed.

7. Re tanks, Shah said he goes along with Jablonsky's proposals for holding density to present M–60's, rehabbed M–47's and eventually 250 Sheridans. Threat to Iran in Gulf, he said, is more apt to require naval or air force counter-action than tank action. When I said presumably his naval requirements will be met by British, Shah said there were some items such as ship missiles which he would like from US.

8. When Shah referred to argument that Turkey has large tank complement, figures which Dept so helpfully provided in State 90119[3] were given to Shah. It was emphasized that this info was for his personal info only. He was obviously impressed that Turks are not nearly as well off as he had thought.

9. When question arose as to possible tank production. Shah once again registered resentment toward Paks. According to Shah, Paks are declining to cooperate in project where British tank factory would be established in Iran to produce tanks for Pakistan, Saudi Arabia, Kuwait and Iran. Pakistani reluctance makes whole project dubious. Shah said that Paks are showing active interest in British proposal for building five-ton tanks in Pakistan. Shah regards such project with great disdain. He described five-ton tanks as useless "mosquitoes."

Meyer

---

[3] Dated December 27. (Department of State, Central Files, POL IRAN–US)

---

257. Telegram From the Department of State to the Embassy in Iran[1]

Washington, January 12, 1968, 8:13 p.m.

98267. Subject: Iranian Financial Problems.

1. In discussion January 12 of certain Iranian financial problems with Under Secretary Rostow, Iranian Ambassador Ansary expressed hope recognition would be given to role Iran must play in area. Rostow

---

[1] Source: Department of State, Central Files, PET 2 IRAN. Confidential. Drafted by Eliot, cleared by Special Assistant to the Under Secretary for Political Affairs Robert T. Grey, Jr., and approved by Rockwell.

said Shah can have no doubt of our appreciation of role Iran playing and we will support Iran in every way we can.

2.   Ansary said oil revenues are key. Rostow expressed pleasure concerning settlement devaluation issue and said our impression of general tone of companies' attitude on offtake issue is positive.

3.   Rostow indicated while we still looking into various legislative aspects our arms sales program we are confident we will be able sell arms to Iran on substantial scale and are working on that premise. We hope be able take some action this spring on basis studies of military and economic aspects of situation which are now in progress.

4.   Ansary raised matter of controls on private US investment, speaking as he has elsewhere about bad timing of application of these controls to Iran which is only just beginning major effort with US encouragement attract investment in non-oil sectors. He said Iran special case due to recent termination AID program, fact Iran paying for own defense needs, has substantial development program, needs American capital and has unbalanced trade with US favorable to US. Once again saying he not asking for specific action at this time, Ansary asked for special consideration of any problems which may arise.

5.   Rostow stressed we can evaluate effects controls on investment only after we learn from companies of their investment plans within program. We must make clear to speculators and financial community that we mean business. We will watch with greatest possible concern effects of program and within program's limits will attempt facilitate investments companies wish make. He said Iran's and other countries' representations have been well received and convey realities which we wish take into account. If program hurts Iran we will give most sympathetic consideration to Iran's problems at a later point. But this does not necessarily mean we will make changes in program. Rostow added best procedure for taking care of problems which may arise is through arrangements for special licenses if they become possible. He pointed out Iran is in favored category because it can receive AID investment guarantees.

Katzenbach

258.   Telegram From the Embassy in Iran to the Department of State[1]

Tehran, January 16, 1968, 0900Z.

2897. Subject: Iranian Arms Procurement.

1. Arms procurement was only cursorily discussed during my audience with Shah 15th.

2. In discussing future Persian Gulf security (Tehran 2886),[2] Shah categorically asserted that despite implications of British withdrawal he is determined not to augment five-year military program beyond scope already planned, except for few minor revisions. This conclusion is explicable by virtue of fact that in formulation five-year program Shah undoubtedly assumed British would be withdrawing by end of that period.

3. General Jablonsky had seen Shah previous day and had some luck in further reducing Shah's shopping list, e.g. re artillery. Meanwhile Shah been consulting with Samii in anticipation latter's discussion re possible credit arrangements with Kuss in Rome.

4. While we gratified by interest being shown in Washington in direction responsiveness to Shah's requirements, we trying be careful here and we trust Kuss will do same in talking with Samii to remind Iranians current discussions re military credit sales dependent on Congressional concurrence.

Meyer

---

[1] Source: Department of State, Central Files, DEF 12–5 IRAN. Secret; Priority; Limdis. Repeated to CINCSTRIKE and to Rome for Henry Kuss.

[2] Dated January 15. (Ibid., POL 33 PERSIAN GULF)

259.   Telegram From the Department of State to the Embassy in Iran[1]

Washington, February 28, 1968, 0045Z.

121476. Ambassador Ansary asked to see Undersecretary Rostow urgently and alone on February 26. He said he had had a disturbing telephone call from the Shah asking him to come to Switzerland at once for consultations. Two issues were mentioned: a rumor that Americans had been seeing former Prime Minister Amini, and that we had not been neutral, but pro-Saudi, in the median line dispute in the Gulf.

Rostow saw Ansary again on February 27, after urgent checks. He said the episode was instructive and useful. For him the moral was that the Shah should feel solid confidence in the stability of American policy, despite the sometimes frenetic atmosphere of rumormongering on the part of those who were anxious about their careers or interested in creating difficulties between the United States and Iran. Our policy was clear and simple—it was one of friendship and confidence for the Shah and for Iran. We also had friendly relations with Saudi Arabia and with King Feisal, and we hoped that developing cooperation between Iran and Saudi Arabia could become the nucleus for stability and progress in the Persian Gulf. In this process, naturally, patient and statesmanlike leadership on the part of the Shah was indispensable.

Rostow said that according to the information we had been able to assemble overnight, no American had seen Amini for two years at least, and probably three years. This fact as he knew was contrary to our usual policy of staying in touch with a wide range of opinion. But we were aware of sensitivities between the Shah and Amini, and wished to do nothing to create difficulties for the Shah. There were even rumors in Tehran that I had seen Amini during my recent trip to Tehran.[2] As he knew, this was nonsense. I had seen a former student, Parvez Saney, who called on me at the Embassy when he saw that I was in the city. I told the Shah about the young man, and he said he was interested in hearing his ideas.

As for the median line dispute, we had taken exactly the same line in both countries, stating our interest in a peaceful resolution of the conflict, and urging both parties, in the same words, not to take steps that would make it worse. Both Ambassadors were experienced and first-rate men, and had carried out their instructions fully. There were no currents of dis-

---

[1] Source: Department of State, Central Files, POL IRAN–US. Confidential; Exdis. Drafted and cleared by Eugene V. Rostow on February 27.

[2] Rostow visited Tehran February 7–9 and met with the Shah. (Telegram 3258 from Tehran, February 9; ibid., POL 7 US/ROSTOW)

sent about our Persian Gulf policy, so far as Rostow could tell, within the Department or the government.

Ansary asked whether we had messages for the Shah on other subjects. Rostow reviewed the present state of the Jarring mission, and suggested that the Shah might wish at this point to do everything he could, as we and the British are doing, to support Hussein, and to urge him not to go to the Security Council on the Jerusalem question. Rostow asked for any suggestions the Shah might have as to what could be done to improve the chances of peace in the Middle East.

Rusk

260.   Telegram From the Department of State to the Embassy in Iran[1]

Washington, March 2, 1968, 0807Z.

123602. Subject: Iran Oil.

1. Fulmer, Texaco, McDonald, Mobil, Hedlund, Esso New York, and Clark, Esso London Office, called on Eliot at their request March 1, to review oil situation Iran.

2. Point of meeting was to ensure that Department informed why companies had to reply negatively to requests for larger offtake or cost oil. Re offtake companies cited extraordinary recent increases from Iran, especially in 1967, limit to size of overall market for ME crude, and competition from other areas that cannot be ignored. Re cost oil, companies said that since GOI not investing any capital or paying royalties, supply such oil would be tantamount to partial expropriation. Furthermore, oil to bloc countries, oil surplus area, would push out oil into consortium sales area and bloc may in any case be within consortium sales area in future. Giving in to Iran would also result in similar demands from other countries. Companies pointed out their strenuous efforts to find solution to Shah's demands and had made progress; this should be appreciated.

---

[1] Source: Department of State, Central Files, PET 6 IRAN. Confidential. Drafted by Walter M. McClelland (NEA/IRN), cleared by Akins, and approved by Eliot. Repeated to London and Paris.

3. Important other points emerging were a) companies not asking USG/HMG intervention at this time, just keeping us informed, and b) there is some confusion as to whether GOI demands for $5.9 billion oil revenue over next five years includes revenue from other companies as well as consortium. Eqbal, both in October and in his recent letter, has said that the 5.9 figure applied to consortium only; however Shah told Bridgeman in early January, and consortium reps on January 31, that figure includes all oil revenues, and Fallah recently said same thing to reps in US.

4. As to future steps, Clark said companies hopeful Shah will want to talk further. Consortium had not yet decided whether or not to send written reply to Eqbal letter, but sentiment in favor of keeping disagreement oral growing among members.

5. CFP reported to be "as responsible as anyone" for consortium rules, solidly behind decision not to sell cost oil, and relented only at last minute to allow additional refinery throughput. Nevertheless, CFP "oil hungry" and wants all the oil it can get.

Rusk

---

261.   Telegram From the Department of State to the Embassy in Iran[1]

Washington, March 5, 1968, 0125Z.

124570. Eyes Only for the Ambassador. Ansary called for a private meeting with Rostow as soon as he arrived back from his meeting with the Shah in St. Moritz. Ansary appeared very concerned and made following points with great emphasis.

1. He said that according to Iranian sources it appeared that some of our people had contacted former Prime Minister Amini. More importantly, he passed on story to effect that Ambassador Meyer had said to General Amini's widow that he would like to meet with former Prime Minister Amini and suggested meeting at dinner at her house.

---

[1] Source: Department of State, Central Files, POL IRAN–US. Secret; Priority; Nodis. Drafted by Grey on March 4, cleared by Eliot, and approved by Under Secretary Rostow.

2.   Ansary noted that there had been some student unrest in Tehran recently and passed on the report that some of our people had been in contact with the students involved.

3.   Ambassador stated that Rostow's position on closeness of US-Iranian relations had been accepted by Shah but that Shah noted that some people appeared to take a slightly different view of this relationship and had been less than neutral in median line dispute, Gulf problems and consortium discussions. Shah had pointed out that his government was after all a nationalistic one and it would be disastrous both for himself personally and for US Government's interests in area if he were to give up Iranian claims to $2 billion worth of oil in dispute in median line area. Ultra Nationalists, people out of sympathy with his regime, and Communists would exploit such concessions on his part to detriment of both his and our interests.

4.   As example of types of stories circulating in Tehran which tended to erode basic US-Iranian understanding was report Ansary had heard from two sources which indicated that US Ambassador had said that he thought cancellation of Shah's visit to Saudi Arabia was a mistake. Ansary added that stories to this effect would provoke an emotional reaction both from Shah and from his immediate entourage.

5.   Ansary stressed that we should not underestimate the seriousness of the Bahrein problem, and that he was most concerned by reports that Bahrein and Qatar were contemplating becoming members of Gulf federation.

6.   Ansary reported that Shah was extremely disturbed by status of consortium negotiations and he felt that some movement on part of companies was badly needed. Shah had pointed out to him that Iraqis had taken away large part of consortium concession in Iraq but consortium was still producing oil in Iraq at relatively satisfactory rate.

7.   On arms sales negotiations, Ansary said Shah was extremely disturbed because after several months of negotiations no draft agreement had been produced. He pointed out to Ansary that Iraq and Saudi Arabia were buying arms elsewhere and that his reasonable requests for purchases from the US had not yet been honored. He wished to do business with us and he hoped that he would be able to continue to do so, but there would come a time when his patience would be exhausted.

8.   In conclusion, Ansary stressed fact that in a period of increased nervousness in Tehran when there were even unfounded rumors of a change in government, it would be wise for US diplomatic establishment to proceed cautiously as suspicions and fears were heightened.

9.   Rostow made appropriate responses to all points covered.

10. Rostow expects see Ansary again March 6 and would appreciate comment on above beforehand.

Rusk

---

262.   **Telegram From the Department of State to the Embassy in Iran**[1]

Washington, March 5, 1968, 0123Z.

124569. Eyes Only for Ambassador. For Ambassador from Under Secretary Rostow. We are concerned about the atmosphere and the implications of these charges and rumors. On their face, they are absurd. But what do they mean? We want not simply the factual ammunition required by the situation but your full evaluation of what these démarches represent, and your advice on how they should be handled. Needless to add, we do not take these transparent attempts to drive wedges seriously. But how serious are the suspicions and fears they represent?

Rusk

---

[1] Source: Department of State, Central Files, POL IRAN–US. Secret; Priority; Nodis. Drafted and approved by Rostow on March 4.

263. Telegram From the Embassy in Iran to the Department of State[1]

Tehran, March 5, 1968, 1350Z.

3619. Eyes Only for Under Secretary Rostow. Ref: State 124570.[2]

1. Shah's grievances, as reported by Ansary, strike me as ill-founded and over-dramatized. Gratifying, however, they are now on table. Hopefully frank discussion such as you with Ansary and between Shah and me when he returns can clear the air and restore mutual confidence. Point by point comment substance reftel follows:

A. In casual dinner conversation with General Amini's widow some time ago possibility of seeing Amini some time was mentioned. If necessary to take up specifics of these allegations, perhaps you could say plain fact is we have had no contact with Amini. Given present sensibilities this is probably not the time to dwell on broader issues. Shortly after my arrival I tried to persuade Shah, apparently without success, that it is in his interest for true friends like ourselves to maintain contact with people out of power. I noted how helpful it had been in Lebanon in bringing the govt and outsiders together and in preventing explosions. I made clear to Shah all of this was done with full knowledge and confidence of President Chehab. Unfortunately traditional Persian disposition is to suspect and then eliminate, or at least quarantine, any diversity of thought. Incidentally, one reason for not pursuing this broader question more recently was our assumption, until present flurry, that political opposition was insignificant.

B. Any contact we have had with students had been most casual and normal. If there are any specific allegations of questionable contact, we should like to have them.

C. Having assisted Shah in satisfactory solution re four major points in crisis with consortium just over year ago, plus consortium's subsequent concessions re OPEC discount, devaluation problem, refinery throughout, etc., it difficult to understand charges of being less than neutral re oil problems. Re median line, we have not even suggested position that GOI must ratify initialled 1965 line. We have, however, expressed impartially to both sides our hope that further confrontations can be avoided and reasonable mutually satisfactory solution found at early date.

D. Re cancellation of Saudi visit, Shah's primary impression obviously derives from fact we worked so hard to try to have visit material-

---

[1] Source: Department of State, Central Files, POL IRAN–US. Secret; Priority; Nodis.

[2] Document 261.

ize. "Two sources," to which Ansary refers, could be FornMin Zahedi and Alam, to both of whom, in discussions after visit cancelled, I voiced view that on this issue we had obviously had honest difference of views but assumed our friendship strong enough to withstand some diversity of opinion. Around town, including Diplomatic Corps, we have sought carefully to avoid any implication we lobbied for visit, for we fully aware that key factor in Iranian policy-making is posture of "national independence."

E. Re Bahrein and Gulf federation, this first inkling we have had re Shah's embryonic reaction. (This may be Ansary's own initiative.) Obviously we here have no comment.

F. Re present consortium problem, our effort been directed to obtaining clearer understanding and good will both sides. FYI. It not unnatural consortium becoming increasingly impatient Shah's incessant demands, and our fear is that there only limited further give possible by member companies. My talk with Alam (Tehran 3587)[3] was designed to be helpful, including implicit suggestion that gap-narrowing concessions, e.g. elimination OPEC discount, increased refinery output, best foot forward, etc. might serve as face saving device for getting GOI out of box if it so wishes.

G. Re arms, I have informed Samii that we are proceeding along lines recommended by PriMin in our talk February 25 (Tehran 3471).[4] I have added that everything seems be on rails, i.e. Jablonsky having extensive review of shopping list in Washington light [list?] is coming out in couple of weeks, and "pacing factor" is progress on annual economic review. Samii assures us he hopes have data available by March 9 so we can try to meet Department's March 15 deadline (State 123603).[5] Undoubtedly one of key factors behind Shah's present questioning of our integrity here is report from Iran Embassy Washington (perhaps delivered to Shah by Ansary), which has been cited to us by Samii, that Pentagon has confirmed draft agreement re new five-year military program was sent to Embassy "some time ago." Under Department's guidance, we been telling Iranians we had no such draft. Ted Eliot can fill you in on details. It is quite likely Shah suspects I personally have blocked this action so dear to his heart, perhaps because of chagrin over cancellation of Saudi visit. At least Embassy been cast in role of prevaricators.

H. Re rumors of possible change of govt, we heard nothing about them until reading stories in press and PriMin Hoveyda's public remarks.

---

[3] Dated March 31. (Department of State, Central Files, PET 6 IRAN)

[4] Dated February 25. (Ibid., DEF 12–5 IRAN)

[5] Dated March 2. (Ibid.)

2.   Assessment of what is behind this obvious attempt to dredge up unsubstantial grievances will follow tomorrow as will recommendations for counteraction. Meanwhile, Embassy's airgrams (A–417[6] and A–465[7]) may be useful to you as background.

Meyer

---

[6] Dated February 10. (Ibid., POL 33 PERSIAN GULF)
[7] Dated March 3. (Ibid., POL 12 IRAN)

---

264.   Telegram From the Embassy in Iran to the Department of State[1]

Tehran, March 6, 1968, 0730Z.

3626. Eyes Only for Under Secretary Rostow. Deliver at 8:00 a.m. Wednesday morning.

1.   Recalling your congenial and constructive audience less than a month ago, Shah's present state of mind, as reflected by Ansary, is indeed puzzling. Since Shah arrived on ski slopes, some spark must have ignited his cogitation, e.g. inflammatory reporting from Tehran or irritation over London *Economist* article re "The Intemperate Shah." In any case Shah is brooding.

2.   We not only one baffled. As you know, Alam continues not to consider situation serious. SAVAK called in CAS to ask what is behind all this and categorically assured CAS that SAVAK has no reports of our misbehavior. Hoveyda's public remarks signalled Shah's unhappiness, but even Hoveyda seems puzzled. He has invited me to en famille dinner, which is scheduled for Friday evening.

3.   In analyzing cancellation of Saudi visit (A–417) and attack of Amini (A–465),[2] Embassy conjectured re motivations behind Shah's current behavior. These included: a) his penchant for moodiness with which my predecessors have also had to cope; b) chronic Persian tendency to

---

[1] Source: Department of State, Central Files, POL IRAN–US. Secret; Immediate; Nodis.

[2] See footnotes 6 and 7, Document 263.

impute foreign hand behind any unpleasant development; c) intoxicating effect of such successes as last August's visit to US, coronation panoply, and current economic boom; d) Shah's almost messianic desire to transform Iran into a country as modern as any European during days of power remaining to him; e) sycophantism which tends to inure Shah from reality; f) escalation of inflammation by Foreign Ministry and, in case Amini, perhaps by Prime Minister; g) tendency of Persian monarchs to "show their teeth" and success of that tactic in recent devaluation issue with consortium; h) Shah's desire to be world and Mideast leader; i) eagerness of all Iranians from Shah down to prove their "national independence" which here means from the US; j) cover Russian tactics of putting Iranians increasingly on defensive (particularly as prelude to Kosygin's visit) by shrill broadcasts, overtly and clandestinely, to effect Iranian regime is stooge of Americans, etc.

4.   All of these are contributing factors to present state of affairs. Undoubtedly the event which has catalyzed them and caused them to peak at this moment is British announcement of withdrawal from Gulf. It is important to make clear that in a sense Shah welcomes British departure as a new era with glorious possibilities for Iran. Thus to tell him we urging British to continue to play influential role in Gulf is of little beneficial effect.

5.   Prompted by factors in para 3, Shah's initial responses to challenge of Gulf's future were gun-boat diplomacy in median line and "showing of teeth" by cancelling Saudi visit. While news of these sallies was carefully managed, many Iranians have reservations, including even some Cabinet ministers. Except from official organs and agents, plaudits to which Shah accustomed not been forthcoming. Although unexpressed, thinking Iranians are questioning government by whim, e.g. one day papers printed letters from heads of Parliament and Senate forswearing pilgrimage and three days later PriMin Hoveyda publicly bade farewell to first batch of pilgrims. Inevitably there is some concern about too close an embrace with Soviets. Sharp increase in government budget, especially military, is causing some grumbling as tax collection becomes more strong armed. Meanwhile, presumably for apolitical reasons, strikes are occuring in Iranian universities; they have been disturbingly well-coordinated. This adds to worries of Shah and GOI.

6.   Outside Iran, Shah's initial sallies in Gulf been greeted with disapproval, notably in British press. (NYT may follow suit as energetic Tom Brady was here last week.) Officially, Shah knows USG disappointed re cancellation of Saudi visit and Median Line confrontation. Vis-à-vis US, he has guilt complex.

7.   Shah knows Iran becoming somewhat isolated. Ostensibly honeymoon with Russians continues but frictions developing and Shah realizes Moscow is mortal enemy his regime. Nasser is his bete noir. Other

Arabs, including Faisal, are in Shah's view Nasser's hostages and vulnerable to overthrow by radical Arabism. Shah is at odds with Ayub. Turkish friendship is not warm. Israel is convenient friend but not in same league with US.

8. Urgent questions are burdening Shah on Swiss ski slopes: Whether to authorize IPACI proceed with drilling on Saudi side of 1965 initialled line; whether to score fait accompli by occupying Tunb and other mid-Gulf islands; whether to oppose confederation of Gulf sheikhdoms; whether to take more active measures to demonstrate patriotism re Bahrein, etc. If he takes such steps, he jeopardizes relationship with US, the one country from which he can least afford to be isolated.

9. Key to US–Iran relationship is, of course, arms supplies. Shah vividly recalls American embargo on arms to Pakistan during latter country's 1965 hostilities with India. He must be painfully weighing whether reorientation his arms procurement is practical possibility and if not how he can fashion Gulf policy without alienating Americans. Neither option is easy. Beyond military field, Shah realizes cooperation with US commercially and otherwise is sine qua non if Iran is not to become another Finland.

10. Meanwhile, Shah is in jam with consortium, which provides more than 50 percent of GOI's income, this year around $800 million. Public bravado re intolerability of consortium irresponsiveness necessitates either new consortium concessions, which unlikely, or face-saving exit for Shah. Either way Shah will wish USG assistance.

11. How foregoing analysis reduces to Shah's suspicions of American collusion with Amini only Byzantine, or perhaps Persian, mind can fathom. Certainly, one explanation is that best defense is good offense. Shah's remonstrances through Ansary are in other words tactical, i.e. rationalization to US and to himself for actions he has recently taken, and for actions he may take in near future; also a pressure tactic on US vis-à-vis his problems such as arms, consortium and Gulf policy.

12. Perhaps silver lining is that Shah is coming to grips with reality. He is generating his own turbulence, which is preferable to our doing it. Situation is, of course, very delicate and our job is to deter Shah from irrational actions. At stake is future of Gulf, role Shah will play and our relationship with Shah as he plays it. Our recommendations are set forth in separate telegram.[3]

Postscript: There no objection your eliminating nodis label from this telegram if you so wish. Might also be worth repeating to London and other interested posts.

Meyer

---

[3] Document 265.

265.   Telegram From the Embassy in Iran to the Department of State[1]

Tehran, March 6, 1968, 0750Z.

3627. Eyes Only for Under Secretary Rostow. For delivery at 8:00 a.m. Wednesday.

1. Based on evaluation in Tehran 3626,[2] and recognizing our problem as psychological and tactical, as well as political, I offer following recommendations in treating suspicions and fears reflected in Shah's démarches via Ansary:

2. Play it cool. If Shah thinks he has US on defensive, he is apt to become even more temperamental.

3. Apply appropriate massaging. Early indication through me via Alam that President will have Shah to lunch when he comes for Harvard degree would be very helpful. Periodic correspondence with President, as well as high-level USG visits, also indicated.

4. Do what we can to placate grievances. Make clear Embassy has not been in contact with Amini, nor encouraged striking students. Neither have we sided with Aramco; on contrary our record in Shah's behalf quite extraordinary. Might note Saudis are alleging Iran is our favorite.

5. Both here and in Washington (and probably in consultation with British) we should address ourselves intensively to critical problems in Gulf area in wake of British departure, i.e. Median Line, Tunb and other mid-Gulf islands, and, of course, Bahrein. Purpose to facilitate solutions with which Shah can live. While these problems may seem minor on world scene they are of type which breed major confrontations if not resolved.

6. Remind Shah consortium has made remarkable number of concessions to Iran in past two years and that in short span of less than 15 years Iran has catapulted from Mosadeq's abyss to front rank in Mideast oil production. Should also point out that while Iraq is now increasing production their demagogic tactics, e.g. unilateral legislation and taking away proven fields, have dropped them way behind in Mideast oil derby. Their performance not worthy of emulation. (Meanwhile, we should seek from Mobil some useful explanation, if there is one, to counter Iranian annoyance at Hungarian reports that Mobil has tried to undercut NIOC.)

7. Request Henry Kuss to correct report given to Iranian Embassy, Washington, that draft military agreement was sent to Embassy "some

---

[1] Source: Department of State, Central Files, POL IRAN–US. Secret; Immediate; Nodis.

[2] Document 264.

time ago." Fact is that what we received was an uncleared piece of paper. Meanwhile, assure Iranians along lines reported in para 1.g of Tehran 3619.[3]

8. Seek diversions. Shah is presently all tied up in knots re his own problem. To extent we can, we should draw his attention to world problems, e.g. Mideast and Viet Nam, and invite his thoughts. Incidentally, special Viet Nam briefing team will be coming here in few days and our hope is Shah will agree to receive them.

9. To extent possible enlist cooperation of Israelis (possibly also Turks) to disabuse Shah of suspicion that USG has turned against Iran. Separate airgram reports Israeli attitudes here.

10. Assure Shah of complete USG confidence. This means all agencies, including CAS and Embassy. Make clear there is absolutely no possibility of separate clandestine policies.

11. To extent you feel possible declare your full confidence in US Ambassador in Tehran and your disappointment that in spirit of frankness, suspicions and allegations have not been taken up directly with him. If feasible, you could point out that Ambassador in Tehran has presented Iranian case in fashion more formidable than Shah apparently appreciates and that he deserves Shah's full trust. *Note:* Alam once delightfully described me as Iran's best Ambassador to Washington and he implied Shah felt that way too.[4]

12. Here in Tehran, I intend to have heart-to-heart talks with Hoveyda and Zahedi, as well as with Shah when he returns. I confident we can lay to rest suspicions against Embassy even though Shah's deeper concerns may be more difficult. Big challenge is to inspire Iranians to follow up their successes to date by playing leading constructive role in future of Persian Gulf area.

Meyer

---

[3] Document 263.

[4] In telegram 125954 to Tehran, March 7, Under Secretary Rostow thanked Meyer for his suggestions and said that he had consistently expressed his confidence in the Ambassador, which was shared by all of them there, and would continue to do so in talks with Iranian officials. (Department of State, Central Files, POL IRAN–US)

266.   Memorandum From the President's Special Assistant (Rostow) to President Johnson[1]

Washington, March 6, 1968.

SUBJECT

Appointment for the Shah of Iran

The Shah is coming to receive an honorary degree at Harvard on June 13. He would naturally like to drop in for a short chat with you.[2] With the British withdrawal from the Persian Gulf now a certainty, he will want to stay in close touch with you, and we have an interest in his cooperation with his Arab neighbors to prevent an undue increase in Soviet or Arab radical presence.

Secretary Rusk recommends that you invite the Shah to an office meeting and a small working lunch either June 12 (Wednesday) or 14 (Friday) so he can stop in on his way to or from Cambridge. We realize you just had him for a more formal visit last August and would not have recommended another meeting so soon. But since he's coming on a private invitation for a laudable purpose, it's hard not to pay him some attention.

An additional reason for the meeting is that, as you know, we maintain our relationship with the Shah via periodic contact of this sort—more frequent than is normal in other cases. Right now he is having another periodic case of annoyance and nervousness over some serious problems and decisions he faces.

In short, he's at another point of needing reassurance that he can count on us. He isn't getting what he wants from the oil companies; the British are vacating the Gulf leaving him face to face in a dispute with Saudi Arabia over tremendous oil reserves under the Persian Gulf; his military sales agreement with us is pending; Kosygin is coming in April, and the Communist clandestine radio is raking him over and appealing to his opposition; he's not doing too well with the Arabs, and he may be feeling generally isolated at the moment.

Your schedule would permit an office chat and small lunch on either June 12 or 14.[3]

Walt

---

[1] Source: Johnson Library, National Security File, Country File, Iran, Memos & Miscellaneous, Vol. II, 1/66–1/69. Confidential.

[2] In telegram 3437 from Tehran, February 21, Meyer had reported that the Shah had decided to accept the invitation to receive an honorary degree at the Harvard commencement, and that Court Minister Alam had expressed the belief that the Shah would also want to meet with the President. (Department of State, Central Files, POL 7 IRAN)

[3] Approved for June 12.

267. Telegram From the Department of State to the Embassy in Iran[1]

Washington, March 8, 1968, 0030Z.

126616. 1. Rostow called in Ansary March 7 and made following points:

2. In the nature of the relationship of confidence and trust between our two countries and the respect and admiration we feel for the Shah, it is gratifying and right that we clear away any doubts, misunderstandings or suspicions that may arise between us. It is natural, given the complexity of some of the problems we face together, that such misunderstandings can arise from time to time. We appreciate the spirit that led Shah to ask the Ambassador to raise with us the problems we discussed at our last meeting.

3. We have rechecked the points raised. We are glad to assure the Shah that so far as we can find out from all sources there is no substance to any of the rumors that have been given us. No one at the Embassy has been in contact with Amini, nor has any American connected with other official groups. It is true that the possibility of a social meeting with Amini was mentioned at a dinner party some time ago, but it was not followed up. From the point of view of our normal diplomatic policy, as the Ambassador knows, we would see such meetings as normal. The problem of contacts has been fully and amicably discussed by Ambassador Meyer with the Shah. If you have more concrete evidence, we should be glad to consider it. But it is hard to check on vague and general rumors.

4. Any contacts Embassy officers or other officials have had with students, through Student Center at university or otherwise, have been most casual and normal. The idea of Americans being involved in any way in student movements or demonstrations is fantastic, and has no foundation.

5. With regard to the cancellation of the Shah's visit to King Feisal, our views were thoroughly and frankly discussed with the Shah. While we were somewhat disappointed, we understood his decision, and there was no criticism of it. We did not discuss our views in public, or outside a very tight circle in the government.

6. On broader issues, Rostow said he had been unable to detect any rebels against the President's policy. In every agency, and at every level, there was a unanimity remarkable in the American government, and not very typical of the American mind—a unanimity of enthusiasm for what

---

[1] Source: Department of State, Central Files, POL IRAN–US. Secret; Nodis. Drafted by Under Secretary Rostow on March 7, cleared by Eliot, and approved by Grey.

Iran is accomplishing, and of confidence in the Shah's leadership, at home and abroad—in the Persian Gulf, in the Middle East, and in world affairs.

7.   On oil questions, we have indeed been neutral. The Saudis think we favor Iran. Our efforts with the Consortium have been addressed to facilitating clearer understanding and good will on both sides. The Consortium has made major concessions to Iran in past two years, and their performance over the last 15 years has been spectacular, and has helped make possible the Shah's program of economic and social development. So far as Iraq is concerned, their behavior over the years has reduced both investment and their share in production.

8.   With regard to the arms supply problem, Rostow said he had checked on the status of plans. Draft military agreement had not been sent to Embassy some time ago. Nothing more than an uncleared sketch had been received. But a directive has now been issued to have the entire matter prepared for action very quickly. Ways and means of financing the transaction are being studied. We have every reason to expect an answer within a short period. We must of course bear in mind the history of Congressional interest in arms sales generally.

9.   About the Gulf, we stand ready to examine problems of cooperation and stabilization in that vital area with GOI, here and in Tehran. We realize the sensitivity and importance of the issues involved, and will do our best to facilitate their solution. The problems of the Gulf are of critical importance. The latest Soviet statement on the subject is serious. It asserts that our interest in the safety of the region is directed against the security of the southern borders of the Soviet Union. It endorses national liberation movements in the area, and attacks "imperialist and neocolonialist regimes." And it offers Soviet protection to the governments of the area in order to safeguard them against imperialist encroachments. Rostow said there was no need to stress the implications of this bold public statement, as published in *Pravda* on March 4.

10. Our government is unanimous in its admiration of and respect for our Ambassador. He has been doing an extraordinary job. Ansary warmly and enthusiastically agreed and said he knew Shah had great confidence in Ambassador Meyer. Rostow said we were glad to be assured by the Ambassador that Ambassador Meyer enjoys the confidence of the Shah. We believe that confidence is fully merited. Ambassador Meyer presents the Iranian viewpoint to us with great force and understanding. We are glad there is no misunderstanding between us on this point. Rumors of this kind would normally be cleared up in frank talks with the Ambassador in Tehran, and we are sure this practice will continue to be the rule when the Shah returns to his capital. Ansary agreed with Rostow that undoubtedly reason why these issues were raised in Washington rather than Tehran at this time was their sensitivity. In view of

probable sources of reports, it would have been difficult for Shah to handle problem by cable to Tehran.

Rusk

268.   **Telegram From the Embassy in Iran to the Department of State**[1]

Tehran, March 14, 1968, 1650Z.

3767. Shah's Preoccupations.

1.   Zahedi Tour. Shah 14th told me major purpose FornMin Zahedi's visit to Washington is discuss Persian Gulf. Oil consortium problem also.

2.   Angry at British. Shah said his Isfahan statement (Tehran 3754)[2] was directed at British. He refuses accept their non-responsibility for creation of FAA. He has reached conclusion that Bahrein's inclusion in FAA, plus implication that British will deliver Tunb Islands and Abu Musa to sheikhdoms, is intolerable. Shah said he waiting to hear from British following Zahedi's talks. He considers Brenchley as chief HMG culprit with George Brown not far behind. If British, who are allegedlly allies, persist in present course, Shah said, Iran will not sit at same table with them, e.g, CENTO.

3.   Wants not to be pressed re Bahrein. Shah said he had previously suggested formula for dissolving Iran's claim to Bahrein, i.e. plebiscite, but that would not be possible now given present excitement on Bahrein question. If issue could be put in ice-box for two years, plebiscite might be possible then. I noted Sheikh of Bahrein himself has problems and referendum might only succeed in stirring up rabid Arab nationalists. Basing remarks on State 128944[3] re nebulous nature of FAA until now, I urged Shah to relax a bit. Noted public denunciation of FAA by Iran could have unhappy repercussions, i.e. drive Bahrein more solidly into

---

[1] Source: Department of State, Central Files, POL IRAN–US. Secret; Limdis; Noforn. Repeated to Dhahran, Jidda, Kuwait, London, Moscow, and CINCSTRIKE/USCINCMEAFSA.

[2] Dated March 14. (Ibid., POL 15–1 IRAN)

[3] Not found.

FAA, open opportunities for exploitation by radical Arabism etc. Concluded it behooves all of us to buckle down to see if some mutually satisfactory resolution can be achieved for knotty Gulf problems precipitated by departure of British.[4]

3 [sic]. Oil Consortium. Shah seemed relatively relaxed re consortium. He has impression consortium will meet his demands for 1968 or gap will be so narrowed that it acceptable. Problem is oil income for remaining four years of fourth plan. Shah concentrated particularly on inter-participants agreement, proudly reporting that through various sources he has received secret info re attitudes of various companies. He repeated what we had heard from consortium reps, that previously internal regulations "absolutely impossible" but now they merely "impossible." He believes obstructive underlifting companies are concerned that overlifters might steal some of their markets. Shah believes underlifters can be mollified by setting limit, e.g. 15 percent as to how much overlifting oil hungry companies, e.g. Iricon, will be allowed to take if and when restrictions can be loosened further. I pointed out what one rep had told me that obviously oil hungry companies will say revised regulations are still prohibitive so long as they think further liberalization is possible. Also went to considerable lengths to suggest offers by East Bloc and CFP have ulterior motives, i.e. shaking the normal oil industry in Mideast for their own political and economic benefit. Cited phoney Hungarian report against Mobil, and fact that as soon as Shah got special price to barter oil to Romania and other East Bloc countries Romanians raced to Saudi Arabia, Libya, Egypt and other oil producing companies offering barter deals for oil—with none of them, including deals with Iran, resulting as yet in moving one drop of oil to East Bloc. Re Mobil, Shah said Iran can not object to consortium companies trying to sell additional oil including in East Bloc but it does object if an NIOC price is undercut. Shah said in Washington Zahedi will make point that Iranian liftings only 130 million tons per year while Arab states moving around 600 million, but West would be well advised to work toward better balance in view of uncertainty of Arab behavior.

4. Soviet Hostility. Referring to recent Soviet communiqué, [garble] Iran broadcasts, Soviet diplomatic démarche etc., Shah said it is "clear as daylight" Soviets have their own plans for Persian Gulf. He annoyed by overtones of "sphere of influence" in communiqué. Not only

---

[4] In telegram 3774, March 15, Meyer reported that his audience with the Shah had convinced him that his analysis in telegram 3626 (Document 264) was "right on the button." He suggested that the Shah might be satisfied by a package deal including: 1) clear cession to Iran of the Tunb and Abu Musa Islands (through British auspices); 2) a joint Saudi-Iranian venture in the mid-Gulf for exploiting oil resources on both sides of the 1965 initialed line; and 3) relinquishment by Iran of its claim to Bahrein. (Department of State, Central Files, POL IRAN–US)

has Communist expansionism been added to Czarist designs for warm water port, Shah said, but their major strategy is to control valves of Mideast oil. Soviet system has failed in competition with West, Shah said, and world war is out of question for them, so they trying to dominate Mideast and its oil as means for destroying West European industry and thereby systems of government. Shah said he has ordered Zahedi to have Iranian diplomats in Western Europe emphasize this point.

5. Relaxed re Arms Program. Shah seemed content with status of negotiations re continuation our military credit sales. He was particularly pleased when I noted annual economic review which was held with PriMin that morning had taken place May 3 year ago. Shah seeing Jablonsky Sunday.[5] Incidentally, PriMin had already apprised Shah of our discussion, including pitch we had made (with which both PriMin and Shah agree) for encouragement of copper development and other private enterprise joint ventures.

6. U.S. Collusion. Began conversation by expressing gratification that small irritants which had been mentioned by Ambassador Ansary to Under Secretary Rostow been cleared away and mutual confidence fully restored, including with this Embassy. Shah still thinks we side with Saudi Arabia but only because of his partisan evaluation of events leading up to cancellation of Saudi visit. As I was leaving he mentioned Amini and I reviewed details, also my conviction that our being in touch with outsiders is to his advantage. Cited how well this worked when I was in Lebanon, also how helpful it was (and he agreed) when I took on Iranian students across from Blair House last August. He then professed there no objection to our seeing even Amini "every night" (but of course he does not mean it). Shah (as Hoveyda had done before) said what caused concern was coincidence of events, e.g. student unrest, Amini's increased activity, etc., which resembled developments in 1961 prior to Amini's coming to power. His view now is that student unrest was definitely Communist inspired and other disturbing events also had nothing to do with USG. Conversation ended most amicably with Shah jokingly agreeing I not persona non grata.

Meyer

---

[5] March 17.

269.   Telegram From the Department of State to the Embassy in Iran[1]

Washington, March 16, 1968, 0048Z.

131326. Subject: Zahedi's Washington Visit.

1. Following summary FYI, Noforn, uncleared and subject revision upon review.

2. *Summary.* Zahedi stressed seriousness to Secretary of Iran's interest in obtaining more oil revenues and in protecting its interests in Gulf. He blamed British for formation FAA and indicated necessity for GOI be able respond to desires Iranian people in settling problems of Bahrein, Tunb and Abu Musa. Secretary urged Iran consider its actions in context total dangerous world situation.

3. Iranian FonMin Zahedi called on and lunched with Secretary March 15 accompanied by Amir-Teimur, Fartash, Ansary and Batmanglidj. Under Secretary Rostow, Davies, Farley, Saunders and Eliot also present.

4. Zahedi made lengthy presentation to Secretary on oil and Persian Gulf.

a. On oil Zahedi reviewed Iranian need for revenues to support development program and military requirements which have increased as result British decision withdraw from Gulf. He stressed Iran's helpfulness in keeping its oil available during last June's crisis. He asked whether it wise for oil companies depend so heavily on Arab oil and on Aden refinery. Iran thought that alliance and friendship with US and UK, actions in June crisis, and constructive attitude on many international problems would have resulted in different response. Iran doesn't wish put oil companies in corner and threaten them and is open to suggestions. Consortium has been told what Iran's requirements are and has been asked raise offtake and/or provide cost oil for Iran to market and/or invest in Iran. If Consortium unable respond, it must think of consequences.

b. Zahedi reviewed his discussion with Brown in London (State 130381).[2] Said Iran hurt by UK's recent actions. Iran doesn't desire anyone's land, wants strong and healthy states on other side of Gulf and wants resolve small problems so that true friendship will prevail. Will not take Bahrein by force and will even risk wrath of public opinion by agreeing to plebiscite or some other way to solve problem. Zahedi re-

---

[1] Source: Department of State, Central Files, POL 7 IRAN. Secret; Limdis. Drafted by Eliot on March 15 and approved by Davies. Repeated to Dhahran, Jidda, Kuwait, London, and CINCSTRIKE/CINCMEAFSA.

[2] Dated March 14. (Ibid., POL 15–1 IRAN)

viewed Saudi–Bahrein communiqué, Fartash mission, cancellation Shah's visit, Amir–Teimur mission, noting all instances of alleged Saudi misbehavior. He then mentioned formation of FAA,[3] accusing British of double-cross. Problem with federation not only inclusion of Bahrein but also inclusion of Ras-al Khaimah and Sharjah and with them of Tunb and Abu Musa Islands. He said Iranian public cannot accept this and that if FAA is formally inaugurated on this basis March 31 British will have to accept consequences. He asked how Iran can stay allied to country which behaves in such a way. British tell Iran be patient, but for how long? In response Secretary's question concerning role of British in formation FAA and expression of doubt British planned it, Zahedi and Amir-Teimur reiterated belief they had hand in it, citing Roberts' telling Shah that UK favored federation of some of Sheikhdoms. Secretary also asked if FAA more shadow or substance and whether its formation would affect Iran's relations with individual components. Zahedi indicated formation FAA on present basis would indeed interfere with Iran's relations with Sheikhdoms.

5. In response Secretary said he hesitated give off-the-cuff response to such serious and far-reaching problems. He mentioned number of world problems, including Vietnam, Laos, Cambodia, Thailand, Burma, Korea, stirrings in Eastern Europe, economic situation in Free World. He noted that following June war Soviets felt sense of panic and loss of prestige. Stresses in Communist world and judgments they make concerning Free World produce situation pregnant with possibilities of crisis. Secretary said hard for us think about problems Zahedi raised except in framework world situation. We would be disturbed if Iran and UK at odds. Would be serious if Iranian actions would create inflammation in Arab world against Iran causing Arabs to look to Soviets for assistance. He expressed understanding how serious these problems are for Iran but stated they also grave in terms total world situation. It would be easy, he said, for US to counsel patience, but instead we ask Iran examine all consequences and alternatives in current dangerous world situations where clarity and wisdom in high demand. Secretary reviewed our strenuous efforts dissuade British from early withdrawal from Gulf. He mentioned knowledge some Iranians feel we not neutral in Iranian-Saudi problems and assured Zahedi this not so and that in fact we believe good Iranian-Saudi relations prerequisite to peace in Gulf and that they have identity of interest in preventing expansion Soviet influence in area. He said we deeply concerned about any match being applied to gunpowder anywhere. Shah one of best informed men in world and also wise man.

---

[3] The Federation of Arab Amirates (FAA) was formed in February 1968 by the rulers of the nine Gulf States—Bahrain, Qatar, Abu Dhabi, Dubai, Sharjah, Ajman, Umm al-Qaiwain, Ras al-Khaimah, and Fujairah.

Hopefully Iran would look at its problems in widest context. Secretary concluded by saying he could not speak from Mount Olympus and hoped discussions these subjects would continue through Ambassadors.

6.   On oil, Secretary said we cannot dictate to companies. We hope both parties will continue to promote their mutually beneficial relations. We will keep in touch with companies. Rostow mentioned our strong interest in mutually satisfactory solution and asked if Iranians had discussed offtake from Abu Dhabi with British.

Rusk

---

270.   Memorandum From Harold H. Saunders and John W. Foster of the National Security Council Staff to the President's Special Assistant (Rostow)[1]

Washington, March 18, 1968.

SUBJECT

Hoveyda's "Strange Series of Coincidences"

You asked if there is anything in the "strange series of coincidences" cited by Iranian Prime Minister Hoveyda in the attached cable.[2] We can't rule out the possibility that something is going on, but this looks more like a case of adding two and two and getting sixteen.

There has been student unrest. It started because of difficulties with university administrators and the political content has been low.

There was a teacher's strike, but as far as anyone knows, pay was the only issue.

The Iranian government is worried about former Prime Minister Amini's activities, but we are unaware that he has done anything, and there is no indication that he is involved with the mullahs.

Many of the mullahs have always been anti-Shah, but there doesn't appear to be any unusual activity.

---

[1] Source: Johnson Library, National Security File, Country File, Iran, Memos & Miscellaneous, Vol. II, 1/66–1/69. Secret; Nodis.

[2] Telegram 3681 from Tehran, March 9, is attached to the source text but not printed.

The Iranians are having trouble with the oil consortium, but no one has discovered any tie between the oil companies and either Amini or the mullahs.

The odds are that Hoveyda—and probably the Shah—have, in typical Iranian fashion, combined a few unrelated events, some rumors and their own unfounded suspicions into a conspiracy. They had suspected the US government was involved, and, despite what Hoveyda told Armin Meyer, our protestations of innocence are unlikely to have convinced them completely. But Armin's latest audience with the Shah suggests that we've quieted suspicions for the moment.

The best explanation of all this Iranian edginess is Armin Meyer's guess as to why the Shah called his ambassador to meet him in Switzerland and then had the ambassador bring back a bag full of crazy charges against Armin. If you haven't seen this, it's worth your time as background eventually for the Shah's visit (also attached).[3]

John
Hal

---

[3] A copy of telegram 3626 from Tehran (Document 264) is attached.

---

271.   Telegram From the Department of State to the Embassy in Iran[1]

Washington, March 22, 1968, 0125Z.

134583. For Ambassador from Battle.

1. Inter-departmental regional group for NEA considered military sales program for Iran March 21. No conclusions reached and IRG will resume discussion March 25.

2. Some concern was voiced in IRG meeting particularly as to implications of any kind of "commitment" for 5-year period following 1968. Possible that IRG may decide some further study required, e.g. on

---

[1] Source: Department of State, Central Files, DEF 19–8 US–IRAN. Secret; Priority; Limdis. Drafted by Eliot and Sober, cleared in draft by Rockwell and Battle, and approved by Eliot.

nature and requirement of military threat facing Iran and impact on Iranian economic situation of program of this magnitude. In that event, possible that final IRG recommendation on 1969–73 program might be delayed for some time which we can now not precisely estimate. Could be as much as several weeks. Given that contingency, I would appreciate your personal views on desirability your presenting Shah in near future firm USG offer regarding $100 million credit sale for FY68, indicating decision on remainder of Shah's request would be forthcoming as soon as possible. (As you well aware any IRG recommendation concerning FY68 program would still require approval by higher authority and we could not guarantee timing.)

3.   Would also appreciate your view as to whether political objectives of program would be achieved if it were to be reduced to $50 million or $75 million annually.

4.   Would appreciate your answer soonest prior to March 25 IRG meeting.

Rusk

---

272.   Memorandum From Harold H. Saunders of the National Security Council Staff to the Assistant Secretary of State for Near Eastern and South Asian Affairs (Battle)[1]

Washington, March 22, 1968.

SUBJECT

IRG Discussion on Iran

On mulling over our discussion of the military threat to Iran, I should like to come back to one major point. You said several times you could not find anybody around the room who challenged the military justification for the package. I wish now that I had, because I feel that a basic challenge was implicit in everything that was said. For instance:

—Stuart Rockwell led off by saying quite accurately that what we are coping with here is the *Shah's* assessment of what he needs. This political reality is our central problem.

—Harry Schwartz, when you asked him to discuss the specific questions of Iranian absorptive capacity and the like, said quite frankly that he could not provide this kind of justification for the package. As I under-

---

[1] Source: Department of State, Central Files, DEF 12–5 IRAN. Secret. Copies were sent to Rockwell, Schwartz, Critchfield, Clark, Williams, Eliot, Sober, and Brigadier General Doyle.

stood him, he said that the package is the sum of a lot of elements—the Shah's assessments of his needs, our assessment of what he can afford, our estimate of what we can afford, our estimate of what Congress will stand for, etc. But nowhere did I hear him say anything about the kinds of wars he might have to fight with the Arabs—Harry excluded the Soviet threat—and the specific kinds of equipment he'd need to fight those wars.

—Jim Critchfield's eloquent description of the threat was largely a description of the world as the Shah sees it emerging. This is valid, and we have to cope with it. But there was no intelligence estimate, such as we are striving for on the Israeli-UAR front, that the Iranians could defeat the Iraqis in five days, that the balance between Syria–UAR–Iraq and Iran would tip in the radicals' favor by January 1970 or any of the other measurable dangers one might conceive if one tried to war-game the threat against Iran precisely.

In short, while there was some side-talk about naval needs, no one at the meeting challenged the military element of the package. Someone said that the Shah's main objective is to be so strong as to deter attack, but we didn't take the next logical step to admit that there really isn't a pure military justification.[2] While no one challenged, nobody really justified either. What we have done is started with the Shah's first bargaining shot of $800 million and squeezed the most obvious bargaining components out of that package. Now we have reached a hard collection of items that the Shah says he needs.

Like you, I don't question for a moment the political rationale for the program, but I think we ought to be quite candid with ourselves in admitting that the political rationale is also pretty much the military rationale. Unquestionably, the Shah needs some modernization, and I'm sure General Jablonsky must have some military rationale, but it hasn't surfaced in the IRG. You'll recall that no one argued against your 5–7 year idea on military grounds at all. All of the arguments were related to "reliability", bargaining, Congress, etc.

I'm not sure that it is possible to be more precise on the military side, although I think there may be some virtue in trying. The economic problems which Maury Williams mentioned are much more measurable and do warrant a real review. But if in the course of the next two weeks, no one in the Pentagon can give us a military picture comparable to the economic one, I think we ought to reduce the military aspects of this problem to the political question of how far we can safely bargain the Shah down.

Hal

---

[2] A handwritten notation next to this sentence reads: "none."

273.   Telegram From the Embassy in Iran to the Department of State[1]

Tehran, March 23, 1968, 0850Z.

3869. Ref: State 134583.[2] For Assistant Secretary Battle. Summary: While conscious of problems involved, Embassy believes we should proceed with arms cooperation with Iran. Any "hitches" in US attitude likely to have severe repercussions and defeat our purposes. We still can cut off arms supplies, as we did Pakistan, if Shah misbehaves in Gulf area. He is fully aware of this, but still wishes to work in harmony with us.

1.   Given unhappy addition of Persian Gulf to many frustrations which are confronting our country these days, I am not surprised that some concern being voiced by our IRG colleagues re proceeding with military credit sales program of Iran. Frankly, these concerns are shared here at Embassy. However, after weighing all factors, we continue convinced we have no choice but to proceed with program promptly, if we are to retain healthy friendship with Iran and if we are to maintain effective influence not only on Shah's armament but on key role which he will inevitably play in Gulf.

2.   Our manifest displeasure when British projected their exit from Gulf testifies to our expectancy that major trouble could ensue; thus, it seems to us, we should not be too astounded by initial inter-riparian frictions which so quickly erupted. No doubt we shall witness more, but despite stridency which has characterized some of Shah's initial sallies, I definitely sense restraining effect which our influence has on Shah. This is worth preserving.

3.   A few straws in the wind. Shah is actively interested in rescheduling Saudi visit and Foreign Ministry is going out of its way to keep us posted. Reasonably effective Kuwait–Iran dialogue continues. Shah has reiterated instructions to IPAC to desist from drilling F–7. Admiral Rasai has told General Jablonsky and me he will not again hi-jack Americans in Gulf. When disclosing how Italians offered attractive helicopter deal while he was in Switzerland, Shah made clear to me 14th he awaits General Jablonsky's advice, another testimonial to key role which ARMISH/MAAG Chief until now plays in military decision-making process here. This too is worth preserving.

4.   Curbing Shah's military appetite has been chronic problem and over years our record has not been without success. During past two years we dissuaded Shah from: two additional squadrons of F–5's, all

---

[1] Source: Department of State, Central Files, DEF 19–8 US–IRAN. Secret; Priority; Limdis.

[2] Document 271.

Hawk missiles (he wanted three battalions), costly Vulcan anti-aircraft, etc. More recently we have reduced his estimate of additional needs for next five years from $800 to $500 million; we have cut tank program from 1,500 to under 1,000 including holding on to OLM M–47's; we have again talked him out of land-based surface-to-surface missile system; we have reduced his desire for self-propelled Howitzers from 222 to 50; etc. In general, we have succeeded in shaping his program to scope below armament levels of his neighbors, notably his potential enemies who are being heavily supplied by Soviets (Arabs have SAM's, bombers, etc., which Shah does not have and will not be getting).

5. Three weeks ago Shah suspected that US-Iranian military relationship, which he so much values, was on verge of rupture. His concern was prompted by reports that this Embassy was interdicting draft five-year agreement. Thanks to masterful endeavors of Under Secretary Rostow, Shah's irrational reaction was mollified. Both General Jablonsky and I have found Shah on his return to be relatively relaxed, confident in faithfulness of his American friends. Make no mistake about it, however, Shah expects early positive decision.

6. If as reftel implies we are now to suggest, no matter how indirectly, that new hitch has developed in trust which Shah has placed in USG, consequences are apt to be quite seismic. While Shah may have undue preoccupation with things military, he is probably most serious and realistic leader in all Middle East. As he sees it, vacuum which will be created in Gulf with departure of British cannot remain so. He prefers full collaboration with Saudis and other riparian regimes, but realistically assessing their capability as minimal and their longevity as questionable, he will assuredly prepare Iran for its role, hopefully in harmony with USG but if necessary alone. Thought of Russian-backed Arab radicals in Gulf is intolerable to him (as it is to us).

7. Shah is only too conscious of leverage which his purchasing US arms provides US. Most electrifying moment during my three years here was when at height of Indo-Pakistani hostilities Shah learned firmly from me that no Iranian arms could go to Pakistan, which was already suffering from USG arms embargo. Pakistan's plight made indelible impression on Shah. Fact that he is still prepared to do most of his arms business with US, knowing the restrictions to which he becomes committed, is in itself testimony to his wanting to play game our way.

8. During past weeks, I have carefully not threatened Shah. To do so could easily precipitate irrational reactions. At same time, I have assured through several intermediaries—e.g., Alam, Hoveyda, Samii, Afshar—that Shah is cognizant of fact that USG will not fuel hostilities between Iran and its trans-Gulf Arab neighbors. I am sure Shah has this message and that this is responsible for restraints noted in para 3 (as well as his crotchetiness while he was in Switzerland). Meanwhile, same mes-

sage was mutually understood when in our economic review with Pri-Min Hoveyda I led off with point that basic assumption for our discussion must be that "stability" presently characterizing this country and Gulf region would continue.

9. In our view, it is far better to preserve our conditioning influence in foregoing positive way than by negative threats, strings and hesitancies which can only offend Iranian sensitivities and defeat our purposes. Shah can easily be driven to other suppliers, and wide diversification of his arms sources is costly, e.g., increased expense caused by influx of Soviet arms. Buying helter-skelter (we favor some diversification to Western sources) multiplies wastefully the drain on Iran's economic resources.

10. Two years ago, we in Washington made decisions re scope of Shah's military program which he thought were decisions to be made here. This precipitated his kicking over traces by making first arms purchases from Soviets. Kosygin is coming and undoubtedly will be making syrupy new offers. As long as Shah remains optimistic re American cooperation, we doubt Soviet offers will receive markedly affirmative response.

11. Re one thing we must be clear. We are not only pebble on beach. Arms peddlers galore are invading Iran. It may be sacrilegious in some American quarters to relate arms sales and balance of payments, but given critical nature of latter problem for us I wonder re wisdom of rejecting $100,000,000 per year income which is certain to go elsewhere, probably in larger measure, if we be too prudish.

12. Before submitting recommendations, it is worth noting that in world increasingly unfriendly to USG, Iran's friendship is worth keeping. There is much truth in proposition that militarily Iran is only significant Gulf riparian power. There have been no demonstrations here against US policy in Viet Nam. We still profit immeasurably from vital strategic facilities here. USAID has bid adieu. More normal trade and cultural ties are blossoming. But key to healthiness of our friendship remains military cooperation.

13. All foregoing is simply prelude to expression of hope that our IRG friends will find it possible to agree ASAP:

A. To recommend to President importance of maintaining Shah's good will, key to which is our arms cooperation.
B. To authorize in principle extension of our military cooperation through FY73. Realizing that should Shah's behavior in Gulf become too reprehensible we have numerous loopholes, of which Shah only too keenly aware, for suspending our cooperation. (This point should reassure those in IRG who are concerned about long-term "commitment".)
C. Above all, to authorize earliest discussion with Shah of $100,000,000 FY68 tranche. If IRG cannot be persuaded re 5-year program at next sitting, least I should be authorized to do is to tell Shah ex-

tension of agreement to FY73 is awaiting outcome of current Congressional deliberations so as to assure most advantageous terms for Iran.

14. To suggest at this time reduction of annual tranche below $100,000,000 (para 3 of reftel) would under circumstances invite disaster. We do not rule out possibility that if area conditions change and if we maintain our capability for influence, ARMISH–MAAG Chief in coming years will have opportunity to keep expenditures under $100,000,000 level.

15. In short, I feel strongly present circumstances commend carrot more than stick. Latter is already understood. At stake is our relationship with Shah, our ties with Iran, and future of Persian Gulf area, re which Shah is bound to play key role.

Meyer

---

274. Research Memorandum From the Director of the Bureau of Intelligence and Research (Hughes) to Secretary of State Rusk[1]

RNA–12   Washington, March 27, 1968.

SUBJECT

The Shah of Iran as a Nationalist

The Shah's personal rule of Iran is probably more secure now than at any time since he succeeded to the throne in 1940, and a primary reason for this is his conscious avowal of nationalistic policies during the last six years. This paper examines the policies followed during that period and estimates the degree of success achieved by the Shah in his search for support for his program of "positive nationalism."

Abstract

In 1962 the Shah formulated a six point reform program which has been broadened since then to twelve points, some of them very extensive

---

[1] Source: Department of State, Central Files, POL 15–1 IRAN. Secret; No Foreign Dissem; Controlled Dissem; Limdis.

in scope. These reforms define the Shah's concept of "positive national-ism" and are intended to gain the support of Iranians for the Shah's re-gime while cutting the ground from under any opposition groups which might seek support openly or clandestinely. The reforms are also in-tended to give the Shah the image of a modernizer in foreign countries. Although the reform program is by no means complete, it has already ac-complished some of the goals the Shah set for it.

In Iran's dealings with the Western oil Consortium, the Shah has cul-tivated the image of a nationalist hero fighting against foreign exploita-tion and has striven to succeed the late Mosadeq in that role. Since about 1962 Iran has gradually moved to downplay its ties with the West and to establish an independent foreign policy. The Shah has visited seven Communist countries in the last three years. This period has enabled the Shah to stress the benefits to Iran of his "positive nationalism", and the coronation of October 1967 symbolized and highlighted his accomplish-ments. The coronation also demonstrated the Shah's resolve to provide for continuation of the Pahlavi dynasty and played up the cultural heri-tage of Iran. The Shah's determination to provide a strong defense in the Persian Gulf to back up Iran's involvement in the area has been publi-cized as a national mission, and there is a danger that a serious oil dispute in the Gulf or a clash between Arab and Iranian residents of Bahrein (which Iran claims and which is to be a member of the prospective Fed-eration of Arab Amirates) could prompt the Shah to involve Iranian forces to protect Iran's national honor.

Despite growing prosperity and dwindling opposition activity the Shah has not permitted Iranians to involve themselves in free political ac-tivity on an organized basis. The New Iran Party, established in 1963, soon lost its pretension of representative political activity and became simply a creature of the government in power. Opposition parties have been persecuted and in turn weakened by internal dissension over what reaction they should have made to the persecution. The Shah seems to have made a conscious decision to emphasize the pursuit of higher standards of living in order to keep Iranian minds off any movement to secure participation in the political process. If the current campaign against former Prime Minister Amini is any indication, political criticism may be subject to attack in the future as a threat to Iran's material pros-perity. Perhaps the Shah will allow limited political participation when he feels he has gained broad support of the people.

The Shah has been able to remove from his regime the stigma of be-ing subservient to the West, and the opposition no longer has a monopo-ly on nationalism. There is little doubt that the Shah's position has been strengthened. The greatest weaknesses of his regime are probably the continued rift between it and most intellectuals, and the fact that the gov-ernment is highly personal, with the Shah in the central role. Removal of the Shah from political life would probably cause a major crisis and might seriously affect Iran's stability.

[Here follows the body of the paper.]

---

275. Telegram From the Department of State to the Embassy in Iran[1]

Washington, March 30, 1968, 0049Z.

138990. 1. In a meeting with top executives of Esso, Mobil, Standard Oil of California, Texaco, Gulf and Iricon (morning March 28) Undersec Rostow said USG wished to have candid exchange of views with them about Iranian oil negotiations in their full political context. We did not wish to cross the delicate line between political and commercial considerations nor did we wish to take responsibility for the negotiations. But there was a deep national interest in a mutually satisfactory outcome for the negotiations at this time. The Consortium came into being with special anti-trust and other privileges by reason of such political considerations. He wished to discuss directly with the responsible leadership of the companies the political factors we saw impinging on the negotiating process.

So far as the Persian Gulf was concerned, we faced a national security problem in view of the British withdrawal, and the risk of penetration of weak Gulf States by movements of radical Arab nationalism, as well as by more direct Soviet interventions. In that perspective, Iran was the keystone of American plans. We wished to have equal friendship with Iran and with Saudi Arabia, and close cooperation between them. At this point, Iran was clearly the stronger partner, progressive and developing. But Saudi cooperation with Iran was indispensable from every point of view, political, psychological and geographic, if stability in the Persian Gulf was to be assured. Rostow reviewed recent history and present prospects of efforts to bring Shah and Feisal together, and stressed importance of an oil settlement compatible with the necessities of that process.

---

[1] Source: Department of State, Central Files, PET 6 IRAN. Secret; Limdis. Drafted by Akins and Rostow on March 29; cleared by Deputy Assistant Secretary for International Resources and Food Policy George R. Jacobs, Oliver, and in draft by McClelland; and approved by Rostow. Repeated to London, Kuwait, Jidda, and Dhahran.

But Persian Gulf problem was intimately linked to Middle East crisis as a whole. After reporting on problems of M.E. since Nov. 22 S.C. Resolution, Rostow said we regarded the situation as increasingly grave. UAR was blocking progress on the Jarring Mission. And Syria—perhaps UAR as well—was training and sending out terrorists on a very dangerous scale. Jordan had a Vietcong on its territory, as Laos does, and could no longer control it. In the absence of peace negotiations, Israeli reprisals were inevitable, despite our urgent efforts to prevent them. As a result, there was a serious possibility of renewed general hostilities in the Middle East, with incalculable potentialities. We were working on a crisis footing to head off hostilities, but we could not be sure of the outcome.

2. Rostow referred to Shah's statements that he cooperated with West at his great risk during crisis last June. If he felt this cooperation not recognized through favorable treatment by Consortium, there was possibility he would not cooperate with West in new crisis. Rostow also said withdrawal of British from area made it necessary for Iran to cooperate with Arabs in Gulf and in a new round of hostilities he might not be willing risk their wrath by breaking Arab blockade again. As companies knew, even temporary boycott of Middle East oil, if it included Iranian production, would be catastrophic.

3. Iran, he said, has written $5.9 billion into its development plan and Shah would not change it. We know companies cannot give Iran all it wants for its plan but we also believe that if there is some increase in earlier estimates there will be chance of averting confrontation and new crisis in Iran this year.

4. Rostow asked without prejudice about possibility of investment commitments, raising APQ, altering over-lift arrangements to permit crude-hungry companies to take more oil, on equitable terms, increasing refinery throughput, and making special allowances for British Petroleum if it decided to reduce Abu Dhabi production in favor of Iran. Desirability of equality of treatment between Iran and Saudi Arabia was stressed, and generally accepted. Companies said they are examining all these possibilities and said all offered some room for adjustment but they gave no definite assurances on any.

5. They pointed to certainty more favorable treatment Iran would result immediate demands from Arab and other producing countries which they could not meet. In reference this as well as to willingness French other "oil hungry" companies to take more cost oil, they said such oil could only be sold at expense current marketing since demand was being fully met. Rostow said USG recognized all alternatives were impossible, but we would weigh the political value of a settlement with Iran very highly.

6. Companies asked USG attempt convince Iran that Consortium trying help it meet development goals. Rostow said we had done this re-

peatedly and would do so again, if companies assured us they would make genuine effort to reach satisfactory agreement. This assurance was given. To be effective, companies would probably have to improve their estimates and do everything economically feasible to help Iran. Companies said they knew any approach would have to be on this basis.

7. At end of meeting question was asked whether USG seriously thought risk of confrontation, and of rash and destructive action by Shah, was high. Rostow answered affirmatively, and said our concern over this risk was the subject matter of meeting, and the reason it was called.

8. Company position throughout meeting was neither hostile or negative and we believe they will endeavour seriously to devise new offer before April 20. Clearly any new offer will be below Iranian demands but we hope enough will be offered to avert crisis this year.

Rusk

---

276.   Telegram From the Embassy in Iran to the Department of State[1]

Tehran, April 3, 1968, 0910Z.

4015. Persian Gulf. Summary: Shah reviewed with John McCloy his concern re Persian Gulf and re Soviets in Mideast. McCloy urged statesmanship. Shah is particularly disturbed re future USG policy.

1. During hour and half discussion with John McCloy at Caspian April 1, Shah set forth his well-known views re Persian Gulf. McCloy received impression Shah more interested in mid-Gulf islands than Bahrein. Shah claimed islands are Persian and for British to turn them over to amirs would be "affront." Stressing Faisal is his friend, Shah gave impression his irritations directed more at British than Arabs.

2. Shah reviewed danger of Soviets gaining control of Mid-East oil spigots in order to compel Western Europe to dance to Soviet tune. Expressing view Europe is far too complacent and De Gaulle merely serving as "jackal" for Soviets, Shah deplored build-up of Soviet fleet in

---

[1] Source: Department of State, Central Files, POL 7 US/McCLOY. Secret. Repeated to Dhahran, Jidda, Kuwait, London, and Ankara.

Mediterranean, conversion of fertile crescent to "red crescent," Soviet exploitation of Arab-Israel conflict with imminent threat to Jordan and King Hussein. He urged USG support "regional strength," particularly Greece, Turkey (which is unfooled by Soviets) and Iran.

3. Shah seemed shaken by prospective loss of President Johnson's leadership. He hoped President's move does not foreshadow shirking by USG of its key responsibilities in Viet Nam and in world. Any "uncertainty" re USG's "steadfastness" would cause loss of faith in US commitments with devastating effect worldwide. Shah urged there be no diminution of USG's statesmanship, vigor and decision.

4. McCloy in turn urged Shah to demonstrate statesmanship in keeping Persian Gulf from being added to major problems which confront US. He reminded Shah Iran is big progressive country and Shah a respected leader who could afford to be big in dealing with his neighbors. Shah contended political concessions are difficult if he is to retain respect and leadership capability.

5. While consortium problem was scarcely mentioned by Shah, Alam later outlined in detail Iran's needs as well as alternatives which GOI considers open to consortium. McCloy reiterated what he had told Hoveyda that GOI should avoid any "rupture" in its profitable relationship with oil companies.

Meyer

---

277. Record of Meetings of the Interdepartmental Regional Group for Near East and South Asia[1]

IRG/NEA 68–16   Washington, April 5, 1968.

Record of IRG Meetings—March 21 and April 3, 1968

The IRG devoted both meetings to a consideration of *proposed arms credit sales to Iran.*

The IRG reviewed the analysis and recommendations of the various interested agencies as well as of Embassy Tehran, directed primarily to a

---

[1] Source: Johnson Library, National Security File, NSC Files of Harold Saunders, Iran, 1/1/68–1/20/69. Secret; Limdis. Drafted by Sidney Sober.

proposal for a $600 million, six-year (FY 1968–FY 1973), credit sales package. (See attachments to IRG/NEA 68–13 and 68–14 for pertinent papers.)[2]

Political Factors. The IRG *agreed* that our arms supply relationship has a vital importance in our overall ties with Iran, and that—given the Shah's great concern over Iran's security problems—our response to the Shah's current request for arms sales in the years immediately ahead will have a decisive influence on the pattern of our overall relationship with Iran for the next several years. The benefits of our relationship with Iran run the gamut from valuable collaboration with our own military and intelligence endeavors based in Iran, to the intangibles of friendly cooperation of an ally on the international scene. Although the Shah has desired to evince a greater degree of "independence" in his foreign policy and has taken steps to improve Iran's relationship with the USSR, Iran remains a loyal supporter of CENTO, retains a realistic awareness of long-range Soviet intentions, and has made it clear it wishes to keep its close ties with the United States. It was noted that our relationship with Iran assumes added importance in light of the increased Soviet threat in the Middle East and the continuing instability in the Arab world. The Shah is concerned over the implications of strong Soviet support for the radical Arab states, with whom he sees Iran potentially in conflict. It was noted that the forthcoming British withdrawal east of Suez will enhance Iran's importance in future developments in the Persian Gulf area, in which the United States has key strategic and economic interests.

Military Factors. The CIA member cited various recent developments which have affected the Shah's view of Iranian security problems and which have impelled him to modernize and strengthen Iran's security forces. These developments include the USSR's supply of the radical Arab states with modern weapons; the UK's announced withdrawal from the Persian Gulf by 1971; increased Soviet naval activity in the Mediterranean, and the assumption that the Soviets will seek to extend their influence as broadly as possible east of Suez; the pressure on existing US military forces in connection with the situation in Southeast Asia and the Shah's probable concern as to our ability and willingness to provide rapid support to Iran in the event of an external aggression.

The JCS member noted that Iran must orient a large portion of its military defense against the potential Soviet threat, although no Soviet military action against Iran is foreseen in the years immediately ahead. The Shah's major external security concern is for the threat posed by the UAR and other radical Arab nationalists to the oil-rich Khuzistan area.

---

[2] IRG/NEA 68–13, "Proposed Arms Sales to Iran," March 21, and IRG/NEA 68–14, with the same title, April 3, are in Department of State, NEA/RA Files: Lot 71 D 218, IRG/NEA Basic File, 1966–68 (Final).

The Shah is anxious to procure sufficient air defense aircraft, antiaircraft and naval equipment to counter a potential UAR or UAR/Iraqi air and naval threat to southeast Iran and the Persian Gulf. His reorganization of the Iranian Ground Forces, with greater emphasis on armor and mobility, stems from the size of his country and the diversity of the current threat in general—in particular the tank threat posed by a potentially hostile Iraq.

The IRG *agreed* that it was impossible to relate any projected level of arms supply precisely to any given threat or combination of threats. It is uncertain, for example, to what extent radical Arab forces constitute a real military threat; what combination of radical Arab forces might threaten Iran; and just what military capability Iran would require, at a given time, to counter such a threat. These questions involve both quantitative and qualitative issues. Recognizing these uncertainties, the JCS member concluded nevertheless that Iran needs solid US support, in the form of modern arms and equipment and appropriate military training and advice, in order effectively to deter or defend against potential military action by radical Arab forces.

The JCS member noted that the currently proposed program for modernizing and building up Iran's military establishment over the next half-decade has been developed in close consultation by the Chief of the US Military Assistance Advisory Group and Iranian authorities. Iran's ability to absorb the equipment in question was implicit in the development of the program. In summary, the JCS member stated, the program made sense from a military viewpoint.

Economic Factors. The IRG devoted considerable attention to the question of Iran's economic situation and its ability to finance a major program of military reinforcement. It noted Iran's impressive record of an 8–9% annual economic growth in real terms in the last three years in a climate of price stability. Rising oil revenues have permitted a steady increase in expenditure for economic development as well as for defense. It noted that Iran's new Five Year Development Plan, which went into operation on March 21, 1968, aims at increasing GNP at an average annual rate of 9.3%. This Plan foresees a rise in the proportion of fixed public and private investment to GNP from 21% in 1967 to 25.3% over the 5-year period.

The members *agreed*, however, that many uncertainties and intangibles make it impossible to predict with assurance the precise course of Iran's economy over the next several years. A major uncertainty is the GOI's projection of oil revenues, which depends on the outcome of discussions now under way with the Oil Consortium. It was agreed that the GOI projection of a 17% average annual increase is too high, but that there would nevertheless be an appreciable rise in Iran's oil revenue, perhaps at a 12% annual rate. Doubts were also expressed as to whether

Iran's non-petroleum exports will rise as fast as projected by the GOI, and whether the GOI could hold down its defense expenditures as planned. The AID member expressed particular concern that a shortfall of oil revenue could force a cutback in proposed development expenditure by Iran's Plan Organization; such a cutback could have internal political repercussions as well as economic implications, since it could reduce government investment for the next few years below the rate estimated for 1966 and 1967.

The IRG *agreed* that, although there was cause for optimism as a result of Iran's past record and that, although there was no cause for concern as to the $100 million military sales program proposed for FY68, it is most important that the GOI arms program not interfere unnecessarily with Iran's economic development and progress. The actual course of Iran's economic expansion will have to be kept under careful review, particularly regarding Iran's ability to finance an arms buildup such as it proposes. The balance between economic progress and defense outlay will continue to be a prime factor in our consideration of Iran's specific request for arms each year.

Congressional Factors. The IRG noted recent Congressional concern over arms races and over possible excessive expenditure on defense by foreign countries with which we have an aid or supply relationship. It also took note of the fact that our ability to supply arms on credit to a country such as Iran after the end of this fiscal year will depend upon passage of new military sales legislation now before the Congress, and also on the availability of appropriated funds to support annual credit sales programs. It was *agreed* that these factors tended to militate against our seeking to enter into any more or less firm "commitment," however hedged, involving precise credit sales levels for several years beyond the current fiscal year. The Chairman noted that any type of multi-year proposal would probably have to be discussed with Congressional leaders.

The AID member raised a question as to the need for a Presidential determination in the event of an increase in the military credit sales program for Iran in FY 1968, above the illustrative $50 million presented to the Congress last year, under the final proviso in the military assistance item of the Foreign Assistance and Related Agencies Appropriation Act, 1968. There is a difference of view among legal experts in State, Defense, and AID on this question. It was agreed that this issue should be clarified, but that it was not substantively critical to the larger question before the IRG inasmuch as any recommendation on the FY 1968 credit sales tranche would require Presidential approval.

Annual Review. The members attached crucial importance to the annual review of political, military, and economic factors to be considered prior to a decision on each annual tranche of military sales to Iran. It will be necessary, for example, to have in mind the development of relations between Iran and Saudi Arabia and the other Persian Gulf entities; the development of the threat from the radical Arab states; the economic situation in Iran, and particularly the effect of defense outlay on Iran's economic development program; and our own military requirements, financial situation and credit availabilities. The Chairman emphasized that the annual review will be a key part of any multi-year arrangement with Iran. The precise level and composition of each annual sales program would be decided upon the basis of the annual review.

Conclusions and Recommendation. The IRG considered a proposal for a six-year (FY 1968–FY 1973), $600 million military credit sales proposal for Iran, as well as various alternatives, in the light of the above factors. It was *agreed* that we have an overriding political interest in offering to the Shah an arms supply proposal that would be adequate to bolster the Shah's confidence in our desire to retain our intimate military relationship with Iran; to keep him from feeling that he had no choice but to turn to the Soviets for sophisticated arms; and to support continuance of our present close and constructive overall ties with Iran. It was *agreed* that some form of multi-year understanding is essential for this purpose. It was also *agreed* that it would be desirable, if possible, to conclude such an arrangement with Iran before the Shah's expected visit to Washington on June 12, 1968.

The IRG *agreed* to recommend to higher authority a proposal as follows:

To protect our important interests in Iran, to assist the maintenance of stability in the Middle East, and to ensure the continuation of the valuable U.S.-Iranian relationship in the military field, while at the same time maintaining a requisite degree of flexibility, the U.S. should before June 1:

1. Offer Iran a credit sales program for FY 1968 on concessional terms for a minimum of $75 million and, subject to the availability of necessary additional funds, a maximum of $100 million. (This to be dependent on funding arrangements and global availability of funds.)
2. Tell the Shah that we recognize his desire to work for the five-year plan he developed with the Chief of our MAAG as Iran's program for modernization for the next five years, and engage to cooperate with him in his attaining this goal on the following basis:

Governed by an annual review by each government of the political, military, and economic factors bearing upon the size, nature, and funding of each annual program, the U.S. declares its intention each year to seek Congressional authority and appropriations for such cash and credit sales as both governments would agree were indicated to move toward accomplishment of the Shah's program.

The IRG also *agreed* that it would be necessary for the U.S. to undertake intensive annual internal studies on the political, economic, and military implications of the Shah's military program, commencing with timely preparation for the FY 1969 tranche.

SS
Staff Director

MEMBERS PRESENT

    Executive Chairman: Mr. Battle
    AID: Mr. Williams
    CIA: Mr. Critchfield (3/21); [*name deleted*] (4/3)
    DOD: Mr. Schwartz
    JCS: Brig. Gen. Doyle
    NSC: Mr. Saunders
    USIA: Mr. Carter

    ACDA: Mr. Van Doren
    BOB: Mr. Clark
    Eximbank: Mr. Middleton (3/21); Mr. Carlisle (4/3)
    Treasury: Mr. Albright

    State: Mr. Rockwell; Mr. J. Wolf; Mr. Eliot; Mr. J. Campbell (4/3)
    DOD: Mr. Reed; Mr. Olney (3/21); Mr. Ligon (4/3)
    SIG: Mr. Ruser
    Staff Director: Mr. Sober

---

278. Telegram From the Embassy in Iran to the Department of State[1]

Tehran, April 9, 1968, 1005Z.

4118. For Assistant Secretary Battle. Summary: Prompted by his concerns re Persian Gulf security in future, Washington delays, and his profound shock at President's decision not to seek re-election, the Shah is anxious for a yes or no from USG re his five-year military program. Two temporizing alternatives are suggested in absence of greenlight from IRG.

1. Alam called me in evening eighth (for third time in five days) to convey Shah's anxiety re our military credit program. Alam spoke from notes taken at Shah's direction.

---

[1] Source: Department of State, Central Files, POL IRAN–US. Secret; Priority; Noforn; Limdis.

2.   Alam said Shah still concerned re delay in Samii's visit to Washington and New York. My previous endeavors to counsel patience have only had limited effect.

3.   According to Alam, Shah wishes to know as soon as possible whether he can count on US for his military needs in next five-year period. Shah reiterated he wished to retain US orientation as far as Iranian military is concerned. He is buying arms, not seeking grant assistance. He has committed himself not to acquire sophisticated weapons elsewhere, but he must know whether he can rely on US, not just for one year, but for implementation his five-year program. (My impression was that he may have had some info from Ansary indicating USG present thinking concentrating on FY68 tranche.)

4.   Alam went on to say that Kosygin offered provide any of Iran's military needs, whether planes, tanks or ships, and Russians prepared to make firm unlimited commitment through 1975. Of course, Shah had ignored this Soviet ploy.

5.   Recalling Alam's report to us on Shah–Kosygin talk (Tehran 4039),[2] I noted Alam had not mentioned arms as having been discussed, even though I had asked specifically re that subject. Alam surmised that Kosygin had made pitch to Hoveyda.

6.   Obviously detecting some annoyance on my part at what appeared to be crude intimidation, Alam assured me Shah's mentioning Soviet offers was not an attempt at "bullying." Alam did, however, followup this part of conversation with Shah-suggested disclosure re probable Moscow visit in July (Tehran 4116).[3]

7.   In concluding discussion re military, Alam noted Shah will certainly discuss this subject with President Johnson in June. He went on to say how devoted Shah is to President and cited how Shah was affected by President's cautions against excessive ($800 million) arms expenditures in most recent communication this subject.[4]

8.   *Comment:* Although reaction to a pitch of this kind is always visceral, one must resist saying "go ahead deal with Russians" and try to understand Shah's present deeply felt dilemma. I need not repeat our analysis (Tehran 3869)[5] here, but points made remain valid. Announcement of British withdrawal from Persian Gulf has plunged Shah into profound preoccupation with Iran's role in preserving security and stability of that area, in the face of radical Arab adventurism and historic Russian aims.

---

[2] Dated April 3. (Ibid., POL IRAN–USSR)
[3] Dated April 9. (Ibid., POL 7 IRAN)
[4] Document 254.
[5] Document 273.

9. On top of that has been added an equally profound factor which it is impossible to overestimate. The Shah probably more than any other world leader has been shaken by the President's announcement not to seek re-election. He considers President true personal friend in whom he has utmost confidence. He cannot envision any successor so well disposed to maintenance of Iranian-US relations, including in field of military cooperation. On contrary, he despairs that successor President may curtail arms cooperation which is core of current US-Iranian relationship.

10. It is because of this uncertainty, coupled with fact that Shah has already been waiting for some six months for answer to his question, that Shah will insist on reasonably clear statement of US intentions over next five year period. Without it, he is fully capable of taking undesirable steps. It was my hope (Tehran 3869) that we could convince our IRG colleagues of importance of favorable decision, at same time assuring them that no one knows better than Shah that we have adequate loop-holes to curtail our military cooperation any time Shah misbehaves or we run into Congressional troubles.

11. Since there has been no greenlight yet received here pursuant to two recent IRG meetings, I would suggest either of following actions:

A. Arrange for early visit of Mehdi Samii to Washington to discuss commercial credit in general and preliminary terms.

B. Letter from President to Shah referring to Shah's démarches to me, counselling patience, assuring Shah that five-year program is receiving close and expeditious attention, expressing hope for an affirmative response before June and indicating President looks forward to discussing this and other subjects with Shah in June.[6]

Meyer

---

[6] In telegram 4125 from Tehran, April 10, Meyer reported that for the moment, the Shah's temperature regarding the military credit program had subsided a bit. (Department of State, Central Files, DEF 19–8 US–IRAN)

279. Telegram From the Department of State to the Embassy in Iran[1]

Washington, April 9, 1968, 2226Z.

144116. Ref: Tehran 4073;[2] CHARMISH/MAAG ARCG 7076.[3]

1. We are proceeding urgently toward decision on US military credit sales program for Iran. No final decision on program has yet been reached but we hope to obtain such decision shortly. Until program approved, would be premature commence negotiations with GOI officials including Samii.

2. FYI. IRG/NEA agreed recommend modified program April 3. We plan submit program for approval by higher authority this week. Congressional consultations would follow this approval. (Summary of IRG meeting decisions being pouched.) End FYI.

3. Battle told Ansary April 9 that while we have many problems connected with Congressional and legislative considerations, there is no disagreement within executive branch on basic issue of our wanting continuing relationship with Iran in military field. Battle advises Ansary not to worry, including about time it will take us reach decisions, and said Shah could be reassured.

Rusk

---

[1] Source: Department of State, Central Files, DEF 19–8 US–IRAN. Secret; Priority; Limdis. Drafted by McClelland; cleared by Eliot and Rockwell and in substance by Sober, G/PM Director for Operations Joseph J. Wolf, Jack Reed, and Ligon (OASD/ISA); and approved by Battle. Repeated to CINCSTRIKE/CINCMEAFSA.

[2] Dated April 6. (Ibid., DEF 12–5 IRAN)

[3] Not found.

280. Memorandum From Secretary of State Rusk to President Johnson[1]

Washington, April 19, 1968.

SUBJECT

Approval of a Program of Military Credit Sales to Iran

Recommendation:

With the concurrence of the Secretary of Defense, I recommend that you approve, subject to the satisfactory conclusion of Congressional consultations:

1. An offer to Iran of a military credit sales program for FY 1968 on concessional terms for a minimum of $75 million and, subject to the availability of necessary additional funds, a maximum of $100 million. (This is to be dependent on funding arrangements and global availability of funds.)

2. Informing the Shah that we recognize his desire to work toward a program of military modernization for the next five years and that we engage to cooperate with him in his attaining this goal on the following basis:

The United States Executive Branch declares its intention each year to seek Congressional authority and appropriations for such credit sales as both governments would agree were indicated to move toward accomplishment of the program mentioned above. On the part of the United States the amount of authority and funds sought, and the amount of sales made for cash, would be subject to the results of a yearly review, with the Government of Iran, including reviews of Iran's economic development and military programs, as well as an assessment of the effect of military purchases on the Iranian balance of payments and budgetary situation. The actual amount of credit made available to Iran in each year will of course depend on the amount of credit authorization and appropriations approved by the Congress and on other U.S. requirements worldwide. If the amount of credit authorization and appropriations approved by the Congress proves in future years to be insufficient for the mutually agreed needs of Iran, the Executive Branch declares its intention to do what it can to help Iran obtain credits from non-Governmental banking sources.

Discussion:

Since military credit sales were introduced in 1964 as a way to shift Iran from grant aid to self-financed procurement, U.S. equipment cost-

---

[1] Source: Johnson Library, National Security File, Country File, Iran. Secret.

ing some $300 million has been sold to Iran. Two credit tranches of $50 million each remain to be released under the 1964 U.S.-Iranian Memorandum of Understanding; recommendation 1 (above) proposes to combine them for release in FY 1968 as the first increment of a $600 million, six-year procurement program developed by Iran to provide for Iranian military needs after U.S. grant aid terminates in FY 1969.

There are no political, economic or military reasons not to proceed with a $75–100 million credit in FY 1968, and we recommend offering it to Iran at terms of 5-1/2 percent interest, with seven years to repay. Several possible funding alternatives are enclosed.[2] Equipment to be purchased is designed to modernize the Iranian military forces and is planned to include F–5 aircraft, M60 and Sheridan tanks, armored personnel carriers, a surface-to-air missile unit for Iran's destroyer and self-propelled artillery.

Since last summer, the Shah has been pressing us for a new commitment on credit sales in the 1970's. The comprehensive program he has developed in conjunction with his U.S. advisers is a logical follow-on to our grant aid program, and we believe it essential, in order to protect our important interests in Iran and to assist the maintenance of stability in the Middle East, that we be forthcoming in response to his requests for military credits to support it. Our arms supply relationship is of decisive importance to our overall ties with Iran. These ties bring us important benefits, including collaboration on military and intelligence operations, and the intangibles of friendly cooperation with an ally on the international scene. Moreover, the importance of our ties with Iran has increased as a result of the announced British withdrawal from the Persian Gulf, the growing Soviet threat in the Middle East, the continuing instability of the Arab world, and real doubts about long term continuance of U.S. facilities at Peshawar.

Nevertheless, I cannot recommend that the United States undertake at this time a firm commitment for the full $500 million additional credit program (FY 1969–73). Uncertainties about Congressional authorization of future arms credits and the level of appropriations, about the effect of future defense spending on the Iranian economy and about the development of Iranian-Arab relations make it prudent to base the program after FY 1968 on the outcome of thorough annual political, military and economic reviews.

Some form of multi-year understanding for future years is, however, essential to meet our objectives in Iran, and we believe that recommendation 2 (above) should achieve this purpose while at the same time maintaining a requisite degree of flexibility. We are fully aware that, by

---

[2] Attached but not printed.

adopting this cautious policy, we run the very real risk that the Shah may consider the proposed arrangement too indefinite and therefore insufficient. This could trigger another round of bargaining or, alternatively, might cause him to turn to other arms sources, including the USSR and Eastern European countries. Should the Shah react in this manner, we believe your June 12 luncheon with him could be critical, and we would, if it proves necessary, propose additional course of action for your consideration prior to that date.

The foregoing recommendation has been submitted by the Interdepartmental Regional Group for the Near East and South Asian Affairs under Assistant Secretary Lucius D. Battle's chairmanship after a careful review of the factors involved and of our interest. The record of the IRG/NEA meetings on the subject is enclosed.[3]

After satisfactory informal Congressional consultations, we will send a letter formally advising the Congress of your decision to increase the program for FY 1968 and the major reasons for doing so.

Nicholas deB. Katzenbach[4]

---

[3] See Document 277.

[4] Katzenbach signed for Rusk.

---

281. Memorandum From the President's Special Assistant (Rostow) to President Johnson[1]

Washington, April 29, 1968, 12:55 p.m.

SUBJECT

New Military Credit Sale for Iran

Shortly after his visit last August, the Shah wrote you[2] that he intended to embark on a new five-year $800 million program for further

---

[1] Source: Johnson Library, National Security File, Country File, Iran. Secret. Attached to a May 1 memorandum from Rostow to the President that reads: "You should know that there is some urgency in connection with a decision about the Iranian arms package. There was considerable delay in the bureaucracy in developing an agreed position. Meanwhile, the Shah is becoming restless, having had reason to expect a response earlier. You will recall that he mentioned the matter to John McCloy, underlining that he was, after all, willing to pay for these arms and that our common strategic interest in the area required him to be strong."

[2] Document 242.

modernizing his armed forces. He is now down to $600 million for six years, and this will be uppermost in his mind when he sees you June 12.

There is no question that the Shah will go ahead with some such program. The issues are how to keep it from slowing his economic development and how to keep him from turning to other suppliers.

No one has serious reservations about going ahead with the proposed $75–100 million program for FY 68. Nick Katzenbach recommends you approve this subject to satisfactory Congressional consultations. He would start at $75 million and hold the additional $25 million for you to throw in when the Shah comes.

The real issue is how we assure the Shah that we will participate in this program without actually committing ourselves. He says he has to know what he can count on. We can't say for sure, and we have good reason for not wanting to jump in all at once even if we could:

—We don't know what military sales authority Congress will approve or how much it will appropriate. We don't want to tie up funds until we see how much we have to divide worldwide.
—We're wary about Iran's committing so much to military expenditures so far ahead. We'd like to go year by year.
—When the British withdraw from the Persian Gulf, Iran and Saudi Arabia face a number of difficult issues there. We want to be careful about how we build up a new sub-regional super-power.

Offsetting these reservations is our need to maintain a close relationship. Now that AID has phased out, our military program is the major concrete manifestation of that relationship. We look to the Shah to maintain a pro-western Iran and depend on him for even expanding our sensitive intelligence collection activities.

The Shah believes he must be strong enough militarily to deter any attack—overt or subversive—by the Arab radicals. He is worried, as he told John McCloy, about Soviet gains in the area. He knows the British are pulling out. He fears even more that our policy since last June indicates diminished US interest in the Mid-East. Therefore, he wants to modernize his forces but, perhaps even more important, he wants some reassurance of our continuing concrete interest in his security. It's quite possible that we may not be able to satisfy him.

To tread the narrow line between general assurance and specific commitment for the next five years, State and Defense have devised the finely worded paragraph under recommendation #2 in Nick Katzenbach's attached memo.[3] Essentially, it says we'll do what we can to help with his five-year program but we just can't commit ourselves that far ahead. We'd declare Executive Branch intention to push ahead year-by-

---

[3] Reference is to Document 280.

year toward accomplishment of the Shah's program. You will want to read the fine print.

The real problem is not the approval of this well-hedged formula. The problem will be whether you feel you can make this stick with the Shah when you see him on June 12. You will have the tough job of trying to persuade him of the continuity of the US-Iranian relationship without knowing either what the Congress will do or who your successor will be. Your line will have to be that (a) anyone who sits in your seat will be impressed with the necessity of a strong continuing US–Iran relationship and (b) we hope he will bear with us through this transitional period.

In the face of this difficulty, I recommend you approve this approach as a start. Regrettably, there seems little chance of devising a more flexible position for you, at least until Congress acts.

You will want to read the attached memos from Charlie Zwick[4] and Nick Katzenbach.

Walt

Approve the $75–100 million sale for 1968 and the hedged assurance that we will try to help with the rest of the program[5]

See me

Put on Tuesday lunch agenda

---

[4] Attached but not printed.
[5] The first and last options are checked.

---

282. Telegram From the Department of State to the Embassy in Iran[1]

Washington, May 2, 1968, 2350Z.

157500. Ref: Tehran 4506.[2] Eyes Only Ambassador from Under Secretary Katzenbach.

---

[1] Source: Department of State, Central Files, DEF 19–8 US–IRAN. Secret; Exdis. Drafted by Katzenbach; cleared by Battle, Walt Rostow, Deputy Assistant Secretary for Politico-Military Affairs Philip J. Farley, and Warnke; and approved by Katzenbach.
[2] In telegram 4506 from Tehran, May 2, Meyer reported that Alam had told him the Shah's patience regarding the arms package was wearing thin. Meyer also expressed his own concern over the package tentatively approved by the IRG. (Ibid.)

1.   Military credit program may have struck you as "typical IRG lowest common denominator product" but it has in fact received my closest attention and study, incorporates the strongly held views of the Deputy Secretary of Defense and has now been approved by the President.

2.   We are about to take next step of Congressional consultation and if all goes well, we will be instructing you shortly. In the mean time, as indicated, we are in process of determining whether additional funds, over $75 million, are available so that offer can be raised to $100 million. I cannot tell you today if that decision will be made prior to sending your initial instructions.

3.   The Shah is not the only one with political problems.

Rusk

---

283.   Telegram From the Department of State to the Embassy in Iran[1]

Washington, May 18, 1968, 1921Z.

166827. Subject: Military Credit Sales Program for Iran.

1.   The President has approved, Congressional consultation has been completed, and you are hereby authorized to inform the Shah of USG approval of the following Military Credit Sales Program for Iran:

a)   USG offers to Iran a military credit sales program for FY 1968 on concessional terms for a minimum of $75 million and, subject to the availability of necessary additional funds, a maximum of $100 million. (This is to be dependent on funding arrangements and global availability of funds.)

b)   You should tell the Shah that we recognize his desire to work toward a program of military modernization for the next five years and that we engage to cooperate with him in his attaining this goal on the following basis:

---

[1] Source: Department of State, Central Files, DEF 19–8 US–IRAN. Secret; Immediate; Limdis. Drafted by McClelland on May 17; cleared by Eliot, Rockwell, and Saunders and in draft by Sober, Schwartz, Kuss, Assistant AID Administrator for Near East and South Asia Maurice J. Williams, Lewis D. Junior (G/PM), Knute E. Malmborg (L/E), and Assistant to the Secretary of Treasury for National Security Affairs Raymond J. Albright; and approved by Katzenbach. Repeated to CINCSTRIKE.

The United States Executive Branch declares its intention each year to seek Congressional authority and appropriations for such credit sales as both governments would agree were indicated to move toward accomplishment of the program mentioned above. On the part of the United States the amount of authority and funds sought, and the amount of sales made for cash, would be subject to the results of a yearly review, with the Government of Iran, including reviews of Iran's economic development and military programs, as well as an assessment of the effect of military purchases on the Iranian balance of payments and budgetary situation. The actual amount and terms of credit made available to Iran in each year will of course depend on the amount of credit authorization and appropriations approved by the Congress, on prevailing credit market factors, and on other US requirements world-wide. If the amount of credit authorization and appropriations approved by the Congress proves in future years to be insufficient for the mutually agreed needs of Iran, the Executive Branch declares its intention to do what it can to help Iran obtain credits from non-Governmental banking sources.

2. You should also tell the Shah that we are anxious to complete the credit negotiations for the FY 1968 increment as soon as possible and must complete them prior to June 30. We therefore propose that a U.S. negotiating team be sent to Iran about June 15 for this purpose. If the Shah prefers, however, the USG would be pleased to receive an Iranian negotiating team in the United States at that time. (FYI. Negotiations should commence after June 12. End FYI.)

3. You should inform the Shah that the President's action is a token of our confidence in the Shah and in Iran, that the equipment we are providing will be responsibly employed to the maintenance of peace and stability in the area. We further hope that with this arrangement made, Iran can devote the fullest possible resources to economic development and social reform.

4. You should tell the Shah that as in former years we have carefully reviewed the economic data provided by the Central Bank and congratulate Iran on its continuing economic progress. Although we have concluded that Iran's economy is making good progress and warrants a large credit increment this year, there are a few points of concern. For example, we note that security expenditures have grown very rapidly over the last few years and we hope it will be possible for the GOI to keep the increase closer to the growth in the economy and, in any event, no higher than that projected in the Central Bank figures (11.6 percent increase per year) in future years. We are also concerned that increasing payments for arms purchases may reduce total public investment and thus reduce the rate of economic growth. We believe economic improvement and social betterment are best assurance of security in long run against threats to

Iran and urge that Iran's economic progress not be adversely affected by her military expenditures.

Rusk

---

284.   Telegram From the Embassy in Iran to the Department of State[1]

Tehran, May 20, 1968, 1745Z.

4857. Ref: State 166827.[2] Subject: Military Credit Sales for Iran.

1.   Although at first insisting he must have iron-clad five-year commitment, Shah 20th eventually bought my thesis that USG is treating him very well and that in reality qualifications attached to proposed credit sales program are consistent with constitutional factors which have heretofore regulated successful US-Iranian military cooperation.

2.   Shah said Iran's immediate military needs would exceed 100 million but agreed confer further with ARMISH/MAAG Chief Jablonsky re essential FY69 requirements. If USG credit restricted to $75 million, Shah said, obviously orders for at least $25 million must be placed elsewhere.

3.   Telegraphic reports on this[3] and other subjects covered during two-hour conversation will be forwarded tomorrow. In general, all went well and Shah remains solid friend.

Meyer

---

[1]   Source: Department of State, Central Files, DEF 19–8 US–IRAN. Secret; Immediate; Limdis. Repeated to CINCSTRIKE.

[2]   Document 283.

[3]   In telegram 4866 from Tehran, May 21, Meyer reported in detail on his May 20 discussion of the military credit sales program for Iran with the Shah. (Department of State, Central Files, DEF 19–8 US–IRAN)

285. Memorandum From John W. Foster of the National Security Council Staff to the President's Special Assistant (Rostow)[1]

Washington, May 21, 1968.

SUBJECT

The Situation in the Persian Gulf

One problem you might like to begin thinking about again as we prepare for the Shah's visit (June 12) is the situation in the Persian Gulf. It's bound to come up.

As you know, both the Shah and Faisal understand that they must cooperate to prevent outside interference in the Persian—or "Arab"—Gulf. The two rulers have much in common—especially a dislike for Nasser—and, aside from dividing valuable underwater oil concessions which could be worked out, no specific bilateral problems in the Gulf.

There is a basic conflict, however, between the Iranian assumption that Iran has the mission of controlling the Gulf, and the Saudi assumption that Saudi Arabia is responsible for everything on the Arabian peninsula. This has led to Saudi support for the Arab sheikhdoms on the Gulf and the sheikhs do have conflicting claims with Iran.

The nine British protectorates in the Gulf recently formed a Federation of Arab Amirates. So far the organization has not found workable machinery, but the nine rulers keep holding meetings in an effort to create a viable confederation. Apparently they are going to get King Faisal's blessing. The trouble is that the Shah claims part of their territory.

Iran has a longstanding claim to Bahrain, one of the nine Amirates. The Saudis have tried to play down Bahraini participation, and the Shah says he won't push his claim if he isn't challenged directly on it. But as the amirs organize, the challenge becomes clearer. The news of the FAA's latest meetings has led the Shah to consider the cancellation of a proposed November visit to Saudi Arabia. (You will remember that the Shah "postponed" his visit last January after a Saudi-Bahraini communiqué spoke of the "Arab character" of the Gulf.)

The other territorial disagreement hasn't yet become a major problem, but could be as serious. Iran claims some islands in Hormuz Strait (the Tunbs and Abu Musa) which leads from the Gulf to the Arabian Sea. As long as the British held the Islands, the Shah was content to let the claim lie dormant. He is now afraid that if the Arabs get the islands, it will only be a matter of time before Nasser establishes a naval base there and

---

[1] Source: Johnson Library, National Security File, Country File, Iran, Memos & Miscellaneous, Vol. II, 1/66–1/69. Secret.

blockades Iran. His fears may be groundless, but for him this is a real danger.

Hopefully, the Shah and Faisal will let their common interest overcome minor territorial disputes, but it won't be easy. Our policy is to stay out of the middle but to keep reminding both of them that the best way to keep Nasser and the Russians out is to work together. State has been back and forth over this problem and decided that our main effort should be gradually to expand our representation in the Gulf to make our views heard but generally not to think in terms of major US programs.

John

286.   Action Memorandum From the President's Special Assistant (Rostow) to President Johnson[1]

Washington, May 22, 1968.

SUBJECT

Dinner for the Shah

You asked whether we could have a big dinner for the Shah to which he might bring his wife, instead of the small working luncheon we had planned for him on June 12.

Both your schedule and the Shah's would permit our having a large dinner on June 11. Everyone here and at State feels that, from the foreign policy viewpoint, this would be a good thing to do. The only reason we had not suggested it before was that the Shah had been here on an official visit just last August and, since he is coming this time on a private visit to receive an honorary degree, we did not want to impose on you for another dinner. However, if you would like to have him, we would all be delighted.

We cannot be sure that his wife could come. She has decided not to accompany him on this trip. However, she will just have been to Ethiopia with him, will come as far as Europe with him and then will go on to Morocco with him after his visit here. The Shah has never told us exactly

---

[1] Source: Johnson Library, National Security File, Memos to the President, Walt W. Rostow, Vol. 78, May 20–24, 1968. Confidential.

why she did not wish to come here, but we believe that her unpleasant experiences with demonstrating students in Berlin on a previous trip may have made her wary of coming here, where Iranian students usually demonstrate against the Shah when he comes. She might reconsider and come just for the White House part of the trip, but we cannot guarantee this.

If you would like to invite the Shah to dinner on June 11 in hopes that the Empress can come too, we would propose the attached message[2] from you suggesting this change in plans and making a special point of your wish to entertain the Empress before you leave the White House.

If you wish to wrap this all up in one day, we could reschedule the office visit to 5:30 P.M. on June 11. If not, we would leave it scheduled for 12:30 P.M. on June 12.

Once we have your preference and the Shah's acceptance, we will work out the announcement with George Christian.

W.W. Rostow[3]

Approve dinner Tuesday, June 11, with office meeting at 5:30 P.M. same day

Approve dinner Tuesday, June 11, with office meeting at 12:30 P.M. the next day[4]

Leave schedule as is with office meeting at 12:30 P.M. Wednesday, June 12, followed by small working lunch

---

[2] Attached but not printed.
[3] Printed from a copy that bears this typed signature.
[4] This option is checked.

287.   Telegram From the Department of State to the Embassy in Iran[1]

Washington, May 22, 1968, 0031Z.

168328. Subject: Iranian Arms Program.

1. Assistant Secretary Battle briefed Iranian Ambassador Ansary May 21 on our arms program for Iran, stressing that briefing was for Ambassador's background as Ambassador Meyer had made formal presentation to Shah.

2. Battle also briefed Ansary on Congressional consultations on arms program. He said that two principal areas of Congressional interest were Iranian-Soviet relationship and Iran's relations with its Arab neighbors. He said he had indicated to Senate Foreign Relations Subcommittee that Shah is well aware of Soviet aims and that although there are frictions in Gulf, we believe our arms program for Iran will assist area stability. Battle also said there had been questions about nature of military threat to Iran. He stressed that atmosphere of consultations had been very good and that there is warm feeling for Iran and Shah on Capitol Hill.

3. In discussing Congressional consultations, Battle indicated there may be some Congressional repercussions as result forthcoming Soviet fleet visit to Iran.

4. Battle also mentioned that *New York Times* has apparently acquired from Congressional sources information on our proposed arms program. He said it is likely story will appear May 22.

5. Only point Ansary raised on arms program was Shah's disappointment with $75 million limitation this fiscal year. Battle indicated that as Ambassador Meyer had told Shah we are trying to find additional funds.

Rusk

---

[1] Source: Department of State, Central Files, DEF 19–8 US–IRAN. Secret; Priority; Limdis. Drafted by Eliot on May 21 and approved by Battle. Repeated to CINCSTRIKE.

288. **Telegram From the Embassy in Iran to the Department of State**[1]

Tehran, May 28, 1968, 1345Z.

5007. Ref: Tehran 4993.[2] Subj: Soviet Military Equipment Offers.

1. Shah informed ARMISH/MAAG Chief Jablonsky that Zakharov (returned USSR May 27 after 10-day visit in Iran) had offered wide variety military supplies with early delivery. Specifically Zakharov offered destroyers, submarines, missile boats and MIG–21s. MIG–21 price of $700,000 quoted and Zakharov reportedly pointed out contrast with price of $3 million for US sale of F–104's to West Germany. When Jablonsky commented there was no requirement for such equipment, Shah replied "I agree and it will not happen unless you help them" (alluding we suppose to possible U.S. failure to satisfy his requirements).

2. In separate conversation Jablonsky had earlier with General Toufanian latter disclosed Zakharov had also offered 200–300 spaces in Soviet military academy for Iranians, plus accommodation 15–25 in war college and 200–300 in infantry, artillery and armored schools. Toufanian rejected offer, but confirmed IIA sending 12 trainees to Soviet Union for six months' training. Russians told Toufanian they still not prepared to sell Iran radar-guides 23 mm. anti-aircraft weapons.

Thacher

---

[1] Source: Department of State, Central Files, POL 7 USSR. Confidential; Limdis. Repeated to CINCSTRIKE and Moscow.

[2] Dated May 28. (Ibid.)

289.   Telegram From the Embassy in Iran to the Department of State[1]

Tehran, May 29, 1968, 0830Z.

5016. Subj: Shah's Visit. Ref: State 172125.[2]

1. Alam informs me Shah is quite agreeable to dinner on June 11 in place of lunch June 12.

2. Ansary has apparently succeeded in stirring up a lot of concern here about possible threat to Shah's personal safety, at Harvard ceremony. According to Alam, Ansary has been to Cambridge and personally walked through the proposed proceedings. These would require Shah pass in procession down a street lined with buildings where students live and to be in very exposed position at ceremonies themselves. FBI, Alam says, believes it very difficult provide proper security measures. I said I was sure Department studying problem very thoroughly and would take every possible precaution. Alam himself leaves June 1 to arrive in U.S. June 3 and plans visit both Washington and Cambridge for personal study of situation. Department will wish no doubt do whatever it can calm Ansary's fears.

Alam informed me also there has been leak here re Harvard ceremony. *Peigham-Emruz*, left-leaning small circulation Persian daily, ran story afternoon May 28 referring to a ceremony to be held at Harvard shortly honoring the Shah. No date given. Alam has instructed press here give no further circulation to report and wire service reps also told not to run it. Alam acknowledged leak had occurred at Pahlavi University where Shah's speech sent for translation.

Thacher

---

[1] Source: Department of State, Central Files, POL 7 IRAN. Confidential; Priority; Exdis.

[2] Telegram 172125 to Tehran, May 28, reported that Ansary had relayed a message from the Shah accepting the invitation and conveying the Empress' regrets. (Ibid.)

290.   Memorandum From Secretary of State Rusk to President Johnson[1]

Washington, June 7, 1968.

SUBJECT

Your Meeting with the Shah of Iran, June 12, 1968, at 12:30 P.M.

Our aim during the Shah's visit will be *to reassure* him that despite the forthcoming change in our Administration and despite our involvement in Vietnam and with our domestic problems, *we wish to continue the intimate relationship we have with Iran.* To this end, you might:

1.   Speak to him of your conviction that no matter who succeeds you in the Presidency, *our fundamental policy toward Iran will continue.*

2.   Tell him that *we will do our best to continue our close military cooperation with Iran:*

—After careful review, we have determined that *we can make available $100 million in credits for FY 1968.*
—*For the longer term* we must continue to have the support of the Congress for authority and funds to carry on the credit program, and *we will do our best to convince the Congress of its desirability.*

3.   *Take the Shah into your confidence* on major world problems:

—*Vietnam.* The Shah has played a helpful role in trying to bring about peace talks.
—*The Arab-Israeli problem.* The Shah is concerned about King Hussein's position.
—*US–USSR relations.*

4.   *Congratulate the Shah* on Iran's domestic progress and on its self-reliant foreign policy:

—*We hope that Iran's military procurement will not impede its spectacular economic development.*
—*We are confident that the Shah's awareness of long-term Soviet objectives will* cause him to *continue to limit Iran's involvement with the Soviet Union,* especially in the military and political fields.
—*We do not desire to replace the British in the Persian Gulf, but strongly hope* that the littoral countries, especially *Iran and Saudi Arabia, can cooperate* to ensure the Gulf's security and progress. The *recent visit of the Shah to King Feisal* in Jidda on June 3 *is a welcome step* in this direction.

Dean Rusk

---

[1] Source: Johnson Library, National Security File, Country File, Iran, Visit of Shah of Iran, 6/11–12/68. Secret.

Attachment

POINTS THE SHAH MAY RAISE AND SUGGESTED RESPONSES

1.   *United States Military Credit Program for Iran*

a.   The Shah may indicate concern about the *uncertainty of our commitment* to assist Iran with military credits in future years. You might respond by saying that *all of our previous military credit agreements with Iran have been conditioned, like the latest one, on Congressional authorization, the availability of funds and annual economic reviews.*

b.   The Shah may ask that the FY 1968 credit finance *patrol craft (PG–84's) armed with Tartar ship-to-ship missiles,* which he desires to defend against similar craft the Iraqis are to receive from the USSR. You might respond that the PG–84 armed with Tartar missiles is *still in the development stage* and that it would *therefore be premature* to fund them this year. We are examining other possible systems which could meet this requirement.

c.   The Shah may ask for assurances that we will supply him with the *two additional squadrons of F–4's* which he desires in the early 1970's. You might respond that we have *no objection* to supplying these aircraft *if Congressional action and our annual reviews permit.*

d.   The Shah might ask again about *training for Iranian pilots.* You might respond that per his request last summer we have allocated 75 spaces for Iran annually through 1970—half of the available pilot training spaces for all allied countries—and that *any further increase would be extremely difficult.*

e.   The Shah might ask that we supply *US Air Force technicians* to maintain the F–4 aircraft he will start receiving from us this fall. You might respond that even aside from the demands of the Vietnam war on our Air Force, we could not do this under our military assistance program, and *suggest that Iran hire civilian technicians,* possibly from McDonnell–Douglas Aircraft Corporation which the Shah will visit on June 14.

2.   *Oil*

a.   The Shah may ask your assistance in persuading *American oil companies to lift more Iranian oil* so that Iran can obtain more oil revenues for its development program. You might respond that *this is a matter for our private oil companies,* adding that the statistics indicate that their performance in recent years has been to the great benefit of Iran as well as themselves.

b.   The Shah may ask assistance in *opening up the American market to more Iranian oil.* You might respond that *U.S. oil import quotas are issued to domestic refiners who are free to procure their imports from any producing country*; increased participation in the U.S. market for Iranian oil can best be obtained by the GOI's ensuring, in collaboration with producing companies, that Iranian production is economically attractive to American refiners who have the allocations to import crude oil.

---

291. Supplementary Memorandum From Secretary of State Rusk to President Johnson[1]

Washington, June 7, 1968.

SUBJECT

Your Conversation with the Shah of Iran, June 12, 1968 at 12:30 P.M.

Discussion:

We do not propose that you raise it, but the Shah may raise with you the subject of our installations at Peshawar and the Pakistani request that we leave there by July 1969. Implied in any such question will be whether we are thinking of increasing our facilities in Iran as a result of the loss of Peshawar.

In accordance with a decision you made in the spring of 1966, we have been taking steps, on a contingency basis, to make possible the transfer of some of the Peshawar operations to Iran. We have not yet decided, however, when any such transfers should be made or the extent to which it would be politically feasible to make such transfers, in the light of our relations with Iran and our desire to retain our existing facilities in Iran.

Recommended Talking Points:

You might tell the Shah, if he raises the matter, that we are still studying the situation caused by Pakistan's request that we leave Peshawar and have not yet reached any firm conclusion. You might assure him that if it turns out that we would desire to increase our operations in Iran, we would of course discuss the matter with him beforehand, any such in-

---

[1] Source: Johnson Library, National Security File, Country File, Iran, Visit of Shah of Iran, 6/11–12/68. Top Secret; Nodis.

creases would be minimal and inconspicuous, and we would hope that he would be able to accommodate them, as before, in the interest of the security of the Free World. (*[less than 1 line of source text not declassified]* will be speaking to the Shah along these lines on June 12 and before you see the Shah.)

Dean Rusk

---

292.   Memorandum From the President's Special Assistant (Rostow) to President Johnson[1]

Washington, June 11, 1968.

SUBJECT

The Shah's Visit

Your office visit with the Shah will be Wednesday[2] at 12:30 p.m., but before the dinner and meeting tonight you will wish to know what is on his mind. As usual, he will wish to hear your views on major world issues, but three specific subjects especially concern him:

1. He hopes for as much assurance as you can give on the continuity of US policy toward Iran. He was badly shaken by your March 31st announcement.[3] Armin Meyer has told him that any American President looking at the Middle East will recognize Iran's importance to us, but it will help for him to hear this from you.

2. Related to this, he will try to find out how much he can count on us for arms supply. You have just agreed to the first $75–100 million sale in a $600 million six-year program. We stated our intention to go ahead year by year, but we had to say we can't commit ourselves ahead until Congress gives us new authority. The one thing you can do is to start off the conversation by telling him that we can go all the way to 100 million this year. (We had told him "$75–100 million" pending final review of funding possibilities.)

---

[1] Source: Johnson Library, National Security File; Country File, Iran, Visit of Shah of Iran, 6/11–12/68. Top Secret; Sensitive.

[2] June 12.

[3] On March 31 President Johnson announced that he would not run for re-election.

3. Whether or not the Shah talks much about the Persian Gulf, we want to urge him to cooperate with King Faisal. The British pull-out by 1971 leaves Iran, Saudi Arabia and the little Arab principalities face-to-face with a series of conflicting claims over territory and oil rights. We want the leaders on the ground to get together rather than looking to us to arrange a settlement. The Shah understands our position, but knowing you are watching will underline it. He apparently had a good airport talk with Faisal on his way here, and we hope he'll follow up.

The one other matter that may come up—[1 line of source text not declassified]—is the fact that we may wish to move [less than 1 line of source text not declassified] intelligence facilities to Iran if Pakistan closes us down at Peshawar. Your best response is to affirm the importance of these activities and let [less than 1 line of source text not declassified] carry the ball.

Walt

---

293. **Memorandum From the Director for the Near East and South Asia Region of the Office of International Security Affairs, Department of Defense (Newcomer) to the Assistant Secretary of Defense for International Security Affairs (Warnke)**[1]

I–23182/68   Washington, June 12, 1968.

SUBJECT

Discussions with Shah of Iran

The Shah told President Johnson last night at dinner[2] that he plans to raise two military supply topics at their 1230 meeting today: (1) additional U.S. advisors/maintenance personnel to help Iran's armed forces assimilate advanced equipment being purchased from the U.S. and (2) the Peace Ruby air control and warning system which is to be constructed along the Persian Gulf. The Shah may also discuss his desire to buy fast

---

[1] Source: Washington National Records Center, RG 330, OASD/ISA Files: FRC 72 A 1498, 333 IRAN, 12 June 1968. Secret.

[2] No record of this conversation has been found.

gunboats with surface-to-surface missiles and/or his plan to purchase a national integrated communications system.

1. *U.S. Advisors.* The Shah wants to take delivery on two more squadrons of F–4 interceptors as quickly as possible. ARMISH/MAAG has developed a training plan which should permit the Iranian Air Force to operate and maintain these aircraft by 1971. The Shah wants these aircraft earlier, has investigated contract maintenance (by McDonnell) but finds it extremely expensive ($10–12 million per year).

The Shah therefore concludes that we could save him this $10–12 million per year by adding about 200 U.S. airmen to our advisory mission to maintain the new aircraft. We are seeking to discourage this corruption of the role of the advisory mission (and the concomitant acceleration of Iran's procurement program), citing Vietnam requirements and our general cutbacks in U.S. personnel overseas. This point is adequately covered in the President's talking paper.

2. *Peace Ruby.* This four-station addition to the limited air control and warning system, built by the UK and the US, was purchased by Iran in 1966 to extend radar coverage and communication along Iran's Persian Gulf coast. Since that time, the delivery schedule has slipped nearly two years (1970 to 1972) owing to unforseen path testing difficulties and unrealistic production leadtime estimates, and costs have increased sharply ($21.3 to $37.8 million) as a result of faulty initial estimates, system changes and equipment price increases.

Iran has indicated that it plans to shift the program from a government-to-government arrangement to a direct contact with a US manufacturer. This would eliminate the time required for competitive bidding and restore the original schedule, but it would cost Iran a bit more than the USAF contract. We have no objection to this shift and have made certain changes in our joint credit arrangements to permit Iran to go this route if it desires.

3. *PG–84 with missiles.* The Shah is pressing to buy four of our new PG–84 (165, 240T) fast patrol boats with a General Dynamics-developed surface-to-surface configuration of the Tartar missile as its principal armament. We have sought to discourage this sale, at least for this year, noting that the missile has not been mated to the PG–84 by the US Navy, that the West German Tartar program is still in the development stage, and that we are not yet convinced that missile boats represent Iran's best defense against the Iraqi Komar threat (aircraft may well prove the most effective and least expensive response).

4. *National Military Communications System (NIMCOMS).* Iran presently has no effective national communications system. We have studied the situation for Iran and have made several recommendations as to an integrated military system. None of these has been accepted.

With the Shah's agreement, Page electronics is now surveying at its own expense Iran's needs in depth and drawing up a program proposal. When this study is completed, Iran is expected to choose a contractor to build the system. If an American firm is chosen, we would expect to fund NIMCOMS under the credit sales program in future years, subject to Congressional approval.

The White House Staff has asked that you and Mr. Schwartz be available to answer questions that may arise during the President's 1230–1400 meeting with the Shah today. We have passed your telephone number at the Madison to Mr. Sanders at the White House for his use, if necessary. Mr. Schwartz and Mr. Reed of my staff plan to stand by in their offices.

Henry C. Newcomer[3]
Brigadier General, USAF

---

[3] Printed from a copy that indicates Newcomer signed the original.

---

294.   Memorandum From the President's Special Assistant (Rostow) to President Johnson[1]

Washington, June 12, 1968.

SUBJECT

Checklist for Your Talk with the Shah—12:30 p.m. Today

We hope the following will have been covered in your talks:

1.   We will stretch this year's arms sale to the full $100 million. (You approved $75–100 million. Defense has found funding for the full amount, and Secretary Rusk recommends you tell the Shah.)

2.   We'll do our best to help with his future arms purchases, though we can't commit ourselves beyond what Congress authorizes. You're confident any US Administration will recognize Iran's importance.

---

[1] Source: Johnson Library, National Security File, NSC Files of Harold Saunders, Visit of Shah of Iran, June 11–June 12, 1968. Top Secret.

3. You're glad the Shah saw King Faisal. Stability in the Persian Gulf depends on their cooperation. (When they had a tiff earlier this year, you urged cooperation. This will show your approval.)

4. Approve attached joint statement.[2]

Here are answers on subjects the Shah raised last night:

1. If he asks about USAF technicians for Phantoms, you might suggest he hire civilians. Even aside from Vietnam demands, we can't do this under our military assistance program.

2. We're not sure which telecommunications problem he'll raise:

—If it's financing his new national military communications system, we could consider military credit.
—If it's aircraft control and warning, he could shave a few months by dealing directly with US suppliers rather than through USAF.

3. He may ask you to lean on American oil companies to lift more Iranian oil. We want Iran's revenues to increase, but we stick to the line that we have to leave this to our private companies. He may also ask help in letting more Iranian oil into the US to barter for US goods. We'd hate to commit ourselves on an oil import quota without knowing what he proposes. You might suggest that the oil expert with him (Mr. Fallah) talk to Tony Solomon.

W.W. Rostow[3]

---

[2] Attached but not printed; for text, see *Public Papers of the Presidents of the United States: Lyndon B. Johnson, 1968–1969,* Book I, p. 712.

[3] Printed from a copy that bears this typed signature.

295.   Memorandum of Conversation[1]

Washington, June 12, 1968, 11 a.m.

SUBJECT

Iran's Military Needs

PARTICIPANTS

H.I.M. Mohammad Reza Pahlavi, Shahanshah of Iran
H.E. Hushang Ansary, Iranian Ambassador

The Secretary
The Honorable Lucius D. Battle, Assistant Secretary, NEA
The Honorable Armin H. Meyer, Ambassador to Iran
Mr. Theodore L. Eliot, Jr., Country Director for Iran

The Shah said that it is necessary for Iran's defense forces in the Persian Gulf area to be ready by the time the British leave the Gulf. He expressed particular concern about Iran's having the capacity to deal with the missile boats that Iraq is receiving and to be able to counter the psychological boost given the Soviet Union through their fleet visits. He could not foresee Iran's having in the near future sufficient naval forces to cope with these problems because Iran has insufficient trained manpower. He looked instead to a combination of naval craft, aircraft and land-based missiles to take care of his country's needs in the Gulf.

The Shah referred specifically to his need to obtain technicians from the US to assist Iran in maintaining the F–4's which will soon be received from the United States. He also referred to the need to carry through with the aircraft control and warning project in south Iran and also the national communications project.

The Shah stressed that he must be able to plan militarily several years in advance and therefore needs assurance from us that we will be able to meet his needs over such a period. Responding to the Secretary's comment that we are now in our annual hassle with the Congress on our military assistance and sales programs, the Shah said that he had two suggestions. One is for the Defense Department to include Iran's requirements in its orders of equipment for American forces. This would tend to keep the prices for Iran down. Alternatively, the Defense Department might be able to persuade American arms manufacturers to give Iran special favorable prices. In either case, favorable prices would serve to offset the cost to Iran of financing it might have to obtain from commercial banks.

---

[1] Source: Department of State, Central Files, POL 7 IRAN. Secret. Drafted by Eliot and approved in S/S on June 25. The meeting took place at the Blair House. The source text is Part II of II; Part I is ibid., S/S Conference Files: Lot 70 D 418, Visit of the Shah of Iran, June 11–12, 1968, Vol. I of II.

The Secretary indicated that after our nominating conventions, it might be useful for the Executive Branch to discuss this subject with the candidates of both parties. He said that he believed the present leading candidates favor our program of military cooperation with Iran, and the Shah said that he also believes this to be the case.

---

296. Memorandum From the President's Special Assistant (Rostow) to President Johnson[1]

Washington, June 12, 1968.

SUBJECT

Arms Agreement with the Shah

After hearing the warmth of your statement to the Shah, I'm sure this is just a formality.

However, we reserved for you the final go-ahead on making this year's military credit sale to Iran the full $100 million. You earlier approved $75–100 million assuming available funds.

The Shah's negotiator is here and will sign an agreement Friday if you approve. Secretaries Rusk and Clifford recommend you do so. Funds are available.[2]

Walt

---

[1] Source: Johnson Library, National Security File, Country File, Iran, Memos & Miscellaneous, Vol. II, 1/66–1/69. Secret.

[2] The "Approve" option is checked on the source text and handwritten notes indicate that Harold Saunders was notified on June 12 and that he notified the Iranian desk the same day.

297.   Telegram From the Department of State to the Embassy in Iran[1]

Washington, June 13, 1968, 2025Z.

182515. Subject: Shah's Visit to US.

1. Shah arrived New York June 10, Washington June 11, proceeds Cambridge for Harvard honorary degree June 12, St. Louis to visit McDonnell–Douglas Aircraft Corp June 13, Chicago University June 14 to dedicate building in his name and financed by him, and New York June 15.

2. New York visit June 10–11 highlighted by background conference with leading editors, meeting with top-level financial men, and lunch with U Thant. Financial meeting was especially useful in terms drawing attention to Iran's burgeoning economy and investment opportunities, although Shah made special point that foreign firms investing in Iran can have no better than 50–50 arrangement.

3. In Washington President gave large dinner June 11 in Shah's honor and had discussions with him that evening and also following morning. Public remarks at dinner and private discussions reflected warm and close friendship of the two men and their countries. Shah also met with Secretary Rusk and with Dillon Ripley of Smithsonian Institution in connection with scientific cooperation between Iran and US.

4. Principal substantive subjects on Shah's mind in Washington talks were (a) need to bolster Iran's defense capabilities in light forthcoming British departure from Persian Gulf and (b) desire of Iran to sell additional oil to US on barter basis. Talks also reviewed general world situation including Soviet policies in Eastern Europe, Korea and Vietnam, and current situation in Near East. As in previous visits of Shah to Washington, exchanges on world affairs were full and frank, with basic similarity of views on both sides.

5. In light private nature of visit, press coverage has not been as great as during last August's official visit. Press has speculated primarily on military discussions.

6. About 100 students demonstrated on Shah's arrival at Waldorf in New York but were not seen by Shah or party. Two or three students appeared opposite Blair House on one occasion when Shah was departing for Blair House.

Rusk

---

[1] Source: Department of State, Central Files, POL 7 IRAN. Secret. Drafted by Eliot on June 12. Cleared by Rockwell and Saunders and approved by Battle. Repeated to London, Jidda, Ankara, Rawalpindi, Kuwait, and CINCSTRIKE.

298.   Memorandum of Conversation[1]

Washington, June 13, 1968.

PARTICIPANTS

Mehdi Samii, Governor of the Central Bank of Iran
W.W. Rostow
Harold H. Saunders

Mr. Samii came in just to wind up a general discussion of economic development in Iran which he and Mr. Rostow had begun at the dinner for the Shah.

Mr. Rostow began by placing Iran at that point on the development ladder where the "take off" is just about finished and the nation is beginning to diffuse its resources and technology into a broad range of new industries. He likened Iran somewhat to Mexico, noting that Iran was still just a little bit behind. Looking to the future, he felt that Iran's greatest increase in revenue would come not from pressing for marginal increases in oil earnings, but would come from the widespread expansion of processing industries. The important principle will be for Iran to reap the profits of value added to its raw materials rather than to let these profits go to processors outside Iran.

Mr. Samii asked what he thought Iran should do in mining its metal ores. Mr. Rostow said he could not be sure without studying the resources and markets in detail, but in general he felt that Iran might look at the example of Sweden. He felt it would make sense for Iran to move gradually from selling raw ore into various stages of processing. He urged that Iran, in developing new processing industries in all fields, not be afraid of foreign capital to start with but to be sure in its initial agreements with foreign investors to provide for the gradual transfer of management and control to Iranian hands. He felt this would undercut much domestic opposition to the suspected "new-imperialism" of foreign capital and would avoid embarrassing political problems for both sides later.

Mr. Rostow, as he had promised Tuesday night, gave Mr. Samii a collection of memoranda and articles on the need for high protein additives to improve nutritional levels (copies provided to NEA). Entirely apart from the human obligation to do our best by each child that is born, he said it makes sense purely from the hard-headed planner's point of view to insure that a developing country will have the best minds it can develop, and we have now learned that adequate diet is an essential part

---

[1] Source: Johnson Library, National Security File, Country File, Iran, Memos & Miscellaneous, Vol. II, 1/66–1/69. Confidential.

of producing those minds. Mr. Samii expressed his gratitude and asked whether we would be able to send someone out to help develop a project in this field, once his government had decided what it needed. Mr. Rostow said that Ambassador Meyer would certainly be prepared to discuss this when Mr. Samii was ready.

Mr. Rostow also stressed the possible importance of educational television. He said that a country like Iran must learn to develop talent within the country and not to rely entirely on education abroad. Where there is a shortage of teachers, educational television can bring the best teachers to even the remotest areas. He recommended that Mr. Samii talk with Mr. McGeorge Bundy or David Bell at the Ford Foundation.

H.H.S.

299. Memorandum for the Record[1]

Washington, June 14, 1968.

SUBJECT

The Shah's Visit—Follow-up Actions

As a result of his talk with the Shah on June 12,[2] the President requested that memoranda be written on the following subjects presenting the basic proposition on each, the pros and cons and recommendations. The President would like to be as forthcoming as possible.

1. Can the US buy more oil from Iran on the basis of its being 100% tied to US procurement? One aspect of this is whether the Defense Department might buy more oil for Vietnam from Iran. The main problem is to assure that any sales would be incremental.

---

[1] Source: Johnson Library, National Security File, Country File, Iran, Memos & Miscellaneous, Vol. II, 1/66–1/69. Secret. Copies were sent to the Secretaries of State and Defense, the Bureau of the Budget Director, and the AID Administrator.

[2] Attached to a copy of this memorandum in Department of State files is a typewritten note that reads: "Meeting between the President and the Shah, June 12, 1968: President Johnson had a private meeting with the Shah of Iran and no formal memorandum of conversation was prepared. However, the attached memorandum for the record from Walt W. Rostow concerning follow-up actions for the Department of State was prepared as a result of the meeting." (Department of State, S/S Conference Files: Lot 70 D 418, Visit of the Shah of Iran, June 11–12, 1968, Vol. I of II)

2.   Can the US provide USAF technicians in support of the F–4 aircraft that Iran is buying? The President wishes to give this sympathetic high priority consideration. What are the possibilities for meeting the Shah's concern?

3.   Can we meet the Shah's concerns about his radar and military telecommunications systems, with particular reference to the slippage in time? Since this was not spelled out in detail, it may be best to do a memo on each as a separate problem, noting the Shah's concern and what the possibilities are of meeting it.

4.   How can we give the Shah assurance that he can plan on obtaining arms from the US for his five-year program, i.e. that his planning can be long range, not on a year to year basis? The President made it plain in general terms that, within the limits of our world-wide arms sales program, he felt that Iran should enjoy high priority and be able to buy high quality modern equipment from us.

5.   What role can the Northup 530 aircraft play in the development of Iran's air force? What are the facts on the development and financing of this project and could Iran participate in any consortium type arrangement for its further development?

6.   What is the best military way of dominating the entrance to the Persian Gulf? The Shah expressed his concern about the Russian Fleet and the Persian Gulf and asked whether we could fix surface-to-surface missiles owned and controlled by Iran on the islands in the Straits of Hormuz to dominate it.

7.   The President asked the Shah to consider shifting some of Iran's dollar holdings from short term to a longer term basis to aid our balance of payments. The Shah, without committing himself, agreed that Governor Samii of Iran Central Bank should follow this up with the Treasury Department.

I believe it is permissible, if the Shah's proposals as described are not clear enough to make possible an adequate response, to seek clarification of his concerns through Ambassador Ansary or Ambassador Meyer.

WW Rostow

300.   Memorandum From the Joint Chiefs of Staff to the Assistant Secretary of Defense for International Security Affairs (Warnke)[1]

DJSM 790–68   Washington, June 25, 1968.

SUBJECT

The Shah's Visit—Follow-up Actions (U)

1. (U) Reference is made to a memorandum by the Assistant Secretary of Defense (ISA), dated 19 June 1968, subject as above.[2]

2. (S) During the recent talks with the President, the Shah of Iran raised the question of the best military way of dominating the entrance to the Persian Gulf. The Shah also expressed his concern about the Russian Fleet and the Persian Gulf and asked whether the United States could fix missiles owned and controlled by Iran on the islands in the Strait of Hormuz to dominate it.

3. (S) By his concern, the Shah identified the major threat to the Persian Gulf as the Soviet Navy. However, this threat is not considered immediate and therefore all elements of the problem should be thoroughly examined before changing the proposed sales program, which was recently developed in response to previous requests by the Shah.

4. (S) Considering the range, nature of the target, usual temperature and environmental factors, it would seem that the Nike Hercules is the only missile in the United States inventory that would approach the Shah's requirements. One or two batteries (nine launchers each) located on the mainland or on Larak or Qeshm Islands, could deliver 500 pounds of high explosive to any point in the strait with an estimated 200 yard circular error probable (CEP). A guided missile system would have the advantage that such a system could probably be established without the undue irritation that would be caused by measures such as mining. Disadvantages of the system would be the high cost (probably at least $4 million per battery), the need for another variety of specialized personnel, and the susceptibility to enemy destruction. Production lines of this missile are presently shut down. In addition, experience in use of the Nike Hercules in the surface-to-surface role is considered inadequate to justify expenditure of funds to employ this missile as possibly envisioned by the Shah.

5. (S) Presently Iran has a well motivated, competent Air Force which could operate with good effect in the Strait of Hormuz. This capa-

---

[1] Source: Washington National Records Center, RG 330, OSD Files: FRC 73 A 1250, Iran 400, 25 June 68. Secret.

[2] Not found.

bility will be greatly improved with the programmed acquisition of F–4 aircraft.

6. (S) The Shah has also sought to procure PGM–84 missile boats with a surface-to-surface capability. These are also considered more practical, when available, than an island based missile system.

7. (S) Iranian control of the Strait of Hormuz will not in itself keep the peace in the Gulf or maintain its Western orientation. Also, if the USSR should decide to move into the Persian Gulf, Iranian missiles would not be a deterrent. It is therefore recommended that an attempt be made to dissuade the Shah from procuring an island based surface-to-surface missile system.

B.E. Spivy
Lt. General, USA
Director, Joint Staff

---

301.   Letter From Secretary of Defense Clifford to the Shah of Iran[1]

Washington, June 29, 1968.

Your Imperial Majesty:

Since your departure from Washington, my staff has looked carefully into the pricing of F–4 aircraft.[2] As a result, I can assure you that Iran has paid no more than the costs our armed services would incur in purchasing the same number of aircraft at the same time. I do not expect this situation to change in the future.

I have asked Mr. Henry Kuss of my staff to discuss this matter in some detail with Governor Samii in order to resolve any questions which he may have on either past or future procurement.

It was indeed a pleasure to see you again. The occasion gave me an opportunity to re-acquaint myself with the great advances Iran has made in recent years under your wise leadership.

Sincerely,

Clark M. Clifford

---

[1] Source: Washington National Records Center, RG 330, OSD Files: FRC 73 A 1250, Iran 452, 29 Jun 68. No classification marking.

[2] A June 20 memorandum from Warnke to Clifford noted that in response to the Shah's questioning of Clifford about aircraft prices paid by the U.S. Air Force versus those paid by Iran, Warnke wrote that Iran had paid no more, and in one case paid less, than the costs that the U.S. armed services would have incurred in purchasing the same number of aircraft of the same configuration at the same time. (Ibid.)

302. Memorandum From Harold H. Saunders of the National Security Council Staff to the President's Special Assistant (Rostow)[1]

Washington, July 1, 1968.

SUBJECT

Your appointment with Ansary—Tuesday,[2] at 11 a.m.

Attached is State's briefing paper.[3] Following are the main points you might make to Ansary:

1. We are just about finished with *the studies the President promised* the Shah. It will take us a couple of more weeks and the President will be in touch. Some of these involve difficult problems for us but we have made every effort to be as forthcoming as possible.

2. You could say how much the *President enjoyed the Shah's visit* and how much the President has enjoyed his association with the Shah.

3. You might say the *President appreciates the Shah's agreement to consider shifting dollar holdings to longer term basis.*

4. You might ask Ansary to *tell Prime Minister Hoveyda how much we are looking forward to his visit in December.* (The purpose of that visit will be to broaden our current praise of Iranian leaders. We don't want the Shah to think that he is the whole show. Having Hoveyda here, with the possibility of meeting the President-elect, will serve this purpose.)

5. You might *chat about the Persian Gulf* in the light of its experiment in sub-regional relationships. The main point we want to make is the importance of the Shah working out these arrangements with other leaders in the Gulf, especially Faisal.

6. You might *chat about the Arab-Israeli problem* (keeping your comments general since everybody reads Ansary's reports and he isn't always too accurate).

State recommends that you not foreshadow our response on any of the specific requests the Shah made so we can save the full impact for the President. For your information, however, here are the conclusions on the points the President asked to have studied as they stand in draft:

1. Assuring the Shah of our *support for his five-year program.* The best we have been able to come up with so far is a promise by the President to speak to his successor about the importance of our continuing

---

[1] Source: Johnson Library, National Security File, Walt Rostow Files, Visitors, 1968. Secret.

[2] July 2.

[3] Attached but not printed.

cooperation with Iran. We would also reiterate the assurance we have already given—that the Executive Branch will continue to try to persuade Congress of the importance of our ability to participate in Iran's military development program.

2. *USAF technicians to support F–4 aircraft.* The USAF has surprisingly come up with a proposal to send 40–50 supervisory personnel for maintenance management. However, this still is not final because we haven't resolved the major question of who would pay.

3. *Dominating the entrance to the Persian Gulf.* The proposal so far is that we offer the Shah a study of this problem. I don't think this is quite enough by itself, and I will urge that this be beefed up.

4. *Radar and military communications systems.* Our next step will be to outline the alternatives to the Shah to make clear what he still needs to decide. Once there is a definite plan, we will see how we can help, but the issue is just not precisely enough defined yet.

5. *Northrop 530 Aircraft.* We would give the Shah the facts, telling him that we think it is premature for Iran to invest because the plane has not even been design-tested yet.

6. *US to buy more oil from Iran.* This is the toughest. The proposal is to invite Iran to work through companies that have US oil import permits, since the USG can't engage directly in barter without upsetting the whole quota system. Iran could also bid on the sale of refined products to Defense (though it's not clear yet what this would add up to).

As I say, these are still tentative, and we will be sharpening them in the next few days.

Hal

303.   Telegram From the Embassy in Iran to the Department of
       State[1]

Tehran, July 7, 1968, 0825Z.

5600. Subject: Student Unrest. Ref: State 186094.[2] Summary. Iran
would have to be unearthly if student problems did not exist. However,
for the moment at least, potential student demagogy is having trouble
tilting against Iran's economic boom and Shah's "independent nationalism" policies. So student problems will probably remain low key, although in long run student unrest could erupt, particularly if Shah's
present highly successful policies should begin to falter.

1.   Compared with recent events at Columbia University, Berkeley,
Paris and Rome, student situation in Iran is at least for moment tranquil
and well-controlled. Several minor student upsurges occurred this
spring (A–476, A–520, A–539, and A–647),[3] which surprised GOI and
prompted charges of foreign inspiration but as reported by Embassy
(A–576)[4] these upsurges gained little momentum and were effectively
brought under control by GOI.

2.   In Iran, student unrest is largely function of political status quo.
Politically, Shah and his regime have never been more firmly in saddle.
As result of "white revolution" and "independent nationalism" policies,
wind has been taken out of sails of opposition, i.e. remnants of Tudeh and
National Front parties can no longer effectively accuse regime of being
feudalist or US puppet, meanwhile, economic boom, premised on $800
million oil revenues, leaves oppositionists, past or potential, with few
flags to wave.

3.   This is not to say that younger generation in Iran is less restive
than youth elsewhere. Rebellious adolescent instincts exist. They are encouraged by epidemic of student unrest elsewhere in world, including
even in Communist Bloc. They should never be judged as less than incipient. It must be remembered that massive student uprisings against
Shah's regime did occur here in early 1950's, cleverly manipulated by
demagogic leader, Mosadeq. As recently as 1963, major uprising occurred at Tehran University, which was quelled by rather ruthless police
action.

4.   Present day Iran affords some special opportunities for student
unhappiness. Despite economic boom, there is almost legendary lack of

---

[1] Source: Department of State, Central Files, POL 13–2 IRAN. Confidential.
[2] Dated June 19. (Ibid.)
[3] Dated March 9 (ibid.), April 6 (ibid., EDU 9–3 IRAN), April 17 (ibid.), and June 6
(ibid., POL 13–2), respectively.
[4] Dated May 6. (Ibid., EDX 12 IRAN)

identification. Decisions are made by Shah or not much lower than cabinet-technocrat level. There is thus little feeling of participation in decision-making, least of all among student groups. This frustration is, however, for the moment considerably offset by prospects of personal economic gain and by vague awareness (and pride) that compared with other countries in Mideast Iran is somewhat a model of economic development and social progress. Dissatisfaction which exists tends to be less focussed on Shah and has become more of an amorphous discontent with political structure. Specific issues for stirring up dissidence are, however, quite unpromising. In short, instead of passionate student hostility there is student apathy, which is less but still worrisome.

5.   In Iran, Shah monarchy has 2500-year tradition. It may one day give way to liberal democracy, but it is institution which still is effective, particularly as so cagily manipulated by present Shah. Mosadeq sought to tilt with this institution and Shah as its personification with 20th century weapons, but, as so often happens in emerging societies, Mosadeq employed totalitarian tools as much or more than regime against which he tilting. Still today there is some lingering pro-Mosadeq sentiment. For example, there seems to be goodly number of secondary school teachers who mostly due to limited qualifications have never risen to prominence and who still tend to carry Mosadeq torch. Their teaching has some influence on university enrollment (which knew not Mosadeq), with sort of greener pastures overtones. But this sentiment, as all other oppositionism, bucks national self-congratulation induced by Iran's present manifest prosperity and progress.

6.   Some controversy inevitably develops over manner in which GOI copes with student manifestations. Thanks largely to university leadership, peaceful student marches have been condoned, but any activism is quickly suppressed by police (and SAVAK) action. This, of course, reaps student resentment. In case of Pahlavi University unrest several students were locked up and accused under highly questionable pretexts of being ChiCom agents. In future, ruthless police methods could contribute to student explosion. However, GOI leadership is convinced that strong police action is in keeping with exercise of authority as historically practiced in Iran. Its belief in efficacy such measures has only been strengthened by dramatic reports of recent student riots in US/other countries where in GOI eyes administration has been too lax.

7.   Fact that Shah has always been good America friend, and in particular prevailed over Mosadeq with American blessing, tends to associate Shah's regime, despite its flirtations with Soviets, with US. Since he is riding high, US is for present in relatively good position, although among student groups there is inevitably unhappiness over Shah's military expenditures, as well as US role in Viet Nam. Nonetheless, there have been no demonstrations in Iran re Viet Nam, even by students.

Therefore, under present circumstances chances of student revolt being centered on anti-Americanism are not bright.

8. Student problem was reported in greater detail in A–576, along with GOI and USG activities connected therewith. Of course, student situation could explode at moment's notice. However, our best guess is that student troubles in Iran will at least for present remain at relatively low key. Student grievances are apt for the present to center on university policies. In long run, however, political frustrations could mount up, particularly if Shah's dream of transforming Iran into political entity with Western European standards of living does not materialize.

Meyer

---

304.   **Telegram From the Embassy in Iran to the Department of State**[1]

Tehran, July 12, 1968, 0905Z.

5666. Shah's Defense Concepts. Summary. In tour d'horizon re Iran's defense program, Shah emphasized vital importance of security of Gulf and Iran's key role in attaining that objective. Kuss succeeded in securing Shah's consideration of cost effectiveness and of need for gearing shopping list to other factors such as supply of technicians.

1. Shah 11th opened two-hour conversation with Defense Deputy Assistant Secretary Kuss and me by contrasting Iran's military posture with that of its neighbors. Question he emphasized is not merely preparing against threats but maintaining military "balance" so as to deter adventurous aggression.

2. Doubting Soviets would risk world war by direct attack on Iran, Shah said Iran would nevertheless resist as long as it could should Soviet aggression take place. More likely, however, would be "wars by proxy."

3. Shah noted Afghanistan has MIG's, SAM's (which Iran does not have), and Soviet technicians. Iraq, he said, is "big question mark," capable of going either anti-Communist or to chaos. He noted Iraq has more

---

[1] Source: Department of State, Central Files, DEF 1–5 IRAN. Secret; Priority; Limdis. Repeated to CINCSTRIKE/CINCMEAFSA.

fighters than Iran plus sixteen Sukhoy bombers with sixteen more to come. Radical Arab states have vast quantities of Soviet arms, supported by Soviet technical personnel (3,000 in UAR alone). More recently Saudi Arabia has bought Hawks and Lightnings, Kuwait and even Qatar are seeking arms deals with British. When Kuss pointed out none of these countries serious military threat because of personnel incompetence, Shah noted they hiring mercenaries. Discussion re British, FAA and Bahrein being reported separately.[2]

4. Shah stressed vital importance of Persian Gulf to Iran. It simply not possible to permit vacuum which will occur by British withdrawal to be filled by irresponsible forces. To assure Iran's interest and, therefore, Gulf security Iran must play role consonant with its size and capability. Most effective means for doing so would be potential control of Strait of Hormuz. Knowledge that Iran has such capability would in Shah's view serve as most effective deterrent. We emphasized Iran must be prepared by end of 1971, date of British withdrawal.

5. Shah placed highest priority on air defense, radar and navy. Army requirements could if necessary be to some extent deferred.

6. Noting Iran not interested in fighting Iraqi KOMAR ships but is more concerned re larger vessels (such as UAR destroyers coming around Arabian peninsula). Shah discussed merits of land-based missiles at mouth of Gulf. He felt they would have maximum optical impact of deterrent nature. If land-based missiles (he has impression Tartar missiles have 40 mile radius) unfeasible, missile-carrying boats would be alternate. He mentioned possibility of Bagrielle missiles and expressed belief their Israeli origin could be successfully camouflaged by saying they were French-made.

7. Noting this is complicated question, Kuss said thorough study being made by DOD experts. Meanwhile, we called Shah's attention to fact that air force is potent weapon indeed in handling threat from enemy navy. Nothing could give greater optical impact than Phantoms screaming across horizon. Shah was concerned that air force could not do job at night or during inclement weather. But readily agreed that air force would be primary instrument inside Gulf.

8. Throughout conversation Kuss stressed trained manpower as limiting factor. Shah reported his discussion with President re possible USAF technicians as soon as some could be spared from Viet Nam scene. Shah hinted he might pick up at least part of tab for USAF technicians. He also mentioned possibility of "mixture" of USAF technicians with some civilians hired under contract.

---

[2] Not found.

9. Shah affirmed Iran must avoid duplications in country-wide communications systems. He reiterated, however, that air defense communications must be independent, mentioning again the ease with which potential enemy can knock out microwave pylon. Kuss pointed out no nation has completely separate military communications and noted that if pylon knocked out alternative routings would be possible. Shah eventually concurred that PTT should be backbone of basic military system and even that separate air defense communications be installed in order of priority, utilizing at least temporarily such PTT links as are already available. Kuss stressed saving in money is secondary to economic utilization of Iran's limited supply of technicians. He also noted that TOPO communications centers just as vulnerable as microwave centers. Re Peace Ruby, Kuss agreed USAF would complete "statement of work" within three months. Shah at least tentatively decided to save time by negotiating with sole source rather than resorting to competitive bidding.

10. Recalling how two years ago USG cut back Iranian pilot training slots to five, Shah expressed gratification for 75 slots provided as result his discussions with President year ago. He expressed unhappiness with training of 25 pilots in Pakistan, on grounds program is inferior, trainees being supplied with ChiCom propaganda, and Paks are even asking Iran for training equipment and instructors. Shah stated he prepared to postpone expensive present plans for developing pilot training in Iran if there is assurance that USG will continue to train pilots to meet Iran's needs. Kuss agreed question reasonable and would take up with Chief Air Force and other US authorities.

11. After extensive discussion of tank situation, Shah tended to agree to slippage, if necessary, of Sheridan tank procurement, provided few such tanks could be made available for advance training. Kuss noted how Shileleigh also would be drain on technician supply. Shah stressed Sheridans needed for tank destroyer mission. He agreed to Gen. Twitchell reviewing situation to insure best equipment for this mission. Re M–47, he has decided Swingfires too expensive ($140,000) and tends toward use of 105 mm gun with perhaps some of M–47's retaining 90 mm gun. Re engines for retrofit, Shah tends toward Continental because it is identical with engine in M–60, but will await results of test runs made in Italy. Kuss agreed obtain test data and provide.

12. Shah stressed his need to have firm commitment for five year program. Kuss reiterated standard USG position re our "intention" and noted qualifications which we have mentioned have been present in previous years but they particularly delicate this year because of legislation before Congress. Kuss recognized five year plan worked out with ARMISH/MAAG but urged Shah's support for going beyond "shopping list"

type planning to broader joint planning which delineates manpower, training, operations, and financial requirements in keeping with material timing.

Meyer

---

305.   Memorandum From Secretary of State Rusk to President Johnson[1]

Washington, July 17, 1968.

SUBJECT

The Shah's Visit—Follow-up Actions

Recommendations:

That you approve the enclosed letter to the Shah of Iran.[2]

That you approve the enclosed instructions to Ambassador Meyer.[3]

Discussion:

When he visited with you on June 11 and 12, the Shah made six specific requests for various types of American assistance, largely in the military field (see Mr. Rostow's memorandum, enclosed).[4] In response to your instructions to be as forthcoming as possible to these requests, each one of them has been reviewed in detail and the suggested letter to the Shah incorporates the principal conclusions of these reviews. As you further instructed, memoranda, one on each request, have been prepared and are enclosed:[5]

I believe that the suggested response to the Shah is as forthcoming as we can be at this time, will serve to convince the Shah of our desire to

---

[1] Source: Department of State, Central Files, POL 7 IRAN. Secret; Limdis. Drafted by Eliot and McClelland on July 11, cleared by Rockwell and Battle, and in draft by Wolf, Soloman, Akins, and Warnke.

[2] Attached but not printed. A typed notation on the source text states that the President signed a revised letter to the Shah; see Document 307.

[3] See Document 307.

[4] See Document 299.

[5] Attached but not printed.

maintain our close military relations with Iran, and will therefore contribute to the strengthening of our overall relationship with that important country.

Some of the questions raised by the Shah are complex and I also enclose, for your approval, suggested instructions that you may wish sent to Ambassador Meyer in order that he may explain the background and various considerations underlying your letter.

The Secretary of Defense concurs in this memorandum and the background memoranda enclosed have been coordinated with the Department of Defense. The paper on the Shah's proposal to barter Iranian oil has also been coordinated with the Treasury Department and the Department of the Interior. The Treasury also concurs in your reminding the Shah of your hope that Iran will shift a portion of its dollar reserves into long-term United States assets.

Dean Rusk

306.   Memorandum From the President's Special Assistant (Rostow) to President Johnson[1]

Washington, July 24, 1968, 5:15 p.m.

SUBJECT

The Shah's Visit—Follow-up Actions

You will recall that the Shah put six specific questions to you. Attached are (1) a letter for the Shah answering these questions and (2) instructions for Armin Meyer to use in explaining your answers.[2] We have been relatively responsive, but we have not been able to do everything the Shah has asked us to do. Therefore, the letter is straightforward in saying what we can and cannot do. Following is the reasoning behind each of our answers, arranged in the same order as they are mentioned in your letter:

---

[1] Source: Johnson Library, National Security File, Special Head of State Correspondence File, Iran, 7/1/68–10/31/68. Secret.

[2] See Document 307.

1.   *What assurance can we give the Shah so he can plan on obtaining arms on good financial terms from the US for his five-year program?*

It is still not possible for us to give the Shah any categorical assurance that he can depend on USG credit in the future since we do not know what authority Congress will give us to sell arms on credit. We believe the best offer to make right now is for you to promise the Shah to speak to your successor about your relationship with him and the importance of our continuing cooperation. We have already given him a general assurance that the Executive Branch will urge Congress to fund a continued program, but your personal offer to intervene with your successor might be a sufficiently attractive new element to make him feel that we are doing everything possible.

2.   *Can the US provide USAF technicians to help Iran learn to maintain the F–4 aircraft it is buying?*

We are prepared to send fifty supervisory-level personnel for a one-year period to begin with if the Iranian Government will pay for them. We had already planned to send three USAF mobile training teams for a shorter period to help Iran handle its first F–4's this fall, but we could send a mission for longer. However, with limited military aid funds and our balance of payments problem, it would be hard to justify to Congress our paying for these extra people over a period longer than that required for familiarization with the new equipment.

3.   *What is the best military way of protecting the entrance in the Persian Gulf against the Soviet fleet?*

JCS does not like the Shah's proposal to station land-based missiles at the entrance to the Gulf because they are too expensive, too uncertain, and too vulnerable to attack. JCS would rather see the Shah rely on a combination of his Air Force and some good missile gun boats. We would give the Shah this preliminary JCS reaction and offer to study the question further with him if he wishes.

4.   *How can we speed up planning and construction of the Shah's radar and military communications systems?*

Both of these projects still require decisions by the Shah's Government. We have already turned over several preliminary engineering studies. We do have proposals for helping the Shah decide exactly what he wants and for speeding completion. But your best response to his question, rather than get into these details, is to offer full discussion of these alternatives by our Ambassador and military chief in Iran.

5.   *What role can the Northrop 530 aircraft play in the development of Iran's Air Force?*

We would keep the door open for Iran's possible participation in this plane's development. But since it is still in the design stages and is not planned for production before 1975, we would suggest that the Shah move cautiously before committing much money.

6. *Can the US buy more oil from Iran?*

This is the toughest. The best we can tell the Shah is that the Defense Department would buy more refined products at competitive prices if such products are available. This would not amount to too much because we already have a long-term contract with ARAMCO to buy Saudi products through the refinery on Bahrain. What the Shah really wants is for us to increase purchases of crude oil from the National Iranian Oil Company. Theoretically, we could do this by giving Iran a special import quota or by bartering Iranian oil for US exports. The main problem with both methods is that we would have to change our whole import quota system and would thereby open ourselves to requests for similar treatment from our other oil-producing friends, upset Venezuela and stir up a domestic hornet's nest. He will be disappointed, but we suspect he will be prepared for this answer.

I believe the Agencies have given these questions a fair look. The answers are not entirely what the Shah might hope for. But they are reasonably responsive and he should recognize this. The attached letter is for your signature if you approve, and beneath it are more detailed instructions for Armin Meyer.

Walt

Approve[3]

Disapprove

Call Me

---

[3] This option is checked on the source text, and a handwritten note indicates the Department of State was informed that the President signed the letter on July 25.

307.   Telegram From the Department of State to the Embassy in Iran[1]

Washington, July 26, 1968, 1716Z.

209512. Subject: Shah's Visit Follow-up Actions.

1. The President has approved and you are hereby instructed to transmit the following message to the Shah:

"Your Imperial Majesty: I must say once again what a great pleasure it was to see you in Washington last month and to have the opportunity to share thoughts with you and to seek your counsel on matters of mutual concern. My admiration for your country's progress under your leadership continues to grow.

During our conversation, you mentioned a number of specific matters on which you indicated a desire for further consultations. We have reviewed these matters in detail, and I am now in a position to give you additional thoughts on all of them. Ambassador Meyer will also be prepared to discuss them further with you.

I fully understand your concern and need for long-term military procurement plans. Although our past undertakings to cooperate with Iran in the military field have, like our present one, been conditioned on Congressional action, they have come to fruition. It is my desire that we continue this cooperation in the future and my hope that the Executive Branch, in accord with the Congress, will continue the agreed programs of military cooperation with Iran. I will discuss this subject with my successor and inform him of the importance I attach to continuing close cooperation with Iran in all fields.

In connection with your request for additional technical advisers for Iran's F–4 aircraft, I am pleased to inform you that we will be able to provide, on a reimbursable basis and initially for a one-year period, up to 50 additional United States Air Force personnel if they can be of substantial assistance to advise and assist in providing maintenance management for these aircraft. I suggest that the details of this arrangement be worked out between your military people and the Chief of our Military Assistance Advisory Group in Iran.

You mentioned your concern about defense arrangements in the Persian Gulf. Our military people have made a preliminary investigation which reveals a number of problems and indicates that a land-based missile defense of the Strait of Hormuz would probably not be feasible. If

---

[1] Source: Department of State, Central Files, POL 7 IRAN. Secret; Limdis. Drafted by McClelland on July 11; cleared by Eliot, Rockwell, Battle, Wolf, and Saunders; and in draft by Warnke, Solomon, and Akins; and approved by Rusk. Repeated to CINCSTRIKE.

you desire I shall be pleased to direct that a detailed study be prepared for you on this subject, including possible alternatives which might assist your future planning.

Your concern to have the most efficient radar and communications system, at the lowest cost, for your southern defense, is of course a matter on which our military people have been working together for some months. I have asked the Department of Defense to consider urgently how we can assist Iran's needs in this connection. Our Ambassador and the Chief of our Military Assistance Advisory Group in Iran will be prepared to pursue this matter with your people, and we will be as helpful as we can to you in exploring possible alternatives.

I am currently having an evaluation made of the plans for the new aircraft being developed by the Northrop Corporation that you mentioned to me. I understand that it is now planned that this aircraft will be ready after 1975. The work on it is still in an early stage, but if it develops that a consortium is to be formed and the aircraft lives up to design specifications, Iran might give further consideration to participation in this project. At that time perhaps our military planners could consult with you as to what alternatives would be available for the further modernization of the Iranian Air Force.

We have also looked into the possibilities for expanding the purchase of Iranian oil by American companies or the American government, possibly on a barter basis. I regret that there seems to be very little that can be done in this regard outside of normal, existing trade channels. To give special quotas to Iran for the import of petroleum into the United States or to enter into special arrangements for the exchange of Iranian oil for American goods would raise grave problems for our worldwide oil policy. On the other hand, the Department of Defense regularly purchases refined oil products for our forces in East Asia on the basis of competitive bidding, from a number of sources, and if Iranian companies can supply the required quantities at competitive prices we would be pleased to purchase them.

Finally, I appreciate your willingness to consider shifting a portion of Iran's dollar reserves into long-term United States assets which will assist our balance of payments, and I look forward to hearing further from you about this at your convenience.

I take deep satisfaction, Your Majesty, in the warm relations between our countries and look forward to doing what I can to strengthen these relations still further in the future. You and the people of Iran can continue to depend on the sympathy and support of the people of the United States as you strive to build the kind of prosperous and secure Iran that you want.

With my warmest personal regards,

Sincerely,

Lyndon B. Johnson"

2. When presenting President's letter to Shah, or at appropriate time thereafter, Ambassador Meyer may state that President authorized him to make following comments concerning letter:

a) *General:* President's reply is based on most careful examination of Shah's various requests by all agencies concerned. It takes into consideration not only President's desire to maintain close ties with Iran in all fields, but also our own domestic problems and political system. All subjects raised by Shah will of course be subjects of continuing consultations in the future.

b) *Five-Year Commitment:* President hopes Shah fully understands why US cannot, in view of our legislative system, give any more definite assurances than he has already given. Congressional situation requires us to consider our military credit program on annual basis. This, however, has been true in past, and our past record bears witness to our understanding of importance of our military cooperation with Iran and clearly indicates our desire to continue this cooperation in future.

c) *Technical Advisers:* Although President wants to be helpful in providing additional MAAG personnel in connection with Iran's F–4 aircraft, we are uncertain exactly what Shah has in mind. As Chief, ARMISH/MAAG has informed Shah in past, we cannot supply MAAG technicians to perform direct support for foreign forces. If, on other hand, IIAF has requirement for supervisory-level personnel, we could supply up to 50 such people, initially for one-year period, with extension possible for one more year. We would want this program to be on a fully reimbursable basis. We estimate 50 USAF personnel would cost, on this basis, no more than $1,000,000 per year or substantially less than cost of similar personnel hired on commercial basis. Moreover, effectiveness of such personnel, operating as integral part of MAAG, would be far greater than that of personnel operating outside MAAG. Our MAAG Chief can work out details with IIAF.

d) *Persian Gulf Defense:* President will be pleased to have more detailed study conducted if Shah desires one. Such a study would consider not only question of land-based missiles but also of cost and effectiveness of alternative air and naval defense systems for Gulf. Preliminary investigation referred to by President revealed number of problems concerned with capability and characteristics of land-based missiles for defense of Strait of Hormuz. Furthermore, it indicated that if powerful enemy forces should decide to move into Persian Gulf, Iranian land-based missiles would not be a deterrent since they would be susceptible to enemy destruction. On other hand, Iran has well-motivated, competent air force whose capability will soon be greatly improved with acquisition of F–4 aircraft, and this force could operate with good effect in area.

e) *Radar and Communications Systems:* President has instructed DOD to ensure full information on various alternatives is made available to Irannian authorities and every assistance given them, through MAAG, to enable GOI to decide on specific courses action for these projects. When decision taken USG will lend every assistance it can to expedite projects. If US contractor is selected to carry them out, USG will do its best to provide necessary military credits to cover future year program costs within present arrangements as communicated to Shah on May 20, 1968.

f) *Northrop 530:* DOD is considering support for this aircraft for production in US if the aircraft lives up to design specifications. If a consortium is formed Iran would certainly be welcome to join, but it is not expected aircraft would be available until after 1975.

g) *Oil Barter:* President realizes importance the Shah attaches to his proposal to barter or sell Iranian oil for American goods. Accordingly, USG has made a careful review of all alternatives open but has not found any encouraging avenue.

i.   *Special Quota for NIOC:* Quotas are currently given to importers. There are no restrictions on where they get their oil. They could not be instructed to take oil from any specific country, nor could NIOC be given special quota without fundamental revision of US oil imports program. USG has been asked to grant, but has declined, special quota treatment for other countries in the past.

ii.   *Barter or Sale of Iranian Oil for American Products:* NIOC is free now to barter oil with American companies if there are any companies with import permits willing to make such arrangements. On the other hand, any arrangement with Iran to accommodate barter of Iranian oil outside US oil import program would require modification to program and would cause us very difficult problems with other oil-producing countries and in our domestic oil market. Such arrangement, in effect, would require USG give Iran special country quota with problems explained above.

iii.   *Increased Military Procurement from Iran:* DOD purchases refined oil products, on basis of competitive bidding, from a number of sources. In first half of 1968, it purchased significant quantities from Iran and would be pleased to take additional quantities from companies concerned if suitable products are offered at competitive prices. Ambassador Ansary has been given full information on this procurement. Unfortunately this requirement is only for refined products at relatively low prices, and Iranian companies may prefer to sell elsewhere.

3. Signed original of letter being pouched.

Rusk

308.   Telegram From the Embassy in Iran to the Department of State[1]

Tehran, July 29, 1968, 1250Z.

5881. Shah's Visit—Follow-up Actions. Ref: State 209512.[2] Summary. Although deeply disappointed over bleak prospects for selling oil to US, Shah welcomed aspects of President's letter which indicate continued fruitfulness of US–Iran military collaboration. For the moment, we seem to be over the hump.

1. President's message (reftel) conveyed to Shah at Caspian morning 29th. After reading it, Shah was told President's reply reflects most careful study of various subjects raised during Shah's Washington visit. I added that as usual diplomacy is continuing process and Shah, General Twitchell and I would be consulting re these matters on continuing basis.

2. Oil Deal. After expressing appreciation for President's attention to Iran's problems despite heavy preoccupations such as Honolulu Conference, Shah's initial comment was re oil deal. Apparently he already alerted by Reza Falla (probably Ansary) re bleak prospects his barter proposal. I explained why USG cannot tamper with import quota nor dictate to authorized importers countries from which oil must be bought.

3. On commercial side, Shah felt Planet would find it most difficult to break into our import market at profit. He noted contract been initialed with General Electric for $70 million worth GE products if barter oil transaction consummated. I gave Shah background re Planet (State 208708).[3] He smiled and said he wished he had bought stock. We agreed Allen et al. respectable entrepreneurs.

4. Shah pointed out how he had hoped to do $800 million worth business in US over next five years, and he mentioned capital goods, arms, and USG securities. In passing he expressed amazement at USG policy which restricts cheap oil from Mideast while consuming US's precious and dwindling reserves.

5. Shah still saw ray of hope via program which Falla had reported whereby foreign oil imports are permitted to petrochemical industries provided products are exported. Without closing door to this possibility, I recalled recent PIW report which indicated Interior Dept running into trouble with this program due to strong resistance from domestic producers.

---

[1] Source: Department of State, Central Files, POL 7 IRAN. Secret; Priority; Limdis. Repeated to CINCSTRIKE/USCINCMEAFSA.

[2] Document 307.

[3] Dated July 25. (Department of State, Central Files, PET 6 IRAN)

6. Re DOD purchasing, Shah was surprised to learn that via consortium substantial quantities of Iran oil are moving to Far East. He did not pursue this subject further.

7. USAF Technicians. Shah was pleased that despite Viet Nam, President prepared to make 50 USAF technicians available, initially for one year. Noting our Balpa difficulties, I pointed out technicians would be on fully reimbursable basis to which he agreed. Also stressed they would be supervisory-level, working within ARMISH/MAAG framework. He thought this best utilization of technicians. It was left that General Twitchell would work out timing and other details.

8. Gulf Defense. Shah requested DOD proceed with full study of Hormuz defense weaponry and expressed hope results would be available expeditiously. If land-based missiles are out, he hinted he might purchase certain hardware from Israelis (with whom, he disclosed, he recently signed secret general credit agreement). When I referred to Gabrielle missiles, Shah merely noted that there is some doubt as to their range.

9. Telecommunications. I pointed out various reps, both private, PTT and military, began meeting this morning to determine best integration of communications systems in Iran. Shah said it already decided that Peace Ruby with its communications would go to Philco as sole source. He also disclosed he has decided (whether it is irrevocable, I do not know) to purchase mobile TOPO units from Northrop for $8,000,000. He noted they are almost immediately available and eventually when land-based stations are completed mobile units would be valuable reserve. I urged we see what emerges from current deliberations.

10. Northrop P–530. Shah had already heard that Europeans are banding together to produce their own fighter for mid-seventies and this would probably rule out P–530 project. He was interested that DOD taking interest in P–530 and we agreed to stay in touch re this subject in coming months. If P–530's unavailable, Shah is considering possibility that rehabbed F–4-C's might eventually replace current F–5 squadrons.

11. Long-term Commitment. Although obviously disappointed Shah did not make issue of five-year commitment. If military credit is unavailable via USG sources in coming years, he said, he would seek to purchase directly from American companies even using cash if necessary. I explained USG record vis-à-vis Iran in field of military collaboration is impressive. Also emphasized that given Congressional and other problems in Washington these days USG, with concurrence of all Washington quarters, is again treating Iran very well indeed. I added that this unique treatment reflects confidence which USG has in Shah's constructive, non-demagogic, and peaceful policies.

12. *Comment:* At Caspian, Shah tends to be calm and relaxed. We shall be hearing more on all these subjects in weeks ahead, but for mo-

ment we seem to be over the hump. In reporting to Ansary it is suggested we downplay our optimism for if he reports that we think Shah is satisfied Shah may seek ways to dispel our temporary complacency.

Meyer

309.   Letter From the Shah of Iran to President Johnson[1]

Tehran, August 2, 1968.

Dear Mr. President,

I thank you most sincerely for your detailed letter of 24th July,[2] in which you have stated your opinions and enlarged upon various topics that I had the pleasure of discussing with you during my recent visit to Washington.

Once again, I would like you to know how glad I was to have had the benefit of a frank and valuable exchange of views with you on matters affecting the interests of our two countries.

I too, am highly gratified to observe the amicable relations and the good understanding that exist between Iran and the United States of America, which I trust will continue to be further consolidated to our mutual advantage in the years that lie ahead.

As you, Mr. President, are no doubt aware we have already drawn up our military defense plans which, as you will agree, are absolutely vital and of paramount importance to the maintenance and the safeguarding of the interests of an independent sovereign state. You will also concur with me that we cannot rely on one-year military programmes, but must envisage effective long-range plans for our defence. It is my hope that your Government will be able to continue to meet our requirements as before. I look forward to receiving, as soon as is convenient, the results of the detailed technical evaluation which your experts are carrying out on the project for the defence of the Strait of Hormuz.

I had also hoped that by selling Iranian oil on the American market on a barter basis, this would have facilitated our purchase of American

---

[1] Source: Johnson Library, National Security File, Special Head of State Correspondence File, Iran, 7/1/68–10/31/68. No classification marking.

[2] See Document 307.

goods, while at the same time enabling us to invest part of our capital in the United States. But, to my regret, this does not, owing to certain difficulties that you have indicated in your communication, seem feasible at the present time.

The matter concerning the shifting of a portion of my country's dollar reserves into long-term United States assets is under careful study and serious consideration at the moment, and I shall be pleased to apprise you of the outcome in due course.

I wish to express my gratitude for your thoughtful offer of up to 50 additional United States Air Force personnel as advisors for Iran's F–4 aircraft on a reimbursable basis. This, I am convinced will be of great assistance to us.

In conveying my deep appreciation of the kind and friendly sentiments that you, Mr. President, have expressed on your personal behalf and on that of the People of the United States of America in regard to my country and myself, I send you my cordial and heartfelt good wishes for your continued success in the great task that lies on your shoulders of leading your Nation towards an ever brighter and more prosperous future.

With kindest regards to you and Mrs. Johnson from the Empress and myself,

Sincerely,

M.R. Pahlavi

310. Action Memorandum From the Assistant Secretary of State for Near Eastern and South Asian Affairs (Battle) to Secretary of State Rusk[1]

Washington, August 22, 1968.

SUBJECT

[1 *line of source text not declassified*]

Background

NSAM 348,[2] approved by the President in May 1966, authorized the construction of a facility [*less than 1 line of source text not declassified*] which could be used in the event our Peshawar facility became unavailable. In accordance with the NSAM, we are about to begin the construction of a warehouse [*3-1/2 lines of source text not declassified*].

On August 19, Mr. Helms wrote you a letter (Tab B)[3] suggesting that it might be inadvisable in terms of our relations with the Shah and our overall intelligence interests in Iran to proceed with the facility as planned. The main issue to be resolved is the political advisability of proceeding with the plan. In addition there are some questions about how much intelligence effort in Iran is needed to substitute for Peshawar. Mr. Helms suggests that construction of the facility be suspended until a review of the issues has been completed and suggests that I coordinate this review. I am having an inter-agency meeting on the matter today.

Recommendation

That you sign the attached reply (Tab A)[4] to Mr. Helms indicating that you have asked me to coordinate action on this matter.

---

[1] Source: Department of State, Central Files, BG 16 TEHRAN. Top Secret. Drafted by Eliot and cleared by Handley and in draft by Deputy Director of the Bureau of Intelligence and Research George C. Denny, Jr.

[2] For text of NSAM No. 348, see footnote 2, Document 146.

[3] Not attached. A typed notation on Rusk's reply to Helms (Tab A) reads: "Sensitive incoming letter retained by INR/Richard Curl."

[4] Attached but not printed. Rusk wrote Helms that he agreed that it would be useful for all concerned to review these plans once again, and that Battle should coordinate action on this matter.

311.   Telegram From the Embassy in Iran to the Department of
State[1]

Tehran, September 17, 1968, 1600Z.

6606. Subject: Shah's USSR Visit. Summary. Shah himself is aware
there may be some adverse public reaction in West to his Moscow visit.[2]
However, he believes visit ultimately will benefit Iran and free world
causes. Certainly he is under no illusions as to Soviet aims.

1.   Shah and I 17th discussed at length his forthcoming USSR visit.
He said developments in Czechoslovakia had caused him to consider in
depth pros and cons of proceeding with trip as scheduled. He had concluded life must go on. He noted USG announced continued support for
NPT and had indicated contacts with Soviets would continue. It clear Soviet actions in Czechoslovakia not going to be reversed by outside powers and canceling his visit would certainly not do it. Meanwhile, he
hoped his speaking frankly to "those damned people" might do a little
good.

2.   Providing him with President's speeches re US–USSR relations
and following other suggestions from Dept, I urged Shah to convey to
Soviets his own views re détente and bridge-building, re Czech invasion,
re Viet Nam, re Arab-Israel situation, etc. He promised to report to us his
impressions re all these subjects, as well as re state of play inside Kremlin
leadership.

3.   Re Arab-Israel situation, Shah said he had been encouraged by
his talks with King Hussein but this was offset by report that Arab Forn-
Mins had decided on military rather than political action. Nasser's
speech had conciliatory note but current Arab arms and propaganda
build-up very disturbing. Shah reiterated his view that Israeli demand
for direct negotiations unwise. He also recalled Kosygin's telling him
that Arab arms supplies had been replenished after June disaster. Shah
said he now questions assumption that Soviets will or can control irrational Arab action, i.e. early resumption of hostilities with Israel.

4.   Shah said he also haunted by another remark by Kosygin i.e.,
Western powers are organizing for world war. Shah realizes this is nonsense but fears Soviets as is typical may be projecting their own intentions. Shah noted reports that Soviets have virtually closed ballistic

---

[1] Source: Department of State, Central Files, POL 7 IRAN. Secret; Limdis. Repeated to
Moscow.

[2] On September 5 Ambassador Ansary informed Under Secretary Rostow of the
Shah's decision to make a visit to the Soviet Union beginning September 24. (State Depart-
ment Activities Report, September 6; Johnson Library, National Security File, Agency File,
State, Department of, President's Evening Reading, Vol. IX)

missile gap and that they may feel desperate in their efforts to hold Commie Bloc together. If Kosygin reiterates suggestion that West, particularly Germans, are bent on war, Shah said only response he can think of is that there is no imaginable reason why West should invite mass destruction. I ventured suggestion that when Kosygin made that remark he undoubtedly preoccupied how Kremlin was going to bring Czechs in line and might have been concerned that military move by Soviets would precipitate world conflict; thus accusing West was smokescreen. Shah agreed this might be explanation.

5. Noting how Sovs will seek maximum exploitation his visit to restore their image, I urged Shah to avoid Commie lingo which characterized Kosygin visit communiqué, e.g. "atmosphere of friendship," "together with other peace-loving countries," similarity of views re European security, belief of signatories in "non-interference," etc. Shah showed clear desire to avoid playing this Soviet game to extent possible. Re European security, he did, however, reiterate his belief in nuclear-free zones, e.g. Central Europe (he believes we also do not wish Germans to have nuclear weapons), as well as for Mideast countries ("those crazy Arabs").

6. In discussing value of neighborly relations (within limits) with Soviets, Shah noted such relations forestall Soviet clamor against Iran's building up military strength in interest of Persian Gulf security. This opened opportunity to suggest that it is not necessary to punch US in nose when target is USSR, e.g. Hoveyda's statements and DPA quotations of Shah that Americans will not be permitted to replace British colonialism in Iran and in Gulf area. Shah agreed it preferable to refer to other powers in general.

7. Opportunity was also afforded to point out that real Soviet aim, as is so clear from Soviet broadcasts, is ouster of US presence and driving USG back into isolationism. Shah agreed, saying Soviets would then have free hand. He added that his own regime is equally target of clandestine broadcasts but agreed with my view that Soviets are "cultivating the land" for day when Shah's firm hand is no longer at tiller.

8. *Comment:* My impression is that Shah realizes there may be raised eyebrows in West re his USSR visit, but he hopes to prove that visit ultimately is to free world benefit. FornMin Zahedi tells me no other Cabinet minister except himself will accompany the Shah, thus limiting scope for Soviet propaganda exploitation. Ali Khani, Minister of Economy, was originally scheduled to go to expand economic cooperation further. Also Toufanian who is arms purchaser has been eliminated from entourage.

Meyer

312.   Telegram From the Embassy in Iran to the Department of State[1]

Tehran, October 19, 1968, 0755Z.

1735. Iranian Arms Procurement.

1.   In course of two-hour discussion 18th, Shah made clear that just as Iran is launching $10 billion fourth five-year plan in economic field Iran is also projecting five-year military program at only fraction economic plan's cost. Naturally, he said, he wishes to maintain American orientation of his military establishment but if present Congressional discussions restrict credit sales to Iran he intends to purchase elsewhere. He hopes at least, he said, to keep Iran Air Force American-oriented.

2.   Without any taint of blackmail, Shah reported Soviets are almost daily manifesting eagerness to expand arms sales program begun year ago, with repayment in natural gas. Shah frankly acknowledged Soviet purpose is to wean Iran away from Americans. My impression is that Shah is well aware not only of Soviet purposes but of inferiority of Soviet equipment.

3.   Shah noted French also are eagerly making sales pitches. Their aircraft are high quality, he said, but their other wares are exhorbitant (probably referring to helicopters and tanks).

4.   Shah expressed his conviction that USG after Viet-Nam not likely to come to Iran's support in case of trouble. He also reiterated his long-held view that Iran must take care of itself and that Iran itself is in better position to ascertain its military requirements than outsiders. He noted that five-year military plan is being worked out with ARMISH/MAAG.

5.   Once again Shah referred to size of Turkish establishment, almost four-fold that of Iran and heavily supported with MAP grant funds. He said it is difficult to understand American hesitation to sell arms to credit worthy country like Iran which has almost entirely American-oriented military establishment.

6.   Shah expressed great concern over influx of Soviet arms to Arab neighbors. He said UAR Air Force been 80 percent replenished. Syrians have been re-equipped beyond pre-hostility capacity, and Iraqis too receiving abundant arms including Sukhoy bombers.

7. I did my best to urge Shah to keep military expenditures to minimum, noting wastefulness of Arab military build-up and lesson taught by Israelis that equipment is much less important than quality of personnel.

---

[1] Source: Department of State, Central Files, DEF 19–8 US–IRAN. Secret; Limdis.

8. I also explained in detail present state of play in Congressional Conference Committee re military credit sales. Shah said he willing to wait another month but if it develops that procurement from U.S. is not feasible we should not be surprised if he places orders elsewhere.

Meyer

---

313.   Telegram From the Department of State to the Embassy in Iran[1]

Washington, October 30, 1968, 2059Z.

263948. Joint State/Defense message. Subject: Iranian Military Sales.

1. State and Defense have reviewed problems posed by (a) order deadline of December 1968 for 10 C–130 aircraft desired by Iran and (b) Iranian desire have third and fourth squadrons of F–4's delivered by end 1971.

2. Under existing policy, we see no choice except to include C–130 aircraft in sixth (FY 1968) tranche. We cannot permit GOI order these aircraft in expectation credit funds will be forthcoming because decision on credit comes only after annual review. Cash purchase of this magnitude also must await annual review or special authorization. Including C–130's in sixth tranche can be accomplished by reducing number of Sheridans to 16 at $10 million. We reluctant postpone purchase of M–60 tanks because this would undoubtedly lose present favorable price.

3. In order deliver two additional F–4 squadrons to Iran by end 1971, two possible funding programs suggest themselves: (a) ordering all 32 aircraft plus long-lead support items at cost of $100 million in FY 1969 tranche and balance of support items ($30 million) in FY 1970 tranche. This would absorb all of planned credit in seventh (FY 1969) tranche. (b) Ordering long-lead items and AGE for all 32 aircraft ($24.5 million) in FY 1968 (sixth tranche), rest of third squadron ($41.8 million) in FY 1969 (seventh tranche), and rest of fourth squadron ($63.7 million) in FY 1970 (eighth tranche).

---

[1] Source: Department of State, Central Files, DEF 12–5 IRAN. Secret. Drafted by Eliot; cleared by Schwartz (OASD/ISA/NESA), and in draft by Reed, Alne (ISA/ILN), Lewis D. Junior (G/PM), and Director of the AID Office of Near Eastern Affairs John Eddison; and approved by Rockwell. Repeated to CINCSTRIKE.

4. Our present policy, however, precludes our adopting either of these suggestions. Under present policy, we cannot commit ourselves to more than one year's financing each year following annual review. Funding of F–4's per para 3 above implies commitment to future year funding because first increment would fund only part of equipment needed for a squadron and implies obligation continue funding in future. In addition, suggestion (a) would preempt entire seventh tranche and postpone funding of other items, such as NIMCOMS, Sheridans, Persian Gulf defense items as recommended by Richmond report and other items which have high priority for Iranians. Suggestion (b) would require postponing items from sixth tranche in addition to Sheridans or decision sell C–130's for cash; the latter being unacceptable under current policy as mentioned in para 2 above.

5. Another possibility would be raising planning ceiling for FY 1969 program above $100 million. This would require policy change, including Congressional consultations, and might in any case not be possible given present limitations on credit availabilities.

6. In absence compelling political justification we are reluctant undertake steps to alter present policy. We note in this connection recent sharp decline in Iranian foreign exchange reserves. We question desirability change in policy so soon after Shah's USSR trip. In any case, policy reconsideration could not be undertaken without reviewing political factors and completing economic study, which would have to take into account forthcoming IBRD and IMF reports.

7. Another alternative is of course to postpone delivery fourth squadron. Under this alternative, third squadron could be funded in seventh tranche and fourth in eighth tranche, and additional funds would be available in both tranches for other high priority items even if ceiling remained at $100 million each year. Principal difficulty with this alternative, in addition postponement delivery of fourth squadron until 1972, would be fact fourth squadron could cost an additional $4–$10 million.

8. Embassy/MAAG comments requested on following points: (a) Political, economic and financial factors involved in possible change of policy to permit incremental financing of F–4's, increase in $100 million ceiling, or substantial cash purchases in FY 1969. (b) Timing of annual review preceding seventh (FY 1969) tranche. When does Embassy believe economic data will be available? (c) Impact on Iran's force structure and political-economic factors involved in postponement delivery fourth F–4 squadron to 1972. (d) Substitution of C–130's for Sheridans (except 16) in sixth tranche.

Rusk

314.   Memorandum From the Executive Secretary of the Department of State (Read) to the President's Special Assistant (Rostow)[1]

Washington, November 7, 1968.

SUBJECT

Military Credit Sales to Iran

In your memorandum of May 2, 1968,[2] you outlined the President's understanding, in approving the FY 1968 military credit sales program for Iran, that State, Defense, and AID would go ahead with further in-house economic and military studies in order to provide the best possible estimates of military credit requirements for the FY 1970 budget and the basis for our joint review with the Iranians next year. As you suggested, we have been in touch with the Bureau of the Budget on this matter.

The requested reviews have now been completed and are enclosed for your information.[3] Our review revealed many political and military reasons for continuing to plan on the basis of $100 million in annual U.S. military credits to Iran. However, the economic study points out several problem areas for the future and recommends that these be kept under review. Our recommendation is, therefore, that the FY 1970 budget estimate for military credit sales to Iran should be set at $100 million, up to half of which might be from commercial credit funds as indicated in the attached report of the financial study group. The final figure would be subject to the results of the annual military, economic and political review to take place during FY 1970.

John P. Walsh[4]

---

[1] Source: Johnson Library, National Security File, Country File, Iran. Secret. A copy was sent to Zwick in the Bureau of the Budget.

[2] Not printed. (Ibid., NSC Files of Harold Saunders, Iran Military, 1/1/68–1/20/69)

[3] Attached to the source text but not printed.

[4] Walsh signed for Read.

315.   Memorandum From the Assistant Secretary of State for Near Eastern and South Asian Affairs (Hart) to the Executive Secretary of the Department of State (Read)[1]

Washington, November 19, 1968.

SUBJECT

Desire of Iranian Prime Minister to Meet with President-elect Nixon

Prime Minister Amir Abbas Hoveyda of Iran will be in the United States on an official visit beginning Tuesday, December 3, 1968. He has expressed a desire to call on President-elect Nixon.[2]

The Prime Minister met Mr. Nixon in Tehran on April 22, 1967 when they were both guests at a dinner at the home of the Iranian Foreign Minister. During that visit, Mr. Nixon also had lunch with the Shah.

NEA strongly recommends that the President-elect receive the Prime Minister. Our interests in Iran would be well served by such an indication that the new Administration will want to maintain our close ties with Iran. These interests include our ability to influence an increasingly powerful Iran to play a constructive role in the Middle East and Persian Gulf and our ability to retain certain strategic intelligence facilities whose importance is increasing as our facilities in Pakistan are being closed down. Should the President-elect not see the Prime Minister the Shah is likely to be concerned that the new Administration may not want to continue our present intimate relationship with Iran.

The Prime Minister will be in New York on December 4, in Washington December 5 and 6, in Florida December 7 and 8 and in Los Angeles December 9–11 and would be available for a meeting with the President-elect on any of those dates.

---

[1] Source: Department of State, Central Files, POL 15–1 IRAN. Secret. Drafted by Eliot and cleared by Rockwell.

[2] A handwritten notation on the source text reads: "Nixon will NOT see. RHoudek."

316. Telegram From the Department of State to the Embassy in Iran[1]

Washington, November 21, 1968, 0443Z.

275285. 1. Embassy requested deliver following message from President-elect to Shah of Iran: "Your Imperial Majesty: I thank you for your congratulations and your good wishes on the occasion of my election to the office of President of the United States. In view of the close relations between our two countries, I am especially grateful for your kind words and your expression of continuing support for our mutual efforts for peace and for better lives for all mankind.

On my part, I assure Your Majesty that I will continue to do all in my power to forward and strengthen the close ties between our two governments and people. I remember with pleasure your wonderful hospitality to me in Tehran in April 1967 and have continued to follow with admiration your country's progress at home and constructive statesmanship internationally. Thank you again for your message.

Sincerely yours, Richard M. Nixon."

2. Following FYI is text of message to President-elect from Shah: *Begin text:* Excellency, I take great pleasure in expressing my sincere congratulations and those of my people on Your Excellency's election to the high office of U.S. President. I sincerely wish you success in discharging your critical responsibilities as a President and in our ever-increasing mutual efforts toward world peace and the freedom and happiness of mankind. I strongly hope that the long-standing friendship and cordiality which has always existed between Iran and the United States on the basis of cooperation, mutual belief, and goodwill will further strengthen and expand in the future. With my best greetings. Mohammad Reza Pahlavi. *End text.*

Rusk

---

[1] Source: Johnson Library, National Security File, NSC Files of Harold Saunders, Visit of Amir Hoveyda, Prime Minister of Iran, December 4–5, 1968. Limited Official Use. Drafted by Robert G. Houdek of the Executive Secretariat Staff, and approved by Ambassador William Leonhart in S/NL. Another copy of this document is in Department of State, Central Files, POL 15–1 US/NIXON.

317. Telegram From the Department of State to the Embassy in Iran[1]

Washington, November 23, 1968, 0037Z.

276775. 1. At Ansary's request Secretary received him alone November 21. Following points were covered.

A. Ansary said Shah understands US providing Turkey with M–60 tanks in place of M–47s to go to Pakistan. Shah wanted to know why Iran could not get M–60 replacements for its own older models. Secretary said he did not think M–60s were involved but he would pass request to his colleagues. (FYI. Plan is for US to provide Turkey with rehab M–48s in place of M–47s which would go to Pakistan. End FYI.)

B. Shah wanted us to know he making every effort eliminate outstanding problems between Iran and Afghanistan.

C. Ansary made two suggestions about oil which he said Prime Minister would raise during his visit to US. First, was that US buy Iranian oil for Vietnam and sequester proceeds which could be used for Iranian arms purchase in this country. Second, was that US should buy Iranian oil for stockpiling. Secretary said he would ask his colleagues consider latter suggestion which he had not heard of before.

D. Ambassador said Shah was concerned lest US in order maintain a certain balance give undue support to Saudi Arabia. Secretary probed without much success for what was behind this suggestion but got impression Shah feels that undue American support for Saudi Arabia would create problems of prestige in the Middle East for Iran. Net impression Secretary received was that Shah rather hoping that US will pick Iran as its "chosen instrument" in the Middle East.

Rusk

---

[1] Source: Department of State, Central Files, POL IRAN–US. Secret; Priority; Nodis. Drafted by Rockwell on November 22 and approved by Rusk.

318.   Telegram From the Department of State to the Embassy in Iran[1]

Washington, November 24, 1968, 0042Z.

277012. Subject: Hoveyda and President-elect. Please inform PriMin that President-elect will not be able meet with him during his US visit next month. President-elect hopes that PriMin will understand that during next few weeks he must devote his full time and attention to preparing for his administration. He has therefore decided that he will not be able to receive any foreign visitors in this period. You may tell PriMin that President-elect remembers with pleasure his talks with the PriMin in Tehran in April 1967, that he has warm admiration for the PriMin and for his role in Iran's great progress in recent years, that he looks forward to strengthening the already close ties between our two countries and that he very much regrets not being able to meet with the PriMin in December.

Rusk

---

[1] Source: Department of State, Central Files, POL 7 IRAN. Confidential. Drafted by Eliot on November 22, cleared by Leonhart, and approved by Rockwell.

---

319.   Telegram From the Embassy in Iran to the Department of State[1]

Tehran, November 24, 1968, 0745Z.

7433. Subject: Military Sales to Iran. Summary. Shah's complaint about projected delay in delivery of Sheridan tanks has been seized as opportunity for trying to divert him from virtual obsession with date of Dec. 31, 1971. That is date when British will have withdrawn from Persian Gulf. In effect Shah is trying to compress 5-year military purchasing into intervening three years. Specifically, case was made for deferring

---

[1] Source: Department of State, Central Files, DEF 12–5 IRAN. Secret; Limdis. Repeated to CINCMEAFSA/CINCSTRIKE.

delivery schedule of fourth F–4 squadron. Shah was non-committal except to attach hope to oil barter deals with GM and other American companies.

1.   After noting 16 Sheridans included in sixth tranche, Shah 23rd expressed concern that additional Sheridans not projected for delivery until 1972 or later. Suggesting General Twitchell more familiar with technical aspects such as two-year lead time, I said Shah's question, however, raises broader issue of future program projection.

2.   Describing as understandable his keen interest in end of 1971 target date (when British will have withdrawn from Gulf), I said in effect he is trying to compress five-year military program into three years. This in turn is incompatible with our projected $100 million annual credit availability. Shah agreed this is problem, adding if choices have to be made his air force and navy needs must come first.

3.   I said I wondered whether precise date of December 31, 1971, is all that critical. Iran's military strength is obviously capable of handling any currently envisaged threat in Gulf area. Moreover, if threat arises it will probably be as result of ferment of several years after British leave.

4.   Thus I questioned whether having both third and fourth F–4 squadrons on hand by end of 1971 is really necessary. Shah himself had observed at Lavan Island that Iran's international prestige has soared as result of news that Iran has Phantoms. As Kuss had said, their chief value is deterrence through "eye impact". It seemed to me that essentially this objective can be served as well by three squadrons as by four by the end of 1971.

5.   I told Shah I not questioning military value of four squadrons but merely whether their delivery might not be spaced out so as to give us elbow room to include in future tranches, if they are approved, other items which are important to five-year program. Meanwhile, we would be keeping options open for such things as possibly acquiring rehab F–4's after Viet Nam conflict ceases.

6.   Shah's response tended to center on his confidence that oil barter deal with US companies may come to fruition. He obviously places great hope in Jim Zand's proposals for exchanges with General Motors, adding that one of attractive aspects is GM will give sizeable discounts on hardware it sells. In short, he has vaguely in mind getting Sheridans via barter deals which he contends would be incremental to normal Iranian imports from US.

7.   In addition to financial bind, I told Shah there is always problem of human resources. He readily agreed, commenting this is point with which he cannot argue. I pointed out still to arrive are 155 M–60 tanks whose payment included in sixth tranche. According to General Twitchell, I said, absorption capability of ground forces for tank is already over-

strained. Shah indicated agreement but did not necessarily agree to translate this into lengthy delay in receipt of Sheridans.

8. In concluding general argument for easing up pressure to crowd as much hardware as possible in before end of 1971, I told Shah he should take long-view. USG has treated him well in past and all indicators are good for future. FMS legislation has been passed. Thanks to deliberations re FMS, our Congressional friends, as reflected in several personal letters I have received, are now more fully conscious of Shah's fine leadership as well as Iran's needs. Furthermore, his good friend, from whom only previous day he had received warm telegram, will be in White House. In a sense, I said, when USG made tough decision to let Iran buy Phantoms (first foreign release except for Britain), it was political decision. We betting on Shah to continue to exercise, as Nixon said in his telegram, "constructive statesmanship internationally".

9. *Comment:* While all the points were made, discussion was not as neat and articulate as reported above, for Shah kept interrupting and going off on tangents. Therefore, it was a no-decision affair. But in my view ground has been prepared and perhaps seed planted. I pointed out that with sixth tranche out of way we now have time to ponder these things while undertaking next annual review and determining seventh tranche next June. Shah corrected me to say F–4 order must be placed by May.

Meyer

---

320. Memorandum From Secretary of State Rusk to President Johnson[1]

Washington, December 2, 1968.

SUBJECT

Your Meeting with the Prime Minister of Iran, December 5, 1968, at 12:00 noon

Our aim during the Prime Minister's visit will be to assure him, and through him the Shah, that despite the forthcoming change in our Ad-

---

[1] Source: Johnson Library, National Security File, Country File, Iran, Visit of Prime Minister Hoveyda of Iran, 12/5–6/68. Secret. Drafted by Eliot; cleared by Rockwell, Chapman, Eddison (AID), Reed (DOD/OASD/ISA), Akins, and Country Director for Saudi Arabia William D. Brewer.

ministration, we will wish to maintain our present intimate relationship with Iran. We also wish to give recognition to the important role played by the Shah's advisers, as represented by the Prime Minister, in Iran's domestic progress and international statesmanship. To these ends you might therefore:

1.   Tell him of your conviction that the new Administration will have the same regard for Iran and the Shah and the same interest in preserving our close ties as your Administration has had.

2.   On Iran's domestic progress:

a.   Express your admiration for the strides that have been made, in which the Prime Minister has played a major role.

b.   Indicate your belief that private American enterprise will continue to be attracted by investment opportunities in Iran.

c.   While referring to our desire to maintain our close military relationship with Iran: (1) express the hope that Iran's military procurement will not impede its spectacular economic development and (2) indicate that any compression of the currently planned five-year military procurement program would have financial and economic implications and would also not seem to be warranted by the military situation.

3.   On international issues:

a.   Take him into your confidence on our view of the situation with respect to Vietnam, the Arab-Israeli problem and Soviet policies in eastern Europe and elsewhere.

b.   Indicate pleasure concerning the Shah's recent visits to Saudi Arabia and Kuwait and confidence that the security of the Persian Gulf area following the British departure in 1971 will be assured by cooperation among the littoral countries.

Dean Rusk

Attachment

POINTS THE PRIME MINISTER MAY RAISE AND SUGGESTED RESPONSES

1.   *United States Military Cooperation with Iran*

The Prime Minister may raise specific problems connected with our military credit sales program for Iran. He may indicate a desire to have our planned five-year program compressed into three years. For example, he may ask that the delivery of the two additional squadrons of F–4 aircraft desired by Iran be advanced from the currently contemplated 1971–72 period to 1971 when British forces are scheduled to leave the Persian Gulf.

You might respond that within the bounds set by Congressional authority and appropriations, you expect our military cooperation with Iran will continue. On specific problems, you might say that they are being communicated to us through Ambassador Meyer and that you expect they will be considered during our joint annual review of our military credit sales program this coming spring. You might say that while we understand Iran's concern for the security of the Gulf, Iran's military strength is capable of handling any currently envisaged threat in that area. Any acceleration of presently planned Iranian military procurement or compression of the planned program into less than five years would not only have economic and financial implications but would also not seem to be warranted by the military situation.

2.   *Oil Matters*

The Prime Minister may ask assistance for Iran to sell additional oil to the United States under barter arrangements, to sell additional oil products for our Far Eastern Defense forces or even to sell oil directly to a U.S. stockpile.

You might respond that sales of oil to the United States are governed by our oil import policy under which import quotas are given to domestic refiners and not to foreign countries. Increased participation in the American market for Iranian oil can best be obtained by Iran's ensuring, in collaboration with the producing companies, that Iranian oil is economically attractive to those American refiners who have import allocations. Likewise, the Department of Defense purchases oil products on the basis of competitive bidding, and if Iranian companies can supply the required quantities at competitive prices, the Department of Defense would be pleased to purchase them. There are no plans at the present time for either civilian or military stockpiling of petroleum or pretroleum products in the United States.

321. Memorandum of Conversation[1]

Washington, December 5, 1968.

PARTICIPANTS

President Lyndon B. Johnson
Prime Minister Hoveyda of Iran
Harold H. Saunders

PLACE

The President's Oval Office

The President welcomed the Prime Minister, and the Prime Minister extended the Shah's greetings. The Shah had asked him to express his hope that the President and Mrs. Johnson would have an opportunity to visit Iran again soon. The Prime Minister went on to express appreciation that the "American Government under your leadership" had always extended the support Iran needed. He felt Iran is on the right track and "things seem bright." "What we need is peace in the world; we have stability at home." There are no problems between Iran and the US. We have been good friends. The US has supported Iran's development, and the time has come to broaden economic relations between the two countries. He hoped that more US firms would come to work in Iran. "Development is not only government-to-government business but concerns the peoples of our countries as well. Iran has all the facilities for investment of capital and feels that if private firms make money, Iran makes money."

The President said that is a very enlightened viewpoint. As a result, he felt development will come more rapidly. He said he did not know any country—and he has been in dozens—where the leadership has been wiser or more effective. "Some people talk about development. Some people do it." The Prime Minister said that if Iran continues at its present speed, it will double GNP in seven years. Iran is even reaching the point where it could begin to think about assisting its neighbors.

The President said that Iran could be a constructive force for peace. The Prime Minister said that the state of the world compels Iran to responsible leadership. Irresponsible leadership could lead to war. Iran must provide its people the insurance that military strength gives. Iran has to modernize its forces. The Iranian taxpayer expects this kind of security. But equally important, the defense of an area should be the burden of the people of the area. Iran has no interest in attacking anyone.

---

[1] Source: Johnson Library, National Security File, Country File, Iran. Secret; Exdis. Drafted by Saunders. Copies were sent to Rostow and Read. According to the President's Daily Diary, the meeting took place from 11:57 a.m. until 12:45 p.m. (Ibid.)

Iran understands that the British have to leave the Persian Gulf. "I don't say we appreciate it, but we understand it. Now it is up to the people of the Persian Gulf, and their understanding and cooperation can provide stability there." One of the problems is that some of the regimes on the other side of the Gulf are unstable. He mentioned principally Iraq but also Syria and the UAR. He said "we have to look for peace and count on it. We have to build the monument of peace." This is the policy the Shah has followed.

The Prime Minister continued, saying that relations between Iran and the US have developed nicely. Never in my four years as Prime Minister has there been any serious problem with the US. We have been real friends—not only in days of happiness but in difficult days. He is happy that Iran does not need any more grant aid but he is thankful for continuing US support with Iran's military development and for the presence of the US military mission in Iran.

The Prime Minister hoped that the seventh tranche in the military sales program could be signed as soon as possible. That includes two squadrons of Phantoms. The area is more and more filled with armament and one never knows whose hand is on the trigger. The Prime Minister said we usually have an economic review before signing new military sales agreements. "I have many people with me and they will be happy to sit down in the Pentagon and have this review." He specifically mentioned Iran's need for more technicians "on levels 7 and 9." Iran is preparing its own manpower and needs this help. The Prime Minister recalled that the Shah had raised the question of oil during his last visit. Arrangements are progressing and Iran knows that a new oil import quota for it is out of the question but hopes that maybe something can be worked out within the existing quota.

He mentioned that South Africa was stock-piling oil in its old empty coal mines. He would like to raise this possibility with the US Government in hopes that the US might buy from Iran for this purpose. Iran would also like to sell more JP–4 fuel for the US Navy and is ready to make certain concessions on price.

The President said that our people will be "happy and willing to explore" all these matters while the Prime Minister is here.

The President said further that, while he will be in Government only a short time longer and could not speak for the next administration, he believed that US interests are such that a close relationship between the US and Iran will continue. He understood that President-elect Nixon had already sent a message to the Shah saying this. "We want to do all we can to help."

The President further said that we planned to continue our role in Iran's military development as far as Congress will permit. The President said he had always been concerned that Iran's military expenses not become so great as to undercut economic development.

The Prime Minister said, "There I can assure you that they are balanced." The Prime Minister said Iran understands the importance of keeping these things in balance. Disarmament is the ultimate key to these problems and Iran would be happy to disarm tomorrow if that were possible. The President said that we were trying to work along these lines with the Soviet Union. The Prime Minister said that the cost of one plane could build three hospitals. But, he asked rhetorically, "What is the use of the hospitals if you do not have the planes to protect them?"

The President said that we cannot change our oil import policy but we would certainly consider the purchase of Iranian products wherever their prices are competitive. We favor whatever barter arrangements Iran can work out with the private US companies and hope that Iran can increase its opportunities that way. The President said that there may be a time when the US will not be in the same position it is now on oil and we may have to do what South Africa is doing. We are fortunate to have friends like Iran. [Comment: The implication was friends who have oil if we need it some day.][2]

The President said that in the years left to him he hoped he could return to Iran. He remembered the warm welcome he had received there and expressed the deep affection he felt for the Iranian people. He expected to be busy in the next couple of years with his library but he expected that he and Mrs. Johnson would have time to travel. He hoped that the Prime Minister would tell His Majesty the Shah that the President recalls the "gorgeous" reception the Johnsons had received on their last visit to Tehran and he is looking forward to seeing Iran again and to going out in the countryside and seeing how Iran's land reform program has gone.

The Prime Minister said he hoped the President would keep his promise and "come and see us." The people of Iran have "the greatest regard for your courage." He spoke of how the people in Iran had watched the March 31 speech on television and felt "a great deal of tension" [comment: presumably over the thought that the President would leave office]. He spoke of the President's great responsibilities for the peace of the world and how greatly Iranians had appreciated his handling of those responsibilities.

The President said he had made every effort not to expand the war in Southeast Asia by involving the USSR or Communist China. At the same time, he could not stand by and let aggression go unopposed. The only US objective is to see the people of the area determine their own fu-

---

[2] All brackets are in the source text.

ture. The US will come home as soon as that is possible. We don't want to change governments or destroy North Vietnam or kill another person.

The President said people from all over the US would be coming to the dinner for the Prime Minister tonight. This was the next to last official visit during his Administration and it turns out that the last two—Iran and Kuwait—are with neighbors and good friends.

The conversation turned again to the Iranian economy. The President asked about Iran's agricultural and land development. The Prime Minister said the Shah is never satisfied with Iran's achievements. The President referred to his remarks at the arrival ceremony and said that the key to development is the human process he had described there— the distribution of the land and education and, above all, giving the father the hope that his son's life can be just a little bit richer than his own. Once you get human beings involved this way, you have something very exciting going.

The President promised to review his conversation with the Prime Minister with Secretaries Rusk and Clifford later in the day and would encourage them to be as helpful as possible.

The Prime Minister returned to the question of peace and stability in his part of the world. He mentioned a disturbing report that the Iraqis are trying to develop a capacity to wage germ warfare. The Soviets had refused help, but the Iraqis are approaching Bulgaria now. The thought of germ warfare in the hands of such an unstable government made him shudder.

The President asked what the population of Iran is now, and the Prime Minister replied, "close to 26 million" with a 2.7% growth rate. He said his government had launched a highly successful family planning program without fanfare—"we have done it without talking about it, without fuss." The problem is not that they don't want more Iranians, he said, but they want better balance in the population since 48% of the population is now ages 0–14.

The President asked about fertilizer use. The Prime Minister said Iran is building new plants, one with Allied Chemical. Iran in a recent six-month program had demonstrated the capacity to increase its rice crop from 2-1/2 tons per hectare to 4-1/2 tons. When the Prime Minister mentioned Allied Chemical, the President checked and said that Mr. John Connor of Allied would be at the dinner tonight. The President described a new liquid feed Allied had developed that the President had tried on his Ranch.

The Prime Minister, picking up the President's description of the liquid feed, said Iran is now trying to develop protein products from oil. He cited the problem of land erosion that arises when animals are allowed to overgraze on the grasslands and agreed with the President that it is important to find other means of feeding until the grass is established. The

President commented that fertilizing these lands to get grass started is expensive, but the results justify the expense. He gave an example of his experience in starting grass on some of his own eroded land in Texas.

The President then said that it had been called to his attention in connection with the recent monetary crisis that Iran had not yet ratified the Special Drawing Rights Amendment to the IMF. The President pointed out that the amendment would not go into effect until 67 countries with 80% of the votes had ratified it. The US had been among the first to ratify. He very much hoped Iran would ratify in the near future. The Prime Minister took a piece of paper out of his pocket, made a note and said he would look into it.

The Prime Minister said further that the recent monetary crisis had been distressing. He told the President that President DeGaulle, whom the Prime Minister had just seen in Paris on the way to Washington, had been grateful for the President's message at the height of the franc crisis. The Prime Minister had asked President DeGaulle what he thought the results of his monetary reform program would be, and DeGaulle had declined to predict. The President explained how he had come to send the message to DeGaulle, saying that it was a word of encouragement at a difficult time for DeGaulle and not a recommendation or endorsement of his program. Once DeGaulle had crossed the bridge of decision, the President felt our role was to help him succeed rather than to make life difficult for him.

The President then invited Mr. Walt Rostow to bring in Dr. Henry Kissinger to meet the Prime Minister. The President informed Dr. Kissinger that he had told the Prime Minister that he felt close relations would continue to exist between the US and Iran in the new administration. The President cited President-elect Nixon's message to the Shah saying this. Dr. Kissinger said that he had "spoken to Mr. Nixon about Iran yesterday" and he could reiterate Mr. Nixon's earlier words to the Shah today in behalf of the President-elect. The President told the Prime Minister that Dr. Kissinger had served both Republican and Democratic Presidents faithfully and well and that the US is fortunate and proud to have men of his stature who lend their great abilities to the Government regardless of partisan positions. The President then told the Prime Minister that he would be talking further with him this evening and would be glad to take up any further issues that might emerge in the course of the Prime Minister's discussion here.

Comment: The discussion flowed easily. The Prime Minister was relaxed, informal, responsive and friendly. The President spoke with warmth and good feeling about his past and present relations with the Shah and other Iranian leaders. They had no trouble keeping the conversation moving, and one could only judge the meeting thoroughly satisfactory on both sides.

Harold H. Saunders[3]

---

[3] Printed from a copy that indicates Saunders signed the original.

---

322.   Memorandum of Conversation[1]

Washington, December 6, 1968, 10 a.m.

SUBJECT

    U.S. Military Sales Program for Iran

PARTICIPANTS

    H.E. Amir Abbas Hoveyda, Prime Minister of Iran
    H.E. Hushang Ansary, Iranian Ambassador
    H.E. Mehdi Samii, Managing Director, Plan Organization, Iran

    The Hon. Dean Rusk, Secretary of State
    The Hon. Armin H. Meyer, American Ambassador to Iran
    Stuart W. Rockwell, Deputy Assistant Secretary, NEA
    Theodore L. Eliot, Jr., Country Director for Iran, NEA

The Prime Minister asked the new Managing Director of the Plan Organization, former Central Bank Governor Mehdi Samii, to join the discussion and to raise certain matters connected with our military sales program for Iran. He explained that Mr. Samii would, in his new job, continue to be responsible for military credit negotiations with the United States.

Mr. Samii said that Iran needs to place orders for the additional two squadrons of F–4 aircraft it desires in order to have these squadrons delivered by the end of 1971 when the British forces leave the Persian Gulf. A problem arises, however, because the planning ceiling of $100 million for the FY 1969 (seventh) credit tranche will not be sufficient to cover the

---

[1] Source: Department of State, Central Files, DEF 12–5 IRAN. Secret. Drafted by Eliot and approved in S on December 11. The source text is labeled "Part 3 of 4." The time of the meeting is from Rusk's Appointment Book. (Johnson Library)

F–4's and other requirements. He asked if there could be some flexibility, for example exceeding in this year the planning ceiling. As an alternative, he mentioned the possibility of spreading out the credit requirements. (*Comment:* Here he was clearly referring to what we would term "incremental funding.") In addition to the F–4's, he mentioned the need to fund 100 additional Sheridan tanks, 200 recoilless guns and communications equipment in the seventh tranche.

Mr. Samii also said that we have informed Iran that after FY 1969 it must purchase all the ammunition previously supplied on a grant basis despite the fact that the 1966 amendment to our 1964 Memorandum of Understanding extended our grant program an additional two years. Ambassador Meyer and Mr. Eliot stated that the 1966 amendment of the 1964 Understanding extended the credit but not the grant program beyond FY 1969.

The Secretary said that he recognizes that it is necessary to think ahead but that our Congressional requirements make it necessary for us to plan on an annual basis. He said that if Iran wishes to increase the size of a tranche, we would have to ascertain whether the understanding between us would be firm over a number of years, so that we wouldn't find ourselves being asked to increase later tranches and hence being asked to increase the total program.

Mr. Samii said that if we can reach an agreement on a total program, there would be no need to increase the size of later tranches.

The Secretary said that some of this may be easier for us in later years after the end of the war in Vietnam. He stressed that there is one serious aspect of the matter that must be kept in mind. Although we of course do not wish to infringe on the sovereignty of Iran, our ability to obtain the resources we need for this program depends on our examining the relationship between Iran's military and development expenditures. The Secretary said he understood the Government of Iran would be supplying us with some figures.

Mr. Samii expressed the hope that we could advance the timing of our review of the economic factors. Hopefully, reports now being prepared by the IBRD and the IMF could serve as a basis. The Central Bank of Iran would also supply some data. All this information should become available in December.

Ambassador Meyer said that the economic review has usually taken place in the spring. He said that there are two important problems to be considered. One is whether incremental funding is possible. The other is whether the fourth squadron of F–4's is really needed by the end of 1971. He asked whether delivery of the fourth squadron could be put off a year. This would assist solution not only of financial but also of manpower problems.

The Secretary said that it would be useful if the economic figures could be made available as soon as possible so that he could brief his successor. He doubted it would be possible to have formal negotiations within the next few weeks but said he would like to discuss the matter with his successor.

Mr. Samii said that the annual economic review has become a normal thing. The reports due from the IBRD and the IMF in December and January will cover the economic situation pretty thoroughly. In response to Ambassador Meyer's remarks, he said that he did not believe that delivery of the fourth squadron of F–4's could be postponed because once the British leave the Persian Gulf, Iran had to be ready for anything. Mr. Rockwell interjected that there was nothing four squadrons could do that three couldn't do at that time. Mr. Samii reiterated that the fourth squadron was not just for "window dressing." The Prime Minister added that Iran must be able to have teeth available.

Ambassador Ansary then mentioned that the Iranian Air Force also has a requirement for additional technicians at higher levels and asked if they could be made available. He said that the requirement is for more than the 50 the USAF has already made available and perhaps goes as high as 221. These technicians would supervise and train Iranians in maintaining F–4's.

The Secretary said that we will look into this matter. He said that it presented no great problem in principle but posed a practical problem. He concluded this part of the discussion by saying that our military people on both sides might wish to review the military contingencies to see how many squadrons of F–4's are really needed.

323.   Memorandum of Conversation[1]

Washington, December 6, 1968.

SUBJECT

Oil Matters

PARTICIPANTS

H.E. Amir Abbas Hoveyda, Prime Minister of Iran
H.E. Hushang Ansary, Ambassador of Iran
H.E. Mehdi Samii, Governor of the Central Bank of Iran
Dr. Reza Fallah, Director, National Iranian Oil Company

The Hon. Dean Rusk, Secretary of State
The Hon. Armin H. Meyer, American Ambassador to Iran
Mr. Stuart W. Rockwell, Deputy Assistant Secretary, NEA
Mr. Theodore L. Eliot, Jr., Country Director for Iran, NEA

The Prime Minister asked Dr. Fallah to join the meeting for a discussion of oil matters. He said that Iran has no problems in the current year with the Oil Consortium but that it hopes for one billion dollars in oil revenues next year. (*Comment:* presumably the Iranian year beginning March 21, 1969.) The member companies of the Consortium are considering this request, but have not yet responded. Last year, he said, the Shah told the companies that if they could not meet Iran's requirements, Iran would find its own markets. He decried what he described as the companies' policy of supporting such states as Abu Dhabi and Kuwait that either have no useful way to employ their oil revenues or use them to support radical Arabs.

The Prime Minister went on to say that Iran is now looking at the American market. One way to sell oil to the United States would be through the present American quota system, using the proceeds to purchase American goods. Iran might possibly buy into an American firm having an import quota. In any case, the Prime Minister said, two aspects of this situation deserved special mention. One is the fact that the United States needs additional oil reserves. Iran has entered into a contract with another country (*comment:* South Africa; see below) desirous of stockpiling oil and has asked a private firm for a study on a similar possible contract with the United States. Iran would give this study to the United States Government for its consideration. Iran could use the proceeds from such sales to the United States to buy American products. The second aspect of the matter was possible sales of petroleum products to the Department of Defense.

---

[1] Source: Department of State, Central Files, PET 6 IRAN. Confidential. Drafted by Eliot on December 8 and approved in S on December 12. The source text is labeled "Part 4 of 4."

Dr. Fallah said that sales to the Department of Defense pose a problem because DOD purchases on the basis of public tender. The Secretary asked if Dr. Fallah meant that Iran could not meet the price competition. Dr. Fallah said that the National Iranian Oil Company (NIOC) would act as the Consortium's agent. The Prime Minister said that the NIOC would find a market for the Consortium. The NIOC would make no money as an agent, but Iran would profit through the taxes the Consortium would pay on higher production. Dr. Fallah said that Iran desires a three-year contract with DOD, but the latter won't go beyond six months. This and not price is the problem. The Prime Minister said that Dr. Fallah would be talking with DOD officials. The Secretary said that we can be sympathetic provided that the price is right, but we do not want to subsidize the seller.

Dr. Fallah said that on the other aspect of the Iranian plan to sell oil to the United States, Iran believes that it is in the US interest to buy inexpensive Iranian oil. The Secretary asked how such purchases would be financed. He said that he couldn't imagine the Congress financing an oil stockpile. Dr. Fallah said that at some time in the future, the United States, like South Africa, might finance a stockpile. Iran could provide credit for that part of the sale whose proceeds would go to Iran.

The Secretary said that from the standpoint of national resources policy there was some logic in the Iranian proposal. But to translate the proposal into financial and political terms would be difficult. He asked if such a proposition might not be more attractive for Western Europe. Dr. Fallah replied that Western Europe is already a market for Iranian oil. The Secretary commented that in our case, the proposal would appear to hurt our own producers who wouldn't trust their government to keep the stockpile locked up. Dr. Fallah said that the major American companies would like the proposal.

The Secretary said he was interested in the subject and would give it more thought, but there are political and financial problems. Dr. Fallah said that Alaskan finds are not the permanent answer to American oil needs and added that the Iranian proposal would not hurt the American balance of payments. The Secretary repeated that the proposal is politically very difficult. He asked that Iran provide us with its studies informally and that future discussions be on an informal basis.

324. Telegram From the Department of State to the Embassy in Iran[1]

Washington, December 9, 1968, 2212Z.

284246. Subject: Hoveyda Visit.

1. *Summary.* Hoveyda's December 3–4 visit to New York and December 5–6 visit to Washington eminently successful in further improving climate our relations with Iran. It provided us with opportunity give recognition Iranians in addition to Shah who playing important role in their country's development. We also conveyed to Hoveyda fact that our desires for close ties with Iran transcend partisan American considerations. For his part, Hoveyda's warm and frank personality made excellent impression on Americans he met. Principal substantive discussions were on Mideast problems and Iranian desires speed up military purchases from US and sell oil to US market.

2. During course his New York and Washington visits Iranian Prime Minister Hoveyda had half-hour meeting with President, hour and half meeting with Secretary, in addition formal dinner at White House and lunch at Dept. Hoveyda greatly pleased by special attention of President who attended Iranian Embassy reception in Washington. He also met in New York with Ambassador Murphy and while with President had brief discussion with President-elect's newly appointed foreign policy assistant Henry Kissinger. At private social occasions he was guest of David Rockefeller in New York, with Governor Rockefeller present, and of Senator Percy in Washington. At National Press Club speech in Washington and off-the-record appearances before Council on Foreign Relations in New York and Washington Institute of Foreign Affairs Hoveyda stressed Iran's internal progress and stability and pointed to importance for peace and stability of Middle East of a strong Iran. Press coverage was moderate but favorable. No student or other demonstrations.

3. In substantive discussions Hoveyda reviewed full range of Iranian policies toward its neighbors along familiar lines. We provided him with our current views on Arab-Israeli and Vietnam problems. Hoveyda pressed for speedy completion arrangements for next increment our military sales credit, stressing need place orders for additional two squadrons of F–4's so as to meet desired 1971 delivery date. In this connection he also mentioned Iranian need for more USAF technicians. Further discussions these subjects will be held in Washington December 13–16 with

---

[1] Source: Department of State, Central Files, POL 7 IRAN. Confidential. Drafted by Eliot on December 7, cleared by Saunders, and approved by Rockwell. Repeated to CINCSTRIKE.

PlanOrg Managing Director Samii. In addition discussions with oil companies in New York (septel), Hoveyda in Washington discussed possibilities for Iranian sales of oil to US and of oil products to DOD. Discussions these possibilities were inconclusive. Memcons follow.

Rusk

325. Telegram From the Department of State to the Embassy in Iran[1]

Washington, December 18, 1968, 2346Z.

289317. For Chargé. If you are questioned about fact President-elect did not receive Prime Minister Hoveyda but subsequently received Israeli Defense Minister Dayan and the Amir of Kuwait, you should say that you have no information on this subject. If pressed for explanation by high-level Iranian officials, you can suggest they await return of Ambassador Meyer who you are certain will be in a position to discuss this matter with the Prime Minister.[2]

---

[1] Source: Department of State, Central Files, POL 7 IRAN. Confidential; Limdis. Drafted by Eliot, cleared by Meyer (draft) and Leonhart, and approved by Rockwell.

[2] Printed from an unsigned copy.

Index